CASES

IN

MARKETING MANAGEMENT

CASES IN

MARKETING MANAGEMENT

FIFTH EDITION

KENNETH L. BERNHARDT
COLLEGE OF BUSINESS ADMINISTRATION
GEORGIA STATE UNIVERSITY

THOMAS C. KINNEAR
GRADUATE SCHOOL OF BUSINESS ADMINISTRATION
THE UNIVERSITY OF MICHIGAN

IRWIN
Homewood, IL 60430
Boston, MA 02116

© RICHARD D. IRWIN, INC., 1978, 1981, 1985, 1988, and 1991

Senior Sponsoring editor: Stephen Patterson
Developmental editor: Andy Winston
Project editor: Rita McMullen
Production manager: Bette K. Ittersagen
Designer: Jeanne M. Oswald
Compositor: Better Graphics, Inc.
Typeface: 10.5/12 Times Roman
Printer: R. R. Donnelley & Sons Company

Library of Congress Cataloging-in-Publication Data

Bernhardt, Kenneth L., 1944–
    Cases in marketing management / Kenneth L. Bernhardt, Thomas C.
Kinnear.—5th ed.
        p.   cm.
    Includes index.
    ISBN 0-256-08832-2   0-256-10139-6 (PC disk version)
        1. Marketing—Management—Case studies.   2. Marketing—Decision
making—Case studies.   I. Kinnear, Thomas C., 1943–   . II. Title.
    HF5415.13.B448   1991
    658.8—dc20   90–26291

Printed in the United States of America
2 3 4 5 6 7 8 9 DOC 8 7 6 5 4 3 2 1

To Kathy and Karen
To Connie, Maggie, and Jamie

Preface

Marketing is an exciting and dynamic discipline. Unfortunately, much of the excitement is hidden among the definitions and descriptions of concepts that are a necessary part of basic marketing textbooks. We believe that one way to make the study of marketing exciting and dynamic is to use cases. Cases allow the student to work on real marketing problems, to develop an appreciation for the types of problems that exist in the real world of marketing, and to develop the skills of analysis and decision making so necessary for success in marketing and other areas of business. Cases represent as close an approximation of the realities of actually working in marketing as is possible without taking a job in the field.

Your task as a user of this casebook is to work hard to develop well-reasoned solutions to the problems confronting the decision maker in each of the cases. A framework to assist you in developing solutions is presented in Part 1 of this book. Basically, you will be using this, or some other framework suggested by your instructor, to analyze the cases in this book. By applying this framework to each case that you are assigned, you will develop your analytic skills. Like all skills, you will find this difficult at first. However, as you practice, you will get better, until it will become second nature to you. This is exactly the same way one develops athletic or musical skills.

The cases in this book represent a broad range of marketing problems. The book contains consumer and industrial cases, profit and nonprofit cases, social marketing cases, specific marketing area cases, and general cases, plus cases on marketing and public policy. Each case is designed to fit into a specific section of a course in marketing management. The cases are long and complex enough to require good analysis, but not so long and complex to be overly burdensome. Within sections, cases do vary in terms of difficulty and complexity.

Users of the first four editions will note that the fundamental thrust and positioning remains the same in this edition. However, we do note the following changes. First, 14 new cases have been added. Second, a number of cases with greater complexity have been added to allow more in-depth work.

This book contains 46 cases and 2 case-related exercises. Twenty-three of the cases and both exercises were written by the authors of this book. In some instances we had a coauthor, and we have noted the names of the coauthors on the title pages of the cases concerned. We wish to thank these coauthors for their assistance and for allowing us to use the cases: Richard Aiken, Eric Andrew, Bruce Bassett, Stephen Becker, Danny Bellenger, Merle Crawford, Sarah Freeman, Matthew Hausmann, Tom Ingram, Susan Johnstal, Constance Kinnear, Ludwig Laudisi, Joanne Novak, James Novo, Martin Schreiber, Craig Uhrnst, Jos Viehoff, and John Wright.

We would like to thank the executives of the organizations who allowed us to develop cases about their situations and who have released these cases for use in this book.

The remaining 19 cases were written by many distinguished marketing casewriters. We appreciate them allowing us to reproduce their cases here. The names of each of these persons are noted on the title page of the cases concerned. They are: John Bargetto, Daniel Bello, Mort Ettinger, Kenneth Hardy, Cleon Hartzell, James Henderson, C. B. Johnston, Fred Kniffin, Aylin Kunt, Zarrel Lambert, Lawrence Lamont, Daniel Lindley, Eleanor May, Roger More, Rowland Moriarty, Patrick Murphy, James Nelson, Douglass Norwell, Michael Pearce, Adrian Ryans, Anne Senausky, Larry Uniac, Carloyn Vose, Charles Weinberg, and John Wright.

We were helped in selecting cases for this edition by the following people who responded to our survey:

Earl D. Alberts, *Moorhead State University;* Julian Andorka, *DePaul University;* William D. Ash, *California State University at Long Beach;* Amardeep Assar, *State University of New York at Binghamton;* Thomas J. Babb, *West Liberty State College;* George W. Boulware, *David Lipscomb University;* Betsy V. Boze, *University of Alaska-Anchorage;* Richard Brand, *University of Colorado-Denver;* Jerry Breuer, *Lawrence Technological University;* Gene Brown, *University of Central Arkansas;* Henry C. K. Chen, *University of West Florida;* William D. Coffey, *Saint Edwards University;* Jerry A. Cooper, *Southern Oregon State College;* Gerard R. DiBartolo, *Salisbury State University;* Matt Elbeck, *University of North Dakota;* Gary Ernst, *North Central College;* James Finch, *University of Wisconsin-LaCrosse;* Gary T. Ford, *American University;* George Galiourdis, *Webber College;* John Gwin, *University of Virginia;* Alfred G. Hawkins, Jr., *Rockhurst College;* Donald W. Hendon, *Northern State University;* Thomas Hitzelberger, *Southern Oregon State College;* John C. Howard, *Pennsylvania State University;* Jarrett Hudnall, *Stephen F. Austin State University;* Irving C. Jacobs, *State University of New York College at Fredonia;* Jerry W. Johnson, *Baylor University;* Anthony C. Koh, *University of Toledo;* Greg Lessne, *University of Rhode Island;* Frank Kattwinkle, *Saint Leo College;* Sylvia Keyes, *Bridgewater State College;* Robert Brock Lawes, *Chaminade University of Honolulu;* Richard C. Leventhal, *Metropolitan State College;* William P. Lovell, *Cayuga County Community College;* Michael Luthy, *University of Illinois at Urbana-Champaign;* Donald

A. McCall, *Southern Arkansas University;* P. H. McCaskey, *Millersville University;* H. B. McIntire, *Mesa State College;* Stephen J. Miller, *Oklahoma State University;* Charles R. Patton, *University of Texas at Brownsville;* Christopher P. Puto, *The University of Arizona;* L. D. Redinbaugh, *Creighton University;* S. V. Scott, *Boise State University;* Margery Steinberg, *University of Hartford;* Richard R. Still, *Florida International University;* Bill Tadlock, *University of Arkansas at Little Rock;* James Thomas, *Peru State College;* Zafar Uddin, *State University of New York College at Fredonia;* Stephen Warfield, *University of Southern Colorado;* Charles W. White, *Hardin-Simmons University;* Attila Yaprak, *Wayne State University;* George M. Zinkhan, *University of Houston;* and Thomas M. Zygmunt, *Webster University.*

We would also like to thank our colleagues at Georgia State University, the University of Michigan, and the Case Research Association for their helpful comments and their classroom testing of cases. Finally we want to acknowledge the help in the many tasks associated with the editing and production of the book we received from Vicki Einhorn and from Rita McMullen, Steve Patterson, and Andy Winston at Irwin.

Kenneth L. Bernhardt
Thomas C. Kinnear

Contents

Part 1

An Orientation to the Case Method

Chapter 1

Note to the Student on the Case Method

The case method is different from other methods of teaching, and it requires that students take an active role rather than a passive one. The case method places the student in a simulated business environment and substitutes the student in the place of the business manager required to make a set of decisions. To define it, a case is:

> typically a record of a business issue which actually has been faced by business executives, together with surrounding facts, opinions, and prejudices upon which the executives had to depend. These real and particularized cases are presented to students for considered analysis, open discussion, and final decision as to the type of action which should be taken.[1]

With the case method the process of arriving at an answer is what is important. The instructor's expectation is that the student will develop an ability to make decisions, to support those decisions with appropriate analysis, and to learn to communicate ideas both orally and in writing. The student is required to determine the problem as well as the solution. This method of teaching thus shifts much of the responsibility to the student, and a great deal of time is required on the part of the student.

The case method often causes a great deal of insecurity on the part of students who are required to make decisions often with very little information and limited time. There is no single right answer to any of the cases in this book, an additional source of insecurity. The goal is not to develop a set of right answers, but to learn to reason well with the data available. This process is truly learning by doing.

Studying under the case method will result in the development of skills in critical thinking. The student will learn how to effectively reason when dealing with specific problems. The development of communication skills is also

---

[1] Charles I. Gragg, "Because Wisdom Can't Be Told," *Harvard Alumni Bulletin*, October 19, 1940.

important, and students will learn to present their analysis in a cogent and convincing manner. They must defend their analysis and plan of action against the criticism of others in the class. In the class discussion, individual students may find that the opinions of other members of the class differ from their own. In some cases this will be because the individual has overlooked certain important points or that some factors have been weighted more heavily compared to the weighting used by other students. The process of presenting and defending conflicting points of view causes individual members of the class to reconsider the views they had of the case before the discussion began. This leads to a clearer perception of problems, a recognition of the many and often conflicting interpretations of the facts and events in the case, and a greater awareness of the complexities with which management decisions are reached.

In preparing for class using the case method, the student should first read the case quickly. The goal is to gain a feel for the type of problem presented in the case, the type of organization involved, and so on. Next, the student should read the case thoroughly to learn all the key facts in the case. The student should not blindly accept all the data presented, as not all information is equally reliable or relevant. As part of the process of mastering the facts, it frequently will be desirable to utilize the numerical data presented in the case to make any possible calculations and comparisons that will help analyze the problems involved in the case. The case will have to be read a number of times before the analysis is completed.

The student must add to the facts by making reasonable assumptions regarding many aspects of the situation. Business decision making is rarely based on perfect information. All of the cases in this book are actual business cases, and the student is provided with all the information that the executives involved had at their disposal. Often students cannot believe the low level of information available for decision making, but this is often the case. What is required in those situations is the making of reasonable assumptions and learning to make decisions under uncertainty. There is often a strong reluctance on the part of the student to do this, but the ability to make decisions based on well-reasoned assumptions is a skill that must be developed for a manager to be truly effective.

Once the student has mastered the facts in the case, the next step is to identify and specify the issues and problems toward which the executive involved should be directing his or her attention. The issues may be very obscure. Learning to separate problems from symptoms is an important skill to learn. Often there will be a number of subissues involved, and it will be necessary to break the problem down into component parts.

The next step in the student's case preparation is to identify alternative courses of action. Usually there are a number of possible solutions to the problems in the case, and the student should be careful not to lock in on only one alternative before several possible alternatives have been thoroughly evaluated.

The next step is to evaluate each of the alternative plans of action. It is at this stage of the analysis that the student is required to marshall and analyze all the facts for each alternative program. The assumptions the student is required to make are very important here, and the student must apply all the analytical skills possible, including both qualitative and quantitative.

After all the alternatives have been thoroughly analyzed, the student must make a decision concerning the specific course of action to take. It should be recognized that several of the alternatives may "work," and that there are a number of different ways of resolving the issues in the case. The important consideration is that the plan of action actually decided upon has been thoroughly analyzed from all angles, is internally consistent, and has a high probability of meeting the manager's objectives.

Once an overall strategy has been determined, it is important that consideration be given to the implementation of that strategy. At this stage, the student must determine who is to do what, when, and how. A professor may start out a class by asking the question, "What should Mr. Jones do tomorrow?" Unless the students have given some thought to the implementation of the strategy decided upon, they will be unprepared for such a question. Improper implementation of an excellent strategy may doom it to failure, so it is important to follow through with appropriate analysis at this stage.

During the class discussion the instructor will act more as a moderator than a lecturer, guiding the discussion and calling on students for their opinions. A significant amount of learning will take place by participating in the discussion. The goal is for the students to integrate all their ideas, relating them to the goals of the company, the strengths and weaknesses of the company and its competition, the way consumers buy, and the resources available. A suggested framework for the integration of these ideas is presented in the next chapter of this book in the appendix titled "Outline for case analysis."

The student's classroom discussion should avoid the rehashing, without analysis, of case facts. Students should recognize that the professor and all the other students in the class have thoroughly read the case and are familiar with the facts. The objective, therefore, is to interpret the facts and use them to support the proposed plan of action. The case method obviously requires a great deal of preparation time by the student. The payoff is that, after spending this time adequately preparing each of the steps described, the student will have developed the ability to make sound marketing management decisions.

Chapter 2

Introduction to Marketing Decision Making

In Chapter 1, you were introduced to your role in the execution of an effective case course in marketing. In summary, the primary task is to complete a competent analysis of the cases assigned to you. If you have never undertaken the analysis of a marketing case before, you are probably wondering just how you should go about doing this. Is there some framework that is appropriate for this task? Indeed, there are a number of such frameworks. The purpose of this chapter is to present one such framework to you. We think you will find it useful in analyzing the cases in this book.

An Outline for Case Analysis

The appendix to this chapter is the summary document for the approach we believe that you should use for case analysis. We suggest that you apply the types of questions listed there in your analysis. Figure 2–1 provides an overview of this outline. Basically, we are suggesting that you begin by doing a complete analysis of the *situation* facing the organization in the case. This *situation analysis* includes an assessment of (1) the nature of demand for the product, (2) the extent of demand, (3) the nature of competition, (4) the environmental climate, (5) the stage of the life cycle for the product, (6) the skills of the firm, (7) the financial resources of the firm, and (8) the distribution structure. In some cases legal aspects may also form part of a good situation analysis. The premise here is that one cannot begin to make decisions until a thorough understanding of the situation at hand is obtained.

Once a detailed situation analysis is prepared, one is in a position to summarize the *problems* and *opportunities* that arise out of the situation analysis. These problems and opportunities provide an organized summary of the situation analysis. This in turn should lead to the generation of a set of *alternatives* that are worthy of being considered as solutions to the problems and actualizers of the opportunities.

FIGURE 2-1   Overview of a framework for case analysis

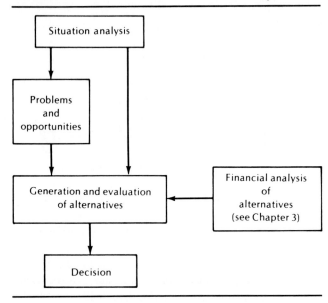

These alternatives are then *evaluated* using arguments generated from (1) the detailed situation analysis, (2) the summary statement of problems and opportunities, and (3) relevant financial analysis (break-even points, market shares, and so on). The use of financial analysis is discussed in Chapter 3. The point here is that we use the situation analysis to generate and evaluate alternative programs. The pros and cons of each alternative are weighed as part of this evaluation and a *decision* is then reached.

A Good Case Analysis

The question naturally arises: In applying the outline in the appendix to a case, how do I know when I have done a good analysis? The purpose of this section is to raise some points that are often used by instructors to evaluate either an oral or written analysis.

1. Be complete. It is imperative that the case analysis be complete. There are two dimensions to this issue. First is that each area of the situation analysis must be discussed, problems and opportunities must be identified, alternatives must be presented and evaluated using the situation analysis and relevant financial analysis, and a decision must be made. An analysis that omits parts of the situation analysis, or only recognizes one alternative, is not a good analysis. Second, each area above must be covered in good depth and with insight.

2. *Avoid rehashing case facts.* Every case has a lot of factual information. A good analysis uses facts that are relevant to the situation at hand to make summary points of analysis. A poor analysis just restates or rehashes these facts without making relevant summary comments. Consider the use of a set of financial facts that might appear in a case:

Rehash: The current ratio is 1.5:1, cash on hand is $15,000, retained earnings are $50,000.

Analysis: Because of a very weak financial position, as demonstrated by a poor cash position and current ratio, the firm will be constrained in the activities it can undertake to ones requiring little immediate cash outlay.

3. *Make reasonable assumptions.* Every case is incomplete in terms of some piece of information that you would like to have. We would, of course, like to have all the necessary information presented to us in each case. This is not possible for two reasons. First, it would make the cases far too long to be capable of being analyzed in a reasonable period of time. Second, and more important, incomplete information is an accurate reflection of the real world. All marketing decisions are made on the basis of incomplete information. Often, it just costs too much or takes too long to collect the desired information.

A good case analysis must make realistic assumptions to fill in the gaps of information in the case. For example, the case may not describe the purchase decision process for the product of interest. A poor analysis would either omit mentioning this or just state that no information is available. A good analysis would attempt to present this purchase decision process by classifying the product (a shopping good?) and drawing on the student's real-life experience. Could you not describe the purchase decision process for carpeting, even though you have never read a research report about it?

The reasonableness of your assumptions will be challenged by your fellow students and instructor. This is one of the things that makes case discussions exciting. The point is that it is better to make your assumptions explicit and incorporate them in your analysis than to use them implicitly or not make them at all. If we make explicit assumptions we can later come back and see if our assumptions were correct or not.

4. *Don't confuse symptoms with problems.* In summarizing a firm's problems a poor analysis confuses the symptoms with real problems. For example, one might list two problems as (1) sales are down and (2) sales force turnover is high. This would not be correct. These are symptoms. The real problem is identified by answering the question: Why are sales down or why is sales force turnover high? For example, sales force turnover may be high due to inadequate sales training. But this may not yet be the root problem. You still need to ask: Why is sales training inadequate? It may be that the sales manager has ignored this area through his or her lack of knowledge of how to train people. What you do is keep asking ''why'' until you are satisfied that you have identified the root problem.

5. *Don't confuse opportunities with taking action.* One can recognize an opportunity but not take any action related to it. For example, a large market for a product may exist. This is an opportunity. However, a firm may decide not to compete in this market due to lack of resources or skills or the existence of strong competition. Decisions involve the complex trading-off of many problems and opportunities. Thus, don't make statements that direct action—''target to . . . , promote as . . . ,'' and the like—as opportunity statements.

6. *Deal with objectives realistically.* Most cases present a statement from management about their objectives. For example, it might say they want a sales growth rate of 25 percent per year. Good analysis critically evaluates statements of objectives and revises them if necessary. Then it uses these revised objectives as part of the argument about which alternative to select. Poor analysis either ignores the stated objectives or accepts them at face value.

7. *Recognize alternatives.* A good analysis explicitly recognizes and discusses alternative action plans. In some cases, these alternatives are stated in the case. In other cases, the student must develop alternatives beyond those stated in the case. A poor analysis explicitly recognizes only one or two alternatives or only takes the ones explicitly stated in the case.

8. *Don't be assertive.* In some case analyses, the decision that was made is clear to the reader or listener in about the first sentence of the situation analysis. The whole rest of the analysis is then a justification of the desired solution. This type of analysis is very poor. It has asserted an answer before completing a situation analysis. Usually, other alternatives are ignored or treated as all bad, and the desired solution is treated as all good. You must do your situation analysis and recognize alternatives before evaluating them and reaching a decision.

9. *Discuss the pros and cons of each alternative.* Every alternative always has pros and cons. A good analysis explicitly discusses these. In a poor analysis there is no explicit discussion of the pros and cons of each alternative. Problem and opportunity statements serve as the basis of your pro (opportunities) and con (problems) discussion. Different ones relate to specific alternatives.

10. *Make effective use of financial and other quantitative information.* Financial data (break-even points and so on) and information derived from other quantitative analyses can add a great deal to a good case analysis. Totally ignoring these aspects or handling them improperly results in a poor case analysis. This analysis should be presented in detail in a written appendix or in class if asked for. However, in the body of a paper or in an oral discussion present only the summary conclusions out of the analysis. Say "The break-even point is 220,000 units," and be prepared to present the detail if asked.

11. Reach a clear decision. You must reach a clear decision. You might like to hedge your bets and say "maybe this, maybe that." However, part of the skill of decision making is to be forced to reach a decision under ambiguous circumstances and then be prepared to defend this decision. This does not mean that you do not recognize limitations of your position or positive aspects of other positions. It just means that despite all that, you have reached a particular decision.

12. Make good use of evidence developed in your situation analysis. In reaching a decision, a good analysis reaches a decision that is logically consistent with the situation analysis that was done. This is the ultimate test of an analysis. Other students may disagree with your situation analysis and thus your resultant conclusion, but they should not be able to fault the logical connection between your situation analysis and decision. If they can, you have a poor case analysis.

The "Outline for case analysis" contained in the appendix is designed to assist you in doing case analysis. You should keep the points stressed in this section in mind when you apply this outline.

Appendix

Outline for case analysis*

Overview of Analysis Structure

   I. Situation analysis
      A. Nature of demand.
      B. Extent of demand.
      C. Nature of competition.
      D. Environmental climate.
      E. Stage of product life cycle.
      F. Cost structure of the industry.
      G. Skills of the firm.
      H. Financial resources of the firm.
      I. Distribution structure.
  II. Problems and opportunities
      A. Key problem areas.
      B. Key opportunities.
      C. On balance, the situation is.
 III. Generation and evaluation of alternative marketing programs
      A. Objectives defined.
      B. Marketing mix/program decisions.
 IV. Decision

Details of Analysis Structure

I. SITUATION ANALYSIS

A. Nature of demand

The purpose of this section is to make *explicit* your beliefs and assumptions regarding the nature of the purchase decision process (consumer or industrial) for the goods or services under investigation. In case analysis we are concerned primarily with developing your *skills* of analysis to identify areas of problems and opportunities and in developing well-supported marketing program recommendations. Conflicting student beliefs and assumptions should lead to interesting and enlightening class discussion regarding the nature of the purchase decision process and its implication for marketing programs. We hope that through this type of class discussion, you will increase your sensitivity to, and understanding of, buyers and

---

* This outline is adapted from an unpublished note by Professor James R. Taylor of the University of Michigan. Used with permission.

their behavior. Again, the value of this type of analysis concerns its application to better *reasoned* and *supported* marketing program decisions. Hopefully, the development of your skills in this area has value in improving your *judgment capabilities* and in increasing your understanding of marketing decision making.

Analysis areas and questions

1. How do buyers (consumer and industrial) **currently** go about buying existing products or services? Describe the main types of behavior patterns and attitudes.
   a. Number of stores shopped or industrial sources considered.
   b. Degree of overt information seeking.
   c. Degree of brand awareness and loyalty.
   d. Location of product category decision—home or point of sale.
   e. Location of brand decision—home or point of sale.
   f. Sources of product information and current awareness and knowledge levels.
   g. Who makes the purchase decision—male, female, adult, child, purchasing agent, buying committee, so on?
   h. Who influences the decision maker?
   i. Individual or group decision (computers versus candy bar).
   j. Duration of the decision process (repeat, infrequent, or new purchase situation).
   k. Buyer's interest, personal involvement or excitement regarding the purchase (hairpins versus trip to Caribbean).
   l. Risk or uncertainty of negative purchase outcome—high, medium, or low (specialized machinery versus hacksaw blades) (pencil versus hair coloring).
   m. Functional versus psychosocial considerations (electric drill versus new dress).
   n. Time of consumption (gum versus dining room furniture).

   Basically, we are attempting to determine the *who, what, where, when, why,* and *how* of the purchase decision.

   Note: The key to using the above analysis is to ask what are the implications for marketing programs? For example, if the purchase (brand) decision is made in the store and branding is not important to the buyers, what implication does this have for national TV advertising versus in-store display? Do you see how you might *use* this information to support a recommendation for intensive distribution and point-of-purchase promotion and display?

2. Can the market be meaningfully segmented or broken into several homogeneous groups with respect to "what they want" and "how they buy"? Criteria:
   a. Age.

> *b.* Family life cycle.
> *c.* Geographic location.
> *d.* Heavy versus light users.
> *e.* Nature of the buying process.
> *f.* Product usage.

Note: For each case situation, you should determine whether a more effective marketing program could be developed for each segment versus having an overall program for all segments. The real issue is whether tailoring your program to a segment will give you a competitive advantage. Of course, there may be negatives to this strategy in terms of volume and cost considerations.

B. Extent of demand

The purpose of this section is to evaluate demand in an aggregate and quantitative sense. We are basically concerned with the actual or potential size of the overall market and developing sound estimates of company sales potential.

Analysis areas and questions
1. What is the size of the market (units and dollars) now and what will the future hold?
2. What are the current market shares, and what are the selective demand trends (units and dollars)?
3. Is it best to analyze the market on an aggregate or on a segmented basis?

Note: We are basically concerned with making *explicit* assumptions regarding primary and selective demand trends. These estimates are critical to determining the profit (loss) potential of alternative marketing programs.

C. Nature of competition

The purpose of this section is to evaluate the present and future structure of competition. The key is to understand how the buyer evaluates alternative products or services relative to his or her needs.

Analysis areas and questions
1. What is the present and future structure of competition?
   a. Number of competitors (5 versus 2,000).
   b. Market shares.
   c. Financial resources.
   d. Marketing resources and skills.
   e. Production resources and skills.
2. What are the current marketing programs of established competitors? Why are they successful or unsuccessful?
3. Is there an opportunity for another competitor? Why?

4. What are the anticipated retaliatory moves of competitors? Can they neutralize different marketing programs we might develop?

Note: Failure to correctly evaluate demand and competition is one common reason for unprofitable marketing programs. Also, Sections A, B, and C are analysis areas particularly important in making decisions concerning "positioning" your product and developing the marketing program to support your positioning strategy.

D. Environmental climate

It's not hard to identify current marketing programs that have been highly disrupted by a changing environmental climate. The energy crisis together with pollution, safety, and consumerism concerns, can bring many such examples to mind. We are sure you can identify firms who have benefited from the energy crisis. The point is that the environment is constantly changing and those organizations which can adapt to change are the ones which enjoy long-run success.

Analysis areas and questions
1. What are the relevant social, political, economic, and technological trends?
2. How do you evaluate these trends? Do they represent opportunities or problems?

E. Stage of product life cycle

The purpose of this section is to make explicit assumptions about where a product is in its life cycle. This is important because the effectiveness of particular marketing variables may vary by stages of the life cycle.

Analysis areas and questions
1. In what stage of the life cycle is the product category?
   a. What is the chronological age of the product category? (Younger more favorable than older?)
   b. What is the state of the consumers' knowledge of the product category? (More complete the knowledge—more unfavorable?)
2. What market characteristics support your stage of life-cycle evaluation?

F. Cost structure of the industry

Here we are concerned with the amount and composition of the marginal or additional cost of supplying increased output. It can be argued that the lower these costs, the easier it may be to cover the costs of developing an effective marketing program (see accompanying table). Basically, one is relating the level of fixed cost to variable cost.

	Marginal costs	
	High*	Low†
Selling price per unit	$1.00	$1.00
Variable costs per unit	0.80	0.10
Contribution per unit	$0.20	$0.90

* Such as the garment and auto industries.
† Such as the hotel and telephone industries.

G.   Skills of the firm

The purpose of this section is to critically evaluate the organization making the decision. Here, we effectively place limits on what they are capable of accomplishing.

Analysis areas and questions
1.   Do we have the skills and experience to perform the functions necessary to be in this business?
  a.   Marketing skills.
  b.   Production skills.
  c.   Management skills.
  d.   Financial skills.
  e.   R&D skills.
2.   How do our skills compare to competitors?
  a.   Production fit.
  b.   Marketing fit.
  c.   Etc.

H.   Financial resources of the firm

Analysis areas and questions
1.   Do we have the funds to support an effective marketing program?
2.   Where are the funds coming from, and when will they be available?

I.   Distribution structure

The purpose of this area is to identify and evaluate the availability of channels of distribution.

Analysis areas and questions
1.   What channels exist, and can we gain access to the channels?
2.   Cost versus revenue from different channels?
3.   Feasibility of using multiple channels?
4.   Nature and degree of within and between channel competition?
5.   Trends in channel structure?
6.   Requirements of different channels for promotion and margin?
7.   Will it be profitable for particular channels to handle my product?

II. PROBLEMS AND OPPORTUNITIES

Here we prepare a definite listing of *key* problems and opportunities identified from the situation analysis which relate to the specific issues or decision questions faced by management.

A. Key problem areas

B. Key opportunities

C. On balance, the situation is:
1. Very favorable.
2. Somewhat favorable.
3. Neutral.
4. Somewhat unfavorable.
5. Very unfavorable.

Note: At this point, the critical issue is whether a profitable marketing program can be formulated or whether a current marketing program needs to be changed in order to overcome the problem areas and/or take advantage of opportunities.

III. EVALUATION OF ALTERNATIVE MARKETING PROGRAMS

A marketing program consists of a series of marketing mix decisions which represent an integrated and consistent "action plan" for achieving predetermined goals. Different marketing programs may be required for various target segments. For a given target segment, alternative programs should be formulated and evaluated as to the effectiveness of each in achieving predetermined goals.

A. Objectives defined
1. Target market segments identified.
2. Volume to be sold (dollars or units).
3. Profit analysis (contribution analysis, break-even analysis, ROI, etc.).

B. Marketing mix/program decisions
1. Product decisions
   a. Develop new product(s).
   b. Change current product(s).
   c. Add or drop product from line.
   d. Product positioning.
   e. Branding (national, private, secondary).
2. Distribution decisions
   a. Intensity of distribution (intensive to exclusive).
   b. Multiple channels.
   c. Types of wholesalers and retailers (discounters, so on).
   d. Degree of channel directness.
3. Promotion decisions
   a. Mix of personal selling, advertising, dealer incentives, and sales promotion.

 b.   Branding—family versus individual.
 c.   Budget.
 d.   Message.
 e.   Media.
4. Price decisions
 a.   Price level (above, same, or below).
 b.   Price variation (discount structure, geographic).
 c.   Margins.
 d.   Administration of price level.
 e.   Price leadership.

Note: The above four decision areas involve specific strategy issues which together form a marketing program.

The key to effective marketing decision making is to evaluate alternative marketing programs using information from the situation analysis. The pros and cons for each alternative should be presented and discussed.

IV.   DECISION

The outcome of the evaluation of alternatives is a decision. You must make a decision. Case analysis is designed to develop your skills in making well-supported and reasoned marketing decisions. The quality of your reasoning is much more important than reaching any particular decision. Generally, if your situation analysis is different (you perceive the facts differently and have made different assumptions) from someone else's, you should reach different decisions.

Chapter 3

Financial Analysis
for Marketing
Decision Making

In Chapter 2, we laid out an approach to marketing decision making. The "Outline for case analysis" summarized this approach. There is, however, one more important aspect of a competent case analysis that was not presented in that outline. This is the financial analysis of the alternatives presented in a case.

The ultimate goals of all marketing activities are usually expressed in financial terms. The company has a particular return on investment in mind, or growth in earnings per share. Proposed marketing activities must thus be evaluated for their financial implications. Can you imagine asking your boss for $1 million for a new distribution center or an advertising program without having to present the financial implications of such a request? It does not happen in the real marketing world, nor should it happen in a good case analysis.

Financial analysis can be complex. Our purpose here is to present some simple financial calculations that can be useful in case analysis. More sophisticated financial techniques are left to courses in financial management. Basically, the advanced techniques add little to the understanding of the cases in this book and take too much time and effort for the reader to implement.

It should clearly be understood that financial considerations are only one aspect in the evaluation of marketing alternatives. Marketing alternatives cannot be reduced to a set of numbers. Qualitative aspects derived from the situation analysis are also relevant. Sometimes the qualitative aspects are consistent in terms of pointing to an alternative to select. In other cases, they may point to different alternatives. The task of the student is to formulate both types of arguments for each alternative, and to select an alternative based upon which arguments the student thinks should carry the most weight.

This chapter assumes that the student is familiar with elementary financial accounting concepts. What we will present here are some useful concepts not usually presented in basic accounting courses.

Contribution

Contribution per unit is defined as the difference between the selling price of an item and the variable costs of producing and selling that item. It is in essence the amount of money per unit available to the marketer to cover fixed production costs, corporate overhead and, having done that, to yield a profit. So, if a manufacturer sells an item for $12.00, and the variable costs are $8.40, then

$$\text{Contribution per unit} = \text{Selling price} - \text{Variable costs}$$
$$= \$12.00 \qquad - \$8.40$$
$$= \$\ 3.60$$

Each unit this company sells gives it $3.60 to cover fixed costs.

Total contribution is the contribution per unit times the number of units sold. So, if this firm sold 20,000 units:

$$\text{Total contribution} = \text{Contribution per unit} \times \text{Units sold}$$
$$= \$\ 3.60 \times 20,000$$
$$= \$72,000$$

If the total relevant fixed costs of this product were $42,000, the *profit* earned by this product would be:

$$\text{Profit} = \text{Total contribution} - \text{Fixed costs}$$
$$= \$72,000 \qquad - \$42,000$$
$$= \$30,000$$

Costs

In determining contributions and profit we used the terms *variable cost* and *fixed cost*. At this point we want to define them more formally. Variable costs are those costs that are fixed *per unit* and, therefore, vary in their total amount depending upon the number of units produced and sold. That is, it takes a certain amount of raw materials and labor to produce a unit of product. The more we produce, the more total variable costs are.

Fixed costs are costs that remain constant in *total amount* despite changes in the volume of production or sales. These costs would thus vary per unit depending upon the number of units produced or sold.

Sorting out which costs are variable and fixed is important in good case analysis. The rule to apply is: if it varies in *total* as volume changes, it is a variable cost. Thus, labor, raw materials, packaging, salespersons' commissions would be variable costs. Note that all marketing costs except commissions would be considered fixed costs. Don't be fooled if a marketing cost or other fixed cost is presented in a per unit form. It may look like a variable cost, but it is not. It is only that much per unit at one given volume. For example, if we are told that advertising cost per unit will be $1, this means that at the end of the year when we divide total sales into advertising expenditures the result is expected to be $1 per unit. What we must be told is at what volume advertising is expected to be $1 per unit. If the expected volume level is 300,000 units, we then know that the firm intends to spend $300,000 ($1 × 300,000 units) on advertising. This $300,000 is a fixed cost. Note that if they sold less than 300,000 units, the cost per unit would exceed $1 and vice versa. So beware of fixed costs that are allocated to units and presented in a per unit form.

Break Even

A solid perspective on many marketing alternatives can often be obtained by determining the unit or dollar sales necessary to cover all relevant fixed costs. This sales level is called the break-even point. We define

1. Break-even point in units $= \dfrac{\text{Total fixed costs}}{\text{Contribution per unit}}$

2. Break-even point in dollars $= \dfrac{\text{Total fixed costs}}{1 - \dfrac{\text{Variable cost per unit}}{\text{Selling price per unit}}}$

or

$$= \begin{matrix}\text{Break-even point} \\ \text{in units}\end{matrix} \times \begin{matrix}\text{Selling price} \\ \text{per unit}\end{matrix}$$

Let's illustrate these definitions. Suppose that (1) direct labor is $7.50 per unit, (2) raw materials are $2 per unit, (3) selling price is $22 per unit, (4) advertising and sales force costs are $400,000, and (5) other relevant fixed costs are $100,000.

$$
\begin{aligned}
\text{Contribution per unit} &= \text{Selling price} - \text{Variable costs} \\
\text{Contribution per unit} &= \$22.00 - (\$7.50 + \$2.00) \\
&= \$22.00 - \$9.50 \\
&= \$12.50
\end{aligned}
$$

$$
\begin{aligned}
\text{Break-even point in units} &= \frac{\text{Total fixed costs}}{\text{Contribution per unit}} \\
&= \frac{\$400,000 + \$100,000}{\$12.50} \\
&= 40,000 \text{ units}
\end{aligned}
$$

$$
\begin{aligned}
\text{Break-even point in dollars} &= \frac{\$500,000}{1 - \dfrac{\$9.50}{\$22.00}} \\
&= \frac{\$500,000}{1 - 0.4318181} = \$880,000
\end{aligned}
$$

Alternatively

$$
\begin{aligned}
\text{Break-even point in dollars} &= 40,000 \times \$22.00 \text{ per unit} \\
&= \$880,000
\end{aligned}
$$

Profit Targets

Breaking even is not as much fun as making a profit. Thus, we often want to incorporate a profit target level into our calculations. Basically, we are answering the question: at what volume do we earn X profits? Covering a profit target is just like covering a fixed cost. So in the previous example, if we set $60,000 as our profit target we would have to sell an additional number of units equal to:

$$\text{Units to cover profit target} = \frac{\text{Profit target}}{\text{Contribution per unit}}$$

$$= \frac{\$60,000}{\$12.50} = 4,800 \text{ units}$$

Total units to reach this target is

$$40,000 + 4,800 = 44,800 \text{ or } \frac{\$500,000 + \$60,000}{\$12.50} = 44,800$$

Break-even analysis is a useful tool for comparing alternative marketing programs. It tells us how many units must be sold but does not help us with the critical question of how many units will be sold.

Market Share

$$\text{Market share} = \frac{\text{Company sales level}}{\text{Total market sales}}$$

This calculation adds perspective to proposed action plans. Suppose that the total market sales are 290,000 units and our sales level needed to break even is 40,000 units. Thus, the required market share to break even is:

$$\frac{40,000}{290,000} = 13.8\%$$

The question then to ask is whether this market share can be obtained with the proposed marketing program.

Capital Expenditures

Often a particular marketing program proposes expenditures for capital equipment. These would be fixed costs associated with the proposed program. Typically, they should not all be charged to the relevant fixed cost for that proposal. For example, suppose that $5 million are to be expended for equipment that will last 10 years. If we charge all this to the break-even calculation in year one, it will be very high. Further, for years 2 through 10, the break-even point will fall substantially. It is better to allocate this $5 million equally over the 10 years. Thus, $500,000 would be a relevant fixed cost in each year associated with the equipment. What one needs to do is to make some reasonable assumption about the useful life of capital assets and divide the total cost over this time period.

Relevant Costs

The issue often arises as to what fixed costs are relevant to a particular proposal. The rule to use is: A fixed cost is relevant if the expenditure varies due to the acceptance of that proposal. Thus, new equipment, new research and development, and so on, are relevant. Last year's advertising or previous research and development dollars, for example, do not vary with the current decision and thus are not a relevant cost of the proposed program. Past expenditures are referred to as *sunk costs*. They should not enter into current decisions. Decisions are future oriented.

Corporate overhead presents a special problem. Generally, it does not vary with a particular decision. We don't fire the president in selecting between marketing programs. However, in some instances, some overhead may be directly attributable to a particular decision. In this instance, it would be a relevant cost. We should recognize that to stay in business a firm must cover all its costs in the long run. Also, from a financial accounting point of view, all costs are relevant. This type of accounting is concerned with preparing income statements and balance sheets for reporting to investors. In marketing decision making we are interested in managerial, not financial, accounting. Managerial accounting is concerned with providing relevant information for decision making. It, therefore, only presents costs that are relevant to the decision being considered. Such things as allocated overhead or amortized research and development costs only serve to confuse future-oriented decisions.

Margins

Often a case will present us with a retail selling price, when what we really want to know is the manufacturer's selling price. To be able to work back to get the manufacturer's selling price, we must understand how channel margins work.

When firms buy a product at a particular price and attempt to sell it at a higher price, the difference between the cost price and the selling price is called margin or markup or mark-on. Thus,

$$\text{Selling price} = \text{Cost price} + \text{Margin}$$

An example could be:

$$\$1.00 = \$0.80 + \$0.20$$

So a company has bought a product for $0.80, added on a $0.20 margin and is charging $1.00 for the product.

Margins are usually expressed as percentages. This raises the question as to the base on which the margin percentage should be expressed: the cost price or the selling price. Here, if the $0.20 margin is expressed as a percentage of selling price the margin is $0.20/$1.00 = 20 percent. If it were expressed as a percentage of cost price, the margin is $0.20/$0.80 = 25 percent. The most common practice in marketing is to express margins as a percentage of selling price. Margins expressed in this fashion are easier to work with, especially in a multilevel channel situation. Unless explicitly stated otherwise, you may assume that all margins in the cases in this book use selling price as the relevant base.

A number of different types of margin-related problems arise. They include:

1. Determining the selling price, given you know the cost price and the percentage margin on selling price.
Suppose that a retailer buys an appliance for $15 and wants to obtain a margin on selling price of 40 percent. What selling price must be charged? The answer $21 is not correct because this margin ($6 = $15 × 0.4) would be on cost price. To answer this question we must remember one fundamental relationship. This is that

$$\text{Selling price} = \text{Cost price} + \text{Margin}$$

Here we are taking selling price as the base equal to 100 percent, so we can write

$$100\% = \$15 + 40\%$$

That is, the cost price plus the margin must add to 100 percent. Clearly the $15 must then be 60 percent of the desired selling price. Thus,

$$\text{Derived selling price} = \$15/60\%$$
$$= \$25$$

The dollar margin is then $10 which is $10/$25 = 40 percent of selling price.

The general rule then is to divide one minus the percentage margin expressed as a decimal on selling price, into the cost price. For example, if cost price is $105 and the margin on selling price is 22.5 percent, then the desired selling price is $105/(1 − 0.225) = $105/0.775 = $135.48.

2. Conversion of margin bases.
Sometimes a margin is given on a cost price basis, and we wish to convert it to a selling price base or vice versa. How do we make the conversion? Suppose that a product costs $4.50 and sells for $6.00. The margin is $1.50. On a selling price basis, the margin is $1.50/$6.00 = 25 percent. On a cost price basis, the margin is $1.50/$4.50 = 33.33 percent. The conversion from one percentage margin to the other is easy if we remember that selling price is composed of two parts: margin and cost.

For selling price base.

$$\text{Selling price} = \text{Margin} + \text{Cost}$$
$$\$6.00 = \$1.50 + \$4.50$$

or more important

$$100\% = 25\% + 75\%$$

For cost price base.

$$\text{Selling price} = \text{Margin} + \text{Cost}$$
$$\$6.00 = \$1.50 + \$4.50$$

but here the cost is the 100 percent base, so

$$\$6.00 = \$1.50 + 100\%$$

or

$$133.33\% = 33.33\% + 100\%$$

That is, the selling price should be thought of as 133.33 percent of the cost price. *Conversion from selling price to cost price base.*

$$\text{Selling price} = \text{Margin} + \text{Cost}$$
$$100\% = 25\% + 75\%$$

So, if we want to convert the 25 percent margin to a cost price basis, the 75 percent that is the cost becomes the relevant base and

$$\text{Margin as a percentage of cost price} = \frac{25\%}{75\%} = 33.33\%$$

Note that this is exactly the same as dividing $1.50 by $4.50.

A simple formula for making this conversion is

$$\text{Percentage margin on cost price} = \frac{\text{Percentage margin on selling price}}{100\% - \text{Percentage margin on selling price}}$$

In our example, this is

$$\frac{25\%}{100\% - 25\%} = \frac{25\%}{75\%} = 33.33\%$$

Note that the only piece of information that we need to make this conversion is the margin percentage on selling price.

Conversion from cost price to selling price base.

$$\text{Selling price} = \text{Margin} + \text{Cost}$$
$$133.33\% = 33.33\% + 100\%$$

The margin is 33.33 percent and the relevant selling price base is 133.33 percent, so

$$\text{Margin as a percentage of selling price} = \frac{33.33\%}{133.33\%} = 25\%$$

Note that this is exactly the same as dividing $1.50 by $6.00.

A simple formula for making this conversion is

$$\text{Percentage margin on selling price} = \frac{\text{Percentage margin on cost price}}{100\% + \text{Percentage margin on cost price}}$$

In our example, this is

$$\frac{33.33\%}{100\% + 33.33\%} = \frac{33.33\%}{133.33\%} = 25\%$$

Note that the only piece of information that we need to make this conversion is the margin percentage on cost price.

Multiple Margins

Often a manufacturer gives a suggested retail selling price and suggested retail and wholesale margins. For example, the suggested retail price may be $7.50 with a retail margin of 20 percent and a wholesale margin of 15 percent. To determine the manufacturer's selling price in this situation, we simply take the appropriate margins off one at a time. Thus,

Retail selling price	$7.50
Less retail margin (20% of $7.50)	1.50
Equals retail cost price or wholesale selling price	6.00
Less wholesale margin (15% of $6.00)	0.90
Equals wholesale cost price or manufacturer's selling price	$5.10

No matter how many levels there are in the channel, the approach is the same. We simply take the margins off one at a time. Note that we cannot just add up the margins and subtract this amount. Here 20% + 15% = 35%, and 35% of $7.50 is $2.63, making the manufacturer's selling price $7.50 − $2.63 = $4.87. This is not correct.

This chapter has outlined some financial concepts that add greatly to our abilities to make sound marketing decisions. These concepts should be applied where needed in the cases in this book.

Chapter 4

A Case with a Student Analysis

The fundamental premise of this book is that one learns by doing. However, one can also learn from example. The purpose of this chapter is to give an example of a case analysis. The framework of analysis presented in the previous two chapters will be used here in order to clarify how one can use the framework.

The case presented in this chapter, "Crow, Pope, and Land," is a broad issue marketing case that has no textbook or single "correct" answer. A student analysis of the case follows the case presentation, and in the last section of the chapter we present our commentary on the case analysis.

We suggest the following steps in using this chapter:

1. Read and prepare your analysis of "Crow, Pope, and Land." This will give you a better perspective on the case analyses presented in this chapter.
2. Read and evaluate the analysis presented here. You may wish to use the points that constitute a good case analysis as presented in Chapter 2.
3. Read our commentary on the case analysis. Compare our view with yours.

Case

Crow, Pope, and Land Enterprises*

In early August 1973, Mr. Dan Thatcher, vice president of CPL Condominium Enterprises, a subsidiary of Crow, Pope, and Land Enterprises, was planning his strategy for a new condominium project in Jacksonville, Florida. The project was an important one, since it was the company's first attempt to diversify out of the Atlanta area with nonresort condominiums. Earlier in the year, Mr. Thatcher had arranged the purchase of an option on a 40-acre tract just outside the city limits of Jacksonville, and the company had to renew the option in the next week or they would lose their earnest money. Before the senior officers of the firm would approve the final purchase of the land for approximately $700,000, Mr. Thatcher had to prepare a report discussing the proposed marketing strategy for the condominiums to be built there. His report was to include discussions of the target market, the specifications of the units to be built, the price range of the condominiums, and the promotional strategy to be used in marketing the units.

Company Background

Crow, Pope, and Land Enterprises, Inc., is a developer of residential, commercial, and motel/hotel real estate property, with projects located throughout the world. Headquartered in Atlanta, Georgia, the company was incorporated on January 14, 1967, under the name Lincoln Construction Company. Trammell Crow of Dallas, Ewell Pope of Atlanta, and Frank Carter of Atlanta were the shareholders of the company. Mr. Pope and Mr. Carter had been partners in the real estate brokerage firm, Pope and Carter Company, which had acted as the leasing agent for several of Trammell Crow's developments, namely, Chattahoochee Industrial Park and Greenbriar Shopping Center. These two adventures had proved so successful that the three men decided to strengthen their association and form Lincoln Construction Company.

---

*This case was written by Kenneth L. Bernhardt and John S. Wright, Professor of Marketing, Georgia State University. Copyright © 1975 by Kenneth L. Bernhardt.

In June 1972, Mr. Pope and Mr. Carter decided to establish separate organizations, both of which were formed in association with Mr. Crow. Crow and Carter started Crow, Carter, and Associates, Inc., and Crow and Pope, in association with A. J. Land, Jr., became owners of the continuing company, Crow, Pope, and Land Enterprises, Inc.

The company is organized on a project-management basis, with a managing partner who oversees and is responsible for every phase of the development assigned to each project. The manager of each project acts very much like the president of a small company, with the exception that he has the resources of a much larger corporation to draw upon when it is felt that added expertise would be of assistance. Most of the project managers, including Mr. Thatcher, are young, aggressive MBA graduates from leading schools of business administration.

The projects in which the company is involved range from the development of apartment complexes, condominium complexes, office parks, and shopping centers, to "total community" complexes complete with apartments, condominiums, single-family houses, retail outlets, parks, schools, office buildings, and recreational facilities. The firm has recently become active in the development of urban community centers containing a mixture of such features as commercial high-rise office buildings, luxury hotels, retail shopping facilities, and other pedestrian conveniences designed for high architectural impact in downtown environments. Examples of some of the company's projects include the $100 million Atlanta Center project (a large Hilton Hotel together with office buildings and shopping areas in downtown Atlanta), the $40 million Sheraton Hong Kong Hotel and shopping mall complex, and the Cumberland, Fairington, and Northlake total community complexes in Atlanta. Cumberland, a $65 million joint venture development with the Metropolitan Life Insurance Company, will, upon its completion in 1978, include a 1 million-square-foot enclosed shopping center, 750,000 square feet of office space, 1,800 apartments and condominiums situated around a 17-acre lake, an indoor tennis center, and hotel/motel facilities.

Crow, Pope, and Land has built a number of condominium and apartment complexes in Atlanta and has built more condominiums than any other developer in the area. Among the projects currently being sold in the Atlanta area are projects oriented toward retired couples, young swingers, sports-minded couples and families, and couples who want to own their own residence but cannot afford single-family detached housing. The company also has several resort projects in Florida.

Background on the Jacksonville Project

The original idea for the Jacksonville project came out of a meeting Mr. Thatcher had in early 1973 with Lindsay Freeman, another vice president of CPL Condominium Enterprises. In discussing the future goals and directions for the subsidiary, they decided that a high priority should be placed on reducing their dependence on the Atlanta condominium market where all nine of their projects were located. Since different geographic areas often were at different stages of the business cycle, they felt expansion into new geographical areas would provide a hedge against economic downturns as well as opening up profitable new markets for their products.

The first decision made was that they should concentrate on the Southeast, within a 400-mile radius of Atlanta, allowing greater control from the Atlanta headquarters. Also, projections of housing market demand indicated that this region of the country would experience rapid growth in the coming few years.

A number of cities, including Memphis, Louisville, Chattanooga, Mobile, and Birmingham, were investigated as possible sites for a condominium project. Several criteria were established. The area had to have several condominium projects already in existence since they did not want to be the first project in the area. Their experience had shown that the pioneers had to undertake a large educational effort, which usually took two years and a lot of money. The city should have a population of at least 250,000 so it would absorb a large number of condominiums if the company decided to add other projects at a later date. Lastly, the area should have a large number of residents in the target market for condominiums—young married couples and "empty nesters," couples whose children are grown and have moved out of the home.

Using census data, information obtained from Chambers of Commerce, and other real estate research sources, Thatcher narrowed the choice to Charlotte, North Carolina, and Jacksonville, Florida. In both places, condominiums had been marketed for two to three years, and a number of developments were being built. In Charlotte, however, the only land that was available for immediate development was not particularly well suited for multifamily building. It had been decided that land that had been zoned for condominium development, with utilities easily accessible, would be favored to avoid the normal two-year period to get undeveloped raw land ready for development. Therefore, it was without reservation that Thatcher made the decision to expand into the Jacksonville market.

Background on the Jacksonville Area

Jacksonville is the most populated city in Florida and ranks second in the Southeast and 23rd in the United States. In October of 1968, the city adopted a new charter which consolidated the city and county governments. All of Duval County is now operated as one government, and the consolidation made the new city of Jacksonville the largest city in the continental United States with 840 square miles (537,664 acres). To put the figures into comparative terms, the city is two thirds the size of the state of Rhode Island.

Recent growth has brought many young people to the Jacksonville area. In 1970, the median age of the population was 26 years, compared to 32.3 years for the state of Florida and 28.3 years for the total United States. Duval County has a large, rapidly growing economy, with a balanced employment profile and a rather diversified economic base. This diversification has produced a stable economy by minimizing its sensitivity to both industrial and national business cycles.

For a distance of approximately 100 miles in all directions, the area surrounding the city is predominantly rural in character. With over 500,000 residents, Jacksonville is the commercial and cultural center of northeast Florida and southeast Georgia. It is one of the principal distribution, insurance, and convention centers in the Southeast.

One of the major impacts on the city's economy is the presence of three large military installations in the area, particularly the Jacksonville Naval Air Station located in the southern part of the county on the St. Johns River just north of the city of Orange Park. This facility is one of the largest naval air bases in the United States. It is supported by a smaller air station, Cecil Field, located in the western part of the county, where several air squadrons operate in preparation for air carrier qualifications. The third facility, the Mayport Carrier Basin east of Jacksonville, has berthing capacity for three of the country's largest aircraft carriers. The military installations employ approximately 34,000 people including some 5,000 civilians, 9,000 shore-based military personnel, and 20,000 mobile/afloat military. Another 5,000 military employees are expected to be transferred to these facilities in the next year or two.

Extensive bedroom areas are forming just outside Duval County, reflecting lower tax rates, lower land prices, an absence of restrictive zoning ordinances, and a preference for suburban living. Also, the city of Jacksonville was busing children to achieve racial integration in the schools, and many residents were moving to Orange Park and other areas of Clay County (just south of Duval County) where there was no busing of students. The impact of all these factors made Clay County, and the Orange Park area in particular, a rapidly growing area.

The city of Orange Park lies adjacent to and south of the Duval County line, and is approximately 15 miles from the central business district of Jacksonville. Exhibit 1 presents a map of the area showing the location of Orange Park in relation to the naval air station, Cecil Field, and the business district of Jacksonville.

After talking with many real estate people in the area, and after reviewing the statistics presented in Exhibit 2, Mr. Thatcher decided to obtain an option on a 40-acre tract of land just west of the city limits of Orange Park. As shown in the exhibit, the residents of Orange Park had an above-average median family income for the area and were better educated than Duval County residents. Also, over half the population in the area worked outside the county (principally in Duval County). Thatcher thought the higher-income, better-educated people would be receptive to condominiums. Also, he felt that the close proximity to Duval County would be attractive to many potential purchasers.

Access to the site is off Blanding Boulevard (State Road 21 on the map), a heavily traveled two-lane thoroughfare with development, for the most part, consisting of commercial and single-family residential development. Within the

EXHIBIT 1
Map of Jacksonville and Orange Park area

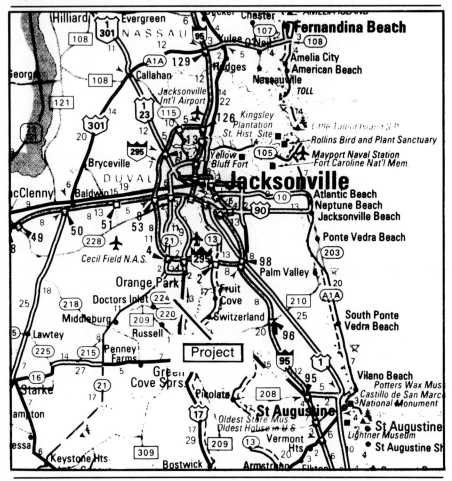

EXHIBIT 2
Selected statistics for Orange Park, Clay County, and Duval County/Jacksonville

	City of Orange Park	Clay County	Duval County/ Jacksonville
Total population, 1970	7,677	32,059	528,865
Median family income, 1970	$10,021	$8,430	$8,671
Median school years completed— 1970, adults	12.5	12.1	12.0
Percent of residents who work outside the county	—	53.5%	2.6%
Percent of residents who have lived in the same area for five years or more, 1970	30.0%	45.6%	67.1%

past year a considerable amount of multifamily development had occurred, but it was mainly concentrated further northeast in the vicinity of U.S. Highway 17.

Within one mile of the site to the north is a minor shopping center with a Winn-Dixie supermarket as the cornerstone tenant. Two and one half miles north, a 1 million-square-foot regional shopping center is being developed and is scheduled to open in 1975. The school system in the area is rated excellent, and several elementary schools as well as junior and senior high schools are in close proximity to the site. Churches of all denominations and hospital and recreation facilities are all well represented in the area.

The current housing market in the Orange Park area is composed substantially of single-family houses, with prices of these units beginning at $32,000. Apartments in the vicinity of the site have achieved 100 percent occupancy, with many of the apartments renting for between $150 and $200 per month. There are a number of condominium projects in the area, as shown in Exhibit 3, although almost all of them are situated much farther north. The price range on these condominium projects typically begins in the low $30,000 range and goes up to almost $60,000.

Marketing Strategy

The first question Thatcher had to resolve concerned the target market for the condominiums. There were three basic strategies he had been considering: (*a*) a specialty type product with a large amenity package oriented toward active, young "swinging" couples; (*b*) a project oriented toward the retiree market; or (*c*) a project oriented toward families who wanted to purchase their residence but could not afford a single-family house. Crow, Pope, and Land had considerable experience in building all three types of condominiums in the Atlanta area, and Thatcher was reluctant to consider other types of condominiums that the company had not had experience with. He reasoned that taking a product that had worked elsewhere would reduce some of the risk of entering a new, relatively unknown market. Also, use of a product that the company had built in Atlanta would save the cost of architect's fees, and he would be in a better position to negotiate with a contractor to build the units because he would know in advance what the costs should be (building costs in the Jacksonville area were virtually the same as costs in Atlanta).

EXHIBIT 3
Condominium projects in the Orange Park area

Project	Rooms	Square feet	Price range
Bay Meadows	2BR,2B –3BR,3B	1,350–2,243	$34,850–$48,300
Solano Grove	1BR,1B –3BR,3B	874–2,006	26,100– 58,200
Regency Woods	2BR,2B –4BR,2½B	1,456–2,102	35,500– 45,900
Sutton Place	2BR,2½B–4BR,2½B	1,366–1,842	31,500– 38,000
Baytree	2BR,1½B–4BR,3½B	1,404–2,214	32,000– 46,750
The Lakes	2BR,2B –3BR,2½B	1,330–2,050	37,500– 59,400
Oxford Forest	2BR,1½B–3BR,2½B	1,282–1,622	28,500– 35,500

Thatcher had located a site along the St. Johns River that would be suitable for the specialty, high-amenity product. There might be some environmental problems with the Army Corps of Engineers, who had jurisdiction over the site, but he thought these could be worked out. The Orange Park site under option would not be suitable for this type of project, which Thatcher thought should be built around a body of water. With the high land cost for an appropriate site, and with the high cost for all the recreational amenities, the company would have to price the condominiums under this strategy at about $40,000 (the same price charged for the comparable Riverbend Condominiums in Atlanta).

The optioned site was also not acceptable for the second alternative, a project oriented toward the retirees' market. Experience in Atlanta had shown that retired couples preferred to purchase condominiums with a golf course on site, and the present site was not suited for development of a golf course. Thatcher had located several possible sites suitable for this alternative several miles south of the property under option. Because of the very large investment involved in building a golf course, he felt that a project oriented toward this market would have to be a large one to support the high fixed cost of the golf course.

If the company decided to purchase the property under option, about 12 units per acre could be constructed, or about 480 in total. As they did with almost all their projects, the units would be built in several phases, with phase I consisting of 50 units. Thatcher had determined that units built in the Fairgrounds project in Atlanta could be built and sold profitably in Orange Park for $24,900 for a 1,040-square-foot, two-bedroom unit, and $29,900 for a 1,265-square-foot, three-bedroom unit. The price per square foot was comparable to the other condominium projects in the area, and the total price was well below most of them because of the smaller size. In addition to the difference in square footage and price, the Fairgrounds models also had different exteriors than the typical ones sold in the Jacksonville area; the Fairgrounds units used brick and aluminum siding, whereas most of the others had a stucco exterior. Although he basically believed that the Jacksonville condominium prospect was very similar to the Atlanta prospect, he wondered whether he should incorporate some stucco treatment into the exterior of the units if he should decide to follow through with this strategy.

Another issue he had not resolved concerned the extent to which the strategy should be oriented toward the large (and growing) military market. If he did define his target market as the military market, what impact would this have on the physical product and on his promotional strategy, which was still to be determined? Close to half of the residents of Orange Park worked at one of the three military installations in the area, and both the naval air station and Cecil Field were within seven miles of the proposed site. He was aware of the large word of mouth influence in the Navy—an apartment project not far from the site which was just beginning to lease new units had gone from 5 percent Navy to 30 percent Navy in less than two months.

Another question which concerned Thatcher was the low sales rate of the other condominiums in the area. He thought the reason was the relatively high prices, which caused them to compete directly against single-family housing. Also, he had shopped all the projects and found the on-site salesmen to be very uninformed and uninterested in selling the condominiums. He felt certain that this was hurting sales but was still not sure that the consumers in the Jacksonville/Orange Park area would buy condominiums, even in the price range he was proposing.

The senior officers of Crow, Pope, and Land would also expect a detailed promotional strategy as part of his report. In working with budget figures, he had determined that he could afford to spend $22,000 for promotion (1.5 percent of sales) for the first 50 units, which would be about 12 months' projected sales. Brochures, signs, business cards for salesmen, and other miscellaneous items would cost about $2,000, leaving $20,000 for media and production costs.

Crow, Pope, and Land used a small local advertising agency for all their apartment and condominium advertising in Atlanta. Thatcher was uncertain about the role he wanted the agency to play in this project and was worried that the agency was not attuned to the Jacksonville market. He wondered whether he should try to hire a Jacksonville agency but was afraid that the account was too small for anyone to pay much attention to it. Also, he felt that the retainer that any decent agency would want to handle the account, about $3,000, could be better spent on media. He had studied advertising and promotion in courses in college and thought he should consider creating the advertising himself.

There were really only two alternatives for media strategy in the Jacksonville area—radio and newspaper. There were nine AM radio stations and four FM stations. The rates for the four largest stations were all about the same, between $25 and $30 for a one-minute spot during drive time (6–10 A.M. and 3–7 P.M.) and about 20 percent cheaper at other times, assuming 12 spots per week for 13 weeks. There were two daily newspapers in Jacksonville, a morning paper with 210,000 circulation and an evening paper with 148,000 circulation. As a result of common ownership, there was a combination rate available which was only 10 percent higher than the $13.16 per column inch rate for the morning paper alone. The morning paper had a Sunday edition, with a circulation of 182,000 and a cost per column inch of $13.72.

Mr. Thatcher was also concerned about what message to use in his promotional campaign. He was uncertain to what extent they should mention the fact that there was no busing to schools, an important advantage for many potential buyers. He was worried that other people might be upset with the implied racism in such a campaign. He was also concerned with the implications for the advertising creative strategy as a result of the target market decision concerning whether or not to concentrate on the military market. Another advertising issue was the extent to which the copy should promote the fact that Crow, Pope, and Land was a large Atlanta developer, and that this was their first North Florida project.

The one decision Thatcher had made was that there was much opportunity for the company in the Jacksonville market, and, therefore, much opportunity for him personally to expand his responsibilities in the company. As a result, he wanted to make a recommendation that the company definitely enter the market; the only uncertainty was the strategy to be followed. The company had paid $1,000 for the initial option on the Orange Park property. Next week they had to either pay $20,000 to renew the option for 90 days or lose their $1,000 investment. If they decided to renew the option, this would give them time to arrange for the financing of the project and to arrange a production schedule with the contractors. They had to begin this planning immediately since it usually took at least six months to build condominiums, and that meant that they would have to act fast if they wanted to be selling condominiums by the height of the selling season in June. As he sat down to write the report containing his recommendations, Thatcher realized that a decision to renew the option would be a commitment to actually build the units he recommended.

Example Situation Analysis of Crow, Pope, and Land Enterprises (CPL)

CPL Condominium Enterprises, a subsidiary of CPL Enterprises, Inc., a residential housing and commercial builder, had built a number of *condominium* complexes in Atlanta, designed for specific segments such as retired couples, young swingers, families, and low-middle-income couples. In addition, they had several resort projects in Florida.

In order to reduce their dependence on the Atlanta condominium market, a *goal* of expanding into new geographic areas where profitable markets were opening up was developed by two CPL Condominium Enterprises VPs. The *tactics* were to choose a city of at least 250,000 population within a 400-mile radius of Atlanta, since forecasts of the housing market projected rapid growth in this general region in the coming few years. Dan Thatcher was to put together a marketing *strategy* discussing product, price, place, and promotion to pursue in reaching this goal. Since this discussion is centered around Dan Thatcher's review of the Orange Park condominium market, it will be assumed here that the product is *condominiums*. In the larger context of the company, which will be touched on at the end of this paper, the product considered is *housing*.

A.   NATURE OF DEMAND

1.   How do buyers currently go about buying condos?

In the search for housing, buyers will generally define the neighborhood they are interested in, then select among the alternatives within their price range. The decision to buy a condominium, rather than a single-family detached dwelling, may be influenced by several factors—price, ease of maintenance, amenities, and the like—which are discussed more thoroughly in part 2. The buyer will seek information to a high degree through media, family, friends, co-workers, real estate brokers, and, if available, reports on developers of other condominium projects to ascertain their reputation and workmanship quality. After looking at a number of developments, the decision of which condo to buy will probably be made at home or after a second or third look at the property under consideration. Sources of information about condos in the Jacksonville/ Orange Park area are probably newspapers, some broadcast coverage, and word of mouth. Although condos have existed for more than two years in this area, awareness level seems low due to the slow sales of condos in the area. In 1973, condos were not in vogue, and hence buyer knowledge and acceptability were not particularly well developed. The decision to purchase is made by the adults; if a couple, by a joint decision. This is the most important major purchase decision in most people's lives, thus much time, thought, and effort goes into the decision process. The buyer is highly influenced by the salesperson, the physical plant itself, friends, the real estate broker, and possibly the bank loan officer. This is usually a new purchase situation, evoking high interest, personal involvement, and excitement by the buyer. All of these factors contribute to a high risk associated with a poor purchase decision—it's hard to get rid of a condo that no one else wants either! A number of functional considerations enter into the decision, such as location, utilities, and convenience (more on this in part 2). A number of psychosocial considerations also enter into the decision, such as aesthetics, social contact, safety, prestige, and self-esteem. This being a durable good, the consumption time is long term.

2.   Can the market be meaningfully segmented?

Due to CPL Condominium Enterprises' expertise in building condo complexes geared toward specific segments, and since Dan Thatcher desires to use an existing set of plans for the new condo development, it seems best to segment the market into those areas CPL can build for— namely, singles, retired couples, and young (low-middle-income) families. In addition, due to the demographic composition of the area (50 percent employed by the Navy), a Navy/military segment is also relevant. Attributes important to each segment are ranked in Table 1. Table 2 then ranks these attributes together with the housing options in the area, limited here to condos, single-family homes, and rental apartments, since these are the housing types mentioned in the case. Since the median age of Jacksonville is 26, below both the Florida and national medians, we can probably safely assume that there are many young couples and singles associated with the large military labor base, perhaps a growing number of babies and children (helping to lower the median), and that the family life-cycle stage is generally early. Additional data on average household size, the age distribution, and income versus age would be helpful in this analysis. The high turnover rate of Orange Park residents suggests either a very mobile population or a very fast-growing area.

Comparing Tables 1 and 2, there is not a one-to-one correlation

TABLE 1

Attributes	Segments			
	Singles	Retirees	Young families	Navy (families)
Price	+ + + +	+ + + +	+ + + +	+ + + + +
Size	+	+	+ + + +	+ + +
Neighborhood	+ +	+ + +	+ + + +	+ +
Convenience to shopping	+ +	+ + +	+ + +	+
Schools	+	+	+ + + +	+ + +
Social acceptability	+ + + +	+ +	+ +	+ +
Social interaction	+ + + +	+ + +	+ +	+ +
Recreation/amenities	+ + + +	+ + + +	+ + +	+ + +
Safety	+ +	+ + + +	+ + + +	+ +
Low tax base	+	+ +	+ +	+ +
Accessibility to work	+ +	+	+ +	+ + + +
Mass transportation	+ +	+ + +	+ +	+ +
Access to entertainment	+ + +	+ +	+ +	+ +
Maintenance	+ + + +	+ + + +	+ + +	+ + +
Financing convenience*	+ + + +	+ +	+ + +	+ + +
Public works	+	+ + +	+	+
Land availability	+ +	+ +	+ + + +	+ +

* Defined as renting versus down payment/monthly mortgage commitments.

between all the boxed attributes of option: condo and segment. Note, however, that there is a correlation between options: apartment and singles segment.

B. EXTENT OF DEMAND
1. Sufficient demand for more condo housing?

Although there is limited information, one can still make some estimate of the total demand in the Jacksonville market. It is well known that nationally about 20 percent of the population moves each year. We also know from Exhibit 2 in the case that 32.9 percent of the population of Duval County (and a much higher percentage of Clay County) have lived there five years or less. On the basis of this information, we might expect about 5 percent of the households to be looking for a house; and, with an average of about 2.5 children and 4.7 people per family, the number of houses shifting hands may equal about 1 to 1.5 percent of the population or in the neighborhood of 6,000 to 7,000 homes. Even if we recognize that a

TABLE 2

	Options		
Attributes	Our condo	Rental apartment	Single-family home
Price	$\boxed{+\,+\,+\,+}$	$\boxed{+\,+\,+\,+}$	+ +
Size	+	+ +	$\boxed{+\,+\,+\,+}$
Neighborhood	+ + +	?	?
Convenience to shopping	+ + +	?	?
Schools	+	?	?
Social acceptability	+ +	+	$\boxed{+\,+\,+\,+}$
Social interaction	+ + +	+ + +	+
Recreation/amenities	+ +	+ + +?	+
Safety	+ +	+	+ +
Low tax base	$\boxed{+\,+\,+?}$	+?	+ + +?
Accessibility to work	$\boxed{+\,+\,+?}$	+ +?	+ +?
Mass transportation	+	+	+
Maintenance	$\boxed{+\,+\,+\,+}$	$\boxed{+\,+\,+\,+}$	+
Financing convenience*	+	$\boxed{+\,+\,+\,+}$	+
Land availability	+ +	+ +	$\boxed{+\,+\,+\,+}$
Equity	$\boxed{+\,+\,+\,+}$	+	$\boxed{+\,+\,+\,+}$

* Defined as renting versus down payment/monthly mortgage commitments.

large proportion of the 20 percent of the population that move in a typical year consists of young people moving from one apartment to another, it would seem that this estimate of 6,000 to 7,000 homes is extremely conservative. Since Jacksonville is a very rapidly growing area full of economic activity, and since the ''baby boomers'' are just entering the age where they will be buying houses, we might raise this estimate to around 10,000 homes. With projected sales of 50 units the first year, Crow, Pope, and Land is trying to achieve around .5 percent of the market.

What part of this will be condos is the next issue to judge.

2. Current market shares

We have no information to judge this. It appears that single-family home purchases dominate the purchasing mode and that apartment rentals are 100 percent occupied. There may exist excess demand for apartments. This can raise apartment rents (if no new apartments will soon be built), making the price advantage of renting less of a factor over time. Selective demand trends suggest that consumer awareness of condo developments is increasing and, along with that, public acceptance. Since single-family homes start selling at $32,000, it could be that condos are not selling because people can just as easily afford single-family homes. Banks usually like housing to account for only 25 to 30 percent of one's gross income; hence these could be too high priced, even though they are less than the other alternatives. Purchasing the smaller condo at $24,000 would lead to the following results:

a. 12 percent, 20-year mortgage:

$$\frac{\$24,000}{7.469} = \$3,213.28 \text{ or } \$267.77/\text{month} = 32.1 \text{ percent of income.}$$

b. 8 percent, 20-year mortgage:

$$\frac{\$24,000}{9.818} = \$2,444.49 \text{ or } \$203.71/\text{month} = 24.4 \text{ percent of income.}$$

It would be difficult for the average person to finance anything but the lower-priced condo at the lower interest rate. Of course, when Thatcher needs to make his decision, he cannot foresee possible future increases in interest rates.

C. NATURE OF COMPETITION

1. Present and future structure of competition

Seven other condo projects in the general area as well as numerous single-family home developments exist. Market shares are unknown, although we know that rental apartments have 100 percent occupancy. Financial resources of competitors are unknown. Marketing resources and skills of condo competitors, judged by their salespeople, are poor. They lack interest, enthusiasm, and knowledge of the projects they are trying to sell. Production resources and skills of competitors are unknown.

2. Current marketing programs of established competitors

We do not know much but, judging from the slow sales, it might be reasonable to suppose that consumer awareness is low, knowledge of market needs is poor, and the salesperson's role is a very critical part of the competition's marketing program, although it seems to be unsuccessful.

3. Opportunity for another competitor?

The fact that the property Thatcher has an option to buy is *zoned* for condos indicates that the planning body of the county feels that condos will serve as one of the housing mixes for the area. Since the opportunity for CPL to drastically price cut the market exists, there does seem to be opportunity for another competitor. Whether buyer demand exists is another question, however.

4. Retaliatory moves of competitors?

Competitors can probably drop their prices somewhat. The other developments appear to be a few miles away from this one, though, so perhaps another condo development may not greatly affect the competitors.

D. ENVIRONMENTAL CLIMATE
1. Relevant social, political, economic, and technological trends

Since this project is located in the South, busing is a hot issue. People opposed to busing (which is taking place in Jacksonville/Duval County) will want to live in an area with no forced busing. Condominiums are just hitting the market—they are in a young product life-cycle stage; thus social acceptability is currently in the developing stage.

The last lottery for the Vietnam War draft took place in 1973. The war is starting to wind down. In 1975, some military ships were mothballed. Hence the lifeblood of Orange Park, which is over half military, will soon be in a transition stage. Basing a project on military personnel housing demand is probably very risky at this time.

Some of these factors may increase the attractiveness of condos. People will want to live closer to work but in an area with low land rates and a low tax base due to the ever-increasing squeeze on their pocketbooks. A condo may be easier to keep cool; the accessibility to a pool, which a condo development in Florida is likely to have, may further increase its attractiveness.

E. STAGE OF PRODUCT LIFE CYCLE

The product category, condominiums, is at an early life-cycle point. Some people are aware of their existence, but the concept is not yet so well tested that people are rushing out to buy condos. As the product ages and more people begin purchasing condos, social acceptability will increase. The slow sales of the present condo developments in the area are indicative of this lack of social acceptability due to the product's early life-cycle stage. Of course, other factors that are perhaps more important (price, location, etc.) enter into this, too. The fact that one of CPL's development criteria was that other condo projects should have existed in the area for at least two years supports the argument that an educational and acceptability process must first take place before the product sells well. The more knowledge the consumer has, the more he/she will want to buy this product.

F. COST STRUCTURE OF THE INDUSTRY

Comparing our project to the other projects' $/square feet range, the CPL project is about average in $/square foot price, although lower in total price due to the low square footage of the units. A comparison with competitors is presented in Table 3. The highs and lows are boxed. We know that $22,000 of selling costs equals 1.5 percent of sales. Hence, the first 50 units will bring in an expected revenue of

$$\frac{\$22,000}{.015} = \$1,466,667.$$

For sale of 480 units, total revenues would equal

$$\frac{480}{50} \times \$1,466,667 = \$14,080,003.$$

TABLE 3 Comparison of cost by competitor

Project	Rooms	Sq. ft.	Price range	$/Sq. ft. range
Bay Meadows	2B2B/3B3B	1,350–2,243	$34,850–$48,300	$25.81–$21.53
Solana Grove	1B1B/3B3B	879–2,006	26,100– 58,200	29.86– 29.01
Regency Woods	2B2B/4B2½B	1,456–2,102	35,500– 45,900	24.38– 21.84
Sutton Place	2B2½B/4B2½B	1,366–1,842	31,500– 38,000	23.06– 20.63
Baytree	2B1½B/4B3½B	1,404–2,214	32,000– 46,150	22.79– 21.12
The Lakes	2B2B/3B2½B	1,330–2,050	37,500– 59,400	28.20– 28.98
Oxford Forest	2B1½B/3B2½B	1,282–1,622	28,500– 35,500	22.23– 21.89
CPL	2 Bdr	1,040	$24,900	23.94
	3 Bdr	1,265	$29,900	23.64
Single-family home		Assume 1,400	$32,000	$22.86

Other costs we know of:

Land = $721,000 (include $1,000 + $20,000 in option).
Selling costs = 1.5% = $210,000 ($14 million × .015).

Assume construction is approximately $20/square foot:

1,000 square feet × 480 condos × $20/square foot
= $9,600,000 per condo, approximately.

Sales	$14,080,000	100%
CGS	9,600,000	68%
Gross margin	$ 4,480,000	32%
Sales	210,000	
Land	721,000	8%
Other (guess)	100,000	
Net profit (pretax)	$ 3,449,000	24%

The project looks profitable at this point, if these assumptions are valid. If the company highly leverages the development, this would be a very attractive investment indeed.

G. SKILLS OF THE FIRM
1. Marketing

Apparently the firm as a whole has been quite successful, and much of this success for a real estate company must be attributed to marketing. A small Atlanta advertising agency is used for the Atlanta apartment and condominium advertising, but Thatcher is not sure the agency will be able to adequately and successfully come up with a Jacksonville marketing plan. To hire a local Jacksonville agency, about $3,000 would need to be spent on a retainer, which Thatcher thought could be better spent on media.

Since he had studied advertising and promotion in college courses, Thatcher thought he had the skills to create the advertising himself. If CPL commonly has its project managers create the advertising for projects, then

I would question whether the marketing skills of the firm were really very good. I do not think Thatcher is who we want promoting a $14 million condo complex!

We do not know how successful CPL has been with its condo developments, but we can only assume that continued existence and expansion in the business means that it has been successful thus far, and hence its marketing is good.

2. Production

Again, we don't have too much data to access this, but judging from the size of some of the projects, such as the Atlanta Center Project, the Sheraton Hong Kong Hotel, and the Cumberland, Fairington, and Northlake total community complexes, CPL must be able to "produce" buildings or else it wouldn't be undertaking such large efforts. Thatcher says that CPL has experience building the three condominium types in Atlanta (swinging couples, retirees, and young families) and could thus negotiate well with the contractor in Jacksonville, since he would have a good idea of what the actual costs would be. He also mentioned that this "product had worked"; therefore, he thought it could work again. Also, perhaps the use of brick and aluminum siding exteriors is popular and well liked, thus helping the firm to sell a slightly different product better than the stucco exterior norm in Jacksonville.

3. Management

Apparently, the company has a lot of MBA types and, due to the project-management emphasis, fairly aggressive self-starters. Crow and Pope had a good record of success in the real estate brokerage business prior to their forming CPL. It looks like we can assume the company has good management skills and talented, although perhaps overly confident, people on staff.

4. Financial

Their financial skills are probably very good, since the owners have over five years of experience in the business and the project managers, similar to Thatcher, have business training backgrounds/education. Due to the size of the projects the parent company is undertaking, we can assume it has a good financial relationship with its bank and must be doing well to continue getting large sums of financing. The subsidiary, CPL Condominiums, is thus backed by a strong parent company. The parent company is probably making nice profits from its hotel operations, as high margins are typically the rule in this area.

5. R&D

R&D in terms of a popular product design appears to be good, since it sounds like a brick and aluminum siding exterior condo is an attractive and long-lasting exterior. Modifying their developments to meet the needs of particular market segments in terms of amenities shows good insight in producing a product to meet the needs of the consumer.

However, the background research Thatcher has performed for judging the Jacksonville condo market is quite limited. He is basing his decision on very limited data. A much better decision could be reached with more research into demographic trends in the area, determining the mobility of the Navy personnel, and finding out how future road work will favorably or adversely affect this proposed condo development. The fact that apartments are 100 percent occupied but condo sales are slow should cause Thatcher to question whether condos are what is needed here. Perhaps apartments would be a better fit to community needs.

As far as comparing CPL's skills to the competitors, we do not know enough about the competitors, except that their marketing seems weak, to make a particularly valid comparison.

H.   FINANCIAL RESOURCES OF THE FIRM

As the calculations in part F show, the financial return on this investment looks very attractive. Since CPL Condominium Enterprises has the backing of the parent company, I think it is safe to assume that financing this project will pose no problem.

I.   DISTRIBUTION/PROMOTIONAL STRUCTURE AVAILABLE

Classic distribution institutions are not a directly relevant dimension here. However, the existence of an institutional structure for promotion is important.

This is where media advertising comes in: a number of types could be utilized, under the constraint of $20,000 for the first year's promotional activities after spending $2,000 for brochures, wages, and business cards. Advertising on commute time radio could take up most of this budget, if four radio stations are used, with 12 spots a week for 13 weeks (4 stations × $30/minute × 12 spots/week × 13 weeks = $18,700). Advertising in the newspaper only, using the Sunday rate of $13.72/column inch would allow $\frac{\$20,000}{13.72/\text{col. in.}} = 1,455$ inches over 26 weeks. This is 56 column inches per week, which seems like a lot of newspaper coverage. A combination of these two mixes would probably be good. The Atlanta advertising agency would be able to determine what would be best. In addition, the agency might try to find a Navy newsletter to advertise in because this market, if encouraged to investigate the condo alternative, might through word of mouth be a very helpful advertising method. Also, the use of coupons in the paper to be exchanged for a gift upon coming to look at the development may further increase buying traffic. These media institutions are available for CPL use.

Problems and Opportunities

A.   Problems
1.   Dan Thatcher:
   a.   His inexperience in the Florida condominium market.
   b.   His ambitiousness, possibly causing him to miss opportunities as he sees the "success" of this project promoting his career.

      c. His shortsightedness in only considering condominiums rather than apartments also, which may be more suited to the community needs.

2. Economic dependence of the areas on the three military installations.
3. Availability of close substitutes to condos, namely, similarly priced single-family housing.
4. The instability of the Orange Park housing market, symptomized by the high turnover/mobility.
5. Advertising agency located in Atlanta, with no promotion experience in this Florida, highly military market.
6. High prices of the projects.
7. Low social acceptability, as shown by the low demand.
8. Transportation:
   a. The project under consideration is located on a heavy use corridor. More development will cause traffic problems.
   b. New freeway allowing easy access to the navy base is under construction, thus easy accessibility to work is not yet present.
9. If the young swingers or retirees are the chosen market segment, need more land to put in amenities. Army Corps of Engineers may not approve other option plot if that one is pursued.
10. Need better demographic data to properly evaluate the market, demand, and supply.
11. Public still needs educating about the product itself.

B. Opportunities
1. Very attactive area to build, as there are low taxes, low land rates, and no busing.
2. Military market is large.
3. The aluminum siding and brick exterior condo can provide a new look and style to the Jacksonville condo market.
4. Market for rental housing is excellent, due to low vacancy rates, a large influence of relatively mobile military personnel, and low median age of the area.
5. Good reputation and experience of CPL. They know housing construction and costs. Financial strength of CPL.
6. Market open to new competitor; fast-growing regions are the Southeast and Florida.
7. The plot under option is zoned for condos.

C. On balance, the situation is:
1. Very favorable for *housing*.
2. Neutral for *condo*.

Commentary on the Case Analysis

Table 4 presents our point-by-point summary evaluation of the case analysis. In our view, it is very well done, and our guess is you will agree. We should point out, however, that it is far easier to evaluate an analysis than to do one.

TABLE 4 Summary of the evaluation of the case analysis

Criteria	Analysis
1. Completeness	Very complete on all aspects of situation analysis structure Reasonable depth of analysis
2. Avoids rehash	Good Most points are made with an analysis purpose
3. Makes reasonable assumptions	Excellent
4. Proper problem statements	Excellent; has not confused them with symptoms Somewhat incomplete; e.g., competitors
5. Proper opportunity statements	Good; has not given action statements
6. Deals with objectives realistically	Very good; has questioned this issue Alternatives given and discussed
7. Recognizes alternatives	*
8. Is not assertive	Generally OK Some actions are implied in situation analysis, but not a big problem here
9. Discusses pros and cons of alternatives	*
10. Makes effective use of financial and other quantitative information	Excellent All options are given a good quantitative appraisal
11. Reaches a clear and logical decision	*
12. Makes good use of evidence developed in situation analysis	*
13. Overall appraisal	A very good situation analysis of a tough situation

* Not applicable as only situation analysis is presented.

Part 2

Introduction to Marketing Decision Making

In Part 1 of this book you have studied how marketing decisions should be made. The cases in this section are designed to let you begin to apply this approach in decision making. These cases should be viewed as an opportunity to practice your skills on some broad issue marketing cases before we go to other sections of this book, where we study cases that are more specifically tied to product or distribution, and so on.

Case 1

General Motors: Cadillac*

When Executive Vice President Lloyd Reuss took his job as the head of all North American car operations for General Motors (GM) in February 1986, he had a four-item list of goals. One of the four—clearly of the highest priority for GM—concerned a single division, Cadillac. The words were strong and simple: "Restore Cadillac products and image to where they are the standard of the world."[1] The task before Reuss was an ominous one. The U.S. auto market, General Motors, and Cadillac had all changed significantly since he joined GM in 1959. At that time, the U.S. market largely belonged to the "big three" domestic producers (GM 42 percent, Ford 28 percent, Chrysler 11 percent), and Cadillac *was* the "standard of the world." Now, 30 years later, things had changed. The three major domestic producers' market share has fallen to 67.8 percent, and Cadillac's share and reputation in the luxury market is being challenged not only by domestic competition but also by European and Asian competitors as well.

In order to analyze Cadillac's position in the market, Reuss must seek the answers to several questions. For example: Is it selling the right products? Are its products targeted at the right market? Does its image appeal to the buyers Cadillac seeks? Does Cadillac's advertising effectively reach the right market and convey Cadillac's desired image?

Current Environmental Factors

Throughout the 1950s and 1960s, while energy was plentiful and inexpensive, American car manufacturers enjoyed great success building cars that were large and powerful. During the 1970s, energy prices increased—the product of temporary shortages in the supply of oil. As a result, import manufacturers,

---

* This case was prepared from public sources by Eric P. Andrew, under the supervision of Thomas C. Kinnear. Copyright © 1989 by Thomas C. Kinnear.

[1] Jerry Flint, "Hold the Velveeta—Please Pass the Brie," *Forbes* 8 (September 1986), p. 30.

many of which were building small, fuel-efficient automobiles, were in prime position to take advantage of the situation. With the influx of these fuel-thrifty imports, the domestic portion of the U.S. automobile market began to shrink from approximately 96.5 percent in 1957 to 85 percent in 1973, to 77 percent in 1979, and finally to approximately 68 percent in 1987.[2] Most of these imports were coming from Japan (Toyota, Nissan, Honda, etc.), now the world's largest producer of motor vehicles.

Western European countries also have been major suppliers of automobiles to the U.S. market. Makers such as Volkswagen, Mercedes-Benz, and BMW from West Germany; Volvo and Saab from Sweden; to a lesser degree, Peugeot and Renault from France; and sporadically, Fiat, Lancia, and Alfa Romeo from Italy. Also, during the 1980s the Yugoslavians (Yugo) and the Koreans (Hyundai and partnerships through Ford and GM) began exporting cars to the United States. (See Exhibit 1 for 1987 import sales.)

Throughout the energy shortage and until the mid-1980s, the Japanese enjoyed favorable yen/dollar exchange rates and were, therefore, in large part able to offer vehicles that cost less than comparable U.S. or West European products. The Japanese manufacturers also had significant success in producing

EXHIBIT 1   Selected 1987 U.S. import sales

Manufacturer	Country	Sales
Acura	Japan	109,470
Alfa Romeo	Italy	6,320
Audi	West Germany	41,322
BMW	West Germany	87,839
Eagle/Renault	France	13,991
Ford/Kia	South Korea	26,750
Honda	Japan	312,218
Hyundai	South Korea	263,610
Isuzu	Japan	39,587
Jaguar	Great Britain	22,919
Mazda	Japan	206,354
Mercedes-Benz	West Germany	89,918
Merkur	West Germany	14,301
Mitsubishi	Japan	67,954
Nissan	Japan	405,996
Peugeot	France	9,422
Saab	Sweden	45,106
Subaru	Japan	175,864
Toyota	Japan	583,809
Volkswagen	West Germany	130,641
Volvo	Sweden	106,539
Yugo	Yugoslavia	48,812

Source: *Automotive News, 1988 Market Data Book.*

---

[2] Sales/Registrations, "Market Shares for 36 Years," *Automotive Industries—1988 Market Data Book Issue,* May 25, 1988, p. 32.

these small, fuel-efficient automobiles with high quality. However, the U.S. government, pressured by GM, Ford, and Chrysler, imposed a "voluntary restraint," or quota, on the number of Japanese cars which could be exported to the United States. With this quota and with the appreciation of the yen, which occurred in the mid- to late-1980s, Japanese manufacturers began to lose their ability to sell large volumes of small cars and still make desirable profit margins. These factors began to force the Japanese to adjust their product mix to include a greater percentage of the more profitable larger, upscale, and specialty automobiles.

While the Japanese first concentrated on small, fuel-efficient cars, the European car manufacturers, with Volkswagen as the possible exception, have targeted distinct market niches. Mercedes-Benz, BMW, Audi, Saab, and Volvo have all, to varying degrees, concentrated on the upper segments of the market. The Koreans and Yugoslavians have targeted the low-end market and, due to the strength of the Japanese yen against the U.S. dollar and other currencies, have replaced Japan as the low-cost automotive exporters to the U.S. market.

In response to the high cost of fuel in the mid-1970s, the U.S. big three began to downsize their products and increase the number of small and fuel-efficient models. As a result, cars in the 1980s are generally smaller and more fuel efficient than earlier models. However, when fuel prices in the mid- to late-1980s stabilized, manufacturers began to build and consumers began to purchase the larger and more powerful models as they had in previous years. These cars were, however, still more efficient than the vehicles of the 1960s.

Car sales are a function of the economy. When work forces are employed and the economic outlook is favorable, sales will more than likely be healthy. If gasoline prices are perceived as high or not stable, sales of small, fuel-efficient vehicles will rise. In the mid-80s, during a period of high interest rates and a slow economy, domestic automobile manufacturers offered large cash rebates and attractive low-interest financing (as low as 0 percent on a 24-month term by American Motors) to spur sales. During this period, when customers shopped, they not only shopped for the best model but for the best sale incentive.

Developments in the Luxury Car Market

Traditional versus Functional Luxury

The U.S. luxury car market can be classified into two segments: traditional and functional. U.S. manufacturers have typically produced entries to the traditional segment, and the Europeans, the functional segment. Traditional luxury cars have been represented primarily by Cadillacs and Lincolns in the first tier and Oldsmobile, Buick, Mercury, and Chrysler in the second. The functional luxury cars of Europe were primarily made up of Germany's Mercedes-Benz, BMW, and Audi; Britain's Rolls-Royce and Jaguar; and certain models of Sweden's Saab and Volvo.

Traditional luxury cars strive to make the driving experience as effortless as possible. This has been accomplished by providing passengers with plush, living-room-style interiors and rides so smooth that Mercury commercials of the mid-1970s boasted that a Cartier jeweler could flawlessly cut a diamond while riding in the back seat of a Mercury luxury car. The functional luxury car, on the other hand, attempts to put the driver in touch with the road via steering and suspension systems that inform the driver of the immediate environment.

Throughout Cadillac's history, the division has had a variety of competitive products to contend with. In the 1930s, brands such as Packard, Pierce-Arrow, Auburn, Cord, Imperial, and Lincoln were vying for a piece of the luxury car market. By the early 1960s, most of these great marques had become memories with only Ford's Lincoln division and Chrysler's Imperial (until 1985) left to offer a measurable amount of domestic competition.

Domestic Competition

As Cadillac plotted its strategy for the luxury car market, Ford's Lincoln wasn't far behind. In 1979, the Town Car/Coupe, Lincoln's equivalent to the de Ville, was downsized to dimensions similar to the Cadillac. (See Exhibit 2 for a description of models.) In that same year, the Mark V, competitor to the Eldorado, was also downsized. The new Mark VI (each new design of the Mark series advances one Roman numeral) in fact shared the same platform as the

EXHIBIT 2 Descriptions of models, domestic comparison

	1978 target	*1988 target*
Cadillac		
de Ville/Fleetwood	Traditional large, 4-door, 6-passenger, rear wheel drive, V–8	New size traditional, 4-door, 6-passenger, front wheel drive, V–8
Brougham	N/A	Traditional large, 4-door, 6-passenger, rear wheel drive, V–8
Eldorado	Traditional large, 2-door, front wheel drive, V–8	International size, 2-door, front wheel drive, V–8
Seville	International size, 4-door, front wheel drive, V–8	International size, 4-door, front wheel drive, V–8
Allante	N/A	2-seat, coupe/convertible, functional
Lincoln		
Town Car	Traditional large, 4-door, 6-passenger, rear wheel drive, V–8	Traditional large, 4-door, 6-passenger, rear wheel drive, V–8
Mark V/VII	Traditional large, 2-door, rear wheel drive, V–8	Smaller, functional 2-door, rear wheel drive, V–8
Versailles/Continental	International size, 4-door, rear wheel drive, V–8, traditional market	International size, functional, 4-door, front wheel drive, V–6

Town Car; therefore, it shared similar overall dimensions and was now for the first time available with four doors. In 1982, Lincoln introduced the Continental, the replacement for the poor selling Versailles. Both cars were direct competition to Cadillac's Seville and attempted to emulate virtues of the Seville. The new Continental went so far as to borrow certain styling cues from the Seville, particularly the "bustle" style trunk.

In 1984, Lincoln's strategy began to change. This year Lincoln introduced the Mark VII. No longer built off the Town Car/Coupe chassis, the Mark VII was back to purely a two-door body style and offered two distinct versions: the traditional luxury model based on the Designer Series, and the functional luxury model—the LSC. The Mark VIIs used a newly developed air suspension system not found in any other car in the United States. The LSC version came with upgraded sport-oriented appointments such as European-style seats and a firmer version of the air suspension. Over the following years, a tachometer and a higher output engine were also added to the LSC to increase its functional appeal.

In 1988, Lincoln introduced an all new design for the Continental. (See Exhibit 3.) Borrowing heavily on the functional theme of the Mark VII LSC, the Continental now seemed as eager to differentiate itself from the Seville as it was earlier to emulate it. According to Maryann N. Keller, automotive industry analyst and vice president of the New York brokerage firm Furman, Selz, Mager, Deltz and Birney, ". . . Lincoln's new Continental, priced just under $30,000, is demonstrating that an American car maker can produce an automobile that combines appealing features from two continents [Europe and North America]. The body style and interior appointments have a definite European flavor. The size and generous complement of creature comforts are distinctly American. Though it could use a more powerful engine, the Continental signals Ford's arrival as a real challenger in the functional luxury car market."[3]

Foreign Competition—European

As Cadillac moved through the 1960s and 70s, the European luxury cars were emerging as serious alternative types of luxury automobiles. Rolls-Royce of England, long recognized as providing expensive, hand-built luxury cars, was never a Cadillac alternative. Mercedes-Benz, however, was a different kind of luxury car. If Cadillacs were as plush as fine living rooms, the Mercedes-Benz was as functional as a well-appointed study. The Mercedes-Benz mission was not to surround the driver or passengers in cushions of soft velour or provide them with a silky smooth ride, but to provide firm, supportive seating and a controlled ride in an automobile engineered for traveling at high speeds on the German autobahn.

---

[3] Maryann N. Keller, "Streetwise Showdown in the High-Priced Sector," *Motor Trend*, October 1988, p. 138.

EXHIBIT 3   1988 Continental

The heritage of today's Mercedes-Benz can be traced back to 1885 and the streets of Mannheim, Germany. It was then that Carl Friedrich Benz produced the world's first motor car. While others had pioneered and patented the gas engine, Benz applied it to a passenger-carrying vehicle.

Since the very beginning, Mercedes-Benz has stood for solid engineering. All of the company's automobiles are targeted to various price points in the functional luxury segment. While a $30,980 entry-level 190–D 2.5 model may share components with the top of the line $79,840 560–SEC, there are no other "lesser" divisions that might require Mercedes-Benz components. This also affords Mercedes-Benz the luxury of maintaining a single automobile focus. However, the company is also one of the world's largest medium- and heavy-duty truck manufacturers.

As the 1970s progressed and the 1980s approached, additional European manufacturers began to market their products in the functional luxury segment. Bavarian Motor Works (BMW) of West Germany moved from importing primarily two-door sports coupes to vehicles similar to Mercedes-Benz. BMW's strategy differed from Mercedes in that BMW catered even more so to the sport-oriented functional luxury buyer. The BMW product offerings begin with the small two- and four-door 3 series, the four-door midsize 5 series, large four-door 7 series, and the two-door 6 series. Over the past few years, BMW has broadened its product offering by introducing the previously mentioned 3 series four-door. The all new 1987 BMW 7 series includes a replacement for the 1986 735i model as well as an all new model for 1988, the 750iL. The 750iL is the largest, and at $70,000 the most expensive, sedan BMW has ever sold in the United States. The 750iL is unique from the lesser 735i in its 4.5-inch-longer wheelbase, distinctive hood and grille treatment, and most notably its 12-cylinder engine. The 750iL is $13,000 more expensive than the 735i and is the only five-passenger sedan in the world to offer a 12-cylinder engine. (See Exhibit 4.)

As the functional luxury market has developed, Mercedes-Benz has also become considered by many to be the ultimate car in the luxury market. (However, it is recently being challenged by BMW.) According to the automotive research company, J. D. Powers and Associates, Mercedes-Benz owners rated their cars and dealer service higher than Cadillac owners did when asked to rate the level of satisfaction of vehicle ownership and dealer service.[4] The Mercedes-Benz line is similar to that of the BMW. The 190 Class is similar in size to the BMW 3 series, the 300 Class the 5 series, and the S Class the 7 series. Mercedes-Benz also offers various two-door coupe and convertible models. In 1987, the combined U.S. sales of Mercedes-Benz and BMW reached approximately 178,000 vehicles, over half of Cadillac's current volume. (See Exhibit 5 for complete market segment sales analysis.)

---

[4] J. D. Powers reports from various years.

EXHIBIT 4 1988 BMW 735i and 1987 Mercedes-Benz S-Class

THE LUXURY CAR AS ONLY BMW COULD ENVISION IT.

When most automakers speak of vision, it's usually to discuss the rake of a windshield.

When BMW employs the term, it's to expound a philosophy.

One of unremitting zeal for performance, for which there is no greater thesis than the new BMW 735i.

A car which emerged after seven years, three million test miles and over 400 prototypes as not just a new luxury car. But a new conception of the luxury car.

LUXURY RETHOUGHT FROM MACROCOSM TO MICROCOSM

That the BMW 735i heralds a new vision of the luxury car is proclaimed in every feature, from its largest component to its minutest detail.

From a torque-rich new 208-horsepower engine whose catalytic converter paradoxically enhances both fuel economy and performance; to electronic variable assist power steering that provides something rare in ultra-luxury cars, a feel of the road.

From a veritable brain trust of technology that optimizes driver, engine and brake performance (the check control alone monitors 26 functions on a single readout); to 9-mph bumpers at a time when the industry standard has dropped to 2.5 mph.

From computer-perfected front and rear crush zones; to a seat belt that adjusts itself automatically to the size of the driver.

From an elegantly sensuous interior swathed in supple, hand-crafted leather, to a buffer between suspension and chassis that banishes road noise from an already serene interior.

From air-conditioning considered the world's strongest and most automated ("Auto Motor und Sport), to an electronic automatic transmission that lets you choose sport, economy or manual shifting modes.

And, finally, from a wider, longer, lower, more feline and aerodynamic body, to seats that "remember" positions for three different drivers, including outside mirror settings.

A 3,800-POUND WATCH.

To manufacture such a total rethink of the luxury car mandates a

rethink of the whole assembly process. Engine tolerances one-fifth the thickness of a human hair.

A rigorous 37-step rust-proofing and painting regimen.

Inquisition-like inspections, demanding not a hundred or even a thousand steps, but a torturous 7,000-step process.

With a daily average of one quality control inspector for every car off the assembly line.

The result is the new BMW 735i. A luxury sedan more akin to a 3,800-lb. Swiss watch than an automobile.

A creation which could only be the handiwork of visionaries.

A group of whom invite you to relish in their vision. Which can be accomplished by a test drive of the new BMW 735i at your authorized BMW dealer.

THE ULTIMATE DRIVING MACHINE.

EXHIBIT 4   *(concluded)*

THE MERCEDES-BENZ S-CLASS:
THE ONE THING MORE IMPORTANT THAN THE
TECHNOLOGY INSIDE IT IS THE TRADITION BEHIND IT.

A "big Mercedes" has crowned the line for almost as long as there has been a Mercedes-Benz.

This is Mercedes-Benz engineering at its most ambitious. And at its most assertive. From the 540K of 1936 pictured at left, to the S-Class sedan of 1987 shown above, every big Mercedes and its performance has seemed to scale slightly larger than life.

The 540K, for example, thundered into legend on the power of a supercharged eight-cylinder engine and the flamboyance of low-slung roadster coachwork. Half a century of technological progress later, the S-Class seems to glide rather than thunder over the road; in the case of the flagship 560 SEL Sedan on the roads of its native Europe, two tons of S-Class authority, capable of gliding along at 142 mph all day.

The Mercedes-Benz impulse to engineering masterstrokes marks the S-Class in other ways as well. In a body design that brilliantly combines large dimensions and low aerodynamic drag. In handling agility that large sedans have seldom aspired to, much less achieved. In vital technological innovations—an Anti-lock Braking System (ABS); and a Supplemental Restraint System (SRS) with driver's-side air bag and knee bolster, and emergency tensioning retractors at both front seat belts — that are gradually being emulated by other large sedans.

And laid over this bedrock of technical excellence, a thick layer of civilization and creature comfort. Experienced within a spacious cabin redolent of fine leathers, plush with velour carpeting, garnished with precious handworked woods.

Part limousine, part performance car— the uncommon versatility of the S-Class is reflected in its selection not only by connoisseurs of automotive luxury, but also by most of today's top-ranked Grand Prix motor racing fraternity.

The S-Class is available in three distinctive sedan models and as a two-plus-two closed coupe. You will find nothing to compare with them, in form or in function, wherever you look in the automotive world. They are unique, as is the tradition that spawned them.

Engineered like no other car in the world

EXHIBIT 5 Calendar year U.S. car sales

	1987	1986	1985	1984	1983
	Domestic luxury markets (units)				
Cadillac	261,284	304,057	298,762	320,017	300,337
Lincoln	166,037	177,584	165,138	151,475	101,574
Total domestic sales	7,081,262	8,214,897	8,204,542	7,951,523	6,795,295
	Luxury market (units)				
Domestic					
Cadillac (C)	261,284	304,057	298,762	320,017	300,337
Lincoln (L)	166,037	177,584	164,868	151,475	101,574
Import					
Acura (A)	109,470	52,869	*	*	*
Audi (AU)	41,322	59,797	74,061	71,237	47,936
BMW (B)	87,839	96,759	87,832	70,897	59,242
Jaguar (J)	22,919	24,464	20,528	18,044	15,815
Mercedes-Benz (M)	89,918	99,314	89,098	79,222	73,692
Total (C,L)	427,321	481,641	463,630	471,492	401,911
Total (A,AU,B,J,M)	351,468	333,203	271,519	239,400	196,685
Total luxury market	778,789	814,844	735,149	710,892	598,596
Total U.S. car sales	10,225,304	11,453,705	11,045,784	10,393,230	9,181,036

* Not in production.

Source: *Automotive News, 1988 Market Data Book. MYMA Motor Vehicle Facts & Figures '88*

The third German player in the luxury car market is Audi. Audi reached an all time high U.S. sales volume of over 74,000 units in 1985 due in large part to the sleekly styled 5000 series (48,057 units). The size of a mid-Mercedes and BMW offering, the 5000 was priced lower and could be purchased with one of the first applications of four-wheel drive in a passenger car. However, in 1986 under reports that 5000s equipped with automatic transmissions could unintentionally accelerate, sales began to slide. In 1987, sales were off 44.2 percent from just two years earlier.

For the 1988 model year, in an effort to restore Audi's presence in the luxury car market, the company introduced an all new replacement for the 4000 series, now dubbed the 80 (as it is in Europe). For the 1989 model year, the Audi 5000 has been relaunched as the Audi 100 and 200 (depending on engine size). The 100 and 200 models do not differ from the 5000 series before them in exterior appearance. However, the interior has been redesigned, and the Audi engineers are quick to point out the new engineering developments that differentiate the 100/200 Audis from the old 5000 series.

Foreign Competition—Japanese

The mid- to late-1980s have been accompanied by generally stable fuel costs. As a result, manufacturers are again offering larger models and more powerful engines. In addition, the late 1980s has also included a weaker dollar against other Western currencies such as the West German mark and the Japanese yen. A weak dollar makes buying West German or Japanese imports more expensive. In an effort to maintain acceptable margins on their automobiles, many of the foreign manufacturers have raised prices. This upscale movement in prices by these manufacturers is accompanied, in many cases, by efforts to market models that are also further upscale in class and content.

In the late 1980s, a strong Japanese yen helped create a situation in which the Japanese were no longer the low-cost producers. No longer were the Japanese able to build entry-level cars and price them as competitively against domestic, Korean, and Yugoslavian entries as they had in previous years. The Japanese, unable to make their desired profit margins on these vehicles, began to expand their product line upward to include a greater proportion of compact and midsize cars. These cars include larger models of Honda Accord, Toyota Camry and Cressida, and Nissan Maxima.

Watching the Germans move further upscale in image and in price, Honda saw an opportunity to provide European-style functional luxury cars, but at the price of traditional domestic luxury models. Acura also places emphasis on dealer service. In combination with product quality, dealer service accounted for the number one rating in the 1988 J. D. Powers Consumer Satisfaction Index.

Acura, and other soon-to-be-released Japanese luxury cars from Toyota (Lexus) and Nissan (Infiniti), hope to appeal to those import buyers that have bought nonluxury imports in the past and now want to move upscale but maintain certain import virtues. Acura models include the midsize Legend. The Legend comes well equipped with four-wheel power disc brakes, air conditioning, power door locks and windows, and stereo radio with cassette tape deck—all standard. Like the European functional luxury cars, Acura also pays special attention to the vehicle's handling and performance. To that end, the Legend carries a high-tech racing-bred multivalve V–6 engine and a suspension not found in any other Honda vehicle. Of the Acura Legend, automotive analyst Maryann N. Keller said, "In less than three years, Honda's Acura division will surpass the magic 100,000-unit mark, which means it will outsell every high-priced European brand in the market."[5] Hans Jordan, head of U.S. marketing for Mercedes-Benz says, "Acura is a legitimate contender in the $20,000 to $30,000 price range."[6] (See Exhibit 6.)

As Acura continues to establish itself in the U.S. luxury car market, Toyota and Nissan are in the process of launching their own luxury car divisions: Lexus and Infiniti, respectively. These new offerings will follow Acura's lead by initially introducing two products for each of the new divisions and selling them only in dealerships dedicated to that division. Acura, Lexus, and Infiniti will not share facilities with the lesser Hondas, Toyotas, or Nissans

---

[5] Maryann N. Keller, "Streetwise Showdown in the High-Priced Sector," p. 138.
[6] Alex Taylor III, "Detroit versus New Upscale Imports," *Fortune*, April 27, 1987, p. 78.

EXHIBIT 6   Acura Legend

MOST AUTOMAKERS WOULD CALL THIS A VERY GOOD YEAR. WE'D CALL IT A VERY GOOD START.

Number one in the J.D. Power Customer Satisfaction Index. Number one in Auto Age's first annual Dealer Satisfaction Index. Number one in sales for all luxury imports.*

There's no two ways about it: Acura automobiles and their dealers were an overwhelming success in 1988. But to our way of thinking, last year's performance is only the beginning.

From the day the very first Acura rolled off the assembly line, we've had a reputation for being innovative. And we have every intention of keeping it that way. Not only by continuing to improve the technology and craftsmanship that give Acura automobiles their edge, but also by striving to provide the highest level of satisfaction to our customers as well as our dealers.

Maintaining that reputation won't be easy. But we feel we already have the keys.

Namely, strong dealers whose sales, service and parts departments have consistently made customer satisfaction their top priority. Not to mention products of uncompromising quality.

1988 was unquestionably a year to remember. But the fact is, even if we wanted to rest on our laurels, we couldn't.

We're too busy working on next year.

© 1988 Acura Division of American Honda Motor Co., Inc. Acura is a trademark of Honda Motor Co., Ltd.
*1988 and 1987 CSI Customer Satisfaction with product quality and dealer service. 1988 Dealer Satisfaction Index survey. *Auto Age,* 12/88. 1988 calendar year to date luxury import sales. *Automotive News,* 12/12/88.

as Lincoln does with Mercury or as Cadillac is allowed with other GM divisions. The Lexus and Infiniti models will also follow Acura by offering a high degree of Lexus/Infiniti ''only'' content and distinct styling not to be shared by Toyotas or Nissans.

Lexus' initial offering in 1990 will be an all new sedan with a modern multivalve V–8. (See Exhibit 7.) According to *Automobile Magazine,* the Lexus LS 400 ''is a large, roomy, rather conservatively styled four-door sedan that appears to be an amalgam of BMW and Mercedes-Benz design cues, given an American spin with a Cadillacesque egg-crate grille, Detroit-style wood trim, and wrinkled leather upholstery. Its drag coefficient makes it the slipperiest of production sedans, and its four-liter, four-cam, 250-horsepower V–8 engine will push that slippery shape through the air at speeds guaranteed to keep Mercedes-Benz, BMW, and Jaguar engineers working late for the next decade

EXHIBIT 7 1990 Lexus LS 400

or so.''[7] The LS 400 is expected to be priced at approximately $35,000, roughly half of a comparable-size Mercedes-Benz or BMW.

Lexus will also introduce a midsize sedan derived from an existing Toyota, the midsize Camry. The ES250 will be powered by a high-tech multivalve V–6 similar to the Acura Legend. A year later Lexus will debut a new coupe model.

Nissan's Infiniti brand will be introduced at roughly the same time as the Lexus. The introduction of the Infiniti brand will begin with a large sedan similar to the Lexus LS 400. The Infiniti Q45 will be powered by a 4.5 liter V–8 and sell for approximately $35,000. (See Exhibit 8.) Commenting on the image intentions of the sedan, Takashi Oka, senior project manager of the Q45 said, ''We want to create a new definition of luxury and establish an international image beyond that of BMW and Mercedes.'' The Q45 will be joined at introduction with a smaller, less expensive two-door model based on the Japanese market Nissan Leopard. The new coupe will be powered by a multivalve V–6 and sell for around $25,000. A third model will join the Infiniti brand in 1991. A multivalve V–6 powered midsize sedan, based on the Nissan Maxima, will go head-to-head with the Lexus ES250 as well as the Acura Legend.

EXHIBIT 8   1990 Infiniti Q45

─────────
[7] David E. Davis, Jr., ''First Look at Toyota's New Lexus,'' *Automobile Magazine*, January 1989, p. 74.

EXHIBIT 9 Comparison of key specifications

	Lexus LS 400	Infiniti Q-Series	BMW 735i	Mercedes 300-E	Cadillac de Ville	Cadillac Seville	1989 Lincoln Continental
Wheelbase	110.8	113.4	111.5	110.2	113.8	108	109
Length	197.6	199.8	193.3	187.2	205.3	190.8	205.1
Width	71.7	71.9	72.6	68.5	72.5	70.9	72.7
Height	55.1	56.3	55.6	56.9	55	53.5	55.6
Weight	3,800	3,860	3,835	3,195	3,470	3,449	3,626
Engine	V–8	V–8	I–6	I–6	V–8	V–8	V–6
Size (liters)	4	4.5	3.4	3	4.5	4.5	3.8
Horsepower	250	270	208	177	155	155	140

Source: *Automotive News*, December 5, 1988.

(See Exhibit 9 for a key specification comparison between the new Lexus/Infiniti models and selected competition.)

Both Lexus and Infiniti have targeted to sell approximately 100,000 units each when the full range of models is available. This contrasts to Acura's estimated sales of 300,000–400,000 by the mid-1990s.[8]

Cadillac

Cadillac Motor Car Division of General Motors got its start in 1899 as the Detroit Automobile Company and was renamed Cadillac in 1902. The car was named after the French adventurer who founded Detroit 200 years earlier. The force behind Cadillac's early years was Henry M. Leland, operator of Leland & Faulconer Mfg. Co., a precision manufacturer of automotive components. Unlike Henry Ford, who once worked for Leland, Leland was not interested in building an "everyman's" car. Leland and his company were devoted to building the best and "despite record production of 4,307 vehicles in 1906, Cadillac management disregarded the lure of volume sales and dedicated the company to making quality automobiles. This lost Cadillac its position as a high-volume producer, but led to engineering accomplishments that made Cadillac one of the leading fine-car manufacturers."[9]

In 1909, Cadillac was purchased by the young General Motors Corporation. The Lelands, Henry and son Wilfred, stayed on to run Cadillac exactly as if it were their own. They did so until 1917 when they left to begin the Lincoln Motor Co. which was later sold to the Ford Motor Company.

The Lelands had left their impression on Cadillac. Their commitment to quality and innovation propelled Cadillac's status as the "standard of the

---

[8] Jesse Snyder, "INFINITI: Nissan Screening Luxury-Line Dealers," *Automotive News*, July 27, 1987, p. 65.

[9] Frank Gawronski, "Detroit's Oldest Auto Manufacturer," *Automotive News*, September 16, 1983, p. 98.

world.'' Innovations that helped to build this reputation included the self-starter in 1912, America's first V–8 engine in 1914, synchromesh gear boxes, and safety glass as standard equipment in 1929–30. In those same years a V–12 and the world's first production V–16 automobile engine were offered. In the late 1930s, as traditional coach building died out, GM used the Fisher and Fleetwood names to maintain the quality image of its prestige models. In 1941 Cadillac was the second manufacturer to offer a fully automatic transmission. In the 1950s Cadillac styling reigned supreme in the art of tail fins. (See Exhibit 10.) The 1960s brought longer, even more powerful luxury cars, and in 1966 Cadillac introduced its first front wheel drive (FWD) vehicle, the Eldorado, years before FWD was offered by any of Cadillac's non-GM competitors.

EXHIBIT 10   1959 Cadillac

Through the ''longer, lower, wider'' years of the 1960s to late 1970s Cadillac remained a distinguished luxury automobile. The Cadillac de Ville of the day weighed over 5,000 pounds, measured over 230 inches long, and was powered by an 8.2 liter engine. In comparison, the 1988 de Ville weighs only 3,437 pounds, is 196.5 inches long, and is powered by a V–8 engine that is 45 percent smaller than the 1976 model it replaces.

The trend toward smaller Cadillacs began in 1977, in reaction to the first oil embargo of 1973. The new de Villes and Fleetwoods were 8 to 12 inches shorter and averaged 950 pounds lighter than their 1976 counterparts. These models represented the first of the downsized Cadillacs. In 1979, the Eldorado received similar treatment. For 1979, the Eldorados were 20 inches shorter and 1,150 pounds lighter than the 1978 models. In 1985 and 1986, respectively, the de Ville and Eldorados underwent yet another round of downsizing to approximately the size they are today.

Cadillac customers are those who have demanded the best in traditional luxury cars. These traditional Cadillac consumers were most often professionals, above average in income and education, and in recent years an average of 58 years of age. (See Exhibit 11 for a demographic profile of the luxury car market.) These Cadillac buyers had also been accustomed to buying the biggest and most powerful. This, however, had begun to change over the course of the 1970s and 80s.

EXHIBIT 11 Demographics

	Median Age	Age percent < 35	Median income ($000)	Percent college grad +
		Industry		
Domestic				
Cadillac	62	2.5%	$61.1	38.4
Lincoln	59	4.4	66.3	39.9
Import				
Acura	35	50.4	55.5	74.6
Audi	41	27.7	78.4	70.8
BMW	42	24.0	98.4	68.3
Jaguar	50	7.9	>150.0	64.6
Mercedes-Benz	45	14.9	117.7	61.7
Saab	38	39.4	69.2	78.1
Volvo	38	36.0	61.7	67.5
		Domestic		
Cadillac				
Sedan de Ville	62	6.9	61.0	40.3
Brougham	65	0.3	53.2	27.4
Eldorado	60	4.1	70.2	39.7
Seville	63	1.6	90.0	47.2
Allante	54	6.1	150.0	47.1
Cimarron	60	9.5	45.2	47.0
Lincoln				
Town Car	60	3.2	58.6	35.6
Mark VII	50	10.2	71.3	45.0
Continental	61	3.6	95.2	49.6

Source: *Meritz 1988 Second Quarter Buyers' Study*

In an effort to appeal to the younger upscale consumers who were not a part of the traditional Cadillac market, GM offered a new Cadillac in the 1970s. In May 1975, the Seville was a smaller, international-size Cadillac. Featuring a fuel injected 5.7 liter V–8 as standard equipment along with a long list of other features, the Seville was one of the most well-equipped cars in the world. In 1981, GM introduced the smallest Cadillac ever, the Cimarron. Built on the ''J'' chassis shared by the Chevy Cavalier and Pontiac 2000, the Cimarron was introduced to take on the small ''near luxury'' imports such as the BMW 320 and later 325i. In 1985, the standard Cadillac, the Sedan de Ville/Coupe de

Ville, was thoroughly redesigned. The de Ville series was shortened and placed on a front wheel drive chassis shared with the Buick Electra and the Oldsmobile 98. (Sharing the chassis, or platform, among car divisions is a common automotive industry practice, particularly among U.S. manufacturers. Henry M. Leland recognized that this sharing of parts, or what he referred to as the "true interchangeability of parts," was the key to a great future for the automotive industry.)[10] In 1986, in a further attempt to appeal to the younger and the more functional-demanding customers, Cadillac began offering a functional luxury version to its de Ville series, the Touring Sedan. The Touring Sedan came complete with front air dam, fog lamps, rear deck lid spoiler, blackwell performance tires on 15-inch aluminum alloy wheels, higher spring rates, and faster ratio steering.

In 1986, Cadillac downsized its Eldorado and Seville (the Seville had grown larger from the 1979 model to the 1980 model year) models back to the international size. These two Cadillacs continue to share common platforms with Oldsmobile and Buick models.

Speaking of the 1986 Eldorado/Seville (E/S) models, Braz Pryor, Cadillac's general sales manager says, "We [are] after a contemporary statement with international appeal for buyers young and old who want the luxury of a Cadillac in a more personal package."[11] GM's director of design, Chuck Jordan, calls the fourth-generation Eldorado "Cadillac's youthful sporty car," adding that "sporty elegance was the design theme."[12] Peter Levin, director of special marketing projects at Cadillac, offered some pertinent insights about the basic market philosophy behind the E/S models when he said, "Today, we're going through a revolution in customer expectations. We're after buyers of a certain mindset. . . . The challenge we gave our engineers was to create vehicles that were more responsive and refined but still retained outstanding comfort, because our buyers demand it."[13]

The 1987 model year Cadillac debuted one of its most unique automobiles, the Allante. The Allante, a two-seat, coupe/convertible, is built on a shortened Eldorado/Seville chassis that is assembled and mated in the United States to bodies and interiors that arrive twice weekly, via 747 cargo jets, from their designer/manufacturer, Pininfarina, in Italy. The Allante assumes the position as the flagship model in the Cadillac line. With a 1988 base price of $57,183 and limited to a supply of 6,000 units, it is the most expensive as well as one of the most exclusive Cadillacs ever produced.

Implementing this new strategy and striving to regain the aura of quality, technology, and exclusivity now associated with European luxury cars is not an

---

[10] Ibid.
[11] Mary Ann Angeli, "'86 Eldorado/Seville: Caddy's New Yuppie Lures?," *Automotive Industries,* November 1985, p. 40.
[12] Ibid.
[13] Bob Nagy, "Cadillacs across America," *Motor Trend,* June 1986, p. 91.

easy task. John Grettenberger, Cadillac's general manager states, "We have to be very careful that we offer the right balance. If you go too far in either direction, a manufacturer like Cadillac could lose on either end of the spectrum. If we go too far in the high-tech direction, we could turn off some of our traditional buyers, but if we stick where we are then we won't appeal to the younger ones."[14]

To help achieve Cadillac's strategy of maintaining the traditional, as well as capturing new customers, Cadillac's 1987 advertising emphasized the "Spirit of Cadillac." (See Exhibit 12 for Cadillac's 1987 model line.) All Cadillac models shared a number of common themes including: making an "eloquent design statement," providing customers "worldwide Cadillac exclusives" (e.g., transverse mounted V–8 engine), balanced performance, a commitment to security, and "the ultimate comfort: peace of mind" via "quality crafts-manship" and extensive warranties.[15]

From this common basis each Cadillac model has its own individual spirit. For example, the Allante is the "new spirit of Cadillac." The Allante was positioned to create a new class of performance that merges European road manners with Cadillac comfort and convenience.[16] The Sedan de Ville and Coupe de Ville are Cadillac's "contemporary spirits representing Cadillac's belief that today's luxury cars should reflect today's values."[17] The Fleetwood d'Elegance and Fleetwood Sixty Special are the "sophisticated spirits" of Cadillac. The d'Elegance's formal Cabriolet roof and opera lamps and the Sixty Special's five-inch extended wheelbase make these the most luxurious of the Cadillac "C-bodies" (chassis shared with the de Ville, Buick Electra, and Olds 98). Eldorado is the "driving spirit" while the Seville is the "elegant spirit." Sharing the same chassis, the Eldorado is a two-door coupe with a suspension system that delivers control with a minimum of body roll and sway, while the Seville is a four-door sedan that emphasizes supreme comfort and an exceptional array of standard luxury features. The Brougham d'Elegance is the "classic spirit" for this large, rear wheel drive Cadillac. It is a carryover from the model that the "C-body" cars were to have replaced. Because it and its competitor, the Lincoln Town Car, are in high demand, the Brougham has lived three years past its originally scheduled termination and will likely live on until the early 1990s. Last and certainly least in terms of size is the "sporty spirit" of Cadillac, the Cimarron. In 1988, the Cimarron was discontinued due to poor sales. In 1988, the spirit theme of Cadillac was also discontinued.

In all of 1987, Cadillac spent $35,334,300 on TV advertising to promote the "spirit of Cadillac," a 32.5 percent increase from the previous year.

---

[14] John McElroy, "Cadillac's Grettenberger: Resetting the Standard," *Automotive Industries,* November 1985, p. 36.

[15] *Cadillac 1987* (Detroit, Mich: Cadillac Motor Division, General Motors Corporation, 1986), pp. 2–3.

[16] Ibid.

[17] Ibid.

EXHIBIT 12 1987 Cadillac Line

Allanté shown at the Music Center of Los Angeles County, Los Angeles, California.

Sedan de Ville shown at the Detroit Institute of Arts, Detroit, Michigan.

EXHIBIT 12 1987 Cadillac Line *(continued)*

Fleetwood d'Elegance shown at the High Museum of Art, Atlanta, Georgia.

Eldorado shown at the Kitt Peak National Observatory, Kitt Peak, Arizona.

EXHIBIT 12 1987 Cadillac Line *(concluded)*

Seville shown at the Adler Planetarium, Chicago, Illinois.

Cimarron shown at the Laumeier Sculpture Park, St. Louis, Missouri.

However, BMW's TV total was $45,498,700, and start-up Acura was almost even with Cadillac at $34,478,500.[18] Cadillac's TV budget in 1988 increased to $54,126,200.[19]

Cadillac is GM's luxury market division. Where it actually fits among the other GM divisions can be seen in the market plots of Exhibit 13. In 1986, Cadillac was positioned as the highest-priced division, offering the consumer automobiles that are conservative but not far from an even split between conservative and aggressive, and family and personal orientations. GM's goals

EXHIBIT 13   GM plots its markets

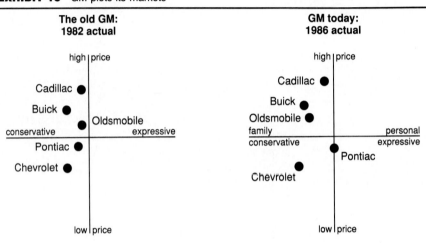

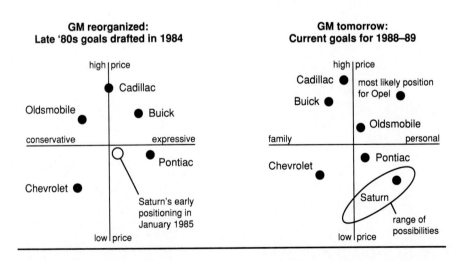

AUTOMOTIVE NEWS/CHARLOTTE WINTER

---

[18] "Et Cetera," *Automotive News, 1988 Market Data Book*, p. 208
[19] Ibid.

for the 1988–89 model year show Cadillac maintaining its basic position except in terms of price, where it continues to move further upscale. According to General Manager Grettenberger, "Our vision is to move every Cadillac upscale in terms of its expressiveness, image, distinctiveness, and overall content. I don't see us having a sale-weighted average of $43,000–44,000 like Mercedes-Benz. But I would like to see Cadillacs move upscale."[20] Cadillac's 1989 model line ranges in price from approximately $25,000 for a Coupe de Ville, $26,000 for the Brougham, and $30,000–34,000 for the Fleetwood. The Eldorado begins at about $27,000 while the Seville begins at $30,000. The Allante is, of course, the high-price leader at $57,183.

The Problem

Throughout most of its existence, Cadillac has been synonymous with the finest in luxury automobiles. In the early years under the Lehland family's leadership, the company won the Dewar Trophy from the Royal Automobile Club. Cadillac not only won this coveted prize for engineering excellence and innovation once but also was the only car company to do it twice. After the Lehlands left, and for quite some time, Cadillac managed to keep its eye trained on building the best luxury cars possible.

By the 1978 model year, Cadillac sales had hit an all time record of 350,813 units. At that time and as recently as 1983, Cadillac accounted for over one third of all luxury car sales. In 1987 Cadillac made up less than one quarter of all such sales. Models that had been previously very popular were selling

EXHIBIT 14 Cadillac 15-year sales trend by model

Year	Cadillac	Eldorado	Seville	Cimarron	Allante
1987	203,487	21,470	24,266	12,295	2,517
1986	235,206	24,266	21,150	23,435	*
1985	187,664	58,310	29,034	23,754	*
1984	195,177	70,577	35,349	18,014	*
1983	176,003	71,624	33,522	19,188	*
1982	148,211	55,761	23,030	13,195	*
1981	134,765	53,233	23,054	13,406	*
1980	126,145	51,065	35,347	*	*
1979	202,681	61,000	44,216	*	*
1978	238,976	43,681	52,396	*	*
1977	238,066	45,206	42,452	*	*
1976	214,649	39,333	39,734	*	*
1975	189,034	44,363	22,738	*	*
1974	183,633	36,360	*	*	*
1973	235,504	50,205	*	*	*

Note: Sales for years 1973–1983 are represented by registrations.
* Not in production.
Source: *Automotive News Annual Almanac Issues/Market Data Books*

---

[20] Dave Zoia, "Cadillac Eyes an Allante Sedan," *Automotive News* 16 (February 1987), p. 37.

poorly. In 1985 the Eldorado and Seville had sales of 66,863 and 32,986, respectively. During the following year, the smaller, redesigned models sold only 45 percent of the 1985 models they replaced; 1987 sales fared somewhat worse. Sales of the exclusive Allante have also been disappointing. The two-door coupe/convertible was expected to be a sellout its first year at 6,000 units, but by year's end the Allante tallied just over 2,500 units. (See Exhibit 14 for Cadillac's 1973–87 sales figures and Exhibit 15 for announced 1988 competitive car prices.)

EXHIBIT 15   1988 Luxury car manufacturers' suggested retail prices

U.S. domestic	4-door	2-door	European import	4-door	2-door
Cadillac			Audi		
Cimarron V-6	$16,071		80 Series 4	$18,600	
de Ville V-8	23,404	$23,049	80 Quattro 5	22,700	
Fleetwood d'Elegance V-8	28,024		90 Series 4	24,330	
Fleetwood Sixty Special V-8	34,750		90 Series 5	24,330	
Brougham V-8	23,846		90 Series Quattro 5	27,720	
Eldorado V-8		24,891	5000S 5	22,850	
Seville V-8	27,627		5000S Quattro 5	27,280	
Allante V-8		56,533	5000CS Turbo 5	30,910	
			5000CS Turbo Quattro 5	34,810	
Lincoln					
Town Car V-8	24,373		BMW		
Town Car Signature V-8	27,374		325 6	25,150	$24,350
Town Car Cartier V-8	28,520		325is6		28,950
Mark VII LSC V-8		26,380	325i6	28,950	
Mark VII Bill Blass V-8		26,380	325ix6		33,290
Continental V-6	26,078		M-3 4		34,800
Continental Signature V-6	27,944		528e6	31,950	
			535i6	36,700	
			535is6	37,800	
			M-5 6	47,500	
			635CSi6		46,000
			M-6 6		55,950
			735i6	54,000	
			750iL 12	69,000	
			Jaguar		
			XJ-6 6	43,500	
			Vanden Plas 6	47,500	
			XJ-S V-12		47,000
			XJ-SC V-12		50,450
			Mercedes Benz		
			190-E 2.3 4	29,190	
			190-D 2.5 5	29,960	
			190-E 2.6 6	33,500	
			260-E 6	37,845	
			300-E 6	43,365	
			300-CE 6		53,340
			300-SE 6	49,900	
			300-SEL 6	53,490	
			420-SEL V-8	59,080	
			560-SEL V-8	69,760	
			560-SL V-8		62,110
			560-SEC V-8		77,065

Source: *Automotive News, 1988 Market Data Book.*

What's more important to Cadillac and to Reuss, executive vice president of North American car operations, was the division's steadily declining reputation for luxury car excellence. On the surface the cause for the decline was multifaceted. First, Cadillac suffered from what the press called "look-alike cars." The Cadillac de Villes and Fleetwoods looked like Buick Electras and Oldsmobile Ninety Eights. This perception was even played up in a Lincoln Town Car television commercial where Cadillac, Buick, and Olds owners can't tell their cars apart at a restaurant when the valets bring the three cars forward. Concedes one GM man, "Cadillac, one could say, is selling 300,000 Buicks."[21]

Cadillac innovation in the late 1970s and early 1980s was also a cause for concern. The availability of a V–8 diesel engine, manufactured from a modified gasoline engine, was discontinued when its reliability proved disastrous. This same scenario played a second time, and in the same time period, with Cadillac's exclusive multidisplacement engine. The engine was programmed to run on 8, 6, or 4 cylinders depending on engine load demand. However, as with the diesel, lack of reliability killed the innovative engine.

On September 27, 1988, consumer activist Ralph Nader issued a report called "Cadillac—The Heartbreak of America."[22] According to Nader, "This report was written because of the large volume of mail we have received from indignant Cadillac purchasers who expect better quality from a $25,000 investment."[23] GM called the Nader document outdated, unfair, and inaccurate.

As Reuss looks over these problems and others, his task appears not to be an easy one. Could the quality and design of Cadillac's cars be the sole cause of the division's problems? Maybe advertising and imaging are being directed at the wrong customer, or perhaps the division has lost sight of just who the Cadillac customer is. Seeing the result of the problems may be easy, but finding solutions to their causes will be the real test to restoring Cadillac as the standard of the world.

---

[21] Flint, "Hold the Velveeta—Please Pass the Brie," p. 31.

[22] John E. Peterson, "The Heartbreak of America," *The Detroit News* 28 (September 1988), p. C1–2.

[23] Ibid.

Case 2

Santa Clara Terminals, Inc.*

Ed Zimmer, the president of Santa Clara Terminals (SCT), leaned back in his chair and contemplated the future of his company. He knew that the company was at a crisis point, not for the first time in its history. Sales and orders were down substantially. The future of the marketing organization was in question. Engineering talent was in short supply, and the existing engineering group was stretched to its limits.

The industry in which SCT operated was undergoing major changes and SCT, as a small company, would have trouble keeping up and competing on a general basis. He wondered what was the best direction to take the company—and how to get there. He summarized the situation as follows:

> Our biggest challenge right now is survival. The field has always been extraordinarily competitive, and the last five years it's been impossible. The Koreans are now strongly in the market, along with the Japanese. Everyone else is manufacturing offshore, and I don't want to. I can't compete in the normal CRT market. I compete in a tiny niche characterized by lots of characters on the screen.

The vice president of operations also noted,

> The company is more interested in staying healthy than in growth. Growth is closely controlled in terms of the company's capabilities. We could go to double our current volume in sales without anything except hiring entry-level production people. Beyond that, growth is not planned and would come as a surprise. It would require adjustments.

Company Background and History

General Information

Santa Clara Terminals is a privately held corporation engaged in the manufacture of CRT display terminals for the commercial computer market. The

---

* This case was written by Sarah Freeman under the supervision of Thomas C. Kinnear. Copyright © 1987 by Thomas C. Kinnear.

company was formed in 1970 in Santa Clara, California, and has grown to have 50 employees. No outside venture capital has ever been solicited or used; all growth has been from retained earnings.

SCT evolved from a company that would sell anything to anyone in terms of CRT display electronics to a company that manufactures custom versions of a few basic designs and builds exceptionally high-quality terminals. SCT's products were priced higher than its competition's to allow for this greater flexibility and reliability.

When this approach was no longer feasible, given the greater flexibility provided all manufacturers with the use of the microprocessor, SCT struggled to redefine its niche. That niche is now defined as the very high-end CRT terminal for the professional user. Professional users are defined as those who work with CRTs for a living—not the clerical worker who spends a great deal of time in front of a CRT, but professionals such as programmers and engineers, who often see their terminals as extensions of themselves.

1970-1973

SCT was founded by three engineers, all of whom had worked for other California firms in the computer and electronics fields. Each of the founders put up $5,000 of his own funds to start the company, and they took no salary during the start-up phase. Of the three, Ed Zimmer is the only one still active in the company, and he now owns it in its entirety.

The company's original products were printed circuit board sets and display controllers, aimed at the OEM and industrial markets. These consisted of display electronics only, packaged in a sheet metal enclosure in the case of the controllers, and could be considered a CRT terminal without the CRT, or screen. Although the company offered a broad range of "standard" products, varying mainly by display format (from 8 lines of 32 characters to 24 lines of 80 characters) and data interface (serial or parallel), virtually all products were sold customized according to the customer's requirements.

At this time, most marketing was by word of mouth, reflecting the fledgling company's limited resources and confidence in its ability to deliver quality products. However, SCT did score some success with an unusual approach to promotion. For instance, at the National Computer Conference in 1971, the company was unable to afford or obtain an exhibit booth. The National Computer Conference was, and still is, the main annual trade show for the computer industry, and SCT's founders thought its products should be on display there. They got into the show as attendees, trailing a small red wagon that contained their products. Although show management later forced them to leave, they stationed the wagon at the door of the exhibit hall. In addition to attention at the show, the ploy earned Santa Clara Terminals a front page story in *Electronic News*'s coverage of the NCC.

During these early days, the company also signed up manufacturers' representatives to sell its products to OEMs and large industrial users. The rep firms carried several related product lines, sometimes including a CRT terminal, and received a commission on all sales within their geographic territories. By 1973, SCT had representatives covering the United States, Canada, and most of Western Europe.

1973–1977

In 1973, SCT introduced its first desktop design, with full CRT display and keyboard. Like other new products, the Design III was designed in response to a customer requirement and then broadened into a standard product line. In this instance, the customer was a West Coast think tank that wanted to display 40 lines of data in order to be able to review more text at one time. The terminal included a monitor and keyboard from other manufacturers, packaged with the display electronics in SCT's case. The desktop design was made to accommodate all SCT board sets, giving the company a full line of desktop terminals.

In 1977, the company was still manufacturing these terminals, in both desktop and controller configurations. All products were essentially "dumb" terminals, with just basic input/output and display capabilities. SCT's sales still consisted largely of customized versions of its standard products, sold to OEMs (both manufacturers and systems houses) and to industrial customers who particularly liked the more rugged controllers.

OEMs were in all fields but had the design and manufacture of computer-based systems in common; systems might be for process control, medical diagnostics, or general-purpose computer systems. Systems houses did not manufacture but rather put together a computer and peripherals from several manufacturers, along with their own specialized applications software, to sell to vertical end-user markets. SCT's customizing could consist of anything from a change of the case color, to the addition of a specialized command or emulation of other manufacturers' code sets, to a complete design to the customer's specifications.

After a brief initial campaign to introduce the Design III, SCT did little or no advertising during this period but relied on its reputation as a manufacturer of high-quality, reliable products, especially of custom designs. This reputation was passed along mainly by word of mouth, particularly by job-hopping engineers.

The company considered itself largely a service operation. It prided itself on its excellent reliability and display quality and on its ability to respond quickly and efficiently to special requirements. SCT was set up to handle custom products in low volume at reasonable cost—minor changes were often designed by technicians rather than engineers, and all products were built to order. This makes sense particularly when one notes that "standard" products accounted for only about 20 percent of SCT's sales. Production operated basically as a large job shop, building standard PC boards and then modifying them to the requirements of each order.

During a period in 1973–74, SCT made an attempt at instituting a middle management structure. One of the three founders had left the company, and the remaining two wished to remove themselves from its day-to-day operations.

Managers were recruited from outside the company to be put in charge of engineering, marketing, and production. However, top management found that this approach required more of their attention than anticipated; results were mediocre, and the entire middle management structure was disbanded within nine months.

Around the same time, Ed Zimmer made the decision to pull out of Western Europe and cancel all representation there. SCT would be a domestic company only for the time being. Zimmer had determined that the company was too small to provide the level of support required overseas. However, at least one of the representatives, covering Scandinavia, elected to continue the relationship by buying at a discount and reselling within the area.

1977–1980

Late in 1977, SCT started moving toward vertical integration and more standardized products. The proliferation of the microprocessor was making its terminal designs obsolete and unnecessary for many industrial customers. In addition, functional customization could now be achieved via simple firmware changes (code changes to the memory chip that determined the terminal's functions) rather than the more complex and less reliable wiring changes used in the past.

The Model 400 was introduced at the National Computer Conference of 1977, and shipping started in December of that year. It was a first for SCT in many respects. It used the first monitor of SCT's own design and manufacture, and it was also SCT's first microprocessor-based product. The company designed the keyboard logic into the terminal itself and was able to use a simple switch matrix key array from another manufacturer. Because many fewer components were required, the Model 400 in its new case took up less than half the desk space of earlier terminal designs.

Following the introduction of the Model 400, the company ran into several production and design-related problems. First, SCT quickly discovered that it was not expert at building quality monitors; its reputation for clear display and reliability suffered while the monitor went through many design changes and was reengineered. In addition, production fell behind schedule and deliveries slipped. Finally, the Model 400 was not code compatible with SCT's previous products. This meant that existing customers would have to rewrite their software if they were to switch over to the new product. The older products were still available but considerably more expensive, and were in the process of being phased out.

SCT addressed these problems first by introducing new versions of the older products, using the Model 400 board sets and design. Monitor quality and reliability problems were eventually corrected, although there is little doubt that the sales and irritation levels of existing customers suffered in the meantime.

Delivery problems were not finally corrected until the company moved to new manufacturing facilities in the fall of 1979.

With the advent of the Model 400 and its related products, SCT continued its customization approach. Some of the custom products were microprocessor-based versions of previous products. Others were emulations of other companies' terminals, particularly the VT52 from Digital Equipment Corp. (DEC), which was being phased out but was still in great demand. So, although the company used fewer different PC boards in the manufacture of its products, all were still customized to a great extent, and OEMs and systems houses accounted for most of the company's sales.

Marketing continued to rely mainly on word of mouth, with some limited fractional advertising in electronics trade journals, such as *Electronic Products*, or programmers' computer magazines, such as *Mini Micro Systems* or *Computer Decisions*. The company also issued regular press releases on new products and enhancements, which were sent to a customer mailing list as well as to the trade press.

Selling was handled by the manufacturers' reps organization, which still covered the United States and Canada. The field reps were supported by an in-house staff responsible for answering their questions, providing quotations for custom products, and coordinating all rep- and customer-related activity. Sales calls by SCT personnel, with or without the sales reps, were rare and limited to major prospects.

1980-1984

Things began to change drastically when the SCT Ambassador was introduced in 1980. This product used the code set specified by the ANSI (American National Standards Institute) X3.64 standard. The ANSI standard had been developed to cover most of the functions offered by computerized alphanumeric display equipment. It was intended to address problems encountered by users in switching between or adding equipment from different manufacturers.

Acceptance of the ANSI standard code set would mean that the market for customized terminals could all but dry up. Although the standard allowed a great deal of latitude in how commands were actually implemented, it specified the code structure for over 100 possible commands and functions.

The SCT Ambassador was introduced at the National Computer Conference in the spring of 1980, and shipping started late that year. It was the first CRT on the market to implement virtually the entire ANSI X3.64 code set, although other terminals, most notably DEC's VT100 and its emulations, implemented portions of the standard.

The Ambassador was a high-end product, with many editing and form-filling capabilities, as well as programmable function keys. What made the terminal unique, however, was its display capability. The Ambassador could display up to 60 lines of 80 characters—a full typewriter page. Most CRTs on the market were limited to a 24-line display. In addition, display formats could be selected with the terminal's local "zoom" capability, ranging from 18 to 60 lines. No other CRT on the market at the time offered either 60-line display or a selectable number of lines.

Because of its unique capabilities, the Ambassador was immediately popular among users interested in a high-end, versatile terminal with large display formats. These especially included programmers (who wanted to see more of their program at one time) and others whose work required a great deal of text editing.

However, OEMs did not find the terminal as attractive. This was partly because of its high price tag ($1,395 list price, while low-end terminals had just been introduced at under $500), but also because they did not face the same problems of code compatibility as end users did. Many functions and great flexibility offered little to a company that could accomplish these easily in its own software. Price, reliability, and basic functions were more important to this customer set.

During the same time frame in which the Ambassador was introduced, lower-end terminals were beginning to add more features at lower cost. The dumb terminal became a thing of the past as even the lowest-priced units offered a wide range of "smart" features like editing and programmable function keys.

SCT attempted to address some of this low-end challenge with modified versions of its Ambassador. The Genie and Genie + Plus terminals were introduced in 1982, offering ANSI X3.64 compatible code sets with a reduced set of functions. The Genie + Plus had all the features of the Ambassador except the 60-line display capability; it had 60 lines of memory, but could only display up to 30 at once. The Genie had only 30 lines of memory, and also removed some of the editing capability and function keys.

With the introduction of these products, the Ambassador's price was increased to $1,595, with the Genie and Genie + Plus priced at $1,195 and $1,395, respectively. The price increase had almost no effect on sales of the Ambassador, which continued to rise, but the Genies were not very successful and were purchased mainly by customers who had not been using all the features of the Ambassador.

In 1983, several more new products were introduced. One was a stand that could be added to SCT's products, providing tilt and swivel for operator comfort. It was intended to address complaints about the "industrial box" look of SCT's case while allowing more ergonomic placement of the terminal. The company also started offering the Ambassador in a portrait display (vertical tube) configuration, intended for customers who used the terminal primarily in its 60-line mode. The portrait display more closely resembled an $8\frac{1}{2} \times 11$ page than did the normal landscape, or horizontal, version.

Another new product was the Graphics Master. This was an add-on to the Ambassador, providing it with graphics capabilities that were code compatible with some of the more popular graphics devices in the field. A major problem with the Graphics Master was that it would not function with most of the

Ambassadors already in the field, requiring several internal changes and making retrofits all but impossible for the end user.

The final product introduced in 1983 was the Guru. This product went beyond the Ambassador to include display formats that could be changed both horizontally and vertically—ranging from 20 to 66 lines and from 32 to 170 characters per line. It also included 15 pages of display memory, usable for editing, printing, and transmission. With the Guru, SCT introduced a product as advanced as an alphanumeric CRT terminal could be at the time.

With these products, SCT decided to confine itself to the very high end of the CRT terminal market, offering lower-end products only for customers who wanted to buy a complete line from the same manufacturer. The company's customer base had changed dramatically over the years, to where they were predominantly end users taking standard products that offered some degree of user customization. The users were mainly people who depended on CRTs for their living—programmers, think tanks, and those who did a great deal of screen editing. SCT's products were particularly well known in the artificial intelligence (AI) community, which, although spread throughout the country in many different companies and universities, communicated regularly with each other and had strong opinions about how computer equipment should function.

With the introduction of the Ambassador, SCT was for the first time attempting to market a product rather than respond to the needs of specific customers. SCT had always marketed more expensive products than its competition, but the criteria for what justified a higher price had changed. SCT moved away from customization to high-end, flexible CRT terminals—essentially, terminals with functions that could be customized by the user. With this move, the nature of its customer base changed.

In 1981, the company started selling Ambassadors through distributors of computer peripherals. In 1982, SCT terminated contracts with all its manufacturers' reps and began to sell direct and through distributors. Direct sales were handled by a field representative, as well as by staff located at the factory. At this point, the company would take any order that came to them, although prospects were referred to a local distributor on initial contact. The general intent was for distributors to handle small-quantity customers, whether they were end users or systems houses, while SCT would handle larger accounts.

At this time, SCT also started advertising more heavily, as it felt that it needed to establish its own name and an awareness of its individual products, particularly the Ambassador. Full-page ads were placed in end-user, systems-house, and programmer publications. Regular mailings of press releases to customer and prospect lists continued as well.

The CRT Terminal Industry

Industry Structure

According to a 1981 article in *Computerworld*, there were nearly 200 manufacturers, including computer makers and independents, selling CRT terminals in the United States at that time. However, in a 1985 research study, Datapro found only 100 manufacturers to survey. Although there has been substantial dropout of CRT manufacturers during this time, new producers have continued to enter the market, particularly offshore facilities that may have originally manufactured under contract for U.S. companies.

The Datapro research study lists 91 manufacturers with a total of 361 models of CRT terminals. These terminals cover the range from dumb teletype replacements to sophisticated cluster configurations and editing terminals. However, most are in the middle range. Prices for stand-alone alphanumeric configurations ranged from $325 to $4,600, but most independents (i.e., non-computer manufacturers) have terminals priced in the $600–$800 range for basic alphanumerics, with editing, highlighting, and programmable function keys. Graphics and color capabilities add considerably to the price. A bewildering variety of options and standard features are also available, further complicating the user's choices.

According to a November 1984 article in *Computerworld*, the IBM 3270 and compatible market accounts for approximately one quarter of the installed base of CRT terminals; non-IBM-compatible editing terminals account for an additional 15.5 percent of the base, while conversational CRTs make up 23 percent. The remainder is split between a variety of cluster configurations, graphics terminals, and other special-protocol products.

An International Data Corporation study on the CRT terminal market found the following market segments and breakdown, based on 1983 shipments:

IBM 3270-type	30%
Low-end ASCII	24
Full-editing ASCII	21
IBM GSD-type	13
Cluster processing	7
Non-IBM synchronous (Honeywell, Sperry, etc.)	5

According to the same study, the market share leaders in the low-end ASCII segment were Digital Equipment (DEC) with 28.1 percent, ADDS with 14.9 percent, IBM with 8.6 percent, Lear Siegler with 7.2 percent, C. Itoh with 6.3 percent, and Hewlett-Packard with 5.5 percent.

In the full-editing segment, where Santa Clara Terminals' products belong, eight vendors accounted for more than 60 percent of total shipments. They were Televideo with 20 percent, Hewlett-Packard with 8.7 percent, Esprit Systems with 6.5 percent, Lear Siegler with 5.4 percent, Micro-Term and Liberty Electronics with 5.3 percent each, and Wyse and Visual Technology with 4.6 percent each. A total of nearly 380,000 full-editing ASCII terminals were shipped in 1983.

Market Size and Growth

According to Datapro, there were approximately 10 million CRT terminals of all types installed in the United States as of the end of 1984. In the IDC study cited above, it was found that a total of 1.78 million CRT terminals were shipped in 1983, for a total of $3 billion in sales. This represents an 18 percent increase over 1982 unit volume.

The increase was not even across all segments. Low-end ASCII terminal shipments increased by only 10 percent over 1982, while full-editing ASCII shipments grew by 30 percent. Through 1988, *Mini Micro Systems* predicts annual growth of editing terminals to run at 27 percent, while conversational (low-end) terminal shipments will increase by only 9 percent per year. The continual price cutting is reflected in its forecasts for dollar volume growth—18 percent for editing units, and −0.7 percent for conversational CRTs.

Evidence of Shakeout

There is some evidence of a shakeout within the CRT terminal industry beyond simply noting the estimated number of manufacturers in various years. Several of the major players within the industry have undergone substantial changes in recent years.

In 1982, Applied Digital Data Systems (ADDS), the largest OEM supplier of CRT terminals, was acquired by its main customer, NCR. Since then, ADDS has continued to operate independently, but NCR takes an increasing share of its production.

Three manufacturers have filed for Chapter 11 bankruptcy protection within the last two years. General Terminal is one of these. The other two, Beehive International and Soroc Technology, were in the top five by market share as late as 1979. Hazeltine, which held the number two position among independents in the late 70s, elected to exit the CRT terminal market and sold this business to its managers in 1983; this is now Esprit Systems.

Several CRT terminal manufacturers have attempted to enter the personal computer or small systems markets, but there have been no notable successes. Televideo holds the leading share of ASCII terminals among the independents, but is said to be losing money largely because of its unsuccessful venture into microcomputers. Other terminal manufacturers have attempted mergers, but without bringing them off. Many are rumored to be in financial difficulty.

Other Changes in the Industry

Technological changes and continual feature enhancements have blurred the distinctions between dumb and smart terminals, smart and intelligent terminals, and intelligent terminals and workstations. The introduction and popularity of the personal computer has further confused definitions, particularly when it can be used in local area networks. The ease of adding features with the microprocessor, along with dropping hardware and memory costs, have contributed to the trend for manufacturers to add advanced features to even their low-end products.

Some experts predicted that readily available and inexpensive microcomputers would mean the end of CRT terminals. This has not happened, although microcomputers have made some inroads in the intelligent and high-end segments. Microcomputers can be used in place of CRT terminals to provide more local processing power, but they can still be connected to a host computer. At the present time, CRT terminals are still more cost effective than personal computers for most applications. However, this depends on how much local processing is desired.

Another major change is the number of CRT terminals that, like other electronics, are now being manufactured offshore, primarily in Asia. U.S. manufacturers started moving their production in the late 70s to take advantage of lower labor costs and to try to match falling hardware prices. Most used contract manufacturing, although some have their own overseas manufacturing subsidiaries. Now all the major U.S. companies do at least some portion of their manufacturing offshore.

In some ways, this strategy came back to haunt them when the contractors in Taiwan and Korea began to produce their own brands and market them in the United States. Televideo, the number one independent in ASCII terminals, started by manufacturing monitors for Atari. Liberty Electronics began by manufacturing for Hazeltine.

The price cutting and feature enhancing that have gone on for several years show no signs of abating. CRT vendors are each struggling for their share of the market, accepting lower margins to do so. It was not uncommon for CRT manufacturers to have gross margins as high as 40 percent in 1980; now 10 percent margins are common in the more crowded segments.

Finally, ergonomic features have become a requirement rather than a market advantage. When terminals began to include more function at lower prices, some manufacturers used human engineering (ergonomics) to distinguish themselves from their competitors and create a differential advantage. Features such as tilt and swivel screen, low-profile keyboards, nonglare screens and keytops, and different screen colors were touted for their enhancement of operator comfort. More terminal makers incorporated these features into their designs, so that virtually all now have some aspects that are considered user friendly or ergonomic.

Santa Clara Terminals' Primary Competition

SCT considered just a few companies to be its direct competition, and these it watched more closely than others. The following section contains a brief description of each of these key competitors.

Digital Equipment Corporation

DEC was considered a main competitor, not because its CRT terminals competed head on in the same range as SCT's, but because the majority of SCT customers had DEC computers and were therefore likely to consider and possibly buy DEC terminals.

DEC had been influential in defining and later establishing the ANSI X3.64 standard in the CRT industry. Its VT100 had been "the" ANSI standard terminal for many years. Introduced in 1978, it was estimated that over 500,000 had been shipped as of the end of 1983. In November 1983, DEC introduced its replacement for the VT100—the VT200 line of CRT terminals. These products included ergonomic advances, along with some more functionality, over the VT100.

With the VT200 series, DEC also corrected some mistakes it had made with the introduction of the VT100. When the VT100 was announced, DEC had not anticipated the extent of demand and was unable to produce enough terminals for the first couple of years of production. Consequently, the door was opened to independent manufacturers, many of which came out with VT100 emulations. Generally, the emulations were more readily available and often included more features at a lower price than the DEC unit. However, DEC was able to gear up manufacturing more quickly on the VT200; Dataquest estimates that it shipped between 50,000 and 60,000 of these units in the second quarter of 1984 and predicts that it will be able to retain at least 60 percent of the VT200-compatible market segment.

There are three main models in the VT200 line, with list prices ranging from $1,395 for the basic alphanumeric terminal to $3,195 for a unit with color graphics capabilities. Display formats on the alpha terminals were always 24 lines but could switch between 80 and 132 characters per line.

CIE Terminals

CIE Terminals was a wholly owned subsidiary of C. Itoh Electronics, a large Japanese company, and was formed when C. Itoh bought its exclusive distributor in early 1983. C. Itoh had established itself in the U.S. terminal market with an emulation of DEC's VT100. It was one of the first manufacturers to develop a copycat of this popular unit and emulated it almost completely. In fact, its CIT-100 was so close to DEC's product that DEC sued C. Itoh for copying its case and design.

SCT considered CIE a closer competitor than other companies because it was one of the few that produced a full-page display. The CIT-500 displayed 66 lines of 80 characters, which were not selectable, displayed on a vertical tube. Overall, it has less function than SCT's Ambassador—for instance, it had no form-filling capability. The single-quantity price for the CIT-500 was $2,150. However, in late 1984 there was a rumor that CIE would be discontinuing it and was dumping its stock at $1,200.

Micro-Term, Inc.

Micro-Term was a small, privately held manufacturer founded in St. Louis in 1976. As of 1982, it reported $7 million in sales, with 80 employees. Micro-Term sold through distributors and direct field sales. It was believed that the company would give its distributor price to any bona fide reseller, without requiring stocking or minimum quantities. In 1983, it moved production off-shore, contracting with Sampo Electronics.

The Datapro report of 1985 lists five models from Micro-Term, priced from $399 to $1,595. The one that most interested SCT was the Twist, Micro-Term's top of the line. This unit was actually private-labeled from Facit, a Swedish company. Micro-Term had exclusive distribution rights for the Twist in the United States. The Twist could display a 72-line page in a vertical screen format, or it could be turned 90 degrees to display the more common 24 lines on a horizontal screen.

Micro-Term had made an unsuccessful earlier attempt at marketing its own full-page display terminal, the ERGO 4000. Although the company advertised the product largely on its ergonomic features, it was also pushed as a word processing unit. After introducing the ERGO 4000 at $1,695, Micro-Term dropped the price to $1,195 six months later and finally withdrew it from the market after a little over a year.

Human Designed Systems

HDS was another small, privately held company that was started in Philadelphia in 1975. Its Concept line of CRT terminals was fairly sophisticated and high end in terms of advanced editing capabilities, form-filling, and multiple pages of memory. The 1985 Datapro report lists three basic models, with list prices ranging from $1,295 to $1,895. All were available with extra memory for $150 additional.

Although HDS did not produce a full-page display terminal, SCT considered the company a key competitor because of its reputation within the AI community. Its products were targeted at the high end of the market, and it was known to produce high quality. HDS reported 1982 sales of $7 million, with 35 employees.

SCT's customer service manager had the following to say about its competition and the advantages offered by SCT's products:

> People might buy any one of our competitors' products. DEC, obviously, because it's DEC and the systems and software are known. Others they buy on price and because SCT has too many features they may not need. They buy us because of the flexibility—for instance, the zoom for selectable display formats. People may be using 24-line software today, but they too are thinking ahead to future needs. SCT makes products they can grow into, while using them all along.

The vice president of operations further defined why companies would purchase SCT's products by saying:

Needs don't necessarily dictate what product you buy—money does. Anyone can have high-end needs. A company will allocate more money to an engineer's terminal than to a clerk's. It's a cost-benefit trade-off for the customer. . . . Loosening up the money to buy it determines the sale more than the functionality of the terminal. But it's in terms of *who* you're making more productive. Like company cars—you buy a stripped-down van for the delivery person, and a Mercedes for the salesperson.

Santa Clara Terminals Today

Marketing Approach

In general, SCT continues to target the high-end, sophisticated user of CRT terminals. Its products push the limits of CRT terminal technology; some have hardware that could be used to provide full workstation functions, although there is currently no software to support it. The vice president of operations explained:

> Our basic marketing approach is to provide high-end products not sold on price. They must be sold on a feature level and on a need level—why it's worth the extra money. It's not a commodity sale, like a $500 terminal. We need people who are trained and understand the product, because no one will know it by themselves. . . . We've been reasonably lucky in that the people we sell to aren't shy. They have their own customer network, and it's developed into an underground marketing approach.

Current marketing is limited. An in-house customer service and support staff fields phone calls and requests for information, as well as answers questions about terminal function and operations. The same people provide after-the-sale support over the phone and interface with the company's engineering, production, and service departments to resolve customer complaints. They also provide support to SCT regional sales representatives and distributors. (See Exhibit 1 for SCT organization chart.)

Paid advertising at this time is limited to new product introductions. The company places a block of ads to run for one to two months in trade publications. The last of these ran in March–April of 1985 to introduce the new XL product line. SCT continues to send out mailings of press and product releases to trade publications and a customer/prospect mailing list. It also exhibits at the computer industry's major trade shows.

The marketing director explained some problems with SCT's marketing:

> A small company takes on the owner's personality—and we're engineering, not marketing, oriented. There's reasonable resistance to marketing here. It's owned by one person, who doesn't have a ''big'' or ''growth'' mentality. We're constrained by the current survival mode.

EXHIBIT 1 Organization chart—January 1, 1985

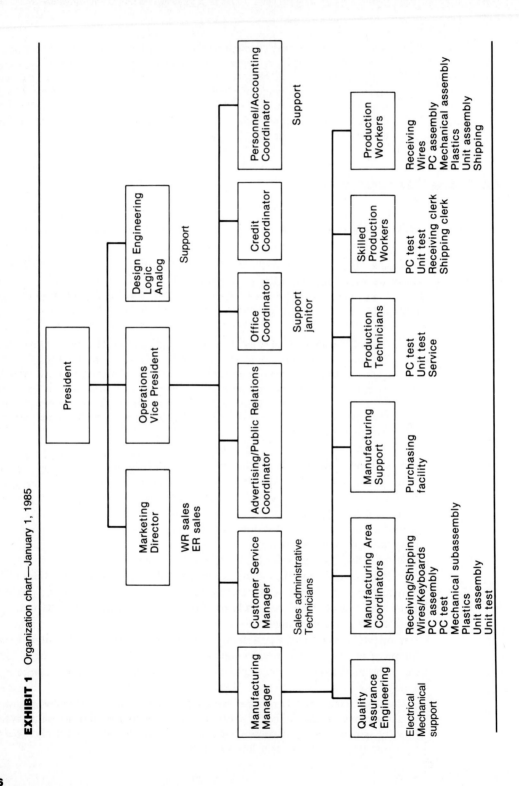

Product

As stated above, SCT's products are at the very high end of the ASCII editing terminal market (see Exhibit 2). It recently introduced the XL series of CRT terminals. These units have the same basic functions as the earlier Ambassador, Genie + Plus, and Guru products, which they replaced. However, they have been repackaged in an updated, more ergonomic case, which features tilt/swivel stand and low-profile keyboard with coiled cable. SCT is also offering the GXL, which is the Ambassador packaged with the Graphics Master introduced earlier as an add-on. This unit is a full graphics display, with resolution of 768 x 600 dots; it can be used with many popular graphics software packages.

SCT has considered bringing out a bit-mapped terminal, which provides much higher-quality display than the dot matrix technique, or a full workstation, but feels it does not have the engineering resources available at this time.

The next new product, the VXL, is scheduled to be introduced in July 1985 at the National Computer Conference. This product goes beyond the current Guru design to provide capabilities for connecting to several host computers at one time, along with multiple windows. This will allow the user to view or edit several files or programs at once, without waiting for the host to complete processing on each one. The VXL will not have local processing abilities.

The marketing director expressed his concerns regarding SCT's product line, saying,

> The product line is too limited, though that depends on the company's objectives. It's all full-page, high-priced—that's a limited market. We need a good, lower-priced terminal, and we could get more business.
>
> Around here you have to prove yourself with increasing sales before you can get the products you want. That doesn't make sense. On the good side, we've addressed some problems. The looks [of the product] were the most important, and we've taken care of that with the XL series. But we could double sales if we had a low-cost, 132-column display.

Distribution

There are currently two regional sales managers, one located on each U.S. coast. They report to the marketing director and are responsible for selling direct to OEMs and large end users, as well as for supporting the distributors in their half of the United States.

There is a network of eight U.S. distributor firms with 25 offices, plus another firm in Canada. The distributors are to sell to smaller-volume (under 100 units) accounts. However, at the current time, SCT will take sales of any volume direct. The company instituted this policy when it was felt that distributors were providing little value-added to the distribution channel. SCT suspected that some distributors were not stocking the products and felt that most were not making the effort to actually sell SCT equipment. In taking

EXHIBIT 2

THE XL SERIES:

A DISPLAY OF EXCELLENCE IN FORM & FUNCTION

Product excellence doesn't happen overnight. _____ we've been designing quality terminals for professionals for over 15 years. We've innovated many of the time- and eye-saving features you now take for granted. And many you don't, if you're not already a _____ user. Now we're unveiling another masterpiece: Our XL Series of ANSI-Standard Terminals.

Designed with you in mind.
The real beauty of the XL Series is its focus on your comfort. Its fully programmable keyboard saves you typing time and effort. Its dynamically selectable display lets you zoom more data onto the screen when you want more context, and less data when you just want bigger characters. With 15-inch or 17-inch portrait or landscape screens, offered in a full spectrum of phosphors, Ann Arbor is easy on your eyes.

Within the XL Series you'll find displays up to 170 characters per line and up to 66 lines per screen.

With plain English setup lines that give you a free hand in feature selection. And a whole palette of diagnostics and data-line monitoring aids to complete the picture.

There's an XL for every application.
Start with the Genie+Plus XL to meet your basic terminal needs. Move to the _____ Ambassador XL when you want a full-page display.

When words alone no longer tell the story, switch to the GXL and add vector graphics. Finally, when you need even more memory and display than any other terminal provides, move all the way to the Guru® XL.

Take a closer look.
Study the specs. View the ergonomic design. See for yourself what it is that makes the _____ XL Series the state-of-the-art display terminal you've been looking for

EXHIBIT 2 *(concluded)*

The XL Series
Features and Capabilities

Industry Standard Interface
- [ ] ANSI X3.64 Standard Controls
- [ ] DEC Software Compatibility
- [ ] EIA RS232 Interface (110-19.2K Baud)
- [ ] Tektronix 4010/4014 Compatibility

Advanced Video Features
- [ ] 15-inch Screen, Portrait or Landscape
- [ ] Slow Scroll
- [ ] Double-Size Characters
- [ ] User-Selectable Display Formats
- [ ] Vertical/Horizontal Keyboard Zoom
- [ ] Up to 28K Memory
- [ ] Paging/Windowing
- [ ] Split Screen Format
- [ ] Pause Key

Enhanced Functional Capabilities
- [ ] Fully Programmable Keyboard
- [ ] 8-Bit Data Mode (Meta Mode)
- [ ] Efficient Forms-Filling Mode
- [ ] Programmable ENQ and DA Responses
- [ ] Fast Editing with Local Move
- [ ] Independent Cursors
- [ ] RS232 Printer Port with Local and Remote Print and Copy Functions

Ergonomic Design
- [ ] Low-Profile Detached Keyboard
- [ ] Non-Glare Screen
- [ ] Mouse Interface (GXL)
- [ ] Tilt/Swivel Base
- [ ] Small Footprint
- [ ] Amber, Green, White Phosphors
- [ ] On/Off and Contrast Controls in Front
- [ ] Operator Convenience Modes
- [ ] English Setup Identifiers

High-Resolution Graphics (GXL)
- [ ] Vector Drawing Speeds of 9600 Baud
- [ ] 11 Line Types (3 User-Defined)
- [ ] Polygon Draw and Fill with 16 Patterns
- [ ] Selective Erase of Vectors, Points, Characters and Windows
- [ ] Alphagraphic Characters with User-Settable Angle, Size and Spacing
- [ ] Viewport Mapping from Drawing Window
- [ ] Print Spooling Mode

Reliability
- [ ] State-of-the-Art Technology in Design, Manufacturing, and Quality Control
- [ ] Internal Test Diagnostics
- [ ] Data-Line Monitor Mode
- [ ] Transparent Test Mode

Maintainability
- [ ] More-than-Fair Exchange Program
- [ ] Economical Factory Service
- [ ] Field Support Program

Note: Not all features are available on all models. Refer to product data sheets for exact specifications.

XL Product Summary
- [ ] The GENIE+PLUS XL is a high performance editing/form-filling terminal with a 30-line display and 60-line memory.
- [ ] AMBASSADOR XL adds a 60-line display capability is available in either a portrait (vertical) or landscape (horizontal) screen orientation.
- [ ] AMBASSADOR GXL adds a vector graphics capability to the standard Ambassador.
- [ ] The GURU XL adds more memory (up to 28K) and more display (up to 66 lines of up to 170 columns), for the most demanding word-processing and text-editing applications.

The portrait display, with the CRT housed vertically, gives the appearance of an 8½" x 11" page, making it appropriate for word-processing applications that involve editing lengthy documents.

The landscape screen display, with the CRT housed horizontally, is well suited to applications involving accounting spreadsheets or vector graphics.

Physical Dimensions
- [ ] XL Terminals—width: 15"; height: 12 3/8"; depth: 13 3/8"
- [ ] XL Stand—footprint: 8 1/2" x 10"; height: 3 3/8"
- [ ] XL Keyboard—length: 16 7/8"; width: 7 3/8"; depth: 1 3/4"
- [ ] 360 degrees of rotation
- [ ] 12 degrees of tilt

orders direct, SCT will discount without a firm volume commitment, more in line with the prices distributors offer to end users.

Previously, SCT had made a greater effort to push products through distribution, except in the case of large-volume and contract orders. Distributors were expected to stock equipment, and all leads were referred to them. The company offered some support in the way of training on SCT's products.

Pricing

SCT's pricing reflects its high-end products. List prices are as follows on the standard product line:

Genie XL	$1,395
Ambassador XL	1,595
Guru XL	2,395
GXL (graphics)	3,590

As noted previously, SCT sells at discounts off these prices, as required. It prefers to sell under an OEM or volume contract, but will give one-time discounts if necessary to get the business, although these are not given out lightly. Distributors' discounts range from 25 to 38 percent off list price.

Service

SCT services all equipment sold by the company, including equipment several generations old, at its facilities in Santa Clara. Recognizing, however, that field service was becoming more important to many end users, the company developed an innovative approach to this problem.

SCT realized that its resources did not make field service outside its own immediate area feasible. At the same time, the specialized nature of its products, along with a relatively small installed base, would make it difficult to attract the attention of a third-party service organization.

To counter these problems, SCT offers the More-Than-Fair-Exchange program for users who require better than normal factory service. For a $25 per unit initial registration fee, the company will ship a replacement unit within 24 hours of being notified of a failure. Returned units are repaired and put back into the replacement pool, with actual repair charges billed to the customer. This approach is much faster than factory service, yet is much less expensive for the customer than full-scale field service.

Engineering

SCT is an engineering-driven company, and a steady flow of new products is vital to its long-term health. Basic research and development engineering is handled by a three-person design group located in Portland, Oregon. This group is responsible for keeping up with the latest computer and display technology and for seeking ways to apply it to SCT's products, both in hardware and software.

Analog (monitor) engineering, as well as manufacturing and product engineering, are located at the Santa Clara factory. These groups "productize" designs. They may be adding refinements requested by the customer, fixing "bugs" that have been found in the firmware, or cleaning up the basic design to get a product to the final production stage.

Finding engineers with experience and high-level capabilities can be a problem for the company. Because of the very sophisticated, state-of-the-art nature of its products, it needs engineers who are not just well abreast of the latest technology but are also able to apply that technology in creative ways to SCT's products.

The customer service manager expressed her concern about the possibilities for growth as follows:

> We need to plan a reorganization if we want to grow. We can handle what we do now, but the current structure isn't viable for heavy growth. . . . We currently have a sales staff, but no marketing staff—no one's in charge of marketing. From an engineering standpoint, we should be telling the engineers what to do and what to build, as opposed to putting the stamp of approval on what they've decided is neat to build.

As Ed Zimmer thought about the future of the company, he had several thoughts:

> Our current marketing approach won't work, but I don't know what will. I see SCT as the only real manufacturer of a full-page terminal. I *know* there's a market out there for it, but I don't know how to reach it.

At the same time, he thought of totally new directions the company could go. For instance, he thought of the printing business and how changes in technology and hardware prices might open it up for creative competitors. He wondered if SCT should be looking at opportunities there or in other segments of the computer industry. Perhaps SCT should get out of manufacturing altogether, or maybe look for another company to acquire it.

EXHIBIT 3
SANTA CLARA TERMINALS, INC., AND SUBSIDIARIES
Consolidated Balance Sheet
As of June 30, 1984, and June 25, 1983

	1984	1983
Assets		
Current assets:		
Cash and cash equivalents	$1,273,643	$1,137,856
Accounts receivable		
Less: Allowance		
for uncollectible accounts of $50,000	1,140,539	973,794
Inventories—at lower of cost		
(first in, first out) or market	611,202	593,714
Refundable income taxes	—	288,000
Prepaid expenses	296,363	284,440
Total current assets	$3,321,747	$3,277,804
Investments:		
Rental property		
Land	161,600	161,600
Buildings	1,000,186	1,000,186
	1,161,786	1,161,786
Less: Accumulated depreciation	205,000	138,322
Total rental at depreciated cost	956,786	1,023,464
Marketable securities	809,536	636,874
Total investments	$1,766,322	$1,660,338
Property and equipment:		
Land	200,283	200,283
Buildings	938,363	938,363
Machinery and equipment	711,789	726,219
Office furniture	125,974	125,974
	$1,976,409	$1,990,839
Less: Accumulated depreciation	903,918	781,110
Total property and equipment		
at depreciated cost	$1,072,491	$1,209,729
Total assets	$6,160,560	$6,147,871

EXHIBIT 3 *(concluded)*

	1984	1983
Liabilities and Stockholders' Equity		
Current liabilities:		
Current maturity of long-term debt	$ 9,606	$ 8,531
Accounts payable	637,654	370,485
Employees' deductions for withheld taxes	8,835	8,949
Accrued expenses		
Salaries, wages, and commissions	232,568	712,430
Taxes, other than income	81,042	152,389
Other	17,600	17,600
Pension plan	—	480,000
Deferred income tax	70,400	—
Total current liabilities	$1,057,705	$1,750,357
Long-term debt:		
Land contract payable		
Less: Current maturity	890,962	901,387
Stockholders' equity:		
Common stock, $0.01 par value, 5,000,000 shares authorized; issued and outstanding 504,000 shares	8,064	8,064
Capital paid in excess of par value	2,354,568	2,354,568
Retained earnings	1,849,261	1,133,494
Total stockholders' equity	$4,211,893	$3,496,126
Total liabilities and stockholders' equity	$6,160,560	$6,147,870

Note: All figures are disguised.

EXHIBIT 4
SANTA CLARA TERMINALS, INC., AND SUBSIDIARIES
Consolidated Statement of Income
for the Years Ended June 30, 1984, and June 25, 1983

	1984	Percent of Net sales	1983	Percent of Net sales
Net sales	$7,959,242	100.0%	$6,821,744	100.0%
Cost of goods sold:				
Inventories,				
beginning of year	593,714		376,483	
Purchases	1,823,819		1,534,394	
Direct labor	519,827		516,454	
Manufacturing expenses	1,595,339		1,689,573	
	4,532,699		4,116,904	
Less: Inventories, end of year	611,202		593,714	
Cost of sales	3,921,497	49.3	3,523,190	51.7
Gross profit on sales	4,037,745	50.7	3,298,554	48.3
Operating expenses:				
Research and development	1,761,747	22.1	765,685	11.2
Selling	682,400	8.6	698,765	10.2
General and administrative	828,429	10.4	1,565,763	23.0
Total operating expenses	3,272,576	41.1	3,030,213	44.4
Income before other income				
or (expense) and income tax	765,169	9.6	268,341	3.9
Other income or (expense):				
Loss from rental operations	(86,082)		(78,051)	
Interest and sundry income	107,080		154,797	
Total other income				
or (expense)	20,998	.3	76,746	1.1
Income before income taxes	786,167	9.9	345,087	5.0
Income Tax—deferred	70,400	.9	—	—
Net income	$ 715,767	9.0%	$ 345,087	5.0%

Note: All figures are disguised.

EXHIBIT 5
SANTA CLARA TERMINALS, INC., AND SUBSIDIARIES
Consolidated Statement of Changes in Financial Position
for the Years Ended June 30, 1984, and June 25, 1983

	1984	1983
Sources of working capital:		
Net income	$ 715,767	$ 345,087
Add: Charge or (credit) to net income not affecting working capital		
Depreciation	207,178	225,186
Gain on sale of vehicle	(6,880)	—
Total provided from operations	916,065	570,273
Transfer of working capital on corporate reorganization	—	1,248,640
Proceeds from sale of vehicle	6,880	—
Total sources of working capital	$ 922,945	$1,818,913
Applications of working capital:		
Increase in investments	172,662	248,018
Acquisition of property and equipment	3,261	34,216
Decrease in long-term debt	10,426	9,232
Total applications of working capital	186,349	291,466
Increase in working capital	$ 736,595	$1,527,447
Changes in working capital:		
Increase or (decrease) in current assets		
Cash and cash equivalents	$ 135,787	$1,137,856
Accounts receivable	166,746	973,794
Inventories	17,488	593,714
Refundable income taxes	(288,000)	288,000
Prepaid expenses	11,923	284,440
Total	43,944	3,277,804
Increase or (decrease) in current liabilities:		
Current maturity of long-term debt	1,075	8,531
Accounts payable	267,197	370,458
Employees' deductions for withheld taxes	(114)	8,949
Accrued expenses	(1,031,210)	1,362,419
Deferred income tax	70,400	—
Total	(692,652)	1,750,357
Increase in working capital	$ 736,596	$1,527,447

Case 3

Atlanta Cyclorama*

The director of the Atlanta Cyclorama was sitting in his Grant Park office speculating over his greatest challenge, namely, devising the 1987 promotional plan for the Cyclorama and long-range strategies for the attraction for future years. Attendance will have to be increased from an estimated 342,000 in 1986 to 500,000 in 1989, and sales will have to exceed $1 million per year by 1990. Attendance in 1982 was 195,000 and in 1983 it reached 300,000. Attendance figures for 1984 through 1986, broken down by ticket class, are shown in Table I.

TABLE I Breakdown of Cyclorama attendance and revenue by ticket class

Ticket class	1984		1985		1986	
	Attendance	Revenue	Attendance	Revenue	Attendance	Revenue
Adult ($3.00)	117,000	$351,000	129,005	$387,015	146,789	$440,367
Adult group and senior citizens ($2.50)	82,463	206,158	77,030	192,575	82,325	205,813
Children ($1.50)	20,446	30,669	22,465	33,698	25,840	38,760
Child group ($1)	7,096	7,096	6,637	6,637	6,122	6,122
Free	41,217	—	37,578	—	42,120	—
Tour groups	30,000	57,483	29,315	67,891	38,900	90,098
Total	298,222	$652,406	279,000	$687,816	342,096	$781,160

The Atlanta Cyclorama

Before the invention of motion pictures, opportunities for the general public to view past events were definitely limited. One vehicle for accomplishing this desire was the cyclorama, which is defined as "a 360° circular painting which when viewed from its interior gives the illusion that the viewer is in the scene."

* This case was prepared at Georgia State University as a basis for class discussion rather than to illustrate either effective or ineffective handling of an administrative situation. All publication rights reserved; copyright © 1987, by John Wright and Daniel C. Bello. Used with permission.

A cyclorama is also sometimes referred to as a panorama. Hundreds of these cycloramas were painted and shown in American cities in the latter half of the 19th century; however, today only 14 survive throughout the world. In the United States, in addition to the Atlanta Cyclorama, a panorama is on exhibit at the Gettysburg Battlefield in Pennsylvania, and another is in the Metropolitan Museum of Art in New York.

The Atlanta Cyclorama was created in 1885 and depicts the 1864 Battle of Atlanta which is familiar to all who have seen the movie *Gone with the Wind*. The masterpiece is a 50-foot-high, 400-foot circumference painting in the round, with a three-dimensional diorama complete with figures added by the WPA in the 1930s. The cyclorama was first displayed in a frame building in Grant Park in 1912. In 1921, the painting was moved to its present building. After years of use and limited maintenance, the attraction had fallen into an advanced state of disrepair so serious that by 1979 the cyclorama had to be closed. Extensive restoration ensued at a cost of $11 million. For two and a half years, workers repaired the tears and flaws in the painting and revamped the three-dimensional diorama that serves as the painting's foreground. The restoration effort also included the installation of a revolving viewing platform as well as the refurbishing of the building that houses the painting. The exhibit reopened to the public in 1982. In addition to the famous painting, visitors can also admire other exhibits related to the Civil War: for instance, the famous locomotive Texas, winner of the "great locomotive chase." It is the same train that a group of Confederates drove to Ringgold to chase Union raiders who had stolen the locomotive General. Thus, the Atlanta Cyclorama is part historical museum, part artwork, and part Confederate memorial. The cyclorama shares its Grant Park location with the Atlanta Zoo, thus providing a combination sightseeing opportunity.

Grant Park is located three miles south of the downtown hotel district. In past years, the zoo had exerted a negative influence on attendance at the cyclorama because local media stories highlighted the fact that the zoo had fallen into a state of disrepair and that animals had been poorly treated. Fortunately, civic pride had lead to a revitalization program for the zoo in 1985, and a major renovation similar to that experienced by the cyclorama had been completed by late 1986. Attendance figures for the zoo are shown in Table II.

TABLE II   Attendance figures for the Atlanta Zoo

Year	Attendance
1978	452,051
1979	388,832
1980	363,433
1981	347,828
1982	402,118
1983	448,397
1984	279,805
1985	344,087
1986	567,269

Zoo attendance had increased steadily with the renovation efforts, growing from 280,000 in 1984 to almost 570,000 in 1986.

The cyclorama is owned and operated by the Atlanta city government. Exhibit 1 is an organization chart for this operation. In addition to a director and an associate director, there is a staff of 17 persons. The director is a professional, chosen by civil service procedures. The city council authorizes the budget and exercises control over other activities.

EXHIBIT 1 Organization chart—Atlanta Cyclorama

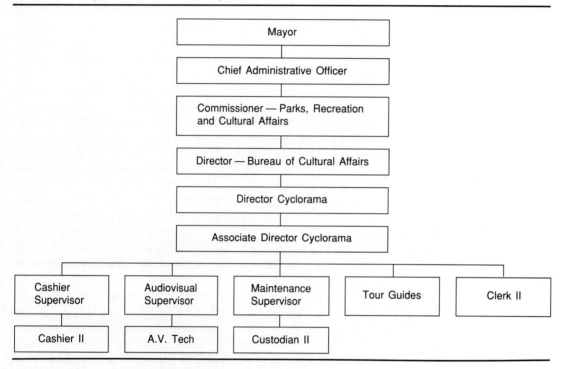

The Product and its Market

Every year, a very diversified crowd visits the cyclorama. The admission price is very reasonable: $3.00 for adults ($2.50 if in groups of 10 or more), $2.50 for senior citizens, $1.50 for children ($1 if in groups of 10 or more), and children under six are admitted free. School groups are also admitted free. Furthermore, there is no charge for parking.

Different groups of people flock to this attraction. The attendance can be segmented into four categories: tour groups (consisting mainly of senior citizens and school groups), conventioneers, visitors and tourists, and finally local residents. These market segments all exhibit particular characteristics.

Tour groups. This segment tends to visit the cyclorama on weekdays. For both segments (school children and senior citizens), the visit usually occurs once a year.

Conventioneers. Atlanta is the third largest convention city in the United States in terms of numbers of conventions hosted. In 1985, 1.5 million conventioneers came to Atlanta. Mostly, they stayed in the downtown area and remained in Atlanta about 3.0 days. Tables III and IV present the conventioneers' attendance growth and their average daily expenditure and length of stay from 1976 to 1985. The main problem they encounter is the lack of activity and entertainment close to downtown. At the heart of the convention world in Atlanta is the Georgia World Congress Center. The Georgia World Congress Center started its operations in Atlanta in September 1976. At that time, it offered 350,000 square feet of exhibition space. But with the convention market booming, it soon proved to be insufficient. In April 1985, the Georgia World Congress Center officially celebrated its expanded opening: 650,000 square feet of exhibition space, and over 1 million square feet of floor space. The center is one of the world's top meeting/exhibit facilities, with its ballroom, auditorium, corporate conference center, and 70 meeting rooms.

TABLE III Atlanta conventioneers' attendance, per year

Year	Conventions Hosted	Attendance
1976	725	635,000
1977	760	760,000
1978	800	850,000
1979	970	876,800
1980	1,090	1,002,900
1981	1,150	1,128,000
1982	1,000	1,150,000
1983	1,100	1,300,000
1984	1,200	1,110,000
1985	1,400	1,500,000

TABLE IV Atlanta conventioneers' daily expenditure and length of stay, per year

Year	Average Daily Expenditure	Length of Stay
1976	$ 70.00	3.2 days
1977	73.50	3.5 days
1978	77.00	3.5 days
1979	81.00	4.0 days
1980	99.00	4.0 days
1981	110.00	4.0 days
1982	126.00	3.5 days
1983	135.00	3.0 days
1984	141.00	3.0 days
1985	141.00	3.0 days

Expanded exhibition space is, of course, only one dimension of the convention business opportunity. To host large meetings requires a sufficient quantity of convenient hotel facilities. Atlanta has also experienced a dramatic increase in the number of downtown hotel rooms, from 9,065 in 1979 to 12,596 in 1985.

The combination of exhibition space and large number of hotel rooms has placed a marketing challenge before the Atlanta Convention and Visitors Bureau. This organization has spearheaded an aggressive program designed to persuade groups to hold their conventions in the city. Atlanta is expected to host even more conventions, thus endowing this market segment with a growth potential.

Tourists and sightseers. This market is more than twice the size of the conventioneer market. Summer is the favorite season to visit Atlanta, since 43 percent of the yearly tourists come to visit during June, July, and August. Table V presents cyclorama attendance figures month by month. Many Atlanta visitors come to meet with family (45 percent); others (39 percent) come to sightsee, with 14 percent specifically mentioning tourist sites and 3.5 percent mentioning cultural sites. Their stay is shorter: one or two days, but many of them enjoy two or three attractions during their visit.

TABLE V Average attendance by month, Atlanta Cyclorama

	Percent of total
January	5%
February	5
March	7
April	7
May	6
June	13
July	14
August	16
September	10
October	8
November	6
December	3

Mention should be made of another tourist group, namely the people who flow through Atlanta as they travel to and from the state of Florida. Atlanta is located on two interstate highways, I–75 and I–85, which provide corridors for traffic to and from the northeast and midwest sections of the United States. Large numbers of tourists living in these regions spend their vacations in Florida, and the State of Georgia has tried for many years to convince these persons to "Stay and See" Georgia. For example, a number of welcome centers were set up at the state borders where information about tourist attractions in the state is distributed. Table VI gives some indication of the magnitude of this opportunity. Sporadically, the state has done media advertising in such areas of

TABLE VI Number of visitors to the Atlanta Welcome Center

Year	Number of visitors
1976	6,605
1977	6,219
1978	5,229
1979	3,498
1980	14,763
1981	5,119
1982	2,035
1983	7,638
1984	10,995
1985	11,600

origin as Ohio and Michigan. In 1985, the state of Georgia tripled its tourist advertising budget to $2.1 million, using "Adventures in the great unknown—Georgia" as a campaign theme.

Local residents and their out-of-town guests. Atlanta and its metropolitan area, encompassing 18 counties, contained an estimated population of 2,326,000 at the end of 1984. This figure can be contrasted with the 1980 population figure of 2,138,231 people, and the 1970 and 1960 figures of 1,684,200 and 1,247,649, respectively. The city is growing rapidly, but the expansion is taking place mostly at the northern perimeter of the city, far from downtown. However, the population in Atlanta is very mobile: Most Atlantans are from other states, and many have been in Atlanta for only a short period of time.

Consumption Patterns and Attitudes

Visitors to the cyclorama seek to fulfill four different types of needs: education, enjoyment of art, history, and entertainment. But each segment exhibits specific trends which affect the attractiveness of the cyclorama.

Conventioneers. One major pattern observed is that Atlanta conventioneers very seldom bring their spouses with them, and only 18 percent bring their children. When planning tours, convention planners seek attractions with overall appeal, uniqueness, ability to accommodate large groups, and accessible parking. The cyclorama fits all these needs remarkably well, plus it has that Old South charm that is so appealing to conventioneers. Furthermore, the cyclorama can be rented to a private group. It will accommodate up to 180 people at a time on its rotating platform.

Tourists and sightseers. Tourists almost always have access to a car, and they are looking for a day-long entertainment schedule. Attributes that are solvent in their choice of attractions are: accessible from freeway, parking, fun for the whole family, near other attractions, and uniqueness. Once again, the cyclorama fares well on all.

Residents and guests. This segment is looking for a full-day experience offering a good time/value ratio. The closeness to the zoo and the low admission price play in the cyclorama's favor. However, it should be remembered that the guests' host will likely influence their choice. Thus, since the cyclorama is visited at most once a year by local residents, this can have a negative impact on the cyclorama.

The cyclorama is a product that is unique. But, it also has many competitors because it belongs in the generic category of tourist and cultural attractions. In the past, the cyclorama had cooperated with other historical/cultural attractions by the use of cross-promotion techniques such as distributing each others' brochures. Additional Atlanta attractions include: (1) Stone Mountain Park, with over 5.6 million visitors; (2) Six Flags Over Georgia, an amusement park that admitted over 2.5 million visitors; (3) Fernbank Science Center which attracted 700,000 visitors; and (4) the Martin Luther King, Jr. Center with its 500,000 visitors. In 1986, the Carter Presidential Library opened to the public and proved to be a popular attraction. Other competing activities in which visitors can participate are shopping, theater, and nightlife.

Trade

The cyclorama is a product that does not lend itself easily to trade activities. However, the cyclorama is a stop on the tour lists of six different Atlanta operators: Atlanta Tours, Arnell Tours, Brewster Motor Coach, Gray Line of Atlanta (a picture of the diorama is featured in their promotional brochure), Metro Tours, and Southeastern Stages. Furthermore, many school groups and senior citizen groups visit the cyclorama.

Past Experience with Communications Elements

Advertising

In 1986, most of the cyclorama's promotional budget was allocated to advertising. Ads were run for three months in *Southern Living* and for seven months in the weekly *Saturday Leisure Guide* of the *Atlanta Journal/Constitution*. In addition, special advertising in connection with special events was scheduled. In total, in 1986 $40,000 was budgeted for routine advertising plus $6,000 for special advertising. Advertising for the cyclorama tends to be simple, staid, and dignified. Print ads are of the reminder type, treating it as a presold product. Exhibit 2 is an example of the print ad run in the local newspaper.

EXHIBIT 2   Sample newspaper ad, 1984

EXPERIENCE THE EVENT
THAT FORGED THE REBIRTH OF

"OUR BRAVE AND BEAUTIFUL CITY"

16 SHOWS DAILY
MONDAY — SUNDAY
9:30 a.m. — 4:30 p.m.

IN HISTORIC GRANT PARK
800 CHEROKEE AVE, S.E.
ATLANTA. GA.

COUPON
ADMIT PARTY AT GROUP RATE
$2.50 – Adults
$1.00 – Child (6 – 13)

Personal Selling

Up to now, the product iself and the budgetary restrictions have prevented the use of this communication tool for the cyclorama.

Sales Promotion

Sales promotion tools used in 1986 were information brochures and cents-off coupons. The brochures are mostly distributed at welcome centers and at Atlanta Convention and Visitors Bureau booths.

The brochures are factual and focus on the historical appeal. They, too, possess the dignity and seriousness of tone generally associated with cultural and historical attractions. Couponing has been directed primarily at conventioneers, and $2,000 of the 1986 budget was spent on media for this purpose. Effectiveness studies have yet to be undertaken.

Publicity/Public Relations

The cyclorama has been the subject of many articles in local magazines and newspapers. It has also been featured in public service announcements on radio and television. The cyclorama is also doing cross-publicity with other national attractions such as the Gettysburg Cyclorama, the Boston Fine Arts Building, the Milwaukee Historical Society, and the Atlanta Historical Society.

Media Cost and Audience Information

The Atlanta area is served by a variety of print and broadcast media. Table VII shows some cost and audience data for the major print vehicles in the Atlanta area. The major newspaper is the *Atlanta Journal/Constitution* which publishes a morning and evening edition. A single three-inch ad costs $277 and runs in both the morning and evening papers. In terms of magazines, *Southern Living* is very popular, containing articles on travel, cooking, and history. An advertiser can place a full or fractional page ad in a statewide edition or a full page ad in a metro Atlanta edition. The three magazines, *Atlanta Magazine, Business Atlanta,* and *Georgia Trends,* are slick periodicals that reach an upscale suburban family or business audience. The two magazines *Where* and *Key* are "What to do in Atlanta" periodicals and are distributed free to hotel guests.

TABLE VII Atlanta area print media cost and audience data for black and white print ads

Newspaper; 3-inch ad	Costs		Number of Readers (000's)		
	1 time	52 times	All Adults	Women	Men
1. *Atlanta Journal/Constitution*	$277	$14,404	963	475	488
Magazines; 1/3-page ad	1 time	6 times	All Adults	Women	Men
1. *Southern Living* Georgia edition	$2,090	$12,540	190	133	57
Atlanta edition, full-page ad only	3,930	21,240	100	70	30
2. *Atlanta* magazine	1,025	5,670	33	—	—
3. *Business Atlanta*	755	4,110	24	3	21
4. *Georgia Trends*	850	4,530	27	—	—
5. *Where/Atlanta*	850	4,260	60	—	—
6. *Key/Atlanta*	115	690	10	—	—

Table VIII shows the cost and audience data for broadcast media. The data for a 30-second television spot on the networks' morning news programs are shown. Also, data for Atlanta's five biggest radio stations are shown for the

TABLE VIII Atlanta area broadcast media cost and audience data for 7:00 A.M. to 9:00 A.M., weekdays

			Number of Viewers/Listeners (000's)		
Television: 30-Second Spot	Cost	Rating*	All Adults	Women	Men
1. WSB (ABC, "Good Morning America")	$350	4.0	108	64	44
2. WAGA (CBS, "Morning News")	125	1.3	36	22	14
3. WXIA (NBC, "Today Show")	375	3.4	92	56	36
Radio: 60-Second Spot					
1. WZGC (Top 40)	$250	1.3	36	19	17
2. WQXI (adult rock)	350	1.9	51	27	24
3. WSB (Contemporary)	200	1.4	38	20	18
4. WFOX (rock oldies)	150	0.9	24	13	11
5. WKHX (Country)	250	1.9	51	26	25

* Rating is a measure of audience size expressed as a percentage of 2,699,800 adults which is the survey area's population base for 1987.

morning drive-time period. The radio stations have different creative formats in addition to different costs and audiences.

A serious constraint facing the director of the cyclorama as he sets about designing the 1987 promotional plan for the cyclorama is in the area of budget. The Atlanta City Council has authorized an expenditure of $50,000 for a publicity fund. The amount is available for media advertising and sales promotion efforts. Personal selling and publicity activities are carried out by the director and associate director as part of their overall duties. A separate printing budget of $25,000 pays for brochures and similar forms of direct advertising.

The director realizes that the budget allocated to the cyclorama is not sufficient given the task of generating an appreciable increase in attendance. Therefore, he is fully aware of the importance of making the right decisions as he designs the cyclorama's 1987 promotional plan.

Case 4

Edgewater Marina*

In early January Captain Nathan Rutledge, proprietor of Edgewater Marina, looked out over the mostly empty docks and remarked to John Burnhart, a graduate student at The Citadel, "I'm starting my second year in this business and I've still got half a mile of empty slips. All I've heard about from Charleston boat owners is that there's a lack of marina space around here, but most of my docks are still empty. I just can't figure out what is wrong with my operation. Any ideas you have, John, would be greatly appreciated."

Background of the Marina

Edgewater Marina, the newest in the Charleston, South Carolina, area, opened for business the previous February (see Exhibits 1 and 2). The proprietor, Nathan Rutledge, was a retired Navy captain who had spent the last six years of his Navy career in the Charleston area. As he was a sailing enthusiast who had spent the greater part of his adult life near ships and the sea, a marina seemed the ideal business to challenge his managerial talents and provide him the less structured lifestyle he was seeking. The apparent lack of marina space in Charleston (the local Municipal Marina had a long waiting list for slips and the others appeared to be always full) plus his love for the Charleston area provided the incentive for him to construct and operate the Edgewater Marina.

To begin the operation, Rutledge purchased a 10-acre plot of land on the Stono River (see Exhibit 3) with 1,200-foot frontage on the river and began construction in January a year ago. The site seemed ideal for a marina as it provided sheltered deep water and was only a quarter mile off the Intracoastal Waterway. The marina is located just off a major two-lane road and is five miles from downtown Charleston. Transit to the ocean could be achieved by either following the Stono River south to its mouth (8 nautical miles) or by following

---

* This case was prepared by Cleon L. Hartzell, Jr., under the supervision of Professor Douglass G. Norvell of The Citadel as a basis for class discussion rather than to illustrate either effective or ineffective handling of an administrative situation. Used with permission.

EXHIBIT 1 Map of the Charleston area

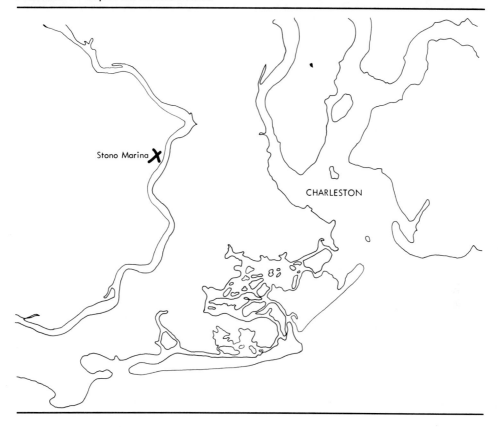

EXHIBIT 2 Charleston area marinas

	Breach Inlet	Mt. Pleasant	Charleston Municipal	Ashley	Ria Scott	Edgewater
Total number berths	6	60	308	92	80*	120
Usually available to transients	0	10	30	12	0	24
Per foot overnight	—	0.25	0.25	0.20	—	0.25
Per foot monthly	1.50	1.50	†	2.00	‡	1.75
Gasoline	X	X	X	—	X	—
Diesel	—	X	X	—	—	—
Water	X	X	X	X	X	X
Electricity	X	X	X	X	—	X
Showers	—	—	X	—	—	—
Laundry	—	—	X	—	—	—
Groceries	X	—	X	—	—	—
Restaurant	—	—	X	X	X	—
Snack bar	X	X	X	—	—	X
Ice	X	X	X	X	X	X
Bait	X	X	—	—	—	—
Boat landing	X	X	X	—	—	—

* Dry stack berths limited to boats under 24 feet.

† Monthly charge averaged $35 per month per berth.

‡ Monthly charge of $50 and one-year lease required.

EXHIBIT 3 Depths of the river near the marina

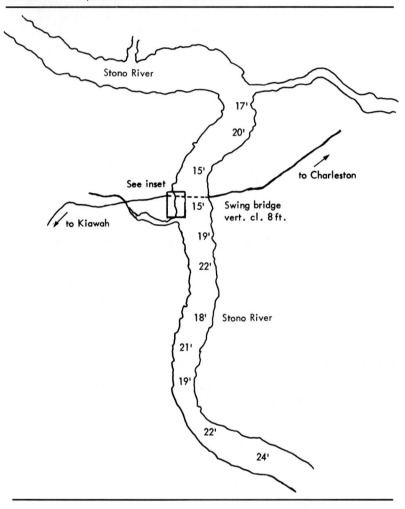

the Intracoastal Waterway to Charleston Harbor and exiting there (13 nautical miles). The Stono River inlet was generally used only by knowledgeable local boaters, as the entrance channel was bordered by shifting sandbars. As a result, marker buoys were always being relocated.

The marina was composed of three 660-foot floating docks connected to the shore by a floating access dock and fixed wharf (see Exhibit 4). Utilities provided on the docks included water (marina well), electricity (110/220), and telephone service (hook-up jacks). A public phone was available at the head of the wharf. The docks were lighted at night, and a dockmaster or assistant dockmaster was always present. The one building constructed at the marina

EXHIBIT 4 Docks and facilities at the marina

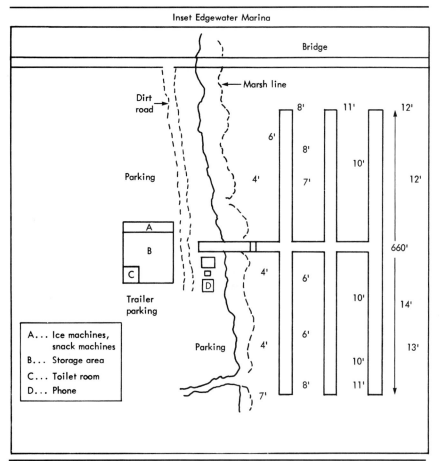

served by partitioning as storage area, toilet facility, and vending machine location. Only one sink and toilet were provided in this building, but facility improvement plans called for the construction of a separate toilet/shower. Captain Rutledge was having problems with the local board of health on this issue and extensive sewage disposal facilities would be required before the additional toilet/shower building could be constructed. Because of the large capital investment required (estimated at $5,000), this project had been indefinitely delayed. The access road was unpaved but well drained. Parking for about 30 cars was provided on an unpaved surface with trees scattered through it. About one fourth of the parking area was unusable after a heavy rain because of the muddy conditions, but this was to be corrected by paving the parking areas within the year. Exhibit 5 shows the financial development plan projected for the marina's first year.

EXHIBIT 5

EDGEWATER MARINA

Financial Development Plan
Pro Forma Statement of Sources and Application of Funds
For the Year Ending December 31

Sources of net working capital:

Net income[1]	$ 24,583	
Depreciation	200	
Issuance of long-term debt	100,000	
Owner input	50,000	
Total sources		$174,783

Applications of net working capital:

Procurement of land	81,950	
Land clearing	1,500	
Installation of electricity	1,550	
Storage/toilet building	2,000	
Auto parking area	4,600	
Septic tank	1,180	
Well and pump	300	
Construction of wharf	1,789	
Construction of docks	43,827	
Installation of pilings	18,000	
Installation of water main	1,000	
Toilet/shower building	2,000	
Fuel pumps and storage tanks	7,000	
Total applications		166,696
Increase in net working capital		$ 8,087

Notes:

[1] Owner agreed to not remove any of the net income from the business during the first year of operation.

Captain Rutledge hoped that the marina would be a family business. His eldest son was to act as dockmaster and live aboard a houseboat at the marina. Also, a second son and a daughter acted as assistants during the peak boating season. All were to be paid wages for their services, and these were deducted from operating revenue as expenses. Because of his independent retirement income from the Navy, Captain Rutledge was to leave the first operating year's income from the marina in the business to build up the net working capital. The dock rental rate structure was based on the prevailing rates at the other local marinas. Charges were $1.75 per month per foot of the boat length plus 10 percent of the boat's length for maneuvering room. Rents were due monthly in advance and no leases were required. The rate for transient boats was set at 25 cents per foot per day with no surcharge for utilities (except telephone). Exhibits 6, 7, and 8 show the projected financial statements of the Edgewater Marina for the first year.

EXHIBIT 6

EDGEWATER MARINA

Pro Forma Cash Budget—First Year

	January	February	March	April
Cash receipts:				
Collection of dock rents[1]	$ 0	$ 1,848	$ 3,696	$ 5,544
Boat care service	0	0	0	0
Fuel, oil, and parts	0	0	0	0
Total cash receipts	0	1,848	3,696	5,544
Cash disbursements:				
Procurement of land	80,000	0	0	0
Administrative services	2,000	50	75	100
Supplies	100	50	50	50
Utilities	50	110	120	170
Loan payments	0	1,170	1,170	1,170
Land improvements	2,100	600	600	0
Facilities				
Wharfs and docks[2]	1,200	35,026	14,195	14,195
Building/equipment	3,830	0	0	0
Insurance	800	0	0	0
Wages[3]	0	0	0	0
Taxes	0	0	0	0
Miscellaneous	0	100	100	100
Total cash disbursements ...	90,080	37,106	16,310	15,785
Net cash gain (loss)	($ 90,080)	($ 35,258)	($ 12,614)	($ 10,241)
Cumulative net cash flow	(90,080)	(125,338)	(137,952)	(148,193)
Analysis of cash flow				
Beginning cash balance[4]	150,000	59,920	24,662	12,048
Net cash gain (loss)	(90,080)	(35,258)	(12,614)	(10,241)
Ending cash balance	59,920	24,662	12,048	1,807

Notes:

[1] Dock rent based on $1.75/foot of dock space at 80 percent usage rate.

[2] Total of 3,960 linear feet of dock space available by April 30.

[3] Wages are for the assistants to owner/manager. Initially these positions are not filled.

[4] Initial cash provided by owner's investment and bank loans.

The First Operating Year

By May all dock construction was complete and utilities installed. Costs for materials and labor used in building the docks ended up being 26 percent higher than was originally planned. As occupancy rate for dock space was only 15 percent, the marina was experiencing a severe cash flow problem. Captain Rutledge contacted an old friend from his Navy days, Captain Alan Jones, and convinced him to invest in the marina. The details of this arrangement are shown in note 2 to Exhibit 8. This provided a fresh infusion of $40,000 into the business and figuratively allowed Rutledge to keep his head above water. All additional facility improvements were deferred until revenues picked up, and costs were closely monitored to conserve cash.

EXHIBIT 6 *(continued)*
EDGEWATER MARINA
Pro Forma Cash Budget—First Year

	May	June	July	August
Cash receipts:				
Collection of dock rents	$ 5,544	$ 5,544	$ 5,544	$ 5,544
Boat care service	700	700	700	700
Fuel, oil, and parts	0	0	0	0
Total cash receipts	6,244	6,244	6,244	6,244
Cash disbursements:				
Administrative services	100	150	150	150
Supplies	50	50	100	100
Utilities	270	380	430	430
Taxes	150	150	200	200
Insurance	150	200	200	200
Wages	1,000	1,000	1,000	1,000
Facilities				
Buildings[5]	2,000	0	0	0
Equipment[6]	0	0	2,700	900
Payment on loans	1,170	1,170	1,170	1,170
Fuel	0	0	0	4,000
Land improvements[7]	0	0	0	1,400
Miscellaneous	200	200	200	200
Total cash disbursements ...	5,090	3,300	6,150	9,950
Net cash gain (loss)	$ 1,154	$ 2,944	$ 94	($ 3,706)
Cumulative net cash flow	(147,039)	(144,095)	(144,001)	(147,607)
Analysis of cash flow				
Beginning cash balance	1,807	2,961	5,905	5,999
Net cash gain (loss)	1,154	2,944	94	(3,706)
Ending cash balance	2,961	5,905	5,999	2,293

Notes:

[5] Additional toilet building to be built in May.

[6] Fuel pumps and storage tanks installed starting in July and ending in November.

[7] Improvements to automobile parking area.

EXHIBIT 6 *(concluded)*
EDGEWATER MARINA
Pro Forma Cash Budget—First Year

	September	October	November	December
Cash receipts:				
Collection of dock rents	$ 5,544	$ 5,544	$ 5,544	$ 5,544
Boat care service	700	700	700	700
Fuel, oil, and parts	300	300	400	450
Total cash receipts	6,544	6,544	6,644	6,694
Cash disbursements:				
Administrative services	150	150	150	150
Supplies	100	100	100	100
Utilities	455	455	530	530
Taxes	200	200	250	250
Insurance	200	200	300	300
Wages	1,500	1,500	1,800	1,800
Facilities				
Buildings	0	0	0	0
Equipment	1,500	1,500	500	0
Payment on loans	1,170	1,170	1,170	1,170
Fuel	0	0	0	4,000
Land improvements	700	700	0	0
Repairs	0	100	100	350
Income tax	0	0	0	200
Miscellaneous	200	200	300	300
Total cash disbursements ...	6,175	6,275	5,200	9,150
Net cash gain (loss)	$ 369	$ 269	$ 1,444	($ 2,456)
Cumulative net cash flow	(147,238)	(146,969)	(145,525)	(147,981)
Analysis of cash flow				
Beginning cash balance	2,393	2,762	3,031	4,475
Net cash gain (loss)	369	269	1,444	(2,456)
Ending cash balance	2,762	3,031	4,475	2,019

EXHIBIT 7

EDGEWATER MARINA

Pro Forma Income Statement—First Year

	Actual	*Pro forma*
Revenues:		
Dock rent	$18,480	$55,440
Boat care service	3,800	5,600
Sales of fuel, oil, and parts	0	1,450
Total revenue	22,280	62,490
Expenses:		
Administrative	1,200	1,425
Utilities	3,100	3,930
Wages	5,000	10,800
Interest	5,534	5,534
Sales tax	600	1,600
Cost of goods sold	0	1,368
Depreciation	200	200
Repairs	400	550
Miscellaneous	1,000	2,100
Insurance	2,550	2,550
Supplies	850	950
Total expenses	20,434	31,007
Earnings before income taxes	1,846	31,483
Income taxes	0	7,100
Net earnings	$ 1,846	$24,383

EXHIBIT 8

EDGEWATER MARINA

Pro Forma Balance Sheet—End of First Year

	Actual	Pro forma
Assets		
Current assets:		
Cash	$ 6,885	$ 2,019
Accounts receivable	1,200	0
Fuel/supplies	700	6,632
Prepaid expenses	315	0
Total current assets	9,100	8,651
Fixed assets:		
Land	84,400	88,050
Buildings .... $ 3,830	$ 5,830	
Equipment 0	7,000	
Wharfs and docks 81,400	64,616	
Less: Accumulated depreciation .... 2,130[1]	200	
Net buildings/equipment/wharfs		
and docks	83,100	77,246
Total fixed assets	167,500	165,296
Other assets:		
Intangible assets	300	300
Total assets	$176,900	$174,247
Liabilities and Net Worth		
Current liabilities:		
Accounts payable	$ 1,390	$ 0
Accrued taxes	0	7,100
Expenses payable	1,000	0
Total current liabilities	2,390	7,100
Long-term liabilities:		
Notes payable	92,664	92,664
Total liabilities	95,054	99,764
Net worth:		
Rutledge, capital	40,923	74,483
Jones, capital[2]	40,923	0
Total capital	81,846	74,483
Total capital and net worth	$176,900	$174,247

Notes:

[1] Depreciation calculated on straight-line basis over 40-year period.

[2] In May Edgewater Marina was changed from a sole proprietorship to a partnership between Captain Nathan Rutledge and Captain Alan Jones. The owners' equity in the marina was recapitalized as follows:

Rutledge, capital $40,000
Jones, capital $40,000

Captain Jones is to be a silent partner. All profits will be equally divided between Captain Rutledge and Captain Jones. As of January 1 Captain Rutledge will receive a salary of $15,000 per year for managing the marina.

It was obvious by July that the marina would not come close to the 80 percent occupancy rate that had been envisioned. While the docks were now half full, many of the boat owners indicated that they would be either moving their boats to warmer climates in the fall or removing them from the water altogether. Until this time Captain Rutledge had relied on word-of-mouth advertising to make the public aware of his marina. The Mid-Atlantic edition of the Waterway Guide made no mention of the Edgewater Marina and only hinted that a marina might be constructed soon along the Stono River. The swing bridge just north of the marina blocked its view from the Intracoastal Waterway, and the few transients that managed to find it were usually boats that had been turned away from the full Municipal Marina. Exhibit 9 shows the breakdown of the boats at the Edgewater Marina in July.

EXHIBIT 9   Edgewater Marina list of boats present (July)

Trailer boats	
14 feet–20 feet	4
20 feet–28 feet	11
Sailboats	
20 feet–30 feet	12
30 feet	5
Pleasure cruisers	
26 feet–34 feet	10
34 feet–44 feet	4
Sport fishermen	
20 feet–30 feet	6
30 feet	3
Yachts	
45 feet	1
Houseboats	3
Total	59

The rest of the first year showed no improvement, and many boat owners left the marina that fall. The occupancy rate averaged out to 27 percent the first year instead of the hoped for 80 percent. No additional facility improvements were accomplished, and this left the marina without a toilet/shower building, paved parking, or fueling equipment. One bright spot had been the demand for boat care service (hull painting, minor mechanical repairs) that had come from the boats that had utilized the marina. If the same demand percentage had occurred from an 80 percent full marina, income from this source would have been twice that predicted. With the start of the boating season only two months away Captain Rutledge was indeed anxious for any ideas to improve marina operations and occupancy rate.

The Market

John Burnhart's interest in boating and a course he was presently taking in marketing at The Citadel motivated him to undertake an analysis of the market for marinas in the Charleston area. He first talked to some of the boat owners who were still present at the marina and asked them how they had come to choose the Edgewater Marina. All were local boat owners and 30 percent indicated lack of space at other marinas caused them to pick Edgewater. Another 40 percent chose Edgewater because it was the most convenient for their needs. The remaining 30 percent were either dissatisfied with something at other marinas (long leases, lack of dredging, lack of personal service) or said they just like the friendly relaxed atmosphere at Edgewater. Many indicated that the lack of fueling facilities was a bother and could cause them to switch marinas at a later date. While this told Burnhart why the present occupants of Edgewater Marina were there, it didn't explain all those empty spots.

A survey of the other area marinas revealed that all of their occupancy rates were at least 75 percent and that the 308-slip Municipal Marina was completely full. A comparison of marinas (see Exhibit 2) showed that Edgewater offered fewer facilities than most other marinas its size. Data from the boating registrations office showed 27,244 powered boats registered in the Charleston area. While most of these boats were not candidates for marina berths, they did use marine supplies. The number of boat registrations had been growing at an average rate of 8 percent over the past five years, and it was anticipated that this trend would continue.

While Burnhart knew that transient boat traffic on the Intracoastal Waterway was seasonal, he learned that both the boating season and the total number of boats traveling was on the increase. In an attempt to gauge this traffic, he examined the records of a bridge across the Waterway near Charleston which had a low vertical clearance. The bridge operator was required to record the name, type, and state of registration of all boats for which the bridge was opened. Results of this examination are shown in Exhibit 10. If the seven busiest months are averaged (April–October) and it is assumed that the bridge acts as a gate for 80 percent of the traffic, then approximately 565 transient boats pass through Charleston per month during the boating season. This does not take into account any boats not using the Intracoastal Waterway by making the outside passage (assumed less than 5 percent). The only marinas presently catering to these boaters were the Charleston Municipal and the Ashley. Only the Charleston Municipal offered showers, laundry facilities, and marine supplies. In the peak months many transients were rafted against one another or were turned away completely at the Municipal Marina because of lack of space.

Advertising by the local marinas was almost nonexistent. Of the local marinas only the Municipal and the Ashley had paid advertisements in the Waterway Guide. Edgewater was now running a daily ad in the classified section of the local paper, and Mt. Pleasant Marina had its fishing supply store

EXHIBIT 10 John F. Limehouse swing bridge
(vertical elevation 12 feet)

Bridge openings for the year. Bridge operator records
name of boat, type, and state of registry.

	Yachts	Sailboats	Monthly total
January	45	32	77
February	24	14	38
March	116	42	158
April	309	167	476
May	511	185	696
June	230	74	304
July	141	66	207
August	244	81	325
September	498	192	690
October	312	152	464
November	101	51	152
December	32	20	52

Note: It is estimated that 80 percent of all transient boats
passing under the bridge require its opening.

advertised in a small local distribution fishing magazine. The Municipal received indirect advertising through yacht brokers and repair facilities who were located near it. No organization existed to represent the interests of Charleston area marinas although there had been talk of organizing one when the city proposed the building of a new city-supported marina. The proposed marina would have 400 slips and be located at a naval museum across the harbor from downtown Charleston. Local private marina operators expressed concern that this constituted unfair competition in that the proposed marina would be subsidized by the city. No action had been taken since the proposal was made, and if such an undertaking was authorized, it would not go into operation for at least three years.

The Analysis

It was now early February and John Burnhart knew Captain Rutledge was eagerly looking forward to his comments and recommendations. As John looked through the data collected (including Exhibit 11), he realized the problems the Edgewater Marina was experiencing could only be solved by a complete marketing analysis and program. Who were the Marina's intended customers, how numerous were they, and what products and services were they seeking? How do you reach and influence this market segment? What would the boating population want in the future and should preparations be made now to meet these needs? These were just a few of the questions that required answering.

EXHIBIT 11 Boating registrations in Charleston County

Boat length	Number of boats	Open	Cabin	House	Other	Outboard	Inboard	In/out	Auxiliary	Other
Less than 14 feet	4,920	4,651	0	0	269	4,127	12	0	13	768
14 feet to less than 18 feet	10,887	10,435	62	1	389	9,601	211	327	35	813
18 feet to less than 22 feet	882	656	179	4	43	506	84	206	29	57
22 feet to less than 26 feet	414	179	200	13	22	141	123	114	7	30
Greater than 26 feet	338	111	173	29	25	21	246	52	10	9
Total	17,441	16,032	614	47	748	14,396	676	699	94	1,677

Case 5

Exercise on Financial Analysis for Marketing Decision Making*

An important part of the analysis of alternatives facing marketing decision makers is the financial analysis of these alternatives. This exercise is designed to give students experience in handling the types of financial calculations that arise in marketing cases. If you can do the calculations in this exercise, you should be able to handle the financial calculations necessary to properly do the cases in this book.

1. You have just been appointed the product manager for the "Flexo" brand of electric razors in a large consumer products company. As part of your new job, you want to develop an understanding of the financial situation for your product. Your brand assistant has provided you with the following facts:

a.	Retail selling price	$30 per unit
b.	Retailer's margin	20%
c.	Jobber's margin	20%
d.	Wholesaler's* margin	15%
e.	Direct factory labor	$2 per unit
f.	Raw materials	$1 per unit
g.	All factory and administrative overheads	$1 per unit (at a 100,000 unit volume level)
h.	Salespersons' commissions	10% of manufacturer's selling price
i.	Sales force travel costs	$200,000
j.	Advertising	$500,000
k.	Total market for razors	1 million units
l.	Current yearly sales of Flexo	210,000 units

* An agent who sells to the jobbers, who in turn sell to the retailers.

* Copyright © 1990 by Thomas C. Kinnear.

Questions
1. What is the contribution per unit for the Flexo brand?
2. What is the break-even volume in units and in dollars?
3. What market share does the Flexo brand need to break even?
4. What is the current total contribution?
5. What is the current before-tax profit of the Flexo brand?
6. What market share must Flexo obtain to contribute a before-tax profit of $4 million?

2. One of the first decisions you have to make as the brand manager for Flexo is whether or not to add a new line of razors, the "Super Flexo" line. This line would be marketed in addition to the original Flexo line. Your brand assistant has provided you with the following facts:

a.	Retail selling price	$40 per unit
b.	All margins the same as before	
c.	Direct factory labor	$ 3 per unit
d.	Raw materials	$ 2 per unit
e.	Additional factory and administrative overheads	$ 2 per unit (at a 50,000 unit volume level)
f.	Salespersons' commissions the same percent as before	
g.	Incremental sales force travel cost	$ 50,000
h.	Advertising for Super Flexo	$600,000
i.	New equipment needed	$500,000 (to be depreciated over 10 years)
j.	Research and development spent up to now	$200,000
k.	Research and development to be spent this year to commercialize the product	$500,000 (to be amortized over five years)

Questions
1. What is the contribution per unit for the Super Flexo brand?
2. What is the break-even volume in units and in dollars?
3. What is the sales volume in units necessary for Super Flexo to yield, in the first year, a 20 percent return on the equipment to be invested in the project?

3. The $40 per unit selling price for Super Flexo seems high to you. You thought you might lower the price to $37 per unit and raise retail margin to 25 percent.

Question
What is the break-even volume in units?

Part 3

Marketing Information and Forecasting

Good information is essential for all marketing decision making. Most cases in this book present some information provided by marketing research. However, they also leave many points of uncertainty. The skill of marketing decision making is the use of the information that is available, along with explicit assumptions about uncertain points to make good decisions. The suggestion that we do marketing research has usually not been allowed in other parts of this text. In this section we turn to the undertaking of marketing research activity.

First, let us define marketing research. It is the systematic gathering, recording, and analyzing of data about problems relating to the marketing of goods and services. There are three kinds of marketing research: (1) exploratory, (2) conclusive, and (3) performance monitoring. Exploratory research is useful for identifying situations calling for a decision and for identifying alternative courses of action. Conclusive research is useful for evaluating alternative courses of action and selecting a course of action. Performance monitoring research is designed to provide the control function over marketing programs.

The marketing research process may be thought of as being composed of the following steps:

1. Establish the need for information.
2. Specify the research objectives and information needs.
3. Determine the sources of data.
4. Develop data collection forms.
5. Design a sample.
6. Collect the data.
7. Process the data.

8. Analyze the data.
9. Present research findings.

The responsibility for the execution of these stages is shared by the marketing manager and the marketing researcher. They both must be sure that the problem has been defined properly, that the objectives make sense, and so on. The researcher holds primary responsibility for the technical details of the study. However, he or she must always be prepared to explain these aspects to the manager in nontechnical terms.

Marketing research costs money. Before it is undertaken, it must be ascertained that the value of the information provided justifies the cost. Also, before research is undertaken, the use to which that research will be made should be clearly understood. A specific decision should be the target of the research, and the way the new information will be used in helping make the decision should be clearly understood.

This note and the cases in this section focus on the managerial aspects of marketing research. The technical details are mostly left for more advanced texts.

Case 6

Bay-Madison, Inc.*

In January 1987, Mr. George Roberts, research director of Bay-Madison, Inc., a large advertising agency, was faced with the problem of how best to conduct a study on Rill, a product of the Ellis Company, one of the agency's clients.

Rill, a powdered cleanser, was first introduced by the Ellis Company in 1966. Its original use was as a heavy-duty cleansing agent for removing dirt and stains from porcelain, metal, and ceramic tile surfaces. A unique bleaching property of the product eliminated the necessity for scrubbing and it contained no abrasive material. In 1976, the company's research department developed and added to the product an ingredient which imparted a light, fluffy texture to textile products washed in a mild solution of Rill. Recognizing the problem of keeping such articles as baby clothes, towels, and blankets soft through repeated washings, the company had promoted Rill both as a cleanser and as a laundry wash water additive since 1977. Over the years, about 50 percent of the company's advertising had featured the product solely as a cleanser, 30 percent as a laundry additive, and 20 percent as a dual-purpose product.

Rill was nationally distributed in a concentrated form in three can sizes— 4 ounces, 8 ounces, and 1 pound. Six other nationally distributed cleansers and two nationally distributed laundry additives posed formidable competition.

The product had sold well during the earlier years, but during the past five years unit sales had declined considerably apparently because of competition, although dollar volume over this period had remained fairly constant.

Company and agency personnel were in basic disagreement as to whether the product should be promoted as a cleanser, a laundry additive, or a dual-purpose product. In order to formulate marketing and advertising strategy for the coming year, the agency personnel believed it was necessary to supplement the quantitative information they had on unit sales, outlets, margins, and distribution with information of a more qualitative nature on consumer attitudes

---

* This case was written by C. B. Johnston, Dean and Professor of Marketing, University of Western Ontario. Used with permission.

toward the product, usage patterns, and opinions on different product characteristics such as strength or concentration, odor, and package size.

In November 1986, Mr. Roberts and his staff had drawn up a research
proposal which they had forwarded to six marketing research firms for detailed
information regarding the following:

1. An appraisal of the proposal and suggestions for any changes.
2. A price quotation on the project (*a*) as outlined and (*b*) including any
   suggested changes.
3. A brief description of the staff who would handle the project.
4. Time required for preparation, implementation, tabulation, and final presentation.
5. Pilot testing suggested.
6. Detailed explanation of suggested sample size.
7. Information on the firm's executive personnel, interviewing staff, and the
   projects handled over the preceding two years.

The research proposal contained a description of the product's marketing
problems, the objectives of the proposed research, broad suggestions regarding
research methodology, and a proposed questionnaire.

In his proposal, Mr. Roberts outlined the major marketing problems as
follows:

1. We really want to know how many people would buy Rill because (*a*) it is a
   cleanser, (*b*) it is a laundry additive, or (*c*) it is a dual-purpose product.
2. How do people buy products like Rill? Is it better to have a strong product
   or a weaker one? What size package should we have? Should it smell like
   soap or like perfume? At what price should it be retailing?
3. Do people see Rill as being a good, average, or poor product? What do they
   like about it? What don't they like about it?
4. Do people want a one-use product or a multi-use product?

By early in January, Mr. Roberts had received the submissions of all six
marketing research firms requested to bid on the job.

Three of these firms were eliminated after preliminary consideration of
their submissions revealed either inadequate staffs, superficial recommendations, or excessively high costs.

In considering the three remaining firms, Mr. Roberts felt he was hampered by his lack of knowledge of the techniques proposed by two of the firms
and his inability to decide whether it was reasonable to expect that a detailed
plan could be drawn up from the information he had provided in his proposal.

Two of the firms under consideration, National Research Associates and
The Progressive Research Group, had outlined quite comprehensive plans for
the research. The third, H. J. Clifford Research, had merely stated that they
would not attempt to formulate any research plans from what they considered
inadequate information. They believed the only way a detailed plan could be

formulated was "through a continuing cooperation, based on mutual confidence, between the research firm, the advertising agency, and the client."

Mr. Roberts knew that many marketing research executives considered the third firm to be the outstanding marketing research company in the country and because of this, he did not believe they could be overlooked.

SUBMISSION OF NATIONAL RESEARCH ASSOCIATES

Introduction

The present research proposal is based upon the assumption that it is crucial to obtain answers to the following marketing problems:

1. Is it advisable to continue to promote Rill as a multipurpose product?
2. If it is, should its various uses be promoted simultaneously or separately and what are the promotional approaches which would be most effective?
3. If it is not advisable to continue its promotion as a multipurpose product, for what uses could Rill be most successfully promoted?
4. What would be the most effective promotional approaches for the uses decided upon?
5. Would it be advisable to launch another product, or possibly the same product under a different name, for either of its uses?
6. What are the ways in which Rill distribution, packaging, pricing, and merchandising could be improved?

Research Objectives

To be able to plan a sound and effective marketing policy for Rill it will be essential to know:

1. The present market position of Rill in relation to its competitors in each of the fields in which it is used.
2. The reasons why Rill is in its present position in each of these markets.

I. Consumer Habits and Practices

The study will provide as complete a description as possible of the cleanser and laundry additive markets. Data will be provided in regard to (1) users and nonusers, (2) brand usage, (3) purchasing habits, and (4) usage habits.

This information will be cross-analyzed by age, socioeconomic status, community size, and level of education of the respondent.

II. Consumer Attitudes, Opinions, and Motivations

The study will thoroughly explore the underlying reasons for the market strengths and weaknesses of Rill in each of the usage categories as completely as possible under the broad headings of:

1. The underlying attractions or resistances to using any product for each of the purposes with which Rill is concerned.
2. The comparative strength of attractions to using Rill and to using competing brands for each of these purposes.
3. The comparative strength of resistances to using Rill relative to competing brands.

Some of the specific topics which will be investigated under these general headings are discussed below:

1. The perceived uses of Rill and its major competitors.
2. Factors affecting the perception of Rill; that is, confusion regarding usage, incompatibility of uses, one use more efficient than the other, and where the attitudes toward the product originated.
3. Attributes of the most desirable product for each of the uses.
4. Common knowledge of the attributes of various brands now on the market.
5. Associations evoked by the brand name Rill and the brand names of competing products.

III. Consumer Knowledge of, and Attitudes toward, Relevant Advertising

1. How far are the terms and phrases currently used in promoting Rill and competing brands seen as (*a*) meaningful, and (*b*) appropriate to the product and its uses?
2. What copy points and adjectives might be most effective for the promotion of each use?

IV. An Evaluation of the Advertising Themes and Approaches Used by Rill

The research will attempt to determine whether the themes and approaches used in past and present Rill advertising are likely to operate toward overcoming resistances to Rill and capitalizing on sources of attraction.

V. An Assessment of the Rill Packages

The Rill package will be tested to determine:

1. Its visual effectiveness as evidenced by its attention-getting ability, its legibility, its memorability, its apparent size.
2. Its psychological effect on the consumer's perception of the brand.

Methodology

Market survey. Face-to-face interviews will be conducted with 2,275 homemakers who will be asked to give factual information about the products they use for each purpose. This survey will show the competitive position of Rill, but will not attempt to provide "reasons why."

Intensive interview study. The "reasons why" Rill is in its present position will be explored in 200 one-and-one-half to two-hour depth interviews which will attempt to discover attitudes, perceptions, and feelings toward the product and its uses.

The depth interview is designed to prompt the revelation of true attitudes and reasons for them by employing projective techniques which, instead of emphasizing personal behavior, invite comment on the behavior of others.

In-depth interviewing takes place in a relaxed, informal atmosphere. Interviews are usually conducted in the respondent's home and her verbatim responses to questions are noted.

The interview schedule contains a large number of open-ended and close-ended queries.

In addition, it employs a variety of techniques, most of which are taken from, or patterned after, standard psychological tests. A description of some of these techniques is given below.

1. The Personification Test. This is essentially an extension of the projective technique employed in psychological testing. It involves an attempt on the part of the respondent to describe certain products in human terms. Such an approach provides an opportunity for the expression of attitudes and opinions not otherwise easily obtainable.

2. The Thematic Apperception Test (TAT). Like the Personification Test, this test is similar to the TAT in psychological projective testing. It consists of presenting to the respondent an unstructured drawing of a particular situation and asking him to "make up a story" of what is happening.

3. Word Association Tests. Respondents are asked to relate what comes to mind when a given word or phrase is read to them. This technique aids in throwing light on areas which may warrant fuller investigation.

4. The Semantic Differential Test. This method, developed by us, has been designed to provide insights and information in regard to the perception of company and product attributes.

Fundamentally, the test consists of having the respondent rate a series of products on specially designed scales. The scales are so designed as to provide an extremely sensitive measure in regard to many dimensions as applied to the various products.

The manner in which these data (along with the data obtained through the use of other techniques) are analyzed makes it possible to determine:

A. The extent to which a given product's image is correlated with the perceived "ideal" product.
B. The desirable direction of change in the perceived product attributes, if such change is found necessary.

Other techniques which may be employed include: (*a*) rank-ordering tests, (*b*) sentence completion tests, (*c*) forced choice tests, (*d*) paired comparison tests, and (*e*) true-false tests.

Laboratory study. Our visual laboratory is equipped to evaluate the relative effectiveness of various merchandising and advertising stimuli. By means of specially designed instruments it will be possible to evaluate the relative effectiveness of the Rill package and label in comparison with those of major competitors.

The various tests which will be conducted include:

1. Attention-getting tests.
2. Product recognition tests.

3. Brand identification tests.
4. Visibility and legibility tests.
5. Memorability tests.
6. Apparent size tests.
7. Color preference and association tests.

Sample

Market survey. For the purposes of economy it is suggested that a quota-controlled, weighted, national sample of 2,275 homemakers be employed. The accompanying table presents an unweighted sample in proportion to household figures and the proposed weighted sample.

The unweighted sample exceeds the number of interviews necessary to ensure reasonable reliability.

However, to allow for a cross analysis of white and black and urban and rural respondents, a total of 3,113 interviews would be required. The weighted sample cuts by 50 percent the number of interviews in the Midwest and the West. The data from these areas will be mathematically converted to representative proportions in the final tabulation.

Intensive study. Quota-controlled samples of 450 white and 150 black homemakers will be used.

Laboratory study. The number of respondents varies from test to test, but the samples will be designed to ensure statistical reliability.

Field Staff

Market survey. Our field staff of 455 interviewers located across the country will conduct the interviews and will be specially briefed and trained for this survey.

Intensive study. Our staff of 88 university-trained depth interviewers will conduct an average of seven interviews each.

Brief Description of Firm

National Research Associates has conducted almost 400 separate and varied research projects since its establishment in 1964. The success of the organization is portrayed by its rapid growth from a small unknown company to a recognized leader in the field in the United States. Further attestation has been the establishment of "continuing relationships" with many clients. The company is an "official training ground" for graduate students in the Department of Social Psychology at a prominent university.

The following individuals will be involved in this project:

R. J. Morrison, PhD, research coordinator and major client and agency contact; academic training—BSc, MSc, and PhD, 1964 to 1969, major universities; research experience—wide experience in research as study director, consultant and research associate in four U.S. universities from 1964 to 1976; teaching experience—seven years of lecturing in psychology at two American universities.

| | Rural | | | | Urban | | Total | |
| | Farm | | Nonfarm | | | | | |
	Unweighted	Weighted	Unweighted	Weighted	Unweighted	Weighted	Unweighted	Weighted
Southeast	44	44	76	76	132	132	252	252
Northeast	101	101	110	110	614	614	825	825
Midwest	126	63	139	70	837	436	1,102	569
West	179	90	107	53	324	162	610	305
South Central	22	22	60	60	242	242	324	324
Total	472	320	492	369	2,149	1,586	3,113	2,275

A. *Milton,* study director; graduate in economics with 10 years' experience in the research field including 3 years with a prominent United Kingdom research firm and a number of years with other English companies.

H. W. *Rolland,* associate study director; senior staff psychologist who will coordinate the intensive study phases of the research. MSc working on PhD.

R. W. *Brown,* associate study director; university graduate in sociology and statistics—10 years' experience in research—will handle tabulation and statistical analysis.

(Four additional staff members were listed, all of whom were university graduates.)

Time and Cost Estimates

The research can be completed in 12 weeks after finalization of the research design. The cost is estimated at $130,000, 50 percent payable upon initiation of the study and 50 percent upon completion.

SUBMISSION OF THE PROGRESSIVE RESEARCH GROUP

Nature of the Problem

It is possible that the two major uses of Rill may, in combination, affect the market negatively. Women may think of it primarily in one sense or the other and those who regard it as a cleanser may not be willing to use it as a laundry additive, or vice versa.

In addition to this possible overall problem, there are certain marketing specifics which may also be important.

1. Is the product right?
2. What about its physical characteristics (strength or concentration, odor, physical form)?
3. What about its psychological connotations?
4. What about the packaging (size of package, nature of package, labeling, and package)?

We propose a consumer study covering the major areas of behavior and attitude including:

1. Brand personality and image for each of several cleansers (including Rill).
2. Brand personality and image for each of several laundry additive products (including Rill).
3. Habit pattern on home cleaning (including products used).
4. Habit pattern on laundry additives (including products used).

Scope of the Study

We see this as a national study as it is entirely possible that varying areas may display differing habits and attitudes.

The section of this proposal dealing with the sample will show the reasons underlying our recommendations. We suggest a total of 750 interviews in this consumer study and the sample will be of a "tight" nature.

The Sample

Type of sample. The sample will be of such a nature that it properly represents the homemaker population in terms of region, socioeconomic group, urban-rural, and the like.

The sample design will be a known probability sample. Primary sampling units will be selected proportionately across the country, and randomly selected starting points will be chosen from which a predetermined path of interviewing will be followed.

Size of sample. We recommend a total sample of 750 homemakers.

There are several reasons. The first concerns our belief that no subsample on which results are based should have fewer than 150 cases.

The other reason concerns overall accuracy with a sample of 750 cases. Better than 9 times out of 10, results based on this total sample should be accurate within some 2.4 percent; this level of sampling accuracy on an overall basis seems highly acceptable for the purposes of this particular study.

Numerical distribution of interviews is indicated in the accompanying table.

	Natural proportional distribution of sample	Proposed sample distribution	Weighting factor	Weighted cases
Southeast	77	125	2	250
Northeast	211	211	3	633
Midwest	265	177	5	885
West	130	130	3	390
South Central	67	107	2	214
	750	750		2,372

Fieldwork

Our field staff is of highest quality. It has been built over a 10-year period, and we spend a sizable amount of money each year on maintenance and development of this staff.

The field staff totals 723 workers, and all states and community sizes are represented.

Supervision

We maintain a staff of 20 salaried regional supervisors across the country. With the exception of a few small remote areas, this means that every interviewer works under the direct control of a regional supervisor.

Qualifications of Interviewers

The average interviewer on our staff has been working for the firm for approximately four years. For our consumer work, we make use of women who, on the average, have the following characteristics: (1) they fall between the upper middle and lower middle socioeconomic group, (2) they have completed some or all of high school, (3) they are extroverted, and (4) they are above the average in intelligence.

The Questionnaire

It is difficult to evaluate your questionnaire without considerable field testing. In the present case, there has been no effort at all to do so. We would save our "criticism" for (*a*) detailed discussion with the agency and (*b*) considerable field testing.

We have conducted a group interview with the subject matter pretty much in its present sequence, though the questions asked were more of an open-minded variety than contained in the questionnaire draft submitted with your specifications.

We do know that the sequence of questions will work. We also know that women can and will answer these questions, despite their nature, if the right approach is used. We further know that while the questionnaire form is quite lengthy, it is still feasible in terms of its length. So it is not as if we know nothing about feasibility of the instrument.

Field Testing

As a result of the group interview, it will be possible—though we have not taken the time to utilize it in such a manner—to study the consumer response to the interview so carefully as to make sure that the phrasings used in the questionnaire follow the words and phrases used in the consumer's actual thinking. The group interview thus means that we are that much further ahead in the phrasings of this questionnaire, even though it so far has not been utilized for such a purpose.

We plan a field test—or perhaps several—with a total of 100 homemakers distributed among people of varying socioeconomic groups, largely concentrated (for efficiency of handling) in the Chicago Metropolitan Area to make sure that the sequence and phrasing are of such a nature as to be understandable, to get cooperation, and to obtain unbiased replies.

Description of the Firm

The Progressive Research Group began operations in 1958 and, as such, is one of the oldest marketing research companies. Over the years the company has handled a large number of projects and has among its clients many of the largest consumer goods manufacturers.

The company possesses the most advanced computer equipment in the country and constant improvements are being adopted to speed up and make more economical, complete, and detailed client reports.

The following persons will direct the project:

A. W. Willis, BA, overall project coordinator; president of The Progressive Research Group and a graduate in economics from a large university.

B. K. Walker, MBA, project director and client contact; vice president and a graduate in business administration from a major university.

R. C. Moffatt, PhD, project adviser; major in sociology—five years' research experience as project director with large U.S. advertising agency before joining The Progressive Research Group in 1967. Three years spent as lecturer and consultant at two large American universities.

Time and Cost

Our report should be available 12 weeks after the finalizing of the project details. Our estimate of the cost of this project is $90,000 plus or minus 10 percent. It is our practice to bill one half of the estimated cost at the time of authorization with the final half billed on delivery of the report.

In discussing these proposals with his assistant, Mr. Jacks, Mr. Roberts wondered whether his own staff could not answer some of the questions if a thorough study of past Consumer Panel reports were conducted. For some 10 years Bay-Madison had received full reports from an independent research company which ran a consumer panel, but these had only been used for day-to-day planning. Never, for instance, had a long-term, thorough study of the trends in Rill sales been compared with the various advertising and promotional campaigns the company had used or to the various price levels that had existed from time to time. Mr. Jacks was particularly enthusiastic about the idea as he had long maintained that the agency was not getting full value from the panel data. He said that he would personally like to work on such a project.

Mr. Roberts, in considering the idea further, estimated that such an analysis could be done for approximately $25,000. He had checked with the research company and found that all past reports were kept on automatic data processing cards. The company was most interested in the idea as an experiment and estimated that all the data required by the agency could be compiled for about $6,500. Mr. Roberts thought he could release Mr. Jacks from his other duties for a period of two months and that the cost of Mr. Jacks' salary, statistical and secretarial help, and other expenses would not exceed $12,000.

It was at this point that Mr. Roberts found himself in January 1987. He knew a decision had to be made quickly as the client was very anxious to get the Rill situation straightened away.

Case 7

*The Atlanta Journal and Constitution (A)**

Mr. Ferguson Rood, research and marketing director for *The Atlanta Journal* and the *Atlanta Constitution,* was still perspiring from the three-block walk in the hot August sun back to his office from the meeting he had just been to at Rich's Department Store. At the meeting, he had been told that Rich's, the newspaper's largest advertiser, wanted to test the effectiveness of TV and radio advertising versus newspaper advertising for its upcoming Harvest Sale. He had promised to make his suggestions for the research plan in 48 hours and felt he had much work to do in that short time. He wondered what recommendations he should make for the study and was concerned that the research design and questionnaire be developed so the study would represent fairly the effectiveness of *The Atlanta Journal* and the *Atlanta Constitution.* As he began to review his notes from the meeting, he picked up the phone to call his wife and tell her he would be home very late that evening.

Background

The Atlanta Journal and the *Atlanta Constitution* are a union of two of the largest circulation newspapers in the South. The *Atlanta Constitution,* winner of four Pulitzer Prizes for its efforts in the area of social reform, was founded June 16, 1868. *The Atlanta Journal,* founded February 24, 1883, became the largest daily newspaper in Georgia by 1889. Also a winner of the Pulitzer Prize, *The Journal* is the Southeast's largest afternoon newspaper.

In 1950, *The Atlanta Journal* and the *Atlanta Constitution* were combined into Atlanta Newspapers, Inc., a privately held company. The two newspapers maintained independent editorial staffs, and there was very little overlap of readers. Exhibits 1 through 4 present data concerning the adult readership of the newspapers, the gross reader impressions, reach and frequency, and readership over five weekdays and four Sundays.

EXHIBIT 1   Gross readership impressions, reach, and frequency of *The Atlanta Journal and Constitution*

Gross reader impressions

The Atlanta Journal and *Constitution* in 15-county metro Atlanta:

During any five weekdays, 864,500 adults read *The Atlanta Journal* or *Constitution* an average of 3.5 times for a total of 3,025,800 weekday gross reader impressions.

During any four Sundays, 907,600 adults read *The Atlanta Journal* and *Constitution* for an average of 3.4 times for a total of 3,085,800 Sunday gross reader impressions.

These newspapers deliver 3,933,400 adult gross reader impressions when one Sunday is added to five weekdays.

Reach and frequency of newspaper reading

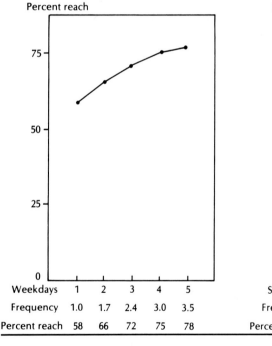

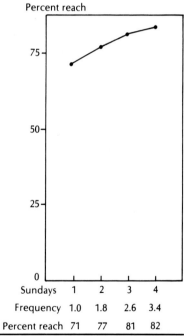

Weekdays	1	2	3	4	5
Frequency	1.0	1.7	2.4	3.0	3.5
Percent reach	58	66	72	75	78

Sundays	1	2	3	4
Frequency	1.0	1.8	2.6	3.4
Percent reach	71	77	81	82

EXHIBIT 2 *The Atlanta Journal* and *Constitution* readership information

78 percent of all daily circulation and 66 percent of all Sunday circulation is within 15-county metro Atlanta.

Of all metro Atlanta adults, 644,400 read *The Atlanta Journal* or *Constitution* on the average weekday. Of this total, 412,700 read *The Journal* and 366,100 read the *Constitution*. 134,400 adults read both. On the average Sunday 782,200 metro Atlanta adults read *The Atlanta Journal* and *Constitution*.

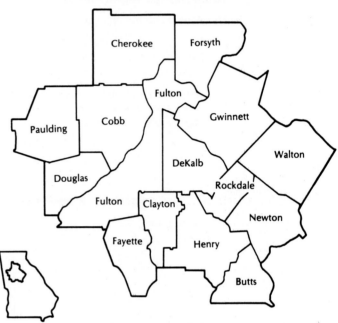

15-county metro Atlanta

Adult readers of *The Atlanta Journal* and *Constitution* in 15-county metro Atlanta

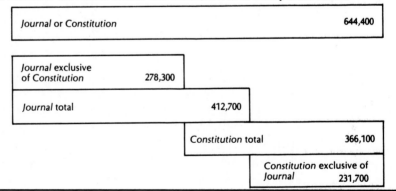

EXHIBIT 3 Readership of *The Atlanta Journal* and *Constitution* over five weekdays

644,400, or 58 percent, of all metro Atlanta adults read *The Atlanta Journal* or *Constitution* on the average weekday. Over five weekdays these newspapers deliver 864,900, or 78 percent, of all metro-area adults with an average frequency of 3.5 days.

	Total metro area adults	Average 1-day readership		Cumulative 5-weekday readership		Frequency
		Number	Percent	Number	Percent	
Total adults	1,105,500	644,400	58	864,900	78	3.5
Sex						
Female	588,500	331,700	56	447,600	76	3.5
Male	517,000	312,700	61	416,800	81	3.5
Household income						
$25,000 and over	104,200	85,900	82	102,700	99	4.2
$15,000–24,999	195,300	146,400	75	181,900	93	4.0
$10,000–14,999	241,900	152,800	63	203,900	84	3.7
$5,000–9,999	334,200	170,600	51	241,800	72	3.5
Under $5,000	229,900	88,500	39	133,000	58	3.3
Age						
18–34	470,500	234,500	50	345,200	73	3.4
35–49	305,600	197,200	65	250,300	82	3.9
50–64	211,900	145,800	69	184,600	87	3.9
65 and over	116,500	66,700	57	84,700	73	3.9
Race						
White	872,800	528,800	61	685,100	78	3.9
Nonwhite	232,700	115,600	50	180,100	77	3.2
Education						
College graduate	173,500	138,000	80	172,600	99	4.0
Part college	194,700	137,600	71	174,100	89	4.0
High school graduate	360,500	225,000	62	302,900·	84	3.7
Part high school or less	365,600	137,000	38	202,200	55	3.4

To provide the advertisers and potential advertisers with information necessary to help them make their advertising media decisions, the newspaper does a considerable amount of research, often approaching $25,000 in a year. Most of the research is designed to be used in selling advertising to a wide range of advertisers, and includes data on retail trading areas, shopping patterns, product usage, and newspaper coverage patterns. In addition to Mr. Rood, the research department had two other trained market researchers and one secretary.

Although there are nine daily newspapers in the Atlanta trading area, all but *The Journal* and the *Constitution* have very small circulations. The principal competition for large advertisers is with radio and TV stations. Exhibit 5 presents information on the circulation of the print media in the Atlanta area. Exhibit 6 contains information on the broadcast media in Atlanta. Although there were 40 radio stations, 28 AM and 12 FM, and 6 TV stations, WSB Radio

EXHIBIT 4 Readership of *The Atlanta Journal* and *Constitution* over four Sundays

782,200, or 71 percent, of all metro Atlanta adults read *The Atlanta Journal* and *Constitution* on the average Sunday. Over four Sundays these newspapers deliver 907,300, or 82 percent, of all metro-area adults with an average frequency of 3.4 Sundays.

	Total metro area adults	Average 1-Sunday readership	Cumulative 4-Sunday readership	Number of Sundays frequency
Total adults	1,105,500	782,200	907,300	3.4
Sex				
Female	588,500	418,800	477,800	3.5
Male	517,000	363,400	429,500	3.4
Household income				
$25,000 and over	104,200	89,100	97,200	3.7
$15,000–24,999	195,300	168,800	180,700	3.7
$10,000–14,999	241,900	190,100	216,400	3.5
$5,000–9,999	334,400	215,600	267,300	3.2
Under $5,000	229,900	118,500	145,600	3.3
Age				
18–34	470,500	313,000	390,000	3.2
35–49	305,600	221,300	248,500	3.6
50–64	211,900	167,000	179,900	3.7
65 and over	116,500	80,600	88,500	3.6
Race				
White	872,800	633,100	727,900	3.5
Nonwhite	232,700	149,100	179,100	3.3
Education				
College graduate	173,500	150,200	163,700	3.7
Part college	194,700	157,300	180,200	3.5
High school graduate	360,500	273,900	313,500	3.5
Part high school or less	365,600	192,300	240,000	3.2

and TV dominated the market. WSB Radio, for example, was consistently rated among the top six stations in the nation and had a greater Atlanta audience than the next four stations combined. WSB-TV and WSB Radio, both affiliated with the NBC Network, were owned by Cox Broadcasting Corporation, which also owns television stations in Charlotte, Dayton, Pittsburgh, and San Francisco and radio stations in Charlotte, Dayton, and Miami. Cox Broadcasting and WSB-TV and Radio stations shared corporate headquarters in Atlanta.

WSB Radio was founded in 1922 by *The Atlanta Journal* newspaper. In 1939, former Democratic presidential nominee and Governor of Ohio James M. Cox acquired the newspaper-radio combine. In 1948, WSB-TV was founded, and two years later the newspapers and broadcast media were separated when Atlanta Newspapers, Inc., was established. Today, there is no relationship between the newspapers and WSB Radio and TV.

Rich's Department Store was the largest advertiser for *The Journal* and the *Constitution,* accounting for almost 5 percent of their advertising revenue, and was WSB's largest local advertiser. Founded in 1867, Rich's by 1970 had

EXHIBIT 5 Circulation of print media in Atlanta

Metro Atlanta newspapers	Edition	Total circulation
Dailies		
Atlanta Constitution	Morning	216,624
Atlanta Journal	Evening	259,721
Journal-Constitution	Sunday	585,532
Gwinnett Daily News	Evening (except Sat.)	10,111
Gwinnett Daily News	Sunday	10,100
Marietta Daily Journal	Evening (except Sat.)	24,750
Marietta Daily Journal	Sunday	25,456
Fulton County Daily Report	Evening (Mon.–Fri.)	1,600
Atlanta Daily World	Morning	19,000
Atlanta Daily World	Sunday	22,000
The Wall Street Journal	Morning (Mon.–Fri.)	16,180
Jonesboro News Daily	Evening (Mon.–Fri.)	9,100
North Fulton Today	Evening (Mon.–Fri.)	2,300
South Cobb Today	Evening (Mon.–Fri.)	2,400
New York Times	Morning (Mon.–Sat.)	500
New York Times	Sunday	3,100
Weekly newspapers		
Atlanta Inquirer		30,000
Atlanta Voice		37,500
DeKalb New Era		16,400
Atlanta's Suburban Reporter		3,900
Lithonia Observer		2,765
Northside News		8,000
Georgia Business News		4,900
Southern Israelite		4,300
Decatur-DeKalb News		73,000
Southside Sun (East Point)		37,700
Tucker Star		10,000
Alpharetta, Roswell Neighbor		6,800
Austell, Mableton, Powder Springs Neighbor		12,123
Acworth, Kennesaw-Woodstock Neighbor		3,242
Northside, Sandy Springs, Vinings Neighbor		20,836
Smyrna Neighbor		6,872
College Park, East Point, Hapeville, South Side, West End Neighbor		18,813
Chamblee, Doraville, Dunwoody, North Atlanta Neighbor		14,963
Clarkston, Stone Mountain, Tucker Neighbor		15,074
The Journal of Labor (Atlanta)		17,500
Austell Enterprise		1,911
The Cherokee Tribune (Canton)		7,100
Rockdale Citizen		6,031
The Covington News		6,000
The Forsyth County News		4,800
Dallas New Era		4,075
Douglas County Sentinel		7,350
South Fulton Recorder (Fairburn)		4,000
Fayette County News		4,500
Jackson Progress Argus		2,635
The Weekly Advertiser (McDonough)		5,650
The Walton Tribune (Monroe)		5,102
Lilburn Recorder		5,000
Lawrenceville Home Weekly		2,000
The Great Speckled Bird (Atlanta)		7,925
The Georgia Bulletin		14,000
The Covington News (Tues. & Thurs.)		6,200
Creative Loafing in Atlanta		30,000

EXHIBIT 5 (concluded)

Metro Atlanta newspapers	Edition	Total circulation
Atlanta area newspapers*		
Cobb		28,000
North Fulton		36,000
North DeKalb-Gwinnett		45,000
South DeKalb		44,000
South Fulton-Clayton		53,000
Major magazines in Georgia		
American Home		70,485
Better Homes and Gardens		145,962
Good Housekeeping		114,045
McCall's		139,728
Ladies' Home Journal		128,331
Family Circle		106,245
Woman's Day		100,566
Redbook		86,354
National Geographic		103,941
Reader's Digest		331,240
Newsweek		41,070
Time		60,438
U.S. News & World Report		40,417
TV Guide		345,871
Playboy		98,389
Sports Illustrated		38,263
Outdoor Life		25,918
True		18,244
Southern Living		95,000
Progressive Farmer		70,000
Cosmopolitan		25,075
Calendar Atlanta		50,000

* These are supplements to *The Atlanta Journal,* and circulation is to *The Atlanta Journal* subscribers only.
Source: WSB Research Department.

grown to a company with seven stores distributed throughout Atlanta, as shown in Exhibit 7. Sales were approximately $200 million per year with earnings after taxes of almost 5 percent of sales. The company was classified as a general merchandise retailer, and carried a very wide line of products including clothing, furniture, appliances, housewares, and items for the home. Rich's dominated the Atlanta market, with close to 40 percent of department store sales and approximately 25 percent of all the sales of general merchandise. The merchandising highlight of the year was the annual Harvest Sale, first held in October 1925. The sale typically ran for two weeks and had become a yearly tradition at Rich's.

Background on the Media Effectiveness Study

Before preparing his proposal to Rich's for the media effectiveness study, Mr. Rood reflected upon the events of the past 24 hours. The day before, he had

EXHIBIT 6 Broadcast media in Atlanta

Location	Station/network	Established	Frequency	Power	Channel	Network
Metro Atlanta AM radio stations						
Atlanta	WSB (NBC)	1922	750 khz	50 kw		
	WAOK	1954	1380 khz	5 kw		
	WGKA (ABC)	1955	1190 khz	1 kw day		
	WGST (ABC-E)	1922	920 khz	5 kw day 1 kw night		
	WIGO (ABC-C)	1946	1340 khz	1 kw day 250 w night		
	WIIN (MBS)	1949	970 khz	5 kw day		
	WPLO	1937	590 khz	5 kw		
	WQXI	1948	790 khz	5 kw day 1 kw night		
	WXAP	1948	860 khz	1 kw		
	WYZE (MBS)	1956	1480 khz	5 kw day		
Decatur	WAVO	1958	1420 khz	1 kw day		
	WGUN	1947	1010 khz	50 kw day		
	WQAK	1964	1310 khz	500 w		
N. Atlanta	WRNG (CBS)	1967	680 khz	25 kw day		
Morrow	WSSA	1959	1570 khz	1 kw day		
East Point	WTJH	1949	1260 khz	5 kw day		
Smyrna	WYNX	1962	1550 khz	10 kw day		
Buford	WDYX	1956	1460 khz	5 kw day		
Austell	WACX	1968	1600 khz	1 kw		
Lawrenceville	WLAW	1959	1360 khz	1 kw		
Marietta	WCOB	1955	1080 khz	10 kw day		
	WFOM	1946	1230 khz	1 kw day 250 w night		
Canton	WCHK (GA)	1957	1290 khz	1 kw day		
Covington	WGFS	1953	1430 khz	1 kw day		
Cumming	WSNE	1961	1170 khz	1 kw		
Douglasville	WDGL	1964	1527 khz	1 kw		
Jackson	WJGA	1967	1540 khz	1 kw day		
Monroe	WMRE	1954	1490 khz	1 kw		
Metro Atlanta FM radio stations						
	WSB-FM	1934	98.5 mhz	100 kw		
	WPLO-FM	1948	103.3 mhz	50 kw		
	WZGC-FM	1955	92.9 mhz	100 kw		
	WKLS-FM	1960	96.1 mhz	100 kw		
	WQXI-FM	1962	94.1 mhz	100 kw		
	WBIE-FM	1959	101.5 mhz	100 kw		
	WLTA-FM	1963	99.7 mhz	100 kw		
	WJGA-FM	1968	92.1 mhz	3 kw		
	WCHK-FM	1964	105.5 mhz	3 kw		
	WGCO-FM	1969	102.3 mhz	100 kw		
	WABE-FM	1948	90.0 mhz	10.5 kw		
	WREK-FM	1968	91.1 mhz	40 kw		
Metro Atlanta television stations						
	WSB-TV	9/29/48			2	NBC
	WAGA-TV	3/8/49			5	CBS
	WXIA-TV	9/30/51			11	ABC
	WTCG-TV	9/1/67			17	IND
	WETV	1958			30	NET
	WGTV	1960			8	NET

Source: WSB Research Department.

EXHIBIT 7 Map of Atlanta and seven Rich's stores

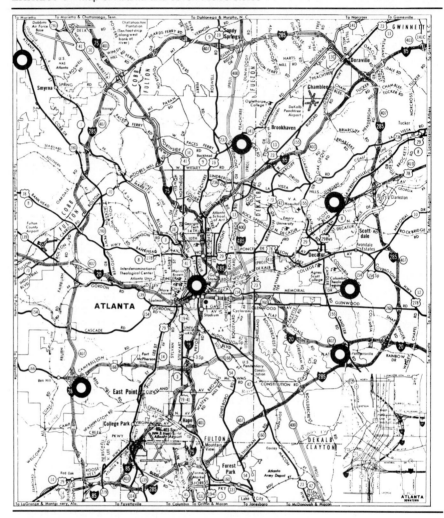

received a phone call from the vice president and sales promotion director from Rich's, inviting him to the meeting at Rich's the next day. Having been told that Rich's research director and the research director of WSB-TV and Radio would also be there, Mr. Rood had been a little apprehensive before going. At the start of the meeting he was asked if the Atlanta newspapers would be interested in participating in a cooperative research study aimed at measuring the effectiveness of various advertising media during Rich's September Harvest Sale, their largest annual sales event. It became immediately apparent that the research director from WSB, Jim Landon, had met with the Rich's people the week before, and was undoubtedly the source of the idea to conduct the study. A document was then passed out that had been prepared by WSB and was entitled "Suggestions for Rich's Media Research." This document is included in the appendix, and outlines the objectives of the study, a suggested methodology, together with a questionnaire.

The suggested objectives for the project were: (1) to measure the ability of TV, radio, and newspapers to sell specific items of merchandise in Rich's seven Atlanta stores; (2) to determine how each advertising medium complements the others in terms of additional units sold to various segments of the customer population (age, sex, charge account ownership, and so on); (3) to determine what each advertising medium contributed in regard to additional store traffic. Mr. Rood's broadcasting counterpart stated at the meeting that "If Rich's is interested in conducting research to measure the effectiveness of various advertising media, WSB-TV and WSB Radio will be happy to assist." Rood had no choice, so he volunteered the support of the newspapers to the study.

The Rich's research manager then asked if the media would participate financially in the study. Mr. Rood suggested that each of the three media participate equally and committed the newspapers to $500 for a study that he figured should cost between $2,500 and $3,000 for interviewing. Mr. Landon indicated that Cox Broadcasting would be willing to put in $500 each for TV and radio.

They then discussed how the research could be conducted. The WSB proposal suggested in-store surveys, with a separate survey conducted for each item of merchandise tested. The survey would be conducted by Rich's employees working overtime in appropriate store locations during the peak shopping hours. The tabulation of the results could be handled by the broadcast station's computer. Care was to be taken to ensure that the TV, radio, or newspaper advertising for the individual items not be "stacked" in favor of one particular medium. The questions in the proposed questionnaire (see the appendix) included questions on how the respondents happened to buy the merchandise at Rich's, if they recalled seeing TV, newspaper or radio advertising, and if they bought anything else. Questions were also asked concerning age and ownership of a Rich's charge account.

Mr. Landon stated that WSB was not trying to take business away from the newspapers and that Rood had nothing to fear. His recommendation was that Rich's not take anything away from the newspaper advertising budget. He suggested that the amount of space purchased in the newspapers be the same as the previous year, with additional monies being committed to the broadcast media. The Rich's sales promotion director then discussed some of his thoughts concerning the study. He indicated that Rich's had been sending 400,000 direct mail pieces to announce the Harvest Sale; this year they would send 200,000, diverting the other money to broadcast. This would make $7,600 available for broadcast, and another $12,000 to $15,000 would be made available to purchase broadcast time.

The Harvest Sale was to open with courtesy days on Monday and Tuesday, September 21–22, with the sale beginning the evening of the 22nd and running for 13 days. While decisions concerning which sales items were to be included in the study and the media schedules to be used were not yet available, some progress had been made. Approximately 10 items were to be researched, and the newspaper ads on Sunday, September 20, would include all or most of the 10 items. Newspaper ads for the items would be repeated Monday and Tuesday with emphasis on *The Journal*. The interviews were to be conducted Monday through Wednesday.

On Sunday and Monday, with a possible spillover to Tuesday due to availability, Rich's would run 120, 30-second TV commercials on all commercial stations except Channel 17. During the same time they would run 120 radio 30-second commercials on a list of stations which had not yet been determined. With both TV and radio, WSB was to get the lion's share if availability could be arranged. Mr. Rood felt certain in view of the client and the research that WSB would manage to come up with several prime-time commercial openings even if it meant bumping some high-paying national advertisers.

Eleven items were mentioned as possible subjects for the research. The 10 final items selected would come mostly from this list, although one or two other items might be chosen. The items mentioned included (1) color TV console at $499; (2) custom-made draperies; (3) Sterns & Foster mattress at $44; (4) carpeting at $6.99 per square yard; (5) Gant shirts at $5; (6) Van Heusen shirts and Arrow shirts at two for $11; (7) women's handbags at $9.99; (8) Johannsen's shoes; (9) pants suits; (10) Hoover upright vacuum cleaner; and (11) GE refrigerator.

Mr. Rood, who had not said very much at the meeting, then asked for 48 hours to review the proposal. Everyone agreed to this, and Mr. Rood promised to present a counterproposal at that time.

Even though it had been rather obvious who initiated the idea for the study and that he at first felt that newspapers were being "set up" by WSB, it had been basically a friendly and relaxed meeting among friends. Mr. Landon and Mr. Rood had worked together in the Atlanta Chapter of the American Marketing Association and had a great deal of mutual respect. Mr. Rood thought Landon was a tough competitor, and understood that he had been successful using awareness-type studies in Cox Broadcastings' other markets to gain additional advertising for broadcast.

When he returned to his office, Rood pulled out some of his files on Rich's. He noticed that the amount of advertising had been fairly constant, approximately 40 pages over the two-week period, during the past three Harvest Sales, and that basically the same products had been promoted. A typical Harvest Sale ad is included in Exhibit 8. He also pulled from the files rate schedules for *The Atlanta Journal* and *Constitution* and WSB (see Exhibits 9 and 10), even though he realized that the exact media schedule would be developed by Rich's advertising agency. Approximately $100,000 would be spent promoting the Harvest Sale, with perhaps a third of this amount being devoted to the sale items.

EXHIBIT 8 Typical Rich's Harvest ad

EXHIBIT 9 *The Atlanta Journal* and the *Atlanta Constitution* retail display rates

Open rate per column inch:*

Constitution	$8.15
Journal	$11.27
Combination	$14.83
Sunday	$15.56

Yearly bulk space rates:

Inches per year	Cost per inch			
	Constitution	Journal	Combined	Sunday
100	$6.21	$8.43	$11.09	$11.65
250	6.16	8.35	11.00	11.55
500	6.10	8.28	10.90	11.45
1,000	6.05	8.21	10.81	11.35
2,500	5.99	8.13	10.70	11.24
5,000	5.93	8.05	10.59	11.12
7,500	5.90	8.01	10.54	11.07
10,000	5.87	7.97	10.48	11.01
12,500	5.85	7.93	10.43	10.96
15,000	5.82	7.89	10.38	10.90
25,000	5.70	7.73	10.17	10.68
50,000	5.61	7.69	10.05	10.61
75,000	5.51	7.65	9.93	10.53
100,000	5.41	7.61	9.81	10.46
150,000	5.21	7.51	9.56	10.31
200,000	5.01	7.41	9.32	10.15
250,000	4.81	7.31	9.08	9.99

* There are 8 columns by 21 inches or 168 column inches on a full page.

EXHIBIT 10 WSB radio and TV advertising rates

	One minute	20/30 seconds	10 seconds
WSB-AM radio: Spot announcements—package plans*			
12 per week	$40.00	$34.00	$24.00
18 per week	38.00	30.00	21.00
24 per week	32.00	26.00	19.00
30 per week	28.00	24.00	17.00
48 per week	26.00	20.00	15.00
WSB-FM radio: Package plan—52 weeks†	16.00	14.00	

WSB-TV
Daytime rates
  60 seconds $ 75–235 depending on program
  30 seconds   40–140 depending on program
Prime-time rates
  60 seconds‡ $540–660 depending on program
  30 seconds   390–725 depending on program

* Available 5:00–6:00 A.M., 10:00 A.M.–3:30 P.M., and 7:30 P.M.–midnight, Monday–Saturday; and 5:00 A.M.–midnight, Sunday. Best available positions in applicable times—no guaranteed placement.

† Quantity discounts available. For example, 18 times per week for 52 weeks is one half the above rates.

‡ Very few available.

Mr. Rood decided that he would have to assume confidence in the effectiveness of the newspapers. He felt if the study were done right he would get his share of media exposure and influence. The other decision he quickly made was that in preparing his comments on the proposed research, he would take Rich's point of view rather than that of *The Atlanta Journal* and *Constitution*. He then began to review the events of the day and the WSB proposal in light of what he felt Rich's needed to know. He also knew that whatever he proposed would have to be acceptable to Mr. Landon. Noting the lateness in the day, he began work on the counterproposal.

Appendix   Suggestions for Rich's Media Research

Objectives

If Rich's is interested in conducting research to measure the effectiveness of various advertising media, WSB-TV and WSB-Radio will be happy to assist. As a basis for discussion, here are suggested objectives for this project:

1. Measure the ability of TV, radio, and newspapers to sell specific items of merchandise in Rich's seven Atlanta metro stores.
2. Determine how each advertising medium complements the others in terms of additional units sold to various segments of the customer population (age, sex, charge account ownership, etc.).
3. Determine what each advertising medium contributes in regard to additional store traffic.

How the Research Could Be Conducted

The project could consist of a series of in-store surveys. A separate survey would be conducted for each item of merchandise tested. The more items tested, the more reliable the results of the overall research project.

If possible, all seven Rich's stores in the Atlanta metro area should participate in the research.

Each survey could be conducted by placing interviewers (Rich's personnel working overtime) in appropriate store locations during "peak" shopping hours with instructions to complete *brief* questionnaires with customers purchasing the item being tested. (See accompanying questionnaire.)

The interview could cover how the customer got the idea to buy the item, other planned purchases in the store during the same visit, charge account ownership, and any other pertinent data. Each interview would last less than a minute and would not bother the customers.

The sample size would vary, depending upon the number of stores participating, the type of merchandise and the sales volume. Interviewers would strive to include all customers purchasing the items during peak hours. Tabulation of the results could be handled by the WSB computer.

Careful Attention to Items and Media Schedules

In order to make the research valid and meaningful, the items to be tested must be selected carefully. In addition, care should be taken to ensure that the TV, radio, or newspaper advertising for these items is not "stacked" in favor of one particular medium. Close attention to the items being tested and the media schedule for each is necessary.

Questionnaire

The proposed questionnaire follows:

(All customers purchasing the item advertised are interviewed.)

1. *How* did you happen to buy this merchandise at Rich's?

   Saw on TV   ( )
   Heard on radio   ( )
   Saw in newspaper   ( )
   TV and radio   ( )
   TV and newspaper   ( )
   TV, radio, and newspaper   ( )
   Saw on display   ( )
   Other: _____ ( )

ASKED OF CUSTOMERS NOT MENTIONING A MEDIUM: (2, 3, 4)

2. Do you recall seeing this merchandise advertised on the TV?
   Yes   ( )
   No   ( )

3. Do you recall seeing this merchandise advertised in the newspaper?
   Yes   ( )
   No   ( )

4. Do you recall hearing this merchandise advertised on the radio?
   Yes   ( )
   No   ( )

5. Are you buying *anything* else at Rich's today?
   Yes   ( )
   No   ( )
   Maybe   ( )
   Don't know   ( )

6. Do you have a charge account at *Rich's*?
   Yes   ( )
   No   ( )

---

7. In which group does your age fall?

   Under 25   ( )
   25–34   ( )
   35–49   ( )
   50 and over   ( )

Store _____

Time of Interview _____

Case 8

The Adirondack Manor*

Burt Gray, director of sales for the Adirondack Manor, could feel the pressure as he was preparing to attend the weekly sales meeting. In just a few months, the manor would be opening a new conference facility designed to enable the resort hotel to better serve the growing meetings and conventions market. Gray knew he would be asked for a marketing strategy to market the resort to the corporations and professional associations who were potential target customers.

Over the past several months, the sales department had been actively recruiting sales personnel and collecting information from trade publications on the meetings and conventions market. Recently, Gray had received a report from a marketing research firm that had been retained to study the buying and decision-making process used by meeting planners for corporations and associations to select locations and facilities for off-premise meetings. He was planning to use the findings from the research study to formulate a marketing strategy. Several questions came to mind as he thought about the marketing issues:

1. Was the resort's present organizational structure satisfactory to enable it to manage its marketing efforts?
2. How should the resort be positioned to best serve the meetings and conventions market?
3. Given the positioning, what marketing strategy would be appropriate to expand the Manor's market?

* This case was prepared by Professor Lawrence M. Lamont, Washington and Lee University, Department of Administration.

The author gratefully acknowledges the research assistance of Steven Daub, Stewart Kerr, and Bennett Ross, all graduates of Washington and Lee University. Assistance in case preparation was provided by Perry Goodbar, also a graduate of Washington and Lee.

Property of the Washington and Lee University Department of Administration. Case material is prepared as a basis for class discussion and not designed to present illustrations of either effective or ineffective handling of administrative problems. Certain names and locations have been changed. Used with permission.

Historical Background

The Adirondack Manor traced its beginning to the summer of 1750, when a local doctor noticed that visitors were attracted to the area for the mineral water from a large hot spring. The doctor began advertising that the spring water was recommended for such maladies as gout, rheumatism, paralysis, and spinal irritations. Later, in 1776, the doctor built a private home and operated it as an inn for visitors.

The inn passed from owner to owner until 1890 when the chief executive officer of a major railroad purchased the property. By 1892, several improvements were under way, and the following year the Adirondack Manor opened its doors as a classic resort hotel.

In 1901, the hotel was destroyed by fire. Before the embers had been quenched, management was making plans for a larger and more modern resort. By the spring of 1902, the main section of the new hotel had been rebuilt, and by 1914, new east and west wings had been added. The Manor was becoming very fashionable for vacationing social guests from Boston, New York, Philadelphia, and Washington, D.C.

In 1959, ski and skating areas were added to improve the seasonal appeal of the Manor. Although the winter weather was somewhat unpredictable, this expenditure was looked upon favorably. It was soon a successful reality, with the installation of snowmaking and icemaking equipment.

The most recent addition to the hotel will be a modern conference facility. It will house additional guest rooms as well as a center capable of accommodating 1,000 people for banquets, conventions, and professional meetings. This addition will enhance the appeal of the Manor to the meetings and conventions market, as well as to the resort's social guests.

Present Facilities

With the completion of the conference facility, the resort's properties will include a luxury hotel with over 500 sleeping rooms, several dining rooms, three swimming pools, and attractive meeting facilities. The 20,000 surrounding acres, also owned by the Manor, contain three championship golf courses, 19 tennis courts, a skeet and trapshooting range, horseback riding and hiking trails, a trout stream, skiing and ice skating facilities, and numerous other recreational amenities.

The Manor directs much of its marketing effort at the social market because its accommodations, dining services, and recreational attractions strongly appeal to the families and individuals in the upper social classes. Most of these customers are destination vacationers who use the resort on a regular basis, while a few are walk-in guests that arrive without reservations. In recent years, the resort has also been somewhat successful marketing to corporations and associations interested in using the facilities for off-premise business meetings and conventions. While these marketing efforts have been modest, the resort has achieved some success in attracting small business meetings and conventions. Management now believed that the addition of the new conference center would enable the resort to substantially improve its competitive position in the market.

Location

Adirondack Manor, one of the largest mountain resorts in the United States, is located in the heart of the Adirondack Mountains.[1] It is surrounded by a small, historic village that has a variety of specialty shops and restaurants that are attractive to visitors and guests. The Manor is located along a two-lane U.S. highway about 20 miles from a major interstate highway.

The Manor is served by nearby McMullen Field which has the capability of handling private and corporate aircraft. The runway is constructed of concrete and is 5,600 feet long, 100 feet wide, and 3,100 feet above sea level, making it the highest air strip east of the Mississippi.

Presently, there are two daily and three weekend flights scheduled into McMullen by an air charter service which operates out of La Guardia in New York. The service takes about 55 minutes and uses Beechcraft 99s with a capacity of 12 passengers. However, four additional planes are available, upon request, when there is a large group needing service. McMullen is located 17 miles from the hotel, but ground transportation is available through the resort.

An alternative method of reaching the resort is to fly into Foxboro Regional Airport, located 60 miles away. Foxboro is served daily with flights by two national carriers using 112-passenger Boeing 737s and a regional airline flying Beechcraft 99s. Again, complete ground transportation to the resort is available at Foxboro.

Climate

While the Manor's location is quite remote, the resort is surrounded by rolling hills and beautiful mountains. The climate is moderate throughout the year with summer temperatures averaging 75–80 degrees and winter temperatures 30–35 degrees. The precipitation varies during the year with an inordinate amount of rainfall during March and April. Business is slower at these times, because social guests and meeting attendees don't want to chance the weather and be unable to take advantage of the recreational opportunities.

The resort has skiing and ice skating, although the weather is not always suitable for these activities. Most of the snow falls from December through early March, and averages 60 to 70 inches a year. In some months, the snow fall is inadequate to support the winter activities. However, snowmaking equipment augments the natural snow to make these activities possible during the winter season.

---

[1] The Manor is a privately owned company. Annual sales are approximately $20 million and employment is 700 people.

Organization and Management of the Adirondack Manor

The Adirondack Manor uses a functional organization to manage its business. The organization chart illustrated in Figure 1 shows the functional departments and elaborates the activities and reporting relationships in the sales department. The president, Les Wright, is responsible for the daily operations of the resort. Several functional department managers report to Wright informally during a weekly staff meeting designed to give each manager an opportunity to review the activities of his department and coordinate them with the other managers. In addition, department managers benefit from Wright's open-door policy which creates an informal line of communication and helps to resolve the day-to-day problems that arise.

Although each department is crucial to the successful operation of the Manor, the sales department has the dual responsibility of selling the resort's meeting and convention capabilities and, through the convention services group, assisting planners with meeting arrangements to ensure that meetings run smoothly. Thus, the sales department has the dual responsibility of sales and customer service.

Burt Gray, director of sales, manages the Manor's sales department. He is knowledgable about the industry, having had 10 years of sales experience in resort hotels. The director's duties include representing the department at staff meetings, preparing budgets for the sales department, and developing sales plans specifying the types of meetings and geographic areas where selling efforts will be concentrated.

FIGURE 1 Formal organization of the Adirondack Manor

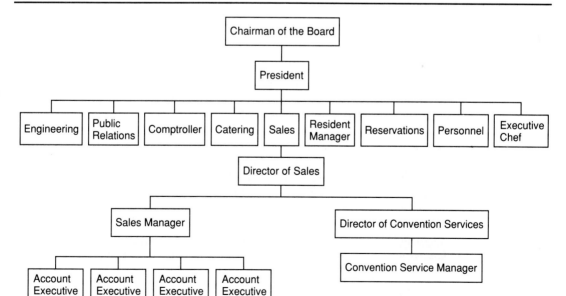

Reporting to Gray is a sales manager and a director of convention services. The sales manager directs the daily activities of the account executives and assists with sales calls and training when necessary. Once a sale is made, responsibility for the customer is transferred to the convention services manager and his staff. As mentioned, this group works closely with the corporation or association meeting planner to finalize the meeting arrangements and attend to any problems that might arise during the meeting at the Manor.

The Meeting and Conventions Market

According to trade sources, the off-premise meetings and conventions market has grown from $8.7 billion in 1973 to $34.6 billion in 1985. Growing at an annual rate of 12.2 percent, the market has become a vital aspect of the nation's economy and increasingly attractive to resort hotels that have traditionally served the needs of affluent families and individuals. A recent survey, covering most of the market, indicates that corporations and associations sponsored over 903,000 meetings in 1985 with annual meeting expenditures exceeding $31.4 billion. As shown in Table 1, the majority of the off-premise meetings were held by corporations; however, they accounted for only 24 percent of the total annual expenditures. In part, this is explained by the fact that many of the corporate meetings are smaller. Attendance at off-premise meetings held by corporations and associations was spread over a variety of different types of meetings. Table 2 shows the attendance by type of meeting in 1985 for both corporations and associations. Regional and national sales meetings accounted for 24 percent of the attendance at corporation meetings, while national conventions were responsible for 43 percent of the attendance at meetings held by associations.

Economic Environment

Generally, the economic environment does not affect the number of meetings and conventions held annually because they are viewed as a necessary expense of conducting business. However, adverse economic conditions have caused corporate and association meeting planners to become concerned about ex-

TABLE 1 Total off-premise meetings and expenditures, 1985

	Off-premise meetings held during year		Total annual expenditures	
Corporate meetings	706,000	(78.0%)	$7,527,800,000	(24.0%)
Association major conventions	12,240	(1.5%)	12,675,800,000	(40.3%)
Association other meetings	185,400	(20.5%)	11,213,300,000	(35.7%)
Total meetings	903,740	(100.0%)	$31,416,900,000*	(100.0%)

* Based on a survey. When projected to the total meetings market, total expenditures are $34,643,100,000.
Source: *The Meetings Market Study, 1985* (New York: Murdoch Magazines Research Department, 1986.)

TABLE 2 Attendance at corporation and association off-premise meetings

Type of meeting	Corporations	Associations
Training seminars	6,868,400 (17%)	
Sales meetings	9,361,000 (24%)	
Management meetings	8,011,300 (20%)	
Professional/technical meetings	3,959,300 (10%)	3,641,000 (11%)
Incentive trips	2,425,300 (6%)	
New product introductions	4,064,600 (10%)	
Stockholder meetings	2,077,300 (5%)	
Educational seminars		6,208,100 (20%)
Board meetings		1,156,000 (3%)
Regional/state/local chapter meetings		4,336,400 (14%)
National conventions		13,537,400 (43%)
Other meetings	3,021,000 (8%)	2,831,200 (9%)
Total	39,788,200 (100%)	31,710,100 (100%)

Source: *The Meetings Market Study, 1985* (New York: Murdock Magazines Research Department), 1986.

penses and to search for ways of reducing the costs. Items such as transportation, room accommodations, meal functions, and receptions have come under careful scrutiny. Many organizations are reducing transportation costs by using central locations or staying closer to headquarters facilities. The cost of meals and banquets is another area for cutting meeting and convention expenses. Many organizations have eliminated cocktail receptions and moved away from meal plans which include three daily meals.

Economic conditions do have an effect on attendance. For instance, during recessions the number of "no shows" at scheduled meetings and conventions is always a problem. Meeting planners are extremely conscious of attendance because a conference that is not well attended is a waste of time and money. To reduce the number of no shows, corporations and associations constantly work to improve the programming and marketing of large meetings and conventions. According to meeting planners, resorts can be more attractive than city hotels because they provide facilities for a serious business meeting while offering enough recreation incentives to act as a lure. Further, the self-contained nature of many resort hotels makes those who attend a captive audience.

Competitive Environment

Competition in the meetings and conventions market is intense and, for any type of meeting or budget, meeting planners have a variety of locations and facilities to choose from. As illustrated in Table 3, facilities range from a midtown hotel or motor inn in cities like New York or Chicago to mountain or ocean resorts in New England and the South.

Resort hotels have always been popular for off-premise meetings. Many resorts, in addition to Adirondack Manor, have built special conference facili-

TABLE 3 Type of facilities used for off-premise meetings

Type of facilities	Corporate planners	Association planners*
Resort hotel	44%	40%
Suburban hotel or motor inn	45	39
Midtown hotel or motor inn	58	70
Airport hotel or motor inn	27	31
Privately owned conference center	17	15
Condominium resort	9	4
Suite hotel	9	5
University-owned conference center	5	10
Cruise	5	1

Note: Totals exceed 100 percent because of multiple response.

* Excludes major conventions, most of which are held at midtown hotels.

Source: *The Meetings Market Study, 1985* (New York: Murdoch Magazines Research Department, 1986.)

ties to accommodate meetings and conventions. The competition has come from other sources as well. The major hotel chains such as Marriott, Hilton, and Westin, which are not typical resort hotels, have concentrated on marketing their hotels and motor inns as such. By offering a meeting and recreation package, they are able to compete in the market as a resort. Many of their facilities are located in urban and suburban areas, often close to airports.

Teleconferencing has become an alternative to extensive traveling for meetings. However, at present it is not a serious competitive threat due to the cost and the slow adoption of the technology. As teleconferencing costs decline, it is likely that meeting planners will make greater use of the technology for future meetings.

Faced with unused capacity in the off-season, resorts often offer attractive rates for meetings. Rates are discounted in the so-called shoulder periods (the weeks immediately before and after a peak season) and the low season (December–February), now popularly called the value season by many resorts.

Seven luxury resorts, all rated as five-star resort hotels by the *Mobile Travel Guide*, are in direct competition with the Manor. In Figure 2, it can be noted that, while the resorts are somewhat comparable in their accommodations, the dining plans vary. Differences are also apparent in the recreational amenities available at each resort. As shown in Figure 3, they generally reflect the unique features of each resort's environment and location.

Of greatest importance to meeting planners, however, is the facilities the resort has for the business sessions of the meeting or convention. Table 4 provides a comparison of the meeting facilities of each resort hotel. These facilities, along with the prices of the resort's accommodations, dining service, and recreational amenities give each resort a somewhat distinctive position in the market. It also makes prices difficult to compare among the competing resorts. Some resorts quoted meeting planners a daily rate that included the room, a meal plan, and use of the resort's meeting and recreation facilities.

FIGURE 2 Accommodations and dining plans by resort

	Accommodations				Dining plan*			
	Single occupancy	Double occupancy	Suites	Cottages	European	Modified American	Full American	Off-season rates
The Arizona Biltmore	X	X			X			X
The Breakers	X	X	X		X	X	X	X
The Broadmoor	X	X	X		X	X†		X
The Greenbrier	X	X				X		X
The Homestead	X	X	X	X		X	X	X
The Lodge	X	X	X		X	X		
Colonial Williamsburg	X	X	X			X‡	X‡	X
Adirondack Manor	X	X	X		X		X	X

* European Plan (Meals not included in daily room rate.) Modified American Plan (Two meals included in daily room rate.) Full American Plan (Three meals included in daily room rate.)

† Available for groups of 350 or more.

‡ Available by arrangement for special conference packages.

Source: Resorts' promotional materials.

FIGURE 3 Recreational amenities by resort

Resort Hotel	Golf	Tennis	Horseback Riding	Swimming	Bowling	Sailing	Trap and Skeet	Skiing	Skating	Fishing	Spa
The Arizona Biltmore	X	X		X							X
The Breakers	X	X		X		X				X	
The Broadmore	X	X	X	X		X	X	X	X		X
The Greenbrier	X	X	X	X	X		X	X	X	X	X
The Homestead	X	X	X	X	X		X			X	X
The Lodge	X	X	X	X							
Colonial Williamsburg	X	X	X	X			X	X	X	X	
Adirondack Manor	X	X	X	X			X	X	X	X	X

Source: Resorts' promotional material.

TABLE 4 Meeting facilities by resort

Resort Hotel	Capacity of largest function rooms †		Number of meeting rooms of various seating capacity*						
	Theater Style	Banquet Style	Total	1,000 +	500–999	250–499	100–249	50–99	49–below
The Arizona Biltmore	1,250	940	17	1	2	3	4	3	4
The Breakers	1,200	1,000	20	1	1	—	2	12	4
The Broadmoor	2,600	1,600	34	2	6	4	4	6	12
The Greenbrier	2,000	1,200	25	1	2	4	8	4	6
The Homestead	1,250	1,020	25	1	2	3	4	2	13
The Lodge	600	400	5	—	1	1	1	1	1
Colonial Williamsburg	850	700	21	—	3	3	6	5	4
Adirondack Manor	1,000	815	23	1	2	3	4	2	11

* Based on theater style arrangement (chairs no tables).

† Banquet style is set for dinner.

Source: Resorts' promotional materials.

Others quoted the various services separately and allowed the meeting planner to construct a package that best met the needs of the meeting.

The manor's prices were based on the full American plan where the rate included the room and three daily meals. For corporations and associations planning a meeting or convention, the per person daily rate also included meeting rooms, audiovisual equipment, receptions, and refreshment breaks. Recreational activities such as golf and tennis were usually priced separately, with group rates available for corporations and associations planning large functions. Off-season rates were also available at the Manor to stimulate demand during the low-occupancy periods. Discounts of up to 30 percent were applied to the regular season rates for groups using the resort's meeting and convention facilities during these times. Following is a brief description of the major competitors offering services similar to those of the Adirondack Manor.

The Arizona Biltmore

The Arizona Biltmore is a luxury resort owned by the Westin chain. It is located in Phoenix, 20 minutes from the Phoenix International Airport, and has over 500 guest rooms and three dining facilities.

The Biltmore's promotional efforts are supported by an extensive advertising campaign designed to build preference for all of the hotels in the Westin chain. It provides a complete conference facility and competes in the higher price, luxury segment of the meetings and conventions market. Sixty percent of the resort's meeting rooms are designed for groups of 50–500 people.

The Breakers

The Breakers is a glamorous ocean resort located on the Atlantic Ocean 15 minutes from the Palm Beach International Airport. It has 568 rooms and two dining facilities. During the hot summer and fall months (July–October), the Breakers offers special off-season conference rates which are generally below the industry average. With 60 percent of its meeting rooms designed for groups of 50 or less, the Breakers is an ideal site for smaller meetings. The resort emphasizes its prestigious location, elegant facilities, and excellent service in promotion to meeting planners.

The Broadmoor

The Broadmoor is a four-season Colorado resort, although it is more popular in the winter months when skiing is available. It is located 15 minutes from the airport serving Colorado Springs and has 560 rooms and four dining facilities. The Broadmoor has pursued a pricing strategy which enables the resort to compete in the lower-price segment of the luxury hotels. It emphasizes a central location and moderate weather in order to attract business. The resort has approximately 25 percent of its meeting rooms designed for groups of 500 or more.

The Greenbrier

The Greenbrier is a mountain resort nestled in the Alleghany Mountains in White Sulphur, West Virginia. It is close to a major interstate highway and 15 minutes from the Greenbrier Valley Airport. The resort has 700 rooms, three dining rooms, three golf courses, and many other recreational attractions. The Greenbrier's dining service emphasizes the modified American plan which does not include lunch. This feature is attractive to health-conscious executives and meeting planners interested in reducing costs by eliminating an afternoon meal.

Information concerning the Greenbrier is contained in an impressive promotional brochure which includes a 43-page meeting planner's manual. Advertisements describing the conference facilities of the Greenbrier have appeared in *Sales and Marketing Management, Dun's Business Month,* and *The Wall Street Journal.* To encourage corporations and associations to plan meetings at the Greenbrier, the resort offers special meeting packages that are available from November through March. With 61 percent of its meeting rooms designed for groups from 50 to 500, it is well suited for moderate size meetings and conventions.

The Homestead

The Homestead, only a short drive from the Greenbrier, is a classic mountain resort, located in Hot Springs, Virginia. The location is somewhat remote, but it is adequately served by Ingalls Field, a small airport 25 minutes away, and Woodrum Field in Roanoke, Virginia, 75 miles away. The resort provides ground transportation from both airports.

The Homestead is self-contained and provides a complete range of services for guests including specialty shops, a theater, night clubs, and live entertainment. The resort has 540 sleeping rooms, three dining facilities, three golf courses, skiing and skating, and a variety of other recreational amenities. Promoted as a resort for all seasons and all meetings, it has received the prestigious Mobil Five Star Award for 21 consecutive years and has been honored with the Gold Key Award from *Meetings and Conventions Magazine.*

The Homestead is also a complete conference facility that operates with both the full and modified American plan. About 65 percent of its meeting rooms are designed for groups from 50 to 500, but it can handle conventions with up to 2,000 people. Special rates are also available from the Homestead for meeting planners who want to plan meetings during the November–March off-season.

The Lodge

The Lodge is a Pebble Beach company resort located in the Del Monte Forest on California's Monterey Peninsula. It is best known for its championship golf courses, Pebble Beach, Spyglass Hill, and Old Del Monte, the first course west of the Mississippi. In addition, the Lodge offers a variety of other recreational, social, and sightseeing activities, benefiting from its proximity to some of the most beautiful scenery and unique tourist attractions on the California coast.

Easily accessible, the Lodge is located just off a U.S. highway and is only eight miles from the Monterey Airport which is served by United Airlines, Air California, and other carriers. Since its beginning, the Pebble Beach Company has tried to develop the Lodge as a resort which provides elegant shopping, fine dining, and excellent recreation facilities to accommodate many types of business meetings. By design, however, it is intended for smaller meetings. The capacity of the largest meeting room at the Lodge is only 600 with banquet facilities for 400. Moreover, the resort offers a selection of only five meeting rooms in which to hold business functions. As a result, the number of conferences and meetings that are suitable for the Lodge is quite limited.

Colonial Williamsburg

Located in historic Williamsburg, Virginia, the Colonial Williamsburg Inn and Conference Center offers professional and business organizations a distinctive and unusual setting for a business conference. The Conference Center is part of a complex which includes the Williamsburg Lodge, the Williamsburg Inn, and the Colonial guest houses. Also, the Williamsburg Motor House and Meeting Center are located just north of the Lodge. In addition to the traditional recreation amenities, Williamsburg has numerous attractions of historical significance to occupy visitors and guests. Guided tours of the historic area may be arranged to suit the interests of a conference group.

Colonial Williamsburg is readily accessible by any mode of transportation, and this feature makes it attractive to meeting planners. The resort can accommodate groups of nearly 900 with banquet services for over 700 guests. The 21 meeting rooms offer a high degree of flexibility and choice for most group customers. However, with over 70 percent of its meeting rooms designed for groups of less than 250, Colonial Williamsburg seems best suited for smaller-scale executive meetings and conferences.

Buyer Behavior in the Meetings and Conventions Market

During the planning for the new conference facility, the Manor retained an independent marketing research firm to study the purchase behavior of the corporations and associations in the meetings and conventions market. Using secondary data and the survey method, the research examined the motives for

FIGURE 4 The buying and decision-making model

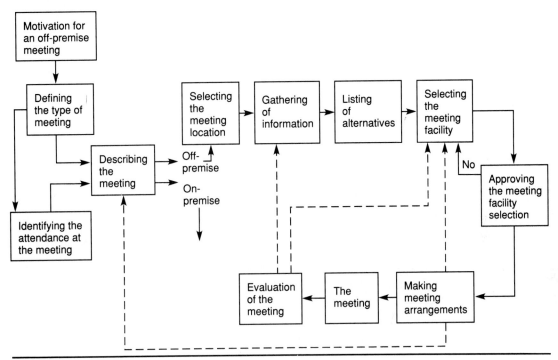

Note: Dashed line indicates information feedback.
Source: Independent marketing research study.

holding off-premise meetings, the information used by meeting planners to plan meetings, the factors used in selecting a meeting location and facility, and many other important aspects of the purchase decision.[2] An important result of the research was a conceptual model of the buying and decision-making process. This model, shown in Figure 4 and discussed in the sections which follow, was expected to be helpful to the Manor in developing the marketing strategy for its meeting and convention services.

The Motivation for an Off-Premise Meeting

Corporate and association meetings are held to communicate the results of operations, to discuss the problems and decisions that arise during the course of business, to train individuals, and to reward outstanding performance. While

---

[2] The survey results are based on a nationwide respondent sample of 303 meeting planners—141 meeting planners for corporations and 162 association meeting planners.

most association meetings are required in their by-laws, the need for many corporate meetings is recognized by the managers of functional areas. For example, an executive may determine that a management meeting is necessary to explain new company policies or introduce a new product.

There are basically two reasons for holding an off-premise meeting. The first is that the organization does not have the capabilities to hold the meeting on its premises. The second is to move the attendees away from the business environment and ensure uninterrupted attendance and attention. In addition, off-premise meetings fulfill certain needs of the organization and the individual attendees. Meetings can improve employee motivation, increase productivity, and satisfy the personal and social needs of those attending. For example, by holding the meeting at a luxury resort, it can satisfy the employees' need for recognition of outstanding personal achievement.

Defining the Meeting

As shown in Table 5, corporations and associations hold a variety of off-premise meetings, each designed to accomplish a specific purpose. Defining the type of meeting to be held is important because it determines who will be responsible for the planning and decision making and the lead time necessary to organize the meeting. Few corporations have employees whose sole responsibility is to plan meetings. The meeting planner's primary job responsibility could be in sales and marketing, public relations, corporate administration, personnel and training, manufacturing and operations, travel, or occasionally meeting planning. The type of meeting to be held usually determines who plans it. For example, 44 percent of the management meetings and 61 percent of the sales meetings were planned by individuals in sales and marketing, while 73 percent

TABLE 5 Numbers and types of corporate and association off-premise meetings

	Corporations	*Associations*
Training seminars	163,500 (23%)	—
Sales meetings	157,400 (22%)	—
Management meetings	178,000 (25%)	—
Professional/technical meetings	63,900 (9%)	31,900 (16%)
Incentive trips	27,600 (4%)	—
New product introductions	67,750 (10%)	—
Stockholder meetings	21,900 (3%)	—
Educational seminars	—	63,300 (32%)
Board meetings	—	37,300 (19%)
Regional/state/local chapter meetings	—	31,900 (16%)
National conventions	—	12,240 (6%)
Other meetings	26,050 (4%)	21,000 (11%)
Total	706,100 (100%)	197,640 (100%)

Source: *The Meetings Market Study, 1985* (New York: Murdoch Magazines Research Department, 1986).

of the stockholders' meetings were planned by corporate administrators and meeting planners. Generally, the decision on a location or facility did not rest entirely with the individual planning the meeting. Many decisions were made in collaboration with department managers or special committees.

The planning of association meetings was often done by an individual whose title might be executive director, meeting planner, administrative assistant, vice president, president, or secretary-treasurer. As with corporate meetings, the type of meeting often indicated who was responsible for planning. Board meetings, educational meetings, and national conventions, for example, are planned primarily by the executive director or the association's meeting planner. Compared to corporate meetings, the individuals planning the association meetings are more likely to have decision-making authority in selecting the meeting location and facility. However, in the case of decisions involving the location of national conventions and board meetings, the association's executive committee may exercise final approval.

Finally, the type of meeting tells the planner the length of time needed for planning and selecting the appropriate facility. The shortest average lead time for off-premise meetings held by corporations is 4.0 months for management meetings, and the longest is 13.1 months for incentive trips (sales award meetings); the overall average for all types of meetings is 7.7 months. The shortest average lead time for associations is 8.1 months for regional or local chapter meetings, and the longest is 38.9 months for national conventions. Excluding national conventions, the average according to association meeting planners, is about 10.2 months.

Identifying the Attendance at the Meeting

Once the type of meeting to be held is defined, it becomes necessary for the meeting planner to determine who will attend. This is important because the attendance often influences the selection of a meeting location and the choice of a facility. For instance, meetings which involve corporate executives are more likely to be held at a resort with recreation facilities than at an airport motor inn. Also, for association meetings, such as national membership conventions where attendance is not mandatory, the selection of a glamorous or popular facility helps to stimulate attendance.

Another important consideration is the number of individuals expected to attend. In Table 6 it can be seen that in general, attendance will depend on the type of meeting being planned. The facility requirements, such as the number of sleeping and meeting rooms, are solely a function of the expected attendance. For this reason, when the meeting planner considers specific meeting or convention facilities, a basic criterion in evaluation is the capacity to accommodate the expected group.

The final aspect of identifying the attendance at the meeting involves considering the areas in which the attendees are located. Meeting planners are

TABLE 6 Average attendance at corporate and association meetings

	Corporations	Associations
Training seminars	33	—
Sales meetings	62	—
Management meetings	40	—
Professional/technical meetings	62	166
Incentive trips	103	—
New product introductions	49	—
Stockholder meetings	85	—
Educational seminars	—	153
Board meetings	—	45
Regional/state/local chapters meetings	—	149
National conventions	—	1,044
Other meetings	97	201

Source: The Meetings Market Study, 1983, *Meetings and Conventions Magazine.*

conscious of the travel time and costs associated with off-premise meetings. Corporations will often arrange a meeting in a central location to reduce travel expenses, while associations concerned with attendance levels are less likely to select a facility that requires members to pay large sums of money to reach the meeting location.

Describing the Meeting

Once the meeting has been defined and its attendance specified, the meeting planner begins to develop the program for the meeting. This process begins with an understanding of the work requirements of the meeting and the need for social and recreational activities to complement the working sessions. Corporate management meetings, for example, usually include presentations and discussions with some time for leisure activities. This blend of work and leisure must be defined before a meeting location is selected. Also, the attendance of spouses at a meeting or convention must be considered early in the planning process. A meeting which includes spouses must provide activities in the program for those not involved in the business sessions.

Meeting length is another aspect that must be considered. In general, the length of either a corporate or association meeting depends on the type of meeting and who is expected to attend. For example, corporate stockholder meetings and association board meetings last less than two days on average, while corporate incentive trips to reward outstanding performance typically last longer than five days. Table 7 gives additional information on the average length of corporation and association meetings.

The final aspect of describing the meeting involves a consideration of any financial constraints. Planners must be aware of the budget and organize meetings within the financial limits imposed by the organization. In addition, meeting planners must be careful when arranging a meeting that might impose a

TABLE 7 Average length (days) of corporate and association meetings

	Corporations	Associations
Training seminars	2.8	—
Sales meetings	2.8	—
Management meetings	2.2	—
Professional/technical meetings	2.3	2.4
Incentive trips	5.5	—
New product introductions	2.0	—
Stockholder meetings	1.4	—
Educational seminars	—	2.3
Board meetings	—	1.9
Regional/state/local chapters meetings	—	2.6
National conventions	—	N.A.
Other meetings	2.8	3.0
Average	2.6	2.4

Source: *The Meetings Market Study, 1985* (New York: Murdoch Magazines Research Department, 1986).

financial burden on attendees by requiring them to draw on personal accounts. Association planners, in particular, must give special attention to the total cost of a meeting or convention package if the members must pay their own expenses.

Selecting a Meeting Location

Given a description of the attendance and the work requirements of the meeting, the meeting planner proceeds to select a location. The marketing research identified seven factors that meeting planners consider in selecting the geographic location: ease of transporting attendees to the location, image of location, environmental setting and climate, transportation costs, recreational activities, sightseeing activities, and distance from attendees. The research also identified the importance that meeting planners attached to the various factors. Table 8 ranks each factor in terms of its importance in location decisions for

TABLE 8 Importance of factors in the selection of a meeting location

Location selection factors	Corporate planner	Association planner
Ease of transporting attendees to location	1	1
Image of location	2	2
Environmental setting/climate	3	3
Transportation costs	4	5
Recreational activities	5	6
Sightseeing activities	6	7
Distance from attendees	7	4

Source: Independent marketing research study.

corporation and association meetings. As can be noted from the table, the most important location factors are similar for both corporations and associations, but some differences do exist, such as the distance of the location from the attendees.

Gathering of Information

As the meeting location is being selected, the corporate or association planner is also gathering information on specific meeting facilities. Meeting planners obtain information at different times from as many as nine sources, as shown in Table 9. The information gathered from an on-site inspection is the most important. An inspection gives the meeting planner an opportunity to sample and evaluate the hotel or resort's services before the facility is finally selected. Some meeting planners spend a majority of their time visiting different hotels and resorts, inspecting them for future meetings. This is encouraged by the sales people in the hotel or resorts, because it is easier to convince someone to bring a meeting to a particular facility if he or she can actually experience what it has to offer. The second most important source of information in the selection of a meeting facility is the organization's previous experience with a specific hotel or resort. A productive meeting previously held at a particular hotel or resort will ensure that the facility is considered again as a meeting site. Conversely, an unsatisfactory experience will reduce the likelihood that the hotel or resort will be considered for future meetings.

TABLE 9 Information sources used to select a meeting facility

Information source	Corporate planner	Association planner
On-site inspection	1 (tie)	1
Previous personal experience with hotel or resort	1 (tie)	2
Personal perception of hotel or resort	2	3
Hotel or resort's sales personnel	3	4
Hotel or resort's promotional material	4	6
Meeting planners' magazines	5	7
Hotel or resort advertisement's	6	8
Meeting planners with other organizations	7	5
Travel agents	8	9

Source: Independent marketing research study.

Although advertising and promotional material ranked low in importance as sources of information used by meeting planners, promotion probably has an indirect effect on the meeting planning process. An effective promotion program can influence a meeting planner's perception of the meeting facility and lead to its consideration as a prospective site.

Listing of Alternatives

Based on the planner's assessment of the information gathered from various sources, and after considering the appropriateness of the hotels or resorts in the geographic location selected for the meeting, a list of individual facilities is compiled for further consideration.

Selecting a Meeting Facility

In selecting a meeting facility, the meeting planner may evaluate the alternative hotels or resorts on several different factors. The nine most important factors, considering all types of meetings, are ranked for both corporations and associations in Table 10. A decision on a specific hotel or resort to be used for a meeting is made when a facility is judged to be superior on the factors appropriate for the meeting being planned.

TABLE 10 Importance of factors in the selection of a meeting facility

Facility selection factors	Corporation planner	Association planner
Quality of food service	1	2
Number/quality of sleeping rooms	2 (tie)	4
Price/value relationship	2 (tie)	1
Efficiency of check-in/check-out/billing	3	5
Number/quality of meeting rooms	4	3
Price of sleeping rooms	5	7
Price of food service	6	8
Price of meeting rooms	7	6
Recreation/shopping/entertainment	8	9

Source: Independent marketing research study.

Individual factors may vary in importance. The most important factors in the selection of a facility for corporate directors' meetings and association board meetings are the number/quality of sleeping and meeting rooms, the quality of food service, the efficiency of check-in/check-out/billing procedures, and the price/value relationship. The least important are the price of meeting rooms, the price of sleeping rooms, the price of food service, and recreation, shopping, and entertainment. This distinction between quality and price is consistent among all types of corporate meetings and reflects a willingness on the part of many corporations to pay for quality meeting facilities and accommodations. The same is true for the board meetings of associations and some national conventions. In this instance, the meeting reflects on the association which necessitates quality facilities and accommodations with less concern about price. The other association meetings such as professional/technical, educational and regional/state/local chapter meetings are more concerned with the prices of meeting and sleeping rooms and the price of food service. The reason is that these meetings are business oriented and the attendees have limited expense accounts or are paying their own expenses.

Approving the Meeting Facility Selection

Following the selection of a meeting facility, approval of the choice is the next step in the planning and decision-making process. In corporations, final approval of the meeting facility often rests with the manager of the functional area holding the meeting. A vice president of sales, for example, will approve a facility recommended by the meeting planner for a sales meeting.

The association facility approval is often a group decision, and many associations have committees for this purpose. Since an association tries to represent the interests of its membership, board meetings and membership conventions are usually moved from region to region. The committee will generally follow the regional members' recommendations for a meeting because they know the facilities in their region that are most suitable.

If a facility is approved, making the meeting arrangements is the next step. However, if facility approval is not obtained, other alternative meeting facilities will be examined, as shown in Figure 4.

Making Meeting Arrangements

Following approval of the facility, the planner, acting as a liaison between the corporation or association and the hotel or resort, makes the arrangements for the meeting. This includes making reservations for the sleeping and meeting rooms and arranging for food and beverage services, audiovisual equipment, and recreational activities. The meeting planner also decides on the registration and checkout procedures, the billing procedure to be followed, the deposit requirement, and the payment procedure. As the details of the meeting are finalized, the meeting planner reviews the program and makes any additions or changes that are necessary. Usually the program is finalized about two weeks prior to the meeting.

As the meeting arrangements are being made, the planner begins to notify the attendees of the time and place for the meeting and appropriate travel arrangements are made. Finally, just prior to the meeting, a package summarizing the program is prepared for all attendees.

The Meeting

During the meeting, the meeting planner or another designated individual acts as a liaison to handle problems that arise and gather information on how those in attendance are enjoying the meeting. This information is useful in evaluating the meeting and deciding whether or not to return to a particular facility. It is also customary for the hotel or resort to designate a member of the marketing staff to serve as a contact person while the meeting is in progress.

Evaluation of the Meeting

At the conclusion of many meetings, the planner may ask the attendees to formally evaluate the meeting. Areas for evaulation are the meeting program and the hotel or resort's performance in such areas as food services, meeting and sleeping rooms, and recreational facilities and activities.

One method of evaluation is to have the planner ask the attendees, on an informal basis, about the meeting. This method is appropriate for the smaller meetings, such as directors' meetings and board meetings, because the executives are treated in a personal manner. The second evaluation technique is having the meeting attendees complete formal questionnaires. Because a large number of responses can be obtained with relative ease, formal questionnaires are suited for the larger meetings such as national membership conventions.

The results of both methods of evaluation will influence the meeting planner's perceptions of a hotel or resort facility. Since personal perceptions are an important source of information in the selection of a facility, a poor evaluation could reduce the likelihood that the facility will be considered or selected for any future meetings.

Evaluation of the Adirondack Manor

A final aspect of the marketing research asked meeting planners to evaluate the Adirondack Manor on several attributes judged to be important in selecting a conference facility. While the meeting planners had not seen the new facility at the time the evaluation was made, many of the planners were familiar with the resort and several had attended small meetings in the previous facility or had visited the Manor as a social guest.

The ratings, shown in Table 11, indicate that the Manor is viewed favorably on many of the factors important to meeting planners. Association planners, in particular, rated the Manor favorably because a higher percentage had planned and attended meetings there and were simply more familiar with the resort than their corporate counterparts who spent less time planning meetings.

The management of the Manor was encouraged by the evaluations, because a number of the factors that were rated highly could be considered competitive strengths. For instance, both corporate and association meeting planners rated the Manor's reputation/image as being almost ideal; the recreational facilities, environmental setting, food services, and overall quality were also rated highly. The fact that the environmental setting was viewed as highly

TABLE 11 Ratings of the Adirondak Manor by corporate and association meeting planners

Aspects of the Manor	Corporate planners	Association planners	All planners
Reputation/image	4.21	4.37	4.30
Recreational facilities	3.95	4.26	4.14
Environmental setting	3.82	4.30	4.10
Overall quality of the Manor	3.97	4.12	4.06
Food	3.78	4.12	4.01
Helpfulness/dependability of sales staff	3.67	4.04	3.88
Courtesy/helpfulness of bellhops, waiters, and maids.	3.77	4.18	3.86
Sleeping rooms	3.31	3.68	3.53
Price/value	3.08	3.49	3.32
Meeting facilities	2.50	2.59	2.55
Location/accessibility	2.25	2.21	2.23

Note: Average scores from a five-point rating scale where 1 = unsatisfactory and 5 = ideal.
Source: Independent marketing research study.

favorable seemed to suggest that, although the Manor was difficult to reach, the seclusion of the resort may be worth the extra travel. Management was not especially concerned about the planners' evaluation of the Manor's meeting facilities. The new facility was expected to accommodate the future needs of meeting planners and remedy this competitive weakness.

Case 9

Greenwood Federal Savings and Loan*

In early October 1986, Ms. Jenny Harris was reviewing the results of the latest research that had been conducted by Greenwood Federal Savings and its advertising agency. Ms. Harris had been asked by the chairman of the board, Paul Robinson, to prepare a strategic marketing plan for Greenwood Federal. Annual marketing plans had been prepared in previous years, but these tended to be tactical in nature. Many changes had taken place in the previous year, necessitating a longer-term look at the organization's marketing planning. Ms. Harris grabbed several items off her bookshelf, including new research study results, last year's marketing plan, and the latest financial reports available documenting Greenwood's recent performance. She then reached for the phone to call her husband to tell him that she would be home very late that evening.

Background

Greenwood Federal Savings (GFS) is one of the nation's larger savings and loan associations. It was founded in 1927 in the largest milk-producing county south of Wisconsin. At the time, the county was beginning to emerge from an agricultural economy into a semi-urban economy oriented toward a major fast-growing city, Sunbelt City, located six miles to the west. The founder was an attorney, state legislator, and business and community leader who was president of the Chamber of Commerce and many civic and charitable groups. The board of directors consisted of a number of leading citizens in the community, and their goal was to make the city the finest residential city in the region. To ease unemployment and provide some new homes during the Depression, the Association pioneered in making construction loans. To ensure the quality of the homes built, the officers of Greenwood developed a code of minimum specifications and named an inspector to see that the homes complied with it.

---

* This case was prepared by Kenneth L. Bernhardt for the purpose of class discussion. Names and selected data have been disguised. Copyright © 1986 by Kenneth L. Bernhardt.

From the beginning, those who directed the policies of Greenwood Federal were concerned with people and the environment in which members of the Association lived. A commitment was made to serve all citizens without prejudice. The first loan to a black citizen was made in 1928. A close relationship with builders and developers was established and has been maintained throughout the years. In the early years, movies and slide presentations of land developments in other parts of the country kept the community's builders abreast of the latest developments. The first branch was established in 1952, when assets had grown to more than $25 million. During the 1960s the Association expanded its services, adding college education loans, home improvement loans, and FHA and VA loans. The officers were concerned that people in moderate and low-income categories should have adequate housing.

Greenwood was seeking to help the people of the community achieve ''the good life,'' including the privilege of home ownership. Over the years, Greenwood was always on the forefront as an ethical, caring organization. For example, it was the last financial institution in the area to raise rates on loan assumptions. All employees were trained and continually reminded that their role was to satisfy customers. Greenwood had a strong corporate creed outlining its commitment to excellence. The officers and employees of Greenwood believed in the creed, which is reproduced in Exhibit 1.

Greenwood Federal Savings grew rapidly during the 1970s and 1980s, mirroring the growth of the city of Greenwood and the metropolis of Sunbelt City. In 1972 the first branch outside the city of Greenwood was opened, representing the Association's 10th office. During the mid- and late 1970s savings offices were opened in four regional malls, and by the end of the decade Greenwood had offices in five counties throughout the metropolitan area. In the early 1980s Greenwood moved statewide through a series of mergers. In 1984, faced with severe losses, the board of directors decided to concentrate on the Sunbelt City metropolitan area and the northern part of the state and sold off some of the offices purchased earlier.

An organization chart is shown in Exhibit 2. Jenny Harris reported directly to the chairman of the board and CEO and was responsible for all aspects of marketing, advertising, and product management. Since her arrival from a major packaged goods company several years earlier, Greenwood had introduced automated teller machines, discount brokerage services, homeowner's and personal lines of credit, automobile loans, credit cards, and checking accounts.

Competitive Environment

Many changes took place in the competitive environment for GFS in 1985. On June 10, 1985, the U.S. Supreme Court handed down a decision upholding regional banking. During the next several months, the major banks in Sunbelt City all merged with or acquired other large banks in surrounding states,

EXHIBIT 1

GREENWOOD FEDERAL
SAVINGS & LOAN ASSOCIATION

Commitment to Excellence: A Corporate Creed

Greenwood Federal Is Committed:

To the pursuit of a leadership position in the delivery of financial services and to the belief that quality is more important than size.

To be innovative in all that we do, including products we design and support services we render.

To understanding the value of customer confidence and realizing that achieving this goal is only outweighed by the need to maintain it.

To the setting of sound financial policies that protect the future while enhancing the present.

To be human, open, friendly, and sincere and to recognize that results should never be achieved at the expense of human dignity.

To specialize in product areas where the future appears strongest and the Association is best able to excel.

To our employees by rewarding merit, by providing an environment for growth, by creating a team spirit by encouraging open, two-way communications, and by enabling them to feel pride in the products and services we provide.

To honest, fair, and enduring relationships with suppliers and associates.

To the concept of corporate social responsibility to our local communities through individual and company participation.

To all of these precepts because they are not only intrinsically right but also happen to be good business.

---

resulting in the creation of "super banks." Other regulations resulted in a blurring of the distinction between banks and savings and loan institutions. In addition, large national organizations such as Sears, CitiCorp, Merrill Lynch, and several major insurance companies all expanded their financial service offerings and entered the Sunbelt City market in a big way.

Like most savings and loan associations, GFS concentrated on the "middle market," which comprised the bulk of its deposits and loans. GFS did not get much patronage from very high-income consumers or from low-income consumers. Competition for this retail middle market had become intense in recent years. There were 20 S&Ls in the Sunbelt City metropolitan area, and most of these, especially the major competitors, concentrated on the middle market. In addition, two of the three largest banks in town concentrated on

EXHIBIT 2 Greenwood's organization chart, 1986

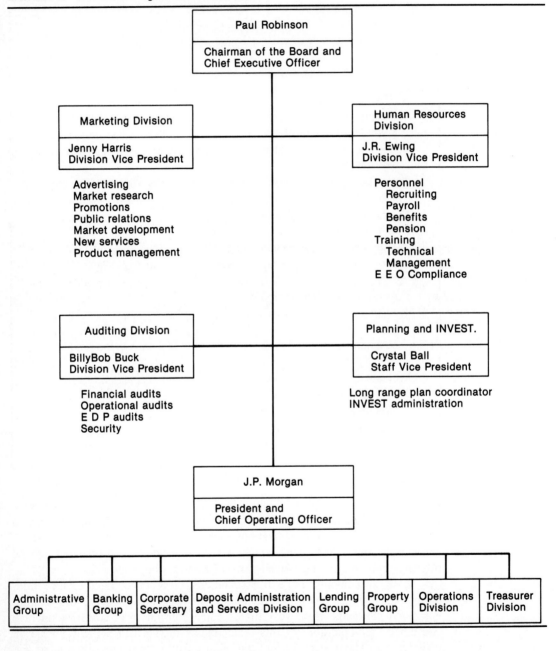

this market, as did many of the national organizations that had recently entered the market. Jenny Harris recognized the problems created by the intense competition for this middle market and knew that it would be important for GFS to segment the market even more finely than it had in the past. The key, she thought, was to identify target markets where GFS could do a better job than competitors in meeting consumer needs.

Exhibit 3 shows GFS's market share and the shares for each of the major competitors. The data in Exhibit 3 comes from a study that GFS had conducted among residents living within three miles of each of its branches. The results show that about one quarter of the people living near its branches have one or more accounts with GFS. Only 9 percent of the residents, however, indicate that GFS is their primary financial institution. Information on each of the major competitors is presented in Exhibit 4. GFS's growth in assets, advertising expenditures, and number of branches are all below those of the major competitors, with the exception of Home Federal.

GFS was a major factor in construction lending due to its long-term strong relationship with builders and its excellent image in the construction community. GFS did not have the lowest interest rates, and over the years had been very conservative in its appraisals and the amount of its loans. It worked with the cream of the builders, catering to them and to the realtors in the community, who recognized that there would be fewer hassles in working with GFS. The organization was very "loan oriented," and almost all the senior management had come from the loan side of the Association.

In 1985 GFS became profitable again, following four straight years of losses. The reserve ratio (net worth/total assets) had deteriorated from 6.3 percent in 1980 to 2.7 percent in 1984. It had increased to 3 percent by the end

EXHIBIT 3 Market share analysis by competitor

	Percent who have relation-ship with institution	Percent indicating primary institution	"Primary" as a percent of "have relationship"
City National Bank	32%	19%	59%
First National Bank	28	10	36
Greenwood Federal	24	9	38
Heritage Trust	24	15	63
Sunbelt Federal	13	5	38
Home Federal	8	3	38
Credit unions	24	7	29
All others	NA*	32	NA*
		100%	

Note: Table is interpreted as follows: 32 percent of the population living within three miles of Greenwood branches have a relationship with City National Bank; 59 percent of those with a relationship with City National (19 percent of the population) indicate City National is their primary financial institution.

*NA = not available.

EXHIBIT 4 Information on major competitors ($ in billions)

	Greenwood Federal Savings & Loan	Sunbelt Federal Savings & Loan	First National Bank	Heritage Trust Bank	City National Bank	Home Federal Savings & Loan
Total assets, 12/31/85	$1.3	$2.0	$12.7	$13.9	$ 9.8	$ 1.4
Percent growth in assets 1985 versus 1984	4.0%	20.6%	12.7%	22.9%	15.3%	5.4%
Total deposits, 12/31/85	$ 1.1	$ 1.5	$ 9.1	$10.6	$ 6.9	$ 1.3
Percent growth in deposits 1985 versus 1984	6.9%	4.0%	13.2%	15.1%	9.3%	4.6%
Net worth/assets, 12/31/85	3.0%	6.2%	5.8%	5.6%	5.9%	1.9%
Return on assets, 1985	.6%	1.0%	1.2%	1.0%	1.0%	(loss)
1985 advertising expenditures ($ millions)	$ 0.7	$ 1.4	$ 1.5	$ 1.6	$ 1.4	*
Number of branches in Sunbelt City area	19	30	55	41	63	15

* Figure not available.

of 1985. Most of GFS's savings and loan competitors had converted to stock organizations or were in the process of converting as a result of the 1985 Federal Home Loan Bank Board Regulations raising the required reserve ratio from 3 percent to 6 percent over the next five years. The easiest way to comply with this regulation would be to sell stock, thus raising a substantial amount of equity. GFS management believed that they could achieve the required ratio if they concentrated on increasing the profitability of the organization. Top management was concerned that if they converted to stock ownership it would not be clear how stockholders would fit in versus employees and customers. They feared they would lose flexibility in marketing and would need to direct a great deal of attention to investor relations and the stockbroker community.

Detailed financial information for Greenwood Federal, its number of accounts, and the structure for its savings and its loans are presented in Exhibit 5. Comments on the competitive situation for each of the major product categories follow.

Savings Certificates

The primary competitors for savings certificates are local banks, savings and loans, and credit unions. In the last year, First National Bank and several of the smaller banks and savings and loans have been particularly aggressive in their pricing. Banks especially are able to pay higher rates on certificates because of their greater ability to match assets and liabilities. Brokerage firms and insurance companies must also be considered competitors for these savings dollars.

EXHIBIT 5 GFS financial data and savings structure, July 31, 1986 (year to date)

Total assets	$1.34 billion
Total savings deposits	$1.18 billion
Number of savings accounts	140,144
Total loans	$1.14 billion
Number of first mortgage loans	27,387
First mortgage loans (average yield 10.0 percent)	$1.07 billion
Second mortgage loans, including home equity loans (home equity yield 10.5 percent)	$24.5 million
Education loans (average yield 10.1 percent)	$11.1 million
Consumer loans (average yield 13.0 percent on unsecured and 11.6 percent on secured)	$19.7 million
Savings account loans	$8.4 million
Other loans	$10.0 million
Operating income as percent of assets	11.75%
Average cost of all funds—July	8.2%
Average cost of new funds acquired—July	6.4%
Operating expenses	2.6%
Return on assets	.6%

Savings structure	Dollars (millions)	Percent of total
Passbook savings	$ 61.2	5.2%
NOW accounts	37.9	3.3
Super NOW accounts	112.0	9.5
Money market accounts	202.7	17.0
Certificates:		
Jumbo	12.8	1.1
3-month	12.6	1.1
6-month	108.2	9.2
12–24-month	145.9	12.5
25–36-month	170.0	14.4
Greater than 36-month	234.7	20.0
Retirement accounts	78.6	6.7
	$1,176.6	100.0%

GFS has always been a leader in the savings certificate product area with high awareness levels. Recent strategy has been to replace 91-day and six-month certificates with long-term certificates in the portfolio.

Checking Accounts

Commercial banks, savings and loans, and credit unions are also direct competitors for both regular checking and NOW accounts. The source of business for checking accounts has been commercial banks, and Sunbelt Federal has been particularly aggressive in its marketing of checking accounts. The banks have a definite convenience advantage, and they possess the majority of checking accounts. Many, however, are demarketing the smaller-deposit checking accounts through the use of high service fees. Ms. Harris felt there was opportunity to attract new checking accounts, with pricing as an important part of the strategy.

Money Market Accounts

Competitors for money market deposit accounts (MMDA) include commercial banks, savings and loans, money market funds, and bond and equity funds. For a large number of consumers the MMDA has actually replaced the passbook as the primary savings relationship. Ms. Harris thought that with its large base of savings customers, GFS had some competitive advantage here, but marketing of the MMDA had not been very aggressive since its introduction in late 1982. Competitors in the Sunbelt City market were not actively marketing these accounts.

Credit Lines

Commercial banks, savings and loans, mortgage bankers, and brokerage firms have all marketed home equity and personal credit lines aggressively during the past two years. GFS introduced its homeowners line of credit (HOLOC) in 1984, and a personal line of credit product was introduced in 1985. Jenny Harris felt that GFS had a tremendous marketing opportunity with the home equity product because of GFS's large pool of mortgage loan customers and because of changes in the federal tax laws expected to occur in 1987.

Residential Mortgage Loans

GFS is the leader among mortgage bankers, savings and loans, and commercial banks in the mortgage loan market. The market has changed dramatically in the past few years, with a large number of new competitors in the local market. Ms. Harris believed the tradition of good service and market leadership at GFS, together with its entrenched position with the real estate professional target market, provided excellent opportunities for continued success for GFS.

Consumer Loans

GFS has a weak competitive position in the consumer loan product area. Commercial banks have much greater experience with consumer loans and higher awareness. Finance companies, credit unions, and other savings and loans also compete for loan volume. GFS has tried in a modest way to build awareness of the availability of the consumer loan product. Ms. Harris thought there were opportunities to build this volume by differentiation based on product features rather than on the interest rate. None of the major competitors had developed an aggressive, innovative way to market consumer loans.

Brokerage Services

GFS was an equity partner in INVEST, a discount brokerage service. The service became profitable for GFS in 1985, with over 2,000 new accounts and $43 million in sales. INVEST was not an exclusive service, and several savings and loans in the area, including Sunbelt Federal, offered the service. The competition for this service included traditional brokerage firms, discount brokers, insurance companies, and depository institutions.

Strategies of Major Competitors

The major competitors employed different strategies and tactics, depending on the product involved. Ms. Harris's perceptions of some selected competitors are discussed below.

Sunbelt Federal Savings operated almost 60 offices in 20 communities, with 30 of the offices in the Sunbelt City metropolitan area. Most of its recent marketing effort focused on checking accounts and consumer loans. It has priced its checking account lower than most competitors and is actively seeking younger checking account customers. Focus groups conducted by GFS showed that consumers perceived Sunbelt Federal as dynamic, progressive, friendly, having low service charges, and a good place for savings.

Ms. Harris felt that First National Bank had earned the reputation as an innovative retail bank and had begun in earnest to cultivate a position as a rate leader. The bank has experienced dramatic growth in consumer deposits during the past year, at the expense of lower interest margins. A major strength is its extensive branching network, with over 75 offices (55 in the Sunbelt City metropolitan area). Its current advertising campaign, "If your bank isn't First, you should have second thoughts," is more aggressive than previous campaigns. In two television commercials First National Bank compares its performance on investment products with that of Heritage Trust and City National Bank. First National aggressively markets VISA cards throughout the South and is among the top 10 VISA banks in the country. Key image attributes for First National Bank mentioned by the participants in the focus groups include efficient, innovative, flashy, colorful, and convenient.

Heritage Trust had successfully positioned itself as the bank for upwardly mobile people, according to Ms. Harris. Its advertising had enjoyed high awareness levels and had served as an umbrella for product advertising, stressing how well the bank suits the needs of its customers. Heritage Trust had aggressively attracted newcomers to the market through strong corporate relationships. Its upscale banking program had been in operation for years and was considered by Ms. Harris as one of the best in the region. Attributes for Heritage Trust identified by the focus group respondents included "pinstriped," educated, professional, confident, successful, convenient, and smart.

City National Bank is the largest commercial bank in the state and has a very strong retail presence through over 75 offices (63 in the Sunbelt City metropolitan area). City National had traditionally been a strong consumer lender and had recently been directing its advertising at the baby boom generation with its campaign, "Think of your future with City National." Product advertising had stressed simple interest loans, discount brokerage services, and Ready Equity (their equity-based credit line). City National's image as profiled by focus group respondents included convenience but also some negative attributes, such as "bully," impersonal, and greedy.

The image of GFS, as perceived by the attendees at the focus group sessions, is "established," conservative, friendly, and older. GFS had, in fact, attracted a market somewhat older than that of the banks.

Exhibit 6 presents data on the importance of various features to consumers, together with the ratings of GFS and four competitors on each of the features. The consumers in the study were asked to rate the importance of each of the features using a scale of 0–10. They were then asked to give a rating to each financial institution on each feature, again using a scale of 0–10 (with 0 being poor and 10 extremely good). Overall, the most important features for a financial institution include:

Seldom make mistakes.

Do a good job overall.

Statements are clear and easy to understand.

Open at convenient hours during the week.

Personnel are polite and courteous.

Long history of financial stability.

Offer all the services I need.

Sufficient tellers to avoid long lines.

GFS is not rated the best on any of these factors, although it is rated better than Sunbelt Federal Savings on six of the eight. It is also rated higher than City National Bank on four of the eight. GFS is rated lower than First National Bank on all eight and lower than Heritage on six of the eight. The biggest "gap" for GFS is in providing consumers with all the services they need. Ms. Harris wondered whether this perception could be changed by increasing the promotion of many of the services currently available at GFS.

Consumer Research

To learn more about what consumers wanted in financial services and how the overall market could be segmented better, Ms. Harris had commissioned, in cooperation with the GFS advertising agency, a major consumer segmentation study. The research was designed to provide several clusters of consumers (segments) based on activities, interests, and opinions rather than on conventional demographic characteristics such as age, sex, or income. Ms. Harris wanted to use the results of the study to help develop a market niche for GFS, to identify appropriate target markets, to evaluate existing and new products, and to improve marketing communications for GFS.

National Family Opinion (NFO), one of the nation's largest marketing research firms, was used to conduct the study. NFO maintains a nationally representative consumer panel of 150,000 households, with over 3,000 in the Sunbelt City metropolitan area. NFO mailed out 1,250 questionnaires, and 57 percent, 712, were returned. In addition, a supplemental sample of 122 GFS

EXHIBIT 6 Importance of features and comparative ratings

	Q:10 Rank	Q10: Importance, scale of 0 to 10:	Ratings of Institutions (poor to extremely good, scale of 0 to 10)				
			GFS	CNB	FNB	HTB	SFS
Seldom make mistakes	1	8.9	6.8	6.1	6.9	7.0	6.6
Good job overall	2	8.8	7.0	6.4	7.1	7.0	6.8
Clear statements	3	8.4	6.5	6.7	7.0	6.8	6.5
Convenient weekday hours	4	8.4	6.9	6.9	7.1	6.9	6.8
Polite and courteous	5	8.3	6.9	6.4	7.1	7.0	6.8
History of stability	6	8.2	7.4	7.7	8.0	7.9	7.1
All services I need	7	8.1	6.6	7.2	7.5	7.2	6.6
Rarely long lines	8	8.1	6.0	5.8	6.2	6.3	5.8
Pay highest rate	9	7.9	6.4	5.4	6.0	5.9	6.4
Conveniently located branches	10	7.9	5.8	7.9	7.4	7.4	6.3
Convenient to live	11	7.9	5.3	7.3	6.9	7.0	6.1
Lowest charges, fees	12	7.7	5.9	4.8	5.4	5.4	6.1
Easily qualify for free checking	13	7.7	5.8	5.2	5.7	5.6	5.9
Tailor services to fit needs	14	7.0	5.4	5.0	5.6	5.5	5.3
Convenient to work	15	7.0	5.0	7.3	6.5	6.5	6.0
Offer consumer loans	16	6.8	6.8	7.6	7.4	7.3	6.8
Convenient Saturday hours	17	6.6	5.4	5.6	5.5	5.5	5.4
Interested in my financial position	18	6.2	5.2	4.8	5.3	5.1	5.0
Interest in me as a person	19	6.2	4.9	4.4	5.0	4.9	4.8
Work with me to achieve goals	20	6.1	5.1	4.8	5.3	5.1	5.0
Offer sound advice	21	6.1	5.7	5.4	5.8	5.7	5.6
Leader among institutions	22	6.0	6.7	7.4	7.5	7.5	6.6
Convenient to shop	23	6.0	5.3	7.0	6.5	6.5	5.6
Develop new products and services	24	5.0	5.5	5.3	5.9	5.8	5.2
Provide non-bank financial services	25	3.3	4.8	5.2	5.1	5.0	4.6

Key: GFS = Greenwood Federal CNB = City National Bank FNB = First National Bank
     HTB = Heritage Trust Bank SFS = Sunbelt Federal Savings

customers also completed the questionnaire. The study included results only from persons primarily responsible for household financial decisions (approximately half male and half female). The median age was just under 45 years old. The proportion classified as "working preferred," that is, employed and reporting a minimum of $5,000 savings, was 40 percent, a level considered normal based on previous studies conducted by GFS.

Slightly over half, 57 percent, used a commercial bank as the main financial institution, 23 percent used a savings and loan, 12 percent used a credit union, and 18 percent listed all other types of institutions. GFS's market share for the main study was 15 percent (having any account, not "primary" institution).

The questionnaire presented 100 opportunities for each respondent to record his or her attitudes or opinions about financial matters and about his or her banking habits and preferences. Examples of questions include "I like to pay cash for almost everything I buy," "I'm always looking for a way to make more interest on my money," and "I need very little advice when making decisions about the types of financial services I should use." In addition, each person was presented with 25 questions concerning the importance to them of individual banking practices and services, together with questions concerning the rating of the individual financial institutions.

A large mainframe computer then was used to perform advanced statistical analysis of the questionnaire data. The objective was to cluster or group the 712 respondents into meaningful segments based on commonality of their attitudes rather than into groups based on age, income, or other demographic characteristics. The computer program identified five clusters or segments similar enough in their attitudes to be classified as distinct survey segments. These segments were then given names to help describe them. Most segmentation studies of this type attempt to group people according to lifestyles, thus ending up with such groupings as "yuppies," "young suburbia," or "gray power." Here the groupings were based on the way the respondents think and act about money, credit, banking, and financial services. Five clusters were identified and named:

Secure Steve (self-confident and self-assured).

Retiring Richard (72 percent employed, but the highest proportion of retirees).

Fast Lane Phil (overspending, undersaving youth).

Minimal Martha (highest proportion of females, but not necessarily female; users of a minimum of products and services).

Single-Minded Sam (desire for one-stop banking at a full-service convenient institution).

Exhibits 7 through 10 present data from the two samples concerning the five segments, including size of the segments, demographics, amount of savings, and financial attitudes. Exhibits 11 through 13 present data from the study

EXHIBIT 7 Descriptions and size of each segment

	GFS customers 100%	Total segmentation study 100%	% of segmentation that were W.P.** 40%
High assets, high checking Wants single account, single interest Wants security, personal attention Organized, disciplined Budgets, saves High TV and radio, high newspaper	Singleminded Sam 7%	Singleminded Sam 11%	32%
Oldest, most affluent High assets Well managed, highly organized Wants security, does not shop No ATM Uses many services Low checking, high savings High newspaper, high magazine	Retiring Richard 17%	Retiring Richard 13%	47%
Middle aged, well educated Good income Technical/Sales/Administrative Undisciplined, uninvolved, wife handles Has difficulty managing, overspends Low assets, low savings High TV, moderate other media	Fastlane Phil 15%	Fastlane Phil 19%	28%
Middle aged Married Likely male Educated Managerial/Professional High income, high savings High investments Self-confident Uses ATM Shops for rate Actively involved in managing finances Low checking balance Likely S & L Customer Age 25 - 49 Low TV and radio, high magazine	Secure Steve 30%	Secure Steve 22%	44%
Decision maker - female Pays cash, avoids credit Distrustful Low ATM usage Offices not convenient Lowest income (51% U 25K) Lowest savings Low education Blue collar Daytime TV, low radio, low news Age 25 - 55	Minimal Martha 30%	Minimal Martha 33%	28%
Base % of total	106 15%	712 100%	* *

*Each segment total

**Note: W.P. means working preferred, those employed with
    at least $5000 in savings.

EXHIBIT 8 Demographics of the segmentation study

Sex of the Segments

	Total survey	Martha	Steve	Phil	Rich	Sam
Women	46%	55	32	48	40	45
Men	54%	45	68	52	60	55
Base:	712	235	158	136	91	78
%:	100.0%	33.0%	22.2%	19.1%	12.8%	11.0%

Age of the Segments

	Total survey	Martha	Steve	Phil	Rich	Sam
65 +	10%	8	8	1	22	21
55 - 64	20%	19	13	15	39	21
45 - 54	14%	16	14	15		12
35 - 44	26%	22	31	35	12	24
18 - 34	30%	35	35	33	14	23
					13	
Base:	712	235	158	136	91	78
%:	100.0%	33.0%	22.2%	19.1%	12.8%	11.0%

Household Income of the Segments

	Total survey	Martha	Steve	Phil	Rich	Sam
$50 +	15%	7	25	12	17	18
$35 - 49.9	23%	22	22	23	31	18
$25 - 34.9	21%	20	26	23	21	12
$10 - 24.9	41%	51	27	42	31	53
Base:	712	235	158	136	91	78
%:	100.0%	33.0%	22.2%	19.1%	12.8%	11.0%

EXHIBIT 8 *(concluded)*

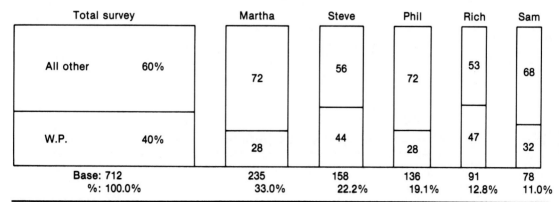

Occupation of the Segments

Total survey		Martha	Steve	Phil	Rich	Sam
Retired	11%	7	8	4		19
Other	11%	13	11	8	27	
			7	12		10
Blue collar	14%	23			11	13
					6	
White collar	64%	57	74	76	56	58
Base: 712		235	158	136	91	78
%: 100.0%		33.0%	22.2%	19.1%	12.8%	11.0%

Savings of the Segments

Total survey		Martha	Steve	Phil	Rich	Sam
$25,000 +	22%	13	24	8		31
				25	53	
$5,000 - 24,999	29%	30	33			25
				67	33	
Under $5,000	49%	57	43			44
					14	
Base: 712		235	158	136	91	78
%: 100.0%		33.0%	22.2%	19.1%	12.8%	11.0%

Working Preferred Status

Total survey		Martha	Steve	Phil	Rich	Sam
All other	60%	72	56	72	53	68
W.P.	40%	28	44	28	47	32
Base: 712		235	158	136	91	78
%: 100.0%		33.0%	22.2%	19.1%	12.8%	11.0%

EXHIBIT 9 Average amount of savings (by study segments)

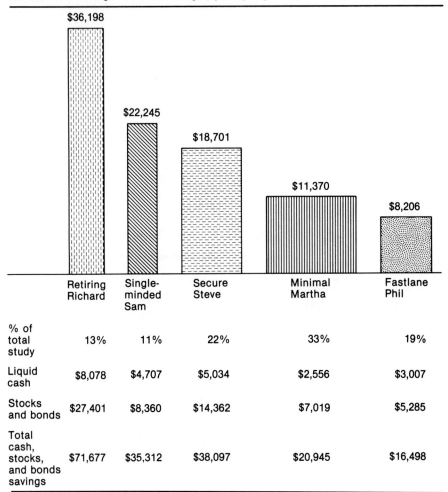

	Retiring Richard	Single-minded Sam	Secure Steve	Minimal Martha	Fastlane Phil
% of total study	13%	11%	22%	33%	19%
Liquid cash	$8,078	$4,707	$5,034	$2,556	$3,007
Stocks and bonds	$27,401	$8,360	$14,362	$7,019	$5,285
Total cash, stocks, and bonds savings	$71,677	$35,312	$38,097	$20,945	$16,498

concerning each segment's rating of Greenwood Federal and usage of various products and services. The share of market for GFS and its major competitors by segment is included in Exhibit 14. Selected findings for each segment are discussed below.

Minimal Martha

This segment was the largest identified, with one third of all consumers and 30 percent of GFS customers included. Minimal Martha had the least usage of financial products and institutions among the five segments. This was the only

EXHIBIT 10 Agreement with various attitudinal statements

		25	50	75	100%	Mean, Scale 1 - 7

Statement	Segment	Value	Mean, Scale 1-7
When it comes to services such as checking accounts, I shop around to find the least expensive provider.	Total	49 GFS = 57	4.3
	Martha	56	4.7
	Steve	73	5.1
	Phil	35	3.9
	Richard	24	3.3
	Sam	31	3.3
I like to try new and different things.	Total	62 GFS = 65	4.9
	Martha	63	4.9
	Steve	77	5.4
	Phil	59	4.7
	Richard	45	4.2
	Sam	59	4.7
I would rather have one place for all my financial needs.	Total	59 GFS = 49	4.9
	Martha	67	5.2
	Steve	50	4.5
	Phil	67	5.1
	Richard	26	3.6
	Sam	78	5.8
It's more important to live well now than to save money for the future.	Total	13 GFS = 10	2.4
	Martha	11	2.3
	Steve	15	2.5
	Phil	11	2.6
	Richard	11	2.3
	Sam	24	2.7
It's important that my financial institution is conveniently located near home.	Total	80 GFS = 84	5.6
	Martha	86	5.9
	Steve	74	5.3
	Phil	83	5.7
	Richard	70	5.2
	Sam	86	5.8

segment where the financial decision maker was most often female and the banking chores were also handled most often by the female head of household. Minimal Martha generally manages her personal finances by paying cash, keeping funds in separate accounts, and avoiding credit. She is less comfortable and trusting of financial institutions. The convenience of a financial institution is probably the major determinant in its selection. Martha has a low income, less education, and is more likely to be married with a larger household and a blue-collar husband than other segments.

EXHIBIT 10 *(concluded)*

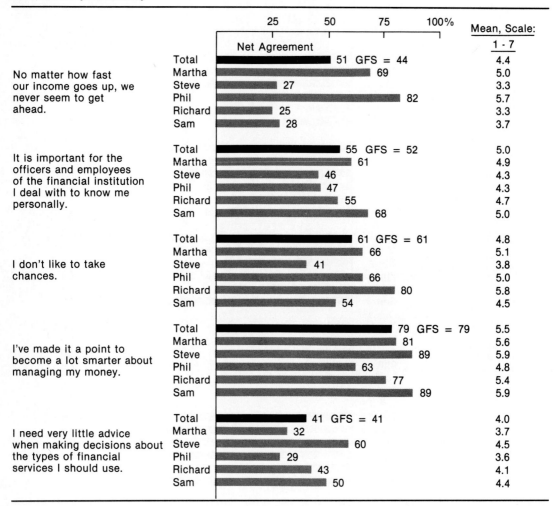

		Net Agreement	Mean, Scale: 1 - 7
No matter how fast our income goes up, we never seem to get ahead.	Total	51 GFS = 44	4.4
	Martha	69	5.0
	Steve	27	3.3
	Phil	82	5.7
	Richard	25	3.3
	Sam	28	3.7
It is important for the officers and employees of the financial institution I deal with to know me personally.	Total	55 GFS = 52	5.0
	Martha	61	4.9
	Steve	46	4.3
	Phil	47	4.3
	Richard	55	4.7
	Sam	68	5.0
I don't like to take chances.	Total	61 GFS = 61	4.8
	Martha	66	5.1
	Steve	41	3.8
	Phil	66	5.0
	Richard	80	5.8
	Sam	54	4.5
I've made it a point to become a lot smarter about managing my money.	Total	79 GFS = 79	5.5
	Martha	81	5.6
	Steve	89	5.9
	Phil	63	4.8
	Richard	77	5.4
	Sam	89	5.9
I need very little advice when making decisions about the types of financial services I should use.	Total	41 GFS = 41	4.0
	Martha	32	3.7
	Steve	60	4.5
	Phil	29	3.6
	Richard	43	4.1
	Sam	50	4.4

Secure Steve

The second largest segment is Secure Steve, who is upscale (managerial, professional, well educated, high income, high savings, high investment) and innovative. Secure Steve shops for low charges and high interest with self-confidence. He rejects frills and is unwilling to pay to get personal attention. Typically, Secure Steve is in the prime of his career, aged 25–49, married, with a confident, ambitious outlook. He maintains the minimum in checking, shops for the best terms, and is willing to try new products. He actively shops around

EXHIBIT 11   Rating of Greenwood Federal Savings (poor to extremely good; scale of zero to ten)

	GFS Rating: Total Study	GFS Rating by Segment				
	Rank (importance) / Rating	Minimal Martha	Secure Steve	Fastlane Phil	Retirng Richard	Single Sam
Seldom make mistakes	1 — 6.8	6.3	7.2	6.7	7.2	6.6
Good job overall	2 — 7.0	7.0	7.0	6.8	7.5	7.1
Clear statements	3 — 6.5	6.4	6.5	6.3	6.9	6.7
Convenient weekday hours	4 — 6.9	7.1	6.6	6.6	7.5	7.1
Polite and courteous	5 — 6.9	6.6	7.3	6.5	7.2	6.9
History of stability	6 — 7.4	7.5	7.2	6.9	8.3	7.8
All services I need	7 — 6.6	6.8	6.9	6.2	6.5	6.4
Rarely long lines	8 — 6.0	5.7	6.1	6.0	6.3	6.0
Pay highest rate	9 — 6.4	6.4	6.5	6.1	6.5	6.8
Conveniently located branches	10 — 5.8	5.7	5.8	5.5	6.5	5.8
Convenient to live	11 — 5.3	5.0	5.6	5.2	6.1	5.1
Lowest charges, fees	12 — 5.9	5.9	6.0	5.6	5.8	5.9
Easily qualify for free checking	13 — 5.8	5.4	6.3	5.3	6.3	6.2
Tailor services to fit needs	14 — 5.4	5.6	5.2	5.3	5.4	5.4
Convenient to work	15 — 5.0	5.1	4.8	4.7	5.8	4.6
Offer consumer loans	16 — 6.8	6.9	6.9	6.6	6.6	7.1
Convenient Saturday hours	17 — 5.4	5.3	5.8	4.9	5.3	5.8
Interested in my financial position	18 — 5.2	5.3	4.8	5.2	5.4	5.3
Interest in me as a person	19 — 4.9	4.9	4.5	4.9	5.1	5.5
Work with me to achieve goals	20 — 5.1	5.2	4.9	4.9	5.1	5.5
Offer sound advice	21 — 5.7	5.8	5.5	5.7	5.5	5.8
Leader among institutions	22 — 6.7	6.7	6.4	6.3	7.3	7.2
Convenient to shop	23 — 5.3	5.1	5.4	5.1	5.7	5.4
Develop new products and services	24 — 5.5	5.6	5.5	5.1	5.9	5.6
Provide non-bank financial services	25 — 4.8	4.9	4.9	4.3	5.0	5.2

EXHIBIT 12 Product usage: Segmentation study: January 25—March 18, 1985

	Total study	GFS Customers	Martha	Steve	Phil	Richard	Sam
M/C Visa card	77	83	64	84	84	90	76
ATM	69	67	60	81	77	55	78
Passbook/statement	69	81	66	67	79	68	65
Home mtg. loan	61	75	58	70	60	62	53
Checking without	60	50	64	48	69	64	58
Checking with	54	69	46	73	41	58	49
Safe deposit	48	61	40	53	38	73	47
Auto loan	42	45	37	49	52	35	35
Stock	35	46	24	55	29	57	17
IRA	35	57	26	47	25	53	37
American Express	27	29	21	33	36	29	18
U.S. Bonds	26	25	24	31	29	25	18
CD More than year	24	46	25	20	13	44	23
Personal instl. loan	23	17	17	25	35	14	29
CD Year or less	23	40	23	22	12	45	22
MMDA BK/S&L	20	26	16	23	15	34	19
Other tax def.	15	22	10	25	13	22	13
MMF, Broker	14	19	9	20	8	29	9
Other mutual fund	13	19	6	17	13	23	12
Second mortgage	11	11	14	11	14	3	12
Corp/Gov. bonds	11	11	10	16	7	20	8
T-bills/Notes	4	3	3	4	2	4	3
Trust service	3	5	2	3	2	6	6

for the "best" financial products and is more willing to change institutions to get the best deal. He represents 22 percent of the sample and 30 percent of GFS customers.

Fast Lane Phil

Phil likely can be found in the fast lane at Household Finance Corporation, but is not found among the jet set in the fast lane at the airport. The segment is

EXHIBIT 13 Service usage

	Total study		GFS customers		Segments				
					Martha	Steve	Phil	Richard	Sam
Automatic deduction from checking	35		34		30	41	45	26	37
Direct deposit of payroll	29		23		7	51	40	31	33
Overdraft protection	29		32		23	35	34	23	39
Unsecured line of credit	19		15		11	27	21	21	25
Stock brokerage other than Bk/S&L	12		14		8	20	9	22	5
Automatic transfer saving to checking	11		6		8	13	12	7	20
Card that automatically deducts purchases	7		4		6	9	7	4	14
Secured line of credit	5		5		4	4	7	1	6
Telephone bill paying	5		2		4	4	4	4	5
Automobile leasing	3		4		3	3	5	2	4
Financial advice and counseling	3		4		2	6	1	3	3
Stockbrokerage at bank or S&L	1		3		1	1	2	2	1
	8								

undisciplined, and they are poor managers of financial affairs. Three out of four in this segment report less than $5,000 in savings. Phil frequently overspends with credit cards and often makes purchases with personal installment loans. He has the highest usage of checking accounts *without* interest and passbook accounts, but the lowest usage of other savings or investment products. This segment represents 19 percent of the total sample and 15 percent of GFS customers.

Retiring Richard

This segment has by far the highest savings. They prefer low risk to high interest and like personal attention. The Richard segment contains the highest

EXHIBIT 14 Share of market (by study segments)

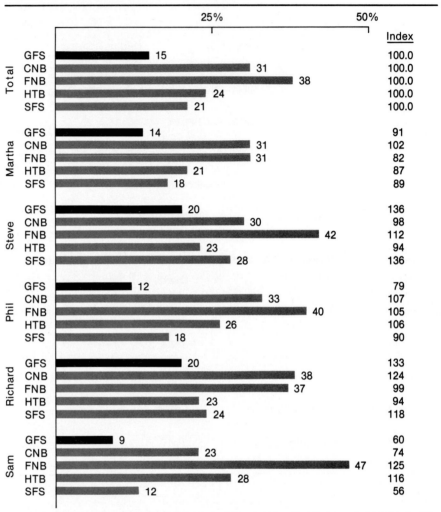

proportion of retirees, 28 percent, more than double the average for the total sample. His financial affairs are well established, and he is somewhat resistant to changing them. Retiring Richard has the highest usage of most financial products and is the oldest and most married of the five segments. The segment represents 13 percent of the total sample and 17 percent of GFS customers.

Single-Minded Sam

This segment, representing 11 percent of the sample and 7 percent of GFS customers, has the strongest preference for a single integrated account with one financial institution. This segment likes the security of a big institution, especially banks, and personal attention is very important. One-stop banking is more important than low fees or a high interest rate on savings. Sam is the second oldest and the most divorced, widowed, or separated of the segments.

Ms. Harris felt that the key to finding a niche for GFS and for differentiating it from the competition could be found in Exhibits 7 through 14. She planned to spend considerable time interpreting the meaning of this data.

Marketing Strategy Considerations

The senior management of Greenwood Federal had recently developed a mission statement. It read, ''The mission of Greenwood Federal is to discover and provide needed financial services to consumers in a manner consistent with their reasonable expectations and consistent with the achievement of reasonable earnings.'' Given the change in regulations that had taken place in the past year and the mission statement, Ms. Harris felt that she should develop a strategic marketing plan to provide ''controlled growth orchestrated to the beat of profitability, protecting assets and net worth while directing a positive course of profits.'' The Association had always used conservative policies, and loan delinquencies over the years had been consistently low because of the relatively strict loan underwriting standards. She felt it was important to maintain a conservative posture but still felt there was considerable opportunity to increase consumer lending with new products, such as the homeowners line of credit, the personal credit line, and a new type of auto loan, the ''Payment Shrinker.'' Exhibit 15 contains copy the ad agency had developed for a brochure to explain how the Payment Shrinker auto loan works.

EXHIBIT 15

Payment Shrinker Auto Financing Cuts Monthly Payments up to 49 Percent

Now you can afford to drive the automobile you really want. GFS Federal makes it possible with Payment Shrinker, the auto loan that can reduce your monthly payments by 25 to 49 percent.

Here's How Payment Shrinker Reduces Monthly Payments

GFS Federal Payment Shrinker combines the lower monthly payment advantages of auto leasing with the ownership and tax benefits offered by conventional car loans.

Depending on your choice of terms, your monthly payments will extend over 24, 36, or 48 months. The final payment amount will be determined at the time you make the loan and will be based on the residual value of the car* at the end of the loan.

Interest is computed on the full amount of the loan, but your monthly payments are lower because the residual car value is subtracted from the purchase price. The monthly principal payments are based upon the difference.

* The residual value of the automobile is determined by *Automotive Lease Guide*, a published residual value book, in effect at the time the loan is originated. The residual value represents the estimated value of the vehicle after the 24- to 48-month loan is completed.

EXHIBIT 15 *(concluded)*

The interest that is charged on the full amount of the loan is tax deductible, as well as any sales tax you pay. This tax benefit is not available for personal automobile leases.

Four Options at End of Loan Term

At the end of the loan term, you'll have a choice of four options regarding your final payment: If you wish to keep your car, you may (1) pay off the residual car value amount figured in with the last monthly payment or (2) refinance the residual. If you would like another car, you may (3) sell or trade your car and keep the profit you make over and above the residual value or (4) return the car in good working condition (subject to condition and mileage requirements) to GFS Federal with no further obligation except to pay a nominal return fee.

Example of How Payment Shrinker Auto Loan Works

Purchase price of the car you want	$13,528
Less: Down payment (10%)	1,353
Amount to be financed over 36 months at	
13¾%† **annual percentage rate**	$12,175
Residual value of car at end of 36 month loan term	$ 6,935

Monthly payments are composed of two parts:
1. Principal and interest payable on $5,240	
($12,175 minus the $6,935 residual value)	$178.44
2. Interest payments on the $6,935 residual car value	$ 79.46
Total monthly payment	$257.90

Monthly payment with conventional auto loan at	
12¼%† **annual percentage rate**	$405.86
Monthly payment with Payment Shrinker	$257.90
Amount saved per month	$147.96

† This is an example. Actual rate may vary.

Compare Monthly Payments—
Payment Shrinker versus Conventional Financing

Amount financed	Conventional auto loan (monthly)	Payment Shrinker auto loan (monthly)
$24,000		
24 months	$1,132.57	$712.24
36 months	$ 800.01	$573.31
48 months	$ 634.96	$501.72
$16,000	—	—
24 months	$ 755.05	$474.82
36 months	$ 533.34	$382.21
48 months	$ 423.31	$334.48
$8,000	—	—
24 months	$ 377.52	$237.41
36 months	$ 266.67	$191.11
48 months	$ 211.65	$167.24

Note: The monthly payment chart shown is based on the following assumptions: Payment Shrinker auto loan: **13.75% annual percentage rate;** Conventional auto loan: **12.25% annual percentage rate.** Assume residual value is 50% of sticker price for 24 months, 45% of sticker price for 36 months, 40% of sticker price for 48 months. Amount financed is 90% of purchase price.

To help determine the relative importance of the various products offered by GFS, Ms. Harris had developed a product hierarchy ranking matrix. This is presented in Exhibit 16, together with the key used to give the ratings. According to her analysis, money market deposit accounts, certificates of deposit, IRAs, mortgage loans, and regular savings accounts were the products that should receive the highest priority. Ms. Harris was very uncomfortable with what she had done and wondered whether the results were accurate. For example, she had weighted each of the factors equally and was now having

EXHIBIT 16 Product hierarchy

	WP* usage	WP hot button	Comp. opp.†	GFS position	Profit	Commitment	Total
MMDA	3	3	3	2	3	2	16
CDs	3	3	2	2	3	3	16
IRA	3	3	1	2	2	3	14
Mortgage loans	3	2	1	3	2	3	14
Regular savings	3	1	3	2	3	2	14
Checking	3	2	2	1	1	3	13
HOLOC	1	3	1	3	3	1	12
INVEST	3	3	1	2	1	2	12
Consumer loans	2	3	2	1	1	3	12
Super NOW	1	2	3	2	2	1	11
Safe deposit	3	2	3	1	2	1	11
Credit card	3	2	1	1	2	1	10
Travel company	1	1	3	1	1	2	9

Product Hierarchy Key

Working Preferred Usage:
　1 = Less than 30 percent use the product.
　2 = 30–50 percent use the product.
　3 = More than 50 percent use the product.

Working Preferred Hot Button:
　1 = Low priority—not likely to move or open account.
　2 = Medium priority—might move or open if offer is strong.
　3 = High priority—will move or open if offer is strong.

Competitive Opportunity:
　1 = Competitors are actively marketing the product.
　2 = Some competitive activity.
　3 = No competitive activity.

Greenwood Federal's Position:
　1 = Weak position.
　2 = Potential for unique position.
　3 = Strong position.

Profitability:
　1 = Significant losses on product.
　2 = Product is losing money but has potential.
　3 = Product is profitable.

Commitment:
　1 = Little or no resources have been committed in the past.
　2 = Some resources have been committed in the past.
　3 = Major resources have been committed in the past.

* WP = Working preferred (employed and savings of $5,000 and up).
† Comp. Opp. = Competitive opportunity.

EXHIBIT 17

Greenwood Federal Announces
A Golden Opportunity.

THE 25K ACCOUNT.

Take a moment to review your investments. If you aren't currently earning a preferred rate on any amount of $25,000 or more, you should consider investing in Greenwood Federal's 25K Account. With 25K you'll earn our highest money market account rate. A fiercely competitive figure you'll rarely find bested. One that changes with market conditions to keep you head and shoulders above the crowd.

Your 25K Account is easily accessible every seven days. And federal insurance makes it as safe as, well, money in the bank.

The 25K Account. It's designed for those who are already experienced in recognizing golden opportunities. And for those interested in smaller investments, we offer competitive rates on a regular money market account with a minimum balance of $2,500. We invite you to come in to any Greenwood Federal office and seize the opportunity today.

your partner

GREENWOOD FEDERAL

Substantial Penalty for early withdrawal.

EXHIBIT 18

AFFORDABLE LOANS.
ACADILLACABLE LOANS.
APONTIACABLE LOANS.
APOOLABLE LOANS.
ANEWPORCHABLE LOANS.
AVACATIONABLE LOANS.
ACOLLEGEABLE LOANS.
ASPEEDBOATABLE LOANS.

Available loans. We've got plenty. Everything from auto loans, boat loans, home improvement loans, lines of credit, and of course, mortgage loans. In fact, we've always been a leader in mortgage lending. And that leadership carries over into all the other loans you need.

Agreeable loans. We're there to make it easier for you. With convenient terms, a variety of services, quick responses, simple interest, no prepayment penalties and service with a smile.

Affordable loans. Don't worry. We'll make sure your monthly payments are well within your reach.

A whatever-you-wantable loans. You'll find all you need at Greenwood Federal.

GREENWOOD FEDERAL

Experience The Partnership.

Member F.S.L.I.C.

some second thoughts about this decision. She vowed to take another look at the product hierarchy rankings as she started to develop the strategic marketing plan.

The advertising agency had recommended several new campaigns for her consideration. The "25K Account" proposal is included in Exhibit 17. The goal of this ad is to attract larger accounts, and the campaign would use the tag line "your partner."

Exhibit 18 contains an ad the agency had developed to attract more consumer loans. This ad made use of the proposed alternative tag line "Experience the Partnership." Finally, Exhibit 19 contains the third proposal from the ad agency, "For the Good Life." This ad was designed to attract high dollar volumes for longer periods of time through the use of attractive premiums. These new certificates of deposit were to be priced 35 basis points below comparable three-, five-, and six-year certificates, with interest to be paid and compounded annually rather than quarterly. The agency proposed that advertising previously scheduled for high-interest checking be switched to this premium promotion and that newspaper ads and radio also be used.

As shown in Exhibit 20, the majority of GFS customers used only one type of product from among the offerings available, although a number of households had more than one account within the type (two or more savings accounts in the household, for example). Ms. Harris thought that there was great opportunity to "cross sell more services to more households." GFS had recently established a small telemarketing operation and she wondered if this might be used for this purpose. She wondered how to direct mail to customers or prospects and if advertising might work to increase cross-selling opportunities. To determine what had happened recently with some of the newer products, she pulled out the report in Exhibit 21 which contained information on new loan production and consumer loans outstanding as of July 1986 (the latest report available).

Lots of things were popping into Ms. Harris's mind. She was concerned about how much attention she should pay to the short run versus the long run. For example, she knew that for GFS to devote strong emphasis to increase its penetration in the small business market would take a long time, given the lack of history in marketing to this segment. Likewise, a strong commitment to home banking using personal computers would be a long-run effort. On the other hand, increasing the emphasis on the Payment Shrinker auto loan, the homeowners line of credit (HOLOC), personal line of credit, or consumer loans would be easy to accomplish in the short run, given that the products had already been developed.

She wondered how much emphasis to put on INVEST, the discount brokerage service. A recent study GFS had conducted showed that 77 percent of the money invested through INVEST came out of other sources and that 23 percent came from GFS accounts. Some of the management at GFS felt that the money pulled out of the accounts would have been invested in stock or bonds

EXHIBIT 19

Gifts for the Good Life.

Get a special bonus now with your new Greenwood Federal savings certificate ... you'll still get interest later.

GIFT DESCRIPTION	7 : Years	5 : Years	3 : Years
Toshiba Gourmet Coffee Maker, OR Pulsar Quartz Watch—Men's/Ladies	$2 500	$3,500	$5,000
Cannon Typewriter w/Adaptor, OR Litton Space-Saving Microwave	$4 000	$5,000	$8,000
GE 13" Portable Color TV	$5 000	$6,500	$10,000
Zenith 13" Color TV w/Remote, OR Magic Chef Deluxe Microwave w/Turntable	$7 000	$9,500	$15,000
RCA 20" ColorTrak TV w/Remote, OR GE VCR w/Wireless Remote	$9 500	$13,000	$20,000
Lawn-Boy Deluxe Self-Propelled Mower, OR Fisher Deluxe VCR w/MTS Stereo	$11 500	$16,000	$25,000
RCA 26" ColorTrak Console TV w/Remote	$14 500	$20,000	$30,000
Pearl Grandfather Clock w/Westminster Chimes	$19 000	$25,500	$40,000
Fisher Stereo Home Entertainment Center	$23 000	$32,500	$50,000
Sony 27" Console TV w/Stereo	$28 000	$38,000	$60,000
Sony 8mm Handycam Camera/Recorder	$32 500	$45,000	$70,000
Apple Macintosh Personal Computer	$35 000	$50,000	$80,000

RCA 20" ColorTrak TV w/Remote.

Sony 8mm Camera w/Recorder.

Pearl Grandfather Clock w/Chimes.

Apple Macintosh Personal Computer.

Litton Space Saving Microwave.

CERTIFICATE TERMS AND DEPOSIT LEVELS

Cannon Typewriter.

Fisher Deluxe VCR.

Lawn-Boy Self-Propelled Mower.

Greenwood Federal announces a new, special kind of savings certificate. It pays you part of your interest income now, in the form of a luxury gift. You'll receive one or more of the gifts listed here, for yourself or to give as a gift. And your money will still earn interest compounded annually. For current rates, call 373-SAVE. So if you have money to invest, come to Greenwood Federal where your investment is rewarded handsomely ... and immediately.

Offer limited. Interest rates, qualifying deposit levels, and items of merchandise subject to change without notice. • Items of merchandise represent interest, therefore, the value of the merchandise will be reported as interest earned in the year received. • Allow minimum of 4 weeks for delivery. • This offer not applicable to IRA or KEOGH accounts. • A substantial penalty, which will include the value of merchandise received, may be imposed for early withdrawal of certificate funds.

GREENWOOD FEDERAL

FOR THE GOOD LIFE

"Why don't you get your grandson a TV set?"   *"I'm giving him the Apple computer."*

anyway, so that at least with INVEST some fees were generated. Also, heavy promotion of INVEST, which had just recently become profitable, could reduce the asset base for the Association while generating some fees, enabling a rise in the reserve ratio. Other GFS managers were more skeptical about this happening.

EXHIBIT 20 Types of accounts held by GFS customers

Account type	Percent of GFS households	Average number of GFS products per household
Savings only	28	
Mortgage only	18	
Checking only	7	
Consumer loan only	3	
Total one product type	56	1.4*
Checking and savings	16	
Mortgage and savings	5	
Consumer loan and savings	3	
Consumer loan and checking	2	
Consumer loan and mortgage	2	
Checking and mortgage	0	
Total two product types	28	3.1
Checking, savings, and mortgage	5	
Checking, savings, and consumer loan	3	
Savings, mortgage, and consumer loan	3	
Checking, mortgage, and consumer loan	1	
Total three product types	12	4.6
All four types	4	6.8
	100	2.5
Any savings	67	
Any checking	39	
Any mortgage	38	
Any consumer loan	21	
Any deposit	83	
Any loan	46	

* This number is greater than 1.0 because many households had more than one account (although all were the same type of account).

Ms. Harris had seen potential in the segmentation study for high-interest checking products with several of the segments. She also thought that the proposed tax law, which would remove deductions for consumer loans, could have a big impact on her strategic planning. Did it mean, for example, that emphasis should not be put on automobile loans (even the Payment Shrinker) and other consumer loans? Did it mean that homeowner equity loans were the wave of the future? She had seen Internal Revenue Service data indicating that only 38 percent of all taxpayers itemized deductions on their 1984 returns. Did this suggest that consumers simply will not care enough about tax savings to establish a home equity credit line when they are ready to buy a car? Homeowner equity lines typically cost $500–$700 in closing cost alone. She had heard rumors that several of the Sunbelt City banks were considering waiving the fees, and wondered how GFS should respond if this in fact happened in the near future. She also had heard rumors that one or more of the banks might lower the rates, currently two percentage points above prime, to prime or even below for several months to attract new accounts with home equity loans.

EXHIBIT 21 Banking group monthly report for July 1986

Consumer loans production:	Number		Total dollar amount
Real estate loans			
Second mortgages	19		$ 358,800.00
Equity line	39		1,145,100.00
Total	58		$ 1,503,900.00
Installment and single pay loans			
Payment Shrinker	10		118,763.86
Auto	184		1,239,500.10
Personal, secured and unsecured	291		2,145,839.73
Personal LOC	80		760,100.00
Total	565		4,264,203.69
Total production for July	623		$ 5,768,103.69

Consumer loans outstanding:	Total available credit	Number	Total dollar amount
Unsecured		1,234	$ 3,280,607.34
Secured other		704	3,718,010.66
Auto		3,106	15,147,248.45
Payment Shrinker		106	1,409,657.19
Subtotal		5,150	23,555,523.64
Equity line	12,493,481.68	1,086	17,383,580.59
Personal LOC	5,348,844.40	760	2,552,124.24
Total		6,996	43,491,228.47

	Number	Total	
2nd mortgages	795	9,219,720.55	
Less participated 2nds	419	−4,956,014.39	
Total 2nd mortgages	376	4,263,706.16	
Grand total	7,372		$47,754,934.63
Second mortgages maintained on mortgage loan system	726	$12,488,112.80	

Credit life insurance − Net income for July: $8,374.52.

Delinquencies:	Over 30 days	Over 60 days
Real estate	11	4
Other	60	27
Total	71 .8%	31 .3%

Charge-offs in July—$11,382.62. Recoveries—$198.00.

Finally, Ms. Harris thought about the advertising agency. It had been bugging her for some time to give it more direction. Did GFS intend to become a full-service financial institution in the mold of a traditional commercial bank, or did it plan to continue to specialize in the consumer savings and mortgage lending areas? Which niche would be appropriate for GFS to seek relative to other financial institutions? What competitive differences could be used to set GFS apart from the competition? She wondered whether it might just be simpler to become a stock company, which would be the quickest and easiest way to raise the net worth/total assets ratio to 6 percent.

Case 10

Modern Plastics (A)*

Institutional sales manager Jim Clayton had spent most of Monday morning planning for the rest of the month. It was early July and Jim knew that an extremely busy time was coming with the preparation of the following year's sales plan.

Since starting his current job less than a month ago, Jim had been involved in learning the requirements of the job and making his initial territory visits. Now that he was getting settled, Jim was trying to plan his activities according to priorities. The need for planning had been instilled in him during his college days. As a result of his three years' field sales experience and development of time management skills, he felt prepared for the challenge of the sales manager's job.

While sitting at his desk, Jim recalled a conversation that he had a week ago with Bill Hanson, the former manager, who had been promoted to another division. Bill told him that the sales forecast (annual and monthly) for plastic trash bags in the Southeast region would be due soon as an initial step toward developing the sales plan for the next year. Bill had laughed as he told Jim, "Boy, you ought to have a ball doing the forecast, being a rookie sales manager!"

When Jim had asked what Bill meant, he explained by saying that the forecast was often "winged" because the headquarters in New York already knew what they wanted and would change the forecast to meet their figures, particularly if the forecast was for an increase of less than 10 percent. The experienced sales manager could throw numbers together in a short time that would pass as a serious forecast and ultimately be adjusted to fit the plans of headquarters. However, an inexperienced manager would have a difficult time "winging" a credible forecast.

Bill had also told Jim that the other alternative meant gathering mountains of data and putting together a forecast that could be sold to the various levels of

* This case was written by Kenneth L. Bernhardt, Professor Tom Ingram, University of Kentucky, and Professor Danny N. Bellenger, Texas Tech University. Copyright © 1990 the authors.

Modern Plastics management. This alternative would prove to be time-consuming and could still be changed anywhere along the chain of command before final approval.

Clayton started reviewing pricing and sales volume history (see Exhibit 1). He also looked at the key account performance for the past two and a half years (see Exhibit 2). During the past month Clayton had visited many of the

EXHIBIT 1   Plastic trashbags—sales and pricing history, 1987–1989

	Pricing dollars per case			Sales volume in cases			Sales volume in dollars		
	1987	1988	1989	1987	1988	1989	1987	1988	1989
January	$6.88	$ 7.70	$15.40	33,000	46,500	36,500	$ 227,000	$ 358,000	$ 562,000
February	6.82	7.70	14.30	32,500	52,500	23,000	221,500	404,000	329,000
March	6.90	8.39	13.48	32,000	42,000	22,000	221,000	353,000	296,500
April	6.88	10.18	12.24	45,500	42,500	46,500	313,000	432,500	569,000
May	6.85	12.38	11.58	49,000	41,500	45,500	335,500	514,000	527,000
June	6.85	12.65	10.31	47,500	47,000	42,000	325,500	594,500	433,000
July	7.42	13.48	9.90*	40,000	43,500	47,500*	297,000	586,500	470,000*
August	6.90	13.48	10.18	48,500	63,500	43,500	334,500	856,000	443,000
September	7.70	14.30	10.31	43,000	49,000	47,500	331,000	700,500	489,500
October	7.56	15.12	10.31	52,500	50,000	51,000	397,000	756,000	526,000
November	7.15	15.68	10.72	62,000	61,500	47,500	443,500	964,500	509,000
December	7.42	15.43	10.59	49,000	29,000	51,000	363,500	447,500	540,000
Total	$7.13	$12.25	$11.30	534,500	568,500	503,500	$3,810,000	$6,967,000	$5,694,000

* July–December 1989 figures are forecast of sales manager J. A. Clayton, and other data comes from historical sales information.

EXHIBIT 2   1989 key account sales history (in cases)

Customer	1987	1988	First six months 1989	1987 monthly average	1988 monthly average	First half 1989 monthly average	First quarter 1989 monthly average
Transco Paper Company	125,774	134,217	44,970	10,481	11,185	7,495	5,823
Callaway Paper	44,509	46,049	12,114	3,709	3,837	2,019	472
Florida Janitorial Supply	34,746	36,609	20,076	2,896	3,051	3,346	2,359
Jefferson	30,698	34,692	25,044	2,558	2,891	4,174	1,919
Cobb Paper	13,259	23,343	6,414	1,105	1,945	1,069	611
Miami Paper	10,779	22,287	10,938	900	1,857	1,823	745
Milne Surgical Company	23,399	21,930	—	1,950	1,828	—	—
Graham	8,792	15,331	1,691	733	1,278	281	267
Crawford Paper	7,776	14,132	6,102	648	1,178	1,017	1,322
John Steele	8,634	13,277	6,663	720	1,106	1,110	1,517
Henderson Paper	9,185	8,850	2,574	765	738	429	275
Durant Surgical	—	7,766	4,356	—	647	726	953
Master Paper	4,221	5,634	600	352	470	100	—
D.T.A.	—	—	2,895	—	—	482	—
Crane Paper	4,520	5,524	3,400	377	460	566	565
Janitorial Service	3,292	5,361	2,722	274	447	453	117
Georgia Paper	5,466	5,053	2,917	456	421	486	297
Paper Supplies, Inc.	5,117	5,119	1,509	426	427	251	97
Southern Supply	1,649	3,932	531	137	328	88	78
Horizon Hospital Supply	4,181	4,101	618	348	342	103	206
Total cases	346,007	413,217	156,134	28,835	34,436	26,018	17,623

key accounts, and on the average they had indicated that their purchases from Modern would probably increase about 15–20 percent in the coming year.

Schedule for Preparing the Forecast

Jim had received a memo recently from Robert Baxter, the regional marketing manager, detailing the plans for completing the 1990 forecast. The key dates in the memo began in only three weeks:

August 1	Presentation of forecast to regional marketing manager.
August 10	Joint presentation with marketing manager to regional general manager.
September 1	Regional general manager presents forecast to division vice president.
September 1–September 30	Review of forecast by staff of division vice president.
October 1	Review forecast with corporate staff.
October 1–October 15	Revision as necessary.
October 15	Final forecast forwarded to division vice president from regional general manager.

Company Background

The plastics division of Modern Chemical Company was founded in 1965 when Modern Chemical purchased Cordco, a small plastics manufacturer with national sales of $15 million. At that time the key products of the plastics division were sandwich bags, plastic tablecloths, trash cans, and plastic-coated clothesline.

Since 1965 the plastics division has grown to a sales level exceeding $200 million with five regional profit centers covering the United States. Each regional center has manufacturing facilities and a regional sales force. There are four product groups in each region:

1. Food packaging: Styrofoam meat and produce trays; plastic bags for various food products.
2. Egg cartons: Styrofoam egg cartons sold to egg packers and supermarket chains.
3. Institutional: Plastic trash bags and disposable tableware (plates, bowls, etc.).
4. Industrial: Plastic packaging for the laundry and dry cleaning market; plastic film for use in pallet overwrap systems.

Each product group is supervised jointly by a product manager and a district sales manager, both of whom report to the regional marketing manager. The sales representatives report directly to the district sales manager but also work closely with the product manager on matters concerning pricing and product specifications.

The five regional general managers report to J. R. Hughes, vice president of the plastics division. Hughes is located in New York. Although Modern Chemical is owned by a multinational oil company, the plastics division has been able to operate in a virtually independent manner since its establishment in 1965. The reasons for this include:

1. Limited knowledge of the plastic industry on the part of the oil company management.
2. Excellent growth by the plastics division has been possible without management supervision from the oil company.
3. Profitability of the plastics division has consistently been higher than that of other divisions of the chemical company.

The Institutional Trash Bag Market

The institutional trash bag is a polyethylene bag used to collect and transfer refuse to its final disposition point. There are different sizes and colors available to fit the various uses of the bag. For example, a small bag for desk wastebaskets is available as well as a heavier bag for large containers such as a 55-gallon drum. There are 25 sizes in the Modern line with 13 of those sizes being available in 3 colors—white, buff, and clear. Customers typically buy several different items on an order to cover all their needs.

The institutional trash bag is a separate product from the consumer-grade trash bag, which is typically sold to homeowners through retail outlets. The institutional trash bag is sold primarily through paper wholesalers, hospital supply companies, and janitorial supply companies to a variety of end users. Since trash bags are used on such a wide scale, the list of end users could include almost any business or institution. The segments include hospitals, hotels, schools, office buildings, transportation facilities, and restaurants.

Based on historical data and a current survey of key wholesalers and end users in the Southeast, the annual market of institutional trash bags in the region was estimated to be 55 million pounds. Translated into cases, the market potential was close to 2 million cases. During the past five years, the market for trash bags has grown at an average rate of 8.9 percent per year. Now a mature product, future market growth is expected to parallel overall growth in the economy. The 1990 real growth in GNP is forecast to be 4.5 percent.

General Market Conditions

The current market is characterized by a distressing trend. The market is in a position of oversupply with approximately 20 manufacturers competing for the business in the Southeast. Prices have been on the decline for several months but are expected to level out during the last six months of the year.

This problem arose after a record year in 1988 for Modern Plastics. During 1988, supply was very tight due to raw material shortages. Unlike many of its competitors, Modern had only minor problems securing adequate raw material supplies. As a result the competitors were few in 1988, and all who remained in business were prosperous. By early 1989 raw materials were plentiful, and prices began to drop as new competitors tried to buy their way into the market. During the first quarter of 1985, Modern Plastics learned the hard way that a competitive price was a necessity in the current market. Volume fell off drastically in February and March as customers shifted orders to new suppliers when Modern chose to maintain a slightly higher than market price on trash bags.

With the market becoming extremely price competitive and profits declining, the overall quality has dropped to a point of minimum standard. Most suppliers now make a bag "barely good enough to get the job done." This quality level is acceptable to most buyers who do not demand high quality for this type of product.

Modern Plastics versus Competition

A recent study of Modern versus competition had been conducted by an outside consultant to see how well Modern measured up in several key areas. Each area was weighted according to its importance in the purchase decision, and Modern was compared to its key competitors in each area and on an overall basis. The key factors and their weights are shown below:

		Weight
1.	Pricing	.50
2.	Quality	.15
3.	Breadth of line	.10
4.	Sales coverage	.10
5.	Packaging	.05
6.	Service	.10
Total		1.00

As shown in Exhibit 3, Modern compared favorably with its key competitors on an overall basis. None of the other suppliers were as strong as Modern in breadth of line nor did any competitor offer as good sales coverage as that provided by Modern. Clayton knew that sales coverage would be even better next year since the Florida and North Carolina territories had grown enough to add two salespeople to the institutional group by January 1, 1990.

Pricing, quality, and packaging seemed to be neither an advantage nor a disadvantage. However, service was a problem area. The main cause for this, Clayton was told, was temporary out-of-stock situations which occurred occasionally, primarily due to the wide variety of trash bags offered by Modern.

During the past two years, Modern Plastics had maintained its market share at approximately 27 percent of the market. Some new competitors had entered the market since 1987 while others had left the market (see Exhibit 4).

EXHIBIT 3 Competitive factors ratings (by competitor*)

Weight	Factor	Modern	National Film	Bonanza	South-eastern	PBI	BAGCO	South-west Bag	Sun Plastics	East Coast Bag Co.
.50	Price	2	3	2	2	2	2	2	2	3
.15	Quality	3	2	3	4	3	2	3	3	4
.10	Breadth	1	2	2	3	3	3	3	3	3
.10	Sales coverage	1	3	3	3	4	3	3	4	3
.05	Packaging	3	3	2	3	3	1	3	3	3
.10	Service	4	3	3	2	2	2	3	4	3

Overall weighted ranking†

1.	BAGCO	2.15	6.	Southeastern	2.55
2.	Modern	2.20	7.	Florida Plastics	2.60
3.	Bonanza	2.25	8.	National Film	2.65
4.	Southwest Bag (Tie)	2.50	9.	East Coast Bag Co.	3.15
5.	PBI (Tie)	2.50			

* Ratings on a 1-to-5 scale with 1 being the best rating and 5 the worst.
† The weighted ranking is the sum of each rank times its weight. The lower the number, the better the overall rating.

EXHIBIT 4 Market share by supplier, 1987 and 1989

Supplier	Percent of market 1987	Percent of market 1989
National Film	11	12
Bertram	16	0*
Bonanza	11	12
Southeastern	5	6
Bay	9	0*
Johnson Graham	8	0*
PBI	2	5
Lewis	2	0*
BAGCO	—	6
Southwest Bag	—	2
Florida Plastics	—	4
East Coast Bag Co.	—	4
Miscellaneous and unknown	8	22
Modern	28	27
	100	100

* Out of business in 1989.
Source: This information was developed from a field survey conducted by Modern Plastics.

EXHIBIT 5 Characteristics of competitors

National Film	Broadest product line in the industry. Quality a definite advantage. Good service. Sales coverage adequate, but not an advantage. Not as aggressive as most suppliers on price. Strong competitor.
Bonanza	Well-established tough competitor. Very aggressive on pricing. Good packaging, quality okay.
Southeastern	Extremely price competitive in southern Florida. Dominates Miami market. Limited product line. Not a threat outside of Florida.
PBI	Extremely aggressive on price. Have made inroads into Transco Paper Company. Good service but poor sales coverage.
BAGCO	New competitor. Very impressive with a high-quality product, excellent service, and strong sales coverage. A real threat, particularly in Florida.
Southwest Bag	A factor in Louisiana and Mississippi. Their strategy is simple—an acceptable product at a rock bottom price.
Sun Plastics	Active when market is at a profitable level with price cutting. When market declines to a low profit range, Sun manufactures other types of plastic packaging and stays out of the trash bag market. Poor reputation as a reliable supplier, but can still "spot-sell" at low prices.
East Coast Bag Co.	Most of their business is from a state bid which began in January 1984 for a two-year period. Not much of a threat to Modern's business in the Southeast as most of their volume is north of Washington, D.C.

The previous district sales manager, Bill Hanson, had left Clayton some comments regarding the major competitors. These are reproduced in Exhibit 5.

Developing the Sales Forecast

After a careful study of trade journals, government statistics, and surveys conducted by Modern marketing research personnel, projections for growth potential were formulated by segment and are shown in Exhibit 6. This data was compiled by Bill Hanson just before he had been promoted.

Jim looked back at Baxter's memo giving the time schedule for the forecast and knew he had to get started. As he left the office at 7:15, he wrote himself a large note and pinned it on his wall—"Get Started on the Sales Forecast!"

EXHIBIT 6   1990 real growth projections by segment

Total industry	+5.0%
Commercial	+5.4%
Restaurant	+6.8%
Hotel/motel	+2.0%
Transportation	+1.9%
Office users	+5.0%
Other	+4.2%
Noncommercial	+4.1%
Hospitals	+3.9%
Nursing homes	+4.8%
Colleges/universities	+2.4%
Schools	+7.8%
Employee feeding	+4.3%
Other	+3.9%

Source: Developed from several trade journals.

Part 4

Product and Brand Management Decisions

The six cases concerned with product strategy decisions in this section involve a number of different kinds of decisions. Many marketers believe that product decisions are the most critical of the marketing mix variables because of their importance to consumers in their decision-making process, and because product decisions, once made, are not quickly or easily reversed or changed. Promotion and pricing changes, for example, can be made much more quickly and with greater ease. Furthermore, most product changes usually require changes in the rest of the marketing strategy—changes in promotion, pricing, and sometimes distribution.

Before examining the various issues in the product strategy area, the concept of what a product is should first be understood. A product is "anything that can be offered to a market for attention, acquisition, or consumption; it includes physical objects, services, personalities, places, organizations, and ideas."[1] A product is thus much more than its physical properties and is everything a consumer buys when he or she makes a purchase. It is a set of want-satisfying attributes. It is important to understand this definition because what the consumer is buying is not necessarily what the company thought it was marketing. So marketers must be aware of consumer attitudes, values, needs, and wants with respect to their products.

The major decisions related to product strategy are:

1. What new products should be developed?
2. What changes are needed in current products?
3. What products should be added or dropped?

---

[1] Philip Kotler, *Marketing Management: Analysis, Planning and Control,* 3rd ed. (Englewood Cliffs, N.J.: Prentice-Hall, 1976), p. 183.

4. What positioning should the product occupy?
5. What should the branding strategy be?

A brief discussion of some of the concepts related to each of these decisions follows.

New Product Development

The sales and profits of a product category tend to change over time. The pattern a product category typically follows is called the product life cycle. It is defined to have the introductory, growth, maturity, and decline stages. Because most products reach the maturity and decline stages eventually, a marketer must continually seek out new products which can go through the introductory and growth stages in order to maintain and increase the total profits of the firm. But what new products should be introduced?

To answer this question, a marketer must consider the objectives of the firm, the resources available, the target markets the firm is trying to satisfy, and how the new product would fit in with other products offered by the company and the competition.

To successfully develop new products, the organization will have to set up formalized strategies for generating new product ideas, means for screening these ideas, product and market testing procedures, and finally commercialization. The objective is to obtain products which are differentiated from those of its competitors and which meet the needs of a large enough segment of the market to be profitable.

Changes in Current Products

The needs, wants, attitudes, and behavior of consumers change over time, and a company must change its products also or risk losing these consumers to a competitor who more quickly responds to these changes in the marketplace.

Should new features be added to the product? Should the warranty be extended? Should the packaging be changed? Should new services be offered? The marketer must continually monitor its target market and the competition to be able to answer such questions.

What Products Should Be Added or Dropped

A marketer must make decisions concerning the product mix or composite of products the firm will offer for sale. This requires decisions concerning the width and depth of products. Width refers to the number of product lines marketed by the firm. For example, General Electric has many lines while Kellogg's has concentrated on breakfast foods. The depth of the product mix is the number of items offered for sale within each product line. Kellogg's, for example, would have a very deep product line with many different alternatives offered for sale.

Whether a product line should be extended or reduced depends on a number of factors, including financial criteria, market factors, production considerations, and organizational factors. The marketer in making these decisions must examine the potential profit contributions, return on investment, impact on market share, fit with consumers' needs, fit with the needs of the channels of distribution, and the expected reactions of competitors. The production and organizational considerations include impact on capacity for other products, and on the goals and objectives of the firm, both in the short and long run.

Product Positioning

Product positioning is defined as that idea that is put into the consumers' minds by telling them how our product differs from its competitors. The position we strive to occupy will depend on the different market segments available, the attributes of our product compared to the needs of each segment, and the positions occupied by our competitors against each market segment.

Branding Strategy

The basic decisions here are whether or not to put brand names on the organization's products, whether the brands should be manufacturers' or distributors' brands, and whether individual or family brands should be used.

These decisions depend on the company's resources, objectives, the competition, and consumer choice behavior. For example, a small firm with few resources and much competition in a product category where consumers perceived small differences in the brands available would probably choose to market its product using private distributors' brands. Family brands such as General Electric and Campbell's are used when the marketer wants the consumer to generalize to the new products all those attributes he associates with the family brand name. The time and money required to establish the brand's name is much lower with this strategy but it does not allow the marketer to establish a separate image for the new product.

Case 11

Amtrak*

In late 1975, the management of Amtrak faced a number of major decisions concerning their Detroit–Chicago route. They were considering purchasing a number of new Amfleet trains to put on this run. There were also questions about what services to offer on these trains if they were purchased.

History of Amtrak

Amtrak was established through federal legislation on April 30, 1971, as a last-ditch attempt to revitalize intercity rail service in the United States. Railroads, during the previous 10 years, had found it difficult to compete with other modes of transportation—in particular, the private automobile (and the new interstate highway system it used), and the jet aircraft in domestic service. Travel by rail in the United States had declined from 70 percent of all intercity travel in 1947, to less than 5 percent in 1971.

Amtrak, a single nationwide passenger rail system, was designed to lure travelers back to the rails. In an era of increasing awareness of energy limitations, and of ever-growing numbers of people utilizing modes of transport other than the auto, revitalization of American rail service was viewed as a necessity. Amtrak's goal was increased ridership through refurbished equipment, modernization of terminal facilities, speed increases, and greater overall convenience.

At the time of the Amtrak takeover, no intercity passenger rail cars had been built in 10 years, and no passenger technology existed in the country to design and build modern cars. Stations were antiquated and without modern facilities of any kind in many cases. Equipment was in an almost constant state of malfunction, and was seldom cleaned. Connections were often impossible, or highly inconvenient. Rail service held little attraction for anyone except fearful flyers and train buffs. The National Railroad Passenger Corporation (Amtrak's official name) had its hands full.

---

* This case was written by Thomas C. Kinnear and G. Ludwig Laudisi. Copyright © 1978 Thomas C. Kinnear.

For the purpose of service development, the various railroad lines and routes were divided into two categories: long-haul services and short- and medium-distance corridors. Long hauls were generally those routes of 700 or more miles, serviced by overnight or two day trains (e.g., The Broadway Limited, 900 miles, 17 hours, overnight between Chicago and New York). Corridors were lines over which several trains a day in each direction were operated. In particular, the corridors of less than 300 miles were thought to be ideally suited for high-quality, high-speed service, which could compete with the airlines. This style service if implemented, it was reasoned, could attract business travelers and others for whom travel time was of great importance. Amtrak had a good reason to believe this would work too: the New York–Washington corridor had offered such service since 1969—the Metroliners—and was very successful.

The Detroit-Chicago Corridor

In the case of the Detroit–Chicago corridor (279 miles), Amtrak saw an opportunity to duplicate the fine operation between New York and Washington. As late as the early 1960s, the New York Central Railroad (which originally operated Amtrak's Detroit–Chicago line) had offered high-quality rail service on the route. Running times between the two cities were as fast as four and a half hours, and luxurious meal and parlor car service was offered. With the completion of Interstate 94 through to Detroit from Chicago, and the introduction of the 727 jet on "short-hop" flights, much of the market for this type of service disappeared. The train was no longer fast enough. As travel volume dwindled, services were cut.

First the parlor cars (first-class service aimed toward business travelers) came off, then the diners with their sitdown meal service. Coaches and snack bars remained. When Penn Central was formed in 1967 (via the merger of the Pennsylvania and New York Central Railroads), high losses were viewed as a reason to further cut service quality. Car cleaning was minimized; maintenance became irregular. In 1969, running times were lengthened to five and a half hours. The Penn Central in its annual report served notice it wanted as few passenger trains as possible. Just prior to Amtrak's takeover of the route, Penn Central offered three trains in each direction a day over the route, one without food service at all, the other two with limited snack service. On-time performance was poor. Rats were once reported in the coaches. The service offered was as poor as it could possibly be.

On May 1, 1971, Amtrak took over this corridor. As with many routes throughout the country, its first major step was to cut the frequency of service. Thereafter, two trains a day in each direction operated between the two cities. It was, according to Amtrak, a temporary economy move to limit the deficit. Further, said Amtrak in newspaper advertising, the remaining trains would be vastly improved.

Improvement was first accomplished by running the trains (the *Wolverine* and the *Saint Clair*) with cars from the C&O Railroad. Its equipment was in far better shape than the Penn Central's, which was immediately withdrawn from service to be rebuilt. The replacement equipment was more comfortable and better maintained, but meal service was still very limited. The schedule remained five and a half hours from endpoint to endpoint. Amtrak also began an advertising program in Detroit, basically just to tell people that the trains were there (many had forgotten or didn't know rail service existed to Chicago). As with other areas of the country, Amtrak promised refurbished cars within a year. The result was a stop in the decline of ridership, and a gradual turnaround by the end of the first year of operation. Unlike the original plans, refurbished cars began to arrive piecemeal—a car here or there, mixed in with older, untouched equipment. But this nonetheless showed good intentions. Schedules were better adhered to as well, and connections at Chicago were improved. This was aided by Amtrak's consolidation of all operations to one Chicago terminal—Union Station—and the elimination of across-town transfers.

But there were many problems with the initial effort as well. Amtrak operated its trains by contractual arrangement with the railroads—in this case, Penn Central. Because of this, they had only indirect control over on-board staff, and the dispatching and running of trains. Problems en route were handled by the railroad in the old manner—which often meant not handling them at all. Amtrak couldn't instruct attendants as to the way to deal with passengers, because the attendants still worked for the railroads. Amtrak, because of the situation, could say little about service quality or uniformity.

Equipment was also maintained by the railroad. Often, after individual cars had been rebuilt (at very high cost), they fell into disrepair because of continued poor maintenance. The age of the equipment was also a problem. The average car was 20 years old. While pleasant inside and comfortable to travel in, they were too old to be completely reliable. Air-conditioning failed or heating gave out while trains were en route. Since no passenger railroad cars had been built in the United States for almost 10 years, no technology was immediately available to construct new equipment.

Stations along the route presented many problems. Without exception, they were run-down, dirty, and without modern facilities. The Detroit station, once a busy rail center, was a decaying edifice, vast and frightening. Serving only four trains a day when Amtrak first took over, it was far too large for its task. Located on the west side of Detroit, it was inconvenient for persons from the east and north suburbs to get to it. The Niles, Michigan, station had no heat, and in Battle Creek the main body of the station had been closed for several years. Conditions were so bad, several of Amtrak's advisory board recommended that three of the stations be ripped down rather than trying to fix them up, and new ones be built in their place.

The Energy Crisis

In 1973, after two years of operation, refurbished equipment ran on the corridor exclusively, stations were painted at last, and on-time operation (on the same slow schedule) became a reality. Then, in the fall of that year, the energy crunch descended on the nation. Gasoline prices and air fares went up substantially, and millions of Americans were forced onto public transportation. Suddenly, Amtrak had its hands full. Trains that were never more than half full were carrying three times their normal load. Overcrowding became commonplace. On the corridor, trains were unreserved (meaning that there was no limit on the number of tickets sold per train). Trains that could comfortably seat 300 people were carrying about 600. Food would run out almost before the trains left their originating stations. Passengers, due to the crowding, sometimes stood for four or five hours, or sat on suitcases in the aisles. Personnel became rude and discourteous. Fistfights broke out on occasion between conductors and irate passengers. The refurbished equipment in many cases couldn't take the abuse and wear it received from carrying this many people. The interiors became damaged and weren't repaired. Heating and air-conditioning were as erratic as ever. Malfunctioning equipment was allowed out on the line for the first time in Amtrak history, so that more cars were available to seat more people.

Amtrak received a ghastly black eye during the energy crunch. It was not able to adequately meet the hordes of people who suddenly came back to the rails. The Detroit–Chicago corridor in particular fared dismally in terms of service, with equipment, food service, and personnel getting more complaints than almost anywhere else in the system. But in two areas, things were positive. On-time performance remained good despite the crowds (which often slowed things down elsewhere), and ridership remained high into the summer of 1974.

The Turboliners

Based on these final two factors, Amtrak made a firm commitment to upgrade service on the route. In late 1973, the corporation leased two French Turboliner trains for experimental use on the St. Louis–Chicago corridor. Since no modern passenger equipment was yet available in the United States, Amtrak went to Europe where new trains could be acquired almost immediately. The Turbos' better schedules, improved food service, and high on-time reliability resulted in greatly improved ridership to and from St. Louis. Amtrak decided to purchase these two and four more sets of Turbo equipment and to place some of them in service between Detroit and Chicago. In April of 1975, the Detroit–Chicago corridor became all turbo. As part of the service improvement program, an additional midday train was added, bringing the number of trains on the route to six daily; that is, in each direction, a morning, noon, and evening train. The new equipment was extremely sleek and modern. Its exterior was reminiscent of the Japanese "Bullet" train, and its interiors were plush, quiet, and featured giant windows and automatic sliding glass doors between each car. Food service was provided cafeteria-style, with an area adjacent to the galley for eating and lounging, and fold-down trays available at each coach seat.

Because of the new technology that the equipment utilized, it was maintained at a special service facility in Chicago constructed specifically for this purpose. Service personnel were specially trained to work on board the new trains and thus the quality level of individual service was vastly improved. The introduction of the new service was accompanied by an innovative and clever advertising campaign on Detroit and Chicago television stations and on local radio stations along the route. Perhaps because of the new trains themselves, or the extensive advertising, or the added service, or the coordination of the entire promotion, ridership on the corridor increased 72 percent the first month, and over 150 percent within three months. The trains ran regularly at their 300-passenger capacity. They were so successful, in fact, that a whole new set of problems arose.

Foremost among them was a problem related to their new technology. Because the equipment was foreign, it was constructed in a manner quite different from traditional American railway design. Hence, the maintenance people ''out on the line'' (that is, anywhere but at the service facility) didn't know how to work on the new trains. The troubleshooting manuals on board each train were no help to them either—they were in French. As a result, if air-conditioning failed on a trip, it probably remained broken until the train returned to its Chicago maintenance facility. Sometimes that meant several trips if loads were heavy, and 300 . . . , 600 . . . , 900 uncomfortable passengers. More than once public address announcements were made asking anyone who could read French to come to the cockpit and translate the manual for the English-only maintenance personnel.

The popularity of these trains led to another problem—overcrowding. Unlike conventional American equipment, cars couldn't be added or removed from the Turbos. They had a fixed number (five) and a standard carrying capacity of 300 people. They ran as unreserved trains, however, meaning that Amtrak would sell tickets to as many people as wanted to ride, and often that was over 300. On weekends, some passengers stood for five and a half hours, all the way to Detroit, or Chicago. Even when there were no technical or capacity difficulties, the sleek, new Turbos still serviced stations in Michigan that were at least 50 years old, and which for the most part hadn't been renovated. Ann Arbor was the single exception, but its refurbished station was far too small for the growing number of passengers using the facility. These difficulties marred the generally good impression the turbotrains gave in advertising and on the many good trips they made. The public failure resulted in a somewhat negative reputation. This was by no means pervasive though, and the trains continued to do well on the route. On subsequent routes where Turbos were assigned, ridership increased as well, seemingly justifying the argument that if modern services were provided, the American public would travel by rail.

The success of this equipment also occurred, it should be pointed out, without great schedule improvement. Due to track conditions, the high-speed capabilities of the new trains could not initially be used, so it was the trains themselves, rather than their speed, that accounted for their popularity. With track improvement, it was reasoned, they would be even more attractive to intercity travelers.

Research data indicated that the average age of Detroit–Chicago train riders was 35 years old, with about 65 percent traveling on vacations, 25 percent on business, and 10 percent for other reasons.

The Decisions to Be Made

In late 1975, the management of Amtrak faced a number of decisions with respect to the Detroit–Chicago route.

1. The first decision concerned the possibility of purchasing a number of Amfleet trains for the route. These trains were being built by the Budd Company of Philadelphia for use on a number of Amtrak routes. Amfleet trains combined the modern aspects of the European Turboliners (speed, new interiors, standardized seating, and food service) with the flexibility of old-style conventional equipment. On an Amfleet train, cars could be added or removed as load factors changed. Since they were American built, the difficulty of foreign technology was eliminated. In addition, Amfleet trains offered the possibility of first-class, daytime accommodations featuring reserved seats and at-seat meal service.

In order to run three trains a day in each direction, Amtrak would have to purchase four locomotives and 24 Amfleet cars. The average Amfleet train on this run was thus expected to have one locomotive and six cars. Each locomotive would cost about $540,000. The price of cars varied depending on whether the car was a coach, first-class, parlor, dinette, and so on. On average the cars would cost Amtrak $425,000 each. A car would hold up to 84 passengers, with 60 in some cars. The useful life of this equipment was expected to be 20 years.

2. The second decision related to whether or not first-class accommodations should be available on the Detroit–Chicago Amfleet trains, if these trains were purchased. This service would include reserved seating and meal service at that seat. Reserved seats were spaced two together and a seat by itself, giving three seats across the car. About 10 percent of the seating capacity of an average six-car train could be available for first-class service. The incremental cost of meals and personnel to Amtrak of each first-class seat sold was estimated to be about $5.

3. A related decision here concerned the price of a first-class ticket, if such service were made available. The price of a coach ticket was $17.50 one way. This compared to $19.50 for the five-hour bus ride, and $39 for a coach seat and $58 for a first-class seat for the one-hour plane ride.

4. At first, the Amfleet trains would continue to take five and a half hours to travel from downtown Detroit to downtown Chicago. They were capable of traveling much faster, but track conditions would not allow this. Amtrak was considering spending $3 million on track and signal improvements in the next year. This money and a great deal more to be put up by Conrail (the regional freight railway of the northeast) could improve the tracks such that travel could be cut to under four hours within a few years. The Amtrak-funded improvements were expected to have about a 10-year useful life. The management of

Amtrak was wondering whether or not they should spend this money, and aim for shorter run times.

5. There were five major stations on the Detroit–Chicago run. Amtrak was considering upgrading them. The cost to Amtrak would be $150,000 per station. The rest of the cost would be covered by the state of Michigan, and local cities. A 20-year useful life was expected on each improved station.

6. Amtrak's advertising agency was Needham, Harper, and Steers. They had developed an advertising campaign for the Amfleet trains in general, and the Detroit–Chicago corridor more specifically. They planned to use a mix of television, radio, and newspapers. The media costs to Amtrak for the Detroit–Chicago run were proposed to be $300,000 per year.

The management of Amtrak wondered what decisions should be made with respect to the Detroit–Chicago corridor.

Case 12

Lotus Development Corporation: Project 3*

The meeting was over, and Steve Jobs, the founder of NeXT, Incorporated, returned to California. Steve Jobs had once again attempted to persuade the management of Lotus Development Corporation to develop a software package for his new NeXT computer. Lotus was presently involved in creating two new spreadsheet products on the OS/2 operating system for the IBM PS/2 personal computer. The first product was a graphical version of its popular 1–2–3 spreadsheet. This product was being developed to take advantage of the OS/2 operating system, which many industry analysts believe will be the most commonly used system in the 1990s. Management was billing the second product, Project 3, as "the next generation in spreadsheets." It is Project 3 that Steve Jobs wants Lotus to develop for his NeXT computer.

Lotus management was now faced with three alternatives. First, Lotus could create a new team to develop a product for the NeXT computer while at the same time continuing development of Project 3 on the OS/2 operating system. Second, Lotus could port Project 3 to the NeXT system and finish the product on that platform. Finally, the firm could ignore the wishes of Steve Jobs and not develop a product on the NeXT system.

Company History

Lotus Development Corporation was founded in 1982 by Mitchell D. Kapor. Its first product was Lotus 1–2–3, a spreadsheet software package designed for the IBM personal computer (PC). Lotus 1–2–3 was well received and helped propel sales of the personal computer. Since 1982, the firm has grown to reach $468,547,000 in sales in 1988.[1] Exhibit 1 provides a five-year summary of sales data, while Exhibit 2 provides the firm's balance sheet for the last three

---

* This case was written from public sources and from interviews with people knowledgeable about this industry by Matthew J. Hausmann under the supervision of Thomas C. Kinnear. Copyright © 1990 by Thomas C. Kinnear.
[1] *Compact Disclosure.* February 1990.

EXHIBIT 1 Lotus Development Corporation five year summary (in thousands)

Date	Sales	Net income	EPS
1988	468,547	58,925	1.29
1987	395,595	72,043	1.58
1986	282,864	48,300	1.03
1985	225,526	38,150	0.77
1984	156,978	36,046	0.75

Source: *Compact Disclosure.*

EXHIBIT 2 Lotus Development Corporation balance sheet (in $thousands)

Fiscal year ending	12/31/88	12/31/87	12/31/86
Cash	192,433	164,909	93,157
Receivables	92,035	45,541	37,844
Inventories	18,088	9,210	6,794
Other current assets	7,430	5,665	6,396
Total current assets	309,986	225,325	144,191
Property, plant, and equipment, net	86,953	51,920	40,964
Intangibles	16,026	32,297	23,270
Deposits and other assets	9,157	8,111	584
Total assets	422,122	317,653	209,009
Notes payable	9,441	7,736	N/A
Accounts payable	45,491	31,685	20,147
Accrued expenses	11,771	15,287	23,883
Income taxes	1,231	19,165	12,055
Other current liabilities	16,592	11,734	6,775
Total current liabilities	84,526	85,607	62,860
Deferred charges/income	10,400	N/A	1,556
Long-term debt	95,000	30,000	N/A
Other long-term liabilities	N/A	N/A	30,000
Total liabilities	189,926	115,607	94,416
Common stock, net	556	546	526
Capital surplus	109,429	83,274	66,624
Retained earnings	266,285	207,360	135,317
Treasury stock	144,030	87,743	83,135
Other liabilities	(43)	(1,390)	(4,783)
Shareholders' equity	232,196	202,046	114,593
Total liabilities and net worth	422,122	317,653	209,009

Source: *Compact Disclosure.*

years. The firm's remarkable growth has been fueled by the popularity of 1–2–3 and its subsequent upgrades. In addition, the firm has developed other product lines including word processing packages, CD–ROM disks, and personal information management packages. These products were developed to change Lotus's one-product dependence. During 1989, however, the firm once again began to focus on its core product: spreadsheets.

Strengths and Weaknesses of Lotus

Lotus has a strong reputation in the industry for the conception and design of products. Many of the firm's latest projects, such as Magellan (a utility program that provides quick and easy access to all the information stored on a PC hard disk) and Notes (an application platform that allows groups to share textual and graphical information across local area networks) are considered to be excellent technical accomplishments. The firm, however, is not considered a technical leader in spreadsheets. A number of software industry observers have been critical of Lotus 1–2–3 upgrades. These critics suggest that 1–2–3 offers poor output and is not user friendly. Many point to Microsoft Corporation's Excel as an example of a product which has been created with an ear to the customer. Yet, Lotus 1–2–3 has an installed base of approximately 4 million users, controls 71 percent of the market in terms of revenues, and boasts 53 percent of units sold. Meanwhile, Microsoft Excel has been able to garner only a 10 percent share of the DOS operating system-based PC spreadsheet market.[2]

Lotus has very strong marketing skills and has been working to make Lotus's customer service the best in the industry. A toll-free number has been instituted, and the service department is carefully monitoring how long customers wait until they speak with a consultant. The goal is to keep waiting time to a minimum and improve customer satisfaction. The firm also has a large, well-trained sales force. The sales force has been extremely effective in pushing Lotus products.

Lotus insiders believe the firm has begun to focus on the customers. As evidence of this, insiders point to the design partner program in which the firm involves select customers in the selection of product features. Lotus is also trying to keep its largest customers abreast of its moves. According to the firm's 1988 annual report, the firm is sharing its product direction and strategy with its biggest customers (under confidential disclosure).[3] Industry analysts believe that this new posture is designed to reverse Lotus's reputation as a brash company that is unresponsive to its customers.

Lotus has had a large problem with product announcements and shipping products. Lotus announced that it was creating 1–2–3 Release 3.0 in 1987 and stated that it would ship this upgrade in the second quarter of 1988. However, the firm experienced major problems with the development process and repeatedly delayed the shipment. (In the industry, this is referred to as vaporware.) Release 3 is now scheduled to be shipped in the second quarter of 1989. Many customers have become angry at the delay and have begun looking at other spreadsheet products. Industry experts, however, say that Lotus has retained most of its user base. According to industry analyst Lincoln Spector, "It is a

---

[2] Ed Scannell. "The Once and Future King?" *Infoworld* (January 23, 1989), p. 41.
[3] Lotus Development Corporation, 1989 Annual Report.

the body what actions to take. In machine vision, the camera (eye) captures an image and transmits it to the controller (brain) via a coaxial cable (optic nerve). The controller sorts relevant from irrelevant data and instructs the machine tool, conveyor, or robot what actions to take.

MVI's Prospectus
September 18, 1985

There are many potential application areas for machine vision in the industrial workplace. Data received by a computer from television cameras viewing an assembly area can be almost instantaneously analyzed so that task performance guidance commands can be sent to a robot. Vision systems can be used in quality control processes to check work in process against required product parameters, which are stored in the system's computer. A vision system can therefore check during production for the proper dimensions and shape of the product, for the presence of all features or parts, and for its general condition including surface flaws. Deviations from acceptable parameters can be brought to the attention of supervisory staff before they cause a substandard product to be produced. Because vision systems can recognize different shapes or identifying markings, production parts can be sorted, facilitating the movement, processing, or assembly of parts. The goals in the use of vision systems are to increase product quality, increase production rates and industrial efficiency, and provide labor savings.

The Market for Machine Vision Products

The machine vision industry did not exist in 1980. In 1981, total industry sales were $7 million. Between 1981 and 1984, sales more than doubled each year, so that by 1984 industry sales totaled $80 million. A compound average growth rate of 60 percent per year has been estimated for the industry as a whole for the period from 1984 to 1990. Estimated sales for 1985 were $125 million. For 1990, the total market was estimated to reach between $750 and $800 million. Machine vision was the fastest growing segment of the factory automation market in the mid-1980s.

Despite all the optimistic estimates for growth in the market, not one competitor in machine vision had consistently made a profit by 1985, though some privately owned companies claimed to have shown a profit in some quarters that year. Between 70 and 100 competitors were vying for the industry's total sales of $125 million in that year, in literally thousands of different applications. The bulk of this revenue was shared among 20 companies. The major competitors in the industry and their sales for the period 1983–85 are shown in Exhibit 1. In 1984, none of these competitors made a profit in this industry. Automatix had a loss of $14.2 million on its sales of $17.3 million. Robotic Vision Systems, Inc. (RVSI), had a loss of $.78 million on sales of $5.1 million in 1984 and a loss of $1.8 million on sales of $9.7 million in 1985. International Robomation/Intelligence (IRI) had a loss of $4.1 million on its

EXHIBIT 1   Competitive sales figures ($ millions)—1983, 1984, 1985

Company	1983 Sales	1984 Sales	Expected 1985 Sales	Type of Financing
Applied Intelligent Systems, Inc. (1976)	$ 0.4	$ 1.4	$ 5.0	Private
Automatix	6.3	17.3	27.0	Public
Cognex Corp.	2.0	5.0	6.0	Private
Diffracto Ltd. (1973)	3.7	5.1	7.3	Private
International Robomation/Intelligence	1.0	2.3	8.0	Public
Itran Corp. (1982)	0.2	1.1	2.2	Private
Machine Vision International	0.5	4.0	10.0	Public
Perceptron, Inc. (1981)	1.0	5.5	15.0	Private
Robotic Vision Systems, Inc. (1977)	1.0	5.1	10.0	Public
View Engineering (1976)	7.5	15.0	19.0	Private
All others	11.4	18.2	15.5	
Total market	$35.0	$80.0	$125.0	

sales of $2.3 million in 1984, but announced in late 1985 that it had been profitable during the first half of 1985.

Analysts of the machine vision industry were hard pressed to pick which companies would survive the early growth years.

> The industry is very fragmented. There are no clear leaders. Although perhaps only 20 companies or so represent the vast bulk of machine vision revenue . . . there are well over 70 companies that call themselves vision systems companies. One only has to go as far down as company number 5 or so in order to be looking at annual revenues of $5 million or less. The revenue gap between the current leaders and those companies really new to the industry is extremely thin. The obvious conclusion seems, then, to be that the industry is entirely up for grabs. Company number 70 or beyond could still easily overtake company number 1 since there is not much that separates them in terms of sales dollars.
>
> Prudential-Bache Securities
> *CIM Newsletter,* February 6, 1985

Industry analysts do point to some industry conditions which will bear on these conclusions. The first, and possibly the most important, of these arises from the newness and difficulty of the technologies involved in making machine vision really work in an industrial environment. The technologies are not yet perfected. The market is often uneducated or unrealistic about the true capabilities of machine vision. Competitors are finding it very difficult to determine all the variables that have to be satisfied and solved to make the products work in a true, operating, industrial environment.

> Experience may represent the single most effective barrier to entry. The vision industry has a lot of companies in it. It is difficult enough to win an order. There are few "easy" wins in the industry. But once you get the order, then the really hard part begins. The winning vendor actually has to deliver a system that works. More often than not, as all the leading companies have undoubtedly discovered, it is simply harder to make the actual system work properly in the real world. There

is no substitute for experience, at least not yet. There may be very few ways for a new entrant to take a shortcut in order to circumvent the pack and leapfrog to the top.

Prudential-Bache Securities
CIM Newsletter, February 6, 1985

Though some large companies, most notably General Electric, Eastman Kodak, 3M, and Owens-Illinois, are competitors in the machine vision industry, none has established itself as an industry leader. There are many technologies applicable to vision applications, and these technologies are still very much in the developmental stage. Possible applications of machine vision can be found in almost any industrial setting where part inspection, part identification, or automated assembly processes are used. This ambiguity in the market is often harder for large companies to deal with than for small ones. Large companies commonly put resources only into areas where large dollar revenues or high profits can be quite reasonably predicted. These usually come from large volume sales of repeatably manufacturable products. At the present, machine vision does not offer these possibilities.

Another development that may have far-reaching impact on the machine vision industry is the involvement of General Motors. GM has become very interested in production automation. This interest was spurred by the results of several automobile industry studies. These studies found that the Japanese had a sizable cost advantage, ranging between $1,500 and $1,800 per car, over U.S. producers in 1985. Also, it was estimated that it took approximately three times as many labor-hours for U.S. automobile manufacturers to produce a car than it did their Japanese competitors. Studies predicted that U.S. car manufacturers would have to reduce their costs by about 25 percent between 1985 and 1990 to remain competitive in the industry. GM's internal studies showed that a lot of the gap between U.S. and Japanese production costs could be corrected with increased automation. Of possible automation alternatives, it was determined that the use of robotics and machine vision were key strategies to use to solve the problem. Forty-four thousand machine vision applications were identified within GM alone by GM analysts.

Taking action on these findings, GM has entered into a joint venture with Fanuc Ltd. of Japan, forming GMF, a highly respected robotics firm. To back its belief that vision was also key to automation, GM invested in five machine vision companies in 1983 and 1984. These were Applied Intelligent Systems (AIS), Automatix, Diffracto Ltd., Robotic Vision Systems (RVS), and View Engineering. The full impact of these investments on the machine vision industry is yet unknown. These investments by GM did give higher credibility and visibility to the entire machine vision industry. They helped the machine vision industry gain awareness among potential users in the marketplace. Within GM, the investments came in conjunction with the identification of GM's needs for vision and brought potential users within GM to search for solutions to those needs. GM's goal became that of filling its 44,000 vision needs by 1990. No five companies within the vision industry would be capable of solving all these applications. Thus, the identification of GM's vision needs opened the door to all vision companies—not just the five GM invested in, although they had an advantage over the others if they could do the application.

The Customers for Machine Vision Products

Though the machine vision market is very fragmented and very new, some information about who the buyers of these products will be has been provided by a report entitled *Vision Systems Survey of End Users,* conducted by Prudential-Bache Securities and published on February 6, 1985.

The report showed several interesting characteristics of present and potential machine vision customers. Sixty-seven percent of the companies surveyed achieved annual gross revenues of greater than $1 billion. Eighty-four percent of the companies had annual gross revenues of greater than $100 million. Fifty-seven percent of the companies interested in vision were located in the Midwest. Another 19 percent were located in the Northeast, with 9 percent on the West Coast. The end users surveyed were in the following industries:

Industry	Percentage of study
Automotive	35%
Electrical/electronics	35
Aerospace	12
Construction	3
Pharmaceutical	1
Other*	14

* Ranges from paper products to metal fabricators.

Ninety-seven percent of the end users surveyed indicated that vision was an important factor in the overall manufacturing process. Sixty-four percent had an actual capital budget for vision system purchases.

Decision makers in the purchasing of vision systems were located in many different levels of the companies surveyed. Sixteen percent responded that the purchase decision was made at the corporate level only, while 29 percent said that the decision was made at the division level. Another 37 percent responded that vision system purchase decisions were made at the department level, with the remaining 17 percent of those surveyed answering that the decision involved more than one level within the company.

The length of present and anticipated future buying cycles for vision systems were as follows:

Buying cycles	Present	Future
Less than 3 months	13%	31%
6–9 months	47	41
9–12 months	23	18
Over a year	9	6

Many customers believed that machine vision systems would not only be installed for production work applications but also for internal development work on automation processes. Nineteen percent of respondents had installed vision systems for development work only, while 54 percent said that they had or planned to install vision systems for both production work and development work.

Fifty-nine percent of survey respondents purchased their vision systems through the direct sales forces of the suppliers. Twenty percent used only OEMs, while 8 percent purchased through distributors. The remaining 13 percent used more than one channel for their purchases.

Vision companies most often mentioned as possible suppliers making the "short list" were: Automatix, View Engineering, Machine Vision International, and Perceptron. The factors most important to purchasers of vision systems, in their order of importance, were: technology, service and support, applications engineering, user friendliness, reputation of vendor, expandability, and price. The companies mentioned as most technically advanced were: Automatix, Machine Vision International, Perceptron, View Engineering, and Diffracto. The companies listed as most user friendly were: Automatix, View Engineering, Itran, Perceptron, and Machine Vision International. The vendors listed as providing the best support/service capabilities were: Automatix, Perceptron, View Engineering, Diffracto, Itran, and Machine Vision International.

The end users were also asked to list areas of application of vision systems in both the present and the future. The responses were:

Applications	Present	Future
Inspection	84%	93%
Gaging	44	60
Sorting	21	35
Process control	37	63
Robot guidance	40	45

The Technologies Employed in Machine Vision

At present, there are four main technologies employed in machine vision systems. These are signal processing, mathematical morphology, statistical pattern recognition, and artificial intelligence. These four and the significant characteristics of each are displayed in Exhibit 2.

The dimensions of the graphic used in Exhibit 2 answer the questions "What is being processed?" on the horizontal axis and "How is this processing done?" on the vertical axis. The "What is being processed?" dimension ranges from images on the left to objects on the right. If images are being processed, the computer converts what the camera sees into an array of different sizes and colors of dots and analyzes the placement of these dots. If an object is being analyzed, then the computer compares measurements of what the camera sees to descriptions of what should be in the camera's view. On the vertical dimension, the image or object can be processed either using arithmetic, linear analysis in

EXHIBIT 2 Vision systems technologies and their characteristics

	Image Based	Object Based	

How Is the Processing Done?	**Signal Processing**
	
	High speed
	Simple discrimination
	Requires special
	   hardware
		Statistical Pattern Recognition
		
		Low speed
		Simple discrimination
		No special hardware
		   required
			Arithmetic
			Computations

	Mathematical Morphology
	
	High speed
	Complex discrimination
	High hardware
	   requirements
		Artificial Intelligence
		
		Low speed
		Very complex
		   discrimination
		Can require special
		   hardware
			Logical
			Computations

What Is Being Processed?

the top two quadrants of the matrix, or using logical, nonlinear analysis in the bottom two quadrants. Arithmetic functions deal with quantities; that is, numbers and equations regarding dimensions or sizes of the image or object are manipulated and analyzed. In logical analysis, binary values that are either true or false are used to determine relationships between what the camera sees and what has been programmed as appropriate.

As shown in Exhibit 2, image processing allows for high-speed analysis but requires extensive hardware to perform its tasks. Object analysis can take place only at slower speeds but does not require as much expenditure in hardware. Arithmetic analysis can perform simple discrimination only; thus it cannot find subtle differences between what is being examined and what is expected. Logical analysis allows for complex discrimination; thus these technologies are capable of handling more difficult or precise problems, and can analyze these with less lighting and placement requirements. The use of statistical pattern recognition produces numerical, quantitative answers, such as "How many parts are present?" or "How big is the part?" The use of artificial intelligence produces qualitative responses, such as "Yes, that is a good part" or "No, that is not properly assembled."

To more fully understand these technologies, it is useful to see what each one is used for in a given application. MVI has a 3-D robot guidance product in which vision is used to direct the robot's placement of windshields in a car moving along an assembly line at the pace of 60 cars per hour. All four technologies are employed in this application. Lighting is used to produce a very sharp, mirrorlike image of the car as it comes into the work area. The bouncing of the light off the car surface to produce this image employs signal processing, a technology developed from radar technology. However, this lighting reflects off more than just the edge of the car body needed to be seen to perform the window insertion task. Mathematical morphology allows the computer control to extract from the image reflected only the part of the image needed for the task, and eliminates the rest from consideration. That is done through complex computer programs that direct the computer to search the image for the exact shape needed for analysis. Statistical pattern recognition is used to take measurements of window position and orientation, since the actual opening size and the position of the car body on the assembly line may vary slightly from car to car. Thus, this technology makes use of another set of computer algorithms to take statistical measurements of the pertinent areas of the problem in question. Artificial intelligence software is used to answer such questions as "Is the window opening the right shape for the windshield that is here?" and "Can the robot reach the opening from its present position?" These questions can all be answered logically; they are either true or false. If corrections are necessary, the computer controls can command the robot to move and change position before actual insertion commands are given.

Exhibit 3 takes the example given above one step further, showing which technologies are necessary to perform the most common applications of vision systems currently on the market. Many applications require the use of only one of the technologies available, while others require multiple technologies. Thus, gauging or fixtured part measurement require only the use of signal processing. Part identification or part positioning require only statistical pattern recognition. Finished surface inspection can be performed with mathematical morphology only, and assembly verification can be done with artificial intelligence alone. On the other extreme, tasks such as 3-D robot guidance and part defect detection require the employment of all four technologies to achieve proper performance. It has been estimated that between 50 percent and 60 percent of the applications in the market in 1985 applied signal processing. Between 20 percent and 30 percent of applications made use of statistical pattern recognition. The remaining 15 percent of applications relied on mathematical morphology to perform the desired task.

Exhibit 4 shows how many of the current competitors in the vision systems market are positioned along technology lines. Most competitors use only one technology. MVI is currently alone in the employment of all four technologies. MVI began as a mathematical morphology company. MVI has consciously developed the use of the other three technologies in order to be able to better handle more difficult industrial problems and to give itself a technology edge over its competition. This was explained in the company's prospectus as follows:

EXHIBIT 3   Technologies used in machine vision applications

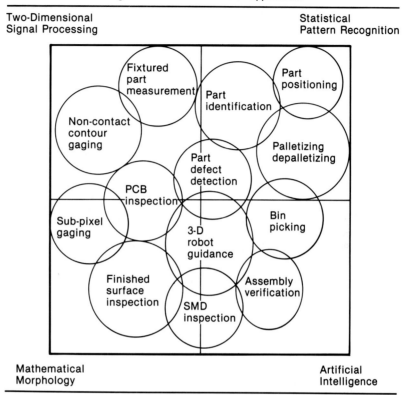

The Company specializes in mathematical morphology which it believes is the most suitable technology for application in machine vision. The Company believes that it has advanced the practice of mathematical morphology . . . such that its utilization in the Company's systems enables application of machine vision to widely varied guidance and inspection tasks in the factory environment. Moreover, the Company is complementing its capabilities in mathematical morphology by establishing capabilities in pattern recognition, signal processing, and artificial intelligence, and believes that the combination of these technologies will enhance the applications of the Company's systems. It is the advanced application of mathematical morphology and the move toward a combination of technologies to complement mathematical morphology that the Company believes differentiates it significantly from its competitors.

Dr. Sternberg explained why it is important to use all the available technologies. He said:

You can force a solution using just one tool, but you end up working 10 times harder than if you use the right tool for the right part of the job. You can find a

EXHIBIT 4 Industry competitors' technology positions

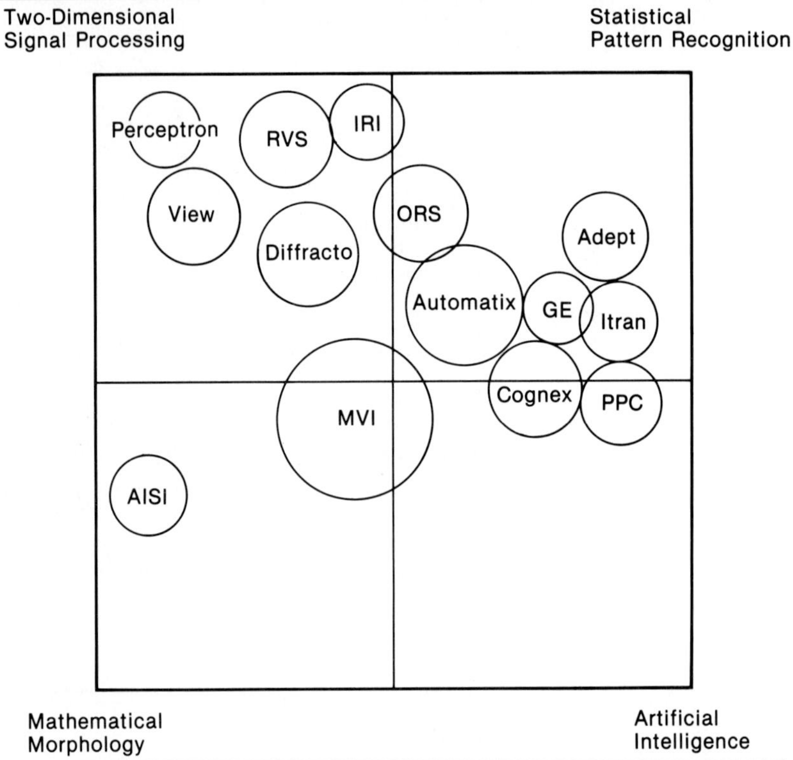

Two-Dimensional
Signal Processing
Statistical
Pattern Recognition

Mathematical
Morphology
Artificial
Intelligence

way to change the spark plugs on your car with just a hammer, but it will take you a lot longer to do it this way than if you had all the right tools for the job.

Machine Vision International—History

MVI was founded as Cyto-Systems Corporation in June 1981 by Dr. Stanley R. Sternberg. Dr. Sternberg had previously worked at the Environmental Research Institute of Michigan, where he was instrumental in the development of the technology of mathematical morphology. Dr. Sternberg's idea was to develop products based on this technology that could be used for measurement, inspection, and control in manufacturing processes. In the fall of 1982, Dr. Sternberg joined with Richard P. Eidswick to develop a plan and strategy to bring this technology to market. Prior to joining MVI, Mr. Eidswick was senior vice president and director of Comshare, Inc., an international computer services company. In May 1983, the company's name was changed to Machine Vision International.

To fund the company, nearly $9.5 million of equity capital was raised through private offerings of MVI securities. Approximately $5 million of these funds were raised through the sale of common stock to Safeguard Scientifics, Inc. In connection with this investment, Safeguard obtained an agreement to make a rights offering of MVI stock to Safeguard's shareholders. This rights offering was completed in November 1985. As of November 5, 1985, MVI was a public company, with its shares traded in the over-the-counter market.

As its strategy in the vision industry, MVI has chosen to focus on three business areas and three specific applications of machine vision. The business areas are automotive, electronics, and general industrial. The applications are three-dimensional robot guidance, surface inspection, and surface-mounted electronic component inspection. The principal component of all systems sold by MVI is the image flow computer (IFC), an image processing computer that uses MVI's proprietary operating software, BLIX, to perform the mathematical calculations necessary for image analysis. MVI markets its products primarily through direct sales groups dedicated to end users in the three business areas. It also markets its products to original equipment manufacturers (OEMs) who specify MVI products in their systems, and through certain specialized sales representatives. Through September 1985, MVI had manufactured and sold approximately 100 machine vision systems for an aggregate sales price of nearly $12 million. Financial statements for MVI are presented in Exhibit 5.

EXHIBIT 5
MACHINE VISION INTERNATIONAL CORPORATION
Statements of Operations

	Period from inception (June 25, 1981) to December 31, 1983	Year ended December 31, 1984	Six months ended June 30,	
			1984	1985
			(unaudited)	
Net sales	$ 541,058	$ 4,011,730	$ 760,807	$ 4,481,476
Cost of sales	338,921	2,536,398	555,891	2,021,068
Gross profit	$ 202,137	$ 1,475,332	$ 204,916	$ 2,460,408
Operating expenses:				
Product development	$ 318,961	$ 1,733,667	$ 610,836	$ 1,354,943
Selling	360,601	1,979,102	652,364	2,011,329
General and administrative	542,101	904,272	420,356	365,184
Total operating expenses	$ 1,221,663	$ 4,617,041	$ 1,683,556	$ 3,731,456
Loss from operations	$(1,019,526)	$(3,141,709)	$(1,478,640)	$(1,271,048)
Other income (expense):				
Interest expense	$ (5,076)	$ (105,089)	$ (15,697)	$ (116,207)
Other	23,342	67,895	64,858	19,410
Total other income (expense)	$ 18,266	$ (37,194)	$ 49,161	$ (96,797)
Net loss	$(1,001,260)	$(3,178,903)	$(1,429,479)	$(1,367,845)
Loss per share	$(.41)	$(.56)	$(.28)	$(.18)
Weighted average number of shares	2,458,495	5,714,391	5,164,775	7,457,460

EXHIBIT 5 *(concluded)*
MACHINE VISION INTERNATIONAL CORPORATION
Balance Sheets

	December 31,		June 30, 1985 (unaudited)
	1983	1984	
Assets			
Current assets:			
Cash and cash equivalents	$ 104,117	$ 191,361	$ 151,601
Receivables—			
Trade, net of allowance for doubtful accounts of zero in 1983, $15,000 in 1984 and 1985	272,945	2,095,875	3,255,081
Inventories	238,772	1,964,951	3,749,191
Prepaid expenses and deposits	8,689	34,961	34,228
Total current assets	$ 624,523	$ 4,287,148	$ 7,190,101
Property and equipment			
Computer and other equipment	$ 221,274	$ 972,614	$ 1,213,574
Office furniture and equipment	91,436	171,737	249,738
Leasehold improvements	6,520	91,665	102,232
	$ 319,230	$ 1,236,016	$ 1,565,544
Less: Accumulated depreciation and amortization	31,154	275,087	470,087
Net property and equipment	$ 288,076	$ 960,929	$ 1,095,457
	$ 912,599	$ 5,248,077	$ 8,285,558
Liabilities and Shareholders' Equity			
Current liabilities:			
Current portion of long-term debt	$ 42,500	$ 74,823	$ 118,000
Note payable	—	675,000	500,000
Accounts payable	246,058	993,292	1,887,677
Accrued liabilities	80,312	155,876	277,417
Accrued payroll	24,228	110,088	262,125
Customer advances	—	141,878	94,167
Total current liabilities	$ 393,098	$ 2,150,957	$ 3,139,386
Long-term debt, less current portion above	$ 118,365	$ 1,671,775	$ 1,205,073
Commitments			
Shareholders' equity			
Preferred stock, no par value, stated value $.001, 10,000,000 shares authorized, no shares issued and outstanding at 1983, 1984, and 1985, respectively	$ —	$ —	$ —
Common stock, no par value, stated value $.001, 30,000,000 shares authorized, 4,017,500, 6,508,620, and 8,213,620 shares issued and outstanding at 1983, 1984, and 1985, respectively	4,018	6,509	8,214
Paid-in capital	1,398,378	5,598,999	9,480,893
Accumulated deficit	(1,001,260)	(4,180,163)	(5,548,008)
Total shareholders' equity	$ 401,136	$ 1,425,345	$ 3,941,099
	$ 912,599	$ 5,248,077	$ 8,285,558

Market Approach

An organizational chart for MVI is shown in Exhibit 6. As the chart indicates, the activities of Mr. Eidswick as chairman and chief executive officer and the

EXHIBIT 6 Corporate organizational chart

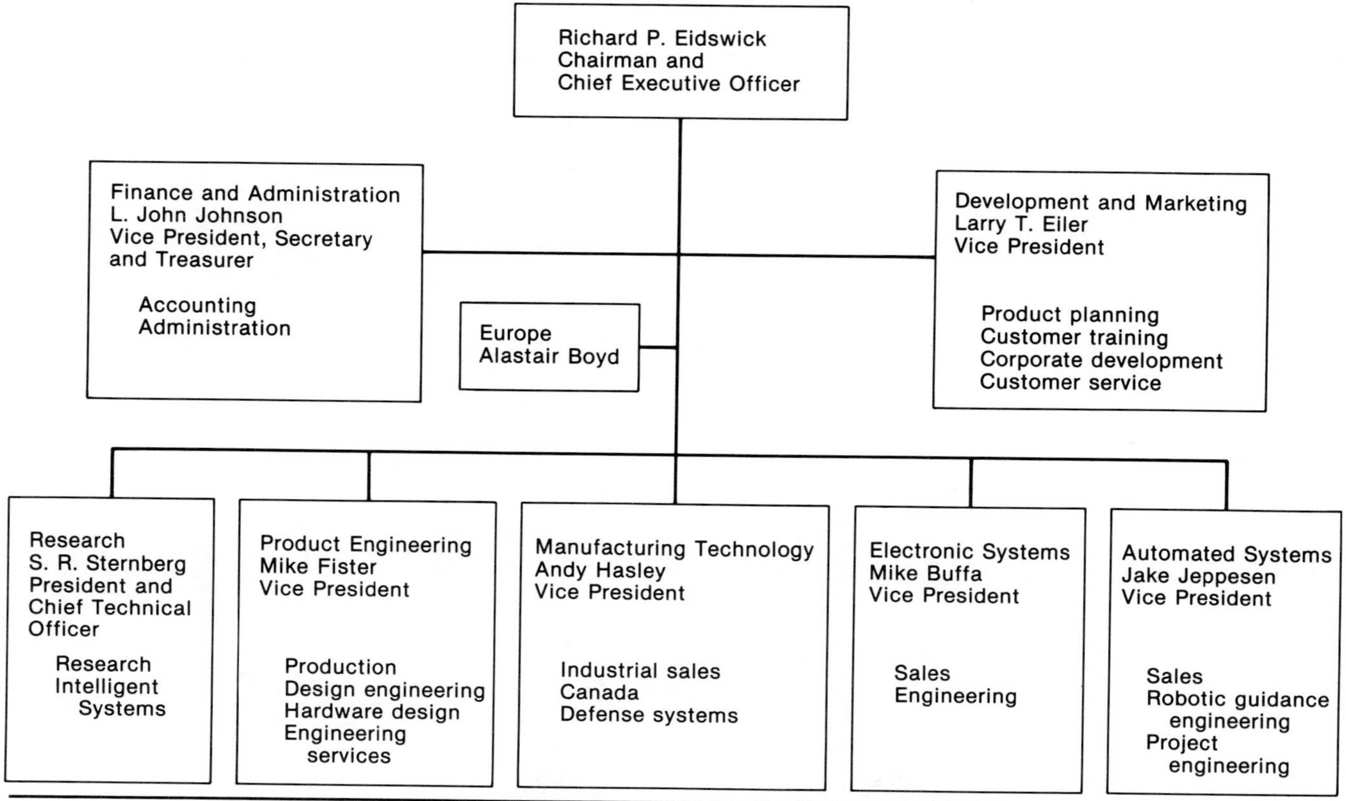

```
                    Richard P. Eidswick
                    Chairman and
                    Chief Executive Officer
```

Finance and Administration
L. John Johnson
Vice President, Secretary
and Treasurer

Accounting
Administration

Europe
Alastair Boyd

Development and Marketing
Larry T. Eiler
Vice President

Product planning
Customer training
Corporate development
Customer service

Research
S. R. Sternberg
President and
Chief Technical
Officer

Research
Intelligent
Systems

Product Engineering
Mike Fister
Vice President

Production
Design engineering
Hardware design
Engineering
services

Manufacturing Technology
Andy Hasley
Vice President

Industrial sales
Canada
Defense systems

Electronic Systems
Mike Buffa
Vice President

Sales
Engineering

Automated Systems
Jake Jeppesen
Vice President

Sales
Robotic guidance
  engineering
Project
  engineering

tasks performed by the finance and administration, development and marketing, and product engineering areas impact all functional areas of the company.

The sales function within MVI is divided along market segment lines. The three current sales divisions—automated systems, electronic systems, and manufacturing technology—mirror those markets pointed out by the Prudential-Bache survey as the major customers interested in machine vision products.

The Automated Systems Division (ASD)

At its inception, MVI was a company with a technology searching for applications. MVI was looking initially for any project that a customer would give them to prove what could be done with the technology at their disposal. MVI began this search in the automotive industry, where executives were already talking about putting resources into finding vision solutions to solve automation problems. Mr. Jake Jeppesen, who joined MVI in June 1983 to head the Automated Systems Division, found a group at GM that had been talking for two years to various vision companies about the possibility of using vision to automate auto glass insertion. The other companies had failed to develop a product that worked. Mr. Jeppesen convinced them to try again with the different technology that MVI offered with its mathematical morphology. The first order for the window insertion product was received by MVI in December 1983. A prototype was working in a GM lab in March 1984, and the first plant installation was made in June 1984. See Exhibit 7 for a representation of how this product works.

EXHIBIT 7   Representation of MVI's window insertion system

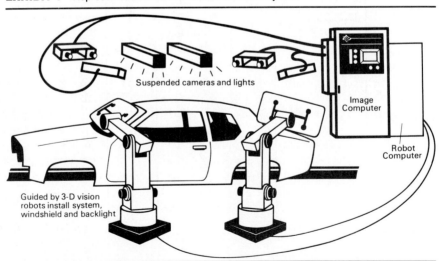

Even though the first vision applications taken on by MVI have shown themselves to be successfully working projects within the automotive industry, the sales process for ASD remains a very complicated one. The division maintains an ongoing educational sales effort, selling everyone from the executive level to the manufacturing staff to the manufacturing research people to plant production people on who MVI is and what the company and machine vision are capable of doing. Since this sales effort is so educational in nature, the decision was made to approach the market on a direct basis; MVI did not want to entrust this type of basic technology and company image selling to any third party. Automotive executives and manufacturing research staff personnel are interested in the technology involved and its advantages over present or alternative assembly automation techniques. However, manufacturing staffpeople are interested in finding ways in which higher-quality cars can be built better, cheaper, and faster. Plant production staff are interested generally in improvements in product quality, but are mainly concerned with production speed so that their quotas can be met. To this group, a product's reliability on the assembly line is of the utmost importance. Since orders within automotive companies come most often from the manufacturing staff or the plant production people, it is the goal of the sales process to give these people confidence that MVI's product ''will do what we say it's going to do forever, first time, every time, and never fail,'' as Mr. Jeppesen put it. These groups are not interested in machine vision for its technology. They want their task performed in the most reliable, fastest way possible. Because of this, Mr. Jeppesen does not describe himself as being in the vision business. He says, ''I am in the surface inspection business and I'm in the automatic assembly business. I use vision to accomplish those very difficult tasks.''

The ASD is currently selling products for two applications in the automotive industry. These are 3-D robot guidance for window insertion and other applications and surface paint inspection. The window insertion product has a selling price of approximately $450,000 per installation. It is only a part of an entire window insertion system that includes robots, body handling equipment, material handling equipment, and controls supplied by other vendors. This total system costs in the neighborhood of $5 million. The surface paint inspection product is currently only used to inspect finished paint surfaces and sells for approximately $500,000 per system. MVI has received seven orders for window insertion systems and one for a paint inspection system.

Though relatively few orders for these products have been received to date, the markets for these products are very large. Mr. Jeppesen sees many application areas for both MVI's 3-D robot guidance and paint surface inspection products beyond those currently being marketed. 3-D robot guidance can also be employed to automate such tasks as automobile wheel and cockpit loading, for the application of paint stripes, and to control many fluid fill operations. Although paint inspection systems are currently only used for finished product inspection, the market could be expanded to inspection of bare metal after frameup, phosphate coating before priming, primer coats, and other checkpoints during automobile production. In total, Mr. Jeppesen currently foresees 10 application possibilities for 3-D robot guidance and 6 application areas for surface inspection in each automobile plant. In 1985, there were 73 automobile assembly plants operating in the United States, and many of these operated with more than one assembly line per plant.

Currently, no other vision company even claims to be able to supply a product that can perform surface inspection. Mr. Jeppesen lists three companies as major competitors in the 3-D robotics business: GMF Robotics, ASEA Robotics, and Automatix. In this area, Mr. Jeppesen said that many companies claim to be able to perform this task, but they really do not have the necessary capabilities. The result of this is a great amount of confusion in the marketplace. There is much misinformation and confusion regarding the cost of a system that really can accomplish what its people say it will do. But Mr. Jeppesen believes that this confusion will soon be dispelled as competitors try to supply the market and fail. He stated it this way:

> There's just enormous confusion out there. Who can do what? Which companies oversell their capabilities? Which don't? The competitors who fail are beginning to get weeded out. All you have to do is tell GM you can do something and fail, and they throw you out pretty quickly.

Electronics Sales Division (ESD)

The electronics market is very different from the automotive area. Therefore, the sales strategy and marketing positioning employed in the electronics market is unique to it. The sales process for the ESD began with marketing research to find out the vision needs in the electronics industry and has been combined with a concerted effort to get to know the decision makers within that industry. In this effort, MVI marketing personnel attend electronics industry meetings, where they get to know the technology leaders within the industry. They gain firsthand knowledge of the industry's technology trends as well as of what the strategies of the major electronics firms will be. The goal of all this is to put the insight MVI gains from firsthand knowledge of plans and trends into the capabilities of MVI's product to produce a better match between that product and its market.

The U.S. electronics industry is currently undergoing a great change in production procedures. In 1985, 90 percent of electronics assembly was being done on lead-through boards. However, overseas, and especially in Japan, nearly 95 percent of electronics assembly was being done on higher-quality, more reliable surface-mounted boards. It is believed that U.S. production will shift to surface-mounted boards very rapidly. This type of production will be highly compatible with automated assembly techniques since the components on surface-mounted boards are much smaller and require greater production sensitivity than lead-through boards.[1]

The total market for surface-mounted inspection systems has been divided into three segments by MVI's market researchers. These segments are: (1) low speed (less than 6,000 parts per hour), high-precision inspection of a broad range of components; (2) high-volume (up to 20,000 parts per hour), low-precision inspection of a limited range of components; and (3) ultra-high-volume (over 20,000 parts per hour), high- and low-precision inspection of a broad range of components. MVI believes its product can be very successful in the first two market segments. For these areas, MVI has made the following total market size projections.

Year	Segment 1 Total no. of vision systems	Segment 1 Total dollar market (in millions)	Segment 2 Total no. of vision systems	Segment 2 Total dollar market (in millions)
1984	30	$ 3.6	7	$ 1.05
1985	65	7.8	20	3.0
1986	90	10.8	130	19.5
1987	125	15.0	340	51.0
1988	350	42.0	525	78.75

MVI has spent two years developing a product that can use vision to control the assembly process and provide inspection for this automated production. MVI believes that the contrast and complexity of the components used in this process require the capabilities of the company's mathematical morphology technology. An effective product for this market must be able to perform three tasks. These are: (1) determine if the correct component (chip, diode, resistor, or capacitor) is present; (2) determine if each part is in the correct position relative to the other components; and (3) check the solder used to attach parts to the board for voids and excess solder material. MVI's vision technology is capable of solving the first two tasks. The third task requires a low-level X-ray capability, which MVI does not currently have but is working to achieve. MVI hopes to eventually be able to market a product that can perform all three tasks required by its users.

Unlike the ASD sales, ESD sales are technology sales. ESD's personnel talk to technical processing engineers, not the traditional purchasing departments within the electronics firms. MVI people talk to these technical people to

---

[1] Surface mount technology (SMT) is an electronic manufacturing method in which miniaturized, prepackaged components are assembled on the top (hence surface) of a circuit. In lead-through assembly, the components have conductors or leads that are inserted through holes that are drilled or punched through the board. These leads are folded or clinched on the back of the board to provide mechanical component attachment. In SMT manufacturing, the components are placed on the board by an automatic mechanism and then soldered in place.

determine their automation needs and to educate them as to the capabilities of MVI's product. The goal is to get to know the people who will use the system and get their support before there is a quotation request made on the part of the electronics firm.

By the end of the third quarter of 1985, MVI had three working surface-mounted inspection systems in the field. The company expected to make deliveries on 9 or 10 more orders before the end of the year. Prices on these systems ranged from $80,000 to $200,000. The hardware used in these systems is priced to closely match the prices of MVI's competition. The software used is specific to each application, and as such is priced to be the profit margin producer for the company.

Competitors in this market are View Engineering, International Robomation/Intelligence (IRI), and Automatix. IRI was mentioned as an aggressive price competitor. IRI's developmental system is priced at between $22,000 and $26,000. This product is sold for applications in which a firm's engineers want to develop automated processes internally. IRI has been said to sell this development system to get a customer interested in vision, with the hope that the customer will return to IRI for more equipment when they are ready to solve their vision needs. IRI's price for an application system competitive with MVI's system would range from $75,000 to $125,000. Automatix' product is really an assembly guidance system, not an inspection system.

The Manufacturing Technology Division (MTD)

MVI's Manufacturing Technology Division is comprised of two sales groups, the Industrial Sales Group (ISG) and the Aerospace Sales Group (ASG). This division has as its goal that of finding new markets for the products developed by the other sales divisions. Manufacturing technology sales groups are to take on applications that require extensions of existing technology or new combinations of what has already been developed by MVI's R&D and engineering personnel. The MTD is headed by Mr. Andrew Hasley.

Industrial Sales Group. MVI receives between 250 and 300 inquiries each month through its marketing work, its presence in several vision shows, and through the references of its present customers arising from the company's reputation as a successful vision system supplier. Many of these inquiries do not come from people within the automotive or electronics industries. Leads from these other nonspecialized industries are turned over to the Industrial Sales Group, which is under the direction of Mr. John Kufchock.

Mr. Kufchock uses three initial criteria to determine whether MVI will pursue these inquiries. The lead must come from a Fortune 500 company; thus, the company must have considerable funds to spend on capital investments. The application being pursued must involve the use of technology already developed by MVI; thus, sales of the ISG are meant to produce a multiplier effect on sales for MVI. Furthermore, the inquiry must come from a company that has an established engineering group capable of understanding both the technology involved and the advantages MVI's technology has over competitors.

The ISG has made sales in many industries, all of surface inspection products that perform very diversified tasks. In the food industry, surface inspection is used to identify foreign objects in produce coming from the fields as well as produce of less than acceptable grade so that these can be eliminated from further processing. In the lumber industry, surface inspection is used to check plywood as it is produced so that its grade and sales quality can be determined. In the rubber industry, tires are checked for flaws and for whether the white-wall rubber has been applied properly. MVI surface inspection systems have also been used to inspect the edges of machine tool inserts and to determine if packages have been correctly sealed. By the end of 1985, the ISG had placed more than 20 systems in industrial workplaces. Mr. Kufchock expects to have nearly 50 more systems on the market in the first six months of 1986. He predicts that ISG can sell over 100 systems per year from a total of only 20 different customer corporations.

The sales process for the ISG usually begins with an inquiry from a prospective customer. Qualified leads are turned over to one of Mr. Kufchock's two sales-oriented application engineers. Through talking with and visiting the prospect, the application engineer studies the customer's vision needs to determine whether MVI's technology can meet the requirements of the task. The application engineer also finds the right people to deal with in the customer's organization. These include those who will understand the technology, those who will use the product, and those who will actually make the purchase decision. All those involved in the decision process must be "put on the team" if the sales process is to be successful. When this has been completed, a test of MVI's product on the prospect's material will be made at ISG's own lab. When the test is successful, the application engineer contacts the customer, asking that they send people to see the test results. Then, a trip is made to the customer's business to determine the actual conditions under which the system must perform and to talk to all the decision makers involved, getting their input on a preliminary sales proposal. After this proposal has had the input of the customer, a final proposal is drawn up and sent to the purchasing department of the customer. This entire selling process takes between three and nine months.

The ISG not only sells through its direct sales force of applications engineers, but also uses distributors in certain industries. These distributors are established machinery and other capital expenditure products suppliers in their industries. MVI uses this type of distribution channel in those industries where customers are geographically distant from the MVI offices and where it is unlikely that there are people within these firms who will understand or need to understand the technologies involved in the system.

The ISG also sells its products to other firms that need vision to make their large automation systems work for their customers. MVI calls these firms strategic partners because often significant development work has been done by MVI's engineering staff to make the vision products work successfully for this partner. These strategic partners have market knowledge that MVI does not possess. Often, the vision portion of the systems sold by these partners composes less than 20 percent of the entire system's selling price.

Prices on vision systems sold through the ISG range from $45,000 to $75,000 each. These prices include the hardware and software necessary for the application plus a training course held in Ann Arbor for the personnel using the system. Fees for engineering services at the customer's plant to get the system up and running are charged separately at an established per diem rate. In the first applications, it was common for MVI to find this engineering support taking more time than expected. This resulted in profit margins less than what was predicted. However, Mr. Kufchock points out that the experience gained from the first applications has made estimating engineering costs on present projects easier.

Aerospace Sales Group (ASG). The Aerospace Sales Group was established in mid-1985. It was spun off from the ISG when it was believed that there was enough business in this area alone to support a dedicated sales effort. The first sales made in the aerospace industry were made by the ISG group.

This group is selling products for many different applications and involving the different technologies developed by the ASD and ESD. These include 3-D robot guidance systems, small parts inspection systems, surface inspection products, and combinations of small parts inspection and 3-D robot guidance in which the system will recognize, inspect, and control the handling of parts. Current applications include turbine blade inspection, surface-coating inspection on space shuttle booster rockets, and 3-D robot guidance used for finding connectors for the assembling of wiring harnesses in aircraft and in the maintenance inspections of existing Air Force fighter planes.

The defense supply industry has different requirements for vision products than do the other industries MVI sells to. Here speed is of less concern than it is in other industrial environments. What is important here is the complexity of the parts to be inspected or assembled. In this area, many different parts must be inspected, as opposed to many of the same part in other industries. As a result, the systems sold by the ASG are complicated and average in price from $400,000 to $500,000.

The impetus for modernizing and automating production in the defense supply industry is coming from the Department of Defense. The government is providing military suppliers with incentives to improve their capital equipment through such programs as the Industrial Modernization Incentive Program (IMIP). The sales process for the ASG begins with contacts within the armed services to find out which firms are actively working on these programs and to learn the names of the IMIP project managers within each company. To help in finding these contacts, MVI has hired Mr. Jack Lousma, a former astronaut, to work as a consultant on a part-time basis. Once these contacts are found, Mr. Bill Wood, the sales manager of the ASG, calls on these project engineers to make initial presentations on the capabilities of the products MVI can offer. Mr. Hasley, director of the MTD, believes that the success of the ASG's first sales will provide new leads within the industry. Other avenues for sales come from contacts with robot manufacturers who need vision to make their robots work.

The defense market includes a wide variety of firms. There are several large military suppliers, such as General Dynamics, Hughes Aircraft, Lockheed, Boeing, Grumman, and Martin Marietta. There are also engine makers, such as TRW, Rohr, General Electric (GE), and GM, to be approached. Many smaller companies are parts suppliers for the military. Another market to be approached includes the repair and maintenance facilities of the armed services themselves. The Air Force alone has seven major repair facilities.

As major competitors, Mr. Hasley mentioned Robotic Vision Systems, Inc. (RVSI), IRI, and View Engineering. As in the automotive industry, no other competitor even claims to be able to perform surface inspection. Mr. Hasley believes there to be little competition in the area of parts inspection. In discussing the competitive environment, Mr. Hasley said,

> In a lot of cases, we don't find we're competing directly with anybody. We still make a lot of cold calls. Selling here is a market development problem really. It's just getting the application defined. Can you do this? Can you do that? It involves a lot of education on what vision can do.

Commonalities of Sales Approach

Though each of MVI's three sales divisions sells to different markets and to different groups of people within customer firms, each application's real bottom line sales approach is similar. What MVI is really selling is improved return on investment (ROI). In some sales, MVI's salespeople may be showing how their product can reduce warranty claim costs. This is especially true in automobile paint inspection since paint flaws are the industry's fourth largest warranty claim cost. Thus, improving paint finish quality is a paramount goal for these firms. In others, it may be improved product quality and customer perception of quality that results from the use of vision equipment. For yet other applications, the main purpose of the vision equipment may be to reduce the costs of inspection, while also providing 100 percent inspection with 100 percent accuracy. In others, the product may reduce direct labor costs because inspection or assembly personnel can be eliminated. For example, Mr. Kufchock pointed out that the plywood inspection system replaced the use of eight inspectors—each earning $21 per hour—in one facility alone. The use of vision equipment may actually increase the production rate of the business, thus improving productivity. All of these benefits impact ROI. Mr. Eiler said that MVI has found that through the improved ROI benefits of its products the company is getting the attention of many of its customers. He said,

> If the customer can get a 15-, 18-, or even 20-month payback on a paint system, for example, you go right to the head of the list for getting their attention. If you've got a three- or four-year payback, they are not really interested and your

product just goes into the pile of other investments with long payback periods. Then you've lost.

Development and Marketing

The development and marketing area serves four distinct functions within MVI. These are product planning, customer training, corporate development, and customer service. These services are under the direction of Mr. Larry Eiler.

The product-planning group is charged with determining the characteristics that will transform a project developed through opportunities discovered by one of the sales divisions into a standard product salable to a defined market. In performing this task, the product-planning group uses market research to analyze a potential market's size, growth rate, opportunities for a given application, and needs of the buyers to be found there. Product ideas are tested in the market so that they can be further specified. The goal is to determine the exact characteristics of a product for that market and then direct engineering to develop that product. Cost and ROI analysis are also done to determine pricing levels. A copy of MVI's product development cycle is shown in Exhibit 8.

The customer-training group provides MVI's customers with courses on the use of MVI's program language, BLIX, and with application-specific courses in the areas of 3-D guidance, paint inspection, and surface mount inspection. MVI employees are also offered courses on vision technologies and presentations on research done to determine the needs and characteristics of targeted customers.

The corporate development group within the marketing area is responsible for the preparation and presentation of financial reports and for all corporate news releases. This group maintains MVI's relationships with industry security analysts, portfolio managers, investment bankers, attorneys, and accountants. They also develop the company's competitive analysis information. The corporate development group is also charged with handling MVI's public relations publications and with maintaining relationships with the technology leaders within the vision industry.

The customer service group has the responsibility of overseeing the actual installation of MVI's products within a customer's facility. They also are in charge of maintenance procedures and the evaluation of the reliability of MVI's products and the components used in their assembly.

Production

For each first-time application, MVI builds whatever hardware and software is needed to make the project work for the customer. For further similar applications, MVI looks for a supplier for the necessary components of the system. Thus, for all of MVI's multiple applications, the optics, hardware, circuit boards, cables, communications devices, and other material handling equip-

EXHIBIT 8   MVI product development cycle

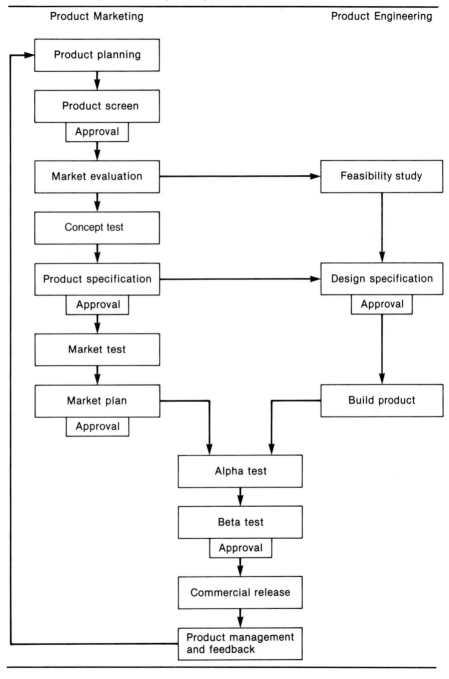

ment are all purchased from outside suppliers. The role of production then becomes that of packaging the optical equipment, the hardware, the software, and the communications materials so that the application works for the customer.

The Future Goals for MVI

Mr. Eiler believes that many of the seeds of MVI's ultimate success in the vision market have already been laid. He believes that the company's early successes have shown customers the "consistency, reliability, and strength of the company. They are learning that MVI is a vendor you can count on; not just a bunch of scientists playing with technology, but businessmen who will be here to stay." He sees that MVI's people have formed a team, and that it is not just strong technology but strong people working with that technology that makes products that perform for the customer.

Mr. Eidswick, MVI's chairman and CEO, has established the company's goal of being a dominant supplier in the machine vision industry. This goal translates into obtaining a 15 percent share of this market within five years and then sustaining that 15 percent share.

Mr. Eidswick has also set achievement goals for each sales division. The ASD and the ESD are to be specialized divisions and, as such, be technology and market share leaders within their industries. Here, there will be a continuing effort to take on new projects that have a strategic purpose. The groups within the Manufacturing Technology Division are to have multiplier strategies; their sales are to come from extensions of products developed by the ASD and ESD. The MTD groups are also to seek out strategic partners, finding companies who need vision in their products and who already have market knowledge and a strong customer base. For this type of customer, MVI would sell its products at a discount from the prices quoted to direct end users since the strategic partners would take over much of the selling process for MVI.

Mr. Eidswick has prepared sales expense breakdowns for the company's two types of sales, those direct to end users and those made through strategic partners, as MVI would like to see them. These expense breakdowns, expressed as percentages of sales revenue, are shown below. The third column shows the breakdown of expenses as percentages of sales for MVI's sales for the first half of 1985.

	End user	Strategic partner	First six months 1985
Revenue	100%	100%	100%
Cost of goods sold	35	55	45
Gross margin	65%	45%	55%
Selling expense	25%	9%	45%
R&D and engineering	10	10	30
Corporate expenses	10	6	8
Total expenses	45%	25%	83%
Profit before taxes	20%	20%	(28%)

These figures tell an interesting story. MVI has not made a profit to date; however, no competitor in the vision industry has been consistently profitable. MVI has bid each project, even the first one for each of its applications, at a price that the company thought would be profitable. However, the number of engineering, selling, and application development hours that these early applications have taken to achieve systems capable of working in real industrial environments and to educate customers on the use of the products has been hard to estimate. These problems have led to the higher than desired selling, R&D, and engineering expenses to date. Mr. Eidswick is most concerned about the high selling expense figure. He is not so concerned about the R&D and engineering expense since this is to be expected in a new, high-technology industry. MVI must, as Mr. Eidswick sees it, find ways to reduce its selling expense.

The Question of Focus

I think the central question right now is, what are we going to be when we grow up? It is not a simple question because the markets right now are small and fragmented. We must be very alert to be successful in the right markets.

Mr. Eidswick

Some vision companies have chosen to be very specialized. They believe that an emerging company cannot afford to spread itself too thin. It must establish a market niche, exploit that niche, make some money, and then go out and spread itself. Others say that this is a new market. No one understands it. What may be a niche one day might just disappear. Some competitors are very specialized. Others are all over the place. Some of each have failed. Why? For the specialized firms, perhaps the market never appeared or the task they chose proved too difficult. For those who were in all markets, each project was different and they had no repeat sales.

Dr. Sternberg

Multiple orders of the same kind of things, that's the kind of result we want to have. We want more repeat orders for the same product, the same application . . . less customization. That way we don't have to keep reinventing the wheel, inventing new technology and engineering new software for every order that we get.

Mr. Eiler

Mr. Eidswick believes that the fact that MVI has ''so much going on, in so many markets, with so many different applications'' is the company's biggest problem right now. But he explains that ''we have to do this if we want to find the applications that will provide repeat business, applications that will establish us as an industry leader.''

MVI has consciously moved its technology position within the industry from a company that employed only mathematical morphology to one that could successfully use all four technologies in its products. Mr. Eiler says this was done as a purposeful marketing strategy because many vision problems cannot be solved by one technology alone. They require capabilities of various technologies. Mr. Eiler also points out that the company has purposefully chosen only very difficult applications, a strategic approach he calls ''a tough jobs positioning.'' That product positioning along with what Mr. Kufchock calls the company's credo that ''There is no unhappy customer'' have been designed to build a strong company image for MVI as ''the company that makes products that work,'' as Mr. Eiler put it.

However, this strategic ''tough jobs'' approach can lead to another set of problems. Because its applications are so difficult, MVI's products are all very highly priced. This may pose a risk in this new industry where there are so many competitors and where each market is undeveloped. As Mr. Eiler said,

> In high tech, everything is too new and the market is too volatile. There are too many factors, too many things driving the marketplace. There are new people coming into this business all the time who think they can make vision systems work. You can lose a job to a low-end, low-price competitor who gets thrown out in three months because his system doesn't work. When others can't do the job, then we all suffer because vision's credibility is questioned.

MVI has not found that it is easy to get a vision application job even after another competitor has failed to provide a product that works. Often customers who have spent thousands and thousands of dollars on vision equipment want to protect that investment by giving their supplier another chance to succeed. Other customers have turned away from vision after initial system failures, waiting for the technology to mature and for the market winners to appear rather than give another company a chance at this time.

The prospectus published by MVI at the time of its stock offering to Safeguard Scientifics, Inc. shareholders states that MVI focuses on three applications. These are three-dimensional robot guidance, surface inspection, and surface-mounted electronic component inspection. Dr. Sternberg believes that, in looking at the company, one should be careful not to confuse its technological diversity with its market position. He said, ''MVI is focused; we are working toward three standardized products.''

Case 14

K mart Corporation*

> Rising in the early 1960s from a mundane variety store chain, K mart set the retail industry on its ear by stamping out enough prototype stores, like so many apple pies, to become the largest discount store chain. It elbowed J. C. Penney aside as the nation's number two, nonfoods retailer. In the first transformation year of 1962, the former S.S. Kresge Co. had sales of $450.5 million and net profits of $9 million. By 1984's end, those numbers had mushroomed to $21 billion in sales . . . and profits rolled in at $499 million.
>
> *Marketing & Media Decisions*
> Spring 1985 Special Edition

The story of K mart Corporation's rise is one of the truly great success stories in the retailing business. The first K mart was opened in 1962. By 1973, there were 745 K mart stores in 47 states. Total sales in that year were $4.6 billion, with $138 million in net income. Stores were added to the chain at a very rapid rate through the 1970s. One hundred and ninety-three new K marts were opened both in 1979 and 1980, with 171 new stores added in 1981. By 1984, there were 2,041 K mart stores throughout the country. The chain enjoyed a compound growth rate in sales of 16.6 percent from 1974 to 1984. Its share of the total mass merchandising market in the United States grew from 1.8 percent in 1972 to 3.7 percent in 1982.

In the company's 1974 annual report, Mr. Robert E. Dewar, chairman of the board and chief executive officer, defined K mart's market position as that of a mass merchandise retailer. He said,

> As mass merchants, we emphasize basic merchandise rather than discretionary purchases and stress value over fashion. . . . Our most important competitive strategy is to use discount pricing. Our store buildings and fixtures are designed and built, our merchandise assortments are selected, and our distribution systems are developed in order to offer a broad range of general merchandise at the lowest possible prices.

---

* This case was written from public sources by Constance M. Kinnear with the assistance of Thomas C. Kinnear. Copyright © 1987 by the authors.

K marts offered everything from clothing to housewares, from delicatessen foods to hardware, from sporting goods to stationery and toys. The product line also included such products as tires, batteries, building materials, and garden supplies not commonly carried by conventional department stores. In the first K marts, national brands composed approximately 50 percent of the merchandise mix, with the remainder being private K mart brands, sold at prices approximately 20 percent lower than national brands. K mart priced its goods with a margin of 25 to 26 percent over cost as opposed to regular retailers that priced at 38 to 40 percent over cost. K mart was not alone in the discount merchandising business. Its competitors included several small regional discount operations such as Mammoth Mart, Unishops, Giant stores, and Arlans. The competition also included new discount chains started by previously regular-only retailing firms. These included Federated's Gold Circle stores, Dayton-Hudson's Target stores, May Company's Venture stores, and Woolworth's Woolco stores. These stores offered little customer service, had a low-overhead, warehouse look, and made their profits through high-volume sales, with inventory turnover rates between six and eight times per year. When these stores were opened, their primary customers were blue-collar families with average to below-average incomes. The discounter's primary goal during this period of quick expansion was to convince its customers that it was safe and smart to save money. To this end, K mart offered only first-quality merchandise and a satisfaction-guaranteed return policy. Using low prices, K mart sought to accustom shoppers to a self-service, low-overhead store. Stores' location decisions were carefully made to make shopping K mart convenient for its customers. By 1984, not only were K marts present in over 80 percent of the standard metropolitan shopping areas of the country, but K mart surveys showed that 52 percent of the people in the country shopped at K mart at least once a month.

The K mart story was not one of totally untroubled success, however. Though sales increased annually, net income growth slowed in 1979 and actually decreased in 1980, 1981, and 1982. In 1982, sales growth itself was flat. Average sales per square foot of sales area were also falling. In 1981, K mart sold an average of $146 per square foot. In 1982, that figure dropped to $132 per square foot. In 1983, K mart average sales per square foot were up to $155, but this figure compared poorly to Target stores' figure of $172 per square foot that year. K mart also faced a falling inventory turnover figure. In 1981, inventory turned over only three and one half times, a sizable drop from the company's six times per year goal. Many factors within the retailing industry were affecting K mart's performance, factors which led K mart management to rethink its chain's position within that industry.

Changes in the Retailing Industry

The area of change in the retailing industry that had the most impact on K mart's performance had to do with an increasing demand on the part of consumers for quality in the products they bought. Mr. Fauber described the change in a speech to the New York Society of Security Analysts in 1983 by saying,

Today's consumer is much more experienced and wiser than in the 60s. Rising levels of education and consumerism and the impact of the media, particularly television, have resulted in a customer who knows how to determine good value for the money to a much greater extent than in the past. The more informed shopper has become a better shopper—not just for price, but also for value. Our research indicates that many more customers today would rather buy a better-quality product with the knowledge that it will provide a more useful economic life. But they still want these products at a good price.

Several different layers of customer wants, desires, and purchase preferences began to appear in the American retail scene. It was impossible for any one store to accommodate all these needs within one building. Many new retailers began to appear on the scene, zeroing in on changing lifestyles and tastes. These new store types were either upscale discounters or off-price specialty retailers, presenting customers with a new ambience and offering brand and designer merchandise priced some 20 to 70 percent below regular retail levels. Consumer loyalty to particular stores and convenient locations began to disappear as buyers shopped around for the best deals. This, in turn, increased competition among retailers to new heights. Retailers cut prices to boost store traffic and build store loyalties, but, in effect, they even further conditioned consumers to shop for value and price. The effects on K mart were expressed in an article in *Fortune,* which said,

> Regional discounters with more attractive stores and more fashionable products began to chip away at K mart's share of the market. New kinds of discounters picked off pieces of the company's domain: specialty stores began selling sports equipment, drugs and beauty products, books, apparel, and shoes. Catalog show-room houses moved in on small appliances and jewelry. . . . In this tough new market, K mart's style and quality did not keep pace with the public's taste.

The success of off-price retailers in the early 1980s rivaled that of K mart itself in the 1960s and 1970s. The total sales of off-price retailers were just $3 billion in 1979, but by 1982 sales totaled $7 billion, or nearly 6 percent of total industry sales in that year. Industry observers believed that this type of retail outlet would continue to grow by 30 to 35 percent annually through the end of the decade. This figure compared with a 10 percent expansion expected for the retail industry as a whole. As a result, it was estimated that off-price retailers could capture as much as 20 to 25 percent of total industry sales by 1987. Within the off-price group, growth rates were expected to be the highest for those retailers who were able to best capitalize on such demographic and economic trends as the new baby "boomlet," increasing numbers of households (especially one-person households), increasing numbers of elderly Americans, and a decline in the teenage population. In 1979, there were only a few hundred off-price retailers in the country. By 1984, it was estimated that there were between 4,000 and 5,000 such outlets operating in the United States. One industry analyst suggested why growth in this area would continue when he said, "I believe that every kind, every conceivable type of 'niche' retailing is going to be tested. More and more people are looking for the successful niche."

In general, off-price retailers served value-oriented middle- and upper-class consumers seeking upscale merchandise at discounted prices. Industry reports profiled the typical off-price shopper as "the suburban female in her 30s with a family income of $35,000."

Most discount retailers made changes that they hoped would appeal to the shoppers moving away from them to off-price stores. "Upscaling" by everyone became the name of the game. For many discounters, upscaling meant changing the selling environment of their stores with improved ambience, comfort, and convenience for shoppers. For most, it meant providing customers with a more appealing product mix with increased value in the products offered. To directly compete with the off-price and specialty discount operations, many discount chains began treating departments that were being chipped away by specialty stores or that fit defined demographic interests as "stores-within-a-store." Special attention was given to the layouts of these departments, giving them a newer, brighter, more separate appearance within the store. Also, the product mix within these departments was made deeper and broader than in departments that faced less competition from new types of retailers.

The goal of upscaling was to enhance competitive positions and attract a broader customer base. Upscaling was not meant to alienate customers who were already shopping discount stores, but instead was intended to make the stores also appeal to customers from higher economic levels. For example, apparel departments in discount stores began carrying an upgraded fashion mix, which included designer and brand name merchandise as well as improved private brands. In hard goods areas, inventories were being weighted more heavily toward branded goods, which provided increased product quality and customer satisfaction. This trend was summarized in the Standard & Poor's Retailing Industry Survey of July 4, 1985, as follows:

> In contrast to their off-price and department store counterparts, discounters have traditionally geared their mix to less affluent, less fashion-conscious shoppers, and stressed price over quality. More recently, however, leading chains have been "upscaling," both to accommodate the higher income level and shopping savvy of today's prototypical discount store shopper and to attract middle-income customers. Upscaling strategies generally entail adjusting the merchandise mix to include more name brands, lacing existing lines with higher-quality, pricier items, and reformatting and sprucing up the stores themselves.

The result of these upscaling activities was that everyone was copying everybody else, and all the stores began to resemble each other. They were all fighting for the same customers. As one president of a discount chain put it, "We are all selling things that can be purchased elsewhere."

All of these changes in retailing were taking place in conjunction with a long-term drop in per capita spending on general merchandise by U.S. consumers. Per capita spending on general merchandise had dropped 24 percent since the mid-1970s. Industry analysts, looking at this trend, pointed to the failure of several marginal retailing organizations and the subpar profitability of many others as proof that the retailing industry as a whole was "overstored."

The growing similarity of merchandise mix within discount stores, the desire to reach the same consumer groups, and the excess retailing space in the country led to a sharp increase in promotional competition within the retailing industry. Discount retailers began lowering prices on already-discounted products to gain customer traffic and maintain market share in dollar sales. This only encouraged consumers to search further for the best value for their dollar, forcing discounters to continue price promotions in order to maintain position within the industry.

K mart's Image

With the arrival of off-price and discount specialty stores, discount stores in general lost ground in the fight for consumer dollars. The situation was summarized by Fred Wintzer of Lehman Brothers' Kuhn Loeb in 1983 when he said,

> Consumers believed the merchandise carried by discounters was of less than high quality and that the stores were too often out of stock. When items were in stock, shoppers found them difficult to locate. Finally, discount stores were perceived as cluttered, as lacking the neatness of other general merchandise outlets. And K mart was the ''king'' of the discounters.

Though all discounters were in a fight to maintain sales and market share, K mart, as the largest discounter, had the most to lose and perhaps had to make the most changes if it was to maintain its leadership position. Mr. Norman G. Milley, K mart's executive vice president of merchandising and subsidiaries, assessed the company's position in the early 1980s when he said,

> We recognized a need to reanalyze the K mart position in the consumer's eyes. We took a great number of surveys and were able to determine that we had the price image but did not have the quality image. We had excellent locations, good traffic and customer acceptance, but we were not selling enough merchandise to many of our customers.
>
> We had narrowly defined the K mart customer and were not accepting the fact that these customers were going elsewhere to buy merchandise that we were not offering. We determined that we could sell those coming to K mart more kinds of products than we were carrying. Why could we not sell much higher-ticket merchandise if we presented it properly?

Low prices had always been K mart's strength. Now the image the company had tried to develop for itself when the chain first began was becoming a liability. Now shoppers were looking for value; yes, they were still looking for good prices, but for quality products at a good price. K mart had a very weak quality reputation among consumers. K mart had to take action in several areas to overcome this low-quality image.

K mart's Changes

K mart's consumer research showed that, although sales were leveling off and net income was falling in the early 1980s, the chain's customer count was not decreasing. Over half the people in the country still shopped a K mart at least once a month. People were still coming to K mart for basic needs, but they were not shopping in the store's more ''ego-centered'' departments like apparel or household furnishings. For these products, K mart shoppers were going elsewhere. The task for K mart was to convince customers to buy more products while in a K mart. The company decided to fight its long-standing image of a low-income, blue-collar store. The goal was to increase sales to the customer group composed of family members aged 25 to 44 with children by offering products that this group wanted. As Mr. Fauber explained it, K mart wanted to increase its interest to its more affluent customers, those who regularly popped into a K mart for the regular price advantage they found for such items as toothpaste or tennis balls. By updating K mart, it was hoped that these customers would stay in the store longer and spend more money on a wider mix of goods.

As a first attempt to reach these goals, K mart's executives felt that all that was needed was an updating of the appearance of the stores and improved stocking methods. It was obvious to them that the stores were dull, and they believed that dull interiors reflected on the quality of the products in the store. Improving the appearance of the stores would improve the impression the stores gave the merchandise. This action was taken first since K mart executives believed that the major advantage regional discounters had over K mart were their clean, bright, modern interiors.

To improve appearance, continuous bands of poppy red, gold, and white were placed in the floor tiles to delineate department areas but yet to encourage shoppers to browse from area to area. Each department was located using the wall signs that continued the color theme used in the floor tile. Individual merchandise signs were standardized and displayed sparingly. Taller, graduated counters were installed. These made better use of vertical space and eliminated visual clutter. They promoted a sweeping view of K mart's merchandise variety. The goal was to present a ''complete store'' message. With a new simplified, low-key atmosphere, the aim was to let the merchandise speak for itself.

K mart management soon found that the decor changes were very unsuccessful. They soon came to the conclusion that the problem did not lie with the way in which the merchandise was displayed, but rather in the merchandise offered in the stores. Mr. Ed Willer, vice president of E. F. Hutton, described K mart's slowness at realizing the true problem when he said, ''For a long time the mousetrap worked so well that it didn't even cross the minds of K mart management to change it. K mart didn't feel it was necessary to fundamentally change what they offered the American consumer.'' Mr. Fauber himself admitted that the company may have become so engrossed with adding square footage that it neglected a more vital ingredient of success, the stores' contents.

K mart's next changes were based on extensive studies of their customers. The management wanted to learn what K mart's customers wanted and what they were likely to want in the future. The first idea to come from these consumer studies was a belief that young homeowners were concerned with maintaining or improving the condition of their homes, as well as getting the best value possible in that work. The result of this was the development of the Homecare Center, a department that was given the status of a "specialty" shop and encompassed 15,000 square feet of space within a K mart store. The Homecare Center consolidated many former departments, including building materials, hardware, power tools, electrical equipment, and lighting, into one area with everything the home do-it-yourselfer would need for fix-up or repair projects. This department was given a distinctive blue-and-white sign to signify its store-within-a-store importance.

The Homecare Center was a great success. Its acceptance encouraged K mart to try other new product mixes. K mart buyers were told to experiment with product purchases and to buy what they thought could be sold. Several different product mix formulations were tried out in prototype stores in different parts of the country. Twenty-five such stores were called "lead stores." In these, new product mixes featured a total selection of name brand products and designer apparel, with the elimination of all private label merchandise. Lead stores were located in higher-income neighborhoods. Other prototype stores, called "future" stores, offered "better-priced" merchandise made by some of the finest manufacturers in the country, but sold under labels other than those normally sold in department stores. The positive responses these trial stores received convinced K mart's management that K mart had not previously carried the products customers wanted on its shelves. The decision was made to stock the K mart chain with a combination of the two trial mixes. K marts would carry more name brand, more designer, and more high-quality private label goods. Although K mart management knew that there was great diversity among the economic status of the neighborhoods their stores served, they were committed to the idea that K mart was a national chain and that the vast majority of the goods carried by one K mart should be in all K marts. Consumers, they believed, should be presented with a national image of the K mart chain, knowing that products they expected in K mart would be found in all stores in the chain. Eighty percent of K mart's merchandise was standardized on a national basis. Store managers were left free to fine-tune 10 to 20 percent of the product mix in their stores in an effort to appeal directly to local markets, be they rural or urban, black or Hispanic, high or low income.

As higher-quality, higher-priced products were added to the K mart line, the traditional products and their low price points were retained. This policy was explained by Mr. Larry Parkin, chairman and CEO of K mart apparel. He said,

> The tactic is to add on at the top of the line, not to abandon the low end. People who bought in the middle of the range, the thinking goes, will step up. K mart will always have the lower price points because if we didn't have the $9 sweater, lots of people would have no sweater at all.

Items that traditional K mart customers expected to find in the store were still there. The new products were added to appeal to customers who wanted higher quality and who had gone elsewhere to find these products in the past.

More national brands began to appear in K marts. It became common to find such products as Armstrong Solarian no-wax tiles, Corelle dinnerware, Rogers stainless flatware, Libbey glassware, Sharp microwaves, and General Electric food processors in K mart stores. Seiko watches were now carried in the jewelry department along with the familiar K mart line of Timex watches. Casio and Sharp calculators could now be found in the electronics departments. Minolta 35-mm cameras were added to the familiar Kodak lines in the camera departments. Now 14k gold jewelry could be found at the jewelry counter near K mart's less expensive merchandise. More fashionable, brand name clothing was added to each apparel department. Brand names with higher price points became the rule and not the exception at K marts.

In order to make room for this line extension program, K mart began to make use of higher display fixtures, which allowed for additional cubic space usage. For example, in apparel departments, "pipe run" displays, which allowed only the shoulders of garments to be readily visible to customers, were replaced with open, circular racks. Using these racks, the entire front of a garment was plainly visible to the shopper. Other new types of fixtures, called "waterfall" displays, were trilevel and allowed the showing of coordinating slacks, blouses, and jackets on one display.

Other specialty departments began to appear and receive a store-within-a-store status. Housewares became The Kitchen Korner. This department now carried more than just low-cost kitchen utensils. Now the shopper could find cookware by such names as Farberware, Revere Ware, and Club Aluminum. Small kitchen appliances carried such brand names as General Electric, Sunbeam, Oster, and Norelco. Mixing bowls and utensils were now Pyrex. The belief was that the more knowledgeable consumer would know these brands and recognize the value that also came with the K mart price.

The linen department was now called the Bed and Bath Shop. This department was greatly expanded, using new display fixtures to better show off the improved variety and quality of the store's selection of sheets, blankets, towels, bathroom rugs, pillows, and bedspreads. Brand names made available included Pepperill and Springmaid.

Totally new product lines were also introduced. The new Home Electronics department carried name brand computer equipment priced below $500. Also carried were nationally advertised computer software, as well as national brand and private label TVs, VCRs, and a wide range of other video and audio equipment. Where it was believed that demand would be great enough, K mart introduced, expanded, or upgraded other departments, such as nutrition and health food centers, wicker shops, unpainted furniture, hard- and softcover book assortments, and stationery and greeting card departments. These were designed to take advantage of demographic trends. An expansion of the number of K mart pharmacies and automotive service departments was also begun.

Changes for K mart Corporation were not limited to adjustments within the company's discount store chain. The corporation began diversifying into other businesses designed to improve the company's profit performance. K mart Corporation purchased two cafeteria-style restaurant chains, Furr's Cafeteria and Bishop's Buffet, and began expanding the number of these outlets. This move was taken because K mart management believed that eating away from the home would continue to be a growing aspect of American life. Furthermore, these restaurant chains offered low-priced, homestyle cooking, something K mart management thought fit well with K mart's image. Following the lead of Sears, K mart introduced K mart Insurance Services to several stores in the South. The corporation was also moving into new forms of retailing to compete directly with the new off-price outlets. In 1982, K mart began opening off-price women's apparel stores, called Designer Depots, which offered only national brand clothing at discount prices. The company was also developing new discount gift shops, called Accents. These stores offered top-of-the-line home fashions and accessories, such as Limoge china and Oneida silver, at discount prices. K mart also entered into a joint venture with Hechinger Company of Washington, D.C., to develop large, free-standing warehouse-style discount home centers, to be called Builders Square.

Changes were also made in the message delivered by K mart's $580 million advertising budget. K mart advertising had long focused on telling customers of special low prices on specific items within the store. The goods advertised were often special loss-leader items designed to bring buyers into the stores, hoping that they would purchase other items while there as well as those products specially priced. In its change in advertising message, K mart began to advertise whole categories of goods or entire departments within the store. Especially featured in the ads were higher-ticketed, upscale merchandise. K mart wanted its customers to know that the chain now carried better-quality merchandise in departments that offered shoppers a wider range of goods to choose from than ever before.

K mart's Concerns

While trying to better attract those customers with higher incomes and an interest in purchasing products of higher price and value, K mart had to be careful not to alienate its traditional customers who came to its stores for low prices. K mart executives were concerned that the firm might have the same problems that W. T. Grant and Sears had when they upgraded the products in their stores. W. T. Grant's image with consumers became confused. Shoppers were not certain whether the chain was still in the discount business or was becoming a regular department store. W. T. Grant went out of business. When Sears increased the quality and price points on its merchandise, lower-income customers left Sears for discount stores. To win these shoppers back, Sears promoted bargains aggressively, but found its traditional shoppers returned to buy the bargains but little else. K mart did not want to confuse or alienate its traditional customer base. K mart's management was strong in its assertion that the chain was not "upscaling" as these competitors had done. It was not trying to bring in new shoppers, but just to provide the merchandise its present customers wanted. As explained by Mr. Fauber in late 1985,

> Many people studying K mart failed to understand the difference between "trading up," offering a higher-priced product at a higher margin, and K mart's approach of "updating," which was selling a higher-priced product, yes, but at our normal markup, and in the process giving the consumer a better value even than before.

K mart management was also concerned that a low-price, low-fashion, low-quality image could not be easily erased, especially during a period of high competitiveness within the industry. It was a difficult problem to balance the need to let consumers know that the stores had new merchandise of higher quality to offer while not stressing this message to the point where it alienated the company's traditional customer base. K mart needed to convince both the customers who had always relied on K mart for price and those that it was trying to attract more spending from that K mart had become a "smarter place to shop." This message would take time to get across to consumers.

The process of establishing a new image for K mart was made even more difficult by the time it took to make the physical changes in store layout, merchandise display, and merchandise purchasing for a chain of over 2,000 stores. One hundred and twenty-six crews were employed to transform the stores. In 1983, 715 Home Electronic Centers were in place, with another 750 planned for that year. In 1984, 650 Kitchen Korners, 125 Homecare Centers, and several hundred Bed and Bath departments were scheduled for completion. The entire changeover of the chain would take more than five years. The cost of refurbishing a store ran between $80,000 and $500,000. Three hundred million dollars was planned for this program in 1983 alone. The total cost of store renovations would be in excess of $1.25 billion for the period 1981 to 1986. Even spending at this pace, the length of time it took to complete the in-store changes delayed K mart's ability to present a new, chainwide image to the public. It would only confuse consumers to see brand name products in K mart ads if these products were not yet in their local store.

The question also remained as to how far K mart could go toward upgrading the quality and price of the products it sold. By 1984, the specialty departments within K marts were achieving and often surpassing management's goal of sales of $200 per square foot of sales space. Could the merchandise mix be even further raised, resulting in even better sales results? By continued merchandise mix trials, K mart management soon realized that there were limits to what consumers were willing to buy in a K mart store. For example, they found customers unwilling to purchase such items as down pillows or $50 blankets in K mart Bed and Bath departments. Shoppers who purchased items like these bought them in regular department stores or in linen specialty shops.

K mart shoppers looked for synthetic-filled pillows and blankets with a top price range of $25. K mart management believed that the stores had to carry predominantly common merchandise mixes across the country. This meant that products that were carried in K marts were carried in all 2,000 stores, and therefore were purchased in massive volumes. There was little room to take gambles on the merchandise to be purchased for the chain. Before an order for a certain product was placed, K mart management wanted to be sure the item would sell.

Opinions of K mart's Success

Opinions expressed in national retailing and business magazines and reports by executives in the retailing industry and industry analysts about what success K mart could expect from all the changes the company had made were as varied as the number of types of retail organizations that existed to serve the American consumer. Excerpts from some of these publications and reports are given below to show some of the controversy that existed regarding K mart's future.

> The hopeful view is that Fauber's moves will yield a resumption of K mart's swift growth and ample profitability. . . . The counterview is that K mart in 1983 is simply grasping for straws. Fauber seems to recognize that the old strategy of forced-draft expansion no longer works. But so far he's replaced it with assorted remedies, not with a well-defined growth strategy. Not with the kind of game plan that made K mart the retailing phenomenon of the 1960s and early 1970s.
>
> Stephen Taub
> *Financial World*
> March 31, 1983

> Other retailers have a stronger position, better profitability, know what they are doing, and have a game plan that's working.
>
> Jeffrey Edelman
> Smith Barney

> Will there be enough off-price merchandise available to meet K mart's huge needs? Will makers of quality-name clothes want to have their merchandise associated with the K mart image? Will the new, more label-conscious customers K mart hopes to attract respond to its bait?
>
> David Taylor
> Prudential-Bache

> The success of private labels hinges on the store's reputation for quality.
>
> Standard & Poor's Industry Surveys
> *Retailing Industry*
> July 4, 1985

The demographic trends are not going K mart's way. To retailing analysts, the most attractive customer group in the near future will be the fast-growing population of 25- to 44-year-old college graduates living in suburbia and making

$20,000 to $35,000 a year from professional and managerial jobs. The typical K mart customer is a blue-collar high school graduate in the $15,000 to $25,000 income bracket. K mart is at the wrong place at the wrong time.

> Fred Wintzer, Jr.
> Lehman Brothers' Kuhn Loeb

On competition, I've seen a definite move toward upgrading. We're not doing that. We're trying to maintain our niche, while several competitors are going after more of the middle- and maybe slightly higher-than-middle-income customer. Hopefully, they will leave more customers on the lower end for us. What we are doing is emphasizing customer treatment, obviously making our store a nicer place to shop in. That's an important factor.

> President of Wal-Mart Stores
> *Discount Merchandiser*
> September 1985

Asked where the blue-collar people will go for their apparel, K mart replies: "We are still going to maintain those price points that K mart is famous for. They may be on the back of the rack, but they are going to be there. We are not going to avoid them."

> *Discount Merchandiser*
> July 1984

K mart sales per square foot improved 9 percent in 1983 to $155, following a 3 percent decline in 1982. A more upward movement is indicated by the 5.5 percent increase in comparable store sales for the first quarter of 1984. In the case of some remodeled stores, sales have been running 40 percent better than a year ago. How much of the improvement is due to remodeling and how much is due to a change in merchandise is a fine point, and not entirely relevant so long as productivity climbs.

> *Chain Store Age Executive*
> August 1984

People usually think of the K mart customer as a blue-collar worker whose wife works and has a household income of about $22,000 a year. But the K mart customer is the customer who works and lives near the store.

> Mr. Samuel G. Leftwich
> President of K mart Corporation

Our stores are changing faster than ever before. We're not doing Saks or Lord & Taylor or an upscale department store. We're upgrading, but keeping within our customers' price point.

> Larry Parkin
> Chairman and CEO of K mart Apparel

K mart feels that it has gained new and better-heeled customers. Citing Simmons' research, the company says that 23.3 percent of K mart customers in 1980 had family incomes from $25,000 to $40,000, but by the end of 1984, the new program and advertising had pushed that customer income figure up to 28.1 percent. Also, in 1980 only 8.3 percent of K mart's customers had annual incomes of $40,000 or more. Now, that share has risen to 18.9 percent, according to the company.

Chain Store Age Executive
August 1984

The notion of quality is, by no means, an easy one to nail down. As Fauber says, it is a concept influenced in a number of ways through "convenience, store ambience, advertising, availability of product, service, and employee attitude."

Discount Merchandiser
September 1985

The difficulty of K mart's task in presenting a new image to America can be shown by the round of applause and laughter the following jokes received when they were included in Johnny Carson's monologue in February 1986:

You know, K mart has made a lot of changes. They now offer valet parking at the front door for your pickup. Inside, I see that they have gotten rid of the used underwear bin. They've made a lot of new room by getting rid of the checkout where you could exchange livestock for household appliances. You notice the change right away—as soon as you walk in, you hear over the loudspeaker, "Pardonez moi, K mart shoppers. . . ."

Case 15

Nigerian Hoechst Limited*

Introduction

In June 1982, Mr. Otto Revier, marketing manager for Nigerian Hoechst Limited (NHL), was preparing his marketing plan presentation for a new pharmaceutical product for the Nigerian market. Before he could proceed with the new product introduction, Mr. Revier had several superiors to satisfy, including Mr. Heinz-Hermann Helms, deputy regional manager (Africa, Central and Latin America) for Hoechst A. G. (HAG), the parent company, which was headquartered in Frankfurt, West Germany. As Mr. Revier looked over his preliminary ideas for the new analgesic product code-named Product H, he decided to review all the data he had on Daga, the product which had been NHL's first venture into the over-the-counter (OTC) market in Nigeria. Daga had been a wonderful success for NHL with first-year sales of ₦1.75 million.[1] Mr. Revier was well aware that not only would Product H's results be compared to Daga's, but also Product H must not unduly cannibalize Daga's sales. Mr. Revier was expected to submit his plans for approval as soon as possible. With this in mind, he began to review all the information he had on the Nigerian market, Daga, and Product H.

---

* This case was written by Professor Michael R. Pearce. It is intended as a basis for classroom discussion, and not as an illustration of effective or ineffective handling of an administrative situation. Some data in this case have been disguised.

Copyright © 1984 by IMEDE (l'Institut pour l'Etude des Methodes de Direction de l'Entreprise), Lausanne, Switzerland, and School of Business Administration, The University of Western Ontario. Used with permission.

[1] Currency: The naira is the official currency of Nigeria, signified by an ₦. One naira equals 100 kobo. Coins are ½ (note there were hardly any ½-kobo coins), 1, 5, 10, and 20 kobo. Notes are 50 kobo, 1, 5, 10, and 20 naira. During the time of most of the case events, the ₦ floated with the U.S. dollar, ranging from $1.83 in 1980, $1.63 in 1981, to $1.47 in 1982. The deutsche mark (DM) was used in most of HAG Group records. The average rate of exchange in 1980 was 1 ₦ = DM3.20, DM3.30 in 1981, and DM3.50 in 1982. Management forecasted an exchange rate of DM3.40 in 1983. Because of uncertainty, NHL company officials typically used a 3-to-1 ratio of DM to ₦ in most of their planning for NHL. Because of the volatile currency situation, naira values have been shown throughout the case.

Hoechst A. G.

Hoechst A.G. was founded in 1863 by two German chemists and two German businessmen in the small city of Hoechst on the banks of the Main River near Frankfurt, West Germany. They began with dyes and colouring agents, entering pharmaceuticals in 1883 with new products to combat fever and headaches. By 1982, the Hoechst Group was involved in a very wide variety of product lines including pharmaceuticals, crop protection chemicals, printing plates, waste water purification methods, disease diagnostic systems, plant and animal nutrition, roof covering and paints for buildings, packaging films, fibres, plastics, facsimile copiers, electronics chemicals, and industrial gases. The Hoechst Group operated in 140 countries, employing 182,154 people in 1982.

In 1981, sales of the entire HAG Group were DM34,435 million and net profit after taxes was DM426 million. Approximately 65 percent of sales were from outside the Federal Republic of Germany. Pharmaceutical sales were very nearly DM6,000 million, representing 17 percent of total Group sales in 1981.

Nigerian Hoechst Limited

HAG started its activities in Nigeria in the mid-1950s using a local importer and distributor called Major & Co. to handle its pharmaceutical products. A representative of HAG was stationed in Nigeria to promote Hoechst products, but soon after local pharmacists were hired to intensify this effort. NHL Limited was formed on December 18, 1963, under the name of Hoechst Products Nigeria Limited (HPN). This company was jointly owned by Hoechst and Major & Co. HPN Ltd. sold the entire HAG product range except pharmaceuticals. The name was changed to Nigerian Hoechst Limited in 1973 to reflect the transfer of Major & Co.'s shares to a local company called Chief Ashamu Holdings. This change was in accordance with Nigerian government indigenization policies, that is, local ownership of companies. Indigenization had been promoted strongly since 1972, with the 1977 decree the strictest yet of three major policy positions on the matter. According to Nigerian law, NHL was classified a "Schedule II local manufacturer and own importer." Foreign equity was restricted to 40 percent. NHL could undertake both local manufacture and import activities and thus could be relatively flexible and coordinate all their activities. There was no pressure on NHL to manufacture or repack all its product range within the country.

Until 1981, the NHL pharmaceutical (pharma) business involved ethical and semi-ethical products such as Novalgin, Baralgin, small spectrum antibiotics, Berenil, Lasix, Reverin, Daonil, and Claforan. NHL pharma business in Nigeria prior to 1974 was handled by an agency, Major & Co., who also handled other pharmaceutical companies. NHL pharmaceutical business up to 1974 did not develop as rapidly in Nigeria as expected. Management of HAG believed the major difficulties had been the agency distribution arrangement, with problems such as conflict with other principals regarding the assortment, shortage of stocks, and delays in payments of accounts receivable. The relative lack of attention Hoechst was receiving prompted HAG management to place the pharma business under the same roof as other HAG divisions in NHL. NHL not only looked after HAG products and subsidiaries (such as Optrex) but also represented three other pharmaceutical companies (Roussel, Schering, and Nattermann) in importing, warehousing, and physical distribution. These companies had their own marketing and sales people in Nigeria. NHL management, as they moved from agency distribution to their own direct distribution, realized that they needed sales branches throughout the country, a qualified sales and promotion force, and their own distribution system.

Establishing its own infrastructure became a clear priority for NHL because of the chaotic market infrastructure in Nigeria. As of 1973, NHL was headquartered at Ikeja, just outside Lagos. Industrial chemicals were produced at Ikeja, and pharmaceutical production began at Otta in 1982. There were five pharma branches—Lagos, Ibadan, Benin, Aba, and Kano—in 1981. Branches were planned for Jos in 1982 and Kaduna and Maiduguri in 1983. NHL staff levels had increased steadily during the 1980s. In 1980, there were 40 field force members and 104 additional staff. By 1982, the field force had grown to 55 and the additional staff had increased to 126.

From 1974 to 1980, NHL pharma sales increased tenfold. NHL was divided into two major divisions, industrial and pharmaceutical. With a 41 percent increase in sales from 1979 to 1980 (partly due to a 25 percent price increase), pharma division with ₦17 million sales[2] (DM51 million) accounted for one third of NHL sales in 1980. Pharma division profits of ₦2.7 million (DM8.1 million) were 65 percent of total NHL profits that same year. Total NHL sales were ₦41.8 million for 1981, and total profit for the same year was ₦4.0 million. This moved NHL pharma sales from 22nd in the Hoechst group worldwide rankings in 1979 to 11th largest pharma operation in 1981. Further data are shown in Table 1.

TABLE 1 NHL pharma sales and profit summary (in ₦ million and percent)

Year	Sales (including agencies)	Growth (percent)	Hoechst pharma sales	Growth (percent)	Hoechst Consolidated profit
1976	4.9	64%	4.2	54%	(.313)
1977	8.4	72	6.1	45	(1.306)
1978	8.6	3	5.6	(8)	(1.572)
1979	12.2	41	8.6	54	330
1980	17.0	41	11.3	31	2.581
1981	23.0	35	15.5	39	4.217

In 1980 dipyrone products (Novalgin and Baralgin) accounted for 48 percent of Hoechst pharma sales. However, there were several concerns being expressed about dipyrone by various international groups, which led NHL

---

[2] Figures include agency operations for Roussel, Schering, Nattermann, and Optrex.

management to believe they should not be so dependent on products containing this substance. Further, Novalgin constituted a substantial proportion of NHL's government business. Government customers had become serious accounts receivable problems—in 1981–82, government outstandings were about 10 months' sales, leading NHL management to believe that reliance on government business had to be reduced.

The Hoechst product line had been predominantly ethical, but this kept NHL out of at least one third of the Nigerian market, that is, the OTC market. Further, new ethical products showed promise only over the mid to long term. Introduction of new ethical products in Nigeria was a slow process because of the substantial conservatism of Nigerian prescribers and dispensers. Further, management believed that the pharmaceutical market would not grow appreciably in the ethical area until there were significantly more doctors in Nigeria. This analysis led management to examine the OTC market.

Nigeria

The Federal Republic of Nigeria in 1982 was the most populous African country, although only the 12th largest geographically. With 923,768 square kilometres in area, Nigeria was about the same size as France, West Germany, and the United Kingdom combined or 50 percent larger than Texas of the United States. Many sources estimated that Nigeria was one of the world's 10 most populous nations and that one in five Africans was Nigerian, although these statements were difficult to confirm. Nigerian population figures were very imprecise because most estimates were still based on the only reliable source, the 1963 census; however, NHL management believed population was growing at an annual rate of 2.7 to 3.5 percent. Using NHL figures, population was 88.2 million in 1980 (the UN estimate was 77.1 million), rising to 94.5 million in 1982.

Half the population was thought to be under 15 years of age. Using the 1963 census applied to the estimated 1982 population, the age structure was as follows:

Age group	Percent
0–4	17.2%
5–9	15.2
10–14	10.7
15–19	9.4
20–24	12.4
25–29	10.0
30–34	7.8
35–39	4.5
40–44	4.3
45–49	2.1
50–54	2.2
55–59	0.8
60–64	1.4
65–69	0.5

There was a very wide range of ethnic, linguistic, cultural, and religious groupings in Nigeria despite efforts of the federal government to create a single national identity. There were some 400 ethnic groups, of which three predominated: the Hausa-Fulani in the north, the Ibo in the southeast, and the Yoruba in the southwest. The north was mainly Islamic and suspicious of westernization (modernization, Christianity, etc.). The north contained 79 percent of the country's area and, in terms of the 1963 census, 54 percent of the population. The western region (which included Lagos) had 8 percent of the land and 17 percent of the population. The eastern region (which had the oil) had 8 percent of the land and 22 percent of the population. The midwest had 4 percent of the land and only 4.5 percent of the population. Often, observers divided the country into north and south. In this sense, the south included the western, eastern, and midwest regions. The south was westernized and moving decades ahead of the north in development. The north was more rural, less industrialized, lower income, about 67 percent in farming, accounted for about 35 percent of national income, and had an illiteracy rate approaching 85 percent. The south was more urban, more industrialized, had higher incomes, had about 45 percent in farming, accounted for 65 percent of national income, and had a lower illiteracy rate. Approximately 34 percent of the adult population were thought to be literate by 1980. The official language was English. Hausa, Ibo, and Yoruba were the principal languages spoken in the north, east, and west, respectively. Exhibit 1 shows a map of Nigeria.

EXHIBIT 1 Map of Nigeria

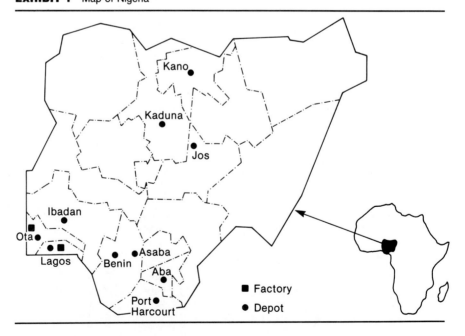

Nigeria has had a great deal of difficulty because of tribalism, which has caused much disagreement about political leaders, territorial divisions, etc., and has often resulted in violence and civil war. Nigeria became independent in 1960. There was a bloody civil war from 1967 to 1970. There have been several coups; of its first four heads of state, three were killed in office and the fourth was deposed and exiled. Nigeria was under military rule for 13 years until 1979.

There were 19 Nigerian states as of February 1982 (24 were proposed by the government in late 1981) and five political parties. The system was patterned after that of the United States, requiring five sets of elections. A general election was coming in August 1983. These would be the first elections organized by civilian as opposed to military authorities. It was the general expectation that the government would be reelected and that its main priorities would be overcoming current economic problems, the shift of the capital to Abuja (a new federal capital territory), and the creation of further states to facilitate better government.

The rate of drift of population from rural to urban was more pronounced than in almost any other developing nation. Exact populations of cities also were unknown. Here is an estimate as of 1982:

City	Estimated population
Lagos	4.5 million
Ibadan	2.3 million
Kano	750,000
Ilorin	600,000
Port Harcourt	450,000
Kaduna	420,000
Maiduguri	420,000
Ogbomosho	370,000
Oshogbo	265,000
Benin City	265,000
Enugu	265,000
Abeokuta	245,000
Sokoto	185,000
Jos	185,000
Owerri	185,000

Nigeria was a member of OPEC and in 1981 was the world's ninth largest producer of oil. Agriculture used to be the mainstay of the Nigerian economy; but after the development of oil, agriculture dropped to about 20 percent of gross domestic product (GDP) by 1981, even though it still employed about two thirds to three fourths of the working population. GDP at current prices was estimated at ₦39,939 million in 1979, ₦43,280 in 1980, and ₦43,450 in 1981. Adjusted for inflation, 1981 was down by 2 percent. GDP real growth averaged approximately 8 percent throughout the 1970s.

Nigeria had become very dependent on oil income (about 90 percent of the country's foreign exchange earnings and 80 percent of government revenues) and experienced a dramatic decline in this between 1980 and 1981. The trade deficit in 1980 was close to U.S. $5,000 million, which, combined with an outflow of service payments, meant a current deficit of over $7,500 million in 1981. For this reason, the government attempted to cut imports by one third in 1982 and to place greater emphasis on developing Nigerian import replacement industries. However, despite the decline in oil income, Nigeria was regarded as the richest country in Sub-Saharan Africa. Roughly 55 percent of revenues went to the federal government, 35 percent to the states, and 10 percent to local governments.

Gross national income was estimated by NHL management to be ₦50,599 million in 1980, ₦60,000 million in 1981, dropping to ₦57,000 million in 1982. Income per capita was estimated to be ₦574 in 1980 and ₦603 in 1982. Estimates of GDP varied remarkably. Nigerian sources estimated 1981 GDP at ₦54,000 million.

The rate of inflation was high. NHL management estimated it to be 20 percent in 1980, 15 percent in 1981, and 12 percent in 1982. *Business International* ranked Lagos as the world's most expensive city in 1981. Using 1975 equals 100, a composite consumer price index combining urban and rural centres showed all items at 189.2 in 1979, 219.5 in 1980, 257.5 in 1981, and 275.7 at the end of 1982.

Nigerians were on balance extremely poor (approximately one car per 1,000 population), had high malnutrition and disease caused by dietary deficiencies, suffered inadequate standards of environmental hygiene and a shortage of medical facilities, and had a life expectancy at birth of 48 years.

The Nigerian Market for Pharmaceuticals

The pharmaceutical market in Nigeria depended on the disease patterns in the country, the health care system, and the activities of the pharmaceutical companies. The health problems of the country were attributed to the poor quality of public works and education. As of 1979, the prevalent illnesses and causes of death were quite different from those in developed countries. According to a *Business International* 1979 report on Nigeria:

Most prevalent illnesses	*Leading causes of death*
Malaria	Pneumonia
Dysentery	Malaria
Gonorrhea	Cerebrospinal meningitis
Pneumonia	Tetanus
Measles	Infectious hepatitis
Tuberculosis	Tuberculosis

Malaria remained the most commonly reported of notifiable diseases in Nigeria, with its incidence in 1981 at 1,694 cases per 100,000 population. The difficulty with any Nigerian health statistic was that less than a third of the population had access to conventional health facilities, so statistics over-emphasized disease patterns in the urban areas. Nonetheless, this pattern of disease meant that the medical needs in Nigeria were for antibiotics, analgesics, vitamins, and tonics. Pharmaceutical usage was quite different from the German market HAG served. For example, various sources compared the market structures in 1981 as follows:

Nigeria	Percent	Germany	Percent
Analgesics	16%	Antirheumatics	6%
Antibiotics	16	Vasodilators	5
Vitamins/tonics	12	Cough and cold	5
Antimalarials	8	Anti-infectives	4
Cough and cold	4	Psychotropics	4
Psychotropics	2	Analgesics	4
Antirheumatics	2	Vasoprotectors	4
Cardiovascular	2	Cardiac-glycosides	3
Antispasmodics	1	Antihypertonics	3

Mr. Jeffrey Ford, marketing manager for the Pharma Division of NHL from February 1980 to March 1982, explained the thinking behind offering a pain and fever remedy in Nigeria as follows:

> Analgesics are a very important product for Nigerians because of the way they live. The Nigerian lives in a climate that contributes to all sorts of exotic tropical diseases. For example, the average Nigerian is stricken with a case of malaria perhaps once a month, diarrhea probably twice a month, and a headache probably once or twice a week. Sanitation is hopelessly substandard, resulting in impure water, proliferation of parasites, and other problems. Further, the average Nigerian has a diet very different from our standards. Instead of a balance of protein, carbohydrates, and minerals, his diet is about 90 percent carbohydrates, which means his body does not get what it should, and malfunction results. Add these factors to the environment of heat, humidity, and dirt and you can see why analgesic consumption is so much higher than in Europe and North America.

Enormous expenditures were planned in public health care in the Nigerian 1975–80 Plan. For example, the plan called for an increase in doctors per million inhabitants from 45 in 1972 to 71 in 1980. Although the Nigerian population was estimated to be nearing 100 million people, only 12 to 20 million Nigerians were thought to have access to the Nigerian governmental medical facilities.

There were free public health care facilities provided at three levels: federal, state, and local. The federal government concentrated much of its expenditure in teaching hospitals at the expense of expanding primary health care. The federal Ministry of Health accounted for roughly half of the total state expenditure on health. The most important federal program for pharmaceutical manufacturers was the Basic Health Service Scheme, which was to initially establish 256 health centres across the country for primary health care. Ultimately, the plan called for about 4,000 health care units and to have the whole population within five kilometres of a dispensary or primary clinic. This program ran into many problems, not the least of which was disagreement among tribal leaders as to where initial units would be located.

The state governments were generally responsible for their own health care outside the teaching hospitals. On the whole, each state was autonomous in health care. There were many malpractices evident to pharmaceutical companies dealing with state health care officials. Some products purchased by institutions were subsequently sold on the private market.

Local governments focused almost completely on prenatal, postnatal, and pediatric activities.

By the end of 1979, Nigeria had a total of 69,670 hospital beds and was expected to have around 82,000 in mid-1982. Facilities as of 1979:

	Hospitals	Health centres	Clinics
North	189	288	4,521
West	196	53	1,850
East	255	197	1,030
Midwest	75	58	611
Total	715	596	8,012

Government hospitals and clinics were chronically short of funds and staff, resulting in less than adequate service levels in the opinion of many. Consequently, private health care facilities were being developed in the major urban areas and particularly in Lagos. Companies in particular were investing in this development.

Undercapitalization of the governmental health care system led to drug shortages and slower than expected development of the institutional market by pharmaceutical companies and led to a substantial growth in the self-medication OTC market. According to *Business International,* there were two principal segments of the Nigerian pharmaceutical market. The urban population, about 10 percent of the total, already provided a considerable and rapidly growing market. As it expanded in size and wealth, it was expected to take a larger share of the total market. The public sector, comprising the federal and state governments and public corporations, was also growing fast and would provide more and more opportunities for the drug companies. On the other hand, the purchasing power of the masses was expected to develop more slowly, with deep-rooted traditions, beliefs, and tastes posing major challenges to consumer goods marketers. For the foreseeable future, according to *Business International,* Nigeria was primarily a market for infrastructure (roads, telecommunications equipment, port installations, schools, hospitals, clinics, hotels, etc.) all over the country. And alongside these capital purchases there would be a market for the supplies used—medicines, hospital and school equipment, books, cables, and so on.

It was very difficult to estimate the size of the market. Not only were population and medical statistics inaccurate and unreliable, but there were problems of definition, such as which products were pharmaceuticals and at what level to examine the market. Perhaps most difficult was the lack of consistency as to what price level to use in calculations. The term *market at wholesale prices* is used very loosely in Nigeria and can refer to market size at price to prime distributor or at price to pharmacy level. Most pharmaceutical companies considered prices to wholesalers/prime distributors to form the best basis for determining total market size regardless of product origin (locally manufactured or imported). See Table 2.

TABLE 2 Estimate of total Nigerian pharma market (in ₦ million)

1978	1979	1980	1981	1982 (est.)
160	200	250	350	370

The pharmaceutical market in Nigeria had grown dramatically with the increase in money available due to the oil boom. Analysts predicted that the overall annual rate of growth for pharmaceuticals in Nigeria would average 20 percent until 1985, then drop to 15–18 percent thereafter. Further, the private market was expected to account for 80 percent of total sales by 1985, and local manufacture to account for 50 percent of supply by 1987–88.

Generally speaking, there had been four phases of development in the Nigerian market for pharmaceuticals over the period 1974–81:

1. *1974–1977—Frantic growth*. Growth in the private sector was more than matched by demand from institutional sources. Many institutional purchases were delayed, lost, or stolen. The boom in demand encouraged many major suppliers to establish their own importation and primary distribution companies. The retail market was undersupplied.
2. *1978–1979—Austerity*. Easing of port congestion and cutback in institutional purchases led to dramatic increases in inventories at all levels. The indigenization program of 1977 changed many distribution arrangements.
3. *1980—Sharp recovery*. Rapidly rising oil revenues allowed many governmental authorities to increase purchases dramatically.
4. *1981–1982—Economic reversal*. Decline in oil revenues, tighter import restrictions, and lower demand reduced pharmaceutical sales growth.

Analgesics

Analgesics accounted for 16 percent of pharmaceutical sales in Nigeria in 1981. Within the analgesics segment, management estimated that 20 percent of sales were ethical products, including injectable analgesics, narcotics, and Novalgin. Novalgin, the third highest-selling analgesic in Nigeria after Phensic and Panadol, was considered by NHL management to be a premium-priced analgesic targeted at the ethical market. Aspirin and paracetamol could not be injected and were not as effective as Novalgin in the case of severe pains. Direct distribution to the public of OTC analgesics such as aspirin, paracetamol, caffeine, and combinations thereof was permitted. De facto, though not allowed, Novalgin tablets were retailed via OTC channels as well.

Analgesics were estimated to account for ₦56 million in sales in 1981. Acetylsalicylic acid-based analgesics made up around 47 percent of the OTC analgesic market, and plain paracetamol preparations accounted for approximately a further 25 percent. NHL estimates of OTC analgesic market shares by product as of the end of 1981 are shown in Table 3.

TABLE 3 OTC analgesic market shares in 1981

Product	Company	Active ingredients*	Share (percent)
Phensic	Beecham	A, Ca	17%
Panadol	Sterling-Winthrop	Pa	14
Cafenol	Sterling-Winthrop	A, Ca	10
Pengo	Christlieb	A, Ca	8
Daga	Hoechst	A, Pa, Ca	4
P.R. Tabs	Boots	A, Pa, Ca	4
Dispirin	R-C	A	3
Aspirin	Boots	A	1
Febrilix	Boots	Pa	1
Top Tabs	Seward	A, Ca	1
Paracetamol	Glaxo	Pa	1
Others			36
Total	50+ products		100

* A = Aspirin; Pa = Paracetamol; Ca = Caffein. Aspirin and paracetamol provided pain and fever relief, while caffeine provided a lift, like a tonic.

Marketing Pharmaceuticals in Nigeria

Reliable market research on the Nigerian market for pharmaceuticals was not readily available. Usually, if a firm wanted in-depth sectoral research, management had to do its own. Even then, management usually found statistical information highly questionable. Consequently, most marketing decisions in Nigeria tended to be made more subjectively than in many other markets. Nonetheless, management believed that the total Nigerian pharmaceutical market could be divided roughly into three equally important customer segments:

1. *Private sector.* Private hospitals, medical doctors, and retail pharmacists purchased directly or via wholesalers approximately an equal value of ethical and OTC products.
2. *Governments.* Federal and state governments purchased almost exclusively on a tender basis primarily ethical products.
3. *Public at large.* Public at large purchased almost exclusively self-medication OTC products via retail patent medicine stores, retail pharmacies, and street vendors.

Traditionally, NHL had been strong through the first two segments; Daga was intended to be NHL's lead product into the third segment.

Local Manufacturing and Importing

Most of the local formulation industry was based on the repackaging of finished pharmaceutical preparations imported in bulk. The reason was that it was far more profitable, except for low-value/high-volume products, to import rather than attempt to manufacture in Nigeria due to the difficult operating conditions there. Nonetheless, the value of local manufacture had been growing rapidly.

The major sources of pharmaceuticals for Nigeria in 1981 were as follows: United Kingdom (48.3 percent), West Germany (17.3 percent), Switzerland (10.2 percent), and France (4.6 percent). U.S. companies traded mostly through European regional centres.

As a direct consequence of dwindling currency reserves and declining oil export levels, the Nigerian government implemented a series of import restrictions of increasing severity with the aim of halving imports. Thus far, Nigeria had adopted a laissez-faire approach to the pharmaceutical industry, but close observers expected this to change in the mid-1980s. As of early 1982, finished pharmaceuticals could still be imported easily, but import licenses were required for some raw materials, auxiliary chemicals, and virtually all packing materials.

The Nigerian Customs and Excise Tariff used the Brussels Tariff Nomenclature (BTN). A single-column, nonpreferential import tariff schedule applied equally to all countries. Duties were either specific or *ad valorem* depending on the commodity. Duties were computed on the cost and freight c.i.f. value, and all imported goods had to be insured by an indigenous insurance company. All import duties were payable on entry in Nigerian currency. Tariff rates by African standards were moderate. These advance payments were made to the importer's bank before a letter of credit was opened. The funds were then placed in a noninterest account with the Central Bank of Nigeria.

However, even tougher measures were to take effect in April 1982. This new procedure would do the following:

1. Increase the level of import duties on many products including pharmaceuticals, i.e., up 5 percent points from 10 percent to 15 percent on cost, insurance, freight (c.i.f. value).
2. Instruct all state authorities to purchase locally produced products unless a certificate of nonavailability is issued.
3. Introduce a 50 percent deposit requirement. This meant that importers must deposit 50 percent of the value of goods on application and then pay the full amount of the consignment before attempting to recover the deposit. This would force many smaller importers out of the market and perhaps affect the level of parallel importation, which was becoming a growing concern.

Distribution

Wholesaling and retailing of all types were an extremely important component of the Nigerian economy, second only to oil in terms of share of gross domestic product. In general, the Nigerian distributive trades performed the same tasks and were structured similarly to the distributive trades in other countries. However, the infrastructural problems of Nigeria resulted in major physical distribution difficulties and resulted in a very complex, multilevel trade system for most products.

Pharmaceuticals were available to the public from a wide variety of sources in addition to government hospitals: dispensing doctors and private clinics, registered pharmacies, patent medicine stores, other stores with a patent medicine license, and itinerant and market traders. NHL executives estimated there were from 30,000 to 50,000 retail outlets and 1 to 2 million street traders selling pharmaceuticals in Nigeria. Exhibit 2 is an attempt to show diagramatically the distribution system for pharmaceuticals in Nigeria.

A central characteristic of the pharmaceutical distribution system was the relative lack of controlled distribution via registered pharmacists. This was caused by the shortage of doctors and pharmacists in Nigeria. With approximately one pharmacist in private practice per 85,000 Nigerians, doctors tended to dispense their own pharmaceuticals. Further, the shortage of official channels for ethical preparations in particular prompted illegal channels and a lot of self-medication. For example, although a patent medicine store had OTC products legally, often it also had ethical products under the counter, which would be sold without prescription. For example, a man with gonorrhea might go to such a store and get an injection of antibiotic through the trousers. Sometimes, these ethical products had been stolen from shipments to government hospitals. Such products were impossible to identify because there was no marking on the packages to distinguish government sales, etc., so tracing could not be done.

A registered pharmacy employed a registered pharmacist selling both ethical and OTC products typically from behind a counter in an outlet no bigger than 25 square metres. This was the upscale end of the pharmaceutical market. There were about 500 outlets throughout Nigeria, of which about 80 percent were in the major cities.

A patent medicine store (sometimes called a chemist) was a store specializing in OTC products. Such stores may or may not be licensed. These outlets were very small but very popular for the high-volume OTC products, such as analgesics, tonics, and glucose preparations. There were an estimated 13,000 patent medicine licenses as of 1982. Some of these licenses were used to establish patent medicine stores, while some were used to enable other types of stores to add OTC products to their assortment of other goods. Again, there were many thousands of outlets that sold OTC products without a license.

The supermarket had not yet really arrived, in part because of the strength of the street traders. As of 1982, there were only a few supermarkets, and these were not important channels for pharmaceuticals. However, there was an enormous market called Onitsha near Asaba on the banks of the Niger River.

EXHIBIT 2 NHL distribution flowchart

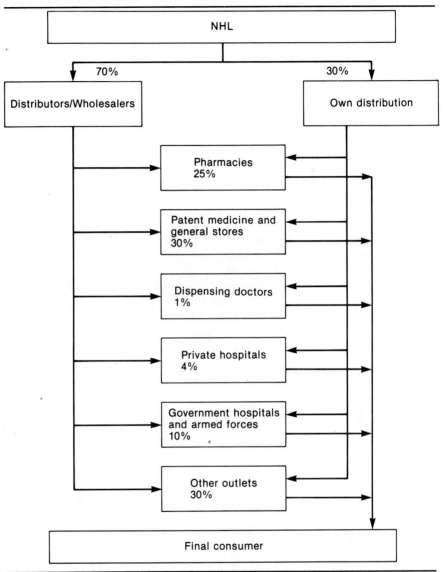

This one market accounted for about one fifth of all pharmaceuticals sold in Nigeria.

A major component of pharmaceutical distribution was the grey market of itinerant and market street traders. There were three types of street traders:

1. Those with a fixed place of business, usually a very small kiosk (usually one metre square), frequently specializing in a particular type of product.

2.   Sedentary traders who spread their wares out beside them on the ground and usually dealt in goods such as cigarettes and sundries.
3.   Hawkers, a large number of whom carried their wares around in the slow-moving traffic of the cities, especially Lagos, selling quite a variety of products.

Pharmaceutical companies called the stationary traders "mammy stalls." For an example, see Exhibit 3. These traders obtained their goods either by treating other retailers as wholesalers (that is, going to a patent medicine store and carrying purchased product back to the stall) or by salespeople who went up and down the streets looking for them. Mammies operated from their stalls in high-traffic areas and moved around the surrounding area with a circular tray on

EXHIBIT 3   Nigerian mammy stalls

their heads, selling cigarettes, or condensed milk, or analgesics, or whatever. Many of their sales were one cigarette at a time or two analgesic tablets at a time. Often they had subhawkers working for them, too.

In the view of many observers, the Nigerian wholesale distribution system for pharmaceuticals had changed dramatically since the mid-1970s. Prior to that time, the trade was dominated by a relatively small number of specialist and multidivisional importation-distribution groups, such as Major & Co. They generally had infrastructural and depot networks covering the various regions and were able to meet the needs of the foreign pharmaceutical companies. Then the market grew so rapidly that several companies began to consider the economics and marketing advantages of their own importation-distribution. Further, the Nigerian indigenization decrees affected the independent importer-distributors dramatically. Because they were importing, these companies had to reduce their foreign shareholding to 40 percent. Relatively few of the major pharmaceutical companies continued to use the services of the independent importer-distributor companies. The initial impact of this change was to weaken the whole pharmaceutical distribution system as the new entrants sought to build systems as good as the original importer-distributors had established. However, despite this change, a great deal of the wholesaling function continued to be performed unofficially by retailers selling to one another.

Pricing

Price controls were introduced in 1977 by the Nigerian federal government on both locally produced and imported goods. These were not uniformly or completely monitored and enforced. Pharmaceutical products were exempt from official price and markup controls. In general, the industry experienced price increases in small installments twice a year. In general, pharmaceutical companies had great difficulty ensuring uniform prices throughout the country.

Wholesale prices of accepted brands in Nigeria tended to be at least 40 percent higher than those same brands in Germany. Retail prices in turn tended to be high in Nigeria due to the substantial distribution costs and markup requirements that arose out of the multilevel distribution system. Generally speaking, the margin structure meant that the price to pharmacy level was about twice c.i.f. levels for locally manufactured products and three times c.i.f. for imported products. Sales to street traders were typically at chemist prices and for cash only. Invoicing was regarded to be out of the question. Very few outlets resold items at fixed prices; most items were bargained for.

Not only were several suppliers faced by increased competition from other products, but many also had difficulties with illegal parallel imports. This problem could not be solved so long as local manufacture meant higher prices and smuggling remained unchecked. Observers believed parallel importation would become more profitable because Nigerian inflation was higher than inflation in other industrialized countries and there was little indication that local manufacturers were going to reduce their margins and prices.

The Nigerian government used three methods for procurement: open competition, negotiated contract, and selective tender. Selective tender was the most prevalent. All bids were required to be sealed in wax and submitted before the deadline. Contracts had been lost because the wax was omitted. According to NHL officials, it was very difficult to get state tenders in particular. These governments tended to purchase from local wholesalers and often provided little or no notice to companies of opportunities to bid. Goods for tender awards could be supplied duty free. The official commission payable to suppliers in respect to state tenders was 10 percent, although exceptions existed.

One major problem for all suppliers had been the increasingly slow payment by customers, especially retailers and governments. Some marketers were less interested in government business for this reason.

Advertising

As of 1982, Nigeria had one of the most developed media systems in developing Africa. There were 14 major daily newspapers, approximately 20 weekly newspapers, and about 25 magazines published in Nigeria. All the dailies were published in English, as were most of the weeklies and magazines. Still, circulation of the newspapers reached very few Nigerians—somewhere in the 2 million range.

Radio was regarded as the best way to reach the Nigerian public. According to a 1979 estimate, there were just over 5 million radios; however, a 1982 estimate said 18 to 20 million radios. There were five federal regional services broadcasting in English and appropriate regional languages, and each of the 19 states had an autonomous radio station. Radio stations accepted commercial advertising.

Each state capital had its own TV station broadcasting in its local language plus the federal station broadcasting in English, making a total of 20 stations. According to a 1980 estimate, there were 450,000 televisions, essentially limited to the urban elite. The number of television sets was growing rapidly and expected to top 2 million in 1983. For transmission purposes, the country was divided into six zones. Commercial television advertising was accepted.

There were few guidelines available concerning how to advertise in Nigeria. Most firms were finding their own way. A *Business International* report on Nigeria in 1979 stated:

> The do-you-good theme exerts strong advertising appeal to a people whose diet has always been short of essential nutrients. A local detergent claims its use has a "tonic" effect. A market survey on smoking motivation shows that some Hausas of the north smoke cigarettes because of their cooling effect during the hot season and their warmth on the chilly days of the harmattan. Responses like these give Western advertising experts new vistas for creative action.
>
> The marketing success scored in Nigeria by Guinness stout is another example. Stout is a heavy, warming beverage seemingly ill-suited to the steamy

climate of West Africa, yet it has swept the market for some years on the platform of "power." Guinness marketing men discovered that power has many subtle interpretations for the Nigerian. The "Guinness gives you power" formula has struck the fancy of the Nigerian consumer and appeals to his more urgent desires. Primarily, it is seen as a body-building aphrodisiac to be taken just before leaving the bar for home. It is also thought to relieve some pains and blood disorders, strengthen the lungs, sharpen the brain, add stature to the puny, and make men more dynamic.

Advertising expenditures for analgesics in 1981, excluding point-of-sale promotion and discounts, were estimated at ₦1,715,000, of which NHL's Daga accounted for roughly one quarter.

Personal Selling

The personal sales force was very important to marketing pharmaceuticals in Nigeria. Detailmen visited doctors, pharmacies, patent medicine stores, and, in some instances, street traders. The sales task involved selling, sampling, debt collection, encouragement of wholesaling, and efforts to learn about opportunities for bidding on state contracts. On average, a detailman could make at least six quality calls per day. In 1982, NHL had 28 OTC salesmen, in comparison with Bayer's 10 and Pfizer's 14.

Pharmaceutical Competitors

The leading local pharmaceutical manufacturers in Nigeria in 1981 in order of size were: Sterling Products Nigeria Limited, Pfizer Products Ltd., Glaxo Nigeria Limited, Embechem Ltd., Beecham Ltd., and Wellcome Nigeria Ltd. (Note: If Glaxo's Glucose D was added to its production figure, it would be largest.)

The OTC emphasis in the Nigerian market was reflected in Sterling's Panadol (largest-selling paracetamol preparation) and Cafenol (third largest-selling analgesic on the OTC market). Panadol was promoted as a pain reliever—it did not relieve fever. Cafenol was a combination of aspirin and caffeine. Both of these products had been available in Nigeria for over 10 years. Sterling-Winthrop was the largest manufacturer of analgesics in Nigeria.

Pfizer concentrated most of its efforts on ethical preparations. Glaxo Nigeria Ltd., on the other hand, concentrated primarily on OTC preparations, such as multivitamins, cough preparations, glucose, and baby foods. Approximately 68 percent of its Nigerian sales were OTC; Glucose D accounted for 37 percent of total company sales. Most of its ethical products were imported.

Beecham concentrated on Beecham's consumer toiletry and food preparations. It established a local plant in 1973 and began to produce locally the Phensic analgesic and Macleans toothpaste. Phensic was not a large contributor to Beecham even though it was probably the largest OTC analgesic preparation sold on the Nigerian market and the oldest available in Nigeria. Phensic was promoted for fever relief.

Boots Company (Nigeria) Limited opened a plant in 1981 to produce PR Tabs and blood tonic products.

NHL management estimates of overall competitive results for 1981 were as follows:

Company	Sales (₦ million)	Market share (percent)
Glaxo	₦19.0	5.6%
Beecham Group	18.7	5.5
Hoechst	15.7	4.6
Sterling-Winthrop	14.6	4.3
Wellcome	14.0	4.1
Pfizer	12.8	3.7
Roche	10.0	2.9
Merck Sharp & Dohme	9.0	2.6
E. Merck	8.5	2.5
Bayer	6.2	1.8

The period 1982–85 was very important for local manufacture because several firms were bringing local plants on-stream. By 1985, at least 17 of the major multinational pharmaceutical firms were expected to have their own local formulation plants operating in Nigeria, meaning about 50 percent of pharmaceuticals sold in Nigeria would be manufactured locally. The major reason for this was that companies had been unable to guarantee enough supply to their sales force due to difficulties getting product into Nigeria. Analgesics in particular were well suited to local manufacture because they were low value, high volume, and relatively simple to formulate and tablet.

According to NHL management, as of the beginning of the 1980s, the main differences between the marketing programs of competing analgesics firms and NHL's Daga were mostly in terms of advertising and promotion and the aggressiveness of the sales force. NHL also had an advantage by virtue of having the most elaborate branch distribution system, which enabled it to provide better service to customers.

Doing Business in Nigeria

Doing business in Nigeria was difficult for many reasons. According to the U.S. Department of Commerce:

> The Nigerian market requires a strong commitment over the long term; it cannot be developed from afar. The business environment stresses personal relationships in both direct sales and major products . . . seriously consider appointing an agent or stationing a company official in Nigeria to stay abreast of current developments and to maintain contacts with government officials and the local business community. . . . Companies, however, should not underestimate the cost of maintaining a representative in Lagos, which for the first year could reach close to U.S. $300,000.

HAG had discovered over the years that it was necessary to pay special attention to physical distribution problems at ports of entry. For example, in its budgeting, HAG allowed about an extra 10 percent, for that was required to get imported goods unloaded and out of the port. NHL had its own facilitator team that was absolutely essential in management's view.

The difficult living conditions in Nigeria and the prevailing customs of the country had a substantial impact on the way business was conducted. Management knew that in every deal, and there were innumerable deals, there were extra payments being made, often back to employees and representatives. As one senior Hoechst executive put it:

> I know that many local people have their fingers in the pie. We don't want the moon from our business there. As long as the overall profit level at the end of the year is OK, we're happy. If our people get a little extra, OK, let them have it. They live under very difficult conditions. It's not like working here in Europe. We know what we expect, and if results are less than that, then we look more closely at what happened and ask questions.

The Daga Story

The decision to introduce an OTC analgesic in the Nigerian market was considered by both NHL and HAG management during 1978–79. NHL's reliance on Novalgin (50 percent of volume and 80 percent of profit) and the ethical market worried senior management. Further, the opportunities in OTC analgesics appeared exciting. The key managers involved in Daga were Mr. A. Woerpel, divisional manager pharma of NHL from mid-1979 (and who had been involved in OTC marketing in Asia), and Mr. H. H. Helms of HAG. See Exhibit 4 for an abbreviated organization chart.

Mr. Ford recalled the circumstances when Daga was introduced:

> I first got involved in Nigeria in February 1980, having come from ethical marketing for Hoechst in the United States. I was in Nigeria for a little over two years and had two major products to introduce. The first was an ethical antibiotic aimed at the gonorrhea problem and the other was Daga. Most of my time and that of the rest of the pharma management was directed at Daga.
>
> In terms of marketing activity, the analgesic market had been quite dormant— the lion's share was held by products that in terms of image, packaging, composition, and advertising and promotion were relatively antiquated and quiet.

However, it proved difficult to convince top HAG management that NHL should be allowed to enter the OTC analgesic market. According to Mr. Helms:

> The American approach to pharmaceutical marketing is very different from the German approach. The traditional German method is to spend a lot of money on research and development to pull out a molecule that has medical benefits, and then think, because of its benefits, it will sell itself in the pharmaceutical market. You'd probably call it a research-driven approach. This means that a shift for us to OTC products with all the attendant marketing skills required is a major strategic change. In fact, we got into other OTC markets by acquisition of OTC companies. The soul of our business has remained ethical.

EXHIBIT 4 Partial HAG and NHL organization chart, 1982

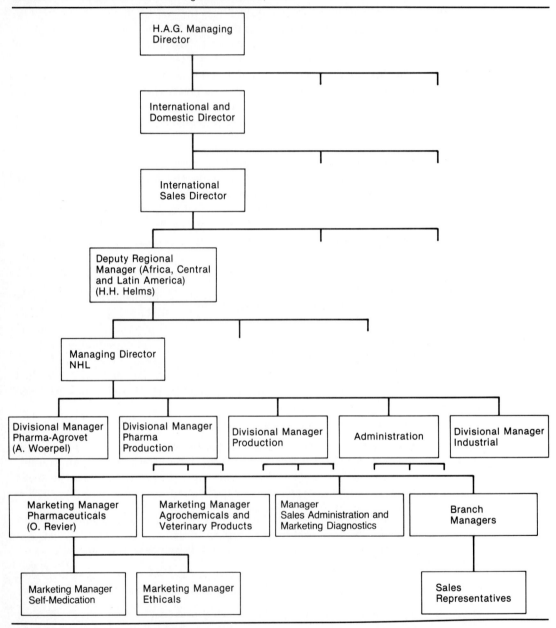

So, when we began to consider OTC analgesics in Nigeria we had two problems. First, prior to 1978, we had really no market data. We knew there was a big market for analgesics, vitamins, and tonics, but we had no figures. Second, and more important, all our senior Hoechst management think in ethical terms. To go to them and say why don't we sell a tonic or an analgesic with a very simple product composition and use modern mass marketing techniques was a risky proposition. They viewed it as being street hawking, not ethical at all. So, our proposal was a significant strategic decision for senior management. We got permission to proceed by mid-1979.

The Product

After receiving approval to put together a detailed plan for the introduction of an analgesic in Nigeria, NHL executives wanted to get into the OTC market as quickly as possible, which argued for using known ingredients. Candidate products and/or ingredients could be sourced within the Hoechst group. The major effort to develop a marketing approach did not begin, however, until the arrival of Mr. Ford.

Pure acetylsalacylic acid products were the least expensive products to offer. NHL management decided they did not want to enter the lowest-price segment ASA market nor to cannibalize their higher-priced segment captured by Novalgin. This left the middle segment of combination products of ASA and paracetamol and/or caffeine. Within the Hoechst group, there already was a product in Afghanistan and Thailand that had the approximate composition NHL executives thought would be appropriate.

Using a product that had already been marketed elsewhere saved a lot of time. Management wanted a product that had proven galenical properties.

Daga was a triple-formulation product. A Daga tablet contained three active ingredients: aspirin (ASA), 225 mg; paracetamol, 250 mg; and caffeine, 30 mg. By comparison, Tylenol was a single-formulation product using paracetamol. Anacin was a dual formulation of aspirin and caffeine. The Daga triple formulation offered advantages to the user: the lower dosage of two analgesic drugs combined gave synergistic analgesic results with reduced side effects from either analgesic. Daga was the second triple formulation on the Nigerian market.

According to Mr. Ford, Daga was introduced as a two-tablet standard dose because of tradition in the market:

> The standard dose is two tablets at a time. We considered this carefully, but the history of Beecham's Phensic was pivotal. That product has been on the market for 25 years in a two-tablet dose form. We decided we had to continue with a two-tablet format because the consumer was so accustomed to it. So, we formulated the product accordingly. We made it cream coloured to differentiate it from all other tablets, which were white. Many Nigerians used analgesics as tonics and as preventative medicine for headaches by taking a morning dose regularly. In addition, after a stressful day they would take analgesics to help sleep, to ward off headaches, before going drinking to prevent hangovers, and, in general, "to strengthen the body."

Pharma management knew that HAG executives would not favour manufacturing Daga in Frankfurt nor would it be possible to manufacture originally in Nigeria. Registration of Daga in Nigeria would be relatively easy, leaving the question of source of supply. Mr. Woerpel had worked in Asia and knew that

Thailand could produce what NHL management wanted, so Thailand was chosen as the initial source of supply for Daga. This continued until the Nigerian factory was ready in 1982.

NHL management had been considering a factory in Nigeria since the latter part of the 1970s but had been waiting for a clearer indication of the future development of the Nigerian market and some way to reduce dependence on the analgesic Novalgin product. The decision to build a factory to produce a high volume of tablets was made in late 1980. This plant was intended to produce Novalgin, Baralgin, Lasix, and Daonil tablets along with the new Daga product; the major justification for the plant was the anticipated volume of Daga product. The foundation stone of the new factory was laid in May 1981, and the factory and central warehouse in Otta were to be officially dedicated in November 1982. The factory was designed to enable liquids production at a later stage with minimal conversion costs.

From the outset, pharma management had conceived line extensions for Daga. The first such product was Daga-Syrup, to be launched in 1982. The Nigerian market was a significant liquid market because of the age distribution of the population. Parents liked liquids to give to children. And although the product was a pure pain and fever medication, parents gave it to their children as a tonic, too. The Daga tablet could also be easily broken in half to give to children. Six to 12 months later, management planned to introduce Daga-Co, which was a Daga and codeine cocktail, to capture a further share in the ethical market since OTC sale of codeine was forbidden. In 1983, the final line extensions would be Daga-Quine—a Daga plus chloroquine combination for malaria relief—and Kiddy-Daga, which was to be a low-dose analgesic for children.

The Name

In March 1980, using personal interviews, 50 Nigerians (half male and half female) were given a choice of three alternative product names, including Daga. Approximately 96 percent chose the Daga name. The attractiveness of the name was apparently due to its simplicity, memorability, and its connotation of force and struggle in Hausa, a major tribal language of the north, and its connotation of violence in the south. The connotation of killing pain and fever with Daga appeared to be very strong.

The Logo and Packaging

Shortly after the product name research, using the same research method, 30 people were asked which of five logos appealed the most. Females were almost unanimous in choosing one logo, so management opted for it because of their significance as customers and traders. Further questioning of consumers revealed that green, yellow, and black packaging was a particularly attractive and appealing combination to Nigerians, who as a group love colour. Management believed that the logo—a black dagger—was related to the concept of killing pain and fever.

Two package sizes were introduced in January 1981. One contained five aluminum foil cards of four tablets each, making it a pack of 20. This package was aimed at the individual user market, while a 200-tablet pack (50 foils of 4 tablets) was aimed at larger-scale institutional markets. The four-tablet foil could be easily divided into two by tearing it down the middle to allow retailers to sell fewer tablets at a time at a greater profit per tablet. The 200-tablet package was the largest on the market. A 50-tablet package was introduced in late 1981 consisting of 25×2 foils to facilitate street trading.

Objectives of the Introductory Campaign

Daga was launched January 5, 1981. The main objectives for the introduction were as follows:

1. To establish a large and profitable participation in the self-medication market sector, to reduce outstandings, and to improve liquidity via cash sales.
2. To create a high-unit-volume tablet demand to more optimally utilize production capacity when local production is undertaken.
3. To lessen dependency on products containing dipyrone.
4. To sell 25 million tablets for ₦650,000, contributing 4 percent to overall Hoechst pharma sales.

Introductory Advertising and Promotion

One of the very first tasks assigned to Mr. Ford was "Go see an advertising agency about Daga" because, from the outset, management was determined to advertise and promote Daga heavily. The objective was as follows:

> To allocate a substantial promotional budget to fund a multimedia advertising campaign as the highlight in a multifaceted promotional mix to rapidly establish awareness, appeal, and usage at all levels of the population.

The total advertising and promotional budget established for 1981 was as follows:

Television	₦170,000
Radio	115,000
Press	35,000
Billboards	30,000
Samples	10,000
Giveaways	235,000
Promotion production	70,000
Total	₦665,000

According to pharma management, while materialism was a very powerful social force and a parameter of status in Nigeria, income levels prevented 90 percent of the population from purchasing desired goods. In addition, imported goods were very expensive. Merchandising and promotional gimmicks were thought to be strong contributors to a marketing effort. As a result, promotion was a very important expenditure and consisted of virtually everything management could think of. About two months prior to the launch date, salesmen began delivering a Daga announcement letter to wholesalers and retailers. There were a wide variety of giveaway items for the sales force to use. About 200,000 rectangular Daga car stickers were distributed and attached, with preference to taxis and public transport vehicles. Each of the pharma branches was given large Daga van stickers to put on its vehicles and to put on wholesaler trucks. Approximately 200,000 plastic Daga shopping bags were distributed to retail and wholesale customers. The salesmen also used 10,000 Daga key rings. Advertising space was purchased on 7.2 million match boxes, which were distributed by the match box manufacturer to supermarkets and other retail outlets. The NHL company football team was renamed The Daga Boys and outfitted with equipment bearing the Daga name. There were also a variety of promotional items tied to stipulated sales levels. These items included 10,000 large Daga umbrellas, 20,000 Daga caps, and 10,000 Daga T-shirts. For example, the umbrellas were offered in the third quarter, which was the rainy season, to the wholesalers as a bonus gift item in quantities pegged to packs of Daga purchased. The umbrella became a marketplace status symbol. Twenty-five thousand Daga carton cutters, 5,000 Daga cigarette lighters, 10,000 Daga signs for retailers, and a large quantity of wall calendars, small diaries, lampshades, waving hands for car windows, and point-of-purchase display stands were designed and ordered for the 1982 promotional effort.

Advertising was done using all major media. Television in particular was a major departure for competitive practice for pharmaceuticals in Nigeria. The initial 45-second commercial showed a Nigerian husband in bed, complaining of fever and not being able to sleep. His wife, concerned, turns on the light and from a drawer next to the bed pulls out some Daga. The husband takes two tablets and falls asleep. Next morning, the husband wakes up refreshed to greet a happy wife. This commercial, however, did cause some Nigerians to believe that Daga was a sleeping tablet, and before the first year of introduction was over, NHL was asked to stop that commercial. The television campaign began the same day the product was launched because management, the sales force, and several distributors wished to indicate to their customers that NHL was strongly backing the new product and would encourage both selling in and selling through. Both the television and radio audio finished with a haunting echo effect of "Daga . . . Daga . . . Daga," which was later mimicked by street hawkers when selling the product.

Table 4 shows the introductory year media mix for Daga.

TABLE 4 Media mix

Medium	Quarter 1	Quarter 2	Quarter 3	Quarter 4
Television:				
National network news at 9 P.M.; in English; 45 seconds each	45 spots	45 spots	45 spots	45 spots
Radio:				
8 regional stations; local dialect; 30 seconds each		8 × 75 spots	8 × 75 spots	8 × 75 spots
Outdoor:				
16-sheet size; in English	110 sites	110 sites	110 sites	110 sites
Press (all English):				
Daily press—3 papers, full page	24	12	12	12
Sunday press—1, ⅛-page strips	0	12	12	12
Monthly Health Journal—1, full page, 2 columns	0	3	3	3

Distribution and Selling Activities

Prior to the introduction of Daga, Hoechst had only developed ethical channels using medical representatives. These 13 medical representatives were used in part to distribute Daga to dispensing doctors, hospitals, and pharmacies. For example, the representatives provided doctors and pharmacies with four-tablet Daga sample packs and distributed samples to all the medical meetings throughout Nigeria.

However, in order to reach the mass Nigerian market, NHL recruited 50 OTC wholesalers and hired 15 new van driver/salesmen, who were provided with vans. Each van cost about ₦8,500. These van salesmen were assigned to branch warehouses. The van sales force called on patent medicine stores, street traders—in fact, anyone who would be interested in reselling Daga. These salesmen provided Daga and other products from the van and collected cash on the spot. They also detailed OTC wholesalers and pharmacies. This sales force was paid salary, with a bonus and a chance to compete for one of six places on a two-week trip to Germany sponsored by the company. In addition, other NHL staff were given the opportunity to buy Daga from the company at wholesale prices in order to resell it in their own communities in their spare time.

The launch manual provided to the sales force said the following about customers other than wholesalers:

> Ensure that all other outlets purchase some quantity of Daga, however small, either from us or from our wholesalers. A fully horizontal spread of Daga must be achieved. Like an oil film on water, it only needs to be thin. Later it can be thickened.

More specifically, NHL distribution objectives were as follows:

1. To achieve cash van sales to all major and large OTC retail outlets.
2. To sell one large pack to 15 different retailers per day from January 5 to February 13, using the special introductory offer.
3. To abundantly stock all OTC wholesalers with both pack sizes.
4. To urge OTC wholesalers to push Daga out into their retail outlet networks.

Pricing

The pricing for Daga was established so that the retail price for one tablet was five kobo, roughly the same price as Panadol. NHL sold Daga with the following suggested price schedule:

Pack size	Wholesale	Patent medicine	Retail
20 tablets	₦0.56	₦0.67	₦1.00
200 tablets	5.10	6.00	9.00

For the first six weeks of the introduction, there was an introductory offer, which meant that each time a retailer purchased a 200-tablet pack for ₦6.00 he received a 20-tablet pack free. If the retailer sold all 220 tablets at five kobo each, he would make a profit of ₦5.00. NHL expected that sometimes the salesmen would not pass on the 20-tablet package but instead sell the package and keep the profit. Management believed that the power of the Nigerian profit motive probably contributed significantly during the selling-in exercise.

A 2½ percent discount for cash payment was available to wholesalers who purchased a specified minimum volume of tablets and paid in cash. Most sales were on a cash, not credit, basis.

At the time of introduction, competitive prices were as follows:

Product	Pack size	Wholesale price/pack
Panadol	24 tablets	₦ 0.67
	96	2.67
Cafenol	50	0.59
Novalgin	10	0.82
(ethical)	20	1.43
	1,000	42.50
Phensic	50	0.53
	144	1.40
PR Tabs	10	0.21
	30	0.47
	50	0.75

Daga Results

NHL management initially hoped that 1981 Daga sales would equal the ₦665,000 promotional budget planned. However, sales developed much faster than anticipated, resulting in temporary stockouts of the small pack on two occasions. By year-end, Daga results were roughly three times better than projected, with about 66 million tablets sold. In its first year, Daga accounted for 13 percent of total Hoechst human ethical and OTC turnover, second only to Novalgin, which accounted for 40 percent of turnover with 72 million tablets sold. Table 5 shows quarterly and year-end results as well as projections for 1982.

TABLE 5 Daga sales results and projections

Quarter	20s volume (000)	₦ (000)	200s volume (000)	₦ (000)	Total ₦ (000)
1	206	₦117	34	₦176	₦ 293
2	334	193	41	213	406
3	264	153	53	274	427
4	688	400	43	222	622
Total	1,492	₦863	171	₦885	₦1,748

	1981	1982 (estimated)
Gross sales	₦1,748,000	₦3,000,000
Gross margin	874,000	1,485,000
Direct costs	40,000	60,000
Interest costs	50,000	75,000
Promotion	665,000	620,000
Contribution to indirect costs and profit	119,000	760,000

NHL management predicted that Daga tablet sales would reach ₦5 million by the end of 1983 and ₦8 million by the end of 1986. Total Daga sales including the line extensions were expected to reach ₦15 million by the end of 1986.

Product H

In late 1981, Mr. Ford and Mr. Woerpel had discussed the desirability of a second NHL analgesic positioned in the OTC market to capture additional market share. Mr. Revier thought of it this way:

> The Daga success was wonderful, and Jeff Ford did a fantastic job. Now that I'm here, I have an even more interesting and complicated marketing job. We've got another analgesic of almost equal composition and cost that we hope to market in

such a way as to be seen as quite different from Daga. We want as high a share of the analgesic market as we can get because the competition has come alive after Daga's introduction and they're beginning to fight back with advertising and promotion, too. The television stations have more than doubled their rates because of the demand for commercial time.

The introduction of Product H will have to be carefully done because of the possibility of cannibalism with Daga. I think some form of marketing research is essential even though it's tough to do in this country.

Product H already existed. Its composition was aspirin, 200 mg; paracetamol, 200 mg; and caffeine, 50 mg. This meant that Product H delivered pain and fever relief roughly to the same extent as Daga. The caffeine gave the user a lift. "There's not that much difference," remarked Mr. Ford. "It's much like the distinction between one and two cups of coffee. But it will be noticeable." NHL management were intrigued by the product in part because there were no other analgesics of comparable composition and in part because they perceived that "fast-acting" would be a claim of interest to Nigerians.

Product H would be produced at the NHL factory, and early indications were that its cost would be less than Daga because the change in formulation favoured the less expensive ingredients. Mr. Revier was working at this point in time with an estimate of 10 percent less for cost of goods sold compared to Daga at its time of introduction.

There were still many questions to answer and decisions to make. For example, Product H could be made in an oblong tablet form and coated with a film to enable easier swallowing. Product H could be packaged in blister packs of clear plastic instead of the aluminum foil packages used when Daga was introduced. Mr. Revier learned that these changes would not change Product H costs in any significant way. Mr. Revier wondered how many tablets should be in a package, how many different package sizes, what name to give the product, and what theme to use to promote it:

My objective is to gain a sales level of ₦1 million for Product H in its first year after introduction. I estimate the OTC analgesic market will be about ₦49 million in 1983 because of import difficulties expected. I'm not sure how to estimate cannibalism. I do want to increase sales of both Daga and Product H; doing anything else will not be accepted by my superiors.

Mr. Revier was particularly concerned about pricing. Daga had been increased in price to 6.5 kobo per tablet in early 1982 without any apparent problem from customers. This meant that as of early 1982, the following retail prices generally prevailed (note: two tablets was the common dosage for all of the brands):

Novalgin	17.0 kobo per tablet
Daga	6.5
Panadol	5.0
PR Tabs	5.0
Phensic	2.3
Cafenol	1.8
Top Tabs	1.0
Pengo	1.0

Mr. Revier felt he should price Product H in relation to Daga, but he had not decided whether to be above, the same, or below Daga:

> I've got to put together a complete marketing plan for Product H because it will be reviewed here by my superiors and back in Frankfurt by Mr. Helms and others. I know of a major Nigerian marketing institute that maybe could do some research for us in six months if I decide what I want, but I can't wait too long before submitting my plan. Even if I order research, I'll have to start now to prepare my first draft of a plan. And, I have to keep working on Daga, too.

Case 16

TenderCare Disposable Diapers*

Tom Cagan watched as his secretary poured six ounces of water onto each of the two disposable diapers lying on his desk. The diaper on the left was a new, improved Pampers, introduced in the summer of 1985 by Procter & Gamble. The new, improved design was supposed to be drier than the preceding Pampers. It was the most recent development in a sequence of designs that traced back to the original Pampers, introduced to the market in 1965. The diaper on his right was a TenderCare diaper, manufactured by a potential supplier for testing and approval by Cagan's company, Rocky Mountain Medical Corporation (RMM). The outward appearance of both diapers was identical.

Yet the TenderCare diaper was different. Just under its liner (the surface next to the baby's skin) was a wicking fabric that drew moisture from the surface around a soft, waterproof shield to an absorbent reservoir of filler. Pampers and all other disposable diapers on the market kept moisture nearer to the liner and, consequently, the baby's skin. A patent attorney had examined the TenderCare design, concluding that the wicking fabric and shield arrangement should be granted a patent. However, it would be many months before results of the patent application process could be known.

As soon as the empty beakers were placed back on the desk, Cagan and his secretary touched the liners of both diapers. They agreed that there was no noticeable difference, and Cagan noted the time. They repeated their "touch test" after one minute and again noted no difference. However, after two minutes, both thought the TenderCare diaper to be drier. At three minutes, they were certain. By five minutes, the TenderCare diaper surface seemed almost dry to the touch, even when a finger was pressed deep into the diaper. In

* This case was written by Professor James E. Nelson, University of Colorado. It is intended as a basis for classroom discussion rather than to illustrate effective or ineffective handling of an administrative situation. The data in this case are disguised. Copyright © 1986 by the Business Research Division, College of Business and Administration and the Graduate School of Business Administration, University of Colorado, Boulder, Colorado 80309-0419. Used by permission from James E. Nelson.

contrast, the Pampers diaper showed little improvement in dryness from three to five minutes and tended to produce a puddle when pressed.

These results were not unexpected. Over the past three months, Cagan and other RMM executives had compared TenderCare's performance with 10 brands of disposable diapers available in the Denver market. TenderCare diapers had always felt drier within a two- to four-minute interval after wetting. However, these results were considered tentative because all tests had used TenderCare diapers made by RMM personnel by hand. Today's test was the first made with diapers produced by a supplier under mass manufacturing conditions.

Rocky Mountain Medical Corporation

RMM was incorporated in Denver, Colorado, in late 1982 by Robert Morrison, M.D. Sales had grown from about $400,000 in 1983 to $2.4 million in 1984 and were expected to reach $3.4 million in 1985. The firm would show a small profit for 1985, as it had each previous year.

Management personnel as of September 1985 included six executives. Cagan served as president and director, positions he had held since joining RMM in April 1984. Prior to that time he had worked for several high-technology companies in the areas of product design and development, production management, sales management, and general management. His undergraduate studies were in engineering and psychology; he took an M.B.A. in 1981. Dr. Morrison currently served as chairman of the board and vice president for research and development. He had completed his M.D. in 1976 and was board certified to practice pediatrics in the state of Colorado since 1978. John Bosch served as vice president of manufacturing, a position held since joining the firm in late 1983. Lawrence Bennett was vice president of marketing, having primary responsibilities for marketing TenderCare and RMM's two lines of phototherapy products since joining the firm in 1984. Bennett's background included an M.B.A. received in 1981 and three years' experience in grocery product management at General Mills. Two other executives, both also joining RMM in 1984, served as vice president of personnel and as controller.

Phototherapy Products

RMM's two lines of phototherapy products were used to treat infant jaundice, a condition experienced by some 5 to 10 percent of all newborn babies. One line was marketed to hospitals under the trademark Alpha-Lite. Bennett felt that the Alpha-Lite phototherapy unit was superior to competing products because it gave the baby 360-degree exposure to the therapeutic light. Competing products gave less than complete exposure, with the result that the Alpha-Lite unit treated more severe cases and produced quicker recoveries. Apart from the Alpha-Lite unit itself, the hospital line of phototherapy products included a light meter, a photomask that protected the baby's eyes while undergoing treatment, and a "baby bikini" that diapered the baby and yet facilitated exposure to the light.

The home phototherapy line of products was marketed under the trademark Baby-Lite.™ The phototherapy unit was portable, weighing about 40 pounds, and was foldable for easy transport. The unit when assembled was 33 inches long, 20 inches wide, and 24 inches high. The line also included photomasks, a thermometer, and a short booklet telling parents about home phototherapy. Parents could rent the unit and purchase related products from a local pharmacy or durable medical equipment dealer for about $75 per day. This was considerably less than the cost of hospital treatment. Another company, Acquitron, Inc., had entered the home phototherapy market in early 1985 and was expected to offer stiff competition. A third competitor was rumored to be entering the market in 1986.

Bennett's responsibilities for all phototherapy products included developing marketing plans and making final decisions about product design, promotion, pricing, and distribution. He directly supervised two product managers, one responsible for Alpha-Lite and the other for Baby-Lite. He occasionally made sales calls with the product managers, visiting hospitals, health maintenance organizations, and insurers.

TenderCare Marketing

Right now most of Bennett's time was spent on TenderCare. Bennett recognized that TenderCare would be marketed much differently than the phototherapy products. TenderCare would be sold to wholesalers, who in turn would sell to supermarkets, drugstores, and mass merchandisers. TenderCare would compete either directly or indirectly with two giant consumer-goods manufacturers, Procter & Gamble and Kimberly-Clark. TenderCare represented considerable risk to RMM.

Because of the uncertainty surrounding the marketing of TenderCare, Bennett and Cagan had recently sought the advice of several marketing consultants. They reached formal agreement with one, a Los Angeles consultant named Alan Anderson. Anderson had extensive experience in advertising at J. Walter Thompson. He also had responsibility for marketing and sales at Mattel and Teledyne, specifically for the marketing of such products as Intelli-Vision,™ the Shower Massage,™ and the Water Pik.™ Anderson currently worked as an independent marketing consultant to several firms. His contract with RMM specified that he would devote 25 percent of his time to TenderCare the first year and about 12 percent the following two years. During this time, RMM would hire, train, and place their own marketing personnel. One of these people would be a product manager for TenderCare.

Bennett and Cagan also could employ the services of a local marketing consultant who served on RMM's advisory board. The board consisted of 12 business and medical experts who were available to answer questions and provide direction. The consultant had spent over 25 years in marketing consumer products at several large corporations. His specialty was developing and launching new products, particularly health and beauty aids. He had worked closely with RMM in selecting the name TenderCare,™ and had done a great deal of work summarizing market characteristics and analyzing competitors.

Market Characteristics

The market for babies' disposable diapers could be identified as children, primarily below age three, who use the diapers and their mothers, primarily between ages 18 and 49, who decide on the brand and usually make the purchase. Bennett estimated there were about 11 million such children in 1985, living in about 9 million households. The average number of disposable diapers consumed daily in these households was thought to range from 0 to 15 and to average about 5.

The consumption of disposable diapers is tied closely to birth rates and population. However, two prominent trends also influence consumption. One is the disposable diaper's steadily increasing share of total diaper usage by babies. Bennett estimated that disposable diapers would increase their share of total diaper usage from 75 percent currently to 90 percent by 1990. The other trend is toward the purchase of higher-quality disposable diapers. Bennett thought the average retail price of disposable diapers would rise about twice as fast as the price of materials used in their construction. Total dollar sales of disposable diapers at retail in 1985 were expected to be about $3 billion, or about 15 billion units. Growth rates were thought to be about 14 percent per year for dollar sales and about 8 percent for units.

Foreign markets for disposable diapers would add to these figures. Canada, for example, currently consumed about $250 million at retail, with an expected growth rate of 20 percent per year until 1990. The U.K. market was about twice this size and growing at the same rate.

The U.S. market for disposable diapers was clearly quite large and growing. However, Bennett felt that domestic growth rates could not be maintained much longer because fewer and fewer consumers were available to switch from cloth to disposable diapers. In fact, by 1995, growth rates for disposable diapers would begin to approach growth rates for births, and unit sales of disposable diapers would become directly proportional to numbers of infants using diapers. A consequence of this pronounced slowing of growth would be increased competition.

Competition

Competition between manufacturers of disposable diapers was already intense. Two well-managed giants—Procter & Gamble and Kimberly-Clark—accounted for about 80 percent of the market in 1984 and 1985. Bennett had estimated market shares at:

	1984	*1985*
Pampers	32%	28%
Huggies	24	28
Luvs	20	20
Other brands	24	24
	100%	100%

Procter & Gamble was clearly the dominant competitor with its Pampers and Luvs brands. However, Procter & Gamble's market share had been declining, from 70 percent in 1981 to about 50 percent. The company had introduced its thicker Blue Ribbon™ Pampers in an effort to halt the share decline. It had invested over $500 million in new equipment to produce the product. Procter & Gamble spent approximately $40 million to advertise its two brands in 1984. Kimberly-Clark spent about $19 million to advertise Huggies in 1984.

The 24 percent market share held by other brands was up by some 3 percentage points from 1983. Weyerhaeuser and Johnson & Johnson manufactured most of these diapers, supplying private-label brands for Wards, Penneys, Target, K mart, and other retailers. Generic disposable diapers and private brands were also included here, as well as a number of very small, specialized brands that distributed only to local markets. Some of these brands positioned themselves as low-cost alternatives to national brands; others occupied premium ("designer") niches with premium prices. As examples, Universal Converter entered the northern Wisconsin market in 1984 with two brands priced at 78 and 87 percent of Pampers' case price. Riegel Textile Corporation's Cabbage Patch™ diapers illustrated the premium end, with higher prices and attractive print designs. Riegel spent $1 million to introduce Cabbage Patch diapers to the market in late 1984.

Additional evidence of the intense competition in the disposable diaper industry was the major change of strategy by Johnson & Johnson in 1981. The company took its own brand off the U.S. market, opting instead to produce private-label diapers for major retailers. The company had held about 8 percent of the national market at the time and decided that this simply was not enough to compete effectively. Johnson & Johnson's disposable diaper was the first to be positioned in the industry as a premium product. Sales at one point totaled about 12 percent of the market but began to fall when Luvs and Huggies (with similar premium features) were introduced. Johnson & Johnson's advertising expenditures for disposable diapers in 1980 were about $8 million. The company still competed with its own brand in the international market.

Marketing Strategies for TenderCare

Over the past month, Bennett and his consultants had spent considerable time formulating potential marketing strategies for TenderCare. One strategy that already had been discarded was simply licensing the design to another firm.

Under a license arrangement, RMM would receive a negotiated royalty based on the licensee's sales of RMM's diaper. However, this strategy was unattractive on several grounds. RMM would have no control over resources devoted to the marketing of TenderCare; the licensee would decide on levels of sales and advertising support, prices, and distribution. The licensee would control advertising content, packaging, and even the choice of brand name. Licensing also meant that RMM would develop little marketing expertise, no image or even awareness among consumers, and no experience in dealing with packaged-goods channels of distribution. The net result would be that RMM would be hitching its future with respect to TenderCare (and any related products) to that of the licensee. Three other strategies seemed more appropriate.

The Diaper Rash Strategy

The first strategy involved positioning the product as an aid in the treatment of diaper rash. Diaper rash is a common ailment, thought to affect most infants at some point in their diapered lives. The affliction usually lasted two or three weeks before being cured. Some infants are more disposed to diaper rash than others; however, the ailment probably affects a majority of babies. The ailment is caused by "a reaction to prolonged contact with urine and feces, retained soaps and topical preparations, and friction and maceration" (*Nelson's Text of Pediatrics,* 1979, p. 1884). Recommended treatment includes careful washing of the affected areas with warm water and without irritating soaps. Treatment also includes the application of protective ointments and powders (sold either by prescription or over the counter).

The diaper rash strategy would target physicians and nurses in either family or general practice and physicians and nurses specializing either in pediatrics or dermatology. Bennett's estimate of the numbers of general or family practitioners in 1985 was approximately 65,000. He thought that about 45,000 pediatricians and dermatologists were practicing in 1985. The numbers of nurses attending all these physicians was estimated at about 290,000. All 400,000 individuals would be the eventual focus of TenderCare marketing efforts. However, the diaper rash strategy would begin (like the other two strategies) where approximately 11 percent of the target market was located— California. Bennett and his consultants agreed that RMM lacked sufficient resources to begin in any larger market. California would provide a good test for TenderCare because the state often set consumption trends for the rest of the U.S. market. California also showed fairly typical levels of competitive activity.

Promotion activities would emphasize either direct mail and free samples or in-office demonstrations to the target market. Mailing lists of most physicians and some nurses in the target market could be purchased at a cost of about $60 per 1,000 names. The cost to print and mail a brochure, cover letter, and return postcard was about $250 per 1,000. To include a single TenderCare disposable diaper would add another $400 per thousand. In-office demonstrations would use registered nurses (employed on a part-time basis) to show TenderCare's superior dryness. The nurses could be quickly trained and compensated on a per-demonstration basis. The typical demonstration would be given to groups of two or three physicians and nurses and would cost RMM about $6. The California market could be used to investigate the relative performance of direct mail versus demonstrations.

RMM would also advertise in trade journals such as the *Journal of Family Practice, Journal of Pediatrics, Pediatrics,* and *Pediatrics Digest.* However, a problem with such advertisements was waste coverage because none of the trade journals published regional editions. A half-page advertisement (one insertion) would cost about $1,000 for each journal. This cost would be reduced to about $700 if RMM placed several advertisements in the same journal during a one-year period. RMM would also promote TenderCare at local and state medical conventions in California. Costs per convention were thought to be about $3,000. The entire promotion budget as well as amounts allocated to direct mail, free samples, advertisements, and medical conventions had yet to be decided.

Prices were planned to produce a retail price per package of 12 Tender-Care diapers at around $3.80. This was some 8 to 10 percent higher than the price for a package of 18 Huggies or Luvs. Bennett thought that consumers would pay the premium price because of TenderCare's position: the pennies-per-day differential simply would not matter if a physician prescribed or recommended TenderCare as part of a treatment for diaper rash. "Besides," he noted, "in-store shelf placement of TenderCare under this strategy would be among diaper rash products, not with standard diapers. This will make price comparisons by consumers even more unlikely." The $3.80 package price for 12 TenderCare diapers would produce a contribution margin for RMM of about 9 cents per diaper. It would give retailers a per-diaper margin some 30 percent higher than that for Huggies or Luvs.

The Special-Occasions Strategy

The second strategy centered around a special-occasions position that emphasized TenderCare's use in situations where changing the baby would be difficult. One such situation was whenever diapered infants traveled for any length of time. Another occurred daily at some ten thousand daycare centers that accepted infants wearing diapers. Yet another came every evening in each of the 9 million market households when babies were diapered at bedtime.

The special-occasions strategy would target mothers in these 9 million households. Initially, of course, the target would be only the estimated 1 million mothers living in California. Promotion would aim particularly at first-time mothers, using such magazines as *American Baby* and *Baby Talk.* Per-issue insertion costs for one full-color, half-page advertisement in such magazines would average about $20,000. However, most baby magazines published regional editions where single insertion costs averaged about half that amount. Black and white advertisements could also be considered; their costs would be about 75 percent of the full-color rates. Inserting several ads per year in the same magazine would allow quantity discounts and reduce the average insertion cost by about one third.

Lately Bennett had begun to wonder if direct mail promotion could instead be used to reach mothers of recently born babies. Mailing lists of some 1–3 million names could be obtained at a cost of around $50 per 1,000. Other costs to produce and mail promotional materials would be the same as those for physicians and nurses. "I suppose the real issue is, just how much more effective is direct mail over advertising? We'd spend at least $250,000 in baby magazines to cover California while the cost of direct mail would probably be between $300,000 and $700,000, depending on whether or not we gave away a diaper." Regardless of Bennett's decision on consumer promotion, he knew RMM would also direct some promotion activities toward physicians and nurses as part of the special-occasions strategy. Budget details were yet to be worked out.

Distribution under the special-occasions strategy would have TenderCare stocked on store shelves along with competing diapers. Still at issue was whether the package should contain 12 or 18 diapers (like Huggies and Luvs) and how much of a premium price TenderCare could command. Bennett considered the packaging and pricing decisions interrelated. A package of 12 TenderCare diapers with per-unit retail prices some 40 percent higher than Huggies or Luvs might work just fine. Such a packaging/pricing strategy would produce a contribution margin to RMM of about 6 cents per diaper. However, the same pricing strategy for a package of 18 diapers probably would not work. "Still," he thought, "good things often come in small packages, and most mothers probably associate higher quality with higher price. One thing is for sure—whichever way we go, we'll need a superior package." Physical dimensions for a TenderCare package of either 12 or 18 diapers could be made similar to the size of the Huggies or Luvs package of 18.

The Head-On Strategy

The third strategy under consideration met major competitors in a direct, frontal attack. The strategy would position TenderCare as a noticeably drier diaper that any mother would prefer to use anytime her baby needed changing. Promotion activities would stress mass advertising to mothers using television and magazines. However, at least two magazines would include a dollar-off coupon to stimulate trial of a package of TenderCare diapers during the product's first three months on the market. Some in-store demonstrations to mothers using "touch tests" might also be employed. Although no budget for California had yet been set, Bennett thought the allocation would be roughly 60:30:10 for television, magazines, and other promotion activities, respectively.

Pricing under this strategy would be competitive with Luvs and Huggies, with the per-diaper price for TenderCare expected to be some 9 percent higher at retail. This differential was needed to cover additional manufacturing costs associated with TenderCare's design. TenderCare's package could contain only 16 diapers and show a lower price than either Huggies or Luvs with their 18-count packages. Alternatively, the package could contain 18 diapers and carry the 9 percent higher price. Bennett wondered if he really wasn't putting too fine a point on the pricing/packaging relationship. "After all," he had said to Anderson, "we've no assurance that retailers or wholesalers would pass along *any* price advantage TenderCare might have due to a smaller package. Either one or both might instead price TenderCare near the package price for our competitors and simply pocket the increased margin!" The only thing that was reasonably certain was TenderCare's package price to the wholesaler. That price was planned to produce about a 3-cent contribution margin to RMM per diaper, regardless of package count.

Summary of the Three Strategies

When viewed together, the three strategies seemed so complex and so diverse as to defy analysis. Partly the problem was one of developing criteria against which the strategies could be compared. Risk was obviously one such criterion; so were company fit and competitive reaction. However, Bennett felt that some additional thought on his part would produce more criteria against which the strategies could be compared. He hoped this effort would produce no more strategies; three were plenty.

The other part of the problem was simply uncertainty. Strengths, weaknesses, and implications of each strategy had yet to be given much thought. Moreover, each strategy seemed likely to have associated with it some surprises. An example illustrating the problem was the recent realization that the Food and Drug Administration (FDA) must approve any direct claims RMM might make about TenderCare's efficacy in treating diaper rash. The chance of receiving this federal agency's approval was thought to be reasonably high; yet it was unclear just what sort of testing and what results were needed. The worst-case scenario would have the FDA requiring lengthy customer tests that eventually would produce inconclusive results. The best case would have the FDA giving permission based on TenderCare's superior dryness and on results of a small-scale field test recently completed by Dr. Morrison. It would probably be a month before the FDA's position could be known.

"The delay was unfortunate—and unnecessary," Bennett thought, "especially if we eventually settle on either of the other two strategies." In fact, FDA approval was not even needed for the diaper rash strategy if RMM simply claimed (1) that TenderCare diapers were drier than competing diapers and (2) that dryness helps treat diaper rash. Still, a single-statement, direct-claim position was thought to be more effective with mothers and more difficult to copy by any other manufacturer. And yet Bennett did want to move quickly on

TenderCare. Every month of delay meant deferred revenue and other postponed benefits that would derive from a successful introduction. Delay also meant the chance that an existing (or other) competitor might develop its own drier diaper and effectively block RMM from reaping the fruits of its development efforts Speed was of the essence.

Financial Implications

Bennett recognized that each marketing strategy held immediate as well as long-term financial implications. He was particularly concerned with finance requirements for start-up costs associated with the California entry. Cagan and the other RMM executives had agreed that a stock issue represented the best option to meet these requirements. Accordingly, RMM had begun preparation for a sale of common stock through a brokerage firm that would underwrite and market the issue. Management at the firm felt that RMM could generate between $1 and $3 million, depending on the offering price per share and the number of shares issued.

Proceeds from the sale of stock had to be sufficient to fund the California entry and leave a comfortable margin remaining for contingencies. Proceeds would be used for marketing and other operating expenses as well as for investments in cash, inventory, and accounts receivable. It was hoped that TenderCare would generate a profit by the end of the fiscal year in the California market and show a strong contribution to the bottom line thereafter. California profits would contribute to expenses associated with entering additional markets and to the success of any additional stock offerings.

Operating profits and proceeds from the sale of equity would fund additional research and development activities that would extend RMM's diaper technology to other markets. Dr. Morrison and Bennett saw almost immediate application of the technology to the adult incontinent diaper market, currently estimated at about $300 million per year at retail. Underpads for beds constitute at least another $50 million annual market. However, both of these uses were greatly dwarfed by another application, the sanitary napkin market. Finally, the technology could almost certainly be applied to numerous industrial products and processes, many of which promised great potential. All these opportunities made the TenderCare situation that much more crucial to the company. Making a major mistake here would affect the firm for years.

Knowles Products: Brand Management System*

In early 1989, Clive Langdon, group vice president—pharmaceutical products of Knowles Products, was reviewing a specially commissioned report on his division's brand management system. Knowles, a major marketer of a well-known brand of analgesic and a number of personal care products and owner of a southern U.S. chain of franchised drug stores, had used a brand management system for more than a decade. This system had worked well for Knowles; however, it seemed to Langdon that a review of this system was appropriate. Consequently, in September he had asked Leslie Nome, as a well-regarded marketing consultant, to conduct such a review. After some discussion, Langdon and Nome agreed that the first stage of the project should be to document the way that brand management system operated at Knowles. Langdon was reviewing that report in anticipation of a meeting the next morning with Nome.

Company Background

In the early 1900s Jason Knowles, a pharmacist by training and traveling salesman by profession, developed a patent medicine that he claimed was beneficial for relieving a variety of ills. Over time, the claims moderated but Knowles' product, sold primarily in tablet form, gained popularity as a headache remedy. Descendants of the original family maintained control of the company until the late 1970s, when the stock was first publicly offered.

Product Line

Prior to going public in 1978, the firm had essentially been a one-product company. Although Knowles analgesic was sold in liquid and tablet form and combined with other ingredients to produce such products as cough syrups and

---

*This case was written by Charles B. Weinberg of the University of British Columbia. Copyright © 1989 by Charles B. Weinberg. Used with permission.

cold remedies, the focus was always on Knowles pills and their promised relief from headaches. Some other brands had been introduced but none had ever accounted for more than 10 percent of corporate sales.

In the late 1970s, Knowles management had begun to plan a major expansion of its product line. In 1980, the company announced a program for growth marked by expansion in four major directions:

1. Health-related products.
2. Personal care products.
3. Franchised drug stores.
4. International markets.

In the immediately ensuing years, Knowles acquired three companies, each with a major well-known brand name of health-related product (an upset stomach remedy, a muscle relaxant, and a treatment for athlete's foot). In addition, Knowles also acquired several small companies that marketed specialty personal care products, such as a dandruff shampoo and a denture cleaner. In the six years ending in 1986, Knowles acquired companies with a total of 15 significant brand names and introduced 3 new internally developed brands as well. Although selling a variety of pharmaceutical and personal care products, the majority of the company's sales was made through supermarkets. In 1986, senior management decided to cease acquiring new companies and concentrate on internal development.

In 1984, Knowles acquired a chain of drug stores, named Southern Star, located in Florida and Georgia. About half of Southern Star's outlets were franchised; the rest were wholly owned. Although some additional smaller acquisitions were made, expansion of the Southern Star was accomplished primarily through opening new outlets and increasing sales per store.

Knowles' analgesics had been sold in Western Europe for almost 30 years. Several of the new brands were also manufactured in Europe or Asia, but most overseas markets were served through export sales.

Overall corporate sales had increased by more than tenfold in the past decade to $1.3 billion in 1988. However, profits had not kept pace. Exhibit 1

EXHIBIT 1 Knowles Products: Corporate performance (by line of business; $ millions)

	1988	1987	1986	1985	1984	1983
Net sales:						
Consumer products						
Pharmaceuticals	513	461	399	338	339	251
Personal care	110	94	86	67	39	31
Subtotal	623	555	485	405	378	282
Drug stores	690	678	596	403	240	—
Total	1313	1233	1081	808	618	282
Net income:						
Consumer products	53	49	41	39	32	29
Drug stores	20	18	16	10	7	—
Total	73	67	57	49	39	29

EXHIBIT 2 Partial organization diagram for Knowles Products

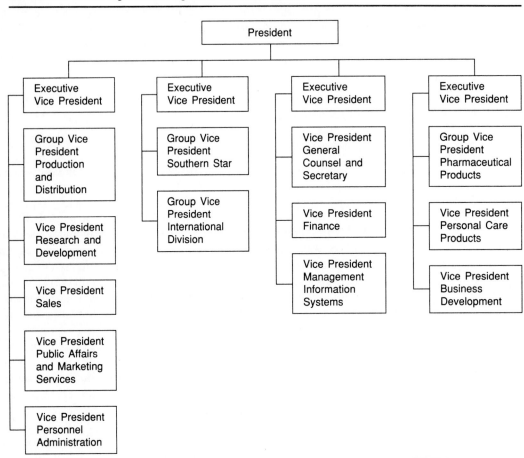

summarizes corporate performance by line of business. An abridged organization chart for Knowles Products is given in Exhibit 2.

The Brand Management System

Knowles had been organized on a product management system, particularly in the pharmaceutical products division as shown in Exhibit 3. There were five job levels in the brand system; brand assistant (BA), assistant brand manager (ABM), brand manager (BM), associate marketing manager (AMM), and marketing manager (MM). The focus of Nome's initial report was on the brand manager and lower levels, that is, assistant brand manager and brand assistant. (See Exhibit 4, 5, and 6, for relevant job descriptions.)

Although Nome's report did not deal extensively with the MM and AMM

EXHIBIT 3 Knowles' marketing organization, Pharmaceutical Products Division

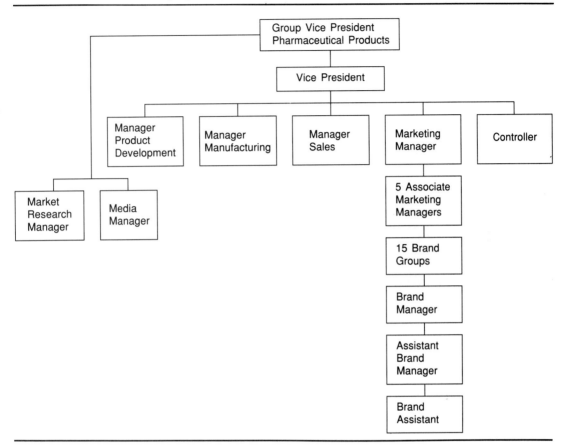

levels of management, these managers played a critical role in brand management. The MM managed all aspects of marketing, except sales execution, for the division. This manager's key objectives were not only achievement of short-term volume and profit goals but also development, testing, and expansion of new products, improved products, and line extensions. These latter goals were emphasized by top management to ensure continued corporate growth. The AMMs largely served coordinating, controlling, training, and strategic overview roles between the AM and BMs. They also had final decision-making authority on promotion activities within existing budgets, and handled many of the administrative jobs in the advertising department.

The entry-level job was that of BA. The BA was primarily responsible for monitoring the product budget, developing sales promotions, and analyzing marketing information (e.g., sales data from the company's management information system, consumption data from the A.C. Nielsen Company, and addi-

---

EXHIBIT 4 Job description—Brand manager

Function: *To contribute to the overall growth of Knowles through development, recommendation, and implementation of effective marketing programs capable of building brand volume, share, and profit for assigned brands. The brand manager is charged to:*

1 Provide management with relevant data regarding the state of the business, serving as management's antennae in the category to identify problems and opportunities.

2 Develop recommendations which are designed to stimulate brand growth.

3 See that all programs are coordinated and run properly, serving as the focal point for all brand-related activity.

4 Ensure that brand personnel learn the skills to handle multifaceted responsibilities of the job.

The brand manager's specific marketing responsibilities are as follows:

1 *Product.* Ensure that the product and package are superior to competition within cost constraints demanded by the marketplace and profit considerations. Requires consumer usage/attitude and product research, establishment of product improvement objectives, and periodic review of progress toward these objectives.

2 *Positioning.* Position the product to maximize volume within the existing consumer and competitive environments. Periodically review marketing strategy in light of changing consumer needs, wants, and attitudes and competitive product positionings and sales. Develop and test alternative copy and promotion strategies attuned to the marketing strategy to improve the brand's overall positioning.

3 *Copy.* Ensure that copy provides the optimum selling power. Demands an ongoing effort in development and testing of new copy pools, different executional formats, and alternative copy strategies.

4 *Media.* Ensure that media plans are designed to deliver advertising in the most effective and efficient manner against the brand's target audience. Requires periodic review of target audience criterion and testing of alternative mixes of media vehicles within budget constraints, as well as testing of different media weights.

5 *Promotion.* Plan, execute, and evaluate, with the assistance of the sales department, consumer and trade promotions, which are cost-effective in increasing brand volume. Demands testing of a variety of promotions each fiscal year and testing, on a periodic basis, alternative annual promotion levels and/or alternative consumer/trade promotion splits within existing budgets.

6 *Volume/Control.* Make adjustments as necessary in fiscal year plans to deliver volume base.

The brand manager's specific management information responsibilities are to identify, analyze, and recommend actions in response to significant developments in the following areas:

1 Realized volume versus budgeted level.

2 Competitive developments.

3 Product and package problems.

4 Problem markets.

5 Implementation delays and cost overruns.

6 Legislative and regulatory activities.

---

tional data from other outside market research services). New projects were added as competence was gained until the BA was sent out for sales training, a 12-week field sales assignment.

Promotion to ABM followed this selling experience. Emphasis was placed upon learning advertising copy and media, developing long-term business-building programs, and assisting and helping train the BA in the area of sales promotion. ABM was a transition job which could last from one to two and a

EXHIBIT 5 Job description—Assistant brand manager

Marketing Responsibilities:

1 *Business Building Plans.* Develop, recommend, and execute those key projects which, long term, will have a major effect on the shipments and consumption of the brand. Examples of these are the introduction of new sizes/products, major distribution building programs, or major trial generating promotions.

2 *Copy.* Work with the brand manager in providing direction to the advertising agency in the development of new executional formats (based on current strategy) and the testing of new copy strategies/executions. Also, work with technical and legal to obtain copy clearance/claim support.

3 *Media.* In conjunction with the brand manager, provide the agency with direction on new ways to more efficiently reach the brand's target audience. This may take the form of media mix tests or testing of different media levels.

4 *Product.* Ensure that a product which fulfills consumer needs and wants is marketed within cost constraints.

5 *Market Research Planning and Analysis.* Initiate and analyze those market research projects which will yield information upon which the brand may act to improve current market position or correct an ongoing problem.

6 *Package Design.* Ensure that the package in the marketplace is appealing, eye-catching, and connotes those attributes of the product most important to consumers.

Management Information:

1 *Market Research.* Analyze research and recommend next steps to correct any problems or capitalize on any opportunities.

2 *Media.* Analyze results of media testing and recommend action to be taken.

3 *Schedule Changes.* Inform brand manager of delays in the progress of key projects in order that management may be apprised of the delay and the reason why.

EXHIBIT 6 Job description—Brand assistant

Marketing Responsibilities:

1 *Sales Promotion.* Plan, in consultation with other brand group members and the sales department, national and test promotions. Write promotion recommendations and issue related feasibility requests and production orders. Implement consumer-oriented portions of promotions (e.g., coupon copy and media, sample drops, etc.) and oversee and/or cooperate with sales department in implementing trade-oriented portions of promotions. Budget and evaluate promotions.

2 *Budget Administration and Control.* Review and code invoices. Reconcile the budget with accounting on quarterly basis. Close out budget with accounting at the end of the fiscal year.

3 *Market Analysis.* Analyze Nielsen data and write bimonthly Nielsen reports. Audit other sources of market information (monthly shipment reports, SAMIs, etc.) and write analytical reports as necessary.

4 *Shipment Estimates.* Prepare monthly shipment estimate which forecasts next three months' shipments with supporting rationale.

5 *Competitive Activity.* Monitor competitive activity reported by sales (promotion and pricing activity), agency (competitive and media spending), and other sources (periodicals, etc.). Write reports on significant developments.

6 *Public Relations.* Cooperate with consumer services in handling special consumer-oriented problems which fall outside normal consumer services activities. Work with research services (home economists) and public affairs on brand-related consumer information projects.

Other areas where brand assistant may contribute, depending upon individual brand assignments, include package design and business-building tests.

Management Information: Report to brand manager on:

1 *Competitive Activity.* Significant competitive developments.

2 *Budget Variance.* Any variations from budget forecasts.

3 *Promotion Problems.* Any problems with implementation of promotions.

4 *Consumer Relations.* Any product problems which threaten volume.

half years, depending on the capabilities of the person and the needs of the company.

When the ABM was promoted to BM, he or she was given overall marketing responsibility for one or more products, including planning, forecasting, and controlling volume and spending for these products. He or she also supervised ABMs and BAs. Due to rotation and normal turnover, not all brand groups were fully staffed with a BA and ABM.

In terms of day-by-day operations, the brand management group considered the other functions as ''staff'' to them. Nonetheless, brand management had no direct authority over sales, manufacturing, market research, and product development. But it did have the responsibility to obtain from staff the inputs necessary for successful marketing. Each functional group, for this purpose, had a representative designated to deal with the brand manager. An integral part of this system of ''responsibility without direct authority'' was the fact that brand management controlled budgets for areas such as market research and package design and represented the staff's channel to top management. For example, a departmental request for information or specific action was typically directed to the brand manager who not only had to concur but was the interface with top management. (See Exhibit 7.)

Excerpts from interviews with several brand managers are given in the appendix at the end of the case.

Corporate Atmosphere

Nome considered Knowles to be an almost classic example of brand management. Brand managers played a ''line management'' role within the marketing function at Knowles. The reasoning for this was that the BM had direct responsibility for the most critical marketing factor—advertising—and had the broadest exposure to the operations of the company and the best overall perspective on his product and markets.

Brand managers were able to accomplish their goals through other people by using their control over the product budget, their position as coordinator of all information, and their interpersonal skills. They had to be successful ''at getting others to do the job.''

But there was even more to the essential nature of the brand manager's job, a perspective that can only be expressed by senior management. These people looked upon brand managers as individuals who could be expected to ask the type of questions a top manager might ask, gather the facts necessary to make a decision, and then recommend a course of action in a very succinct memo. The net effect was that top management's job of managing the marketing of a large number of diverse brands in diverse categories became easier and more effective. The system assured that all brands, even those with small sales, were given attention and that a variety of marketing approaches designed to stimulate growth would at least be explored and recommended.

EXHIBIT 7   Interface matrix

Brand manager responsibilities	Work with these departments	Brand role
Product or package improvement	Sales, R&D market research, manufacturing, and controller	a. Develop objectives for product or package development. b. Approve aesthetics. c. Develop consumer research objectives, fund research, and summarize results. d. Determine unit profit potential and return on investment. e. Recommend test market to management. f. Write manufacturing production orders for test market production of product. g. Analyze test market results and recommend national expansion.
Positioning	Advertising agency, market research, and legal	a. Develop alternative positionings. b. Develop consumer research objectives and fund research. c. Analyze research results and recommend test market. d. Analyze test market results and recommend national expansion.
Copy	Advertising agency, market research, and legal	a. Review agency copy submissions and select copy to be presented to management. b. Approve final production for on-air copy testing. c. Analyze copy test results. d. Recommend national airing of copy.
Media	Advertising agency and media services	a. Review agency media objectives and strategies and recommend alternatives. b. Review and modify agency media plans with help of media services. c. Forward agency media plan to management. d. With help of media services monitor implementation of media plan.
Sales promotion	Sales, manufacturing, promotion development, and legal	a. Develop national promotion plan with help of sales department. b. Recommend loan to management. c. Write manufacturing production order for production of sales promotion product. d. Implement consumer portion of promotion (i.e., coupons, samples, etc.) and fund all trade allowances and consumer promotions.
Volume control	Sales	a. Monitor shipments. b. If undershipment of objectives seems possible, recommend remedial marketing efforts.

The power of the brand managers rested largely in their authority to ask questions anywhere in the company and demand carefully thought out, responsible answers, as long as the questions and answers were limited to matters which either directly affected the consumer of their product or affected their brand's contribution margin (revenue less manufacturing and shipping costs and brokerage commission). In addition, successful brand managers had informal authority arising from their superior knowledge, as compared to that of a functional specialist's, of all consumer aspects of their product, and they had the power to discuss their recommendations (in writing, usually) with top management.

Selection and Screening

Typically, brand assistants were recent MBAs from leading business schools with minimum work experience (See Exhibit 8 for a sample recruitment ad.) In recent years, Knowles had hired some graduates with advertising experience as well as some transferees from other company departments, but these were exceptions. Brand managers were almost always promoted from within. In initial hiring, Knowles sought individuals who were intelligent, trainable, competitive, aggressive, and hardworking. Ideal candidates had qualities which were generalized as: analytical ability; communications skills; the ability to plan, organize, and follow through; the ability to work well with others; leadership, resourcefulness, and ingenuity; decision-making skill; drive and determination; and maturity.

EXHIBIT 8   Sample recruiting advertisement

**Marketing Careers with
One of the Nation's
Leading Companies**

Knowles Corporation manufactures and markets over 15 major consumer brands. Many are among the country's market leaders.

A limited number of entry level positions are available as BRAND ASSISTANT, working within a Brand Group which has responsibility for one or more individual products and is the driving force behind them.

As a Brand Assistant, you will be assigned to a specific product. Your Brand Manager will give you immediate responsibility for a variety of projects and then look to you for leadership, ideas, and results. Some examples of your assignments will be: planning, executing, and evaluating promotions; analyzing business performance; planning and executing a sales presentation for a new market initiative; developing new packaging; and helping to manage your brand's budget.

In addition to individual projects, you will be broadly exposed to all aspects of brand management. As you contribute to the management of your brand and demonstrate your ability to handle additional responsibility, you will be assigned more complex and important projects. Your Brand Manager is responsible for your training and will work very hard to accelerate your personal development. The emphasis, however, is always on you . . . your thinking, your ideas, your contributions. Management career development is excellent. At Knowles, promotion is always from within, and based upon individual performance and contribution.

If you are about to obtain an MBA degree or equivalent and are just starting your career, if you have a background of achievement and can exhibit good analytical and communication skills, and if you are interested in talking further with us, send your resume to:

CORPORATE RECRUITING MANAGER
KNOWLES CORPORATION

Training

The introduction for the new brand assistant was strenuous. Although the initial jobs might range from planning promotions to writing market research summaries, there was a lot of arduous number crunching. Hours were long, often including weekends. There were no shortcuts or special courses and readings that could bypass this breaking-in period. Nor was there much sympathy for the neophyte. Everyone in brand management had been through the same experience, recognized its necessity, and knew the work could be done. "Help" was mainly in the form of providing initial direction, pointing out errors, and suggesting new projects as competence increased. The newer projects were invariably more interesting and challenging, which provided additional incentive to master the earlier tasks. And as new BAs were hired, the more mundane jobs could be passed down.

The purpose of this training was to internalize certain "first principles" which were considered necessary to maintain the brand management system:

1. *All information could be derived from numerical data:* Brand people had minimal contact with either customers or suppliers. Customers were normally represented by market research findings and sales results. Suppliers were represented by specific liaison people. Thus there always had to be an analytic justification for a project or program. Results needed to be summarized in terms of cases of product and net revenue (minus all costs except advertising).

2. *Concern for mistakes:* Brand people were trained to be detail-oriented and concerned about not making errors. No mistake, particularly in a memo, was too small to be noticed. The feedback was intense since memos were commented on in writing as they were passed up and down the distribution chain. If anyone found a mistake, then everyone who missed it was embarrassed.

3. *Brand manager's budget as a control system:* This principle was a bit deceptive, however. While some staff groups—market research, sales merchandising, and package design—were dependent upon brand management for funding of projects, brand management did not use the budgets as a club. The range of interrelationships between brand management and staff was too involved to be reduced to the single lever of money control.

4. *Career success required "the Knowles style":* The Knowles style contributed to the climate and mystique which made brand management successful. This style included memo format, job concept, and attitude. Memos conformed to a particular writing style and format and were not supposed to exceed two pages without an attached summary. Brand people had to be the resident experts on everything affecting their products. Brand managers thought of themselves as the general managers of a very small company. Nonetheless, brand people had to maintain their aggressive, competitive attitude without hurting their relations with staff. The BA might achieve a basic competence in one or two years. The competence was recognized by the addition of more complex assignments. As the BA's credibility and influence increased with the staff, he or she conformed more and more to the corporate style. BMs estimated that they spent as much as

25 percent of their time training BAs and ABMs. In fact, the entire brand management system was a training program. There was no such thing as an old BM; there was no place for the person who didn't want to be promoted.

Management Information Systems

The BM used current data almost exclusively, even though comprehensive historical files were maintained. Meetings were usually frequent and short. Memos were passed through for comment and review by the BM. Magazines might be scanned for ideas but were seldom read. For many BMs, only the Nielsen chart books, the product fact book, and project folders were kept within easy reach.

Tests were used extensively to determine the accuracy of the information routinely received so that results could be optimized and problems avoided. Brand people went out into the field infrequently, yet they had a strong perception about what was happening through their tests and the management information system.

Emphasis had to be placed on the management information system because the BM changed products about every two years and thus lost personal contacts in the agency and staff groups who tended to remain with the products.

Relationship with the Big Five

The five groups which brand management dealt with regularly were the advertising agency, sales, market research, manufacturing, and product development. With each group, there were conflicts which the BM had to resolve. These conflicts might include work priorities, differences of opinion about strategy or objectives, or disagreements over project timing. Brand managers sometimes argued that they had the responsibility for volume and spending without explicit authority to force staff compliance. These other departments, however, saw brand management as more in control due to its final authority to make recommendations to top management as well as its role in setting initial objectives. The other departments would have preferred a better understanding (by brand management) of their role and problems, yet essentially believed in the brand system as the best way to run the company.

Rotation and Promotion

Brand people were expected to shift products about every two years. Due to attrition, new hires, and promotions, the time could vary but seldom exceeded three years. It took a BM several months to become familiar with a new assignment and perhaps a year to implement a major strategy. Thus, the typical BM was working on a predecessor's strategy for much of his or her tenure.

Performance was judged on a number of bases:

1. Did the BM prepare a sound annual marketing plan and was he or she able to sell it to management?
2. How well did the product perform against the volume objective in the marketplace (regardless of who prepared the budget)?
3. What sort of major improvements or line extensions were proposed (though not necessarily implemented)?
4. How well did he or she train others?

In addition, part of a BM's evaluation was based on such factors as: communication, analysis, thoroughness, prioritization, productivity, organization, leadership, work with others, responsibility, ability to accept criticism, motivation, maturity, capacity, judgment, and attitude.

Summary

Brand management at Knowles was a total system. The climate, selection, training, and promotion all tended to encourage the best and brightest people to dedicate themselves to making a product successful.

The people were supported by a management information system and organized structure that allowed them to be trained on the job and rotate from product to product at frequent intervals. The products were all marketed in a similar enough way, e.g., advertising, sales promotions, supermarkets, and retail drug outlets, that the system and organization were the same for each.

The strength of the system lay in the fact that each product had a "champion" who attempted to achieve volume and share objectives, as predicted in an annual plan. The short term was not sacrificed for the long term since the long term generally represented the incumbent's proposed strategy and ongoing business-building tests, and the short term represented a predecessor's strategy. In addition, a pool of potential general management talent was being established and utilized as experienced managers were promoted and new employees added.

Appendix   Selected Portions of Interviews with Brand Managers

Question 1: You typically hire business school graduates with a small amount of work experience. What do you look for and how would you describe their jobs as BAs?

Brand Manager No. 1: I find it takes several months for a BA to become acclimated. New people are usually too theoretically oriented; at this level, pragmatic application of judgment to problems is more important. The most important thing for a

BA to learn is to pay attention to detail. Even typos have a dollar impact. The BA should learn to think things through comprehensively.

The BA begins working about 10 hours per day plus homework, but the time goes down as the job is learned. All marketers are pretty much alike—aggressive, detail-minded—and that's what we look for here.

BM No. 2: The biggest problem a new BA has is to learn how to juggle projects and determine priorities. Business schools teach sequential problem solving but "Brand" requires juggling 15 trivial things and 1 major one. The BA's initial problem is establishing credibility. Brand management requires a mixture of talents but no one specific personality is appropriate. Some brand people do consider themselves prima donnas.

BM No. 3: The BA's problem is simply a lack of experience with our system. The system relies on numbers, and the numbers come from the BA. The BA is constantly calculating and must think in analytic terms. The BA must work very hard, develop rapidly, and learn what brand management is all about. It takes two to six months for the BA to have a good grasp of the job and become acclimated to the system. All training is on the job.

Question No. 2: What is the relationship between brand management and the other departments?

BM No. 1: Brand managers are considered with respect by the advertising agency but brand managers are committed to the agency because the BM cannot fire the agency. Most of the people in other departments do not want to move as fast as brand management. It is a problem conveying the urgency and importance of timing. The BM is responsible for planning, and the other departments for advice and/or execution.

Knowledge is power and the BM is the resident expert on his or her products.

BM No. 2: Brand management is more a line than a staff function.

Brand management has responsibility for achieving volume objectives and keeping profit/case close to target level, but brand management has no direct authority over many other departments which impact on the ability to achieve objectives.

Senior management recognizes that sometimes performance is beyond the control of brand managers.

BM No. 3: Brand managers control the money. Many other departments must rely upon brand management for direction and project funding. The advertising agency has account executives who deal with brand people and the agency's creative and media departments. The agency presents a national media plan once a year. Since the marketing budget is mainly advertising, brand and agency pesonnel write the request. Sales promotions are originated by brand management and proposed to the sales department.

Brand management recommends and analyzes market research and test markets. The purpose of these is to avoid national blunders although the risk is relatively small with ongoing products.

Question 3: How do brand managers spend their time?

BM No. 1: Daily activities are coordination, fielding short questions with answers on the telephone, and commenting on memos passing through. Wide variation exists, but a day might have one hour for thinking and strategy, one hour for standard reports, one hour for the In/Out basket, two hours on the phone, one hour with subordinates, and two hours in meetings.

Dealings are mainly with the "big five"; the account executive at the advertising agency; sales; the manufacturing coordinator; market research; and the product development specialists.

On the average, the BM travels to the field once every three months. Brand management's job is to study the product, determine what is needed, and prioritize projects. The budget for this is set once a year.

BM No. 2: The most important job of a brand manager is the budget request and appropriation. Once each year, a two- to three-hour meeting is held which lays out how and why money is to be spent for the next year. During the period preceding this meeting, much of a BM's time may be spent with the agency. During the remainder of the year, the time falls off with the time spent in once-a-week meetings and telephone calls.

The second major job is the Brand Improvement Objectives meeting which is also held once a year. Brand works with R&D to develop both short-term and long-term product development plans.

Brand strategies require 1½ to 2 years to implement. Long-range planning is important because few changes can be made in the short term due to long lead times in production and media planning.

Most of the BM's time is spent on specific projects.

Heavy use is made of the telephone and many short meetings are held, usually with six people or less.

Brand management has a meeting with the Product Development Center every two weeks.

Question 4: How often does a brand manager change brands?

BM No. 1: All brand people are interchangeable, although it takes about two to four months to become the most knowledgeable. You spend one to two years on a brand.

BM No. 2: Rotation is caused by promotions and departures and occurs every 1½ to 2 years. Continuity is provided by the staggered rotation of BAs, ABMs, and BMs. Once you rotate, you usually do not have time to find out how your old product is doing.

Part 5

Distribution Decisions

Marketers must make decisions on how to present the products they produce to their ultimate purchasers. Most producers do not present their products to end consumers themselves. They tend to make use of wholesalers and retailers.

The marketing decision maker has a number of decisions to make with respect to the distribution of a product. These include:

1. The types of wholesale and retail intermediaries to use.
2. The number of wholesale and retail intermediaries to use of each type.
3. The number of levels in the channel (degree of directness).
4. The ways to motivate existing channel members to perform effectively.

The first cases in this section deal with these issues. Beyond these decisions are a series of decisions concerning the physical distribution of the product. These include: customer service level, inventory size, order quantities, reorder points, warehouse locations, and transportation.

The next section of this note is a short reminder of some of the concepts related to each of these decision points.

Types of Intermediaries

There are many different types of wholesale and retail intermediaries. They vary on the types of products they carry and the services that they are able to perform. The decision on which types of intermediaries to utilize is related to the services that a firm desires to have performed. This is in turn related to the resources and skills of the firm and the needs and behavior of the ultimate consumer.

The Number of Intermediaries

The firm must decide whether to have intensive, selective, or exclusive distribution at the wholesale and retail levels. This decision is related to the quality of support these intermediaries will give in each situation, the ability of the firm to service the intermediaries, and the behavior of the ultimate consumer. For example, a wholesaler whom you want may only be willing to carry your products on an exclusive basis, or you may not be able to afford to contact all the retailers of a particular type. Alternatively, consumers may demand that your product be available at all outlets. This may force you into an intensive distribution situation.

Number of Channel Levels

The decision on how direct a channel from producer to ultimate consumer should be is related to the cost of alternative channels, the service and control provided, the characteristics of the end consumer in terms of their numbers and geographic location, the perishability and bulkiness of the product, plus the characteristics of the firm, and competitive activity.

Motivation

Once a channel is selected, motivating its members to perform effectively is an important activity. Motivating vehicles include monetary things such as margins, allowances, and cooperative programs; service activities such as training and technical advice, inventory taking, and display management; and provision of physical items such as racks. Also important here are the interpersonal relationships among the people in the intermediaries and in your firm.

Physical Distribution Management

Physical distribution management is a complex area where management science techniques have become important. In simple terms, the decision maker sets a customer service level (for example, deliver 95 percent of all orders within seven days) and then makes inventory, warehousing, and transportation decisions to reach this service level at minimum cost. The customer service level is set by considering costs, consumer behavior, and competitive activity.

Case 18

Chaebol Electronics Company, U.S.*

In mid-1984, Mr. Park Sung-Il, grandson of the founder of Chaebol Industries, Inc., and president of Chaebol Electronics Company, U.S., was deciding how his company should enter the U.S. videocassette recorder (VCR) market. As of March 1985, the agreement signed by his company—which gave it access to the proprietary technology of the Japanese company Japan Victor Corporation (JVC) for the manufacture of VCRs but limited sales to only the domestic Korean market—would expire. After that date, Chaebol was free to market VCRs worldwide. The decision had already been made to begin selling Chaebol VCRs in the United States as soon as possible. The decision Mr. Park faced was that of marketing his company's VCRs as it was already selling its televisions or positioning this new product line differently, selling it through different channels of distribution.

History of Chaebol Industries, Inc.

Chaebol Industries, Inc., had its beginnings with a small construction firm started by Mr. Park Kyung-Yung in 1945. After gaining several large port construction projects following the Korean War, Mr. Park expanded the firm into shipbuilding and through this into the exporting business. While Chaebol was growing in these areas, other large Korean conglomerates, such as Lucky-Goldstar, Samsung, and Hyundai, diversified their corporations into such fields as chemicals, oil refining, textiles, appliance manufacture, and electronics manufacturing. Each of these firms developed its own foreign distribution capabilities and became very successful in worldwide markets. As a result, these other Korean firms began to become strong competitors for Chaebol's exporting business.

* This case was prepared by Constance M. Kinnear, Research Associate, with the assistance of Thomas C. Kinnear, Professor of Marketing, both at the Graduate School of Business Administration, The University of Michigan. Copyright © 1986 by the authors.

In 1965, Mr. Park Kyung-Yung retired and his son, Mr. Park Taik-Cha, became president of Chaebol. Looking at the successes of his competitors and their impact on Chaebol's business, Mr. Park decided in 1966 that the time had come for Chaebol to expand its areas of operation into the electronics field. In 1967, Chaebol Electronics Company was established, and began producing black-and-white televisions. Room air conditioners, washing machines, refrigerators, and electric typewriters were added to Chaebol's list of products by 1970. As each new product was added to the Chaebol line, it was marketed only in Korea. However, the Korean market consisted of only 41 million people, with a per capita income of just under $2,000 per year. Faced with intense competition from the other large Korean conglomerates for its domestic market, Mr. Park soon became aware that his company would have to begin exporting its products to gain economies of scale in their manufacture.

Mr. Park hoped that Chaebol's long experience in exporting would give it a competitive advantage in foreign markets. To build on this experience, Chaebol first marketed its black-and-white TVs in the United States in 1975 through Johnson Importers of Atlanta, Georgia, the importer that had handled the export goods the company had transported for years. Since this importer was used to handling only low-cost items carried mainly by discounters, Chaebol offered only its lower-cost, lower-priced 12-inch and 19-inch black-and-white models for export. Johnson Importers found a market for 25,000 Chaebol sets in 1975, sold under the PKY brand name, in discount stores in Georgia, Alabama, and Florida. These stores on average priced the 12-inch sets at $105 and the 19-inch sets at $120 each. These stores included a 20 percent margin in these prices. Johnson Importers made a 15 percent margin on its sales of TVs to these outlets. Chaebol priced its 12-inch sets at $71.50 and its 19-inch sets at $81.50 each. Encouraged by this acceptance, Chaebol increased its production capacity in late 1975 from 300,000 to 400,000 sets per year.

In 1976, Johnson Importers was able to increase the sale of PKY sets to a total of 60,000 sets throughout the South. Mr. Park believed that similar success in the sale of Chaebol's TVs could be found in discount chains in other parts of the country. To achieve this, Mr. Park sent two Chaebol sales representatives to establish a sales office and arrange for warehousing facilities in Atlanta. These sales representatives received $25,000 in salary each, and it was budgeted that their sales expenses would come to another $15,000 each per year. These direct Chaebol employees contacted several large discount chains in the Northeast and Midwest. In 1977, sales to these chains, all employing private labels, were 50,000 units, increasing total company sales that year to 115,000 units. In 1978, Chaebol's salespeople were able to land the sale of 100,000 sets to K mart Corporation under K mart's KC brand name. As part of the arrangement for these sales, Chaebol agreed to open a service center to which sets could be sent by the retailer for repair. This center was located in Atlanta. As a result, total sales in 1978 jumped to 240,000 sets. Korean production capacity was increased to 600,000 units per year to handle these sales. In 1979, sales reached 275,000 units. In 1980, with additional private label sales to discounters in the

West and constantly increasing sales to previous customers, Chaebol sold 375,000 units.

In 1981, Chaebol increased its number of U.S. sales representatives to five and opened a second sales office, warehouse facility, and service center in Chicago. These sales representatives were now being paid a salary of $37,000 per year and had $20,000 a year in expenses each. Chaebol's salespeople began approaching large department store chains, such as Sears and Montgomery Wards, to increase sales. Again, the TVs sold to these accounts carried the retailers' own labels. 1981 total sales were 450,000 units. Of this total, only 100,000 sets carried the PKY brand name, and these were sold primarily to independent discounters who operated only a few stores each in regional areas.

In 1979, Mr. Park had directed Chaebol to begin manufacturing color TVs. As with Chaebol's previous products, these were first marketed only in Korea. By 1981, Mr. Park was ready to bring three color models, 9-inch, 13-inch, and 19-inch sets, to the United States. The decision to introduce color sets was brought on by a shift in sales patterns in the U.S. marketplace. By 1980, annual total sales of black-and-white TVs was dropping, by an average of 6 percent per year. Along with this drop in total sales, black-and-white set prices were dropping steadily, causing profit margins on the products to fall. Nineteen-inch black-and-white models were no longer desired in the market; buyers preferred to spend their money on a smaller color set than on a large black-and-white set. Furthermore, the color TV market was growing steadily, with growth rates of nearly 15 percent per year. Half of Chaebol's capacity was shifted to color TV production, and within black-and-white sets, 19-inch sets were dropped while small, portable 9-inch sets were added to the line. Cost information on Chaebol's export TV product line in 1981 is shown in Exhibit 1.

EXHIBIT 1   Cost information on 1981 export television sets

	Black-and-White		Color		
	9-inch	*12-inch*	*9-inch*	*13-inch*	*19-inch*
Direct material	$ 57.85	$32.70	$102.30	$121.35	$147.05
Labor	1.40	1.00	2.40	2.95	3.45
Overhead	2.50	1.40	4.00	5.00	5.80
Transportation	5.10	6.25	5.20	6.30	6.85
Duty	3.15	1.90	5.35	6.40	7.70
Total costs	$ 70.00	$43.25	$119.25	$142.00	$170.85
Chaebol's selling price to channel	$100.00	$60.00	$195.50	$232.00	$280.00
Average retail selling price of Chaebol sets	$125.00	$75.00	$230.00	$290.00	$350.00
Retail price of leading domestic brand	$156.00	$95.00	$271.50	$345.00	$415.00

Chaebol marketed its color TVs through the same discount channels it was using for its black-and-white models. However, with color, Chaebol's U.S.

EXHIBIT 2 Black-and-white TV market—retail brand shares and market size, 1981–1984

	1981	1982	1983	1984
Domestic manufacturers				
RCA	16.3	16.3	15.5	12.5
Zenith	15.5	15.4	13.6	10.2
General Electric	8.9	8.2	8.4	7.5
North American Phillips	5.8	6.9	8.2	10.3
Other domestic	2.6	2.0	2.7	2.7
Total domestic	49.1	48.8	48.4	43.2
Japanese				
Panasonic	6.0	5.9	7.0	8.1
Sony	4.4	3.9	3.5	5.3
Sanyo	3.6	3.2	3.3	3.2
Hitachi	1.3	0.9	0.7	0.5
Sharp	1.0	1.6	1.0	1.4
Toshiba	0.5	0.6	0.2	0.4
Other Japanese	1.0	1.4	0.8	0.4
Total Japanese	17.8	17.5	16.5	19.3
Far East				
Samsung (Korea)	2.1	2.4	2.9	3.5
Goldstar (Korea)	1.8	1.9	2.3	2.5
Chaebol (Korea)	1.7	1.9	2.5	3.3
Other Far East	0.5	0.6	0.9	1.2
Total Far East	6.1	6.8	8.6	10.5
Private label (Sears, J. C. Penney, Montgomery Ward, K mart, etc.)	20.2	20.0	18.5	17.5
All other	6.8	6.9	8.0	9.5
Market size in units (000)	5,806	5,597	5,488	4,717

salespeople were able to have its sets sold using the PKY label at K mart and two other large discounters. Color TV sales began with 100,000 units in 1981 and grew to 300,000 units in 1982. Forty percent of these color sets carried the PKY label. (See Exhibits 2 and 3 for competitive market shares).

In late 1982, Chaebol drastically changed its approach to the U.S. TV market. Great pressure in the press was being brought upon Korean TV producers, with many accusations of TV dumping by these companies within the U.S. market. In accusing them of dumping, it was being alleged that Korean manufacturers were selling TVs in the United States for prices below those charged for the same product in the domestic market. Mr. Park decided not to wait for the decision from the U.S. International Trade Commission on the dumping charges. He began construction in November 1982 of TV assembly and production facilities in Marietta, Georgia. Initial capacity of 100,000 units per year came online in June 1983. An additional 200,000 units of capacity was scheduled for 1985. Cost figures for 1983 production of 13-inch color TV sets in the United States as compared to in Korea was as follows:

EXHIBIT 3 Color TV market—retail brand shares and market size, 1981–1984

	1981	1982	1983	1984
Domestic manufacturers				
RCA	20.0%	20.1%	18.9%	18.1%
Zenith	18.7	18.9	16.8	16.2
General Electric	8.0	7.8	7.6	6.4
North American Phillips	12.4	11.8	10.5	10.2
Other domestic	4.7	3.8	3.9	3.5
Total domestic	64.0	62.4	57.7	54.4
Japanese				
Sony	7.7	6.9	7.5	6.7
Panasonic	2.6	3.7	4.0	3.9
Sharp	1.4	2.0	2.4	3.1
Hitachi	2.5	2.8	2.8	3.0
Sanyo	1.2	1.2	1.7	1.5
Other Japanese	3.1	3.0	3.0	4.2
Total Japanese	18.5	19.6	21.4	22.4
Far East				
Samsung (Korea)	0.2	0.5	1.6	1.6
Gold Star (Korea)	0.5	0.7	0.8	0.9
Chaebol (Korea)	0.7	1.1	1.3	1.7
Other Far East	0.5	0.8	0.7	0.8
Total Far East	1.9	3.1	4.4	5.0
Private label (Sears, J. C. Penney, Montgomery Ward, K mart, etc.)	13.4	12.7	13.2	12.9
All other	2.2	2.2	3.3	5.3
Market size in units (000)	10,641	11,567	13,608	15,646

	Korean production	U.S. production
Direct material	$101.20	$113.40
Labor	2.40	5.25
Overhead	4.25	5.85
Transportation	5.85	
Duty	5.35	
Total cost	$119.05	$124.50

Even though Chaebol's costs were higher when TVs were produced in the United States, management believed these U.S. costs were approximately 10 percent below those of domestic TV producers.

In conjunction with the establishment of U.S. production facilities, Mr. Park established Chaebol Electronics Company, U.S., and sent his son, Mr. Park Sung-Il, to the United States to head the company. The younger Mr. Park hired six new American sales representatives to work in three new sales offices in Denver, Los Angeles, and New York. Warehouse facilities and service centers were also established in these cities. Chaebol's five warehouses cost an average of $250,000 per year each. Service costs were one-quarter percent of sales in 1984. Mr. Park's goal was to expand TV sales into new markets. In late 1983, Chaebol U.S. succeeded in gaining contracts to sell its TVs in 9-inch black-and-white and 13-inch color to two major catalog showroom companies. These sets were all to carry the PKY label.

Chaebol's sales revenue in 1981 from sales of black-and-white TVs was $36.2 million. In 1983, sales revenue from black-and-white sets was $39.2 million, while sales of color sets brought in $83.75 million. Profit on these 1983 sales was $4.91 million.

The Electronics Market in 1984

Exhibit 4 shows the types of retail stores that sold electronic products in 1975 and 1984. It also shows the number of each type of store and the percentage of total electronic products sold in the United States in that year by that type of store. As the exhibit shows, there has been a significant increase not only in the total number of outlets selling electronic products but also in the variety of store types that carry this kind of product.

EXHIBIT 4 Types of electronics products sales outlets; number and percent of electronics market sales by type

Type of outlet	1975		1984	
	No. of stores	Percent sales	No. of stores	Percent sales
Radio/TV/appliance	50,152	31.4%	30,004	54.1%
Discount chains	17,887	25.0	5,764	12.4
Department stores	11,240	19.7	4,217	9.3
Furniture stores	38,732	15.9	29,609	3.7
Catalog/mail order	7,671	4.8	16,347	11.8
Auto/home supply	—	—	40,729	3.6
Drug/variety	—	—	60,516	3.3
Home centers	—	—	24,837	1.2
Hardware stores	—	—	19,870	0.6
Other	9,874	3.2	—	—
Total	135,556	100%	231,893	100%

Although Exhibit 4 shows that the total number of radio/TV/appliance stores has greatly decreased since 1975, the importance of this type of outlet within the electronics market grew to the point where radio/TV/appliance stores sold more of these products than all the other outlet types combined. The key characteristics of this type of store were wide selection, low price, and high volume. The major appliance stores stocked virtually every model of every major mass market line. It was common to find up to 150 different TV models and 100 VCRs. The stores advertised low prices and often guaranteed that they would meet any price offered by a competitor in their market area. The salespeople were usually quite knowledgeable and were paid on commission. Thus, they were aggressive in selling their higher-margin models. Price cutting was a necessity, and dealers often bought in large quantity lots, watching for deals, damaged-model sales, and other ways to cut costs. The average margin for this type of outlet was about 22 percent. These stores commonly had extensive service departments.

Discount chains, such as K mart stores, had been handling electronic products for 15 years. They bought in large quantity at lowest possible cost. The manufacturers were usually willing to cut prices in order to obtain large volume orders. Some of the larger chains also engaged in private branding, from which they were able to gain very favorable terms from manufacturers. For example, a U.S. manufacturer who engaged in private branding for one of the large chains obtained an average margin of 19 percent versus 34 percent for national brand sales. Chains usually required the customer to contact the company or independent service facility for warranty service. Some stores supported "service centers," which would simply accept the set and send it on to the manufacturer for repairs. With low overhead and low margins (18 percent), the salespeople were usually few in number and rarely informed about electronics or the differences in major lines. These stores also carried very small lines of a few manufacturers, concentrating for the most part on the low end of the model line.

Department stores carried a limited variety of brands and models of electronic products. They usually did not carry either the lowest- nor the highest-priced models, but concentrated on the largest sales models of well-known brand names. The salespeople were quite knowledgeable, and engaged in a fair amount of trying to get the customer to "trade up." Prices were sometimes discounted, particularly in larger chains. The department stores usually got about a 30 percent margin. In addition, they were eager to seek "deals" on quantity buys, closeouts, and so on. Only the national department store chains, such as Sears, J. C. Penney, and Montgomery Ward, had their own service facilities or carried their own private brands.

Furniture stores were involved only in the sales of console model TVs. Their salespeople were well informed about cabinetry and styling, but usually not too knowledgeable about electronics. These outlets usually sold at suggested retail price, and thus gained about a 37 percent margin on their sales. Furniture stores offered no in-store service facilities. With the introduction of the wide variety of electronic products since 1975, the importance of this type of outlet to the total sales of these products had decreased greatly.

Catalog/mail-order sales outlets usually sold a limited range of models from well-known brands. Unlike department stores, the range of models offered by catalog/mail-order stores went from the lower- to mid-priced models. It was also common for catalogs to offer lesser-known brands that could be priced at a significantly lower price than national brands as long as they offered high quality for that price. Catalog/mail-order outlets usually had a 15 percent margin on sales. Little selling at point of purchase was available. No repair services were offered. This type of sales outlet was of increasing importance for electronic product categories that had reached the point of mass acceptance in the marketplace.

Auto/home supply stores tended to carry only specialty products to fit the needs of small segments of the electronics market. Therefore, models and brands offered were limited, and prices and margins were relatively high. Salespeople were very knowledgeable, and these stores often offered repair services.

Drug/variety, home centers, and hardware stores had many characteristics in common. They all carried lower-priced, basic models of electronic products that were commonly purchased only through "special deals" so that low prices were possible. The variety of products and models sold by any given outlet in this group varied greatly from time to time, but usually they carried only radios, small black-and-white TVs, and accessory items like stereo speakers. The salespeople at these outlets had little knowledge of electronics. Margins for this group averaged 25 percent. No service facilities were offered on these products.

The VCR Market in 1984

The VCR market in the United States had grown very quickly from the time of the product's introduction in 1979. In 1981, 1.7 million units were sold. This number grew to 2.0 million units in 1982, 3.75 million units in 1983, and nearly 7.5 million units in 1984. The market shares of the major firms selling VCRs in 1984 are shown in the first part of Exhibit 5. The second part of the exhibit shows the number of brands and models of VCRs sold at each type of electronics outlet and the range of prices charged at each kind of store in 1984. Of the units sold in 1984, 48 percent sold for under $500, 20 percent for between $501 and $600, 17 percent for between $601 and $800, 13 percent for between $801 and $1,000, and only 2 percent for more than $1,000. The average price of VCRs sold in the United States had dropped by over $550 since their introduction in 1979. Typical features offered on low-, medium-, and high-priced VCRs in 1984 are shown below:

Low-priced models *(under $400)*	*Medium-priced models* *($400–$750)*	*High-priced models* *(over $750)*
2 video heads	2 video heads	4 video heads
1 audio head	1 audio head	2 audio heads—stereo, hi-fi
Varactor tuner (preset 12–14 channels)	Varactor tuner (preset 80–99 channels)	Direct access quartz tuner
1-event/7-day programmability	4-event/14-day programmability	8-event/1-year programmability
8-hour/3-speed recording	8-hour/3-speed recording	8-hour/3-speed recording
8-function remote (many wired)	10-function wireless remote	13–17 function wireless remote
Not cable ready	107-channel cable capability	133-channel cable capability

EXHIBIT 5   U.S. videocassette recorder market—retail brand shares, 1984

	1984 share
Domestic manufacturers	
RCA (VHS)	15.1%
General Electric (VHS)	6.2
Quasar (VHS)	5.1
Magnavox (VHS)	4.1
Zenith (VHS/Beta)	3.2
Sylvania (VHS)	1.4
Curtis-Mathes (VHS)	1.3
Total domestic	36.4%
Japanese	
Panasonic (VHS)	12.8
Sony (Beta)	6.8
Sanyo (Beta)	6.3
Sharp (VHS)	4.6
Hitachi (VHS)	3.7
MGA (VHS)	2.7
JVC (VHS)	4.1
Toshiba (Beta)	1.6
Total Japanese	42.6%
Private label	9.5%
Other	11.1%

VCR market—Number of brands and models and price ranges by type of outlet

Type of outlet	No. of brands offered	No. of models offered	Price range
Radio/TV/appliance	12	60	$259–$1,100
Discount chains	5	7	$257–$459
Department stores			
National chains	3	11	$269–$599
Regionals and independents	6	12	$399–$799
Catalog/mail-order stores	6	9	$278–$650

The total U.S. market for VCRs in 1985 was expected to be between 11 and 12 million units. With this level of sales, VCRs will have succeeded in penetrating 25 percent of the product's total market potential (households with televisions) by the end of 1985. Because of the quickness with which VCR sales reached this sales level, industry analysts did not foresee much future growth for the product line, although they did predict sales levels maintaining a 10 million to 11 million unit-per-year pace for the next five years.

The quick growth of VCR sales has had long-reaching effects on the development of the market for these products. After only five years on the market, the demographics of VCR buyers were already broadening. Originally, VCRs were most commonly purchased by upper-income (over $32,000), well-educated, married heads of household between the ages of 35 and 49. In 1984, 27 percent of VCR units were purchased by 18-to-24-year-old singles with average income between $27,000 and $32,000. The amazing sales growth of VCRs attracted many new entrants to the market each year, so that by 1984 there were over 70 VCR brands available. Many brands offered extensive VCR lines. For example, RCA, the market share leader, offered 25 VCR models ranging in suggested retail price from $330 to $1,300. The more entrants there were to the market, the stronger price competition became. This led to progressively lower and lower margins and profitability for both manufacturers and retailers. This margin loss was greatest on the lower-price-range products. To counteract this, many manufacturers were adding VCRs with greater features and capabilities to their lines—VCRs that were higher priced but also more profitable.

In late 1984, market analysts expressed the belief that Korean VCR manufacturers would enter the U.S. market using the same strategy that had gained them market share in TV sales: that of offering low-priced products that would allow them to take advantage of their lower labor costs. Thus, their expectations were that Korean VCRs would be priced $50 to $75 below the 1984 $400 mid-priced Japanese units with the same features. Furthermore, analysts believed that this kind of price differential would require retailers to pick up the Korean models. However, many analysts felt retailers would only carry these models as advertising draws and would often try to get customers to buy up from these low-priced VCRs to more profitable models.

Chaebol's Decision

Mr. Park Sung-Il had narrowed down Chaebol's VCR entry strategy to between one of two alternatives.

Strategy I

The first entry strategy alternative involved using distribution channels and retail outlets for VCRs similar to those Chaebol had employed for TV sales. For VCRs, Mr. Park wanted to limit distribution to only high-volume buyers. Thus, if this strategy was employed, Chaebol would only seek sales to large discount chains and catalog/mail-order retailers. Mr. Park planned to produce three models for these outlets. All would be two video head, one audio head models, with varactor tuning allowing 12 stations to be preset. The lowest-cost model, Model CHA, would also feature one-event/one-week programmability, wired remote, auto rewind, and would not be cable ready. Model CHA would cost Chaebol $143.50 to produce. The next step up in Chaebol's offerings would be Model CHB, which would have 1-event/14-day programmability, an eight-function wireless remote, auto rewind, and be cable ready. Model CHB would cost $201 to manufacture. Model CHC, the highest-priced model offered under this strategy, would feature 1-event/14-day programmability, 12-function remote control, auto rewind, frame advance, a sharpness control, and would be cable ready. Model CHC would cost Chaebol $247.90. Mr. Park believed

Chaebol's costs on these products would allow its customers to price these models 15 percent below similar VCRs on the market.

Since Chaebol salespeople were already calling on these customers, Mr. Park believed this alternative would have few additional costs over Chaebol's present expenses. Additional warehouse space and service personnel would have to be acquired, but no new sales offices would be needed. Mr. Park believed that most of these sales would be low-priced, private brand VCRs, although he hoped that those customers who were purchasing PKY brand TVs would purchase PKY brand name VCRs. Mr. Park estimated he could sell 225,000 VCRs in 1985 with this strategy, 70,000 carrying the PKY name. He believed private label sales would carry a 27 percent gross margin for Chaebol, while the PKY brand sales would bring a 34 percent gross margin.

Strategy II

Mr. Park's alternative to the above strategy was to use Chaebol's cost advantage, arising from lower labor coats than either U.S. or Japanese competitors, to gain admission to the TV/radio/appliance outlets that had the largest share of VCR sales and sold only brand name products. Mr. Park believed Chaebol's cost advantage would allow it to produce VCRs that carried more features than competitors' products at each price point in the market. Selling VCRs in this channel would enable Chaebol's products to be distinguished from the 50 or more brands of low-cost, low-priced VCRs, and firmly establish the PKY brand name. In the future, he hoped to move Chaebol TVs into this channel where there were higher margins for producers and retailers. His dream was to have the PKY brand obtain the same quality reputation that Sony and Panasonic had achieved.

The models Chaebol would offer under this strategy were as follows:

Model	Chaebol cost	Features
CHC	$247.90	Two video heads, 1 audio head, 1-event/14-day programmability, varactor tuning for 12 preset stations, 12-function wireless remote, auto rewind, frame advance, sharpness control.
CH1A	$286.15	Two video heads, 2 audio heads, stereo, 5-event/14-day programmability, varactor tuning for 50 preset stations, 14-function wireless remote, auto rewind, tape memory, memory backup, time-remaining indicator, 107-channel cable ready.
CH1B	$367.90	Four video heads, 2 audio heads, stereo/hi-fi/Dolby, 8-event/1-year programmability, quartz tuning, 133-channel cable ready, 17-function wireless remote, auto rewind, tape memory, time-remaining indicator, one-touch recording, slow motion, frame advance, video dub, audio dub, sharpness control.
CH1P	$388.30	All of the features of the CH1B Model plus portable.

Mr. Park estimated that these models would sell at retail for considerably less than competitive products with similar features. On Model CH1B, he believed the retail price difference could be as much as $350. With this kind of differential, Mr. Park believed he would find many TV/radio/appliance store-owners eager to take on his products since they would allow the retailer to gain larger margins than other brands. Chaebol expected to make nearly a 44 percent gross margin on models sold to this type of outlet.

Mr. Park was considering two approaches to getting his company's VCRs in TV/radio/appliance outlets. The first was to sell directly to the owners of these stores. This approach would require a significant expansion of Chaebol's marketing organization. Since the number of TV/radio/appliance stores to be reached was large and geographically dispersed, new sales offices would have to be established in Boston, Indianapolis, Dallas, St. Louis, and Seattle. Each sales office would have three salespeople. In addition, three regional sales managers would have to be hired to help organize the now diverse and large sales function of the company. Furthermore, the establishment of a high recognition for Chaebol's PKY brand name would have to come from extensive advertising. Mr. Park estimated that the expenditure of $6 million on advertising in 1985 would be minimal to achieve the results he desired.

As an alternative, Mr. Park knew this market could also be approached through the employment of distributors who were already selling the VCRs of other manufacturers to TV/radio/appliance stores. Under this plan, no new sales offices would need to be opened, but one new salesperson would be added to the staff of each existing office. These five salespeople would be charged with maintaining relationships with the 10 geographically dispersed consumer electronics distributors that Chaebol's head office would choose to carry its VCRs. These distributors would work first on getting PKY brand VCRs into the largest regional and national TV/radio/appliance chains. Chaebol's salespeople would also call on PKY retailers in their areas, working on incentive programs with outlet salespeople, solving any problems that might arise, and checking that the services expected from the distributors were being adequately performed. Using distributors would cost Chaebol 11 percent of its margin; that is, the distributors would get an 11 percent margin on sales while Chaebol's margin would drop to approximately 33 percent on these sales. Under this approach, no additional warehouses over those proposed under Strategy I would be required. However, since this approach required the establishment of the PKY brand name, the advertising cost of $6 million would still be necessary.

Mr. Park believed Chaebol could achieve sales of 120,000 VCRs in 1985 using the direct approach and 150,000 VCRs using distributors. Though these figures were lower than the initial sales that could be achieved under the first strategy, Mr. Park believed the long-term strength of the company was better served by the firm establishment of a brand name and a strong position in TV/radio/appliance outlets.

A comparison of the costs involved in the plans considered by Mr. Park is shown in the table below:

Expense area	Cost of each new unit	Strategy I	Strategy II Direct	Strategy II Distributors
Sales offices	$ 25,000/yr.	—	5	—
Salespeople	$ 42,000/yr. salary $ 23,000/yr. expenses	—	18	5
Warehouses	$300,000/yr.	3	5	3
Service facilities		.25% sales	.33 sales	.33 sales
Average margins		27%, 34%	44%	33%
Advertising		$1.5 million	$6 million	$6 million

As Mr. Park worked on estimating the relative costs of these alternatives, he wondered if there was another approach to the market that might lead to success both now and in the future for Chaebol Electronics Company, U.S.

Case 19

Thompson Respiration Products, Inc.*

Victor Higgins, executive vice president for Thompson Respiration Products, Inc. (TRP), sat thinking at his desk late one Friday in April 1986. "We're making progress," he said to himself. "Getting Metro to sign finally gets us into the Chicago market . . . and with a good dealer at that." *Metro,* of course, was Metropolitan Medical Products, a large Chicago retailer of medical equipment and supplies for home use. "Now, if we could just do the same in Minneapolis and Atlanta," he continued.

However, getting at least one dealer in each of these cities to sign a TRP Dealer Agreement seemed remote right now. One reason was the sizable groundwork required—Higgins simply lacked the time to review operations at the well over 100 dealers currently operating in the two cities. Another was TRP's lack of dealer-oriented sales information that went beyond the technical specification sheet for each product and the company's price list. Still another concerned two conditions in the Dealer Agreement itself—prospective dealers sometimes balked at agreeing to sell no products manufactured by TRP's competitors and differed with TRP in interpretations of the "best efforts" clause. (The clause required the dealer to maintain adequate inventories of TRP products, contact four prospective new customers or physicians or respiration therapists per month, respond promptly to sales inquiries, and represent TRP at appropriate conventions where it exhibited.)

"Still," Higgins concluded, "we signed Metro in spite of these reasons, and 21 others across the country. That's about all anyone could expect—after all, we've only been trying to develop a dealer network for a year or so."

---

* This case was written by Professor James E. Nelson and DBA Candidate William R. Woolridge, the University of Colorado. This case illustrates neither effective nor ineffective administrative decision making. Some data are disguised. © 1984 by the Business Research Division, College of Business and Administration and the Graduate School of Business Administration, University of Colorado.

The Portable Respirator Industry

The portable respirator industry began in the early 1950s when polio-stricken patients who lacked control of muscles necessary for breathing began to leave treatment centers. They returned home with hospital-style iron lungs or fiberglass chest shells, both being large chambers that regularly introduced a vacuum about the patient's chest. The vacuum caused the chest to expand and, thus, the lungs to fill with air. However, both devices confined patients to a prone or semiprone position in a bed.

By the late 1950s, TRP had developed a portable turbine blower powered by an electric motor and battery. When connected to a mouthpiece via plastic tubing, the blower would inflate a patient's lungs on demand. Patients could now leave their beds for several hours at a time and realize limited mobility in a wheelchair. By the early 1970s, TRP had developed a line of more sophisticated turbine respirators in terms of monitoring and capability for adjustment to individual patient needs.

At about the same time, applications began to shift from polio patients to victims of other diseases or of spinal cord injuries, the latter group existing primarily as a result of automobile accidents. Better emergency medical service, quicker evacuation to spinal cord injury centers, and more proficient treatment meant that people who formerly would have died now lived and went on to lead meaningful lives. Because of patients' frequently younger ages, they strongly desired wheelchair mobility. Respiration therapists obliged by recommending a Thompson respirator for home use or, if unaware of Thompson, recommending a Puritan-Bennett or other machine.

Instead of a turbine, Puritan-Bennett machines used a bellows design to force air into the patient's lungs. The machines were widely used in hospitals but seemed poorly suited for home use. For one thing, Puritan-Bennett machines used a compressor pump or pressurized air to drive the bellows, much more cumbersome than Thompson's electric motor. Puritan-Bennett machines also cost approximately 50 percent more than a comparable Thompson unit and were relatively large and immobile. On the other hand, Puritan-Bennett machines were viewed by physicians and respiration therapists as industry standards.

By the late 1970s, TRP had developed a piston and cylinder design (similar in principle to the bellows) and placed it on the market. The product lacked the sophistication of the Puritan-Bennett machines but was reliable, portable, and much simpler to adjust and operate. It also maintained TRP's traditional cost advantage. Another firm, Life Products, began its operations in 1981 by producing a similar design. A third competitor, Lifecare Services, had begun operations somewhat earlier.

Puritan-Bennett

Puritan-Bennett was a large, growing, and financially sound manufacturer of respiration equipment for medical and aviation applications. Its headquarters were located in Kansas City, Missouri. However, the firm staffed over 40 sales, service, and warehouse operations in the United States, Canada, United Kingdom, and France. Sales for 1985 exceeded $100 million while employment was just over 2,000 people. Sales for its Medical Equipment Group (respirators, related equipment, and accessories, service, and parts) likely exceeded $40 million for 1985; however, Higgins could obtain data only for the period 1977–1980 (see Exhibit 1). Puritan-Bennett usually sold its respirators through a system of independent, durable medical equipment dealers. However, its sales offices did sell directly to identified "house accounts" and often competed with dealers by selling slower-moving products to all accounts. According to industry sources, Puritan-Bennett sales were slightly more than three fourths of all respirator sales to hospitals in 1985.

EXHIBIT 1 Puritan-Bennett Medical Equipment Group sales

	1981	1982	1983	1984
Domestic sales:				
Model MA-1:				
Units	1,460	875	600	500
Amount ($ millions)	8.5	4.9	3.5	3.1
Model MA-2:				
Units	—	935	900	1,100
Amount ($ millions)	—	6.0	6.1	7.8
Foreign sales:				
Units	250	300	500	565
Amount ($ millions)	1.5	1.8	3.1	3.6
IPPB equipment ($ millions)	6.0	6.5	6.7	7.0
Parts, service, accessories				
($ millions)	10.0	11.7	13.1	13.5
Overhaul ($ millions)	2.0	3.0	2.5	2.5
Total ($ millions)	28.0	34.0	35.0	37.5

Source: *The Wall Street Transcript.*

However, these same sources expected Puritan-Bennett's share to diminish during the late 1980s because of the aggressive marketing efforts of three other manufacturers of hospital-style respirators: Bear Medical Systems, Inc.; J. H. Emerson; and Siemens-Elema. The latter firm was expected to grow the most rapidly, despite its quite recent entry into the U.S. market (its headquarters were in Sweden) and a list price of over $16,000 for its basic model.

Life Products

Life Products directly competed with TRP for the portable respirator market. Life Products had begun operations in 1981 when David Smith, a TRP employee, left to start his own business. Smith had located his plant in Boulder, Colorado, less than a mile from TRP headquarters.

He began almost immediately to set up a dealer network and by early 1986 had secured over 40 independent dealers located in large metropolitan areas. Smith had made a strong effort to sign only large, well-managed durable medical equipment dealers. Dealer representatives were required to complete Life Product's service training school, held each month in Boulder. Life Products sold its products to dealers (in contrast to TRP, which both sold and rented products to consumers and to dealers). Dealers received a 20 to 25 percent discount off suggested retail price on most products.

As of April 1986, Life Products offered two respirator models (the LP3 and LP4) and a limited number of accessories (such as mouthpieces and plastic tubing) to its dealers. Suggested retail prices for the two respirator models were approximately $3,900 and $4,800. Suggested rental rates were approximately $400 and $500 per month. Life Products also allowed Lifecare Services to manufacture a respirator similar to the LP3 under license.

At the end of 1985, Smith was quite pleased with his firm's performance. During Life Products' brief history, it had passed TRP in sales and now ceased to see the firm as a serious threat, at least according to one company executive:

> We really aren't in competition with Thompson. They're after the stagnant market and we're after a growing market. We see new applications and ultimately the hospital market as our niche. I doubt if Thompson will even be around in a few years. As for Lifecare, their prices are much lower than ours but you don't get the service. With them you get the basic product, but nothing else. With us, you get a complete medical care service. That's the big difference.

Lifecare Services, Inc.

In contrast to the preceding firms, Lifecare Services, Inc. earned much less of its revenues from medical equipment manufacturing and much more from medical equipment distributing. The firm primarily resold products purchased from other manufacturers, operating out of its headquarters in Boulder as well as from its 16 field offices (Exhibit 2). All offices were stocked with backup parts and an inventory of respirators. All were staffed with trained service technicians under Lifecare's employ.

EXHIBIT 2 Lifecare Services, Inc., field offices

Augusta, Ga.	Houston, Tex.
Baltimore, Md.	Los Angeles, Calif.
Boston, Mass.	New York, N.Y.
Chicago, Ill.	Oakland, Calif.
Cleveland, Ohio	Omaha, Nebr.
Denver, Colo.	Phoenix, Ariz.
Detroit, Mich.	Seattle, Wash.
Grand Rapids, Mich.*	St. Paul, Minn.

* Suboffice.
Source: Trade literature.

Lifecare did manufacture a few accessories not readily available from other manufacturers. These items complemented the purchased products and, in the company's words, served to "give the customer a complete respiratory service." Under a licensing agreement between Lifecare and Life Products, the firm manufactured a respirator similar to the LP3 and marketed it under the Lifecare name. The unit rented for approximately $175 per month. While Lifecare continued to service the few remaining Thompson units it still had in the field, it no longer carried the Thompson line.

Lifecare rented rather than sold its equipment. The firm maintained that this gave patients more flexibility in the event of recovery or death and lowered patients' monthly costs.

Thompson Respiration Products, Inc.

TRP currently employed 13 people, 9 in production and 4 in management. It conducted operations in a modern, attractive building (leased) in an industrial park. The building contained about 6,000 square feet of space, split 75/25 for production/management purposes. Production operations were essentially job shop in nature: skilled technicians assembled each unit by hand on work benches, making frequent quality control tests and subsequent adjustments. Production lots usually ranged from 10 to 75 units per model and probably averaged around 40. Normal production capacity was about 600 units per year.

Product Line

TRP currently sold seven respirator models plus a large number of accessories. All respirator models were portable but differed considerably in terms of style, design, performance specifications, and attendant features (see Exhibit 3). Four models were styled as metal boxes with an impressive array of knobs, dials, indicator lights, and switches. Three were styled as less imposing, "overnighter" suitcases with less prominently displayed controls and indicators. (Exhibit 4 reproduces part of the specification sheet for the M3000, as illustrative of the metal box design.)

Four of the models were designed as *pressure machines,* using a turbine pump that provided a constant, usually positive, pressure. Patients were provided intermittent access to this pressure as breaths per minute. However, one model, the MV Multivent, could provide either a constant positive or a constant negative pressure (i.e., a vacuum, necessary to operate chest shells, iron lungs, and body wraps). No other portable respirator on the market could produce a negative pressure. Three of the models were designed as *volume machines,* using a piston pump that produced intermittent, constant volumes of pressurized air as breaths per minute. Actual volumes were prescribed by each patient's physician based on lung capacity. Pressures depended on the breathing method

EXHIBIT 3   TRP respirators

Model*	Style	Design	Volume (cm³)	Pressure (cm H₂O)
M3000	Metal box	Volume	300–3,000	+10 to +65
MV Multivent	Metal box	Pressure (positive or negative)	n.a.	−70 to +80
Minilung M15	Suitcase	Volume	200–1,500	+5 to +65
Minilung M25 Assist (also available without the assist feature)	Suitcase	Volume	600–2,500	+5 to +65
Bantam GS	Suitcase	Pressure (positive)	n.a.	+15 to +45
Compact CS	Metal box	Pressure (positive)	n.a.	+15 to +45
Compact C	Metal box	Pressure (positive)	n.a.	+15 to +45

Model	Breaths per minute	Weight (lbs.)	Size (ft.³)	Features
M3000	6 to 30	39	0.85	Sigh, four alarms, automatic switchover from AC to battery
MV Multivent	8 to 24	41	1.05	Positive or negative pressure, four alarms, AC only
Minilung M15	8 to 22	24	0.70	Three alarms, automatic switchover from AC to battery
Minilung M25 Assist (also available without the assist feature)	5 to 20	24	0.70	Assist, sigh, three alarms, automatic switchover from AC to battery
Bantam GS	6 to 24	19	0.75	Sigh, six alarms, automatic switchover from AC to battery
Compact CS	8 to 24	25	0.72	Sigh, six alarms, automatic switchover from AC to battery
Compact C	6 to 24	19	0.50	Sigh, four alarms, automatic switchover from AC to battery

Note: n.a. = not applicable.

* Five other models considered obsolete by TRP could be supplied if necessary.

Source: Company sales specification sheets.

used (mouthpiece, trach, chest shell, and others) and on the patient's activity level. Breaths per minute also depended on the patient's activity level.

Models came with several features. The newest was an assist feature (currently available on the Minilung M25 but soon to be offered also on the M3000) that allowed the patient alone to "command" additional breaths without having someone change the dialed breath rate. The sigh feature gave patients a sigh, either automatically or on demand. Depending on the model, up to six alarms were available to indicate a patient's call, unacceptable low pressure, unacceptable high pressure, low battery voltage/power failure, failure to cycle, and the need to replace motor brushes. All models but the MV Multivent also offered automatic switchover from alternating current to either an internal or an external battery (or both) in the event of a power failure. Batteries provided for 18 to 40 hours of operation, depending on usage.

EXHIBIT 4 The M3000 Minilung

M3000 MINILUNG
PORTABLE VOLUME VENTILATOR

What it can mean to the User...

• The M3000 is a planned performance product designed to meet breathing needs. It is a significant step in the ongoing effort of a company which pioneered the advancement of portable respiratory equipment.

• This portable volume ventilator sets high standards for flexibility of operation and versatility in use. The M3000 has gained its successful reputation as a result of satisfactory usage in hospitals, for transport, in rehabilitation efforts and in home care. This model grew out of expressed needs of users for characteristics which offer performance PLUS. It is engineered to enable the user to have something more than just mechanical breathing.

• Now breathing patterns can be comfortably varied with the use of a SIGH, which can be obtained either automatically or manually.

• Besides being sturdy and reliable, the M3000 can be adjusted readily.

• Remote pressure sensing in the proximal airway provides for more accurate set up of the ventilator pressure alarms.

• This model has the option of a patient-operated call switch.

• AC-DC operation of the M3000 is accomplished with ease because automatic switch-over is provided on AC power failure, first to external battery, then to internal battery.

THOMPSON takes pride in planning ahead

See reverse for specifications.

Innovators in Respiratory Equipment for Over 25 Years
Thompson Respiration Products, Inc.   1680 Range Street   Boulder, Colorado 80301   303/443-3350

M3000 MINILUNG
Portable Volume Ventilator

SPECIFICATIONS:

300 to 3000 ml adjustable volume

10 to 65 cm. water pressure

6 to 30 breaths per minute

Automatic or Manual Sigh

Alarms:
Patient operated call alarm
Low Pressure alarm and light
High Pressure alarm and light
Low Voltage light with delayed alarm
Automatic switchover provided on AC power failure,
   first to external battery, then to internal battery
Alarm delay switch

Pilot lamps color-coded and labeled

Remote pressure connector

Self-contained battery for 2 hour operation — recharges automatically

Power sources:
120 volt, 60 hz, 12 volt external battery; and internal battery

Size: 12⅝ W x 11¼ D x 10¼ inches H

Weight: 39 pounds (Shipping weight: 48 pounds)

Higgins felt that TRP's respirators were superior to those of Life Products. Most TRP models allowed pressure monitoring in the airway itself rather than in the machine, providing more accurate measurement. TRP's suitcase-style models often were strongly preferred by patients, especially the polio patients who had known no others. TRP's volume models offered easier volume adjustments and all TRP models offered more alarms. On the other hand, he knew that TRP had recently experienced some product reliability problems of an irritating—not life threatening—nature. Further, he knew that Life Products had beaten TRP to the market with the assist feature (the idea for which had come from a Puritan-Bennett machine).

TRP's line of accessories was more extensive than that of Life Products. TRP offered the following for separate sale: alarms, call switches, battery cables, chest shells, mouthpieces, plastic tubing, pneumobelts and bladders (equipment for still another breathing method that utilized intermittent pressure on a patient's diaphragm), and other items. Lifecare Services offered many similar items.

Distribution

Shortly after joining TRP, Higgins had decided to switch from selling and renting products directly to patients to selling and renting products to dealers. While it meant lower margins, less control, and more infrequent communication with patients, the change had several advantages. It allowed TRP to shift inventory from the factory to the dealer, generating cash more quickly. It provided for local representation in market areas, allowing patients greater feelings of security and TRP more aggressive sales efforts. It shifted burdensome paperwork (required by insurance companies and state and federal agencies to effect payment) from TRP to the dealer. It also reduced other TRP administrative activities in accounting, customer relations, and sales.

TRP derived about half of its 1985 revenue of $3 million directly from patients and about half from the dealer network. By April 1986, the firm had 22

EXHIBIT 5 TRP dealer locations

Bakersfield, Calif.	Salt Lake City, Utah
Baltimore, Md.	San Diego, Calif.
Birmingham, Ala.	San Francisco, Calif.
Chicago, Ill.	Seattle, Wash.
Cleveland, Ohio	Springfield, Ohio
Fort Wayne, Ind.	Tampa, Fla.
Greenville, N.C.	Tucson, Ariz.
Indianapolis, Ind.	Washington, D.C.
Newark, N.J.	
Oklahoma City, Okla.	Montreal, Canada
Pittsburgh, Pa.	Toronto, Canada

Source: Company records.

dealers (see Exhibit 5) with 3 accounting for over 60 percent of TRP dealer revenues. Two of the three serviced TRP products as did two of the smaller dealers; the rest preferred to let the factory take care of repairs. TRP conducted occasional training sessions for dealer repair personnel but distances were great and turnover in the position high, making such sessions costly. Most dealers requested air shipment of respirators, in quantities of 1 or 2 units.

Price

TRP maintained a comprehensive price list for its entire product line. (Exhibit 6 reproduces part of the current list.) Each respirator model carried both a suggested retail selling price and a suggested retail rental rate. (TRP also applied these rates when it dealt directly with patients.) The list also presented two net purchase prices for each model along with an alternative rental rate that TRP charged to dealers. About 40 percent of the 300 respirator units TRP shipped to dealers in 1985 went out on a rental basis. The comparable figure for the 165 units sent directly to consumers was 90 percent. Net purchase prices allowed an approximate 7 percent discount for orders of three or more units of each model. Higgins had initiated this policy early last year with the aim of encouraging dealers to order in larger quantities. To date one dealer had taken advantage of this discount.

EXHIBIT 6 Current TRP respirator price list

	Suggested retail		Dealer	Dealer price	
Model	Rent/month	Price	Rent/month	1–2	3 or more
M3000	$380	$6,000	$290	$4,500	$4,185
MV Multivent	270	4,300	210	3,225	3,000
Minilung M15	250	3,950	190	2,960	2,750
Minilung M25	250	3,950	190	2,960	2,750
Bantam GS	230	3,600	175	2,700	2,510
Compact CS	230	3,600	175	2,700	2,510
Compact C	200	3,150	155	2,360	2,195

Source: Company sales specification sheets.

Current policy called for TRP to earn a gross margin of approximately 35 percent on the dealer price for 1–2 units. All prices included shipping charges by United Parcel Service (UPS); purchasers requesting more expensive transportation service paid the difference between actual costs incurred and the UPS charge. Terms were net 30 days with a 1.5 percent service charge added to past due accounts. Prices were last changed in late 1985.

Consumers

Two types of patients used respirators, depending on whether the need followed from disease or from injury. Diseases such as polio, sleep apnea, chronic obstructive pulmonary disease, and muscular dystrophy annually left about 1,900 victims unable to breathe without a respirator. Injury to the spinal cord above the fifth vertebra caused a similar result for about 300 people per year. Except for polio, incidences of the diseases and injury were growing at about 3 percent per year. Most patients kept one respirator at bedside and another mounted on a wheelchair. However, Higgins did know of one individual who kept eight Bantam B models (provided by a local polio foundation, now defunct) in his closet. Except for polio patients, life expectancies were about five years. Higgins estimated the total number of patients using a home respirator in 1981 at

Polio	3,000
Other diseases	6,500
Spinal cord injury	1,000

Almost all patients were under a physician's care as well as that of a more immediate nurse or attendant (frequently a relative). About 95 percent paid for their equipment through insurance benefits or foundation monies. About 90 percent rented their equipment. Almost all patients and their nurses or attendants had received instruction in equipment operation from respiration therapists employed by medical centers or by dealers of durable medical equipment.

The majority of patients were poor. Virtually none were gainfully employed and all had seen their savings and other assets diminished to varying degrees by treatment costs. Some had experienced a divorce. Slightly more patients were male than female. About 75 percent lived in their homes with the rest split between hospitals, nursing homes, and other institutions.

Apart from patients, Higgins thought that hospitals might be considered a logical new market for TRP to enter. Many of the larger and some of the smaller general hospitals might be convinced to purchase one portable respirator (like the M3000) for emergency and other use with injury patients. Such a machine would be much cheaper to purchase than a large Puritan-Bennett and would allow easier patient trips to testing areas, X-ray, surgery, and the like. Even easier to convince should be the fourteen regional spinal cord injury centers located across the country (Exhibit 7). Other medical centers that specialized in treatment of pulmonary diseases should also be prime targets. Somewhat less promising but more numerous would be public and private schools that trained physicians and respiration therapists. Higgins estimated the numbers of these institutions at:

General hospitals (100 beds or more)	3,800
General hospitals (fewer than 100 beds)	3,200
Spinal cord injury centers	14
Pulmonary disease treatment centers	100
Medical schools	180
Respiration therapy schools	250

EXHIBIT 7 Regional spinal cord injury centers

Birmingham, Ala.	Houston, Tex.
Boston, Mass.	Miami, Fla.
Chicago, Ill.	New York, N.Y.
Columbia, Mo.	Philadelphia, Pa.
Downey, Calif.	Phoenix, Ariz.
Englewood, Colo.	San Jose, Calif.
Fishersville, Va.	Seattle, Wash.

Dealers

Dealers supplying homecare medical products (as distinct from dealers supplying hospitals and medical centers) showed a great deal of diversity. Some were little more than small areas in local drugstores that rented canes, walkers, and wheelchairs in addition to selling supplies like surgical stockings and colostomy bags. Others carried nearly everything needed for home nursing care—renting everything from canes to hospital beds and selling supplies from bed pads to bottled oxygen. Still others specialized in products and supplies for only certain types of patients.

In this latter category, Higgins had identified dealers of oxygen and oxygen-related equipment as the best fit among existing dealers. These dealers serviced victims of emphysema, bronchitis, asthma, and other respiratory ailments, a growing market that Higgins estimated was about 10 times greater than that for respirators. A typical dealer had begun perhaps 10 years ago selling bottled oxygen (obtained from a welding supply wholesaler) and renting rather crude metering equipment to patients at home under the care of a registered nurse. The same dealer today now rented and serviced oxygen concentrators (a recently developed device that extracts oxygen from the air), liquid oxygen equipment and liquid oxygen, and much more sophisticated oxygen equipment and oxygen to patients cared for by themselves or by relatives.

Most dealers maintained a fleet of radio-dispatched trucks to deliver products to their customers. Better dealers promised 24-hour service and kept delivery personnel and a respiration therapist on call 24 hours a day. Dealers usually employed several respiration therapists who would set up equipment, instruct patients and attendants on equipment operation, and provide routine and emergency service. Dealers often expected the therapists to function as a sales force. The therapists would call on physicians and other respiration therapists at hospitals and medical centers, on discharge planners at hospitals, and on organizations such as muscular dystrophy associations, spinal cord injury associations, and visiting nurse associations.

Dealers usually bought their inventories of durable equipment and supplies directly from manufacturers. They usually received a 20 to 25 percent discount off suggested list prices to consumers and hospitals. Only in rare instances might dealers instead lease equipment from a manufacturer. Dealers aimed for a payback of one year or less, meaning that most products began to contribute to profit and overhead after 12 months of rental. Most products lasted physically for upwards of 10 years but technologically for only 5 to 6. Every dealer's warehouse contained idle but perfectly suitable equipment that had been superseded by models demanded by patients, their physicians, or their attendants.

Most dealers were independently owned and operated, with annual sales ranging between $5 million and $10 million. However, a number had recently been acquired by one of several parent organizations that were regional or national in scope. Such chains usually consisted of from 10 to 30 retail operations located in separated market areas. However, the largest, Abbey Medical, had begun operations in 1924 and now consisted of over 70 local dealers. Higgins estimated 1985 sales for the chain (which was itself acquired by American Hospital Supply Corporation in April 1981) at over $60 million. In general, chains maintained a low corporate visibility and provided their dealers with working capital, employee benefit programs, operating advice, and some centralized purchasing. Higgins thought that chain organizations might grow more rapidly over the next 10 years.

The Issues

Higgins looked at his watch. It was 5:30 and really time to leave. "Still," he thought, "I should jot down what I see to be the immediate issues before I go—that way I won't be tempted to think about them over the weekend." He took a pen and wrote the following:

1. Should TRP continue to rent respirators to dealers?
2. Should TRP protect each dealer's territory (and how big should a territory be)?
3. Should TRP require dealers to stock no competing equipment?
4. How many dealers should TRP eventually have? Where?
5. What sales information should be assembled in order to attract high-quality dealers?
6. What should be done about the "best efforts" clause?

As he reread the list, Higgins considered that there probably were still other short-term-oriented questions he might have missed. Monday would be soon enough to consider them all.

Until then, he was free to think about broader, more strategic issues. Some reflections on the nature of the target market, a statement of marketing objectives, and TRP's possible entry into the hospital market would occupy the weekend. Decisions on these topics would form a substantial part of TRP's strategic marketing plan, a document Higgins hoped to have for the beginning of the next fiscal year in July. "At least I can rule out one option," Higgins thought as he put on his coat. That was an idea to use independent sales representatives to sell TRP products on commission; A recently completed two-month search for such an organization had come up empty. "Like my stomach," he thought, as he went out the door.

Case 20

Laramie Oil Company: Retail Gasoline Division*

In April 1991 George Thomas, vice president in charge of domestic automotive gasoline distribution for the Laramie Oil Company, was considering what action he should take with regard to the company's 12,400 franchised and lessee-operated service stations. A number of developments that indicated discontent among franchisees and lessees had recently occurred. Although he was unsure as to what extent these developments indicated real widespread discontent, Mr. Thomas was wondering what might be causing it, and what action he should take at the present time, and in the long run.

Company Background

The Laramie Oil Company was a fully integrated petroleum company with operations in 21 countries. In 1990 domestic sales were $8.79 billion, and net income was $823.4 million. The Laramie product line included automotive gasoline, aviation fuels, distillates, lubricants, and assorted agricultural and industrial chemicals. Sales of automotive gasoline and related products accounted for 52 percent of revenues earned and 64 percent of net profit.

Both the international and domestic American head offices were situated in New York City. As distribution vice president, George Thomas had responsibility for the overall maintenance of a strong network of retail outlets. This responsibility involved the setting of policies concerning lease terms, the selection of dealers, the training of dealers, the motivation of dealers, the dismissal of dealers, and any other factors involving the maintenance of dealer morale and overall effectiveness. Mr. Thomas had responsibility only for the company's Laramie brand stations. Laramie Oil also operated about 50 discount outlets and expected to open more in the near future. These outlets operated under a different brand name.

* This case was written by Thomas C. Kinnear and C. Merle Crawford, Professor of Marketing, University of Michigan. Copyright © 1991 by Thomas C. Kinnear.

George Thomas described his objective as distribution vice president as follows:

> We've done a great deal of research to determine why gasoline purchasers use one brand of gasoline or another. In almost every instance, the consumer's perception of the gasoline retail outlet was a very significant determinant in brand selection. It appears that we're halfway to first base if we can keep our outlets modern and clean, plus provide the service that the consumer desires. By service, I mean more than just good, fast, competent pump island work. Service includes having outlets open when consumers need them, and making sure that outlets handle our national promotions. There is nothing more irritating to a customer who expects to receive a glass or coupon than to find that the station that he happens to be in isn't participating in the national promotion. That is one of the best ways to lose customers for good.
>
> Our whole retail distribution policy is directed toward providing a consistent type of physical outlet and service from one end of the country to the other. That's how gasoline is sold.

Implementation of Distribution Policies

George Thomas's control over the implementation of his department's policies was quite indirect. A general manager in each of five geographical divisions had responsibility for all marketing activities in his division, including retail distribution. Each division had a distribution manager whose responsibilities included the day-to-day implementation of corporate policies in regard to service station operations. The division distribution manager reported directly to the division general manager. The corporate and divisional distribution managers did, however, maintain informal contact with each other. Each divisional distribution manager had a number of district sales managers reporting directly to him. Direct contact with service station operators was maintained by company sales representatives, each of whom reported to a district sales manager. The sales representative was the final link in the chain of implementation between George Thomas's office and the service station operator. (See Exhibit 1 for a partial organization chart.)

Type of Service Stations

Laramie Oil Company distributed its automotive products through three types of service stations:

1. *Company operated.*   These stations were owned or leased by Laramie Oil who hired the service station personnel to operate them on a straight salary basis. Laramie controlled the retail price and all other aspects of all products sold through these stations. About 100 of Laramie's 12,400 stations were operated in this manner.
2. *Franchised dealers.*   The station site and all physical facilities of franchised dealer operations were owned by the dealers themselves. Laramie

EXHIBIT 1 Partial organization chart

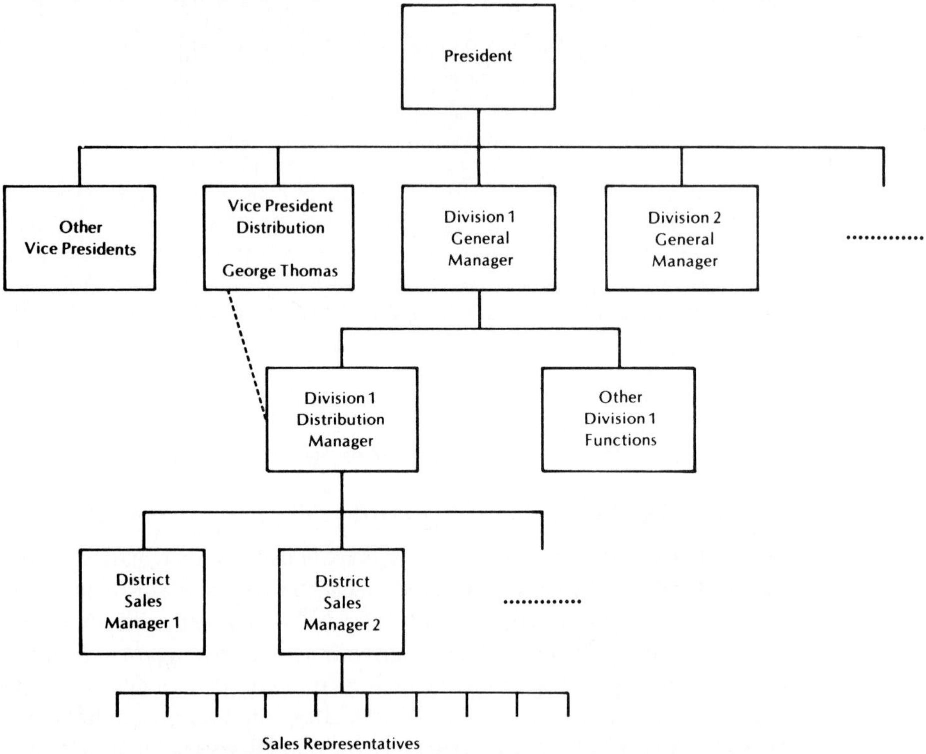

----- Indicates an informal communications link.

did, however, provide financing, so that an individual dealer could commence operation by putting up as little as $2,000. The company, or local financial institutions, held mortgages on the land and physical facilities. About 500 outlets were in this category.

3. *Lessee operated.* Lessee operators were dealers who leased their service station from Laramie Oil. The stations, in these cases, continued to be owned by Laramie Oil. The lessee purchased petroleum products from Laramie but was free to set his own operating policies as related to such things as hours, prices, and brands of accessories carried. The lessee's cost price of gasoline was based on a "tank wagon price" which included all taxes and delivery charges to the lessee's station. Typical lessee operators were charged per gallon, as shown in the accompanying table.

Transport price (except tax)	$0.660
Plus: State and federal taxes	0.450
Transport price (including tax)	1.110
Plus: Jobber margin	0.085
Tank wagon price	1.195
Plus: Rent paid to Laramie	0.055
Lessee's margin	0.070
Retail price	$1.320

The cost price of gasoline to franchised dealers closely approximated the lessee cost arrangement, except that rent charges were not included. For most franchisees, interest charges on their mortgages tended to make up this cost difference.

A Closer Look at Two Laramie Lessee Dealers

1. Jerry Williamson's Laramie service station, Dearborn, Michigan. Jerry Williamson's service station was located at one of the main intersections in the Detroit suburb of Dearborn. His customers were drawn mainly from local residents and commuters who drove through Dearborn on their way to and from their work in Detroit. Williamson was a class A automobile mechanic who had worked for a Ford dealership for eight years before becoming a Laramie dealer in 1974. He had put up $19,500 of his own money to obtain the right to be the Laramie lessee for his Dearborn location. Most of the $19,500 had been used to finance product inventories and tools, while some had been used to physically upgrade the station.

Williamson did a large automobile repair business. Over the years he had built up an excellent reputation among the residents of Dearborn for providing competent and reliable repair service. As a result of this business and his good location for attracting gasoline customers, he did an annual sales volume of slightly over $940,000. His profit statement for 1990 is presented in Exhibit 2.

Williamson took great pride in the fact that he had been able to build a very successful business operation. He thought of himself as being a part of the community as he took part in community work through his memberships in the Lion's Club and the Chamber of Commerce. In the latter organization he had risen to the position of vice president, and was looking forward to being president at some time.

When he was asked if there were any negative aspects to being a Laramie dealer, Williamson replied as follows:

> Well . . . not really; it's tough to complain a lot when you're making $63,000 a year. The only thing I really have to complain about is that Laramie

EXHIBIT 2 Percentage profit statements for Jerry Williamson's and Fred Shaw's service stations for 1990

	Jerry Williamson	Fred Shaw
Sales	100.00%	100.00%
Cost of goods sold	75.36	75.24
Gross profit	24.64	24.76
Expenses:		
Labor for outside work	0.46	0.29
Supplies	0.75	0.79
Wages (excluding owner)	8.38	8.69
Repairs and maintenance	0.34	0.24
Advertising	0.79	0.93
Delivery	0.41	0.42
Bad debts	0.02	0.02
Administrative	0.38	0.35
Miscellaneous	0.96	0.72
Rent	2.60	2.00
Insurance	0.47	0.46
Utilities	0.96	1.00
Taxes	0.74	0.66
Interest	0.10	0.11
Depreciation	0.60	0.65
Total expenses	17.96	17.33
Net profit	6.68%	7.43%
Inventory turnover × 1 year	17.26	12.88

pressures me to buy most of my repair parts and accessories from their own supply company or from company-approved jobbers. I think I could get slightly better margins from other jobbers, as the company takes a percentage rake-off from the approved jobbers. However, it's really a small complaint when you consider all the pluses that Laramie gives. Overall, I'm extremely pleased.

2. Fred Shaw's Laramie service station, Detroit, Michigan. Fred Shaw's service station was located in an industrial section of Detroit, with most of his customers being people who worked in the plants in the surrounding area. Prior to becoming the lessee of his current station, Shaw had worked as an employee in a suburban Laramie station. He had always wanted to be in business for himself, and whenever he heard that a station was available, he would approach the sales representative involved to see if he could obtain the station. Most of the stations had required too much capital, but finally he was able to obtain his current station by putting up $8,500 for the required inventories.

Although managing his station required long hours for Shaw, he preferred it to a very great extent over working for another dealer. It was in a very real sense to him the fulfillment of his dream of being his own boss.

Due to the nature of the surrounding environment, Shaw's station was quiet most of the day except when the shifts changed and then it was extremely busy. This constant changing from feast to famine made proper staffing extremely difficult, and required long hours to cover all shift changes.

Shaw's station was not as productive in either gasoline sales or repair service as was Jerry Williamson's. As a result, his 1990 sales volume was just under $390,000. Exhibit 2 presents his 1990 profit statement.

Hank Homes was the Laramie sales representative in Shaw's district, and on one of his weekly visits recently he asked Fred to take part in a special Bicentennial china giveaway promotion. Part of the conversation between the two men went as follows:

Hank: This looks to me to be one of the best promotions the company has ever put together. They're going to put about $2.5 million in advertising behind it. You should draw a pile of customers.

Fred: Come on, Hank. The type of customer who buys from my outlet isn't interested in bone china. It may be fine for other outlets, but I don't want in on this one. Besides, since the gasoline shortage of '79 and '80, I can't believe anyone wants to start these rotten giveaways again. Also, my customers are really mad about the big jump we've had in gasoline prices since the Kuwait invasion by Iraq.

Hank: I disagree, Fred. I'm sure you'd do well with it. Why don't you let me sign you up. I think you'd be pleased with the results. We pretested this in Denver and it went well. Think about it for a few minutes while we discuss a few other things. It looks to me as if your station could use a new coat of paint this spring. If we let it go any longer, it will chase customers away.

Fred: I don't think I can afford to put out for the paint right now, Hank. You know what a problem I'm having making ends meet here.

Hank: Well, maybe I can help you out on that score. If I work on them at the regional office, they might let me absorb part or even all of the expense for you. . . . Think about the china promotion, Fred, and I'll drop back tomorrow.

Franchisee and Lessee Discontent

The following dealer comments were taken from meetings of several Laramie retail dealer associations in various parts of the United States. Laramie retail dealer associations were groups of Laramie dealers who had gotten together on their own for such purposes as: the discussion of mutual problems, the collective purchasing of products from independent suppliers, and the undertaking of various social activities. Not all Laramie dealers belonged to associations and the strength and activity level of the associations varied greatly.

Lessee 1: The company claims that we can set our own prices, but that damn sales rep comes into my place and tells me I can't sell at more than a four-cent markup. I can hardly scrape from one week to the next at that rate. . . . I know for sure he'll drop my lease if I don't set these prices. Our dealer association has had economists do studies that showed that on the average it takes a gross profit margin of nine cents a gallon to operate profitably. Margins today run from about three cents to eight cents with the average at about five and a half cents. That's just not enough.

Lessee 2: What really bugs me is those stupid premium offers I have to put up with. They advertise them like mad on TV, so I have to carry them or the customers start screaming. . . . I don't get any more business with them—all my competitors are running some premium too—all they do is add to my costs. It's really frustrating. I thought the oil crisis had finished these things. I guess I was wrong.

Lessee 3: I couldn't be more satisfied. I make a really good living. If some of you guys stopped complaining and started working, you could do the same.

Lessee 4: You know I'd really like to close my place down at night . . . the only reason I'm open nights is 'cause the sales rep said he wouldn't renew my lease if I didn't keep his hours—imagine that, I've worked for Laramie for 15 years as a dealer and they'd drop me just like that. I can't afford to lose my station but I'm losing money by staying open.

Lessee 5: What's really got me worried is that they are going to turn my station into a company-owned and -operated outlet. Where would I be then?

Lessee 6: The company is more interested in their gallonage than our profits, and those one-sided leases let them dictate what we'll charge and what products we'll sell. They also use the lease to ride herd on our prices.

Lessee 7: I had hoped that the Supreme Court rulings prohibiting forcing their TBA (tires, batteries, and accessories) brands on us would have helped; however, all it's done is to make their methods more subtle.

Franchisee 1: I thought when I put up my bucks I was going to be in business for myself—fat chance—that sales rep is in my place all the time suggesting what hours to work, how to work, what price to set. . . . If I object, he starts talking about revoking my franchise. I know the Laramie name draws customers but some of his suggestions are unreasonable.

Franchisee 2: This business of them running their own discount stations in competition with me has really got me bugged, too.

Comments of Sales Representatives (SR)

The following comments were taken from individual interviews with selected sales representatives:

SR 1: Sure, I set hours and prices and procedures; if I didn't, some of those dolts would be out of business tomorrow.

SR 2: To get the volume out of my territory that the district manager demands, I have to pressure the dealers. Talking about the lease is always effective. However, I've never actually threatened any of my dealers with the loss of the lease.

SR 3: If you're honest and friendly with your dealers and show them what they will gain from following what you suggest, then you don't have to threaten them to get cooperation.

SR 4: You can bet your life I'm out pushing our TBA line to dealers. That right hasn't been taken away from us. However, that doesn't mean we're going to club them over the head if they don't.

Comments by George Thomas

(Made before a congressional committee.)

> It isn't our policy to require dealers to maintain company-directed hours or prices. The whole idea is that the dealer has the right to establish his own hours and prices.
>
> I'd fire any sales representative found pressuring dealers on matters like prices or hours or contests.
>
> It seems to me that what we have here is a situation completely analogous to the normal arrangement between the landlord and tenant. We have up to $200,000 invested in large stations, and if the dealers are mismanaging them we have a right and a duty to protect our investment.

Developments in 1990

A number of developments that concerned George Thomas took place in 1990.

1. A group of dealers in Chicago filed a suit against Laramie, alleging that Laramie violated the Sherman Act by using short-term leases to intimidate the dealers into following suggested retail prices. No decision had been handed down yet by the court.

2. A Laramie Marketing Research Staff report indicated that the turnover rate among Laramie dealers had increased significantly in the last few years. This problem of dealer turnover was common throughout the oil industry. Estimates indicated that approximately one third of all service stations in the United States change management every year. The Laramie turnover rate was below the national average, but was still very high. This high turnover was considered to be a very serious problem by George Thomas. Also disturbing was the fact that a significant number of long-service Laramie dealers had left to join cut-rate chains who guaranteed station managers at least $2,500 income per month.

3. The Automotive Retail Trade Association had requested the Federal Trade Commission (FTC) to charge the seven major oil companies (including Laramie) with misrepresentation, breach of contract, and promotion of price wars. The writ alleged misrepresentation of "exclusive" franchise agreements and breach of contract because the oil companies have opened "off-brand" stations near franchise service stations. The association charged that the off-brand stations sell at prices lower than the wholesale prices charged to the franchise dealers. The association wants an injunction to stop oil companies from creating subsidiary stations in direct competition with franchised dealers.

   The writ also criticized the oil companies for nondisclosure of fees or profits received by oil companies from firms which supply automobile products to the service stations. The association wanted to know this information since service station lessees are requested to buy the accessories only from designated dealers.

Finally the writ criticized promotional gimmicks and giveaways as a financial burden to operators and alleged that oil companies "demanded" cooperation and participation under threat of nonrenewal of leases.

4. The Central States Automotive Retailers Association presented a brief to the governors of six states asking for legislation to prohibit gimmicks and giveaways connected with gasoline selling. The association alleged that an end to giveaways could reduce the selling price of gasoline by one or two cents a gallon. The brief also asked that oil companies be required to sell gasoline at one price to all customers. At present, wholesale price varies from customer to customer, with the highest charged to leased gas stations.

5. Laramie had recently closed many marginal stations. A group of dealers dispossessed in this process had brought suit against Laramie charging violations of their franchise agreement and conspiracy to restrain trade.

Mr. Thomas reflected on these developments and wondered what alternative courses of action were available to him, and what action he should take both in the short run and in the long run. He also wondered what factors had caused the current problems.

Case 21

American Airlines: Sabre Reservation System in Europe*

Toward the end of 1985, American Airlines decided to enter the European market with its computer reservation system (CRS). Three years before that, it had introduced its first flight to the Old World since September 1950, when American's president C. R. Smith had sold the subsidiary "American Overseas Airlines" to its only direct competitor, Pan American World Airways. Within three years, American offered flights to London, Paris, and Frankfurt. As European airline officials were beginning to talk about the liberalization of their skies, Robert Crandall, the newly elected CEO of the company, looked to gain a foothold in Europe by acquiring landing rights in as many cities as possible. By connecting European travel agents to SABRE, he also hoped to increase the airline's awareness overseas. This case shows the complexity of the CRS business in the rapidly changing airline industry.

The Early Years of American Airlines[1]

The birth of the commercial airline industry in the United States can be attributed in great part to the Kelly Act, which was passed by Congress in 1925. The act turned the airline business over from the Post Office Department to the private sector by requiring contractors to bid for each route. Until then, the U.S. Post Office Department was by far the biggest civil user of airplanes. It had hired 40 pilots in 1919 to fly its mail around the country. (Thirty-one of them had died in crashes by 1925.) There was also a handful of passenger airlines. One private shuttle flew Ford employees between Detroit and Chicago, while a sightseeing airline was run by the brother of Charlie Chaplin. But the number of airlines boomed after the Kelly Act was passed. Within weeks, the federal government received several hundred applications.

* This case was written with the cooperation of American Airlines by Martin Schreiber under the supervision of Thomas C. Kinnear. Copyright © 1990 by Thomas C. Kinnear.
[1] Historical data were found in Robert I. Sterling, *Eagle—The Story of American Airlines* (New York: St. Martin's Press, 1985).

One of the successful applications belonged to Robertson Aircraft Corporation. The company was awarded the route between St. Louis and Chicago (by way of Springfield and Peoria) and began its service April 15, 1926. In an old DH–4 biplane, The Lone Eagle—better known as Charles A. Lindbergh—made what became the first regularly scheduled flight of American Airlines.

American Airlines owes its existence to Sherman Fairchild, head of the Fairchild Airplane Manufacturing Company. In 1929, fearing the loss of a good customer to the competition, he tried to convince his board of directors to help the airline finance the acquisition of additional airplanes to service a recently awarded air mail route. The board of directors went much further: On March 1, 1929, a financing company, The Aviation Corporation (AVCO) was incorporated in Delaware; they sold 2 million shares at $17.50 each, raising $35 million.

Within one year, AVCO acquired majority interests in more than 80 companies: 5 airlines consisting of 13 carriers (one of them being the Robertson Aircraft Corporation of Charles Lindbergh), flying schools, aircraft and engine manufacturers, two airports, one motor bus line, even one broadcasting station. In 1930, AVCO's president, Frederic G. Coburn, consolidated all the domestic air transportation lines into a new corporation: American Airways. Realizing the dependency of the airline on the mail service (75% of its revenues), Coburn also helped develop a passenger plane. The airline, nevertheless, was losing about $1 million every year. The situation deteriorated even more when President Franklin D. Roosevelt cancelled all domestic air mail contracts in February 1934, when a federal investigation discovered that larger airlines had secretly been favored for air mail routes. But six months after the army had been assigned to fly the mail—and 66 of its planes had crashed causing 12 casualities—Congress quickly passed legislation returning the air mail business to the private sector. The Airmail Act, however, reduced the fares to be paid by the Post Office Department from 42.6 cents to 25.3 cents per flown mile. It also included two provisions: first, that airlines had to sell off their aircraft manufacturing subsidiaries; and second, no company involved in prior bidding was allowed to apply for the new air mail contracts. While sounding rather radical, the second provision was easily bypassed by the airlines: American Airways came back to the bidding table as American Airlines, United Aircraft & Transport as United Airlines, Eastern Air Transport as Eastern Airlines, and TWA with Incorporated added to its name.

If nothing else, the carriers had discovered the danger in their heavy dependency on government contracts. American Airlines was losing almost $2.5 million in 1934 and was looking for a strong leader to turn the business around. On October 26, 1934, a Texan was appointed as the new president of the company: Cyrus Rowlett Smith. Except for a period during World War II, he would remain president until 1963, when he became chairman and CEO, a position he held for five years.

C. R. Smith was committed to changing the airline into a passenger transportation business. His strategy consisted of:

- Targeting the business travelers.
- Improving service.
- Replacing old equipment with better and safer equipment.
- Excelling in marketing.

He began by training his employees in what he called esprit de corps. Realizing the importance of the flight attendants, he started a training program designed for stewardesses. In 1936, he convinced Donald Douglas, Sr., to design the DC–3, which became the first profitable all-passenger airplane. In the same year, he offered the first sleeper flights between New York and Los Angeles (via Memphis, Dallas, and Tucson) and introduced the industry to air traffic control systems. He even entered the catering business by opening several restaurants in airports. The strategy paid off: the airline showed its first profit after only two years and within three years, the revenue from mail service decreased from 71 percent to 31 percent of total revenue (Table 1). In 1938, Smith moved American's headquarters from the Chicago Midway Airport to the newly built LaGuardia Airport in New York City. There, he founded the first Admirals Club and opened a reservation school. By then, American's largest reservation office in New York was booking an average of 250 passengers a day.

TABLE 1 American Airways turns into a passenger airline

	Mail revenue	Passenger revenue
1933	$4,728,000	$1,885,000
1937	2,980,000	6,598,000

After serving in the Air Transport Command during World War II, Smith returned to American. He soon dazzled his competitors when he successfully offered the first family fares in the industry. On a 50-acre piece of land in Dallas that he won in a gin rummy game, he built a new learning center, where stewardesses went through a 20-day training program. On January 25, 1959, he introduced the first jetliner, a Boeing 707; seven years later, he retired American's last piston plane.

The Development of SABRE

Until 1946, reservation offices used large display boards, which listed entries and space availability. During the 50s, American introduced the Magnetronic Reservisor to keep track of seat inventories on all flights and to electronically format and send teletype messages to other airlines. This process required that reservations be routed to a keypunch operator, run through a sorting machine, and then processed by another machine which cut the paper tape in order to send the teletype message (prior to being filed).

During a flight in 1953, C. R. Smith met an IBM senior sales representative, R. Blair Smith. As C. R. Smith described the capacity and speed constraints American was encountering with their reservation system, Blair Smith quickly saw a wonderful business opportunity. In November of 1959, American Airlines and IBM announced a joint development project called Semi-Automated Business Research Environment, or in short form, SABRE. Introduced first in 1962 and expanded systemwide two years later, SABRE became the largest electronic data processing system designed for business use. Its computer center was located in Briarcliff Manor, New York. In one day the system could process:

85,000   phone calls.
30,000   requests for fare quotations.
40,000   confirmed passenger reservations.
30,000   queries to and from other airlines regarding seat space.
20,000   ticket sales.

The initial research, development, and installation was estimated at $40 million, the price of four Boeing 707 aircraft.

In the late 1960s, two other airlines came up with their own reservation systems. United introduced APOLLO, while TWA Inc. operated PARS.

Bob Crandall Improves SABRE

By 1974, C. R. Smith had been replaced as president and chairman of American Airlines by Albert V. Casey, a business school graduate with limited prior airline experience. "There are only four jobs in any company, regardless of what kind of business you're in," he once said. "You have one guy in charge of making the product, someone in charge of selling it, the third one's a bean counter who keeps score, and then there's the boss." In June of 1974, he placed Robert Crandall in charge of selling the product by appointing him senior vice president of marketing.

Bob Crandall was determined to utilize American's reservation system as a marketing tool for the airline. He ordered a new and improved SABRE to help analyze collected flight and booking data. American Airlines' yield management system emerged, which could predict booking trends on specific flights and monitor the effectiveness of various marketing strategies. SABRE also introduced new functions such as baggage tracing, crew management, inventory management, and financial analysis.

Together with American's chief of data processing, Max Hopper, Crandall introduced the concept of a joint industry computerized reservation system (JICRS). Travel agents would be able to subscribe to the system and thus quickly access information about any carrier. There had already been several separate efforts to set up an industry system (Table 2). The major purpose was

TABLE 2   Failed attempts to standardize the CRS industry

1967	Donnelly Official Airline Reservation System (BOARS)
1970	Automatic Travel Agency Reservation (ATARS)
1974	Joint Industry Computer Reservation System (JICRS)
1976	United, then American, pulls out of JICRS to market their own reservation systems
1976	Multi-Access Agent Reservation System (MAARS)
1980	American Express makes last major effort to establish an industry system

to eliminate continued duplication of investments and to reduce the reservations and sales cost by shifting the sales efforts from high-cost internal reservation offices to commission-paid travel agencies. Furthermore, before deregulation, all companies charged the same fare for the same service, and it took years to change prices and service. None of the attempts succeeded, however, for lack of capital, lack of agreement, or fear of government suspicions that a joint system would be anticompetitive within the industry. The JICRS concept would die as well, as United started to sell its own system to travel agents. American immediately followed suit and in May of 1976 installed its first SABRE terminal in a travel agency. Other airlines were allowed to offer their services through SABRE and were charged about 35 cents for ticketing through a competitor's system.

Strategically, the distribution of CRSs to travel agents proved to be a very successful move. Not only were airlines gaining increased sales exposure, they also enjoyed high entry barriers against competitors due to travel agency investments in hardware and training, as well as to certain restrictive contract terms.

Although successful, it was not until 1978, when legislation ordered the deregulation of the airline industry, that the reservation systems achieved the importance they enjoy today.

Deregulation

The Airline Deregulation Act of 1978 provided for a phased abolition of regulation on route entry and tariffs. Until then, both of these were issued under the authority of the Civil Aeronautics Board (CAB). However, during its 40-year reign, the CAB had allowed no new major passenger carrier (called a trunk carrier) to enter the industry. Only domestic local service air carriers, commonly called feeder airlines, had been allowed to enter minor markets, as they became uneconomical for trunk carriers to service with their larger planes. Before deregulation, most routes had been served by only one carrier. Prices were set for airlines to obtain a defined industry margin.

As the CAB gradually relinquished authority, the Department of Transportation (DOT) temporarily took over the remaining functions. (The public interest in airline operations was to pass to the Justice Department only in

1989.) New carriers were now allowed to enter the market, not on the basis of "convenience and public necessity," but if they were "fit, willing and able to perform air transportation." In addition, airlines could set their own prices according to supply and demand.

The cooperative attitude prevailing until 1981 quickly disappeared. Many former interline partners went into direct competition with each other. During the four years following deregulation, 119 new carriers entered the industry. As they began offering lower fares, a fierce price competition was launched, which ultimately lowered the average ticket price (Figure 1). In 1982, 80 percent of all tickets were sold at discount fares and the looming question became, who would survive the price war?

FIGURE 1 The effect of deregulation on airline ticket prices

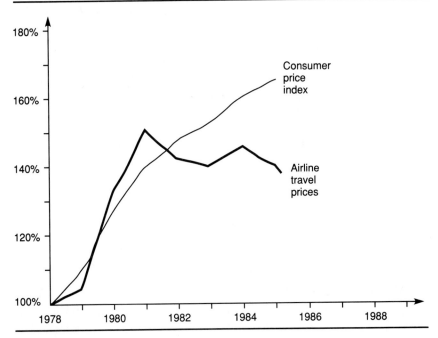

The impact of deregulation on airline operation was as far reaching as it was diverse.

Increase in Productivity

Increased competition forced established carriers to improve their productivity. Using larger, more fuel-efficient jets, they increased their average domestic route length. The incentive to replace their old aircraft with more fuel-efficient planes became even more pressing when fuel prices began to rise at the turn of the decade. Some of the used planes were put on the market and sold to smaller airlines seeking to increase the reach of their networks. Others were simply grounded. Sure enough, when oil prices dropped again, these older aircraft were put back into service.

As smaller, fuel-efficient planes were developed, productivity became less dependent on aircraft size than on maximum aircraft utilization, higher load factors, lower labor cost, and less restrictive work rules.

Lowering of Labor Cost

In order to survive, the large trunk carriers had to cut costs, and fast. With wages being the largest cost component (Figure 2), managers looked for ways to trim the high pre-deregulation salaries down to market rates and to allow for more flexible work rules.

FIGURE 2 American Airline's cost structure during 1985

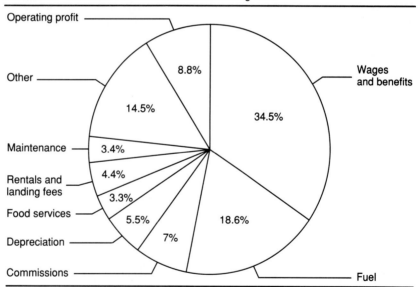

The most common practice was to engage in negotiations with unions. In March of 1983, Robert Crandall of American Airlines first reached an agreement with his employees in a deal that became the basis for negotiations at other carriers. (This is described in a later section.) Other airlines seeking concessions through negotiation were United, TWA, Delta, and Northwest. Pan American and Eastern, which were in more serious financial difficulties, were obliged to offer equity shares (10 percent and 25 percent) to their employees in exchange for wage and work rule concessions.

Two smaller airlines, Texas International and Frontier, tried to bypass the unions by starting their own low-cost nonunion subsidiary. Although initially successful, they were both later acquired by Texas Air Corp. shortly before being forced into Chapter 11 bankruptcy.

Finally, two other airlines, Braniff and Continental, chose the most extreme path to revise their labor costs. Braniff filed for bankruptcy in 1982 and Continental in 1983. In addition to restructuring their debt, both airlines defaulted on their labor contracts and started their operations again as nonunion companies.

Bankruptcies/Mergers

Originally, deregulation was intended to increase competition, but six years after the deregulation act, 75 carriers remained in the market, down from 105. The number contracted due to bankruptcies, mergers, and liquidations. The avalanche of mergers was facilitated by the fact that all regulatory authority had been given to the Department of Transportation, which in several cases overruled objections raised by the Department of Justice.

Pan Am and National were the first airlines to merge. The deal allowed Pan Am, which had been restricted to international air service prior to deregulation, to compete domestically.

Republic resulted from the second major post-deregulation merger. The airline consisted of North Central, Southern, and Hughes Airwest. Republic later merged with Northwest Airlines. Other mergers followed, and in 1985, the trend did not seem to have an end.

Hub and Spoke

As airplanes became more fuel efficient, the load factor became the most crucial variable for an airline's success. To increase the number of passengers per flight, airlines started to expand their hub airport utilization. Hub airports, operating as a central connecting point between city pairs (spokes) offered a competitive alternative to direct flights (Figure 3). By combining passenger traffic from different origins and with different destinations, the airline could increase the number of city pairs served, as well as the average number of passengers and corresponding revenue per flight. For flights to be attractive to customers, the connecting time at the hub had to be as short as possible. Airplanes would land in clusters and wait for all or most of the connecting passengers before taking off. As hubs grew in size and traffic (Table 3), passengers soon faced increasing delays.

FIGURE 3 The use of hub

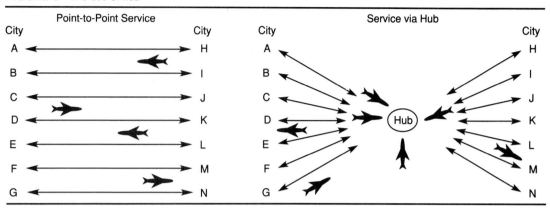

TABLE 3 Increased use of hub airports

Airline	Leading hub city in 1983	Percent of airline's domestic departures at hub	
		1978	1983
American	Dallas-Ft. Worth	11.2%	28.6%
Continental	Houston	12.8	22.9
Delta	Atlanta	18.3	21.4
Eastern	Atlanta	18.3	21.0
Northwest	Minneapolis-St. Paul	16.1	20.7
Pan American	New York	12.3	22.4
TWA	St. Louis	11.9	33.0
United	Chicago	16.0	18.9

International Growth—American Airline's Response to Deregulation

Robert Crandall was named American's president in 1980, three years after he had successfully introduced the Super Saver fares. Even so, as deregulation approached, many analysts predicted the end of American Airlines' existence. In his biography about American Airlines, Robert Serling wrote: "It was like assuming command of the Titanic the day she sailed." Albert V. Casey had tried to limit the damages by moving American's headquarters from New York to the Dallas/Ft. Worth area, but in 1980 the airline reeled under a $111.1 million loss (Table 4).

Crandall's strategy was to "grow a new, low-cost airline inside the old one." He started to lower American's labor cost. Through hard negotiations with unions, Crandall obtained concessions for a two-tiered wage scale, by

TABLE 4 American Airlines' income summary

	1978	1979	1980	1981	1982	1983	1984	1985
Operating results (in millions)								
Revenues								
Passengers	$2,329.5	$2,753.0	$3,154.4	$3,377.0	$3,414.2	$3,885.3	$4,335.8	$4,985.5
Other	$406.0	$499.5	$551.7	$546.6	$563.0	$647.1	$751.6	$873.8
Total operating revenues	$2,735.5	$3,252.5	$3,706.1	$3,923.6	$3,977.2	$4,532.4	$5,087.4	$5,859.3
Expenses								
Wages, salaries, and benefits	$1,083.4	$1,248.5	$1,372.7	$1,417.4	$1,472.9	$1,601.2	$1,748.7	$1,951.9
Aircraft fuel	$514.7	$801.5	$1,114.8	$1,115.7	$1,115.7	$1,038.6	$1,091.8	$1,141.8
Other	$1,018.5	$1,197.6	$1,329.7	$1,346.5	$1,346.5	$1,643.1	$1,907.8	$2,259.1
Total operating expenses	$2,616.6	$3,247.6	$3,817.2	$3,879.6	$3,935.1	$4,282.9	$4,748.3	$5,352.8
Operating income (loss)	$118.9	$4.9	($111.1)	$44.0	$42.1	$249.5	$339.1	$506.5
Operating statistics								
Revenue yield per passenger mile	7.96¢	8.17¢	11.12¢	12.13¢	11.04¢	11.39¢	11.81¢	11.30¢
Revenue passenger miles (in millions)	28,987	33,364	28,178	27,798	30,900	34,099	36,702	44,138
Passenger load factor	63.7%	67.4%	60.4%	61.4%	63.3%	65.0%	62.6%	64.6%
Number of operating aircraft at year-end	251	263	242	232	231	244	260	291

which American would pay newly hired employees only 50 percent of what present employees received. In return, Crandall guaranteed that there would be no layoffs and no pay cuts. His hard negotiating style earned him a reputation of "eating nails for breakfast." With the money saved, Crandall decided to expand the airline dramatically. "The faster we grow, the lower our average cost will be," he argued. Within four years, he bought almost 100 new planes, increasing American's old fleet by 41 percent. American started to build hubs in Dallas/Ft. Worth and Chicago. Both airports accounted for 80 percent of the airline's departures in 1983. The small, semiautonomous commuter airline, American Eagle, operated as a feeder airline funneling passengers from smaller outlying areas into American's route systems.

In 1983, while incorporated under AMR Corp., American began service to Europe with a flight from DFW to London (Braniff left the route open after filing for bankruptcy). By 1985, it had added flights to Paris and Frankfurt. Crandall also consolidated by selling off subsidiaries worth $60.3 million, which included its 45-year-old Sky-Chefs catering company and its AMR Energy Corp. In 1982, American lost $18.2 million, but one year later it registered an operating profit of $249.5 million. By 1985, American was credited with the largest market share (Table 5).

TABLE 5   1985 Market shares in passenger miles

Airline	Market share in revenue passenger miles
American	13.1%
United	12.4
Eastern	9.9
TWA	9.5
Delta	9.0
Pan American	8.1
Northwest	6.7
Continental	4.9
People Express	3.3
Republic	3.2
Western	3.1
USAir	2.9
Piedmont	2.4
Southwest	1.6
Others	9.9

Frequent Flier Programs

Deregulation cannot be discussed without mentioning the frequent flier programs. Designed to entice loyalty to one carrier, they would reward passengers with bonuses (usually a free trip) based on mileage flown and/or fares paid. Obviously, such programs were especially attractive with larger airlines serving many cities. American initiated the frequent flier wars when it introduced its

AAdvantage program. The entire service was run through SABRE.Two years after its introduction, American's competition developed similar programs of their own.

Increased Importance of the CRS Market

With deregulation, the number and complexity of airline fares increased, making reservation systems with their large databases more of a competitive tool. In 1977, before deregulation, travel agencies had booked only 38 percent of all tickets; in 1985, the percentage had jumped to 90 percent. As travel agents booked an increasing share of ticket sales, airlines doubled their efforts to place their CRS terminals with as many agents, particularly business travel specialists, as possible. The commission from ticket sales, which represented the agent's largest revenue source, jumped to 10 percent, even 13 percent in 1985, up from the CAB specified 7 percent. During the same time, the percentage of agencies automated with CRS terminals shot up from 5 percent to 90 percent (Table 6).

TABLE 6 Automatization of travel agencies

Year	Agents	Percent automated with CRS
1976	12,262	*
1977	13,454	5%
1978	14,804	*
1979	16,112	24
1980	17,339	*
1981	19,203	59
1982	20,962	75
1983	23,058	85
1984	25,748	*
1985	27,193	90

* Not available.

These five CRSs competed for market share (Figure 4):

SABRE of American Airlines. SABRE accounted for one third of American Airlines' $506 million in net earnings in 1985. However, as Robert Crandall testified before the Senate Aviation Subcommittee in March of the same year, SABRE had been profitable only since 1983 (Table 7). The accumulated investment in the CRS was estimated at $350 million.

APOLLO of United Airlines. With a 25 percent market share, APOLLO was the second largest system in the country. Along with SABRE, it was the most sophisticated CRS in the market. At the end of 1983, United's total investment in APOLLO was estimated at $250 million.

FIGURE 4 1985 market share of the major CRS vendors' installations

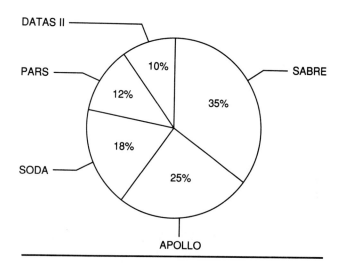

Market Share of the Five Major CRSs

DATAS II — 10%

PARS — 12%

SODA — 18%

SABRE — 35%

APOLLO — 25%

TABLE 7 Estimated operating results of SABRE (millions)

Year	Revenue	Expenses	Operating income (loss)
1976	$ 0.3	$ 4.4	$ (4.1)
1977	2.4	12.7	(10.3)
1978	6.0	24.5	(18.5)
1979	15.6	41.7	(26.1)
1980	32.0	56.6	(24.6)
1981	53.6	68.3	(14.7)
1982	82.9	92.4	(9.5)
1983	124.3	118.8	5.5
1984	179.0	136.2	42.8
1985	483.0	367.0	116.0

PARS of TWA. TWA had unveiled its reservation system to travel agents shortly after American and United had started selling their CRS service in 1976. A decade later, 12 percent of all 32,000 U.S. travel agency terminals were connected to PARS.

SODA of Eastern Airlines. Eastern Airlines had introduced SODA (System One Direct Access) shortly after Congress had passed the deregulation act. Thanks to Eastern's position as the third largest domestic carrier, SODA's market share rose to an impressive 18 percent by 1985.

DATAS II of Delta Air Lines. In 1979, Delta and United entered into an arrangement that allowed Delta to market the APOLLO system using its own name. Delta called its system DATAS. As the advantages of owning a CRS became apparent, Delta developed its own system and called it DATAS II. Its market share in 1985 was 10 percent.

Some other carriers, such as Alaska Air Lines, Pan Am, or USAir also maintained small CRS networks.

Prices charged to travel agents included three components: a one-time installation charge, a monthly hardware fee, and a monthly maintenance charge. To entice travel agents to join their networks, airlines offered financing and booking incentives (free hardware, software, or communication lines when processing a certain level of bookings through the system). Airlines were basing their efforts on the fact that an agent who had opted for their system would find it hard to switch to another system.

With travel agents selling most of the tickets, it became increasingly important for airlines to be listed on other airlines' CRS terminals. CRS vendors quickly raised their fees to about $1.75, up from the pre-deregulation fee of 35 cents. Charges were even higher around hubs of a CRS vendor due to the carrier's—and thus the reservation system's—monopoly position. (Travel agents would subscribe to the CRS that offered the most flights.) Other, mostly new carriers were facing difficulties in obtaining co-host status. Frontier Airlines, for instance, had to wait two years before having its flight information displayed on APOLLO. As travel agents demanded access to all other airlines' flight schedules through their system, CRS vendors were forced to comply.

They soon faced yet another charge: display bias. With many flights available, a standard terminal could not display all of them on one screen. The order by which flights were listed was defined by an algorithm written by the CRS vendor. Usually, nonstop and direct flights were listed first, followed by in-line and then off-line connecting flights.[2] Within each category, systems commonly would give priority to the flights of the CRS vendor. SABRE, for instance, listed the flights alphabetically, putting American with its acronym "AA" at the top of the list. Makes good business sense? Not for subscribing airlines. According to a survey, 90 percent of all travel agents' bookings were made from the first screen. In fact, 50 percent were made from the first line.

To get a more favorable screen display, certain non-CRS carriers offered to pay higher fees to the system operators, contributing to the discriminatory pricing in placement. Other carriers decided they could no longer wait for government regulations or the outcome of lawsuits and started to invest heavily in their own CRS systems. But as they tried to sell their systems to agencies, they faced restrictive contracts prohibiting travel agents from installing more than one system. The only way to gain market share was to convince agencies to change systems. As new systems encroached on their territory, established CRS

---

[2] In-line connections refer to two flights of the same airline. Off-line connections refer to two flights of different airlines.

vendors began to include liquidated damage clauses in the contracts, and sue for damages in case of breach.

In November 1984, six weeks before closing its doors, the CAB issued a final ruling over computer reservation systems.

- The regulation banned both explicit and indirect bias in search routines. CRS vendors were ordered to disclose their algorithms.
- CRS vendors were forbidden to tie travel agents for more than five years. They also were not allowed to force travel agents to book most of their tickets on the CRS's airline.
- Charges to participating airlines could not be ''unfair or discriminatory.''

In spite of these rules, co-host airlines still faced another bias called the halo effect: Travel agents, who were heavily dependent on the CRS vendor for training and maintenance, seemed to favor flights of the CRS vendor over non-vendor flights by a margin of about 10 percent.

The most common algorithms now listed the flights according to flight duration. To be on the top of the list, some airlines published unrealistic flight times, while others focused on shortening connecting times in hubs, causing an inadvertent flood of delays.

Trying to expand their system, CRS vendors enticed hotels and car-rental companies to offer their services through the reservation system. They also added ''backoffice'' software packages that would automate agents' billing and accounting procedures. The airline's task was to create a virtual circle. The more products it could put on its system for people to reserve, the more people would want to hook their terminals to the network. Conversely, the more people on the system, the more economically feasible it would be to offer a diversity of services (e.g., hotel and car reservation). Every new service also increased the dependency of travel agents on their CRS system.

With the increased demand for PCs, dumb terminals were replaced with intelligent workstations. To make the CRS compatible with PCs, connectivity and compatibility problems had to be resolved.

Marketing finally became an integral part of the CRS business. Government agencies and larger agency chains, for instance, were discovered to be very profitable market niches. Both, because of their size, were highly attractive to CRS vendors. On the other hand, they also enjoyed a strong negotiating position.

International Consequences of Deregulation

The international passenger service accounts for a large share of aggregate airline revenue. While the numbers vary among airlines, all U.S. carriers combined have transported roughly 50 percent of all passengers traveling to and from the United States during the last 10 years. An estimated 46.6 million passengers have traveled between the United States and foreign countries (excluding Canada); 40.7 percent of these were crossing the North Atlantic (Table 8).

TABLE 8 International traffic

Region	Passengers (millions)	Share percent
All countries	46.6	100.0%
Central America and Mexico	6.8	14.6
Caribbean	8.8	18.9
South America	2.4	5.2
Europe	19.0	40.7
Africa/Middle East	1.1	2.4
Far East	7.0	15.0
Oceania	1.5	3.2

Bilateral Agreements

In the early days of the airline industry, carriers had to negotiate directly with foreign governments in order to obtain landing rights and to offer services between the United States and a foreign country. It was not until 1943 that the U.S. government took over the responsibility of negotiating bilateral treaties with foreign countries for common air routes. A year later, government representatives from 52 countries tried to define a standard framework for international air service. Because they failed to agree on a multilateral transport agreement, bilateral negotiations between the governments of two countries remained the only way for airlines to obtain the rights to provide service to a foreign country. A typical bilateral agreement would define:

- The right of each government to designate the airline to serve the foreign country.
- The destinations available to the designated airlines.
- The type of traffic the designated airlines are allowed to carry (Table 9).

TABLE 9 The freedoms of the air

1. The right to use the airspace of another country without landing.
2. The right to land in another country for servicing and other noncommercial purposes.
3. The right to discharge in a foreign country passengers and cargo coming from the home country.
4. The right to pick up in another country passengers and cargo bound for the home country.
5. The right to pick up passengers and cargo in a foreign country and convey them to yet another country.
6. The right to transport passengers and cargo from one to another foreign country by routing through the home country.

- The capacity allowed for the designated airlines.
- The pricing of international services.
- Provisions concerning profit repatriation, access to local distribution (CRS) channels, ground handling, airport charges, aviation safety, and other ancillary issues.

Early agreements between the United States and European countries were rather favorable to the United States. One reason lay in the technical superiority of U.S. carriers, which had the capacity to fly more passengers than their European counterparts. Another reason could be found in the large geographical size of the United States. While American airliners could fly to every smaller country with which their government had an agreement, each European carrier was restricted to only a limited number of American gateways.

In an effort to extend deregulation to international air service, the U.S. government in 1978 urged far more liberal agreements. It offered access to new American cities in exchange for fifth-freedom rights. With these rights, American carriers could enter in direct competition with European carriers on inter-European routes. As transatlantic flights were offering high margins, the short flights between foreign gateways would count only as marginal revenue, putting the airline in a position to offer relatively low fares. To no one's surprise, many European airlines opposed the exchange of these rights and instead demanded cabotage rights in the United States (i.e., rights to fly passengers and cargo within the United States). These rights were strongly protected in most countries. Some voices in the EC argued that the European Community was to be regarded as one country, which would change fifth-freedom rights to cabotage rights. But in 1985, a united European transportation system was far from being established.

European Air Transportation

Geographically speaking, Europe consists of 34 countries, each having its own language, currency, and laws. Only 22 of these are listed as members of the European Civil Aviation Conference (ECAC) (Table 10). West Germany, France, and Great Britain represent the largest economies; accordingly, they are also registering the largest demand for scheduled flights. From these countries, most of the tourists travel to the hot spots of Italy, France, and Spain.

Route Length

While the average route length in the United States is over 800 miles, the European average is a mere 465 miles. The longest European route (between London and Athens) is only two thirds the distance between New York and Los Angeles. European carriers thus have a higher percentage of smaller planes than

TABLE 10 ECAC and AEA membership

ECAC members	AEA members
Austria	Austrian
Belgium	Sabena
Cyprus	
Denmark	SAS
Finland	Finnair
France	Air France
	UTA
Greece	Olympic
Iceland	Icelandair
Ireland	Air Lingus
Italy	Alitalia
Luxemburg	Luxair
Malta	
Netherlands	KLM
Norway	
Portugal	TAP
Spain	Iberia
Sweden	
Switzerland	Swissair
Turkey	
United Kingdom	British Airways
	British Caledonian
West Germany	Lufthansa
Yugoslavia	Jugoslav

their American counterparts. They also pay a higher percentage for landing fees and are subject to airspace usage charges throughout the Continent. With these constraints, European airliners are estimated to have operating costs 20 percent higher than U.S. carriers. This is not enough, however, to account for the ticket price difference. During the 1980s, the average ticket price in Europe was 35–40 percent more expensive than in the United States for a comparable stretch.

Government Ownership

In 1985, most European airlines were completely or partially owned by their respective governments and received financial subsidies. In return they were bound to provide a public transportation service. This service included connecting a country's cities, even when demand would not justify it. Government ownership goes back to when operating an airline was thought to add international prestige to the country. Airlines were long considered the commercial ambassadors of their country. This attitude was still predominant during the first half of the 1980s, although some governments, such as Great Britain, were starting to talk about selling a share of their ownership.

Partly because of their relationship with the government, European airlines were heavily unionized. In addition, many countries had strict rules regarding layoffs. In France, for instance, the newly elected socialist government recently passed a law making any firing in the country dependent on governmental approval.

Charter Flights

Passengers in Europe had three options to avoid paying regular fares:

1. Buy a discount ticket offered by regular carriers (Table 11).

TABLE 11 The importance of discount fares in Europe and the United States

	Discount fares issued as a percent off total traffic	Average discount below full fare
Europe	57%	40%
United States	85	56

2. Buy a ticket in the gray market, consisting of second-hand and stand-by tickets.
3. Fly with a deregulated, nonscheduled carrier (charters).

Charters offered complete tours, which included flight and accommodations. Since they were excluded from bilateral agreements, they escaped many price regulations. Unlike in the United States, nonscheduled travel (charter) plays a very important role in Europe. In the United States, the market share of charter service dropped from 27 percent in 1977 to 8 percent in 1985. In Europe, by contrast, 43 percent of all passengers flying within the Continent during 1985 took charters for 55 percent of the total passenger miles. Spain and Greece registered particularly heavy charter traffic. During 1984, 19.9 million passengers used nonscheduled services to visit Spain, while only 4.4 million passengers used scheduled services.

Once scheduled carriers realized the vast opportunity that charter operations could offer, they began buying shares of existing charter carriers. The result was a complicated network of ownership.

Rail Transportation

Europe's air transportation is also exposed to fierce competition from the rail system, particularly over shorter distances. While the U.S. rail system accounts for only 0.5 percent of domestic traffic, European trains carry about 13 percent of all passenger traffic. Like the airlines, the rail systems are regarded as a public utility and, thus, are heavily subsidized by their respective governments. Traveling by train is usually cheaper but takes more time than air travel. With the development of faster trains, rail systems have increasingly been able to compete on longer routes. Probably the most prominent high speed train is the French TGV ("train à grande vitesse") that, at a speed of over 170 mph, connects Paris and Lyon within three and a half hours.

Bilateral Agreements

European bilaterals on scheduled services were relatively rigid:

- Only one airline from each country was usually permitted to service a route.
- The two selected airlines were allowed to offer no more than a designated percentage of the total capacity. Usually, carriers had to share the capacity 50–50; a more liberal bilateral between France and Great Britain allowed for capacity shares between 45 percent and 55 percent.
- The two selected airlines were to share the revenue in proportion to the capacity allocated to them.
- Fares had to be accepted by the regulatory body of both countries.

Liberalization—The role of the EEC

The European Economic Community (EEC) has its origin in the Treaty of Rome, signed in 1957. During the fall of that year, government representatives of 12 countries agreed to work toward economic integration. The community was to establish conditions which would ensure fair competition among businesses of different countries by eliminating state boundaries for businesses. Without directly naming the airline industry, the treaty nevertheless included provisions that applied to any kind of business, like an article guaranteeing the freedom to supply services in any of the given countries. The community also was to establish a common transportation policy. Finally, Articles 85–90 prohibited cartels and anticompetitive practices.

Until 1985, however, the treaty had been mostly overlooked by airline authorities. Most carriers held that the treaty did not address the airline industry. Articles 85–90 applied specifically to acts of enterprises. Carriers, on the other hand, were owned by autonomous governments. Even if the carriers wished to deregulate Europe's skies, they had no authority to do so. The Treaty of Rome had assigned the power of decision over air transportation to a Council of Ministers and not to the AEA. Lastly, deregulation did not make much sense as long as governments were subsidizing their airlines.

Nevertheless, as of 1985, most European carriers agreed to the idea of liberalization, while remaining undecided about the pace by which this liberalization should come about.

The CRS Market in Europe

During the 70s, European airlines had discovered the use of computerized reservation systems. Each carrier had developed its own system offering diverse functions. A 1983 survey on the world's largest reservation systems (Table 12) clearly showed that European CRSs were not as sophisticated as American ones. Backoffice systems, for instance, were not offered by any of the European airlines.

TABLE 12   Survey of major CRSs

	Air France	British Airways	Finnair	Icelandair	KLM	Lufthansa	Sabena	SAS	Swissair	TAP-Air Portugal	American Airlines
Reservations	I	I	I	I	I	I	C	I	I	C	I
Check-in	I	I	C	—	I	I	C	I	I	C	I
Ticketing	I	I	I	—	I	I	C	I	I	—	I
Fare quote	I	I	—	—	I	I	C	—	I	—	I
Hotel reservations	I	I	I	—	I	I	C	—	I	—	I
Car rental	I	C	—	—	I	—	C	—	—	—	I
Baggage trace	I	C	C	—	C	C	C	I	C	—	I
Scheduling	I	I	—	—	I	—	I	I	I	—	I
Crew management	I	I	I	I	I	I	I	I	I	I	I
Flight planning	I	I	I	—	I	I	I	I	C	—	I
Weight and balance	I	I	C	—	I	I	I	I	I	C	I
Inventory management	I	I	I	I	I	I	I	I	I	I	I
Maintenance schedule	I	I	I	I	I	I	I	I	I	I	I
Performance analysis	I	I	—	I	I	I	I	I	I	I	I
Financial	I	I	I	I	I	I	I	I	I	I	I
Cargo control	I	I	I	I	I	I	I	I	I	I	I
Management information	I	I	I	I	I	I	I	I	I	I	I

I = In-house.
C = Contracted.
— = Not available.

Although travel agents accounted for the majority of ticket sales, not all of the airlines offered their systems to travel agents. The airlines that did, did so only to agencies within their respective countries, since the systems generally displayed only flights for the domestic airline. Travel agents wishing to book a reservation on a foreign carrier had to call the other airline's reservation office, ask for seat availability, and if available, ask to have the ticket sent.

SABRE's 1986 European Marketing Plan

Having a 35 percent share of the nearly saturated U.S. travel agency market in 1985, American decided to expand further and to "focus its attention on sales and service of its SABRE system internationally."[3] The 1986 marketing plan for sales and service outlined the strategic steps to successfully enter foreign markets. Besides offering additional revenue generated by new subscribers, the expansion into foreign markets would lead to increased visibility for American Airlines and would generate useful data for yield management concerning international flights.

At American, the foreign network was divided into three areas:

Area I: Central America, South America, and Caribbean.

Area II: Europe, Africa, and the Middle East.

Area III: Australia, New Zealand, Pacific, and South East Asia.

Although trying to expand worldwide, the early phases of the plan concentrated on Europe. Accordingly, we will focus only on the marketing plan as it relates to Europe.

The introduction to the plan also stated the following:

A most effective premise upon which this entire plan is built relates to positive interaction with the International Passenger Sales Division of American Airlines . . . so that, hand in hand, both organizations may identify new opportunities leading to worldwide SABRE distribution.

Competitive Environment

SABRE faced competition from both local systems and CRSs of U.S. carriers. Furthermore, the European market was practically unaware of SABRE. "They may have heard the name, but in their own minds, they do not differentiate its functionality from APOLLO or any other U.S. system."

The marketing plan went on describing several competitive advantages of local systems over SABRE:

- Unlike SABRE, all local systems could issue tickets. Most of them did so through a Bank Settlement Plan (BSP).[4] American was in the process of receiving BSP specifications from each country that offered such a procedure. In non-BSP countries such as France, ticketing capability was administrated through the national carrier.

---

[3] This and the following quotes are taken from the SABRE 1986 Marketing Plan.

[4] The Bank Settlement Plan (BSP) is a unified procedure by which travel agents give the coupons of the tickets they sold to an organization, which manages for a fee the money transfer to the different airlines. In certain cases, a travel agent can strike a deal with an airline and pay the ticket revenue (minus commission) directly to that airline, therefore avoiding the BSP fee.

- Local systems were able to quote fares more accurately than SABRE. To quote fares through SABRE, reliable sources for fare information had to be determined and the information continually updated.

- Most local systems had booking and ticketing capabilities for national rail services. American had just started to negotiate with its first rail participants—the French SNCF and Swiss Rail.

- Local systems maintained nationalistic arguments to promote the use of their systems. They were also backed by the national flag carriers, which objected to the use of foreign CRSs.

Special attention was lavished upon reservation systems in the United Kingdom, Germany, and France, because of the large size of their market (Table 13). In Scandinavia, the reservation system of SAS (Scandinavian Airlines System) represented the major competitor of SABRE. Unknown to American at that time were the operating procedures in Switzerland, Austria, Spain, Belgium, the Netherlands, and Italy.

TABLE 13 Major European CRS competitors

Country	United Kingdom	Germany	France	Scandinavia
CRS	TRAVICOM	START	ESTEREL	
BSP	Yes	Yes	No	No
Special features	Comprehensive fares and quoting capabilities, telex capabilities	Ticketing capabilities for rail system, backoffice system	Ticketing capabilities for rail system	

Other U.S. CRS vendors had already entered the European market (Table 14). United Airlines was by far the most aggressive vendor. Promoting APOLLO, United had placed sales representatives throughout Europe and built a large demonstration facility in Paris. It also offered free installation, several months of free equipment rental, and special override commissions for flight segments booked on United.

TABLE 14 Position of major U.S. CRSs in Europe

CRS	APOLLO	DATAS II	PARS
Airline	United/Covia	Delta Airlines	TWA
Main location	Paris	Germany	London
Comments	Agressive marketing and pricing	Services U.S. military bases	

Objectives and Goals

While never expressively stated, the objectives were obvious: first, to acquire significant international market share to become the worldwide leader in the distribution of travel information; second, to collect through SABRE market information about competitors' operations and pricing, enabling American Airlines to increase its presence on international routes.

> The key is to get SABRE's "foot in the door." As we establish our distribution and enhance functionality, bookings will increase. Optimum revenue potential to American will be long term in nature. Significant booking fee revenue potential exists once the system eases into the role of a primary system and additional CRTs are installed.[5]

The goal was to install SABRE in 310 European locations by the end of 1986 and to achieve a penetration of 4 percent in the worldwide IATA travel agency market (Table 15).[6]

> The focus of the initial sales effort will concentrate primarily on IATA locations. Depending on the particular sensitivities which are present from one country to another, a decision may be reached to automate non-IATA locations as well.

TABLE 15 SABRE's objectives in Europe

	SABRE locations	IATA agencies	Percent
United Kindgom	65	3,155	2.1%
Norway	25	233	10.7
Sweden	25	262	9.5
Denmark	20	150	13.3
Finland	24	300	8.0
Germany	40	1,342	2.9
France	30	1,200	2.5
Switzerland	17	355	5.0
Belgium	14	180	3.0
Holland	20	250	8.0
Other Europe	30	300	10.0
	310	7,777	4.0

Global Strategies

Until SABRE could offer ticketing capabilities and cater to local travel habits, it could be promoted and sold only as a secondary system. Subscribers could only book flight segments in the United States and order tickets to be sent by mail.[7]

---

[5] Cathode-ray tube; commonly used to design computer workstations.

[6] The International Air Transport Association (IATA) is the airlines' own trade association. Until 1984, among other duties, it assumed the jobs of determining equitable fares and controlling the distribution part of the business. It still is assigned to the latter duty. Under its Standard Agency Agreement of 1952, travel agents accredited under the agreement (i.e., those meeting the necessary criteria of competence, financial soundness, and suitable premises) get the right to issue IATA's interlinable air tickets plus the opportunity (if available in their country) to participate in its Bank Settlement Plan (BSP).

[7] Subscribers, such as travel agents, are customers who are using SABRE to process reservations.

While the system would be gradually upgraded to meet the requirements for a primary system, sales were to focus on the technological superiority of the product and price the system at a level competitive with existing U.S. systems. American was considering two ways to enter the local markets: first by getting local travel agents to connect to SABRE, and second, by licensing the sophisticated SABRE software to national carriers. Thus, while advertising the system as a competitive alternative to local CRS systems, the sales and service departments also had to consider every opportunity to make SABRE the CRS standard in each country.

> It should be noted that direct sales activity will be supplemented by on-going Prime Host discussions with key selected carriers. In the event that a Prime Host opportunity is successful, direct sales of SABRE to locations with the national carrier system will cease.

During this early stage, product development was to focus its efforts on:

- Expanding ticketing capabilities.
- Permitting booking and ticketing capabilities for rail and small regional air services.
- Adapting travel agency backoffice accounting software to national standards.
- Offering billing in foreign currencies.

SABRE specialists were scheduled to visit travel agents in order to help them increase their bookings. Agents were also to be offered repeated training and invited to various workshops. Agency sales were also to induce European hotel chains, car rental companies, and other local travel firms to become associates and list their services through SABRE for a fee.[8]

Once all necessary enhancements would be customized for a single-country market, SABRE would finally be promotable as a primary system to compete directly with local CRSs.

Configuration Strategy

Two major competitive disadvantages for SABRE were its high communication costs and its long response time. With the mainframe in Tulsa, Oklahoma, long distances had to be traversed when processing a booking in Europe. The low efficiency was especially evident when an incorrect command was sent by a European travel agent to the mainframe only to be answered, after a long delay, with an error message. It also was very inefficient to have a service used mainly by Europeans (e.g., Swissair shuttle between Zurich and München) being listed and managed in Tulsa. To avoid wasteful communication costs, a European

---

[8] Associates, such as hotel chains, are customers who are offering their services through the reservation system to the subscriber.

mini-mainframe could be designed to filter the messages and send to Tulsa only those which it could not process by itself. Such a system, however, was not feasible in the near future and a study of different alternatives continued.

Initial Research

In March of 1986, three senior analysts were to be hired to conduct a three-month marketing study to determine the potential subscriber base in each region and country. The research would also provide specific country by country information about:

- Current operating methods and procedures for travel agencies.
- Import/export regulations and other documentation requirements.
- Cultural and business practices.
- Communication requirements, and installation and maintenance procedures.
- Language requirements to develop a comprehensive sales, marketing, and installation program.
- Legal ramifications for operations.

The research was also expected to indicate recommendations for:

- Staffing and sales representation.
- Time frames for implementing the sales and installation efforts.
- Training requirements.
- SABRE functional enhancements.
- Promotion strategies.

Sales Staffing

New personnel would be added to headquarters as well as to the overseas staff. Each of the three foreign regions would be controlled by a regional manager. The regional manager of Europe would be based in London and report to the vice president of automation at headquarters. Four country managers would report to the regional manager (Figure 5). They would be responsible for the United Kingdom, France, Germany, and Scandinavia, and oversee one sales and one product specialist as well as one marketing service representative. Further recruiting would be necessary for the product development and training areas (eight analysts) and for the finance department (eight analysts).

Training and HELP Desk

Comprehensive training for travel agents would be crucial for the success of SABRE in Europe. The training had to not only be comprehensive in nature but also be offered in the native languages of travel agents. While located first in

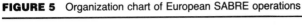

FIGURE 5 Organization chart of European SABRE operations

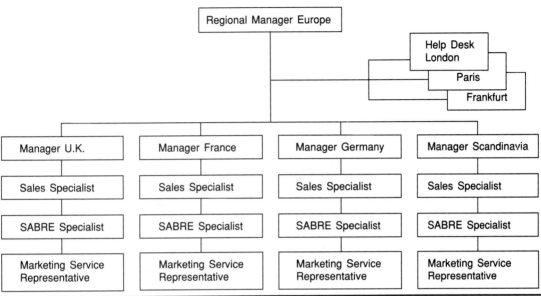

Dallas, the training was later to take place in London. Immediate assistance would be available through Help desks, consisting of two SABRE specialists located in London, Paris, and Frankfurt. The desks could be contacted by phone or electronic mail. "During the third quarter, an in-depth evaluation will be undertaken to determine the feasibility of adding additional Help desks in the cities of Paris, Frankfurt, and Stockholm."

For internal training, regional meetings between the regional manager and all SABRE field personnel would be held on a quarterly basis. "The meetings will be a forum for discussion of current corporate objectives, analysis of results, planning of strategies, and solicitation of feedback and input relating to the international marketplace."

A training session for international passenger sales would also be conducted quarterly to increase awareness and confidence among the sales force.

Advertising and Promotion

New brochures and a video presentation were being developed to highlight the international functionality and the broad features of SABRE for potential subscribers. SABRE was also represented at various air, travel, and computer trade shows throughout Europe. Additionally, the SABRE subscriber conference, which was held in the United States annually, would target international subscribers more actively and highlight its new international enhancements.

During the third quarter, an analyst from advertising and promotion would be charged with the development of international advertising and sales promotion. ''This analyst will address the individual customs, cultures, and language requirements of each respective country and coordinate these efforts with the local advertising agency.''

Legal Issues

The contract administration department of American Airlines faced working around many different contract laws and government regulations in Europe. In conjunction with the legal, financial controls, and international SABRE sales and service departments, it had to ensure the administration of highly comprehensive and enforceable agreements in each country. As SABRE's presence grew in the European market, contract administration would be required to move into each foreign location in order to address the local legal issues more effectively.

The legal and financial control departments were facing yet another issue: foreign currency billing.

Pricing

As noted earlier, SABRE would be priced at a competitive level. The rates of competing U.S. systems had to be matched immediately.

Conclusion

As American prepared itself to relive SABRE's success story in Europe, many questions remained unanswered. Many of them addressed the local marketplace, others were more concerned with global issues. In particular,

- How long would it take SABRE to reach the status of a primary system in each country?
- On which strategy should American focus its efforts, direct sales to travel agents or software licensing to national carriers?
- How would the competition react to SABRE's entry?
- How would the liberalization movements in EEC countries impact SABRE's attempt to become a major CRS in Europe?

''Alea iacta sunt.'' Like Caesar when he crossed the Rubicon, Crandall had thrown the dice in the air; now only the future would tell whether his plans would end successfully.

Part 6

Promotion Decisions

A. Advertising Decisions

Advertising is the most visible and controversial activity carried on in marketing. The first seven cases in this section focus their attention on this function.

Advertising is defined as all paid, nonpersonal forms of communication that are identified with a specific sponsor. It, therefore, includes expenditures on radio, television, newspaper, magazines, and outdoor billboards, plus the Yellow Pages. The largest absolute dollar spenders on advertising tend to be big consumer products companies, like Procter & Gamble, General Foods, and General Motors. The industries that spend the highest percentage of their sales on advertising are the drug and cosmetic companies, followed closely by packaged food products and soaps.

The marketing decision maker has a number of decisions to make with respect to advertising for a product. These include:

1. Setting advertising objectives.
2. Determining the advertising budget.
3. Deciding on what creative presentation should be used.
4. Selecting what media vehicles to use.
5. Selecting what scheduling pattern should be used.
6. Deciding how the advertising should be evaluated.

In the cases that follow in this section, the reader will work to make decisions in most of these areas. The next section of this note is a short reminder of some of the concepts related to each of these decision points.

Advertising Objectives

Advertising objectives should be stated in qualified terms with a specific time period designed for a specific market target. The objective may be in terms of profits, sales, or communications measures such as awareness, interest, and preference. The objective: "increase brand awareness" is obviously not as good a statement as "increase brand awareness to 85 percent of all women 18–40, in the next six months."

Advertising Budgets

Advertising budgets are difficult to set. That is why companies have fallen into using rule of thumb methods such as (1) the "all we can afford" method; (2) the percentage of sales method; and (3) the matching competitors method. We would prefer decision makers to proceed by defining the task they hope to accomplish and then have them calculate the cost of doing this. This is called the task approach. To do this method the advertiser must understand the functional relationship between his or her task and advertising expenditures.

Creative Development

Creative activity is usually done by an advertising agency. The final product is usually the result of much copy testing on dimensions such as attention getting and persuasiveness.

Media Decision

Media decisions are of two types. The first is the selection of broad classes of media to be considered for future analysis. This is done by matching the media characteristics with the needs of the advertiser. For example, television allows for good visual demonstration. This may be a desired characteristic for the campaign at hand.

The second stage involves the selection of specific media vehicles, for example, the NFL football game versus "All in the Family" versus a page in *Fortune*. The procedures for doing this are complex. Simply stated, vehicles are compared on the basis of their cost per thousand (CPM) target audience persons reached. The vehicle with the lowest CPM is selected. Audience sizes are then adjusted to allow for duplication between vehicles and new CPMs are calculated. Then the lowest CPM vehicle at that point is selected. This process continues until the budget is used up. A number of computer algorithms have been developed to handle the many calculations made in this process.

Scheduling Patterns

The advertisers must decide whether to (1) spend their budget continuously throughout the period; (2) concentrate it at a short interval; or (3) spend it intermittently throughout the period. There are no good rules of thumb to answer this question. The advertisers must experiment to find out which pattern makes the most sense for their products.

Evaluating Advertising

If the advertiser has specified quantitative objectives, one is then in a position to measure to see if the objectives were met. The procedure used should be specifically designed to fit the type of objective stated.

B. Sales Management Decisions

The last three cases in this section of the book deal with the management of the personal selling function. Personal selling is defined as all paid, personal forms of communication that are identified with a specific organization.

Organizations in the United States spend over one and one half times as much money on personal selling as they do on advertising. Effective management of personal selling activity is thus very important.

The marketing decision maker has a number of decisions to make with respect to personal selling for a product. These include:

1. Defining the selling job to be performed.
2. Establishing the desired characteristics of the salespersons who will do this job.
3. Determining the size of the sales force.
4. Recruiting and selecting salespersons.
5. Training salespersons.
6. Organizing the sales force.
7. Designing sales territories.
8. Assigning salespersons to territories.
9. Motivating salespersons.
10. Compensating salespersons.
11. Evaluating salespersons.

In the three sales management cases that are in this section, the reader will work to make decisions in most of these areas. Again, the next section of this note is a short reminder of some of the concepts related to each of these decisions.

Definition of the Selling Job

The beginning point of all sales management decisions is the definition of the selling job to be performed. For example, is the job basically just order taking or are there complex engineering presentations involved? In defining a particular selling job, one must keep in mind the role of personal selling in the overall marketing strategy and understand well the needs of the buyer or buyers involved. The competitive and physical environments of the job are also important considerations.

Desired Characteristics for Salespersons

Out of the definition of the selling job, the manager is able to establish a set of criteria for determining the type of person who should perform the selling job. One should list the personal background and individual skills and qualifications that are necessary to effectively perform the defined job. For example, in selling complex electrical equipment, the criteria might include the holding of a degree in electrical engineering, with strong oral communications skills to make presentations to customers.

Sales Force Size

Determining the necessary size of a sales force involves determining the effort level capabilities of an average salesperson and dividing that into a measure of the total selling job to be done. In doing so, judgments must be made on how many total accounts to serve, how often to call on them, and how many accounts an average salesperson can effectively handle.

Recruiting and Selecting Salespersons

The selection of the right salespersons basically involves generating a pool of prospects and evaluating those prospects using the criteria established for the selling job. Information is collected on prospects using application forms, personal interviews, and psychological tests.

Training

The basic objective of training is to bring a salesperson up to the required level of competence in those areas of the defined selling job that were deficient upon hiring. These might include product knowledge, oral presentation skills, field procedures, and so on. Decisions must be made as to who should do the training and where it should be done. Do we let current salespersons do the training in the field or have special people to do it at the office, or some combination?

Organizing the Sales Force

The sales force may be organized on a geographical, product, market, or some combination of these factors basis. If a salesperson can effectively handle all the company's products in a given geographic area, then the geographical structure probably makes the most sense. Otherwise, the product or market basis seem appropriate. The selection between these two approaches depends on whether product or market knowledge is the most important.

Case 22

South-West Pharmaceutical Company*

In August, Frank Van Huesen, vice president of the New Orleans-based advertising agency, Advertising Associates, was sitting in his skyscraper office contemplating a meeting scheduled for the next week. At that time, he was to meet with Mr. Lewis Spring, president of South-West Pharmaceutical Company (S.W.P. Company), to discuss agency recommendations for Gentle Care advertising for the next year. Although advertising expenditures for Gentle Care, a skin conditioner for pregnant women, were relatively small, the client was an important account for Advertising Associates, with about $700,000 in billings. Even though the number of pregnant women had been declining, Gentle Care had been experiencing a sudden, unexpected surge in sales. Therefore, planning its future strategy posed a definite challenge to Van Huesen's marketing and advertising expertise. Before the meeting, he had to come up with sound answers to such questions as: "How much to spend for advertising?"; "What media mix to employ?"; and "What to say in messages for Gentle Care?"

Company Background

The S.W.P. Company of New Orleans, Louisiana, is the oldest manufacturer of proprietary medicine products in the United States. It all began in Iberville, Louisiana, in 1826 when Captain N. L. Denard obtained the "formula" for a tonic from the Choctaw Indians. Formulation took place on south Louisiana plantations for many years until 1860 when Charles Thomas Spring, a pharmacist, bought the formula for $25 and started making and selling bottles of the tonic for $5. The company was moved to New Orleans in 1874 because of the city's better transportation facilities, and growth continued in a sporadic way. In 1955, the Stanfield Company was absorbed and with it another unique product, Gentle Care, joined the S.W.P. product line.

---

* This case was prepared by Kenneth L. Bernhardt and John S. Wright, Professor of Marketing, Georgia State University. Copyright © 1987 by Kenneth L. Bernhardt.

EXHIBIT 1 Product and price list for S.W.P. Company

Wholesale discounts: 18 percent on net billing	Quantity: 150-pound minimum prepaid shipment. Any assortment of S.W.P. Company products in original case lots can be combined to meet these shipping requirements.	Resale to retailers. At list less applicable wholesaler's cash discount when earned. Terms: 2 percent if paid within 30 days from date of invoice. Net and due after discount period.

Product	Unit size	List dozen	List	Packed case	Case weight
Gentle Care liquid	3 oz.	$29.60	$3.70	3 doz.	9½ lbs.
Gentle Care cream	2 oz.	29.60	3.70	1 doz.	3 lbs.

The company now manufactures and sells three principal products: Spring's Tonic, Ease Eye Drops, and Gentle Care. Exhibit 1 shows a partial product list, which includes package sizes, prices charged to retailers per dozen items, suggested "list" prices to be charged customers by retailers, as well as case sizes and weights. Wholesalers selling the products receive an 18 percent discount for performing their functions. Sales volume for the company was at an annual rate of less than $5 million, and had been growing about 10 percent per year.

The firm's products have traditionally been sold in retail drugstores, which received the merchandise through drug and specialty wholesalers. The company employs one salesman who calls upon present and prospective customers, primarily in the Southwest. Mr. Spring is active in several trade associations and spends much time traveling to cement trade relations. Management is keenly aware that customer buying patterns are changing and, therefore, efforts are being made to have company products stocked in discount stores, supermarkets, and chain drugstores. Consequently, many "direct" sales are made to large retailers and to rack jobbers. Of its 3,000 active accounts, 500 are large retail chains, and the remaining 2,500 are to a variety of middlemen including wholesale grocers, rack jobbers, and specialty jobbers.

The Product and Its Market

Gentle Care is also very old as products go, having been first sold in 1869. The product, which is a skin conditioner especially formulated for use during pregnancy to relieve tight, dry skin, was originally provided in liquid form. When massaged on the skin, it has a very soothing and relaxing effect on the muscles. Gentle Care's basic ingredients include winter-pressed cottonseed oil, soft-liquid soap, camphor, and menthol.

In 1967, a line extension of the product was devised in the form of Gentle Care cream, whose ingredients include cottonseed oil, laury, myrestyl, cetyl, stearyl in absorption base, glycerin, sorbitol, perfume, and color. Currently the cream form comprises a small but growing percentage of Gentle Care sales.

Mr. Van Huesen describes the industry as ''body lotions and creams for use during pregnancy.'' Exhibit 2 shows the few other companies in the industry, along with the pricing they employ. It should be noted that the other brands are very small in comparison to Gentle Care, are sold primarily through maternity shops, and have only regional or local distribution. None advertises, nor do the brands pose a competitive threat to Gentle Care, which is believed to have better distribution for its sales volume than any other drug product in the United States. By its very nature, the product is a ''slow-mover'' at the store level, and smaller outlets order the product in half-dozen lots. No deals have been made available to the middlemen in the past; however, an experiment was planned for the fall when retailers would be offered a ''one free in five'' package deal.

EXHIBIT 2 Industry and pricing structure—body lotions and creams for use during pregnancy

Company	Product	Size	Retail price	Wholesale price per dozen
S.W.P. Company, New Orleans, La.	Gentle Care (liquid)	3 oz.	$3.70	$25.60
	Gentle Care (cream)	2 oz.	3.70	25.60
Leading Lady Foundations, Inc., Cleveland, Ohio	Anne Alt Body Lotion	8 oz.	3.00	n.a.
Mothers Beautiful, Miami Beach, Fla.	Mothers Beautiful Body Lotion	8 oz.	2.50	n.a.
Shannon Manufacturing Co., North Hollywood, Calif.	Mary Jane Maternity Lotion	8 oz.	3.00	n.a.
Maternity Modes, Niles, Ill.	Maternity Modes Protein Body Creme	4 oz.	3.00	n.a.

n.a. = not available.

Isolating the target market for Gentle Care may appear to be an obvious exercise—it consists of all pregnant women. Within that category of womankind, however, Mr. Van Huesen thought the prime target for such lotions and creams should be the first-time mother-to-be. If she decides to use such a product at that time, it is quite likely she will again use it during succeeding pregnancies. What role is played by ''influencers'' (the expectant mother's mother, older mothers in the neighborhood, aunts, nurses, maternity shop personnel, and so forth) in the purchase and use decision is not known.

Birthrates in the United States have been declining precipitously, and the United States is approaching a state of zero population growth, a point where

EXHIBIT 3 Birthrate by age of mother and color, United States, 1961–1971

Ago (years)	Nonwhite			White		
	Ten years ago	Now	Percent change	Ten years ago	Now	Percent change
15–19	15.3%*	12.9%	−16%	7.9%	5.4%	−32%
20–24	29.3	18.5	−37	24.8	14.5	−42
25–29	22.2	13.6	−39	19.4	13.5	−30
30–34	13.6	8.0	−41	11.0	6.6	−45
35–39	7.5	4.0	−47	5.3	2.7	−49
40–44	2.2	1.2	−45	1.5	0.6	−60

* Table is read as follows: Ten years ago, of all nonwhite women between 15 and 19 years of age, 15.3 percent gave birth.

deaths and births are in balance. Reference to Exhibit 3 shows, nevertheless, that one woman in seven in the 20–24 age range does have a baby in a given year.

Little is known about the consumer decision to use these lotions and creams during pregnancy. How do women learn about such products? Are influencers important to the decision, or does advertising inform the expectant mother of the product's availability? In the absence of specific research into this area of consumer behavior, it was assumed by both Mr. Spring and Mr. Van Huesen that advertising plays a significant, if not *the* critical, role. The product recently had been experiencing large increases in sales, with this year's sales expected to be about 50 percent greater than the level of two years earlier, in spite of a decline in the market potential for the product category. Exhibit 4 gives the sales of Gentle Care for the previous seven years, as well as the advertising-to-sales ratio for that period. The large sales increases were being achieved by both the liquid and cream forms of Gentle Care.

EXHIBIT 4 Gentle Care—advertising-to-sales ratios

	Sales	Advertising	A/S ratio
Seven years ago	$189,578	$140,512	0.74
Six years ago	195,664	82,092	0.42
Five years ago	205,102	69,390	0.34
Four years ago	250,314	69,050	0.28
Three years ago	253,818	40,902	0.16
Two years ago	264,286	68,176	0.26
Last year	315,918	65,706	0.21
Current year	400,000 (projected)	75,000	0.19

Marketing Strategy

The marketing strategies employed by S.W.P. Company are reflections of the marketing philosophy of its president, Lewis Spring. Before joining the firm in

1969, Spring worked in promotional jobs in the petroleum and entertainment industries and he views promotion as an important part of his job. Technical people are hired to handle the manufacturing and physical distribution sides of the business, while Spring concentrates on the marketing-sales-advertising operations.

This circumstance simplifies Van Huesen's job. There are no layers of bureaucratic approval of S.W.P. Company. Once Van Huesen and Spring agreed on a strategy to be followed, it was implemented. The process involved a combination of Spring's ideas on how proprietary drugs should be promoted and Van Huesen's understanding of how advertising can be used to achieve the company's goals.

For a long time, Spring has maintained great faith in the importance of package design to the sales success of the kind of products manufactured by his company. The company once changed advertising agencies over this issue; Spring thought the Gentle Care package needed changing, while agency personnel felt that such a change would destroy the product's "image with the consumer."

Another of Spring's marketing guidelines is that the smaller company "must find the one single most important use for the product" and build the promotional program around that point. Closely related is another philosophical belief, namely that the firm "should do what the competition is not doing," whether it is in the area of media selection, creative strategy, or other promotional concerns.

The Advertising Budget

The company management does not have any "cut-and-dried" formula for arriving at the advertising budget. Advertising's importance to the sales of company products is recognized by Lewis Spring; nevertheless, as Exhibit 4 reveals, the advertising-to-sales ratio has been declining over the past decade without a consequent decline in sales. The relatively large budget seven years ago was due to the simultaneous introduction of the cream and a change in package design, which was accompanied by an increased budget to help secure greater distribution. The drastic cutback in advertising expenditures three years ago was due to an unsuccessful diversification into the cosmetic business that necessitated a recoupment of financial resources. The relative cutbacks this year and last year were in response to tight money conditions at the time and to a management decision to "make this year a year of profit." Spring believes, however, that such cutbacks can be only a temporary phenomenon; in respect to advertising he holds that "you must be everlastingly at it."

Media Strategy

As has been characteristic of the proprietary drug industry for generations, Gentle Care was traditionally advertised by means of small space ads placed in newspapers. Twenty years ago it was realized that for a product whose market is as highly segmented as that for Gentle Care, this media strategy resulted in a great deal of "wasted circulation" of the advertising message; thereafter, advertising for the product was concentrated solely in magazines.

As shown in Exhibit 5, there exists an appreciable number of magazines which can be characterized as "baby oriented." Of course, within the category, those read during the prenatal stage are desired by the producers of pregnancy body skin conditioners. Once the child is born, the product is no longer needed, although it is possible that the woman will continue to use the product for other skin care purposes.

EXHIBIT 5 Baby-oriented magazines

Magazine	Frequency of publication	Circulation	CPM (B/W)	Page rate (B/W) one insertion
American Baby	Monthly	1,108,700	8.92	$ 9,890
Baby Care	Quarterly	575,785	7.49	4,310
Baby Talk	Monthly	1,021,693	8.28	8,460
Congratulations	Annually	2,624,120*	n.a.†	20,670
Expecting	Quarterly	855,013	9.11	7,790
Good Housekeeping	Monthly	5,703,732	3.94	22,765
Modern Romances	Monthly	752,339	3.48	2,645
Mothers' Manual	Bimonthly	913,085	8.77	8,010
Parents' Magazine and Better Family Living	Monthly	2,017,029	6.52	13,565
Redbook's Young Mother	Annually	1,519,888	4.77	19,345

* Distributed to specific places; CPM not determinable.

† n.a. = not available.

Source: SRDS *Consumer Magazines and Farm Publications.*

For many years, Gentle Care was featured in smaller-sized ads (one-sixth page to one-half page) in 8 or 10 magazines, one or two insertions per year. In other words, the emphasis was placed on the *reach* strategy—trying to get the message before as many different prospects as possible for a given expenditure of advertising dollars. This strategy was replaced with one aiming at greater *frequency;* fewer publications were used with more insertions in each magazine over the year. The rationale behind this change was based on the fact that there is no seasonality in the product's use; women become pregnant throughout the 12 months.

The current advertising schedule for Gentle Care is shown in Exhibit 6. One key change made last year was switching out of *Redbook,* where the product had been advertised every other month adjacent to the magazine's "expectant mother's" column. To ensure that position, larger space had to be purchased, so for the same amount of money, the entire McFadden Group of eight magazines was available, although for small-sized ads. The agency's media department felt that the McFadden Group would be a better match with the target market for Gentle Care than would *Redbook. Parents' Magazine* was

EXHIBIT 6   Gentle Care—current advertising plan

Magazine	Size ad	Cost per ad	Number ads	Total cost
Expecting	½ page (2¼ × 6¹⁵⁄₁₆ inches)	$6,620	2	$13,240
American Baby	1 col. (2⅜ × 5 inches)	3,640	3	10,920
Mothers' Manual	⅓ page (4⁹⁄₁₆ × 5 inches)	3,600	2	7,200
Parents' Magazine	1 col. (2¼ × 5 inches)	5,330	2	10,660
McFadden's Group True Story Photoplay TV-Radio Mirror True Confessions Motion Picture True Romance True Experience True Love Redbook	⅓ page (2¼ × 5¹⁄₁₆ inches)	6,082	4	24,328
Reserve for special regional availabilities				4,000
				$70,348
Estimated production				4,652
				$75,000

included in the media schedule primarily to allow the company to use the seal of approval in Gentle Care advertising, even though its impact on sales was undetermined.

Creative Strategy

Before Advertising Associates took over the account five years earlier, Gentle Care was advertised through ads which featured the product jar. A typical ad, as created by the former agency, is shown in Exhibit 7. This ad shows an attractive woman's head with her hand apparently rubbing her shoulder. The headline is very general in content; it is not until the reader sees the subheading does she learn that Gentle Care is for use during pregnancy. Seals of approval from two well-known certification agencies were also featured, which meant that advertisements had to be placed in *Good Housekeeping* and *Parents' Magazine*. Exhibit 8 shows the first advertisement in company history which prominently displays that the product is for use during pregnancy.

The new campaign inaugurated by Advertising Associates, an example of which is shown in Exhibit 9, was more direct; the reader could readily determine who used the product and for what purpose. One seal of approval, that of *Good Housekeeping* magazine, was dropped in the belief that the magazine's

EXHIBIT 7 Pre-Advertising Associates ad for Gentle Care

EXHIBIT 8   First Gentle Care ad prominently
featuring use during pregnancy

PREGNANT?
MAKE YOURSELF COMFORTABLE.

Treat your skin to a soothing beauty massage with Gentle Care. The rich lubricating liquid helps tight, dry skin stay
soft and supple. It brings you ease and
comfort while you wait. Look for
Gentle Care at your Drug Counter. It's
the Body Skin Conditioner that's especially recommended during pregnancy.

Gentle Care

EXHIBIT 9 First ad in the Advertising
Associates campaign

pregnant?

Make Yourself Comfortable.

Treat your skin to a soothing beauty
massage with GENTLE CARE. It's the
body skin conditioner that's especially
recommended during pregnancy. The rich,
lubricating liquid helps tight, dry
skin stay soft and supple. It
brings you ease and comfort
while you wait. Look for
GENTLE CARE
at your drug
counter.

Gentle
Care

audience was much older than the target market for Gentle Care. The decision was discussed at length because the role of older women in the purchase and use of the product was not known.

Changing standards and values in our society are reflected in the current campaign as shown in Exhibit 10. Here a nude model is seen actually applying the product as it would be done by the purchaser. Furthermore, the headline is direct and to the point. The *Parents' Magazine* seal is again featured, and the product package is illustrated in a subordinate position.

EXHIBIT 10 Example of current advertising for Gentle Care

Don't let your tummy get out of shape while you're pregnant.

Give your tight, dry skin a soothing massage with Gentle Care . Its special formula will help relieve the taut feeling and minimize itching. And it will help your skin stay soft and supple. So make yourself comfortable. Look for Gentle Care in cream or liquid form at your drug counter.

The New Advertising Plan

In mulling over the advertising history of his client, Van Huesen jotted down several questions which he felt needed answering before he could design the new advertising plan for Gentle Care:

1. What level of advertising should be recommended for next year?
2. What changes, if any, should be made in media strategy? Are specialized magazines the best media choice for Gentle Care? If so, are "baby-oriented" publications the best choice?
3. Is the frequency rather than the reach strategy to be continued for Gentle Care advertising next year?
4. Should the *Parents' Magazine* seal be retained?
5. What changes, if any, should Mr. Van Huesen recommend in the creative strategy for the product?

Once these questions were answered, Mr. Van Huesen felt he was ready to meet with Mr. Spring to present his recommendations for the Gentle Care advertising. Van Huesen knew from past experience that he could anticipate some probing questions from Mr. Spring concerning how the effectiveness of the advertising for Gentle Care could be measured.

Case 23

L.A. Gear*

September 13, 1989   The Los Angeles Palladium is packed with reporters waiting for L.A. Gear CEO, Robert Y. Greenberg, to formally introduce their new spokesperson, singer/entertainer Michael Jackson.

Taunted by rumors, the press wants to confirm the two-year, $20 million plus stock option contract Jackson is reputed to have signed in exchange for starring in new commercials, wearing L.A. Gear footwear in his music videos, and designing a new line of apparel and shoes under their new 1990 campaign, UNSTOPPABLE.

Once the star appeared, however, he merely read a prepared statement about the alliance, blew a kiss to the crowd and left the stage, allowing no questions. Industry analyst, Steven Levitt of Market Evaluations, immediately cast doubts on the arrangement, predicting that Jackson would be valuable to L.A. Gear only if he sang in the commercials and if the target were narrowed to 6- to 11-year-old girls.

Thus, without direct confirmation on L.A. Gear's dealings, the press and the public were left to speculate on L.A. Gear's future marketing focus and strategy for the 90s for the $9 billion retail athletic footwear market, and its ability to achieve Greenberg's goal of "building the biggest brand name in the world."

Although Greenberg predicts that L.A. Gear will surpass both Reebok and Nike for sales within the next five years, there is still doubt within the industry that the upstart company will be able to successfully disseminate its trendy styles and its California moniker throughout the world.

Athletic Footwear Industry

The athletic footwear industry, expected to reach $5.4 billion in 1990, has seen rapid growth over the past 15 years, particularly during the past 5 years.

---

* This case was written from public sources and from interviews with people knowledgeable about this industry by Joanne E. Novak, under the supervision of Thomas C. Kinnear. Copyright © 1990 by Thomas C. Kinnear.

Averaging 21 percent growth wholesale and 23 percent growth retail between 1985 and 1990, the forces that have been driving the growth can be identified as:

- *Late 1970s*—The popularity of running.
- *Early 1980s*—The aerobics craze.
- *Early 1980s*—The emphasis on overall health and fitness.
  - —The introduction of specialty shoes for each sport (basketball to boardsailing) or all sports (cross-training).
  - —The emergence of technological innovations in material and design.
- *Late 1980s, early 1990s*—
  - —The use of multimillion-dollar media campaigns and star-studded spokespeople.

From these trends, two distinct market segments have emerged—performance and fashion. There used to be classic, all-purpose, $15 sneakers—such as Converse "Chuck Taylor" All Stars, P.F. Flyers, and Keds—that could easily be replaced once they had worn out and that *never* would label their wearers as slaves to fashion. In the 90s, however, with numerous styles and new players vying for a piece of the market, athletic footwear can cost as much as $170 per pair and new styles appear every 8 to 10 months as manufacturers have decreased their new product introduction cycle. Today, athletic footwear is worn to make a statement.

Emergence of Fashion Segment

The development of the fashion segment began with "the runner's look." Running had become a popular sport, dominated by men, during the early 1970s. After American Frank Shorter won the gold medal for the marathon during the 1976 Olympics, however, many more Americans were inspired to run or jog for exercise. This boom created a demand for runners' apparel and running shoes—supplying growth to the athletic shoe industry from 1977 to 1983. The popularity of the sport eventually reached nonrunners who liked the image of the runner. This image spurred the purchase of running shoes for casual use and reflected the beginning of a nationwide trend toward a more casual lifestyle.[1]

The advent of aerobics in 1983 created a new fashion/fitness trend as women who aerobicized wanted apparel and footwear specific to the sport. They preferred stylish gear that was more comfortable, more colorful, and had more variety than traditional exercise outfits.

---

[1] Angela Hinton et al., "Reebok and Nike: The Athletic Shoe Industry," University of Michigan Research Report for Prof. S. Hariharan, April 18, 1989.

EXHIBIT 1 Males/females purchases of athletic footwear (000s)

	Bought in last 12 months	Bought 1 pair	Bought 2 pairs	Bought >3 pairs
Males				
Total male population = 84,066				
Percent of total male population	20.80%	10.80%	6.00%	4.00%
Total buyers	17,467	9,105	5,027	3,336
Age 18–24	3,915	2,147	1,040	728
25–34	5,910	2,810	2,000	1,099
35–44	3,441	1,668	1,049	724
45–54	2,121	1,259	424	437
55–64	1,155	635	293	227
65+	925	584	220	122
Total shoes	>29,197	9,105	10,054	>10,008
Age 18–24	6,411	2,147	2,080	2,184
25–34	10,107	2,810	4,000	3,297
35–44	5,938	1,668	2,098	2,172
45–54	3,418	1,259	848	1,311
55–64	1,902	635	586	681
65+	1,390	584	440	366
Regions of Buying				
Northeast	4,346	2,258	1,279	809
Midwest	4,757	2,367	1,388	1,002
South	5,276	3,070	1,239	968
West	3,088	1,410	1,121	557
Females				
Total female population = 92,184				
Percent of total female population	28.20%	10.50%	6.30%	11.50%
Total buyers	26,033	9,636	5,827	10,571
Age 18–24	4,263	1,753	677	1,833
25–34	7,874	3,030	1,972	2,872
35–44	6,625	2,325	1,348	2,952
45–54	3,300	1,008	778	1,514
55–64	2,129	775	553	801
65+	1,841	745	498	559
Total shoes	>52,730	9,636	11,654	31,713
Age 18–24	8,606	1,753	1,354	5,499
25–34	15,590	3,030	3,944	8,616
35–44	13,877	2,325	2,696	8,856
45–54	7,106	1,008	1,556	4,542
55–64	4,284	775	1,106	2,403
65+	3,418	745	996	1,677
Regions of buying				
Northeast	6,809	2,449	947	3,413
Midwest	6,986	2,882	1,469	2,634
South	7,718	2,773	1,970	2,975
West	4,520	1,531	1,441	1,548

Source: Simmons, 1988.

EXHIBIT 2 Male/female spending patterns (000s)

Total male population = 84,066

Spending	Buyers	Percent who bought in last 12 months	Percent of total buyers
If men buy athletic footwear			
Spend < $15	4,032	23%	4.80%
Spend $15–$29	6,426	37	7.60
Spend ≥ $30	7,010	40	8.30
Total female population = 92,184			
If women buy athletic footwear			
Spend < $15	9,636	37%	10.50%
Spend $15–$29	5,827	22	6.30
Spend ≥ $30	10,571	41	11.50

77% of men who buy spend over $15.
63.5% of women who buy spend over $15.
Source: Simmons, 1988.

Thus, fashion was brought to the forefront and, for the first time, women were driving the market. By 1987, women bought sneakers more often than men and they bought more of them (Exhibits 1 and 2). The average woman in 1989 owned 2.6 pairs of sneakers compared with 2.5 pairs owned by the average man.

By the end of the decade, athletic footwear manufacturers were facing yet a different market. Inner-city kids began to define territories by brands of sneakers (i.e., on Boston's Intervale Street they would be seen only in Adidas sneakers, whereas Nike streets were Hamilton and Crawford); teenage girls developed sneaker etiquette, shunning boys donning sneakers incompatible with their own; and young urban professionals and teenagers bought several pairs of sneakers to match their wardrobes and their moods. They needed all-night dancing shoes, "impressing the ladies" shoes, and Saturday-at-the-park shoes to let their peers know they had style. As one teen simply said, "If I wear black, I wear black sneakers. If I wear red, I wear red sneakers. If I wear purple, I wear white sneakers."[2]

> Ten years ago, people had an average of 1.2 pairs of athletic shoes in their closets. In 1987, Reebok customers owned an average of 4.5 pairs. By the mid-90s, those same customers will own six to six and a half different pairs of sneakers apiece. Footwear will no longer be an accessory, it will be the main course.[3]
>
> Paul Fireman, CEO, Reebok

[2] "Much Ado About Rubber," CBS's *Sunday Today,* March 25, 1990.
[3] E. M. Swift, "Farewell My Lovely," *Sports Illustrated,* February 19, 1990, p. 80.

These wearers were shifting 40 percent of the athletic shoe demand (30 percent direct demand, 10 percent influential demand) to the 15- to 22-year-old age group and defining athletic footwear as *the* fashion statement.[4]

Acquisitions

Growth in the industry has been the result of not only these trends but also savvy marketing and new product design. Strength abroad and acquisitions of other footwear manufacturers has helped to grow market share (Exhibit 3). Reebok has brought several footwear manufacturers into its corporation: Rockport, 1985; Avia, 1987 (who previously bought Donnor, a hiking/walking shoe company, in 1986); Ellesse, 1987; Frye (boots), 1987; and Metaphors (women's casual shoes), 1987.

EXHIBIT 3   U.S. share of footwear market

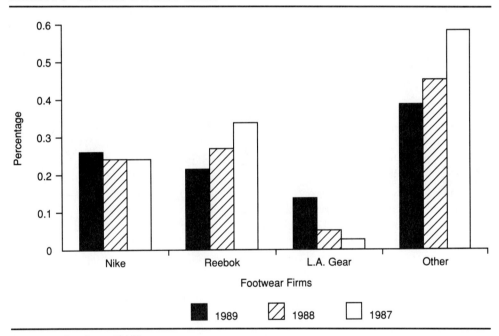

Assumes total market = $9 billion.

Interco, owner of the Florsheim brand, purchased Converse in 1986 and Yarsel Investment Corp. bought Pony (Exhibit 4).

---

[4] Joseph Pereira, "The Well-Heeled," *The Wall Street Journal*, December 1, 1988, p. 1.

EXHIBIT 4 Ownership of athletic footwear brands

Brand	Ownership
Adidas	Private
Autry	Private
Etonic	Private
Fila	Private
K–Swiss	Private
Kaepa	Private
Kangaroos	Private
Lotto	Private
New Balance	Private
Pony	Private
Spalding	Private
Tretorn	Private
Turntec	Private
Hyde	Public
L.A. Gear	Public
Nike	Public
Reebok	Public
Foot-Joy	Public, a division of American Brands
Converse	Public, a division of Interco
Avia	Public, a division of Reebok
Ellesse	Public, a division of Reebok
Keds	Public, a division of Stride-Rite
Brooks	Public, a division of Wolverine
Puma	Public, Germany
Asics Tigers	Public, Japan

Source: Drexel Burnham Lambert Industry Report, December 1987.

Buyers

As the 1990s approach, the athletic shoe manufacturers are forced to address the fashion issue. With their current penetration into the market at only 20 to 30 percent, footwear firms have a great potential to attract new buyers and penetrate the market further.

Buyers are not only serious athletes but also working women, casual or weekend athletes, and casual fashion wearers in search of comfortable, attractive shoes. Within each buyer segment, there are different priorities—performance, fashion, comfort, and price sensitivity—and for each buyer the priorities differ. Currently, 80 percent of all athletic shoe purchases are for casual use.[5]

Additionally, more segments or subsegments have emerged within each segment: male/female; single sport user/multisport user; infant/toddler; young/old. Each of these subsegments has specific needs that they want addressed.

The market also can be segmented according to psychographic profiles. A recent Harvard Business School case study identified segments by athletic

---

[5] Ellen Paris, "Rhinestone Hightops, Anyone?" *Forbes,* March 7, 1988, p. 78.

lifestyles: serious athletes, weekend warriors, and casual athletes. The case identified the serious athletes as the opinion leaders, prompting the manufacturers to cater to them. By satisfying this segment, it is assumed that other types of buyers would follow their lead.

Capabilities

The competition for these buyers has intensified. Nike and Reebok, the number one and number two U.S. market share holders, respectively, are fighting for more share in the media and the stores. They have invested millions of dollars on highly produced, star-studded media campaigns (Exhibit 5) and new product introductions that include air, color and new materials (Exhibit 6). Reebok and Nike have been focused on performance with technological attributes in the lead for product differentiation.

This competition has forced a change to the product development and product life cycle for athletic footwear. The average product development cycle has been trimmed to 6 to 10 months while the product life cycle has been shortened to 8 to 10 months. Nike is using CAD/CAM technologies to shorten their development time for the introduction of new products.

New styles appear with new technologies, materials, colors, or endorsers capitalizing on or creating the latest trends. For the buyer, there is more choice and more confusion about a brand and an athletic shoe's attributes. Also, with the possible eight-month turnaround for new styles—prices can conceivably rise every eight months. The largest retail hike in 1989 has been with basketball pump models retailing between $170 and $180. (Nike's Air Pressure, $175; Reebok's Pump, $170.)

EXHIBIT 5 Advertising and promotional expenditures (in $ millions)

	1986	1987	1988	1989	1990*
L.A. Gear	$ 2.6	$ 5.4	$12.6	$25	$ 50
Reebok		12	35	60	70
Nike	62.5	65.9	85.3	50	100

* Estimated for 1990.
For L.A. Gear, dollars include trade shows, trade and consumer publications (.12), merchandise, TV (.50), and specialty billboards. International advertising of $3 million is not included.

For Reebok, the $70 million is divided between $40 million domestic and $30 million in promotions. International advertising of $20 million is not included. Ten percent of expenditures in 1989 were for children's footwear.

For Nike, $25–$30 million will be spent on promotions in 1990.

Sources: Linda Williams, "On the Right Foot," *Los Angeles Times*, September 31, 1989, s. 4, p. 1.

"Reebok," *Adweek*, February 5, 1990, p. 12.

E. W. Swift, "Farewell My Lovely," *Sports Illustrated*, February 19, 1990, p. 80.

Nike 10–K 1988.

Reebok 10–K 1988.

David Jefferson, "Fashion Victim? L.A. Gear, Highflier in Sneakers, Discovers Perils of Shifting Fads," *The Wall Street Journal*, December 8, 1989, p. A16.

EXHIBIT 6 Reebok energy return system

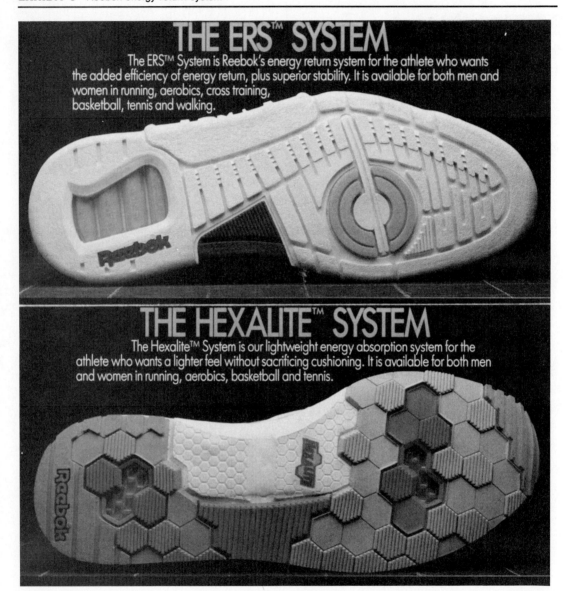

EXHIBIT 6 *(concluded)*

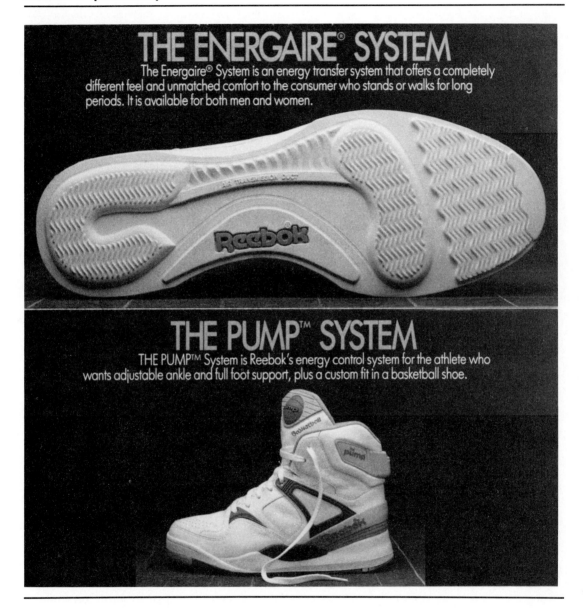

THE ENERGAIRE® SYSTEM

The Energaire® System is an energy transfer system that offers a completely different feel and unmatched comfort to the consumer who stands or walks for long periods. It is available for both men and women.

THE PUMP™ SYSTEM

THE PUMP™ System is Reebok's energy control system for the athlete who wants adjustable ankle and full foot support, plus a custom fit in a basketball shoe.

Considering that the top three manufacturers use low-cost production facilities in South Korea and Taiwan and that it costs only $15 to $20 to manufacture a pair of sneakers that will retail at $60 to $100, in addition to manufacturing, the revenues from these athletic shoes support R&D, advertising and promotion, and company profits.

L.A. Gear, third in retail sales in the U.S. market, replacing Converse in 1989, is growing with the fashion segment (Exhibit 7). As the market expands to new users, however, old competitors (Keds, Converse, Adidas, and designers) are trying to capitalize on the industry's growth to recapture market share.

EXHIBIT 7 U.S. sales of athletic footwear

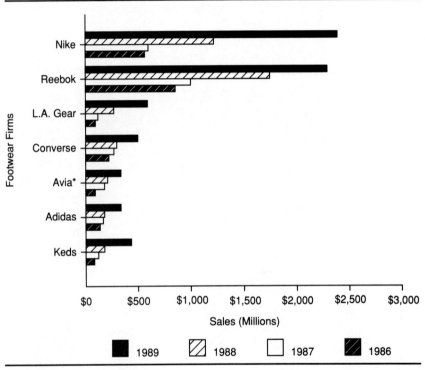

* Avia was purchased by Reebok in 1988.

With buyers willing to purchase several pairs of shoes for different uses, the market for performance shoes overlaps with the fashion shoe market. Thus, the two dimensions—fashion and performance—will not stay separated in the 90s. Manufacturers are faced with positioning themselves effectively in these markets to maintain, grow, or recapture market share.

Driving the 90s

Shoe design—with a technological or fashion emphasis—and advertising become two driving forces in the industry to support manufacturers' positioning. While technological innovations lead to a better-made shoe that has state-of-the-art fit and performance, heavy advertising and promotional activity serves to decrease brand blur and support manufacturers' unique images. The strength of a firm's R&D and image advertising is heavily correlated with leading market share and/or high sales growth.

L.A. Gear's performance over the past four years demonstrates how positioning and strategy can change the perceptions and performance of a company (Exhibit 8).

Net sales increased 217 percent from 1987 to 1988 due to not only higher wholesale prices but also the number of shoes that were purchased—4.4 million units to 10.1 million units (Exhibit 9). Internationally, sales increased from $2.3 million to $20.5 million—a 791 percent gain.

By 1990, sales forecasts for L.A. Gear are projected to exceed $1 billion (Exhibit 10). First quarter 1990 results for revenue already show L.A. Gear

EXHIBIT 8   Statement of operations (in thousands)

	Year ended November 30				
	1988	*1987*	*1986*	*1985*	*1984*
Net sales	$223,713	$70,575	$36,299	$10,687	$9,007
Cost of sales	129,103	41,569	20,880	7,294	6,116
Gross profit	94,610	29,006	15,419	3,393	2,891
General and administrative expenses	54,024	20,559	10,263	2,722	2,685
Interest/factoring expenses	4,102	1,110	686	526	368
Provision for loss from litigation	0	0	2,295	0	0
Royalty income	−856	−604	−1,210	−285	−65
Earnings (loss) before income taxes, discontinued operations, and extraordinary item	37,340	7,941	3,385	430	−97
Income tax benefit (expense)	−15,310	−3,570	−1,634	−199	45
Earnings (loss) before discontinued operations and extraordinary item	22,030	4,371	1,751	231	−52
(Loss) from discontinued operations, net of income carryforward	0	0	−6	−31	−392
Earnings (loss) before extraordinary item	$ 22,030	$ 4,371	$ 1,745	$ 200	($444)
Extraordinary item—use of net operating loss carryforward	0	0	0	133	0
Net earnings (loss)	$ 22,030	$ 4,371	$ 1,745	$ 333	($444)

EXHIBIT 8 (continued) Consolidated balance sheet data L.A. Gear, Inc. and subsidiaries (in thousands)

	November 30	
	1988	*1987*
Assets		
Cash	$ 4,205	$ 3,245
Accounts receivable	49,526	15,148
Inventory	66,556	15,813
Prepaid expenses and other current assets	3,383	951
Total current assets	$123,670	$35,157
Property, equipment, net	3,110	
accumulated depreciation		1,010
Deferred tax charges	1,034	14
Other assets	1,019	613
Total assets	128,833	36,794
Liabilities and Shareholders' Equity		
Current liabilities:		
Line of credit	$ 57,230	$ 7,126
Accounts payable	7,748	3,886
Accrued expenses and other liabilities	10,029	585
Accrued loss from litigation	2,373	2,341
Accrued compensation	5,927	414
Income tax payable	4,217	323
Total current liabilities	87,524	14,675
Shareholders' equity		
Common stock	n/a	n/a
Preferred stock	n/a	n/a
Additional paid-in capital	13,008	15,848
Retained earnings	28,301	6,271
Total Shareholders' Equity	41,309	22,119
Total liabilities and shareholders' equity	$128,833	$36,794

EXHIBIT 8 (concluded) L.A Gear, Inc. and subsidiaries' consolidated statement of income and retained earnings (thousands)

	Three months ended February 28	
	1990	*1989*
Net sales	$187,281	$66,070
Cost of sales	113,605	37,486
Gross profit	73,676	28,584
Selling, general, and administrative expenses	46,498	17,419
Operating income	27,178	11,165
Interest expense, net	4,013	2,118
Income before income taxes	23,165	9,047
Income tax expense	9,266	3,689
Net income	$ 13,899	$ 5,358
Weighted average shares	20,022	17,311
Earnings per share	$0.69	$0.31

Source: L.A. Gear press release, February 1990.

EXHIBIT 9 U.S. sales of footwear market

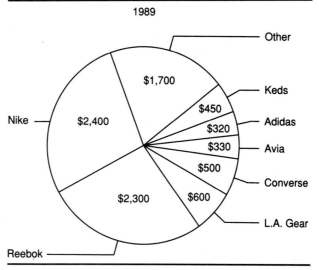

1989

Nike — $2,400

$1,700 — Other

$450 — Keds

$320 — Adidas

$330 — Avia

$500 — Converse

$600 — L.A. Gear

$2,300

Reebok

* Avia was purchased by Reebok in 1988.

EXHIBIT 10 L.A Gear sales

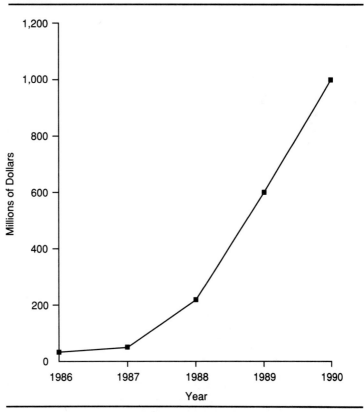

Note: Figure for 1990 was an estimate.

exceeding industry analysts' forecasts of $160 million to $165 million. Their revenue grew 257 percent—from $66.1 million to $170 million.[6]

Greenberg notes, however,

> To achieve increased market penetration and to ensure that we meet the large customer demand for our products, we sold certain styles in the first quarter [1990] at gross profit margins lower than the Company's historic norms.
>
> This decision had its intended effect, increasing market share and retail shelf space for new styles . . . sales during the quarter were substantially in excess of analysts' expectations and the Company's gross and net profit margin percentages decreased somewhat during the period.[7]

By increasing their advertising and trade show presence during the late 1980s and increasing their marketing efforts in large department stores, L.A. Gear developed a stronger push strategy to help increase primary demand for their athletic and athletic-styled leisure footwear.

L.A. Gear's success has been reflected in its stock price (Exhibit 11). Previously considered only a trendy valley girl shoe company, L.A. Gear had the best performing stock in 1989, showing an increase of 185 percent total return to investors.

EXHIBIT 11 L.A. Gear common stock sale prices

	Sales prices	
	Low	High
1987		
First quarter	$ 1.63	$ 3.07
Second quarter	2.32	3.28
Third quarter	2.16	3.16
Fourth quarter	1.72	3.47
1988		
First quarter	$ 1.85	$ 4.47
Second quarter	3.91	6.97
Third quarter	5.82	9.88
Fourth quarter	8.38	11.38
1989		
First quarter	$10.00	$17.56
Second quarter	15.07	26.32
Third quarter	25.75	33.75
Fourth quarter	29.94	45.75

Note: Prices adjusted for an August 1988 and September stock split.
Source: L.A Gear 10–K Report, February 28, 1990.

---

[6] "Nike, L.A. Gear, Reebok are Expected to Post Increaesd 1st Quarter Earnings", *The Wall Street Journal,* March 29, 1990, p. A4.

[7] L.A. Gear Press Release: L.A. Gear Inc., Reports Significant Increases in Revenue and Net Income for First Quarter, 1990.

L.A. Gear

L.A. Gear found a niche in the fashion segment of the 1986 $5 billion athletic footwear industry and exploited it. Known as Good Times Industries until 1985, the company initially designed and sold roller skate shoes and owned roller palaces. In 1983, the company introduced a canvas tie-on shoe with a flat rubber bottom from South Korea and called it The Street Walker. By 1985, the company—now L.A. Gear—had $10.7 million in sales of women's aerobic shoes and leather athletic-styled leisure shoes.

Greenberg says, "I was watching the popularity of athletic shoes as casual shoes."[8] As athletic shoes ceased to be worn for running and jumping, L.A. Gear provided shoes for wearers who chose athletic shoes as their casual shoe of choice. L.A. Gear now has an extensive product line (Exhibit 12).

An entrepreneur by nature, Greenberg began his retailing career in the 1960s selling wigs to beauty shops in Boston. He moved on to selling Wild Oats jeans to department stores in the 1970s, and in 1979 licensed Steven Spielberg's *E.T.* for use on kids' shoelaces. That venture reaped $3 million in 90 days.

Greenberg prides himself on being able to spot trends in his market and continues to introduce products that will appeal to his current customers. He readily acknowledges that designing for trends that take hold of young women can be risky, but he believes that if L.A. Gear stays in close touch with its shoe buyers, the company will only grow. Greenberg himself meets with his customers regularly—when he occasionally poses as a shoe salesman in a nearby mall.

Greenberg hopes to make L.A. Gear "America's No. 1 family brand" and has helped to generate enthusiasm for his goal—beginning with his executive officers (Exhibit 13). He has preprinted tee shirts and caps that say "L.A. Gear 1 in '91" for his executives.

Jonathan Ziegler, industry analyst with Sutro and Company, attributes L.A. Gear's success to good advertising and merchandising in Southern California. By placing their advertisements on MTV and cable stations, he says, L.A. Gear played to their target—the young female who would wear skirts and athletic shoes.[9]

> They identified a niche—the valley girl niche. . . . It's sort of like women in Reeboks and business suits. L.A. Gear hit the juniors with casual clothes and sneakers. It's not a technical shoe that would impress Michael Jordan [Chicago Bulls basketball star], but a fashion shoe that's got more look than technology.[10]
> John Horan—Publisher, *Sports Goods Management News*

As of 1988, L.A. Gear had 4.7 percent market share and currently has a 13 percent share. "There's no doubt that it was the name that caught on," says

---

[8] Linda Williams, "L. A. Gear Posts Huge Increases in Second Quarter Earnings," *Los Angeles Times*, June 29, 1988, s. 4, p. 1.
[9] Ibid.
[10] Ibid.

EXHIBIT 12 L.A Gear, Inc. product mix

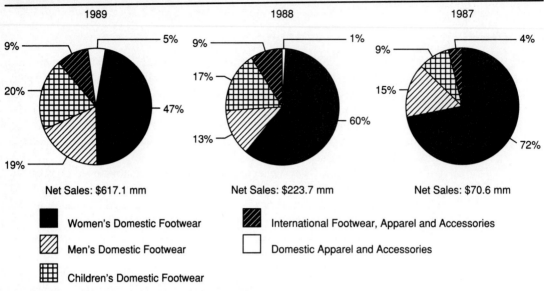

1989	1988	1987

1989: 9%, 5%, 20%, 47%, 19%
1988: 9%, 17%, 1%, 13%, 60%
1987: 9%, 15%, 4%, 72%

Net Sales: $617.1 mm   Net Sales: $223.7 mm   Net Sales: $70.6 mm

■ Women's Domestic Footwear   ▨ International Footwear, Apparel and Accessories

▨ Men's Domestic Footwear   □ Domestic Apparel and Accessories

▦ Children's Domestic Footwear

Note: The product mix is expressed as a percentage of total revenues.

L.A. Gear Product Split—1988

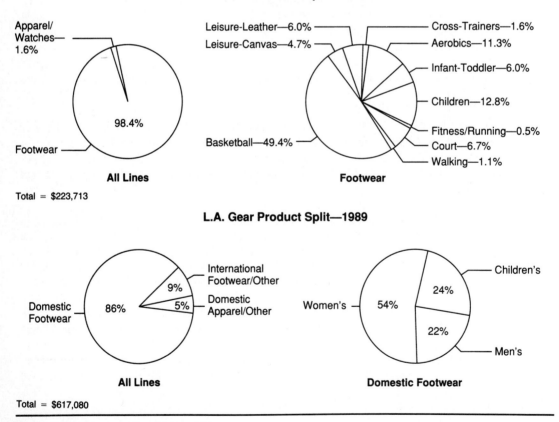

Apparel/Watches—1.6%
Footwear 98.4%
All Lines
Total = $223,713

Leisure-Leather—6.0%
Leisure-Canvas—4.7%
Cross-Trainers—1.6%
Aerobics—11.3%
Infant-Toddler—6.0%
Children—12.8%
Fitness/Running—0.5%
Court—6.7%
Walking—1.1%
Basketball—49.4%
Footwear

L.A. Gear Product Split—1989

Domestic Footwear 86%
International Footwear/Other 9%
Domestic Apparel/Other 5%
All Lines
Total = $617,080

Women's 54%
Children's 24%
Men's 22%
Domestic Footwear

Source: L.A. Gear press release, February 1990.

EXHIBIT 13   Corporate personnel (as of February 1989)

Full-time employees	431
Corporate management	42
Administration	38
Advertising and promotion	13
R & D	16
Sales, customer service	39
Jeanswear	3
Watches	1
International operations	13
Overseas offices	36
Technical reps	4
Warehousing	226
Directors and Executive Officers	*Age*
Allan E. Dalshaug, director	56
Robert Y. Greenberg, chairman of the board, president and director	48
Elliot J. Horowitz, executive vice president, chief financial officer and director	42
Sandy Saeman, executive vice president, secretary and director	41
Richard W. Schubert, director	37
Gil N. Schwartzberg, executive vice president and chief administrative officer	46
Stephen Williams, executive vice president	52
Donald B. Wasley, vice president—promotions	41
Larry Clark, vice president—product sourcing	31
Sudeepto Killick Datta, vice president—international operations and licensing	29
Ralph Hulit, vice president—marketing	45
Angelo Maccano, vice president—research and development	41
Ralph W. Polce, vice president—sales	50

Gilbert Schwartzberg, executive vice president, L.A. Gear. "It has a magic to it . . . we are trying to capture that magic."[11]

Their tactic was to target their products to women, mainly teenagers, and stress the style of California. In its design studio, dozens of artists between age 20 and 30 churn out prototypes with potential fads for the future. Their shoes are splashed with color, multiple laces, inlaid rhinestones, fringes, colored cutouts, neon trim, marbilized leather, vibrant lace colors, silver buckles, and leather lattices.

They exuded the Southern California lifestyle of "fun, colorful, fresh, and young," according to former L.A. Gear CFO Elliot Horowitz. By making themselves popular with trend-seeking women from coast to coast, L.A. Gear has developed a stronghold in the fashion segment.

L.A. Gear attributes their success to their ability to identify and respond promptly to changes in consumer preferences. Sales have skyrocketed from $9 million in 1984 to $223 million in 1988 to $600 million in 1989.

L.A. Gear believes their initial toehold into the market was due to Reebok's initial success in developing the demand for athletic shoes for women. With their soft-leather Freestyle aerobic shoes, they developed a strong niche.

---

[11] Carl Lazzareschi, "A Great Leap Forward for L. A. Gear," *Los Angeles Times*, April 30, 1989, s.4, p. B26.

In 1986, however, when a fire devastated their Korean contract manufacturing plant, they had a shortage of inventory, and L.A. Gear stepped in with its soft-leather fashion shoe. Thus, L.A. Gear entered the industry in the fashion segment and positioned themselves to challenge Reebok on the fashion front.

Manufacturing

L.A. Gear manufactures their shoes using independent producers in Pusan, South Korea, and Taichung, Taiwan. The producers contract the manufacturing on a purchase order basis from L.A. Gear's Korean and Taiwan offices. Specifications for the shoes are predetermined in Los Angeles by management and a production design staff. The 32-member Korean staff and 4-member Taiwan staff only inspect the finished goods prior to shipment and arrange for the shipments.

L.A. Gear does not have a master manufacturing agreement with its producers, and they compete with other shoe companies, such as Reebok and Nike, for production capability. (Adidas, however, is unique and directly manufactures more than 6 percent of its products.) In fiscal 1988, L.A. Gear used 21 producers in Korea and 4 in Taiwan, 6 of which accounted for 57 percent of their total production.[12]

Distribution

L.A. Gear distributes its products in department stores, shoe stores, specialty stores, and sporting goods stores. Unlike its key competitors, Nike and Reebok, who rely on sporting goods outlets for 80 percent of their sales, L.A. Gear does not rely on any customer for more than 10 percent of total sales.[13]

L.A. Gear uses heavy promotions to create brand image and pull the buyers into the stores. Greenberg hopes to export that image and license it, predicting a Japanese opportunity of 500,000 pairs of sneakers sold to young women and teens. Greenberg says, "I want the distributor to set the course for the brand name to grow. If it's in lots of shoe store windows, then people will knock on our door asking to make L.A. Gear products—the name can go on anything.[14] In 1987, seven U.S. licensees put L.A. Gear's name on everything from doll clothes to sunglasses.

Sales

Domestic. L.A. Gear divides their sales into four divisions: (1) department stores and women's shoe stores, (2) sporting goods stores and athletic footwear stores, (3) men's stores, and (4) children's shoe stores. They use 102

---

[12] L. A. Gear 10–K Report, p. 8.
[13] L. A. Gear 10–K Report, p. 7.
[14] Ellen Paris, "Rhinestone Hightops, Anyone?" p. 78.

independent, regional individual sales representatives divided among those divisions and employ their own national sales manager plus three to six regional sales managers per division. L.A. Gear employees sell L.A. Gear merchandise exclusively. This sales force calls on the trade and offers to assist in training their salespeople.

Additionally, L.A. Gear employs five national account managers and 14 technical representatives who assist in marketing. They are responsible for improved product displays and point-of-purchase advertisements.

Since Reebok and Nike are offering the same services, the trade can be overwhelmed with the manufacturers' persistent sales and marketing forces. As the number of styles and shoes increase, their relationship with the trade becomes crucial since they control the limited shelf space. Many small retail outlets cannot stock all of the different footwear categories and hundreds of styles (Exhibit 14).

EXHIBIT 14 L.A. Gear product categories (as of first quarter 1989)

Type	Introduction date	Retail price range for selected styles	
Basketball	Apr. 1986	Shooter	$39.90
		B–424	77.90
Children's	Jun. 1985	Workout	19.90
		B–527	55.90
Aerobic	Feb. 1985	L.A. Impact	43.90
		CMR Trainer	55.90
Leisure	Feb. 1985	Canvas—Workout	21.90
		Surf Cat	37.90
		Leather—Westwood	29.90
		High Beach	53.90
Court (tennis, squash,			39.90
racketball)	Sep. 1985	T Slammer	61.90
		L.A. PRO	
Infant/toddler	Jun. 1986	Gidget	17.00
		Kids Rawhide	47.90
Walking	Dec. 1986	Streetwalker	23.90
		Imperial	59.90
Fitness/running	Aug. 1985 (men)	Skateboard	23.90
	Nov. 1986 (women)	Bandett 2	49.90
Apparel (312 combinations)	Oct. 1987 (men, jr. women)		
	Feb. 1989	Tees	
		Tank Tops	
		Sweatshirts	
		Sweatpants	
		Sweatshorts	
Jeanswear	Aug. 1988 (jr. women)	Pants	
		Jackets	
	Feb. 1989	Shorts	
		Skirts	
Watches (7 styles) (25 combinations of styles and colors)	Nov. 1988 (teen, jrs.)	Quartz/analog	$36–$38

Source: L.A. Gear 10–K, February 28, 1989.

L.A. Gear has only recently been able to penetrate the specialty store. They believe this penetration has been facilitated by their "open stock" system. This system lets retailers order as few as four pairs of shoes in any size, style, or color. According to Schwartzberg, they fill the order from their own inventory instead of reordering from the factory and are able to meet their customers' needs quickly.[15]

L.A. Gear has begun to diversify by entering the men's and children's market in 1986; the apparel market with sweatshirts, T-shirts, and shorts in 1987; and the watch and jean market in 1988.

Their watches are sold through six independent, regional sales representatives and some footwear sales representatives. Apparel is sold through 20 individual, regional sales representatives and some footwear sales representatives. Eight of these independent, regional representatives also sell Jeanswear. L.A. Gear employees sell watches, apparel, and Jeanswear, exclusively.

International. L.A. Gear only began selling overseas to Japan, Switzerland, and Germany in 1987. They now have agreements with 43 distributors in 77 countries for distribution of footwear and apparel. By 1991, they intend to be selling in 100 countries including the Soviet Union. They sell domestic designs in most foreign markets but have occasionally modified their product design in consideration of cultural norms.

After they had put a significant emphasis on international operations in early 1989, net sales from international operations increased from $2.3 million (3.3 percent of net sales) in fiscal 1987 to $20.5 million (9.2 percent of net sales) in fiscal 1988 to $52 million (8.67 percent of sales) in 1989. Killick Datta, vice president in charge of international operations and licensing, expects 1990 sales to reach $110 million. In five years, he predicts sales of $500 million. For 1988, approximately 61 percent of sales were in Canada, Japan, Italy, and England.

In early 1990, L.A. Gear signed a letter of intent with the Asics corporation of Japan for the marketing of L.A. Gear products in Japan. Greenberg indicated that Asics's strong distribution channel, their resources, and their selling experience in Japan would complement L.A. Gear's marketing skills and would help to get L.A. Gear products into the market quickly.

Distributors are given exclusive rights to distribute L.A. Gear to retailers in their specific geographic areas, but to maintain consistency in advertising and promotions, all materials they use must be approved in Los Angeles. Distributors, under the L.A. Gear contract, agree to spend 5 percent of their sales on advertising; they actually spend closer to 10 percent.

Datta believes L.A. Gear's utilization of distributors rather than an international sales force is not a deficiency in their strategy. He believes their distributors know the market "as well as you do or better."[16]

---

[15] L. A. Gear Press Release: Strategies for Continued Growth, 1990.

[16] Rose Horowitz, "Sports Shoe Makers in U.S. Lace Up for Global Race," *Journal of Commerce,* November 27, 1989, p. 5A.

Although L.A. Gear considers their relationships abroad to be strong, they realize Reebok, Nike, and Adidas [industry leader worldwide] are more established in international markets and have greater financial resources at their disposal.

Marketing

L.A. Gear conducts extensive marketing research—product testing, focus groups, store and consumer interviews, and surveys—to help determine designs and technological attributes consumers want and to evaluate the feasibility of expanding existing product lines. Besides point-of-purchase promotions, L.A. Gear channels their research findings into new product designs and image-oriented advertising.

They have developed the 12- to 25-year-old-market with their rhinestone-studded, pink and white basketball shoes, and they continue to make styles incorporating different gadgets. "Technical is another word for gadgetry," says Greenberg, "and we have gadgets in our products."[17] Further, he says, "whether they're technically fashionable or fashionably fashionable, it's all the same thing. . . . Everyone is playing the same game. I just say it."

In 1990, L.A. Gear will spend $50 million on footwear advertising with a heavy concentration on television. The remainder of their dollars will go to trade shows, consumer publications, merchandising, and specialty billboards (Exhibit 5).

L.A. Gear has built a 28,000-square-foot trade show booth with over 50 areas where they can show customers their products and write orders. The booth includes replicas of famous Los Angeles landmarks—the Beverly Hills and Bonaventure hotels, the Forum, the Coliseum, Santa Monica Pier, and City Hall—and illustrates L.A. Gear's commitment to the trade and various shows to spotlight their products.

Reebok and Nike have the resources to outspend L.A. Gear, but in the past, L.A. Gear has been able to effectively target a segment with their fashion message and build product image and brand awareness. As Elliot Horowitz, former CFO of L.A. Gear, says, "You get to a point where you can spend enough money on advertising and promotion that retailers will have to carry the brand. L.A. Gear has passed the critical mark where they are here to stay."[18]

For smaller players, the advertising war means more lost dollars in sales. Gary Jacobson, analyst for Kidder Peabody estimates that the big three—Nike, Reebok, and L.A. Gear—will take another $250 million from the smaller makers. He adds, "If I were a small company, I'd be shaking in my shoes. No small company has the marketing dollars to compete nor the research and development dollars to thrive in a business built on the next big gimmick."[19]

---

[17] Ellen Benoit, "Lost Use," *Financial World,* September 20, 1988, pp. 28–31.

[18] Linda Williams, "On the Right Foot," *Los Angeles Times,* September 31, 1989, s. 4, p. 1.

[19] "Nike, L. A. Gear, Reebok are Expected to Post Increased 1st Quarter Earnings," p. A4.

As a solid player in the fashion segment, getting 75 percent of their sales from 15- to 25-year-old women, however, industry analysts caution that if L.A. Gear intends to go beyond $600 million in sales, they will need to be a major player in the men's market. In 1988, 10 percent of their market was sold to men and 15 percent to children. Industry analysts ask: "How long will women want to wear basketball shoes?"

"I may still have some reservations that they can just go in and penetrate that men's market," says James Hines, vice president and corporate director of marketing for footwear at Oshman's sporting goods chains. "It's pretty hard to

EXHIBIT 15 Reebok product split—1988

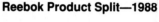

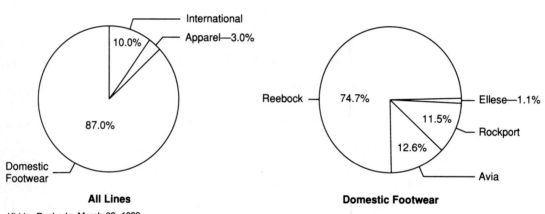

Kidder Peabody, March 28, 1989.

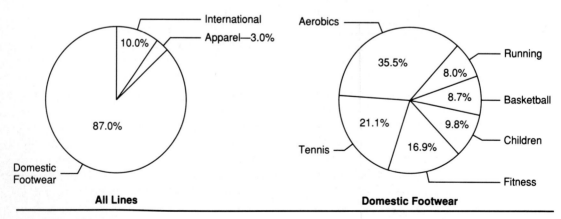

Reebok, 1989 Annual Report.

go in from a dead start and compete.'' Greenberg sees it another way: ''We are predators. Predators look at someone who has a nice big market share, go after it, and take it.''[20]

For 1989, 23 percent of their sales were made to men, up from 10 percent in 1988. That is a small percentage attributable to men compared to their competitors with a 70 percent share. For 1990, analysts predict 40 percent of L.A. Gear's sales will be made up of men's footwear. 15 percent of L.A. Gear's sales are for children's shoes, and most of their buyers (men and women) have been leisure, nonathletic wearers. Competitors' product splits are shown in Exhibits 15 and 16.

EXHIBIT 16 Nike product split—1988

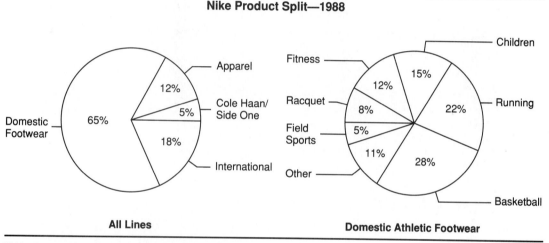

Kidder Peabody, March 28, 1989; Nike, 1989 Annual Report.

Advertising

Greenberg had begun to follow the leaders with high-performance athletes as endorsers in late 1988 when he signed L.A. Lakers Kareem Abdul-Jabbar as spokesman. ''We could have gone out and got some hot shot, but we wanted the Ambassador of Basketball,'' says Sandy Saeman, executive vice president, L.A. Gear. ''Until someone else comes along who has played for 21 years, Kareem will be the ambassador.''[21]

Featured in advertisements for Court Fire, Abdul-Jabbar continues to appear as their performance ambassador in the 1990 UNSTOPPABLE campaign (Exhibit 17). Industry analysts believe, however, ''Jabbar will not be able

[20] Jobeth Daniel, ''L. A. Gear Tries Full Court Press,'' *New York Times,* September 16, 1989, s. 3, p. F4.
[21] ''Even without Layups Kareem Is a Shoo In,'' *Los Angeles Times,* January 17, 1989, s. 4, p. 20.

EXHIBIT 17 L.A. Gear advertising

EXHIBIT 17 *(concluded)*

to persuade serious athletes to wear L.A. Gear. Their male market is the boyfriends of the women buying hot shot—the men more concerned about making a fashion statement.''

Additionally, L.A. Gear has enlisted L.A. Laker, Mychal Thompson; Houston Rocket, Akeen Olajuwon; Utah Jazz, Karl Malone; and San Francisco 49er/Super Bowl MVP, Joe Montana, for their performance image. Montana, signed in 1990, will be marketing their Muscle High cross-training shoes.

Other members of their all star team include: Gary Grant, L.A. Clippers; Winston Garland, Golden State Warriors; Craig Hodges, Chicago Bulls; Scott Hastings, Detroit Pistons; Kenny "Sky" Walker, New York Knicks; Paul Pressey, Milwaukee Bucks; Purvis Short, New York Nets; Jedric Toney, Atlanta Hawks; Byron Nix, Indiana Pacers; and ESPN's "Body in Motion" star, Gil Janklowicz. L.A. Gear also utilizes noncelebrity advertising for 1990 (Exhibit 17).

Even though some industry analysts doubt Abdul-Jabbar's credibility as a performance spokesperson and see L.A. Gear's investment in celebrities as promoting a fashion image, with the signing of athletes L.A. Gear signals a clear indication of its step into the performance arena.

Fashion, however, will continue to be the main thrust of the company, and more ads will appear featuring children (Exhibit 18). Celebrities used to promote the fashion image are Heather Locklear, Priscilla Presley, and Michael Jackson. Greenberg does not see an identity blur for its customers. "This company is not a sporting goods company like Nike and Reebok. It's a fashion company. It's about looking pretty for women and looking good for men." He disagrees with industry analysts who claim the signing of Michael Jackson draws a clear line to teenagers and will clash with the image they are trying to create with Abdul-Jabbar.

For the spring of 1990, L.A. Gear has produced a black and white hightop similar to the space boot worn by Michael Jackson in his movie *Captain Eo* with L.A. Gear embossed on the shoe in five places. More Jackson apparel and footwear under the MJ line will be incorporated throughout the next two years. Jackson's first commercial is scheduled for August 1990.

L.A. Gear produces their advertising in-house under the direction of Saeman, except for Hispanic and international business. Saeman indicated that Michael Jackson made the agreement with L.A. Gear since their creative process is tightly controlled.

Dissatisfaction in early March 1990 prompted Saeman to dismiss their agency with their Hispanic business and to contemplate hiring another agency or also bringing that business in-house.

Competitors

Others with strong positions in the performance arena are Nike, Adidas, and Converse. Nike's million dollar advertising campaigns in the past, Revolution

EXHIBIT 18 L.A. Gear advertising

EXHIBIT 18   *(continued)*

EXHIBIT 18 *(continued)*

EXHIBIT 18 *(concluded)*

in Motion (1988) and Just Do It (1989, 1990) have become the epitome of strong performance positioning.

Nike.   Nike contracted with Chicago Bull's Michael Jordan for another seven-year contract ($19 million) to market their Air line, enlisted baseball/football athlete Bo Jackson to promote their cross-training shoes, and signed Joan Benoit Samuelson to advertise their running shoes. Their past campaigns have stressed their state-of-the-art technology in a superior performance shoe.

Nike CEO Philip Knight, age 52, a University of Oregon graduate, started Blue Ribbon Sports in 1964 with Bill Bowerman, 78, his former track coach, to give the public these state-of-the-art performance shoes. They imported and distributed Japanese-made Tiger brand track shoes, and in 1972 designed and introduced their own line. His goal was to finely tune shoes to human motion and physiology, and he began with a waffle iron sole.

Their sales have grown from $270 million in 1980 to $920 million in 1984 to $2,400 million in 1989. Knight saw his market share sink below Reebok's in 1987 and 1988, prompting him to decentralize decision making to encourage innovation. Realizing that marketing and sales were taking precedence over R&D, he selected a group of his innovators, advance product engineers (APEs), and gave them the mission to create more aggressive designs.

Working in a design shop apart from the main one, they created Nike's Air Pressure by reviving an old idea of incorporating several features of ski boots, basketball shoes, and hockey skates. Also, they created cross-trainers. "What Nike produces depends on whether the consumers will accept innovation in the marketplace," says Dr. Martyn Shorter, Nike sports research lab biomechanic.

Product strategy.   Nike changed its outlook in the 80s from risk averse to adventuresome, prompted by the entrance of Reebok into their market. They became more innovative with new products and big technological changes instead of incremental improvements. "It was healthy for the company to get hit between the eyes," says C. Joseph LaBonte, now former president of Reebok, about Nike. "Nike got hot. God bless 'em."

Nike also changed their strategy. In 1987, Knight said, "For Nike to be a solid company in the long run, we have to concentrate on making the best-quality, best-performing shoe we can. The fashion business is just too hard to manage year in and year out."

In 1988, however, Nike purchased Cole Haan, a dress shoe marketer, and in early 1989 they introduced a new brand of shoes, Side One. These shoes were aimed at junior girls who wore fashion athletic shoes. Nike entered the fashion market—through the side door.

"Now more than ever, we know what the Nike name stands for and how far it can be stretched—and it can't be stretched that far," says Elizabeth Dolan, spokeswoman for Nike. She indicates that Nike has not compromised its name for the fashion segment, but they have entered the market. Side One competes directly with L.A. Gear and Reebok.

In late 1989, Nike had introduced its first non-Nike named brand—i.e., a line of women's casual footwear. For 1990, they plan to add a similar men's casual footwear line in a joint development project with Cole Haan. Keri Christenfeld, an analyst with Needham and Co., indicates both the performance and fashion dimensions are needed for athletic footwear manufacturers to gain market share.

She says that the strategy is a good one and the timing is good, especially as the boundaries blur between athletic and regular street shoes. The manufacturer that is able to capture the sales growth in the blurred area will most effectively be positioned for the growing industry.

Advertising Strategy.   For 1990, Nike has continued to use Just Do It in their television and print executions with Jordan and Jackson depicting hardcore performance and promoting their new technologies. They have expanded that slogan to address the market with a more personal health and personal winning strategy.

In their running and walking print advertisements, they tout exercise as physical therapy and stress management (Exhibit 19). Their Air line of print ads show how the hardcore athlete's driven to perform, but they have developed the runner's drive within a serene context: the busy city runner, the late night loner, and the rural adventurer. The scene is vivid with one serious runner; his or her shoes are not visible (Exhibit 20).

Consumers learn about new technologies from other players, too. Adidas and Converse introduced Torsion and Energy Wave, respectively, which give the consumer new attributes and materials to consider.

The new addition to Nike's 1990 campaigns is a series of Spike and Mike commercials—directed by and starring Spike Lee as a character named Mars Blackmon. Blackmon is a character from Lee's 1986 movie *She's Gotta Have It.* Lee's co-star in the commercials is Michael Jordan.

"We want to show something that conveys the excitement of sports, but still brings our athletes across as human beings," says Dolan. She believes the Spike and Mike advertisements are particularly successful at conveying this with the awestruck fan and the athletic great. "That's kind of how we imagine people are responding to all our ads."[22]

Reebok.   Unlike the successful performance campaigns, Reebok has not been successful with delivering a clear performance message to consumers: Life is not a spectator sport (performance); Let U.B.U. (fashion); Physics behind the Physiques (performance), and Legends (performance) have occurred since the 1983 Freestyle aerobic campaign. In 1988, their lack of success is reflected in

---

[22] Gene Seymour, "Spike and Nike: The Making of a Sneaky Sneaker Commercial," *Entertainment,* March 30, 1990, p. 29.

EXHIBIT 19   Nike Advertising

EXHIBIT 20   Nike advertising

Mothers,
there's a mad man
running in the
streets,
And he's
humming a tune,
And he's
snarling at dogs,
And he still
has
four
more
miles
to go.

Just do it.

There are
clubs you can't
belong to,
Neighborhoods
you can't live in,
Schools you
can't get into,
But
the
roads
are
always
open.

Just do it.

EXHIBIT 20 (concluded)

He's fat and
he's soft,
And he's
wearing your clothes,
And he's
gotten too old,
And he was
born on your
birthday,
And you're
afraid if you stop
running he'll
catch up with you.

Just do it.

Ten million
decibels loud.
And it
doesn't care
you're tired.
Or it's
your birthday,
Or some
holiday honoring
a saint.
So, though
you'd rather
not, you start
down the
road again.
The road
when
it calls,
it screams.

Just do it.

Reebok's first ever decline in earnings. Their campaigns have tried to produce both a performance image and a fashion image but have served to clutter the market rather than draw brand distinction.

In particular, their surrealistic, $10.6 million U.B.U. campaign—with such slogans as, "If U. ain't U., U. ain't nobody"—lasted only six months and was the object of competitors' mockery more than consumer's remembrances. "U. Gotta B. Kidding. Why pay for high performance shoes if U. just want to bang around in sneakers?"(Keds).

With the numerous athletic footwear ads in the media, brand blur occurs where consumers may remember the ads but not the make of the shoe being promoted.

Paul Fireman, CEO of Reebok, acknowledges the problem with UBU. He says, "We had put together a campaign that would bring us awareness, bring us controversy. And that's what 'UBU' came from."[23] He believes Reebok's problem with the campaign was not knowing when to stop it. During its initial phase, in tests compared to Nike's Just Do It, Fireman indicates that consumers had a higher recall of UBU. "The unfortunate thing is that we didn't make a transition. . . . We probably should have shifted to a more normal approach. . . . We did not follow it through into the performance business."

Fireman has built Reebok through knowing when to make changes. His management style includes frequent personnel changes, internal reorganizations, and acquisitions to strengthen their market share. Reebok has had a cash surplus for the past 15 months, and Fireman confirms that if the right acquisition candidate came along, he would continue to build Reebok. "In a perfect world, we'd be in the $300 million-to-$400 million range (for an acquisition) . . . the company could deal with a $1 billion acquisition if we found the right one."[24]

He adds, for 1990, Reebok's most important focus is the international marketplace. He believes the international market has "the opportunity to be as big if not bigger than Reebok USA." He says that they are targeting their wholesale level to be $1 billion by the mid-1990s.[25]

Product Strategy. Until 1989, Reebok had been known and had thought of itself as a "maker of stylish sneakers that give the wearer an edge in social competition."[26] But, in early 1989, while not forsaking the "image drive shoe," Reebok announced its intentions to get a larger piece of the performance driven market. The growth in the market, they believed, was coming from the performance segment.

According to management consultant Heidi Steinberg, "They're defining their strategic outlook . . . And they're now defining themselves as a lei-

---

[23] Pat Sloan, "Reebok Chief Looks Beyond Nike," *Advertising Age,* January 29, 1990, p. 16.

[24] Ibid.

[25] Ibid.

[26] Douglas McGill, "Reebok's New Models, Fully Loaded," *New York Times,* February 14, 1989, p. D1.

sure/lifestyle company. They're not defining themselves as an athletic footwear company any longer."[27]

Advertising Strategy.   For early 1990, Reebok is showing product specific advertisements (Exhibit 21):

- "If it's not one thing it's another" (cross-training).
- "Pump it up" (basketball).
- "Because its never the same game twice" (Energy System—all shoes).
- "Millions of girls want to be in her shoes, but she wants to be in ours" (dance).
- "Wear emblems, not labels" (fashion).
- "It's hard to improve a classic" (aerobics).
- "Go ahead, stick out your tongue" (fashion).
- "Training wheels for the feet" (children).
- "The Pump from Reebok. It Fits a Little Better Than Your Ordinary Athletic Shoe." (performance).

They continue to use Michael Chang, youngest champion of the French Open, as spokesman, and they have added singer/choreographer Paula Abdul to appeal to the younger consumers of their fast-growing competitor, L.A. Gear.

1990 Issues/Competitors' Actions—Reactions

Reebok

January 22, 1990   Reebok announced a split in its U.S. operations. To help keep pace with competitors in both fashion and performance markets, they are splitting into two units so they can focus their actions on performance and fashion, separately.

Citing that the structure will "enable us to move even more quickly to respond to consumer needs," Reebok claims it will shorten its product development cycle to three to six months for its lifestyle footwear. "Fashion is a very quick-moving phenomenon. To be competitive, we have to be able to do this."[28]

Some industry analysts believe the division of function will be a good move since marketing performance shoes is very different from marketing lifestyle shoes. Others, however, disagree saying that with a split personality, Reebok has potential to further confuse the customer, disseminate uncoordi-

---

[27] Pat Sloan, "Reebok May Slip Back into Fashion" *Advertising Age,* September 4, 1989, p. 27.

[28] Joseph Pereira, "Reebok Sets Up Separate Units for Shoe Business," *The Wall Street Journal,* January 22, 1990.

EXHIBIT 21   Reebok advertising

EXHIBIT 21 *(continued)*

While it may appear that we are stretching the truth, surprisingly it's a fact.

Every time your foot strikes the ground, the impact of three times your bodyweight is sent shuddering up your legs.

Armed with this and years of research, Reebok has developed the Sole Trainer™ 5000.

With the impact of three times your bodyweight in every stride, your lightweight shoe better be cushioned.

At only 10 ounces it's a lightweight shoe, but more importantly, it's exceptionally well-cushioned.

The secret lies in the midsole. It's comprised of Hexalite,™ a unique honeycomb of highly resilient yet light thermo plastic.

(Basically, the honeycomb, one of nature's lightest yet strongest designs, absorbs and spreads shock waves over a much larger area than EVA or polyurethane.)

The bottom line is that the Reebok Sole Trainer 5000 lets you run in a durable, lightweight shoe without sacrificing cushioning or comfort.

Now that should take a load off your mind.

EXHIBIT 21 *(continued)*

Training wheels for the feet.™

The revolutionary Agility™ shoes by Weebok® are designed to help beginning walkers the way training wheels help beginning riders – by giving them the extra balance and support they need.

The heart of the Agility system is a series of 10 strategically located pods on the sole. These pods follow the natural weight shift of the child's foot, while a snug-fitting heel cup helps to prevent unnecessary movement inside the shoe. At the same time, Agility shoes provide greater flexibility and breathability for your child's growing feet. Visit your local children's shoe store. Compare Agility™ with other shoes. We think you'll agree that all this comfort and technology is a terrific value.

Agility. It's one of the most important advances in children's footwear in 50 years.

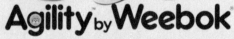

Agility by Weebok®

Weebok® shoes are carefully fitted at select children's specialty and department stores. For more information, call **1-800-843-4444.**

EXHIBIT 21 (concluded)

nated messages and develop a false belief that they can be all things to all people.

To complement the new structural change, the domestic and international advertising accounts are out to bid. There is speculation that two agencies may be assigned to the account, one for fashion and one for performance. Frank O'Connell, Reebok's U.S. division president, says, "We will choose the best creative in terms of advertising. We want spectacular advertising."[29] The company is looking for an umbrella campaign and hopes to have a new domestic agency by May 1, 1990.

February 19, 1990   There is speculation that Reebok's old agency now will be invited to bid for the business from which they were just dismissed. The speculation arose with the appointment of John Duerden as president of Reebok's new global marketing unit.

Duerden, the former international president, replaces Frank O'Connell. O'Connell's departure was due to Reebok's recent consolidation of U.S. and international business into one worldwide unit. This departure follows last December's resignation of C. Joseph LaBonte, Reebok international's president, and Mark Goldston, marketing chief.

March 26, 1990   Reebok's recent Pump advertisement touting the shoe's superior fit has been pulled after airing in only four spots. Reebok pulled the ad in response to customer concerns that people might imitate the bungee jumping sport shown in the commercial.

Once again, Reebok's advertising has been deemed controversial. While Reebok's premise for the ad is fit, for the first time, the company shows a competitor's shoe in the ad. In the ad, two jumpers, one wearing Reeboks, the other Nikes, leap from a Seattle bridge with bungee cords wrapped around their ankles. The elastic cord which is supposed to prevent them from hitting bottom after their thrilling free-fall ultimately works only for the wearer of the Reeboks. The audience sees the Reebok jumper hanging safely upside down while the Nike shoes float—empty—dangling in the wind.

Nike

February 16, 1990   Nike filed a lawsuit accusing L.A. Gear of misappropriating their (Nike's) intellectual property by mimicking Air Jordan's (basketball shoes). The suit cites:

- Trade dress infringement.
- (L.A. Gear style MVP–1:) Mimicking of eight to nine attributes that give Air Jordan's their distinctive recognition.
- Creation of confusion in the minds of consumers.

---

[29] Pat Sloan and Jon Lafayette, "A Race for Reebok," *Advertising Age,* January 29, 1990, p. 3.

Nike representatives state, ''While imitation is a form of flattery, we think they (L.A. Gear) cross the line. . . . It's not one or two, but a bundle of them.''[30]

L.A. Gear's MVP–1 style was introduced in 1989 and has produced $5 million in sales. Nike is asking for a restraining order and as of March 1990 no decision has been reached.

Analysts

Industry analysts believe the high-tech emphasis coming from shoe manufacturers is not significant in creating consumer demand. ''What matters,'' says Samuel Krause of Durham's Athleisure of Drayton Plains, Michigan, ''is that the customer tries it and makes his own decision. It gives the customer a reason to buy the product.''[31]

Analysts continue to speculate how successful footwear firms will be in the 1990s. With more players, the need for more resources and effective advertising and promotions and distribution expertise, they are uncertain as to which firm will take the number one position. Already retailers from a random survey have had their thoughts published in *Sporting Goods Business*'s March 1990 issue:

- 88.3 percent—Nike
- 29.1 percent—L.A. Gear
- 28.1 percent—Reebok

With the results showing retailer's perceptions making L.A. Gear number 1 over Reebok, analysts point to L.A. Gear, in particular, trying to access their performance in the 80s and to project their success in the 90s.

They speculate whether L.A. Gear will have the products that will effectively meet their customers' constantly changing preferences, and if they will be able to keep a strong image in the consumers' minds as advertising wars escalate between the top athletic footwear players and the new entrants that may find a niche with a fad.

Clearly, the effectiveness of their product, marketing, and advertising strategies for the 1990s in developing consumer perceptions and preferences will be their major challenge.

---

[30] Ken Wells, ''Is the Air Jordan Intellectual Property or Just Athletic?,'' *The Wall Street Journal,* February 16, 1990, p. B4.

[31] Douglas McGill, ''Reebok's New Models, Fully Loaded,'' p. D6.

Case 24 _____

Law Offices of Gary Greenwald*

Gary Greenwald leaned back in his chair, daydreaming about what it was going to be like to become a daddy. His law practice had been growing since he started it nearly two years ago, and he was pleased that this year's gross income looked like it would be about 50 percent higher than he earned during his first year. He recognized, however, that he would have to convert some of his excess capacity to increased business if he was to be able to buy a house and adequately support his family. He decided to review the actions he had taken to increase the business over the past 18 months and do some thinking about marketing activities for the next year. He also thought he should review the Bar Association Canon of Ethics regarding marketing practices.

Background

From 1908 until 1977, the legal profession in the United States operated under a canon of ethics that formally banned any method of advertising or client solicitation. The ban, enforced by the American Bar Association (ABA), had historic precedent. Since the days of ancient Greece and Rome, solicitation by attorneys and judges had been both a written and unwritten taboo.

The prohibition of legal service advertising was initiated in the United States in 1908 for several reasons. First, it was felt that the advertising of certain legal services would cause an increase in the events that prompted the need for such service. For example, members of the legal profession thought that advertising of legal services for divorce proceedings would cause an increase in the number of divorces. Second, the American Bar Association felt that the demographic profile of the United States (at that time primarily a rural population) did not have a legitimate need for advertising. Most lawyers were general

* This case was written by Kenneth L. Bernhardt and Bruce Bassett, Graduate Research Assistant, Georgia State University. Copyright © 1984 by Kenneth L. Bernhardt.

practitioners in small communities, and legal services were rendered with a one-to-one relationship between people who were known to each other and the community.

By the mid-1970s, the demographics of the country had changed dramatically from what they were in 1908. An equally important change had occurred in the legal process of society and in the legal needs of the population. Gone were the days of general practitioners and one-to-one relationships between lawyers and clients/friends. Instead, there was a complex society in which legal regulations were rampant and legal specialization was a necessity. One thing that had not changed, however, was the advertising/solicitation prohibition in the ABA Canon of Ethics.

Changes in the Legal Environment

In 1973 and 1974, the ABA conducted a survey to analyze the public's level of knowledge about lawyers, the law, and the legal process. The survey showed that the public had difficulty recognizing when they needed legal services, finding a lawyer to provide such services, and determining what a lawyer would cost. This survey led the ABA to reexamine its restrictions against advertising.

In December 1975, the ABA Committee on Ethics and Professional Responsibility proposed a change in the Canon of Ethics which would allow advertising not containing a false, fraudulent, misleading, deceptive, or unfair statement or claim. However, at the 1976 midyear meeting of the ABA House of Delegates, the advertising proposal was rejected in favor of a limited code amendment. Under the revised amendment, lawyers were allowed to communicate certain information about themselves and their practice (such as name, address, nature of practice, and consultation fees) in legal directories, bar association directories, and the Yellow Pages of telephone books. Concerned that the ABA had not gone far enough, in June 1976, the U.S. Department of Justice initiated an antitrust suit against the ABA, alleging a conspiracy to prohibit advertising.

Responding to changes in the environment, there emerged in the late 1960s and early 1970s clinics of various sorts to meet the needs of society. These clinics ranged from psychological counseling centers to abortion clinics to health services clinics to legal clinics. Each type of clinic had as its avowed purpose the rendering of specific high-quality services to a large number of people at a low cost to the individual. The clinic concept had initially been part of the social and human rights movements and had been financed in large part with government funds. It slowly evolved from a publicly funded orientation into a private enterprise orientation—this was especially true for legal clinics. Private legal clinics sprang up to handle such routine matters as uncontested divorces, adoptions, simple personal bankruptcies, simple wills, and name changes.

The Bates Case

From 1974 through 1976, John Bates and Van O'Steen ran a legal clinic in Phoenix, Arizona. Their clinic handled routine legal matters and was able to keep costs low by utilizing standardized office procedures and forms. They also used automated typing equipment and relied heavily on paralegals.[1] Their idea was to charge low prices for their legal services but to make money by doing a high volume of work.

The issue of advertising was a hot topic in most local ABA circles, and Bates and O'Steen decided to use advertising to secure a steady flow of new business, which they felt was critical to the success of their clinic. They placed an ad in the February 26, 1976, *Arizona Republic Newspaper,* offering "legal services at very reasonable fees." The ad listed their fees for the various legal services they provided (see Exhibit 1). The ad violated the Arizona Bar Association Disciplinary Rule 2-101(B), which prohibited lawyers from publicizing themselves through print, radio, and television advertisements or any other means of commercial publicity.

Bates and O'Steen were summoned before the local ABA disciplinary committee which recommended that they be suspended for six months. The Board of Governors of the Arizona Bar Association, upon reviewing the proceedings, recommended a one-week suspension. The two lawyers took the case to the Arizona Supreme Court which held that the state board had acted within its rights. Bates and O'Steen then sought review of the decision by the U.S. Supreme Court.

In 1977, the U.S. Supreme Court agreed to review the case. In the opinion of the Court, there were several issues that dealt with the U.S. Justice Department's antitrust suit against the ABA and several issues that concerned advertising. It was the opinion of the Court that the public's need for information about availability and costs of legal services outweighed the concerns expressed by the Arizona bar that advertising would have a negative impact on professionalism, on the quality of service provided, and on the administration of justice.

Although allowing lawyers to advertise, there were certain restrictions on legal services advertising that the Court did not strike. The Court allowed continued restrictions on ads that were false, deceptive, or misleading and ruled that the time, place, and manner of lawyer advertising could be subjected to reasonable restrictions. In addition, the Court felt that in order to assume that a consumer would not be misled a disclaimer might be needed. In concluding, the Court avoided a stand on radio and television advertising, stating that "the special problems of advertising in the electronic broadcast media would warrant special consideration." In-person solicitation was not an issue in the Bates case and was reserved for future consideration by the Supreme Court.

---

[1] Paralegals are individuals who have had some specialized legal training but have not graduated from law school and are not certified by the ABA to practice law. They typically are paid much less than a new attorney just out of law school.

EXHIBIT 1

Ad at issue in *Bates* v. *State Bar of Arizona*

ADVERTISEMENT

DO YOU NEED A LAWYER?

LEGAL SERVICES AT VERY REASONABLE FEES

- **Divorce or legal separation--uncontested [both spouses sign papers]**

  $175.00 plus $20.00 court filing fee

- **Preparation of all court papers and instructions on how to do your own simple uncontested divorce**

  $100.00

- **Adoption--uncontested severance proceeding**

  $225.00 plus approximately $10.00 publication cost

- **Bankruptcy--non-business, no contested proceedings**

  Individual
  $250.00 plus $55.00 court filing fee

  Wife and Husband
  $300.00 plus $110.00 court filing fee

- **Change of Name**

  $95.00 plus $20.00 court filing fee

Information regarding other types of cases furnished on request

Legal Clinic of Bates & O'Steen

617 North 3rd Street
Phoenix, Arizona 85004
Telephone [602] 252-8888

Changes after Bates

In August 1977, the ABA responded to the Bates decision by creating the ABA Commission on Advertising. The commission developed two alternative proposals for the regulation of legal advertising, allowing each state bar the option of adopting or not adopting each proposal. The states also had some latitude in changing the recommended codes to reflect their own perceived needs.

Proposal A was described as regulatory. It specifically authorized certain prescribed forms of lawyer advertising, listing the type of information that could be provided in attorney ads. The proposal permitted advertising in print, on radio, and (following a 1978 amendment) on television.

A less restrictive proposal, Proposal B, was also developed. Proposal B, which could be termed ''directive,'' allowed publication of all information not ''false, fraudulent, misleading, or deceptive.'' It provided guidelines for the determination of improper advertisements, which were subject to ''after-the-fact'' discipline by state authorities. Neither proposal allowed one-to-one solicitation.

A majority of states, including Georgia, adopted Proposal A, and developed ''laundry lists'' specifying the terms that could be used in ads. Some state codes included long lists of information about what was permissible within lawyer advertising; others created equally long lists of prohibited information. An attorney from Alabama ran into trouble with his state's regulations, for example, because he included the words *free parking* in his advertising, a term not on the state's list of approved terms.

But in a 1982 case, In re RMJ, the Supreme Court loosened restrictions by state bar associations on legal advertising, stating that they could be no broader than reasonably necessary to prevent deception. The case involved a young attorney who had opened for business in St. Louis, Missouri, in 1978, using advertising containing terms such as *personal injury* instead of the required *tort law*, and *real estate* instead of *property law*.

The attorney also used a mailing that went to potential new customers, not just friends and relatives as required by the Missouri law. After being reprimanded by the Missouri Supreme Court, the attorney appealed to the U.S. Supreme Court, which threw out Missouri's rule limiting lawyer mailings to ''lawyers, clients, former clients, personal friends, and relatives.'' The Supreme Court indicated the state had not justified its interferences with truthful commercial speech and also rejected Missouri's insistence that lawyers limit ad claims to specific state-approved phrases.

In February 1983, the ABA House of Delegates approved a proposal to allow ''written communication not involving personal contact'' but also adopted a proposal that forbids a lawyer to ''solicit professional employment from a prospective client by mail, in person, or otherwise, when a significant motive for the lawyer's doing so is the lawyer's pecuniary gain.'' Direct mail advertising thus would be permitted when distributed to ''persons not known to need legal services, but who are so situated that they might in general find such services useful.'' This was interpreted by legal advertising scholars to indicate that a lawyer could not send direct mail pieces to 50 known survivors in an airplane crash, but he or she could send the mailing to heavy users of airline travel. By mid-1983, direct mail advertising was specifically allowed in only 11 states, with Georgia being one of the ones that had not changed its regulations in response to the Supreme Court decision and subsequent ABA code revision. Greenwald felt sure that the Georgia restrictions against direct mail would be loosened soon. In any case, he believed the restrictions would not hold up if challenged in the courts.

There were substantial variances in legal advertising regulations from state to state. The ABA had no authority to establish advertising policies at the state level, even though they had considerable influence on the state bar associations' decisions regarding advertising policies. The state of Georgia followed the ABA Proposal A closely, requiring that the ads be dignified and allowing the listing of routine services offered. In-person solicitation, direct mail, billboards, handbills, and advertising of contingency fees were all prohibited. TV, radio, Yellow Pages, and newspapers were all specifically permitted.

Most attorneys were still opposed to advertising by lawyers. A recent survey of ABA members funded by the *American Bar Association Journal* revealed that only 3 percent of lawyers had advertised in 1978, only 7 percent had in 1979, and in 1981 only 10 percent had. The percentage had not grown much by the mid-1980s. The bulk of the advertising that had been done had been in the Yellow Pages or in newspapers. Many lawyers, especially established ones, felt that advertising lowers the professionalism of lawyers. The likelihood of advertising decreased as an attorney's income increased, with lawyers earning less than $25,000 five times as likely to advertise as those making over $50,000.

Background on Gary Greenwald

Gary Greenwald moved to Atlanta three years earlier after graduating from Potomac School of Law in Washington, D.C. During his first year in Atlanta, he served as a public defender practicing in the State Court of Fulton County, Georgia. During the first year as a public defender, he handled more than 200 court-appointed cases, with about 80 percent being criminal cases. After two years in business for himself, his practice had changed considerably. He had attained the state bar designation for practice in tax law, had several small-business clients, and had only about 20 percent of his business in criminal cases. His storefront office was on Peachtree Road, the main route from downtown to the affluent residential area called Buckhead.

Within a mile of his office on one side of Peachtree Road were several affluent residential areas made up of single-family homes worth well in excess of $100,000. On the other side of Peachtree Street were many apartments and condominiums housing young urban professionals. All along Peachtree Road were many retailers and office buildings containing small businesses of all types. Although his office was very visible from the street, with "Law Offices of Gary Greenwald" and his telephone number painted in large letters on the window, virtually no clients had come to him as a result of that visibility. Most of the cases that he did have, typically 15–20 at any one time, were referred to him by other attorneys. They sent him certain cases that were types their firms didn't handle, such as criminal and personal injury cases.

In addition to the good location, another advantage of his offices was the low overhead. The rent was $290 per month. Telephone expenses were $200 per month. He spent $200 per month on law books and updates and had spent $5,000 initially for the books in his law library. Other expenses, including a part-time secretary, amounted to about $5,000 per year. The office was not plush, but it was functional. Greenwald believed that it was important for an attorney to meet the expectations people had of a successful lawyer, and therefore he did not see his long-term future in this office. Until he built up the practice, however, the large amount of space and very low rent were extremely attractive.

Greenwald enjoyed the flexibility and freedom associated with running his own law office. Currently, however, his case load was taking only about 25 percent of his time. Greenwald was anxious to increase the business and reduce his idle time and had tried many different things to accomplish this goal.

Recent Marketing Activities

About nine months earlier, Greenwald had put up a poster advertising his services on bulletin boards in about 60–70 locations in the area including supermarkets and apartment building laundryrooms. Each of the posters contained a number of his business cards which could be taken for later reference (see Exhibit 2). Greenwald had paid $100 for 400 of these posters. The effort generated six clients and about $2,000 in legal fees.

Several months earlier Greenwald had distributed 10,000 copies of the $8\frac{1}{2}'' \times 3\frac{1}{2}''$ advertisement shown in Exhibit 3, using a "Dow Pack" mailing for the distribution. The Dow Pack contained 10 other advertisements and cost him $400. Four people had come in for a free initial consultation, but as yet no new clients had been developed from the mailing.

Greenwald had also undertaken some advertising in the Georgia Tech and Georgia State University student newspapers and in *Creative Loafing*, a weekly tabloid newspaper containing entertainment listings which was distributed for free. The ads had not been successful in generating new business. For example, 8–10 weeks of classified advertising in *Creative Loafing*, which cost $100, had generated only one new client—a $650 divorce case.

He had also used a two-line classified ad for 10 weeks at a cost of $75 in a neighborhood weekly newspaper. The ad offered to write one letter on his stationery for a client for $12.50. The series of ads generated demand for five letters and four new clients.

EXHIBIT 2 Poster advertisement

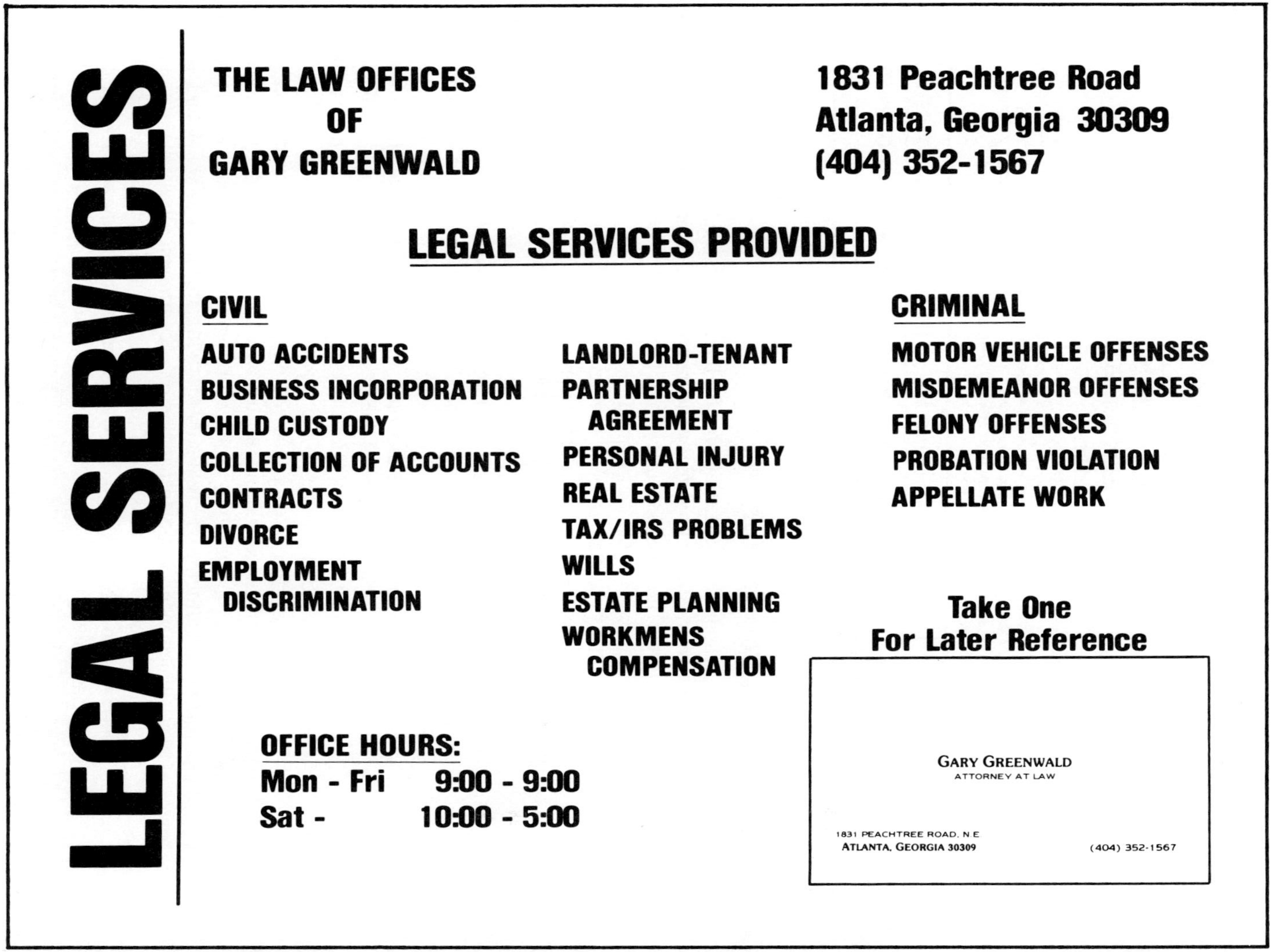

LEGAL SERVICES

THE LAW OFFICES
OF
GARY GREENWALD

1831 Peachtree Road
Atlanta, Georgia 30309
(404) 352-1567

LEGAL SERVICES PROVIDED

CIVIL

AUTO ACCIDENTS
BUSINESS INCORPORATION
CHILD CUSTODY
COLLECTION OF ACCOUNTS
CONTRACTS
DIVORCE
EMPLOYMENT
DISCRIMINATION

LANDLORD-TENANT
PARTNERSHIP
AGREEMENT
PERSONAL INJURY
REAL ESTATE
TAX/IRS PROBLEMS
WILLS
ESTATE PLANNING
WORKMENS
COMPENSATION

CRIMINAL

MOTOR VEHICLE OFFENSES
MISDEMEANOR OFFENSES
FELONY OFFENSES
PROBATION VIOLATION
APPELLATE WORK

Take One
For Later Reference

GARY GREENWALD
ATTORNEY AT LAW

1831 PEACHTREE ROAD, N.E.
ATLANTA, GEORGIA 30309

(404) 352-1567

OFFICE HOURS:
Mon – Fri   9:00 – 9:00
Sat –   10:00 – 5:00

461

EXHIBIT 3 Direct mail ad

LEGAL SERVICES

THE LAW OFFICES OF GARY GREENWALD

A COMPREHENSIVE COORDINATED LEGAL PRACTICE FOR FAMILIES & BUSINESSES
TRIAL PRACTICE IN STATE & FEDERAL COURTS

LEGAL SERVICES PROVIDED

Personal
- Auto Accidents
- Family Law
- Personal Injury
- Estate Planning / Wills
- Taxation / IRS Problems
- Workmen's Compensation

Business
- Contracts
- Collection of Accounts
- Partnership Agreements
- Incorporations
- Taxation / IRS Problems

Criminal
- Traffic Offenses
- Misdemeanor Offenses
- Felony Offenses
- Probation Violations
- Appeals

Present This Ad For Your FREE Initial Consultation

1831 Peachtree Rd. • Atlanta • Mon. - Fri. 9 - 9, Sat. 10 - 5 • By Appointment Only • 352-1567

Current Marketing Considerations

In thinking about his marketing plan for the next year, a lot of things were going through Greenwald's mind. He wondered what rates he should charge, if and how to target his market, and what promotion strategy he should use to communicate to his potential market.

Originally he had offered new clients an initial consultation for free. Recently he had been charging $15 for an initial consultation for individuals and $25 for businesses. His hourly rate varied considerably, depending upon the client and the task. For example, for tax work he charged some clients $40 per hour. He charged others $75 per hour and billed two clients at $120. He was on the list of attorneys taking cases from the juvenile court, and he received only $25 per hour for this work. Greenwald did take a few cases for a fixed fee, typically $500–$600. He did this only when he could accurately forecast the amount of time it would take for the case. Also, he did a number of cases for free when a client could not afford his services, telling the client to pay him when he or she could scrape up the money.

The biggest fee he ever received was $32,000 for a criminal case which lasted 14 months. His next biggest fee was $6,000. He had 10 personal injury cases pending, including a rape, a broken tooth incident, and several car accidents. He anticipated eventually receiving about $20,000 in total from these cases, which were all being handled on a contingency basis.[2]

Greenwald had grossed $40,000 his first full year and expected in the second year to gross $60,000. He knew there was considerable room for growth here, particularly if the number of clients could be increased. That led him to

---

[2] With a typical contingency case, an attorney received no fees if the client lost the case, but received one third of the damages awarded if the client won the case.

thinking about the types of legal services he liked to perform. He had no interest in handling real estate or bankruptcy cases. He felt that the biggest money was to be made in personal injury cases. He liked doing tax work. Greenwald commented that criminal work was fantastic because the work was easy, most cases were plea bargained, and clients always paid in cash. Overall, Greenwald most liked the diversity of work that was possible in his profession.

Advertising

Greenwald reviewed the information he had gathered on various advertising alternatives. He had gathered information on direct mail, newspapers, business publications, radio, television, and the Yellow Pages. Some of this information is presented in Exhibit 4.

There were approximately 10,000 households within a couple of miles of his office. Greenwald could send out a postcard format advertisement, using third-class mail, to 5,000 households for $610, including the cost of the mailing list. He could send out a mailing to 10,000 households for $1,150. It was also possible to include a postcard advertisement in a Valpack. This was a mailing containing the ads from a number of different advertisers who shared the cost of the mailing, resulting in a cost less than half of a solo mailing. Valpack mailings were sent quarterly.

An ad in the Yellow Pages would cost about $4,000 for a small (2" × 2") ad. A large ad would cost approximately $10,000 per year. About 40–50 of the 9,000 lawyers in Atlanta had large ads in the Yellow Pages.

It would cost Greenwald about $1,500 to have a television ad produced before he even ran the ad one time. Ads on the major networks would cost thousands of dollars for each spot, although he could buy time on low-rated stations after midnight for about $50 per spot. Radio advertising was cheaper. He felt that he would have to run an ad at least twice per day, five days per week, for a month to have any impact. This would cost about $3,000, the minimum he felt was appropriate for a fair test. Greenwald knew that Hyatt Legal Services had been very successful with television advertising in Atlanta. Although the six offices in Atlanta had only been open for nine months, he had heard that each office was bringing in about 200 new clients per month as a result of the ads. Hyatt was spending about $8,000 per month on television. In addition, they had a very large ad in the Yellow Pages. Hyatt did not handle personal injury and certain other kinds of cases. They tended to concentrate on simple legal matters like wills, name changes, and uncontested divorces, and Greenwald felt that the average legal fee per client was under $200.

Consumer Analysis

Greenwald had seen the results of several studies that had been conducted to determine the consumer perspective on legal advertising. The studies typically showed that most users of legal services selected their attorney using recom-

EXHIBIT 4 Media costs per advertisement

1. *Atlanta Journal* and *Constitution* (major daily newspapers)

	Sunday	Morning and evening combination
Ad 4¼″ × 3⁷⁄₁₆″	$734.00	$660.96
Ad 2¹⁄₁₆″ × 2″	142.80	128.52
Services classified ad	5.55/line	4.52/line

TV Week supplement:	1 time	2 times	6 times
⅕ page	$735.00	$684.00	$625.00
¹⁄₂₀ page	212.00	197.00	180.00

2. *Atlanta Business Chronicle* (weekly tabloid business newspaper)

	1 time	4 times	13 times
1 inch	$ 49.00	$ 47.00	$ 44.00
⅛ page	290.00	275.00	260.00
Classified 1 inch	24.00	21.00	18.00

3. *Business Atlanta* (monthly business magazine)

	1 time	3 times	12 times
¹⁄₁₆ page	$275.00	$260.00	$225.00

4. Radio

	Morning drive time	Evening drive time
WGST (all news station):		
30 seconds	$ 96.00/spot	$ 68.00/spot
60 seconds	120.00	85.00
WPCH (easy listening):		
30 seconds	88.00	92.00
60 seconds	110.00	115.00
WSB–FM (middle of the road):		
30 seconds	323.00	191.00
60 seconds	380.00	225.00

5. TV (exclusive of production costs)

	Prime time	Late news
WAGA (CBS station):		
30 seconds	$2,200–$7,000/spot	$1,100/spot
WTBS (Channel 17 superstation):		
30 seconds	650–850/spot	450/spot
WANX (Channel 46 independent station):		
30 seconds	150–550/spot	n.a.

n.a. = not available.

mendations by friends or personal acquaintances. Consumers also used the lawyer's area of specialization, integrity, quality of service, past experience, and reputation as selection criteria. Recommendations by other lawyers, promptness of service, and location of office were other selection criteria used. Listings in the Yellow Pages, name of law school attended, years in practice, convenience of office hours, and cost of legal services were not among the top 10 selection criteria used by consumers. Overall, personal acquaintance and recommendation by a friend were overwhelmingly the most frequently used means of selecting an attorney.

It is not clear from the studies exactly why other criteria such as cost or advertising are not used more frequently. Unavailability of these sources of information in the past is one possible explanation. It is interesting to note, for example, that cost of legal services is mentioned as being very important to consumers, yet very few consumers use this as a factor in selecting their attorney.

Conclusion

Greenwald wondered whether he should invest some of the money that he had saved up for the down payment on a house in an advertising campaign to increase his business. With the baby coming, he and his wife really wanted to buy a house, so he didn't want to blow it all on advertising that might not work. He wondered how much he should spend and whether the advertising he had been using could be used or whether he should develop new copy. He wondered what media would be most appropriate and what services would be best to promote. He was also concerned about how big his ads should be and how frequently they should run. He also wondered how he could benefit more from the excellent storefront location he had and how he could generate more referrals.

After thinking about the effort that would be required to generate an effective marketing program, Greenwald wondered whether he should pack it in and go to work for a big law firm instead. He decided that he better not postpone thinking about these issues any longer and reached for the phone to call his wife to tell her that he would be late for dinner.

Case 25

Suburban CableVision*

Kim Harrison had joined Communications Industries, Inc., six months ago, following her graduation from a well-known midwestern business school. Now, in late 1986, she had been promoted to marketing manager for Suburban CableVision, a New England subsidiary of Communications Industries (CI), with the responsibility for marketing cable services in four suburban communities. Suburban CableVision had just been acquired, and a new management team had been put in place.

Ms. Harrison had been assigned the task of developing a marketing plan for 1987. Given that the new year was only a few weeks away, she realized that she did not have much time. The problem was complicated by the regulatory changes that were due to take place on January 1. The new regulations allowed considerably greater flexibility in packaging and pricing cable TV services. As she began to review the marketing files left by her predecessor, she realized that this holiday season was going to be very busy for her and very different than the previous few years when she was on Christmas break from her university studies.

Background on the Cable TV Industry

The cable television industry was born in 1948. At that time, Ed Parsons of Astoria, Oregon, lived at the foot of a mountain. The mountain was between his home, which contained a TV set with nothing but snow on the screen, and the transmitters for the television stations he wanted to watch. Parsons climbed the mountain with antenna in hand, secured it at the top, and strung a wire all the way back down to his TV set. As the only person in town with good picture quality, he soon had friends and neighbors at his house all of the time. When neighbors asked him if he would hook up their sets to his wire, he quickly

---

* This case was prepared by Kenneth L. Bernhardt and James Novo. Copyright © 1987 by Kenneth L. Bernhardt.

agreed, allowing him and his wife to have time alone together for the first time since he had climbed the mountain.

After this birth of cable television, the industry grew very slowly. In areas where TV reception was poor, people put up towers and ran cable to those households willing to pay for better reception. By 1975, only about 10 percent of U.S. television households were cable subscribers. RCA launched the first communications satellite, SATCOM I, in 1975. Programs from the East Coast could now be received by the West Coast instantaneously. Home Box Office became the first company to provide programming specifically aimed at cable subscribers. Others followed, and today there are over 150 programming sources. The rapid increase in programming led to a rapid growth in the number of cable subscribers.

Consumers were expected to spend more than $10 billion on cable television in 1986, more than they spend on going to the movies or renting home video programs. More than 77,000 people were employed by cable systems. The number of subscribers had doubled during the previous five years, and now totaled 42 million. More than three fourths of all TV households now had cable available to them, but only about 60 percent of those households able to receive cable actually chose to buy it.

The number of subscribers had grown at a compound annual growth rate of 14.2 percent between 1980 and 1985. This rate was expected to slow to under 5 percent between 1986 and 1990. An Arthur D. Little study indicated that spending on new cable systems would decline from a peak of $1.4 billion in 1982 to $160 million by 1990. Ms. Harrison recognized that the future of the industry lay in increasing the number of subscribers and revenue from existing systems rather than from laying new cable in areas that previously did not have cable TV available.

Planning for 1987 was complicated by the Cable Communications Policy Act of 1984 (CCPA). The act took away the power of state and local authorities to regulate the rates that cable companies charge subscribers for basic cable service. At the same time, the Federal Communications Commission was phasing out such regulations as the requirement that local cable systems carry all available local channels. Thus, starting January 1, 1987, local systems were free to raise rates and to put whatever programming they wanted on the channels.

The amount of money the average U.S. subscriber paid for cable TV services nearly doubled between 1980 and 1986, to $21 per month. One leading cable TV analyst recently estimated that the average monthly fee would grow to $28 in 1990 and $39 by 1995. Others in the industry were afraid that higher prices could drive away potential new subscribers and cause some existing subscribers to drop cable. A number of premium channels—such as Home Box Office (HBO), Showtime, and The Movie Channel—were already experiencing a slowing in their growth patterns as consumers appeared to be rejecting expensive cable bills that included multiple premium services.

Background on Communications Industries and Suburban CableVision

Communications Industries (CI) owned and operated four cable television systems servicing 43 cities in the states of Delaware, Connecticut, Rhode Island, and Massachusetts. The four systems had cable passing 315,000 homes, 196,000 of which subscribed to basic cable programming services. More than 113,000 (62 percent) also subscribed to premium programming services, such as movie channels or pay sports channels. CI was the 35th largest cable company but was very small compared to the larger firms in the industry (see Exhibit 1). Total revenues for CI were in excess of $100 million from four television stations, six radio stations, and outdoor advertising services in addition to the cable TV revenues.

EXHIBIT 1 1985 Statistics on Communications Industries, Suburban CableVision, and 10 largest cable companies

Rank	Company	Basic subscriptions (million)	Pay units (million)	Homes passed (million)	Percent basic /Homes passed*	Percent premium† /Basic
1	Tel-Communications	3.7	2.7	6.4	57	73
2	ATC (Time Inc.)	2.6	2.3	4.6	56	91
3	Group W	2.0	1.6	3.9	53	76
4	Cox Communications	1.5	1.5	2.7	57	97
5	Storer	1.5	1.5	2.7	56	95
6	Warner-Amex	1.2	.9	2.7	45	75
7	Times-Mirror	1.0	.8	2.0	49	87
8	Continental	1.0	1.1	1.8	54	114
9	Newhouse	.9	1.0	1.5	62	107
10	Viacom	.8	.6	1.5	54	78
35	Communications Industries	.2	.2	.3	62	83
NA	Suburban CableVision	.01	.02	.02	64	119

* Basic penetration $= \dfrac{\text{Basic subscribers}}{\text{Homes passed (those with access to cable)}}$

† Premium-to-basic ratio $= \dfrac{\text{Premium services subscribed to}}{\text{Basic subscribers}}$

Suburban CableVision marketed cable services in four communities. As described in Exhibit 2, the communities had very different profiles. Downing was a blue-collar, industrial town. Suburban had penetrated 75 percent of the homes in Downing with access to cable, which was the highest penetration of any of the cities in the area. However, the number of premium service subscriptions was lower than in the other areas. Some of the Suburban managers attributed this to the lower incomes of Downing's households—many could not afford basic plus several pay channels. They felt that the basic penetration was

EXHIBIT 2 Profile of four towns

	Downing	Anderson	North Lexington–Middletown	
Basic penetration*	75%	58%	61%	
Premium-to-basic ratio†	1.00	1.26	1.26	
Proportion of total households	one third	one third	one third	
Demographics	Blue-collar, industrial	Very white-collar, managerial, elderly	Rural, farm areas rapidly being developed into far-out suburban subdivisions; young families; mixed demographics.	
Number of years system in operation	5	4	3	2

$$* \text{ Basic penetration} = \frac{\text{Basic subscribers}}{\text{Homes passed (those with access to cable)}}$$

$$† \text{ Premium-to-basic ratio} = \frac{\text{Premium services subscribed to}}{\text{Basic subscribers}}$$

high because TV was a major form of entertainment for these people, and they were willing to pay for basic cable service.

The town of Anderson had a high percentage of the population employed in white-collar and managerial jobs. There was also a large elderly population. Suburban managers felt that these people would drive some distance to attend plays and the opera, so TV was less important to them. Those who did subscribe to basic cable, however, were likely to buy more pay services because of their relatively high incomes.

The towns of North Lexington and Middletown were rural, farm areas just beginning to be developed. Although these suburbs were relatively far from the downtown metropolitan area, a number of subdivisions were being created and many young families were moving into the area. The basic penetration and purchase of premium services were similar to the rates experienced in Anderson.

Although the population in Suburban's market area was growing relatively slowly, the company had experienced rapid growth. During 1985–86 the number of households with access to cable increased by only 1.4 percent. The system as a whole comprised 22,675 households, and 14,600 (64 percent) of these were basic cable subscribers. Although the number of basic subscribers had grown by 7.8 percent in the previous year, the number of pay channel subscriptions, 17,200, was up only 2 percent over the previous year.

Channels 2 through 42 contained a wide variety of basic cable programming. Included were several news channels, network and independent broadcast stations, and specialized channels devoted to local programming, movies, children's programs, and music and culture (see Exhibit 3). On channels 44

EXHIBIT 3 Guide to the satellite and premium channels

Channel	Title	Description
2	Local origination	Programming produced locally for all subscribers.
3	Eternal Word	"Inspirational programming"; Catholic Cable Network.
4	Lifetime	Women-oriented programming; many subscriber call-in shows; exercise, lifestyles, star interviews.
5 and 6 (seen on 55 and 56)	Reuters News & Sports	(5 and 6 are a "channel lock," which keeps other channels in tune.) News and financial reports.
7	The Weather Channel	Local and world weather reports.
8	CNN (Cable News Network)	Live coverage of national and world news.
9	CNN Headline	"Around the world in 30 minutes"; for the busy news viewer.
10	C-SPAN (Cable Satellite Public Affairs Network)	Senate and House committee meetings from start to finish; viewer call-in programs.
11	Public access	"Your community channel"; Suburban CableVision supplies the equipment and training free of charge to anyone in the community who wishes to produce and cablecast a television show or event for the community.
12	Educational access	Channel reserved for use by the school system of the community.
13	Middletown College	Channel reserved for use by local college.
14–29		These channels are the network and independent broadcast stations in the area.
30	WOR 9, New York	Movie classics and television programming from the late 60s and 70s; New York news and sports with Nicks, Rangers, Islanders, Devils, Jets, and Mets.
31	CKSH 9, Canada	Canadian television station; broadcasting in French; programming similar to U.S. network stations.
32	WTBS (Turner Broadcast System)	Movie classics and TV programming from the late 60s and 70s.
34	CBN (Cable Broadcast Network)	Family programming; specializes in movies and early television shows from the 50s and 60s.
35	Nickelodeon	Cable channel for kids of all ages; quality nonviolent entertainment.
37	SPN	From movies to music to international entertainment.
38	Nashville Network	Sports, comedy, dance, and news about country-western favorites.
39	MTV–Music Television	Video music, music news, interviews with the stars.
40	Arts & Entertainment	Cultural programming.
41	USA Network	TV series from the 70s no longer seen on broadcast television.
42	ESPN	The total sports network.
44	Sports Channel	The best of Eastern sports; all home Celtics games live.
45	Bravo	International award-winning films; exciting theater productions featuring the world's best performers; opera, symphony, and ballet.

EXHIBIT 3 *(concluded)*

Channel	Title	Description
46	Showtime	Latest box office hits.
47	HBO	Hollywood blockbusters; original HBO premier films.
48	Cinemax	More movies than HBO and Showtime; late-night, adult-only films.
49	TMC (The Movie Channel)	More movies than HBO and Showtime.
50	HTN (Home Theatre Network	Family programming; the movie channel that doesn't have sex and violence.
51	Disney	Disney movies and classic cartoons.
52	NESN	New England's Sports Network; exclusive live coverage of Bruins and Red Sox.

through 52, a number of premium channels were available for an extra charge above the basic cable service.

Pricing

Suburban's pricing structure was very complex (see Exhibit 4). Basic service was broken down into five tiers. The lowest level of service generally available, basic service, consisted of tiers 1 and 2 (channels 2 through 29). Subscribers signing up for this basic service were charged $7.25 per month. The three other tiers available had options to add super stations (tier 3, $2.05 per month), family stations (tier 4, $3.10), and sports stations (tier 5, $2.35). In addition, eight premium channels were available at prices ranging from $7.95 per month to $11 per month.

EXHIBIT 4 Pricing structure

Basic tiers/premium channels	Channels	Service	Cost/month
Tiers 1 and 2	2–29	Basic service	$ 7.25
Tier 3	30–32	Super stations	2.05
Tier 4	34–40	Family stations	3.10
Tier 5	41, 42	Sports stations	2.35
Sports Channel	44	Celtics and eastern sports	6.95
Bravo/HBO/Showtime/ Movie Channel/Cinemax	45–49	Movie channels	11.00 each
HTN	50	Family movies	7.95
Disney	51	Disney movies and cartoons	11.00
NESN	52	Bruins and Red Sox	7.95

Note: If subscribers order basic tiers 1–4, they get a $1 discount off of all $11 services (movie channels plus Disney) and HTN. If subscribers order any three premium channels, they get Bravo free.

Exhibit 5 shows a breakdown by level of service. Only 1,000 subscribers, 6.9 percent, subscribed to tiers 1 and 2 only. Ms. Harrison believed that the

EXHIBIT 5 Breakdown by level of basic service

	Number of subscribers	Percent of subscribers
Tiers 1 and 2 only	1,000	6.9%
Tiers 1, 2, and 3 only	4,550	31.1
Tiers 1, 2, and 4 only	100	.7
Tiers 1, 2, 3, and 4 only	2,950	20.2
Tiers 1, 2, 4, and 5 only	300	2.1
Tiers 1, 2, 3, and 5 only	150	1.0
Tiers 1, 2, 3, 4, 5	5,550	38.0
	14,600	100.0%

current system was much too complicated and caused problems in the development of advertising copy. In addition, it was difficult for Suburban's telephone sales representatives to explain the system to potential new subscribers. Thus, she felt that it was important to create a new system now that the company had the ability to change rates without having to get approval from each city council. She wondered whether she should include tier 3 as part of a basic subscriber package and felt that there was a marketing opportunity to simplify the system into basic and super basic (consisting of all five tiers). Other systems typically charged between $5 and $15 for basic service and anywhere from $7 to $12 for premium channels.

Ms. Harrison believed that Suburban made more money on basic service than on premium channels. The cost to Suburban for most of the premium movie channels was about $4 per subscriber per month, some being slightly more and some slightly less. The premium sports channels cost about $3. Many of the basic channels did not cost Suburban anything, and most of the others only cost about 25 cents per subscriber per month. Counting all costs for billing, maintaining subscriber records, and programming costs, the average variable cost per month for basic subscribers (tiers 1 through 5) was about $5.

Some cable executives believed that "basic subscriptions pay for the fixed costs of the system, and you make your profit from premium channel sales." Others felt that subscribers perceived more value in the basic channels and that premium channels were already priced about as high as they could be. In fact, many felt that if basic channel rates were raised, then premium channel rates should be decreased to prevent pricing people out of the cable market. These managers believed that instead of downgrading their service (for example, having one of the premium channels disconnected), many people would simply have the total cable service disconnected. Ms. Harrison had heard that some systems had substantially increased sales of the Disney channel by lowering the price to $7.95. Ms. Harrison knew that she would have to give considerable thought to the issue of how she packaged the channels together and how she priced them.

Advertising

Exhibit 6 contains a copy of the newspaper advertising that Suburban had been running. The campaign had been only moderately successful, and Ms. Harrison wondered whether newspaper advertising was just not effective or whether it was the copy itself that caused the poor results.

Suburban had been experimenting recently with the use of direct mail in cooperation with premium channel programming suppliers. For example, it had recently completed a test of a promotion with the Disney channel. The promotion, run in September, was centered around a free preview weekend. Direct mail and print ads informed consumers that they could preview the Disney

EXHIBIT 6 Sample newspaper ad

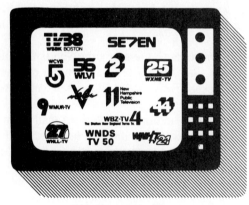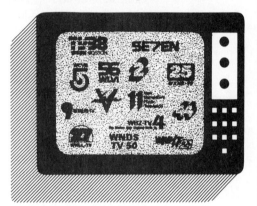

What's the difference between these two pictures?

Cable Channels 2 - 29

SUBURBAN CABLEVISION

All area stations, *and MORE*

Less than 24¢ per day.

Including wireless remote control and monthly cable guide.

channel for free, and if they decided to sign up, a 50 percent discount ($5) was given toward the $10 installation charge. While she had not had time to fully evaluate the promotion, she felt that it had been a success. The advertising and mailing costs had been $2,160, but the Disney co-op rebate had covered $783 of this. The Suburban customer service representatives were given 50 cents per new Disney subscriber as their commission. The gross margin (revenue less cost of programming) was $6 per subscriber per month. In addition, Suburban received the $5 installation fee per new subscriber to the Disney channel and incurred only about 25 cents in actual costs for the installation. Over the course of the promotion, 188 subscribers took advantage of the offer and added the Disney channel to their service. This represented a 14 percent increase in the number of people subscribing to the Disney channel.

A similar offer from HBO and Cinemax was far less successful. This promotion was communicated to subscribers via print advertising only. Only 12 subscribers added HBO as a result of the offer, and nobody added Cinemax.

During the fall, Suburban also tested a heavy newspaper advertising campaign for adding The Movie Channel. New subscribers were given an AM/FM radio premium. Only 18 sales were attributable to the campaign, and Ms. Harrison thus had questions about the effectiveness of newspaper advertising and premiums.

A second direct mail campaign was tested, promoting the Sports Channel and the New England Sports Network. Sales of these two premium channels increased 25 percent and 17 percent, respectively, at a cost per new subscriber of $2.58. No discounts or premiums were used.

As a result of the successes with the premium channel direct mail promotions, Ms. Harrison decided to test targeted direct mail for basic subscriber acquisition. Eleven hundred mailers were sent to apartment addresses that had never had cable service. The mailers cost 25 cents each, and 3 percent of those receiving them signed up. In addition, the mailer was sent to 321 homes where cable had been disconnected because the residents were moving. These homes represented 30 percent of the moves; the other 70 percent had been reconnected when the new residents moved in. One sixth of those receiving the mailing signed up for cable. Ms. Harrison thought that there might be potential with direct mail targeted to subsegments of the nonsubscriber base, including the elderly, educators, managers, and those who disliked network TV.

In the early days of cable, there were a number of "truck chasers"—consumers who would actually chase after the cable television truck when it was in their neighborhood laying cable. They would beg to get hooked up immediately, and direct salespeople were used extensively to make door-to-door sales calls in neighborhoods where cable was being laid. With changing demographics, two-income families, and increased customer sophistication, Ms. Harrison doubted whether door-to-door salespeople would be effective today, but she wondered whether it would be worth testing. A good salesperson would probably cost $25,000, including benefits.

She also wondered whether it might make sense to use public relations to help sell cable subscriptions. She was aware of Toys For Tots campaigns in various cities. In return for bringing in a toy for an orphan, the installation fee for new subscribers would be waived.

Ms. Harrison's predecessor had recommended a public relations program shortly before he left, but a decision had not been made on the program. He had recommended that Suburban sponsor a telethon in North Lexington in support of raising money for the renovation of the local library. There were 1,200 households in North Lexington that had never subscribed to cable, and anyone from these households who donated $25 or more to the telethon would be given free cable installation. Ms. Harrison made a note to review this plan to see whether by changing or keeping its present form it would be a good promotional vehicle for the coming year.

Other Potential Segments

Ms. Harrison was unsure about exactly which segments should be targeted. Much emphasis in the industry had been devoted to increasing the amount of revenue per cable household. Adopting this as a goal would mean that efforts should be directed at increasing the number of services to each current subscriber household, thus increasing the total revenue.

One industry leader believed instead that it's easier to acquire a non-subscriber than to get someone who is already paying $20 a month to pay $30. This person recommended that cable systems target the "Young and Busies," conveying the message that cable provides a sense of control over one's viewing habits. He also recommended going after TV lovers already predisposed to the product category and promoting cable's variety and choices.

Still another target market recommended by others in the industry was videocassette recorder (VCR) owners. A recent study had shown a relationship between VCR ownership and cable subscriptions. Only 18.5 percent of non-subscribers owned a VCR versus 27 percent for basic-only subscribers. The percent owning a VCR increased to 33 percent for those who subscribed to one premium service, and to 34 percent for those who subscribed to two services.

Another recent study indicated that VCR ownership was related to cable subscriber behavior, depending on the degree to which the VCR owner rented tapes. As shown in Exhibit 7, light renters of VCR tapes were more likely than average to upgrade (add premium services), and much less likely than average to downgrade (cancel premium channels) or disconnect the cable service. Ms. Harrison had read in a trade journal about one leading cable company that had been testing a strategy of positioning itself as an expert consultant on video electronics. This cable company promoted a $15 VCR hook up kit, and even offered to come out and hook up a subscriber's VCR for a fee. The company offered technical assistance over the telephone to its subscribers, and had begun selling GE VCRs in several markets. The trade journal article reported that the

EXHIBIT 7 Impact of VCR ownership on subscriber behavior (indexed against all cable subscribers)

	All cable subscribers	Non-VCR owners	VCR owners	Heavy renters	Light renters
Downgrade rate	100	100	100	115	50
Disconnect rate	100	105	89	114	55
Upgrade rate	100	112	88	54	132

Source: *Cable Television Administrative and Marketing Society Newsletter* 1, no. 3 (1985).

company had sold 389 VCRs in one and one half months in a four-market test. Special discounts were offered, tied to a pay channel upgrade campaign. Given that industry projections indicated that 50 percent of the population would soon have VCRs, she wondered whether Suburban should target VCR owners in its advertising and promotional efforts.

Another potential market that she thought should be given some consideration was former subscribers. She thought a direct mail campaign targeted toward these households might have a high payoff. Many in the industry were concerned about "churn." Churn was a result of households downgrading their service or having it totally disconnected, and was computed by dividing the number downgrading or disconnecting each month by the total number of subscribers at the beginning of the month. Depending on the season (it was higher in the summer and lower in the winter), the churn percentage for Suburban had been running between 2 and 3 percent for basic service, and between 4 and 6 percent for premium channels. If she chose to concentrate on increasing retention of subscribers (thus reducing churn), there were a number of promotional techniques that could be used. Some cable systems had experienced success in mailing letters to new subscribers that explained all aspects of cable. Thus these better educated people were able to get more out of their subscriptions. She felt that it would be important to beef up customer service, since some people disconnected in frustration after having trouble getting billing and reception problems taken care of promptly and competently. Finally, she had heard that some cable systems had had some success in reducing churn by using advertising to inform people about programs on cable channels. Apparently, bringing these programs to the attention of subscribers through advertising made them appreciate the service more, and thus they were less likely to downgrade or disconnect. Suburban's churn rate was about average for the industry, and she wondered whether it made any sense to use her promotional budget to reduce churn.

Other Considerations

Suburban's system used the latest technology and was an "addressable" system. This meant that the subscriber's service could be changed by merely pushing a button at the central office. It also allowed the use of pay-per-view

(PPV) television. Basically, PPV is just what the name implies—cable TV customers call their cable company and order a particular movie (or other program, such as a sports event) at one of the times it is offered. The cable company transmits the movie and bills the customer accordingly. This means that cable companies can offer subscribers the ability to watch a movie at home without having to pay a full month's price for such services as Home Box Office or Showtime. It is also more convenient than renting a videotape: You don't have to have a VCR, and you don't have to leave your house.

One leading industry consultant estimated that by the end of 1986, 2.6 million households will have PPV available, and industry revenues are projected to reach $70 million. The same consultant predicts that by the end of the decade, PPV will reach nearly 10 million cable subscribers and generate revenues of more than $350 million. The typical price of a PPV movie is $4.50 (ranging from $3.95 to $4.95, depending on the particular movie).

Currently, movies are shown first in the movie theaters and then are released on videotape to the tape rental stores. Finally, they become available on premium movie channels, such as HBO. With PPV it is sometimes shown on cable TV before it is released on videotape for rental. Suburban's technology would allow the introduction of PPV movies, and Ms. Harrison wondered whether that was the direction in which to go.

Thinking about all of the available alternatives, Ms. Harrison recognized the challenging opportunity in front of her. She realized that putting together the marketing plan for the new management team would be quite a job, and thought that she had better get started.

Case 26

Rich's Department Store*

The Executive Committee meeting had been a lengthy session, lasting through most of the morning, but Mr. Dick Mills, vice president and sales promotion director of Rich's Department Store, had returned to his office knowing that a major advertising decision was still not ready to be made. And Mr. Mills realized that it would be his responsibility to submit a final recommendation on media strategy at the next meeting.

Mr. Mills stared at the two neatly bound research reports that he had placed side by side on his desk. The pair of documents represented summaries of the two presentations that had been made to the Rich's Executive Committee that morning. These studies had been based on exactly the same data, drawn from the same in-store survey of Rich's customers. Each report had been prepared by an experienced and professional marketing researcher. Mr. Mills had expected the strong self-interests of the researchers to be reflected in their presentations and interpretations of the survey results, but he was confident that neither man would misrepresent the actual facts.

Mr. Mills had to admit to himself that he had been very surprised at the apparent major contradictions between the two presentations that he had heard earlier that morning. Mr. Mills and the research director of Rich's, who had also attended the morning presentations by the two outside researchers, had discussed the situation briefly after the meeting. The two men had decided to separately review the written reports and, then, to meet later in the afternoon to decide what additional steps to take.

Before rereading the reports, Mr. Mills thought back over the events of the past three months that had eventually led to this situation.

Rich's Department Store was both the largest merchant and the largest single advertiser in Atlanta, Georgia. The store had been founded in 1867 and had grown to an annual sales volume of approximately $200 million through its downtown store and six branch stores located in major suburban shopping

---

* This case was prepared by Kenneth L. Bernhardt. Copyright © 1990 Kenneth L. Bernhardt.

centers. The Rich's market share was 40 percent of department store sales in Atlanta and 25 percent of all general merchandise sales.

The Rich's advertising strategy in the past had been to emphasize newspaper advertising for specific sales items and to utilize broadcast media primarily for image purposes. Newspaper was also used for some image-oriented advertising, with occasional direct mailings used to promote specific sales items of merchandise. Rich's is the largest local advertiser in both print and broadcast media.

The two principal daily newspapers in Atlanta are *The Atlanta Journal* (evenings) and the *Atlanta Constitution* (mornings). These are two of the largest circulation newspapers in the South, and both have distinguished journalism traditions, including Pulitzer Prizes. Although both newspapers are owned by the same company, Atlanta Newspapers, Inc., there is little overlap of readership except for the combined Sunday morning edition.

There are 6 TV stations and 40 radio stations in the Atlanta market. However, broadcast media are dominated by WSB-TV and WSB Radio, both of which are owned by Cox Broadcasting Corporation.

Mr. Mills recalled that several months earlier, executives of Cox Broadcasting and of their two local stations had met with key executives of Rich's. One topic discussed at that meeting had been possible use of broadcast media to promote individual sales items. WSB had offered to participate with Rich's in a market test to determine the abilities of different media to sell specific items of merchandise.

As a result of these discussions, Mr. Mills had held a series of meetings with Mr. Jim Landon, research director of WSB-TV and Radio, and Mr. Ferguson Rood, research director of the Atlanta Newspapers, Inc., to design the market test. It was eventually decided to conduct the test during Rich's annual Harvest Sale, which has been the merchandising highlight of the year since 1925. This sale runs for two weeks each fall. The test was to center on 10 specific items of merchandise which would be advertised in both print and broadcast media during the first three days of the sale. During this same period, in-store interviews would be conducted by professional interviewers, with all purchasers of these 10 items in three representative stores (see appendixes for detailed survey design, sample questionnaire, and media plan).

At the conclusion of the survey period, the Research Departments of both Atlanta Newspapers, Inc., and WSB were furnished duplicate computer card decks by Rich's containing survey data. It was this data that served as the basis for the presentations that Jim Landon and Ferguson Rood had made to the Rich's Executive Committee. Excerpts from *The Atlanta Journal* and *Constitution* report are in Appendix A, and excerpts from the WSB report are presented in Appendix B.

These were the two presentations that Mr. Mills would have to reconcile to arrive at a decision about future media strategy for Rich's. Mr. Mills knew that a decision would have to be made quickly, in view of TV production lead times, if any change in media mix were to be considered for the upcoming Christmas sales season.

Appendix A

An Analysis of a Rich's In-Store Study of Advertising Effectiveness on Specific Purchase Decisions*

Foreword

This report is the result of an innovative research study conducted by Rich's Department Store in partnership with Atlanta Newspapers, Inc. and Cox Broadcasting Corporation.

The study was designed to measure:

1. The relative performance of newspapers, television, and radio as a source of influence on shoppers' decisions to purchase specific items.
2. Shoppers' exposure to specific item advertising messages.

The advertising period covered in this study consisted of three days (beginning Sunday, September 20) prior to Rich's annual Harvest Sale.

A total of 2,176 interviews were made on Monday and Tuesday, September 21 and 22. The interviews were made in three of Rich's seven stores—Downtown, Lenox Square, and Greenbriar, and focused on the 10 departments in each store where the advertised items were sold.

An Atlanta interviewing firm was employed by Rich's to interview shoppers in each department immediately after they made their purchase. To qualify for the survey, shoppers had to purchase the specific advertised item or a directly related item.

Summary and Interpretation

More than 9 out of 10 shoppers covered in this survey had the specific purchase in mind before going to Rich's, or knew it was *on special*.

Three fourths of all shoppers recalled being recently exposed to advertising messages for specific items.

More than half of all shoppers' decisions to purchase specific items were attributed to advertising.

Attributions to newspapers were more than twice those of television and radio combined in influencing specific item purchase decisions (71 percent versus 33 percent).

Dollar for dollar . . . newspapers delivered more than three times the influence on specific item purchase decisions than television and radio combined.

The advertising schedule placed in newspapers . . . was conspicuously more effective and more efficient . . . in influencing specific purchase decisions . . . than the saturation schedule placed on television and radio.

---

* Presented by *The Atlanta Journal* and *Constitution* Research & Marketing Department.

See Exhibits A–1 through A–16.

EXHIBIT A-1   Newspaper advertising schedule*

	Sunday Journal and Constitution (inches)	A.M. Constitution (inches)	P.M. Journal (inches)
Sunday	1,064		
Monday		172	247
Tuesday	____	0	505
Total	1,064	172	752

* 1,989 column inches, the equivalent of 11.6 pages, made up the newspaper schedule covered in this survey.

EXHIBIT A-2   Broadcast schedule*

	Television			Radio		
	Sunday	Monday	Tuesday	Sunday	Monday	Tuesday
6 A.M.		X			X	X
7		X			X	X
8		X	X		X	X
9		X	X	X	X	X
10		X		X	X	X
11		X			X	X
12		X	X	X	X	X
1 P.M.	X	X	X	X	X	X
2	X	X	X	X	X	X
3	X	X	X	X	X	X
4	X	X	X	X	X	X
5	X	X	X	X	X	X
6	X	X		X	X	
7	X	X		X	X	
8	X	X				
9	X	X				
10	X	X				
11	X	X				
Total spots	42	86	49	53	121	87
Average number per schedule hour	3.8	4.8	6.1	5.3	8.6	7.2

* 438 30-second spots were scheduled to run on five television and five radio stations, for an average of 8 spots per hour, between 6 A.M. and 11 P.M., over the three-day period.

EXHIBIT A-3 Comparison of advertising schedule and buget

	Broadcast spots			Newspaper space (inches)
	TV	Radio	Total	
Hard goods:				
Mattress	12	19	31	35
Carpeting	12	23	35	150
Draperies	16	26	42	407
Vacuum sweeper	15	22	37	172
Color television*	0	0	0	150
Soft goods:				
Handbags	15	27	42	189
Girdles†	15	27	42	0
Shoes	15	27	42	398
Shirts*	56	64	120	86
Pant suits	21	26	47	400
Total 10 departments:				
Sunday	42	53	95	1,064
Monday	86	121	207	420
Tuesday	49	87	136	505
Total	177	261	438	1,989
Budget			$27,158	$16,910

* The original broadcast schedule included 20 TV and 24 radio spots for the color television sets to run Tuesday. Since all the sets were sold on Monday, this commercial time was switches to shirts.

† While no Playtex girdle ads were scheduled to run in newspapers, other foundation advertising during the test period supported the influence.

EXHIBIT A-4 Interviews

	Number	Percent
Total	2,175	100%
Women	1,764	81
Men	380	18
Couples	31	1
Under 35	963	44
35–49	817	44
50 and older	394	18
White	1,966	90
Nonwhite	209	10
Hard goods	527	24
Mattress	71	3
Carpeting	45	2
Draperies	123	6
Vacuum sweeper	134	6
Color television	154	7
Soft goods	1,649	75
Handbags	284	13
Girdles	249	11
Shoes	393	18
Shirts	483	22
Pant suits	240	11
Distribution of interviews by store		
Downtown	683	31
Lenox Square	848	39
Greenbriar	645	30

EXHIBIT A-5

"Before coming to Rich's today, did you have in mind buying this specific brand/item, or did you decide after you came into the store?"

63 percent of all shoppers had the specific purchase in mind before going to Rich's.

These shoppers described the following as sources of influence on their buying decision when asked: "What was it that gave you the idea to buy this brand/item?"

Advertising	52%
Needed or wanted it	23
Past experience with it	16
Outside source suggestion	6
Other	7

EXHIBIT A-6

"Was the store having a special on this specific brand/item today, or were they selling at the regular price?"

84 percent of all shoppers said the brand/item was on special.

These shoppers gave the following sources when asked: "Where did you learn about that?"

Advertising	63%
Store display/crowds	27
Outside source	6
Other	4

EXHIBIT A-7 Advertising influence

55 percent of all shoppers attributed their specific purchase decision to advertising. Of these, 71 percent attributed their purchase to newspapers, 33 percent to broadcasts (28 percent to television and 9 percent to radio), and 9 percent to mail circulars.

Newspapers and broadcast accounted for 94 percent of all advertising influence. 61 percent of these influences were attributed to newspapers exclusive of broadcast. 23 percent were attributed to broadcast exclusive of newspapers, and 10 percent were attributed to both.

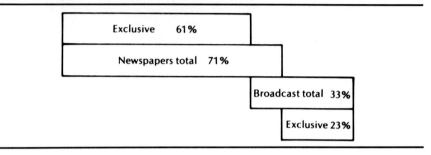

EXHIBIT A-8 Advertising influence

Newspapers and television accounted for 90 percent of all advertising influence. 62 percent of these influences were attributed to newspapers exclusive of television. 19 percent were attributed to television exclusive of newspapers, and 9 percent were attributed to both.

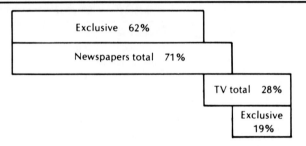

Newspapers and radio accounted for 77 percent of all advertising influence. 68 percent of these influences were attributed to newspapers exclusive of radio. 6 percent were attributed to radio exclusive of newspapers, and 3 percent were attributed to both.

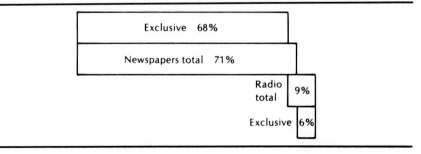

EXHIBIT A-9 Advertising influence—by shopper demographics (among the 55 percent of all shoppers who were influenced by advertising)

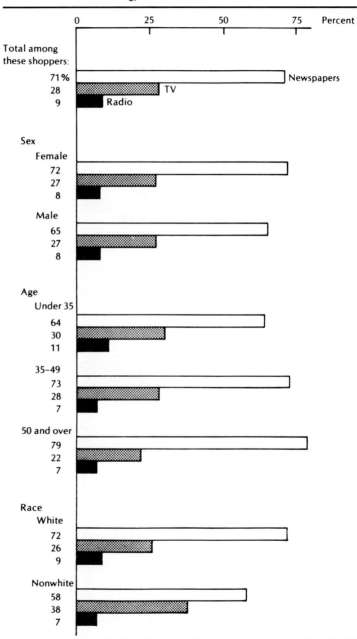

EXHIBIT A-10 Advertising influence—by shopping patterns (among the 55 percent of all shoppers who were influenced by advertising)

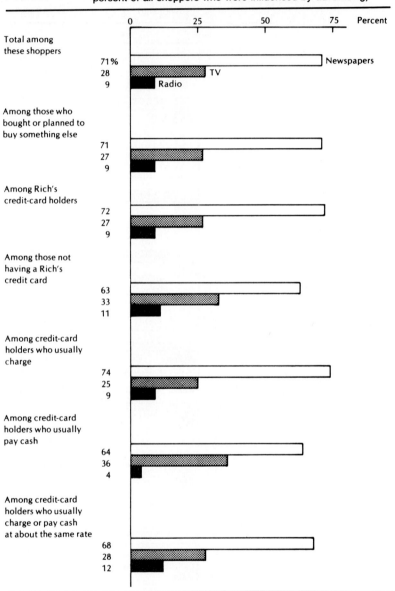

EXHIBIT A-11   Share of budget versus share of influence

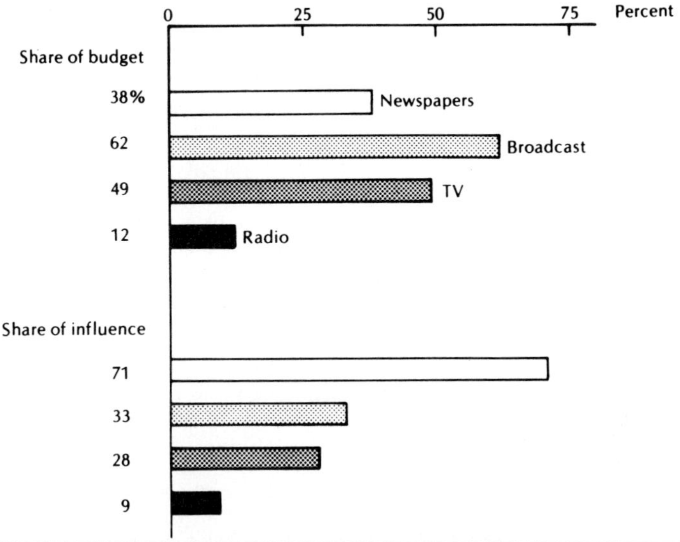

EXHIBIT A-12   Newspapers/broadcast—share of influence versus share of budget by departments

	Newspapers		Broadcast	
	Share of influence	Share of budget	Share of influence	Share of budget
Total	71%	38%	33%	62%
Hard goods	77	45	30	55
Mattress	43	11	69	89
Carpeting	83	39	23	61
Draperies	83	56	22	44
Vacuum sweeper	70	25	45	75
Color TV	99	100	1	—
Soft goods	68	34	34	66
Handbags	68	41	27	59
Girdles	28	—	74	100
Shoes	87	54	25	46
Shirts	63	12	36	88
Pant suits	82	53	16	47

EXHIBIT A-13 Comparison of advertising schedule/budget/ shopper influence*

	Total 10 departments				
	Broadcast spots		Newspaper space		
	TV	Radio	Journal— Constitution	Constitution	Journal
Schedule					
Sunday	42	53	1,064		
Monday	86	121		172	248
Tuesday	49	87		0	505
	177	261	1,064	172	753

* 438 broadcast spots versus 1,989 inches; budget—$27,158 for broadcast spots versus $16,910 for newspaper space; and shopper influence—33 percent for broadcast spots versus 71 percent for newspaper space.

EXHIBIT A-14 Advertising exposure

74 percent of all shoppers recalled being exposed to specific advertising messages within the past day or two. Of these, 79 percent recalled newspapers, 53 percent recalled broadcasts (46 percent television, 18 percent radio), and 24 percent recalled mail circulars.

Newspapers and broadcast accounted for 96 percent of all advertising messages. 43 percent recalled newspapers exclusive of broadcast. 17 percent recalled broadcast exclusive of newspapers, and 36 percent recalled both.

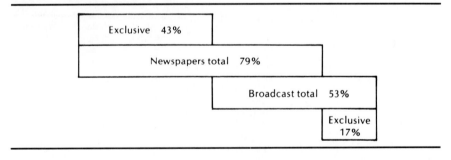

EXHIBIT A-15 Advertising exposure

Newspapers and television accounted for 93 percent of all advertising messages. 47 percent recalled newspapers exclusive of television. 14 percent recalled television exclusive of news-papers, and 32 percent recalled both.

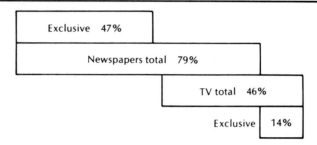

Newspapers and radio accounted for 85 percent of all advertising messages. 67 percent recalled newspapers exclusive of radio. 6 percent recalled radio exclusive of newspapers, and 12 percent recalled both.

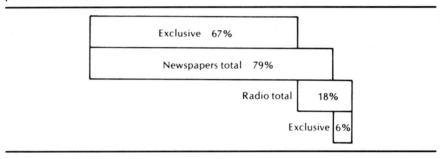

Questionnaire   **HARVEST SALE IN-STORE CUSTOMER SURVEY**

Interviewer Name: _____ (1-2)   STORE: . . . . . . .Downtown . . . . . Lenox . . . . . Greenbriar   (3)
                                                   1   2   3

DATE: M   T   W   TIME OF INTERVIEW: _____ DEPARTMENT: _____   (6)
         1   2   3   (4)   (5)

Hello. We're conducting a short survey among RICH'S customers:

1. What did you happen to buy in this department today? _____
                                             (PROBE, BRAND, STYLE)
                                                                           (7-8)

2. Before coming to RICH'S today, did you have in mind buying this specific brand/item, or did you decide after you came into the store?

         HAD IN MIND. . . .(☐)1   DECIDED IN STORE. . . . .(☐)2   <u>SKIP TO Q. #3</u>   (9)

         What was it that gave you the
         idea to buy this brand/item? _____

         (IF APPROPRIATE, ASK: Where did you learn about that?) _____

                                                                          (10-11)

3. Was the store having a special on this specific brand/item today, or were they selling at the regular price?

         SPECIAL . . . . (☐)1   REGULAR PRICE. . . . . . .(☐)2   <u>SKIP TO Q. #4</u>   (12)

         Where did you learn about that? _____

                                                                          (13-14)

4. Do you recall seeing or hearing any advertising within the past day or two on radio or television or in the newspapers or in a mail circular that may have reminded you or helped you decide to buy this _____ today?

         YES. . . . .(☐)1   NO. . . . .(☐)2   <u>SKIP TO Q. #5</u>   (15)

         a. Where did you see or hear it? _____   (16)

	4a. UNAIDED RECALL	5. AIDED RECALL		
		YES	NO, DK	
RADIO.	1	1	2	(17)
NEWSPAPERS	2	1	2	(18)
TELEVISION.	3	1.	2	(19)
MAIL CIRCULAR	4	1	2	(20)
OTHER, DON'T KNOW	5			

<u>ASK FOR EACH MEDIUM NOT CHECKED IN Q. #4a.</u>

5. Did you happen to see or hear any of the following within the past day or two:
A radio commercial for this specific _____? A newspaper ad for this
specific _____? A television commercial for this specific _____?
A mail circular for this specific _____? _____

6. Have you bought anything else at RICH'S today, or do you plan to buy anything else at RICH'S today?

         YES. . . . .(☐)1   NO. . . . .(☐)2

7. Do you (or your wife/husband) have a RICH'S credit card?   (21)

         YES. . . . .(☐)1   NO. . . . .(☐)2   (22)

         a. Do you usually charge or pay cash for most of your purchases at RICH'S?

         CHARGE . . . .(☐)1   CASH. . . . .(☐)2   SAME. . . . .(☐)3   (23)

8. What is the name of the county where you live? _____ OUT-OF-STATE . . (☐) (24-25-26)

ESTIMATE AGE: UNDER 35 YEARS. .(☐)1   SEX: FEMALE . . .(☐)1   RACE: WHITE . . . . .(☐)1   (27)
                 35 - 49 . . . .(☐)2   MALE. . . . .(☐)2   NON WHITE.(☐)2   (28)
                 50+ . . . .(☐)3   (29)

Appendix B   Analysis of Rich's In-Store Survey*

Introduction

First, we would like to state that WSB television and radio were pleased to have the opportunity to participate in this research effort with Rich's. We have one basic characteristic in common with Rich's—both WSB-TV and WSB Radio, like Rich's, are dominant in the Atlanta market. Like Rich's, we are an Atlanta institution and have enjoyed dominance since our origination.

In this presentation, we will not attempt to interpret the results of your research from a marketing standpoint. You have your own market research department, and we are sure that they have done a capable job of analyzing and interpreting the results of the study from that aspect. Instead, we will concentrate on interpreting the results from a media standpoint, which is our particular area of experience.

The following pages contain our detailed analysis of this research for Rich's management.

Pre-Harvest Sale Advertising Weight

Rich's Pre-Harvest Sale was heavily promoted with a "mix" of three media: radio, TV, and newspaper.

On the broadcast side, Rich's ran 261 radio spots on five stations and 177 TV spots on five stations promoting 10 different items during a three-day period. It can be estimated that the total radio campaign reached about 90 percent of the Atlanta adult metro population, with the average listener exposed to seven commercial announcements (all products combined). The total television campaign also reached an estimated 90 percent of the Atlanta adult population, with the average viewer exposed to 10 commercial announcements.

The newspaper campaign consisted of 13 ads for the specific items and 11 ads for related[1] items, or a total of 24 ads representing 1,987 inches of space in the *Journal* and *Constitution*. Rich's also ran 6,140 inches of other newspaper advertising during the three-day period. We have no way of estimating the reach and frequency of the newspaper ads.

Pre-Harvest Sale a Success

Rich's total advertising effort helped make the store's pre-Harvest Sale a tremendous success.

Monday, September 21, and Tuesday, September 22, were two of Rich's biggest days of the year according to traffic and sales volume. As far as we

---

* Presented by WSB-TV, WSB Radio, and Cox Broadcasting Research.

[1] Same item but different price than in the radio and TV commercial.

know, the departments participating in the test were all up considerably in sales volume compared to a year ago.

Unfortunately, sales results for the *specific items* tested were not available. However, it is our understanding that the departmentwide sales results reflected the success of the individual items in those departments that were tested.

The advertising effort for the pre-Harvest Sale represented one of the few times that Rich's has used a media-mix for *item selling*. Radio and TV have been used extensively by Rich's for institutional advertising and to announce sale events, but item selling has been limited in the past primarily to newspaper and direct mail. *The media-mix for item selling worked from a sales results standpoint.*

Summary of Media Recall Findings

After analyzing the results of the survey, we found the following to be the most significant findings:

1. Because of the confusion and particularly the conditioning factor regarding newspaper, the three media cannot be completely compared in recall.
2. Recall for both radio and TV was significantly higher on Tuesday versus Monday, indicating that the broadcast media were building in impact on customers. Sales results were also generally better on Tuesday versus Monday.
3. Both radio and TV did *best* in recall (compared to newspaper) for items having the *least* amount of newspaper advertising. Radio and TV did *poorest* for items having the *greatest* amount of newspaper advertising.
4. In general, items where radio and TV did *best* in recall (compared to newspaper) had better sales results than items where radio and TV did poorest.
5. All three media performed better among high-priced items and for items where customers decided to buy before coming into the store.
6. Radio and TV balanced newspaper quite well by reaching younger adults than the print medium.

See Exhibits B–1 through B–3.

EXHIBIT B-1   Summary of newspaper recall

Item	Budget	Day/ads	Got idea	Learned of special	Direct recall
Draperies	$4,412	Sun.–2, Tues.–2	48%	68%	81%
Pant suits	3,359	Sun.–2, Mon.–1, Tues.–3	50	56	63
Shoes	2,834	Sun.–1, Mon.–2, Tues.–1	48	55	72
Handbags	1,670	Sun.–1, Tues.–1	30	30	60
Carpeting	1,503	Sun.–1	61	63	80
Color TV	1,503	Sun.–1	62	68	66

EXHIBIT B-1   (concluded)

Item	Budget	Day/ads	Got idea	Learned of special	Direct recall
Dress shirts	859	Sun.–1	40%	40%	54%
Vacuum cleaner	780	Mon.–4	36	62	64
Mattresses	260	Tues.–1	30	37	54
Career shirts	—	—	19	27	45
Girdles	—	—	12	15	16
Averages, all items*			42	51	64

* Excludes girdles (no ads), but includes career shirts because of ads for dress shirts, a related item.

EXHIBIT B-2   Summary of television recall

Item	Budget	Adult audience (000)	Got idea	Learned of special	Direct recall
Career shirts	$2,998	1,373.4	15%	16%	27%
Draperies	2,714	776.5	11	15	37
Pant suits	2,494	885.4	8	9	39
Playtex girdles	2,364	752.1	25	34	32
Dress shirts	2,028	824.8	16	16	29
Handbags	1,922	649.2	10	10	34
Shoes	1,909	724.7	11	14	41
Vacuum cleaner	1,867	627.4	19	36	42
Carpeting	1,790	624.5	8	12	29
Mattresses	1,627	691.9	40	48	49
Color TV	—	—	0	0	5
Averages, all items*			16	21	36

* Excludes color TV (no commercials).

EXHIBIT B-3   Summary of radio recall

Item	Budget	Adult audience (000)	Got idea	Learned of special	Direct recall
Career shirts	$903	489.1	2%	6%	17%
Draperies	560	654.3	1	2	8
Shoes	544	566.8	5	6	14
Pant suits	539	633.9	1	2	12
Carpeting	513	590.9	8	7	24
Dress shirts	498	496.4	4	5	12
Girdles	482	553.0	6	9	11
Mattresses	477	527.6	11	23	29
Handbags	476	475.1	2	3	20
Vacuum cleaner	453	482.1	7	8	10
Color TV	—	374.2	—	1	2
Averages, all items*			5	7	16

* Excludes color TV (no commercials).

Three Types of Media Recall in the Study

The questionnaire used in Rich's in-store survey obtained information about customers' recall of advertising media in three areas:

1. Idea to Buy

For customers purchasing the item being tested, those that indicated having in mind buying that specific merchandise before coming to the store were asked *what gave them the idea to buy the item*. In this question, answers involving media came from top-of-mind recall (not aided). Nonmedia answers to this question, such as ''needed'' item, ''wanted'' item or ''had past experience'' with item were accepted.

2. Learned of Special

Those customers who were aware of the store having a special on the specific item purchased were asked *where they learned about it*. In this question, answers involving media also came from top-of-mind recall and nonmedia responses such as ''saw on display'' or ''friend told me'' were accepted.

3. Direct Recall

Customers were also asked if they recalled seeing or hearing any advertising that may have reminded them or helped them decide to buy the specific item. If they answered in the affirmative, they were then asked *where they saw or heard it*. If radio, newspaper, TV, or mail circular were not mentioned by the respondent, they were also asked if they happened to hear a radio commercial, see a newspaper ad, and so on (aided recall). For purposes of analyzing the results, the unaided and aided answers to direct recall have been combined in this question.

Effect of Confusion and "Conditioning"

First, we would like to emphasize three points that should be taken into consideration when evaluating each advertising medium's performance based on the recall results of the study:

1. Because of the heavy amount of Rich's advertising activity in all media during the three-day period of interviewing, there was a certain amount of confusion that occurred among the customer-respondents regarding where they saw or heard advertising. This fact will be documented in the pages to follow.
2. Because Rich's traditionally has done the vast majority of its *item* advertising in newspaper, customers are ''conditioned'' to this particular medium;

i.e., more inclined to think of Rich's merchandise being advertised in a newspaper.

3. During the three-day period of the study, *other department stores* were also running *newspaper* ads for items similar to Rich's items being tested. Some newspaper ad recall in this study could have been due to confusion with other stores' ads.

These points can all be substantiated by the following results.

Only Slight Confusion for Radio Commercials

There were *no* radio commercials for color TV sets, since the spots were canceled before they were scheduled to run on Tuesday afternoon.

0%	Claimed they got the idea to buy a color TV set from radio commercials.
1%	Thought they learned of color TV sets being on sale from radio commercials.
2%	Said they recalled hearing radio commercials for color TV sets.

Only Slight Confusion for TV Commercials

There were *no* TV commercials for color TV sets, since the spots were canceled before they were scheduled to run on Tuesday afternoon.

0%	Claimed that they got the idea to buy a color TV set from TV commercials.
0%	Thought they learned of color TV sets on sale from TV commercials.
5%	Said they recalled seeing TV commercials for color TV sets.

Some Confusion and "Conditioning" for Mail Circular

In the mail circular that Rich's distributed to its customers the week prior to the survey, there were *no* ads for any specific items, yet among the total sample of customer-respondents purchasing any of the 11 items tested:

3%	Claimed they got the idea to buy the specific item from a mail circular.
5%	Thought they learned of the specific item being on sale from a mail circular.
18%	Said they recalled seeing a mail circular for the specific item.

Greater Confusion and "Conditioning" for Newspaper Ads

There were *no* Rich's newspaper ads for Playtex girdles, yet:

12%	Claimed they got the idea to buy girdles from newspaper ads.
15%	Thought they learned of girdles being on sale from newspaper ads.
16%	Said they recalled seeing newspaper ads for girdles.

There were *no* Rich's newspaper ads for mattresses on either Sunday or Monday of the survey, yet among customers interviewed on Monday:

27%	Claimed they got the idea to buy a mattress from newspaper ads.
30%	Thought they learned of the mattress being on sale from newspaper ads.
49%	Said they recalled seeing newspaper ads for mattresses.

Caution in Comparing Media by Recall!

As you can see, the extent of erroneous recall of newspaper advertising ranged from a low of 12 percent to a high of 49 percent. For this important reason, it is impossible to derive any accurate yardstick for measuring the separate value of each medium, dollar for dollar. In addition, these results cannot be converted to any type of advertising-to-sales ratio.

Radio May Have Been Higher with More WSB Spots

Due to the problem created by trying to find enough availabilities on WSB only in morning and evening drive time (because of the agency's buying criteria) to handle commercials for 11 different items in three days, Atlanta's dominant radio station was not able to contribute as much weight as it should have to most of the media schedules. As a result, a higher proportion of spots ran on WQXI (primarily teens), WAOK (primarily ethnic), WRNG (primarily 50+ listeners), and WPLO (lower socioeconomic level). A brief analysis of the number of radio commercials that ran for each item, showing the light proportion of WSB spots, is shown in the accompanying table.

	Total spots	WSB spots	WSB morning drive spots*
Career shirts	48	10	0
Carpeting	23	6	3
Color TV	—	—	—
Draperies	26	7	2
Dress shirts	15	6	2
Girdles	27	5	1
Handbags	27	5	1
Mattresses	19	6	2
Pant suits	26	8	2
Shoes	27	6	2
Vacuum cleaner	22	5	2
Total	260	64	17

* Monday or Tuesday.

Television versus Newspaper

While TV budgets were fairly even, newspaper budgets ranged from $260 for mattresses up to $4,412 for draperies. TV versus newspaper performance in all types of recall showed a good relationship to the amount of money spent in newspaper. The smaller the newspaper budget versus TV, the better TV performed versus newspaper in recall, and vice versa:

1. TV did *best* in all types of recall *compared to newspaper* for mattresses, career shirts, and vacuum cleaners. These items had the *smallest amount* of advertising space in the newspaper compared to the others.
2. TV did *poorest* in all types of recall *compared to newspaper* for draperies, pant suits, shoes, and carpeting. These items had the *greater amount* of advertising space in the newspaper.

Radio versus Newspaper

Again, radio budgets were fairly even compared to the wide range in newspaper budgets. Radio versus newspaper performance in all types of recall also showed a fairly strong relationship to the amount of money spent in newspaper. The smaller the newspaper budget versus radio, the better radio performed versus newspaper in recall, and vice versa:

1. Radio did *best* in all types of recall *compared to newspaper* for mattresses, vacuum cleaners, and career shirts. These items generally had the least newspaper space.
2. Radio did *poorest* in all types of recall *compared to newspaper* for draperies, pant suits, and handbags. These items generally had the greatest newspaper space.

Less Newspaper Space—No Harm to Sales Volume

We have just indicated that, as newspaper space was reduced, both radio and TV did better in recall.

How about Rich's Sales Volume?

There appeared to be little, if any, correlation between the amount of newspaper space and sales volume as measured by department sales increases. If anything, the reverse occurred:

	Monday	Tuesday
TV and radio did best (least newspaper space):		
Girdles	+7%	+92%
Career shirts	+151	+349
Mattresses	+43	+76
Vacuum cleaners	+98	+222
TV and radio did poorest (most newspaper space):		
Draperies	−0	+9
Pant suits	+17	+46
Shoes	−19	+14
Carpeting	−9	+526

Idea to Buy versus Direct Recall

One probable indication of the "conditioning" of Rich's customers to newspaper advertising comes from comparing initial "idea to buy" recall, where media responses came purely from top of mind, to the direct recall that came later in the interview, concentrating on each medium. All three media gained in regard to the proportion of customers recalling (from idea to buy to direct recall), but newspaper, having been recalled more from top of mind, gained the least, while TV and especially radio, in the background during top of mind "idea to buy," came to the surface more in the direct recall.

	Average recall, all items*		
	Idea to buy	Direct recall	Percent increase
Newspaper	42%	64%	+52%
TV	16	36	+125
Radio	5	16	+220

* Girdles were eliminated for newspaper and color TV sets were eliminated for radio and TV because of no advertising.

First Day versus Second Day Recall

Analysis of the direct recall results by day of interview produced an interesting fact. The impact of newspaper was initial, while both radio and TV performed significantly better on the second day. This is probably due to the nature of the broadcast media, which gain impact and effectiveness with *increased frequency* (as listeners and viewers are exposed to more commercials). In addition, sales results for all items were generally better on Tuesday than on Monday, compared to a year ago. This also indicates that, if spots had been spread more evenly over Sunday, Monday, and Tuesday (rather than concentrated on Sunday and Monday in most cases), and if interviewing had been extended through Wednesday, both radio and TV would have performed better in recall, at no increase in budget for either medium.

	Average recall, all items*		
	Monday	*Tuesday*	*Tuesday percent difference*
Newspaper	66%	62%	−6%
TV	33	38	+15
Radio	13	18	+38

* Mattresses were eliminated for newspaper as an invalid comparison, since there were no ads on Sunday or Monday. However, even though there were no radio or TV commercials for career shirts on Sunday or Monday, and no newspaper ads at all, this item was included in this comparison because there was advertising for dress shirts, a related item. Also girdles were eliminated for newspaper and color TV for radio and TV because of no advertising.

High-Priced versus Low-Priced Items

In order to analyze media performance by item *price range,* the items were divided into either a high-price (carpeting, color TV, draperies, mattresses, and vacuum cleaners) or a low-price (career shirts, dress shirts, girdles, handbags, pant suits, and shoes) group. All three media performed better among high-priced items compared to low-priced merchandise, especially radio and TV. However, the differences were greater regarding "idea to buy" recall and "learned of special" recall than with the direct recall. Customers who had made up their minds to buy a large ticket item were apparently more persuaded by advertising than those coming to Rich's for lower priced merchandise. However, whether in the market for high- or low-priced items, both type customers were exposed to advertising, as indicated in the direct recall.

	High-priced items	Low-priced items	High-priced percent difference
Idea to buy:			
Newspaper	47%	37%	+27%
TV	20	14	+43
Radio	7	3	+133
Learned of special:			
Newspaper	60	42	+43
TV	28	16	+75
Radio	10	5	+100
Direct recall:			
Newspaper	69	59	+17
TV	39	34	+15
Radio	18	14	+29

"Had in Mind" versus "Decided in Store"

In order to analyze media performance by the extent to which customers had in mind to buy the item before coming to the store, the items were divided into two groups: "had in mind" and "decided in store," based on results to the question covering this aspect of purchasing. The four items where roughly half of the customers indicated deciding in the store (pant suits, dress shirts, career shirts, and handbags) were placed in the "decided in store" group. The other seven items, where significantly less customers indicated deciding in store, were placed in the "had in mind" group. All three media performed significantly better among items in the "had in mind" group, that is, for items where a greater proportion of customers made their decision in advance. The differences were greater regarding "idea to buy" and "learned of special" recall than with the direct recall.

	"Had in mind" items	"Decided in store" items	"Had in mind" percent difference
Idea to buy:			
Newspaper	48%	35%	+37%
TV	19	12	+58
Radio	6	2	+200
Learned of special:			
Newspaper	59	38	+55
TV	26	13	+100
Radio	9	4	+125
Direct recall:			
Newspaper	70	56	+25
TV	38	32	+19
Radio	16	15	+7

Broadcast Media Recall Reflected Younger Adults

By analyzing media recall by age of customer, it was determined that radio and TV balanced newspaper quite well by reaching younger adults. In all three types of recall, the under-35 age group was proportionately higher for broadcast, especially radio, than for newspaper. These figures are based on all items combined.

Age	Radio	TV	Newspaper
Got idea:			
Under 35	56%	44%	36%
35–49	31	38	44
50 and over	13	18	20
Learned of special:			
Under 35	50	43	36
35–49	34	41	41
50 and over	16	16	23
Direct recall:			
Under 35	49	44	41
35–49	33	38	41
50 and over	18	18	18

Note: Read table. Of those customers indicating that they "got the idea" to buy an item from radio commercials, 56 percent were in the under 35 age group.

Rich's Dominant Position in Atlanta

In concluding this presentation, we would like to announce the results of separate research that we have just completed that indicates the extent to which Rich's dominates the department store market in Atlanta, a domination that we feel is due to:

Outstanding management.

Quality of merchandise.

Attention to customer service and satisfaction.

Efficient use of advertising and promotion, *especially the use of a media-mix.*

Presentation Summary

1. With use of media-mix for item selling, the pre-Harvest Sale was a success. All departments participating in the test were up in sales volume.
2. Because of confusion and conditioning factors, recall results are not completely comparable between media.
3. In general, as the amount of newspaper space was reduced, the proportion of recall for both TV and radio was increased, and sales results were generally more favorable.

4. Sales volume was up significantly on Tuesday versus Monday in all departments, indicating a relationship with broadcast media recall, also up significantly on Tuesday as frequency increased.
5. All media had higher recall for higher priced items and items where customer generally decided in advance.
6. Separate research confirms Rich's dominance of the Atlanta market, especially versus Davison's. Rich's uses radio and TV effectively, Davison's uses very little broadcast media.

Case 27

Exercise in Print Advertising Assessment*

One of the most important and most difficult marketing decisions is the choice of creative executions in advertising. The purpose of this exercise is to help you develop skills in determining what is a good and a bad creative execution.

In preparation for your class session using this exercise, we would like you to spend time looking at *print* advertising (newspaper and magazine advertising). We would like you to select what you think is the "best ad" you have seen and the "worst ad" you have seen. To aid you in this task you might ask yourself the following questions:

1. What is the sponsor's apparent target segment(s)?
2. What are the objectives of the ad?
3. Is the basic appeal, theme, and copy approach appropriate for these purposes?

To the bottom of each ad you selected attach a small piece of paper containing the following information:

1. Sponsor of the ad.
2. Publication in which the ad appeared.
3. Publication date.
4. Your reason(s) for selecting that ad as the best or worst.
5. Your name.

Staple or tape this information to the bottom of the ad but don't obscure any of the ad. Turn in your ads to your professor as required. In the class session you will get a chance to compare your choice of ads with those of your classmates.

Case 28

Allied Food Distributors*

In April 1990, Ms. Elizabeth Ramsey, the district sales manager for the upper Midwest district of Allied Food Distributors, was preparing to hire a new salesperson for the southwest Indiana sales territory. The current salesperson in this territory was leaving the company at the end of June. Ms. Ramsey had narrowed the list of potential candidates to three. She wondered which of these applicants she should select.

Company Background

Allied Food Distributors was one of the largest food wholesalers in the United States. The company carried hundreds of different packaged food items (fruits, vegetables, cake mixes, cookies, powdered soft drinks, and so on) for sales to supermarkets and grocery stores. Allied carried items in two different circumstances. First, some small food companies had Allied carry their entire line in all areas of the United States. Allied was in essence their sales force. Second, some large food companies had Allied carry their lines in less populated parts of the country. These areas were not large enough to sustain a salesperson for each food company.

Allied operated in all 50 states. The country was divided into 20 sales districts. Ms. Ramsey's sales district included Michigan, Indiana, and Illinois. Each district was divided into a number of sales territories. A salesperson was assigned to each territory.

The Southwest Indiana Territory

The sales territory for which Ms. Ramsey was seeking a salesperson was located in the southwest corner of Indiana. Exhibit 1 presents a map of the territory. It was bordered on the south by the Ohio River and the state of Kentucky, on the west by the Wabash River and the state of Illinois, and on the

---

* This case was written by Thomas C. Kinnear. Copyright © 1990 Thomas C. Kinnear.

EXHIBIT 1   A map of the southwest Indiana territory

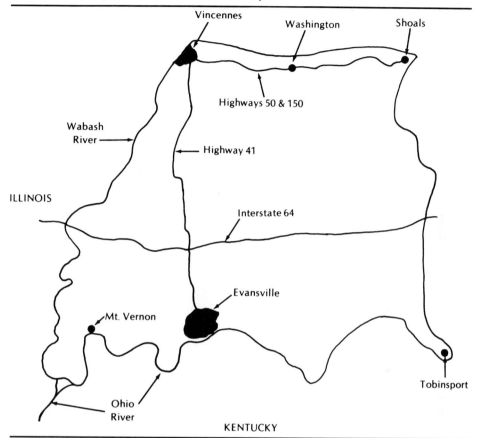

east by the Hoosier National Forest. The northern boundary ran a few miles north of Highways 50 and 150 that ran from Vincennes in the west through Washington to Shoals in the east. Evansville was the largest city in the area with a population of about 140,000. The salesperson for the territory was expected to live in Evansville, but would spend about three nights a week on the road. The only other reasonably large population concentration was in Vincennes with a population of about 20,000. Vincennes was located about 55 miles straight north of Evansville on Highway 41. Interstate Highway 64 ran the 80 miles east-west through the territory about 15 miles north of Evansville. Evansville was 165 miles southwest of Indianapolis, 170 miles east of St. Louis, Missouri, and 115 miles southwest of Louisville, Kentucky. The territory was very rural in character with agriculture being the dominant industry. The terrain was quite hilly, with poor soil. As a result, the farms in the area tended to be economically weak. There were many small towns and villages located throughout this basically rural environment.

The Selling Task

Allied maintained 75 active retail accounts in the southwest Indiana territory. About 10 of these accounts were medium- to large-sized independent supermarkets located in Evansville and Vincennes. The rest of the accounts were small, independent general food stores located throughout the territory.

The salesperson was expected to call on these accounts about every three weeks. The salesperson's duties included: checking displays and inventory levels for items already carried, obtaining orders on these items, informing retailers about new items, attempting to gain sales orders on these items, setting up special displays, and generally servicing the retailers' needs. Often, the salesperson would check the level of inventory on an item, make out an order, and present it to the retailer to be signed. The salesperson generally knew the store owner on a first name basis. The ordered goods were sent directly to the retailer from a warehouse located in Indianapolis.

The Selection Process

The responsibility for recruiting salespersons for the territories within a district was given to the district sales manager. The process consisted of the following steps:

1. An advertisement for the job was placed in newspapers in the state in question.
2. Those responding to the ad were sent job application forms.
3. The returned application forms were examined and certain applicants were asked to come to the district sales office for a full day of interviews.
4. The selection was then made by the district sales manager, or all applicants were rejected and the process started again.

Training

Allied did all its salesperson training on the job. The salesperson on the territory to which a new person would be assigned was given the task of training. Basically, this involved having the new person travel the territory to meet the retailers and to be shown how to obtain and send in orders. The district sales manager usually assisted in this process by traveling with the new salesperson for a few days.

Compensation

The current salesperson on the southwest Indiana sales territory was earning a straight salary of about $43,000 per year plus fringe benefits. Ms. Ramsey indicated that she was willing to pay between $25,000 and $50,000 for a new person depending on the qualifications presented.

The Choices

On the basis of application forms and personal interviews, Ms. Ramsey had narrowed the field of applicants down to three. A summary of the information on their application forms along with the comments she had written to herself are contained in Exhibits 2, 3, and 4. She wondered which person she should select for the position.

EXHIBIT 2 Information on Mr. Michael Gehringer

Personal information

Born July 15, 1948; married; three children ages 14, 16, and 19; height 5 feet, 10 inches; weight 205; excellent health; born and raised in Indianapolis.

Education

High school graduate; played football; no extracurricular activities of note.

Employment record

1. Currently employed by Allied Food Distributors in the warehouse in Indianapolis; two years with Allied; job responsibilities include processing orders from the field and expediting rush orders; current salary $2,600 per month.
2. In 1987–88 employed by Hoosier Van Lines in Indianapolis as a sales agent; terminating salary was $550 per month; left due to limits placed on salary and lack of challenge in the job.
3. In 1985–87 employed by Main Street Clothiers of Indianapolis as a retail salesperson in the men's department; terminating salary $1,500 per month; left due to boring nature of this type of selling.
4. Between 1968 and 1985 held six other clerical and sales type jobs, all in Indianapolis.

Applicant's statement

I feel that my true employment interest lies in selling in a situation where I can be my own boss. This job seems just right.

Ms. Ramsey's comments

Seems very interested in job as a career.
Well recommended by his current boss.
Reasonably intelligent.
Good appearance.
Moderately aggressive.

EXHIBIT 3 Information on Mr. Carley Tobias

Personal information

Born February 12, 1961; married; two children ages 1 and 4; height 6 feet, 2 inches; weight 170; excellent health; born in San Francisco; raised in Cleveland, Ohio.

Education

High school and Community College graduate in business administration; student council president at Community College; plus belonged to a number of other clubs.

Employment record

1. Currently employed by The Drug Trading Company in Cincinnati as a salesperson; job responsibility involves selling to retail drugstores; seven years with Drug Trading; current salary $3,300 per month.
2. In 1981–84 U.S. Army private; did one tour of duty in Germany.

Applicant's statement

I am seeking a new position because of the limited earning potential at Drug Trading, plus my family's desire to live in a less populated city.

Other information

He is very active in civic and church organizations in Cincinnati; he is currently president of the Sales and Marketing Executives of Cincinnati.

Ms. Ramsey's comments

Very personable.

Reasonably intelligent.

Good appearance.

He seems to like Cincinnati a lot.

Good experience.

EXHIBIT 4   Information on Mr. Arthur Woodhead

Personal information

Born May 26, 1968; single; height 6 feet; weight 180; excellent health; born and raised in Chicago.

Education

Will graduate in May 1990 from the University of Illinois, Chicago, with a B.B.A. Active in intramural athletics and student government.

Employment record

Summer jobs only; did house painting and gardening work for his own company. Earned $1,600 per month in summer of 1989.

Applicant's statement

I really like to run my own affairs, and selling seems like a good position to reach this objective.

Ms. Ramsey's comments

Well dressed and groomed.

Very intelligent.

Management potential, not career salesperson.

Not very aggressive.

Case 29

Outdoor Sporting Products, Inc.*

The annual sales volume of Outdoor Sporting Products, Inc., for the past six years had ranged between $6.2 million and $6.8 million. Although profits continued to be satisfactory, Mr. Hudson McDonald, president and chief operating officer, was concerned because sales had not increased appreciably from year to year. Consequently, he asked a consultant in New York City and the officers of the company to submit proposals for improving the salesmen's compensation plan, which he believed was the basic weakness in the firm's marketing operations.

Outdoor's factory and warehouse were located in Albany, New York, where the company manufactured and distributed sporting equipment, clothing, and accessories. Mr. Hudson McDonald, who managed the company, organized it in 1956 when he envisioned a growing market for sporting goods resulting from the predicted increase in leisure time and the rising levels of income in the United States.

Products of the company, numbering approximately 700 items, were grouped into three lines: (1) fishing supplies, (2) hunting supplies, and (3) accessories. The fishing supplies line, which accounted for approximately 40 percent of the company's annual sales, included nearly every item a fisherman would need such as fishing jackets, vests, caps, rods and reels of all types, lines, flies, lures, landing nets, and creels. Thirty percent of annual sales were in the hunting supplies line, which consisted of hunting clothing of all types including insulated and thermal underwear, safety garments, shell holders, whistles, calls, and gun cases. The accessories line, which made up the balance of the company's annual sales volume, included items such as compasses, cooking kits, lanterns, hunting and fishing knives, hand warmers, and novelty gifts.

While the sales of the hunting and fishing lines were very seasonal, they tended to complement one another. The January–April period accounted for the bulk of the company's annual volume in fishing items, and most sales of hunt-

* Adapted from a case written by Zarrel V. Lambert, Auburn University, and Fred W. Kniffin, University of Connecticut, Stamford. Used with permission.

ing supplies were made during the months of May through August. Typically, the company's sales of all products reached their lows for the year during the month of December.

Outdoor's sales volume was $6.57 million in the current year with self-manufactured products accounting for 35 percent of this total. Fifty percent of the company's volume consisted of imported products, which came principally from Japan. Items manufactured by other domestic producers and distributed by Outdoor accounted for the remaining 15 percent of total sales.

Mr. McDonald reported that wholesale prices to retailers were established by adding a markup of 50 to 100 percent to Outdoor's cost for the item. This rule was followed on self-manufactured products as well as for items purchased from other manufacturers. The resulting average markup across all products was 70 percent on cost.

Outdoor's market area consisted of the New England states, New York, Pennsylvania, Ohio, Michigan, Wisconsin, Indiana, Illinois, Kentucky, Tennessee, West Virginia, Virginia, Maryland, Delaware, and New Jersey. The area over which Outdoor could effectively compete was limited to some extent by shipping costs, since all orders were shipped from the factory and warehouse in Albany.

Outdoor's salesmen sold to approximately 6,000 retail stores in small- and medium-sized cities in its market area. Analysis of sales records showed that the firm's customer coverage was very poor in the large metropolitan areas. Typically, each account was a one- or two-store operation. Mr. McDonald stated that he knew for a fact that Outdoor's share of the market was very low, perhaps 2 to 3 percent; and for all practical purposes, he felt the company's sales potential was unlimited.

Mr. McDonald believed that with few exceptions, Outdoor's customers had little or no brand preference and in the vast majority of cases they bought hunting and fishing supplies from several suppliers.

It was McDonald's opinion that the pattern of retail distribution for hunting and fishing products had been changing during the past 10 years as a result of the growth of discount stores. He thought that the proportion of retail sales for hunting and fishing supplies made by small- and medium-sized sporting goods outlets had been declining compared to the percent sold by discounters and chain stores. An analysis of company records revealed Outdoor had not developed business among the discounters with the exception of a few small discount stores. Some of Outdoor's executives felt that the lack of business with discounters might have been due in part to the company's pricing policy and in part to the pressures which current customers had exerted on company salesmen to keep them from calling on the discounters.

Outdoor's Sales Force

The company's sales force played the major role in its marketing efforts since Outdoor did not use magazine, newspaper, or radio advertising to reach either the retail trade or consumers. One advertising piece that supplemented the work of the salesmen was Outdoor's merchandise catalog. It contained a complete listing of all the company's products and was mailed to all retailers who were either current accounts or prospective accounts. Typically, store buyers used the catalog for purposes of reordering.

Most accounts were contacted by a salesman two or three times a year. The salesmen planned their activities so that each store would be called upon at the beginning of the fishing season and again prior to the hunting season. Certain key accounts of some salesmen were contacted more often than two or three times a year.

Management believed that product knowledge was the major ingredient of a successful sales call. Consequently, Mr. McDonald had developed a "selling formula," which each salesman was required to learn before he took over a territory. The "formula" contained five parts: (1) the name and catalog number of each item sold by the company; (2) the sizes and colors in which each item was available; (3) the wholesale price of each item; (4) the suggested retail price of each item; and (5) the primary selling features of each item. After a new salesman had mastered the product knowledge specified by this "formula" he began working in his assigned territory and was usually accompanied by Mr. McDonald for several weeks.

Managing the sales force consumed approximately one third of Mr. McDonald's efforts. The remaining two thirds of his time was spent purchasing products for resale and in general administrative duties as the company's chief operating officer.

Mr. McDonald held semiannual sales meetings, had weekly telephone conversations with each salesman, and had mimeographed bulletins containing information on products, prices, and special promotional deals mailed to all salesmen each week. Daily call reports and attendance at the semiannual sales meetings were required of all salesmen. One meeting was held the first week in January to introduce the spring line of fishing supplies. The hunting line was presented at the second meeting, which was scheduled in May. Each of these sales meetings spanned four to five days so the salesmen were able to study the new products being introduced and any changes in sales and company policies. The production manager and comptroller attended these sales meetings to answer questions and to discuss problems which the salesmen might have concerning deliveries and credit.

On a predetermined schedule each salesman telephoned Mr. McDonald every Monday morning to learn of changes in prices, special promotional offers, and delivery schedules of unshipped orders. At this time the salesman's activities for the week were discussed, and sometimes the salesman was asked by Mr. McDonald to collect past due accounts in his territory. In addition, the salesmen submitted daily call reports, which listed the name of each account contacted and the results of the call. Generally, the salesmen planned their own itineraries in terms of the accounts and prospects that were to be contacted and the amount of time to be spent on each call.

Outdoor's sales force during the current year totaled 11 full-time employees. Their ages ranged from 23 to 67 years, and their tenure with the company

EXHIBIT 1 Salesmen: Age, years of service, territory, and sales

				Sales	
				Previous	Current
Salesmen	Age	Years of service	Territory	year	year
Allen	45	2	Illinois and Indiana	$ 330,264	$ 329,216
Campbell	62	10	Pennsylvania	1,192,192	1,380,240
Duvall	23	1	New England	—	414,656
Edwards	39	1	Michigan	—	419,416
Gatewood	63	5	West Virginia	358,528	358,552
Hammond	54	2	Virginia	414,936	414,728
Logan	37	1	Kentucky and Tennessee	—	447,720
Mason	57	2	Delaware and Maryland	645,032	825,088
O'Bryan	59	4	Ohio	343,928	372,392
Samuels	42	3	New York and New Jersey	737,024	824,472
Wates	67	5	Wisconsin	370,712	342,200
Salesmen terminated in previous year				1,828,816	—
House account				257,384	244,480
Total				$6,478,816	$6,374,816

ranged from 1 to 10 years. Salesmen, territories, and sales volumes for the previous year and the current year are shown in Exhibit 1.

Compensation of Salesmen

The salesmen were paid straight commissions on their dollar sales volume for the calendar year. The commission rate was 5 percent on the first $300,000, 6 percent on the next $200,000 in volume, and 7 percent on all sales over $500,000 for the year. Each week a salesman could draw all or a portion of his accumulated commissions. McDonald encouraged the salesmen to draw commissions as they accumulated since he felt the men were motivated to work harder when they had a very small or zero balance in their commission accounts. These accounts were closed at the end of the year so each salesman began the new year with nothing in his account.

The salesmen provided their own automobiles and paid their traveling expenses, of which all or a portion were reimbursed by per diem. Under the per diem plan, each salesman received $70 per day for Monday through Thursday and $42 for Friday, or a total of $322 for the normal workweek. No per diem was paid for Saturday, but a salesman received an additional $70 if he spent Saturday and Sunday nights in the territory.

In addition to the commission and per diem, a salesman could earn cash awards under two sales incentive plans that were installed two years ago. Under the Annual Sales Increase Awards Plan, a total of $10,400 was paid to the five salesmen having the largest percentage increase in dollar sales volume over the previous year. To be eligible for these awards, a salesman had to show a sales increase over the previous year. These awards were made at the January sales meeting, and the winners were determined by dividing the dollar amount of

EXHIBIT 2 Salesmen's earnings and incentive awards in the current year

| Salesmen | Sales | | Annual sales increase awards | | Weekly sales increase awards (total accrued) | Earnings* |
	Previous year	Current year	Increase in sales (percent)	Award		
Allen	$ 330,264	$ 329,216	(0.3%)	—	$1,012	$30,000†
Campbell	1,192,192	1,380,240	15.8	$3,000 (2d)	2,244	88,617
Duvall	—	414,656	—	—	—	30,000†
Edwards	—	419,416	—	—	—	30,000†
Gatewood	358,528	358,552	(0.1)	400 (5th)	1,104	18,513
Hammond	414,936	414,728	—	—	420	30,000†
Logan	—	447,720	—	—	—	30,000†
Mason	645,032	825,088	27.9	4,000 (1st)	3,444	49,756
O'Bryan	343,928	372,392	8.3	1,000 (4th)	1,512	19,344
Samuels	737,024	824,472	11.9	2,000 (3d)	1,300	49,713
Wates	370,712	342,200	(7.7)	—	612	17,532

* Exclusive of incentive awards and per diem.

† Guarantee of $600 per week or $30,000 per year.

each salesman's increase by his volume for the previous year with the percentage increases ranked in descending order. The salesmen's earnings under this plan for the current year are shown in Exhibit 2.

Under the second incentive plan, each salesman could win a Weekly Sales Increase Award for each week in which his dollar volume in the current year exceeded his sales for the corresponding week in the previous year. Beginning with an award of $4 for the first week, the amount of the award increased by $4 for each week in which the salesman surpassed his sales for the comparable week in the previous year. If a salesman produced higher sales during each of the 50 weeks in the current year, he received $4 for the 1st week, $8 for the 2d week, and $200 for the 50th week, or a total of $4,100 for the year. The salesman had to be employed by the company during the previous year to be eligible for these awards. A check for the total amount of the awards accrued during the year was presented to the salesman at the sales meeting held in January. Earnings of the salesmen under this plan for the current year are shown in Exhibit 2.

The company frequently used "spiffs" to promote the sales of special items. The salesman was paid a spiff, which usually was $4, for each order he obtained for the designated items in the promotion.

For the past three years in recruiting salesmen, Mr. McDonald had guaranteed the more qualified applicants a weekly income while they learned the business and developed their respective territories. During the current year five salesmen, Allen, Duvall, Edwards, Hammond, and Logan, had a guarantee of $600 a week, which they drew against their commissions. If the year's cumulative commissions for any of these salesmen were less than their cumulative weekly drawing accounts, they received no commissions. The commission and drawing accounts were closed on December 31 so each salesman began the new year with a zero balance in each account.

The company did not have a stated or written policy specifying the maximum length of time a salesman could receive a guarantee if his commissions continued to be less than his draw. Mr. McDonald held the opinion that the five salesmen who currently had guarantees would quit if these guarantees were withdrawn before their commissions reached $30,000 per year.

Mr. McDonald stated that he was convinced the annual earnings of Outdoor's salesmen had fallen behind earnings for comparable selling positions, particularly in the past six years. As a result, he felt that the company's ability to attract and hold high-caliber professional salesmen was being adversely affected. He strongly expressed the opinion that each salesman should be earning $50,000 annually.

Compensation Plan Proposals

In December of the current year, Mr. McDonald met with his comptroller and production manager, who were the only other executives of the company, and solicited their ideas concerning changes in the company's compensation plan for salesmen.

The comptroller pointed out that the salesmen having guarantees were not producing the sales that had been expected from their territories. He was concerned that the annual commissions earned by four of the five salesmen on guarantees were approximately half or less than their drawing accounts.

Furthermore, according to the comptroller, several of the salesmen who did not have guarantees were producing a relatively low volume of sales year after year. For example, annual sales remained at relatively low levels for Gatewood, O'Bryan, and Wates, who had been working four to five years in their respective territories.

The comptroller proposed that guarantees be reduced to $250 per week plus commissions at the regular rate on all sales. The $250 would not be drawn against commissions as was the case under the existing plan but would be in addition to any commissions earned. In the comptroller's opinion, this plan

EXHIBIT 3   Comparison of earnings in current year under existing guarantee plan with earnings under the comptroller's plan*

Salesmen	Sales	Existing plan			Comptroller's plan		
		Com-missions	Guar-antee	Earnings	Com-missions	Guar-antee	Earnings
Allen	$329,216	$16,753	$30,000	$30,000	$16,753	$12,500	$29,253
Duvall	414,656	21,879	30,000	30,000	21,879	12,500	34,379
Edwards	419,416	22,165	30,000	30,000	22,165	12,500	34,665
Hammond	358,552	18,513	30,000	30,000	18,513	12,500	31,013
Logan	447,720	23,863	30,000	30,000	23,863	12,500	36,363

* Exclusive of incentive awards and per diem.

would motivate the salesmen to increase sales rapidly since their incomes would rise directly with their sales. The comptroller presented Exhibit 3, which showed the incomes of the five salesmen having guarantees in the current year as compared with the incomes they would have received under his plan.

From a sample check of recent shipments, the production manager had concluded that the salesmen tended to overwork accounts located within a 50-mile radius of their homes. Sales coverage was extremely light in a 60- to 100-mile radius of the salesmen's homes with somewhat better coverage beyond 100 miles. He argued that this pattern of sales coverage seemed to result from a desire by the salesmen to spend most evenings during the week at home with their families.

He proposed that the per diem be increased from $70 to $90 per day for Monday through Thursday, $42 for Friday, and $90 for Sunday if the salesman spent Sunday evening away from his home. He reasoned that the per diem of $90 for Sunday would act as a strong incentive for the salesmen to drive to the perimeters of their territories on Sunday evenings rather than use Monday morning for traveling. Further, he believed that the increase in per diem would encourage the salesmen to spend more evenings away from their homes, which would result in a more uniform coverage of the sales territories and an overall increase in sales volume.

The consultant from New York City recommended that the guarantees and per diem be retained on the present basis and proposed that Outdoor adopt what he called a "Ten Percent Self-Improvement Plan." Under the consultant's plan each salesman would be paid, in addition to the regular commission, a monthly bonus commission of 10 percent on all dollar volume over his sales in the comparable month of the previous year. For example, if a salesman sold $40,000 worth of merchandise in January of the current year and $36,000 in January of the previous year, he would receive a $400 bonus check in February. For salesmen on guarantees, bonuses would be in addition to earnings. The consultant reasoned that the bonus commission would motivate the salesmen, both those with and without guarantees, to increase their sales.

He further recommended the discontinuation of the two sales incentive plans currently in effect. He felt the savings from these plans would nearly cover the costs of his proposal.

Following a discussion of these proposals with the management group, Mr. McDonald was undecided on which proposal to adopt, if any. Further, he wondered if any change in the compensation of salesmen would alleviate all of the present problems.

Case 30

Puritan Drug Company*

On May 1, 1984, David Thomas transferred to the Syracuse Division of the Puritan Drug Company as divisional sales manager. Prior to his transfer, Thomas served as assistant to the vice president of sales in the company's New York headquarters location.

At the conclusion of Thomas' first month-end sales meeting held on June 6, 1984, Harvey Brooks, a salesman in one of the division's rural territories, informed Thomas of his wish to retire, effective the following month. Thomas was surprised by Brooks' announcement because Robert Jackson, the division manager, informed him that Brooks had recently requested and received a deferment of his retirement until he reached his 66th birthday in July 1985. Brooks' sole explanation was that he had "changed his mind."

Brooks' retirement posed a significant territorial reassignment problem for Thomas.

Background of the Syracuse Division

David Thomas became the divisional sales manager at the age of 29. He had joined Puritan Drug as a sales trainee after his graduation from Stanford University in 1978. From 1978 to 1980 he worked as a salesman. In the fall of 1980, the sales manager of the company made Thomas one of his assistants. Thomas assisted the sales manager in arranging special sales promotions of the lines of different manufacturers.

Thomas' predecessor in Syracuse, Harry L. Schultz, had served as divisional sales manager for 15 years before his death in April 1984. "H. L.," as Schultz was called, had also worked as a salesman for the drug wholesale house

* Copyright © 1985 by the President and Fellows of Harvard College

This case was prepared by Rowland T. Moriarty, Jr., as the basis for class discussion rather than to illustrate either effective or ineffective handling of an administrative situation. Reprinted by permission of the Harvard Business School.

that merged with Puritan Drug in 1964 and became its Syracuse Division. Although Thomas had made Schultz's acquaintance in the course of business, he did not know Schultz well. Over the past month many members of the divisional sales force often expressed their admiration and affection for Schultz. Several sales reps made a point of telling Thomas that "Old H. L." knew every druggist in 12 counties by their first name. Schultz, in fact, had died of a heart attack while trout fishing with the president of the Syracuse Pharmacists' Association. Robert Jackson remarked that most of the druggists in town attended Schultz's funeral.

The Syracuse Division of Puritan Drug was one of 74 wholesale drug divisions in the United States owned by the firm. Each division acted as a functionally autonomous unit maintaining its own warehouse, sales, buying, and accounting departments. While the divisional manager was responsible for the performance of the division, there were a number of line functions performed by the regional and national offices of Puritan Drug. As divisional sales manager, for example, David Thomas maintained a relationship with the regional office in Albany, which was responsible for assisting him in implementing marketing policies established by the central office in New York.

As a wholesaler, the Syracuse Division sold to retail druggists a broad product line of approximately 18,000 items. The product line consisted of just about anything and everything sold through drugstores except fresh food, tobacco products, newspapers, and magazines. In the Syracuse trading area, Puritan Drug competed with two other wholesalers; one carried substantially the same line of products as Puritan Drug, and the other carried a more limited line of drug products.

The Syracuse Division operated as a profitable family-owned wholesale drug house before its merger with Puritan Drug in 1964. While the division operated profitably since 1964, it had not shown a profit on sales equal to the average for the other wholesale drug divisions of Puritan Drug. From 1973 to 1984 the net sales of the division rose each year. However, because competitors did not make available their sales figures, it was impossible to ascertain whether this increase in sales represented a change in the competitive situation or merely a general trend of increasing business volume in the Syracuse trading area. While Schultz was of the opinion that the increase had been at the expense of competitors, the Albany office maintained that since the trend of increase was less than that of other divisions in the northern New York region, the Syracuse Division may have actually lost ground competitively. A new technique for calculating the potential wholesale purchasing power of retail drugstores, adopted shortly before Thomas' transfer, indicated that the share of the wholesale drug market controlled by the Syracuse Division was below both the median and the mean for other Puritan Drug divisions.

Only a handful of the division's current work force was employed by the family-owned firm prior to its merger with Puritan Drug in 1964. H. L. Schultz was the one remaining executive whose employment in the Syracuse Division antedated the merger; only two sales reps, Harvey Brooks and Clifford Nelson, had sold for the predecessor company.

Many of the company executives and sales reps, although not employed by the predecessor company, nevertheless had employment histories with Puritan Drug going back to the 1960s and 1970s. Of those employees hired prior to 1974, only Robert Jackson, the division manager, had an undergraduate degree, earned at a local YMCA evening college. The more recently hired employees were, without exception, university or pharmacy college graduates. None of the younger employees were promoted when recent vacancies occurred for the jobs of divisional warehouse operations manager and divisional merchandise manager in Syracuse. Two of the younger employees, however, had recently been transferred to similar positions in other divisions.

The Syracuse Division Sales Force

From the time Thomas assumed Schultz's duties in early May, he had devoted four days a week to the task of traveling through each sales territory with the sales rep who covered it. He had made no changes in the practices or procedures of the sales force. Brooks' retirement request provided the first occasion where Thomas could make a nonroutine decision.

When Thomas took charge of the Syracuse Division sales force, it consisted of nine sales reps and four trainees. Four of the sales reps (Frederick Taylor, Edward Harrington, Grace Howard, and Linda Donnelly) had joined the company under the sales training program for college graduates initiated early in the 1970s. The other five sales reps had been with the company many years. Harvey Brooks and Clifford Nelson were the most senior in service. William Murray joined the company as a warehouse employee in 1960 at the age of 19. He became a sales rep in 1965. Walter Miller joined Puritan Drug as a sales rep in 1965 when the wholesale drug firm that he had previously worked for went out of business. Miller, who was 48 years old, had been a wholesale drug sales rep since the age of 20. Albert Simpson came to Puritan Drug after working as a missionary salesman for a manufacturer. Simpson, who joined the company in 1968 at age 26, had earlier served as an officer in the Army Medical Corps.

The four sales trainees graduated from college in June 1983. When Thomas arrived in Syracuse, they were in the last phase of their 12-month training program and were spending much of their time traveling with the experienced sales reps. Thomas believed that Schultz hired the trainees to cover anticipated turnover of sales reps and trainees and to implement the New York office's policy of getting more intensive coverage of each market area. The trainees expected to receive territory assignments, either in the Syracuse Division or elsewhere, on the completion of their training period at the end of June 1984.

Thomas had not seen very much of the sales reps as a group. His acquaintance with them had been formed by the one month-end sales meeting he attended and through his travels with them through their territories.

Walter Miller. Thomas was of the opinion that Walter Miller was a very easy-going, even-tempered person. He seemed to be very popular with the other sales reps and with his customers. Thomas thought that Miller liked him because he had commented to Thomas several times that his suggestions had been very helpful.

Harvey Brooks. Harvey Brooks had not been particularly friendly. Thomas observed that Brooks was well liked because of his good humor and friendly manner with everyone. Thomas did notice, however, that Brooks intimated that the sales manager should defer to Brooks' age, experience, and judgment. Brooks and his wife lived in the town of Oswego.

On June 4, 1984, Thomas traveled with Brooks, and they visited five of Brooks' accounts. Thomas filed a routine report with the Albany office on the sales rep's field work:

Points requiring attention: Not using merchandising equipment; not following weekly sales plan. Pharmaceutical business going to competitors because of lack of interest. Too much time spent on idle chatter. Only shows druggists what "he thinks they will buy." Tends to sell easy items instead of profitable ones.

Steps taken for correction: Explained shortcomings and demonstrated how larger, more profitable orders could be obtained by following sales plan—did just that by getting the biggest order ever written for Carthage account.

Remarks: Old-time "personality." Should do terrific volume if trained on new merchandising techniques.

On a similar form completed by H. L. Schultz on the basis of his travels with Brooks on March 3, 1984, the following comments were made:

Points requiring attention: Not getting pharmaceutical business. Not following promotion plans.

Steps taken for correction: Told him about these things.

Remarks: Brooks made this territory—can sell anything he sets his mind to—a real drummer—very popular with his customers.

Grace Howard. Grace Howard (age 29) was the oldest of the sales reps who had passed through the formal sales training program. Thomas considered her earnest and conscientious. Howard had increased her sales each year. Although Thomas did not consider Howard to be the "sales rep type," he noted that Howard was quite successful in using the merchandising techniques that Thomas wanted to implement.

William Murray. William Murray handled many of the big accounts in downtown Syracuse. Thomas believed that Murray was an excellent sales rep who considered himself "very smooth." Thomas had been surprised at the affront Murray had taken when he had offered a few suggestions to improve Murray's selling technique. William Murray and his wife were good friends of the Jacksons, as well as the merchandise and operations managers and their wives. Thomas suspected that Murray had expected to be Schultz's successor.

Clifford Nelson. Clifford Nelson appeared to Thomas to be an earnest and conscientious sales rep. He had been amiable, but not cordial to Thomas. Thomas' report on Nelson's calls on 10 accounts on June 5, 1984, contained the following statements:

Points requiring attention: Rushing calls. Gets want book and tries to sell case lots on wanted items. Carries all merchandising equipment, but doesn't use it.

Steps taken for correction: Suggested change in routing; longer, better-planned calls; conducted presentation demonstration.

Remarks: Hard-working, conscientious, good salesman, but needs to be brought up-to-date on merchandising methods.

Schultz's comments on his observations of Nelson on March 4, 1984, were:

Points requiring attention: Uses the want book on the basis of most sales. Not pushing promotions.

Steps taken for correction: Discussed shortcomings.

Remarks: Nelson really knows how to sell—visits every customer each week. Hard worker—very loyal—even pushes goods with very low commission.

On the day Thomas traveled with Nelson, the sales rep suggested that Thomas have dinner at the Nelsons' home. Thomas accepted the invitation, but at the end of the day Nelson took him to a restaurant in Watertown instead, explaining that he did not want to inconvenience his wife because his two daughters were home from college on vacation.

Albert Simpson. Albert Simpson caused Thomas considerable concern. Simpson continually complained about sales management procedures, commission rates, the ''lousy service of the warehouse people,'' and similar matters at the sales meeting. Thomas believed that while most of his complaints were valid, the matters were usually trivial, and that the other sales reps did not complain about any of these matters. Thomas mentioned his difficulties with Simpson to Robert Jackson, the district manager. Jackson replied that Simpson had been very friendly with Schultz. Simpson seemed quite popular with his customers.

Frederick Taylor. Frederick Taylor was, in Thomas' opinion, the most ambitious, aggressive, and argumentative sales rep in the division. He had been employed by the company since his graduation from the University of Rochester in 1980, first as a trainee, and then as a sales rep. Taylor had substantially increased the sales volume of his territory. He persuaded Schultz to assign him six inactive hospital accounts in July 1982. Within six months, he was able to generate sales to these accounts in excess of $50,000. While the other sales reps considered Taylor "cocky" and a "big spender," Thomas regarded Taylor's attitude as one of independence. If Taylor agreed with a sales plan, he worked hard to achieve its objectives; if he did not agree, he would not cooperate. Thomas thought that he had been successful in working with Taylor.

Linda Donnelly. Linda Donnelly impressed Thomas as being unsure of herself, confused, and overworked. Thomas attributed these difficulties to Donnelly's attempts to serve too many accounts in too large a territory. Donnelly was very receptive to Thomas' suggestions on how to improve her work. Thomas believed that, at age 24, Donnelly would improve with proper guidance. Donnelly had raised her sales to a point enabling her to move from salary to commissions in March 1984.

Edward Harrington. Edward Harrington (age 25) was the only sales rep who continued to work on a salary basis. His sales volume was insufficient to sustain the income of $1,500 a month, the company minimum for sales reps with more than one year's experience. Harrington was very apologetic about being on a salary. Thomas believed that Harrington's determination to "make good" would be realized through his conscientiousness. When he was assigned the territory in 1982, it consisted largely of uncontacted accounts. The volume of sales in the territory tripled over the past two years. Thomas felt that Harrington appreciated all the help given and that, in time, Harrington would be an excellent salesman.

Commission and Turnover Rates at Puritan Drug

Sales commission rates were paid to the sales force as follows:

Brooks and Nelson	2.375%
Miller and Donnelly	2.25
Murray and Simpson	2.125
Howard and Taylor	2

Expense accounts amounted to about .75 percent of sales. Thomas explained the differences in commission rates in terms of the differential product commissions set by the company. Higher commission rates were given on items the company wished to "push," such as pharmaceuticals and calendar promotion items.

While all four trainees seemed to be good prospects, they were somewhat of an unknown quantity to Thomas. He had held training conferences with them, and thought they performed rather poorly. He was concerned that Schultz had neglected their training, yet the reps were eager for assigned territories. They indicated this desire to Thomas at every possible opportunity.

The turnover of the Syracuse Division sales force had been quite low among the senior sales reps. Only six of the graduates of the sales training program had left the division since 1979. Two were promoted to department heads in other Puritan Drug divisions. The remaining four left to work for drug manufacturers. Drug manufacturers valued sales reps with wholesaling experience, and wholesalers who competed with Puritan Drug did not offer any training programs. Consequently, there were many opportunities for a sales rep who left Puritan Drug.

Sales Management at Puritan Drug

Throughout the month of May, Thomas devoted considerable thought to improving the sales performance of the Syracuse Division. He had accepted the transfer to this job at the urging of Richard Topping, vice president in charge of sales and his prior boss. Thomas was one of a dozen young employees whom Topping had brought into the New York office as assistants to the top sales executives. None of these young assistants remained in the New York office for more than three years. Topping had made a policy of offering them field assignments so that they could "show their stuff."

Thomas had observed the performance records of other divisional sales managers while he worked in New York. He knew that some sales managers had achieved substantial improvements on the past performances of their divisions. Thomas believed that the sales performance of his own division could be enhanced by improving the sales management plan. He also knew that the share of the Syracuse market for wholesale purchases of retail drugstores[1] held by Puritan Drug was 20.05 percent, compared to a 48 percent share for some of the other divisions.

Thomas remembered that Topping had regularly focused his staff's attention on the qualitative aspects of sales policy. Thomas had assisted Topping in implementing merchandising plans to utilize the sales reps' efforts to minimize the handling cost of their sales, and to maximize the gross margin.

The company promoted a three-step sales plan for increased profitability:

1. Sales of larger average value per line of the order were encouraged because the cost of processing and filling each line of an order was practically constant.
2. Sales of larger total value were encouraged because the delivery cost for orders having a total weight between 20 and 100 pounds was practically constant.
3. Because some manufacturers offered margins considerably larger than others, sales of higher margin items were encouraged. Sales commissions

---

[1] The New York market analysis section calculated the potential wholesale sales for retail drugstores. This market estimate, called the PWPP (potential wholesale purchasing power), was calculated for each county by adjusting retail drugstore sales to an estimate of the purchases of goods from wholesalers.

varied with the margins available to Puritan Drug on the products the sales reps sold.

The headquarters office also sought to increase the effectiveness of Puritan Drug promotions by setting up a sales calendar. The sales calendar coordinated the activities of all Puritan Drug divisions so that during a given calendar period, every company account could be solicited for those specific items which yielded attractive margins. The sales calendar required that the sales reps in each division follow a fairly prescribed pattern in selling to each individual account. The divisional sales managers were responsible for the coordination of the activities of their sales reps. Thomas believed that his predecessor had never really accepted the sales patterns prescribed by the New York office.

The national office also required each division to keep uniform sales and market analysis records. In the New York office, Thomas had developed a familiarity with the uses of these records. He inherited from Schultz a carefully maintained system of sales department records.

The division trading area formed the basis of the sales and market analysis record system. The economics of selling costs, transportation costs of delivery, and sales reps' traveling expenses determined the limits of the trading area. Thomas knew from his own experience, however, that delineation of trading areas was heavily influenced by tradition, geography, number of sales reps, number of possible sales contacts, estimated market potential, competition, and agreements with adjacent Puritan Drug divisions. The Rochester and Albany trading areas bordered the Syracuse Division on the east, south, and west; Canada bordered the division in the north. (A map of this division is included as Exhibit 1.)

Since his arrival, Thomas had formed the opinion that the present territories had been established without careful regard for the number of stores in the area, the sales potential, or the travel involved. Although he had not yet studied any one territory carefully, Thomas suspected that all his sales reps skimmed the cream from many of their accounts. He believed that they simply did not have adequate time to do a thorough selling job in each store. Exhibit 2 provides information on sales and sales potential by county. Exhibits 3 and 4 provide selected data on individual territory assignments and performance.

Sales Territories of Harvey Brooks and Clifford Nelson

Harvey Brooks' sales territory included accounts scattered through small towns in four rural counties northeast of Syracuse (see Exhibit 5). Brooks originally developed the accounts for the predecessor company. At the time he undertook this task in 1954, a competing service wholesaler had established a mail-order business with the area's rural druggists. Brooks "took to the road" to build sales with personal service. He had been hired specifically for this job because he was a native of the area and an experienced "drummer."

EXHIBIT 1 Syracuse Division trading area in upstate New York. Salesmen's assignments

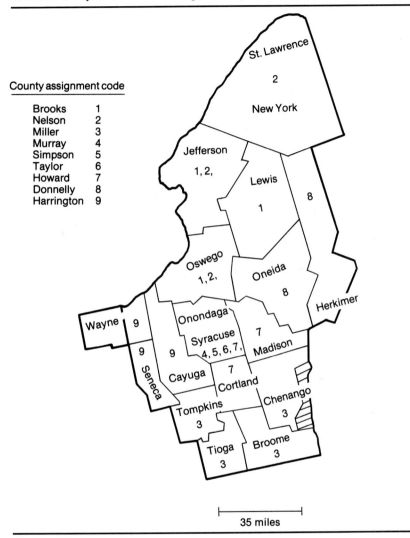

County assignment code

Brooks   1
Nelson   2
Miller   3
Murray   4
Simpson   5
Taylor   6
Howard   7
Donnelly   8
Harrington 9

35 miles

EXHIBIT 2 Selected data on sales and sales potentials, by counties

County	Salesman[a] code	Population (000s)	Percent of division	Retailers								Hospitals			Miscellaneous sales (000s)
				Sold	Inactive accounts	Accounts not sold	Total	Potential wholesale purchasing power (000s)	Percent of division PWPP	Sales[b] (000s)	Sales percent of PWPP	Sold	Not sold	Sales (000s)	
St. Lawrence	2	117.2	6.3%	23	1	2	26	$ 2,725	4.4%	$ 1,020	26.9%	2	4	$ 20	$ 15
Jefferson	1,2	90.2	4.9	34	—	—	34	3,265	5.3	918	28.2	2	2	10	—
Lewis	1	24.8	1.3	8	—	—	8	653	1.0	215	32.2	—	1	—	8
Herkimer	8	69.3	3.7	10	6	1	17	1,560	2.5	245	15.7	—	2	—	—
Oswego	1,2	97.8	5.3	25	1	—	26	3,350	5.5	933	27.1	1	2	—	25
Oneida	8	285.4	15.5	46	14	12	72	8,700	14.2	838	10.5	—	13	—	18
Wayne	9	76.6	4.1	4	—	1	5	618	1.0	138	22.3	—	—	—	—
Cayuga	9	75.6	4.1	12	4	—	16	1,403	2.3	253	18.0	2	—	10	68
Onondaga	4,5,6,7	474.8	25.8	98	9	13	120	19,118	31.2	5,415	28.7	6	9	270	480
Madison	7	59.7	3.2	12	2	3	17	3,125	5.1	653	20.9	—	2	—	60
Seneca	9	34.4	1.9	6	1	3	10	1,395	2.3	210	15.0	2	1	15	—
Cortland	7	45.4	2.5	6	2	1	9	1,275	2.1	403	31.5	—	2	—	—
Chenango	3	48.2	2.6	4	2	6	12	1,420	2.3	158	11.1	—	3	—	—
Tompkins	3	75.7	4.1	9	1	4	14	2,038	3.3	330	16.2	—	5	—	—
Tioga	3	46.2	2.5	4	—	7	11	805	1.3	200	24.8	—	—	—	—
Broome	3	225.3	12.2	22	2	13	37	9,925	16.2	633	6.4	8	8	—	45
Totals		1,846.6	100.0%	323	45	66	434	$61,375	100.0%	$12,562	20.5%	15	54	$325	$719

[a] County assignment code:
Brooks – 1 Murray – 4 Howard – 7
Nelson – 2 Simpson – 5 Donnelly – 8
Miller – 3 Taylor – 6 Harrington – 9

[b] Excludes miscellaneous sales, sales to hospitals, and house sales.

EXHIBIT 3   Selected data on sales reps' territory assignments by county

Sales rep	County	Sales 1984[a]	Active[b] accounts	PWPP[c]	Assigned[b] accounts
Miller	Chenango	$ 154,755	4	$ 1,417	15
	Tompkins	332,250	9	2,038	19
	Tioga	199,195	4	805	11
	Broome	675,750	22	9,928	45
Total		1,361,950	39	14,188	90
Brooks	Jefferson	365,085	16	2,265	18
	Lewis	215,985	8	653	9
	Oswego	924,650	25	2,675	28
Total		1,150,720	49	5,593	55
Howard	Onondaga	572,543	14	2,275	14
	Madison	652,125	12	3,125	19
	Cortland	402,500	6	1,275	11
Total		1,627,168	32	6,675	44
Murray	Onondaga	1,890,383	33	5,563	44
Total		1,890,383	33	5,563	44
Nelson	St. Lawrence	1,020,440	25	2,725	32
	Jefferson	556,298	20	1,000	20
	Oswego	6,950	1	675	1
Total		1,583,688	46	4,400	53
Simpson	Onondaga	1,834,815	29	7,520	48
Total		1,834,815	29	7,520	48
Taylor	Onondaga	1,595,183	29	3,760	29
Total		1,595,183	29	3,760	29
Donnelly	Herkimer	242,650	10	1,560	19
	Oneida	937,500	46	8,700	85
Total		1,180,150	56	10,260	104
Harrington	Wayne	136,000	4	618	5
	Cayuga	317,500	14	1,403	18
	Seneca	271,950	8	1,395	13
Total		725,450	26	3,416	36
Hospitals	Taylor (Syracuse)	270,000			
	Nelson/ Harrington	55,000			
House accounts		$ 1,322,530			
Total division sales		$14,951,910			

[a] The figure by sales rep includes sales to chain and independent drugstores and to miscellaneous accounts, but does not include sales to hospitals or house accounts indicated at the foot of the table.

[b] Includes hospitals and other recognized drug outlets in the territory.

[c] No potential is calculated for hospitals or miscellaneous sales. However, where a county is divided among several sales reps, the potential sales figure for each rep is obtained by allocating the county potential in proportion to the total *number* of potential drugstore and miscellaneous accounts in that county assigned to that rep.

EXHIBIT 4 Summary data on sales reps' performance

	1984 sales (000s)	Percent of total sales	1984 PWPP[a] (000s)	Percent of total PWPP	Sales percent of PWPP	1984 active accounts[b] No.	Percent	1984 assigned accounts[b] No.	Percent	Active accounts percent of assigned	1984 sales per active account	PWPP per assigned account[c]	1984 commissions
I													
Miller	$ 1,363	10.2%	$14,188	23.2%	9.6%	39	11.5%	90	17.9%	43.4%	$35,000	$157,750	$30,675
Brooks	1,505	11.3	5,593	9.1	27.0	49	14.5	55	10.9	89.0	30,750	101,500	35,725
Murray	1,890	14.2	5,563	9.1	34.0	33	9.8	44	8.8	75.0	57,250	126,250	40,200
Nelson	1,585[d]	11.9	4,400	7.2	36.0	46	13.6	53	10.5	85.0	34,500	83,000	38,500
Simpson	1,835	13.8	7,520	12.2	24.5	29	8.6	48	9.5	60.5	63,375	156,750	39,000
Subtotal	$ 8,178	61.4%	$37,264	60.8%	22.0%	196	58.0%	290	57.6%	67.2%	$58,450	$128,500	
II													
Howard	$ 1,628	12.2%	$ 6,675	10.9%	24.4%	32	9.5%	44	8.7%	72.7%	$50,900	$151,500	$ 3,300
Taylor	1,595[d]	12.0	3,760	6.1	42.4	28	8.3	29	5.8	96.5	66,750	129,500	31,900
Donnelly	1,180	8.9	10,260	16.7	11.5	56	16.5	104	20.7	53.8	21,050	98,750	26,550
Harrington	725[d]	5.5	3,415	5.5	21.3	26	7.7	36	7.2	72.3	27,875	95,000	18,000
Subtotal	$ 5,128[d]	38.6%	$24,110	39.2%	21.3%	142	42.0%	213	42.4%	66.7%	$36,188	$113,250	
Total	$13,306[d]	100.0%	$61,374	100.0%	21.7	338	100.0%	503	100.0%	67.0%	$39,325	$122,000	
Hospital sales by:													
Taylor	$ 270												
Nelson	30												
Harrington	25												
House sales:	1,322												
Grand total	$14,953												

a No potential is calculated for hospital or miscellaneous sales. However, where a county is divided among several sales reps the potential sales figure for each rep is obtained by allocating the county potential in proportion to the total *number* of potential drugstore and miscellaneous accounts in that county assigned to that rep.

b Includes hospitals and other recognized drug outlets in the territory.

c Understated since hospitals and miscellaneous accounts are included in the assigned accounts listed but not in the potential.

d Excluding hospital sales.

EXHIBIT 5 Counties sold by Brooks and Nelson

In 1959, Clifford Nelson, a friend of Brooks, became a division sales rep. At the suggestion of Brooks, he covered other accounts in the same four-county area. Nelson previously had been a sales rep for a proprietary medicine firm. He was seven years younger than Brooks. Since 1955, Brooks and Nelson each had had a number of accounts in the four-county area. (The list of their accounts appears as Exhibits 6 and 7.) Thomas noticed that the commission incomes Brooks and Nelson received had been stable over the years.

EXHIBIT 6 Accounts sold by Harvey Brooks, by counties, with 1984 purchases

Jefferson County			Oswego County			Lewis County		
Adams Center	D	$ 8,925	Calosse	D	$ 4,273	Beaver Falls	D	$ 9,525
(Alexandria Bay)	D	45,750	Central Square	D	4,643	Croghan	D	61,493
(Alexandria Bay)	D	39,475	Constantia	M	180	Harrisville	D	46,290
Bellville	D	5,250	Cleveland	M	975	Lowville	D	59,220
(Carthage)	D	152,500	(Fulton)	D	37,800	Lowville	D	10,785
Chaumont	D	1,510	(Fulton)	D	61,275	Lyons Falls	D	15,060
(Clayton)	D	26,575	(Fulton)	D	69,500	Port Leydon	D	5,813
(Clayton)	D	41,000	(Fulton)	D	96,000	Turin	M	7,800
Deferiet	D	923	Hannibal	D	9,725	County total:		$215,986
Dexter	D	29,175	Hastings	M	9,600	Territory total: $1,505,724		
Ellisburg	D	590	Lacona	M	1,155			
LaFargeville	D	1,305	Mexico	D	39,750			
Plessis	D	2,200	Oswego	D	30,188			
Redwood	M	270	(Oswego)	D	51,900			
Rodman	D	8,025	(Oswego)	D	60,250			
Sackets Harbor	D	1,613	(Oswego)	D	102,500			
County total:		$365,086	(Oswego)	D	109,750			
			(Oswego)	D	56,075			
			Oswego	H	38			
			Parish	M	12,900			
			Phoenix	D	24,325			
			(Pulaski)	D	21,875			
			(Pulaski)	D	72,700			
			Sandy Creek	D	35,325			
			West Monroe	D	11,950			
			County total:		$924,652			

Code: D = Independent drugstore; M = miscellaneous account; H = Hospital.

Note: Accounts in parentheses are those indicated by Nelson as the ones he wanted from Brooks. These accounts total $1,044,963 (87.7 percent of Brooks' sales in Jefferson County, 80 percent in Oswego County, or 69.4 percent of the territory total). Added to Nelson's 1983 sales, this would increase his volume 65 percent to $2,658,018. Brooks' old territory would be left with $460,758 in sales.

A Visit from Clifford Nelson

On the morning of June 9, three days after the June sales meeting, Thomas saw Clifford Nelson come in the front door of the Syracuse Division offices. Although Nelson passed within 30 feet of Thomas' desk, he did not appear to notice Thomas. Nelson walked through the office area directly to the partitioned space where Robert Jackson's private office was located. Twenty minutes later, Nelson emerged from the division manager's office and made his way to Thomas' desk.

"Hi there, young fellah!" he shouted as he approached.

"Howdy, Cliff. Sit down and chat awhile," Thomas replied. "What got you out of bed so early?" he asked, knowing that Nelson must have risen at 6 o'clock to make the drive to Syracuse from his home in Watertown.

Nelson squeezed his bulky frame into the armchair next to the desk. "It's a shame Harvey is retiring," he said. "I never thought he could stand to give it

EXHIBIT 7 Accounts sold by Clifford Nelson, by counties, with 1984 purchases

St. Lawrence County			Jefferson County			Oswego County		
Canton	D	$ 98,100	Adams	C	$ 4,713	Pulaski	C	$6,825
Edwards	D	5,040	Carthage	C	5,325			
Edwards	M	14,138	Evans Mills	D	5,525			
Gouverneur	D	1,695	Philadelphia	D	9,450			
Gouverneur	D	70,373	Watertown	D	75,500			
Gouverneur	D	123,898	Watertown	D	11,850			
Heuvelton	D	810	Watertown	D	22,000			
Massena	D	84,443	Watertown	D	76,700			
Massena	D	25,478	Watertown	D	46,100			
Massena	C	18,360	Watertown	D	65,750			
Massena	C	16,688	Watertown	D	95,500			
Massena	H	285	Watertown	D	57,500			
Madrid	D	10,740	Watertown	D	24,250			
Morristown	D	20,483	Watertown	D	2,135			
Norfolk	D	22,463	Watertown	D	28,300			
Norwood	D	23,543	Watertown	C	9,075			
Ogdensburg	D	60,675	Watertown	C	14,925			
Ogdensburg	D	169,163	Watertown	M	1,700			
Ogdensburg	D	54,023	Watertown	H	315			
Ogdensburg	D	25,350	Watertown	H	9,000			
Ogdensburg	M	1,118	County total:		$565,613			
Ogdensburg	H	19,898						
Potsdam	D	115,830						
Potsdam	C	55,283						
Potsdam Falls	D	2,753						
County total:		$1,040,630						
Territorial total: $1,613,068								

Code: D = Independent drugstore; C = Chain drugstores; M = Miscellaneous account; H = Hospital.

up. I never knew anyone who enjoyed selling as much as Harvey—except maybe me.'' Nelson continued praising Brooks and telling anecdotes which illustrated his point until Thomas began to wonder whether Nelson thought that he was biased in some way against the retiring sales rep. Thomas recalled that he had made some critical remarks about Brooks to Jackson, but he could not recall any discussion of Brooks' shortcomings with the man himself, or any of the other sales reps. Nelson ended his remarks by saying, ''Old H. L. always said that Harvey was the best damn wholesale drug salesman he'd ever known.''

There was a brief silence, as Thomas did not realize that Nelson was finished. Finally Thomas said, ''You know, Cliff, I think we ought to have a testimonial dinner for Harvey at the July sales meeting.''

Nelson made no comment on Thomas' suggestion; instead, he went on to say, ''None of these green trainees will ever be able to take Harvey's place. Those druggists up there are old-timers. They would resent being high pressured by some kid blown up to twice his size with college degrees. No sir! You've got to sell 'em right in those country stores.''

Thomas questioned whether Nelson's opinion of the adaptability of the younger, college-educated sales reps was justified by the available evidence. He recalled that several of them with rural territories performed better against their May sales quotas than either Brooks or Nelson. Thomas was proud of his self-restraint when he commented, "Selling in a rural territory is certainly different."

"That's right, Dave. I wanted to make sure you understood these things before I told you." Nelson was nervously massaging his double chin between his thumb and forefinger.

Thomas looked at him with a quizzical expression. "Told me what?"

"I have just been talking to Robert Jackson. Well, I was talking to him about an understanding between Harvey and me. We always agreed that if anything should happen to the other, or he should retire, or something—well, we agreed that the one who remained should get to take over his choice of the other's accounts. We told H. L. about this and he said, 'Boys, what's OK by you is OK by me. You two developed that territory and you deserve to be rewarded for it.' Well, yes sir, that's the way it was."

Without pausing, Nelson went on, "I just told Jackson about it. He said that he remembered talking about the whole thing with H. L. 'Yes,' he said, 'Tell Thomas about it,' he said, 'Tell Thomas about it.' Harvey and I went over his accounts on Sunday. I went over his list of accounts with him and checked the ones that I want. Here is the list with the accounts all checked off.[2] I already know nearly all the proprietors. You'll see that—"

"Wait a minute, Cliff! Wait a minute!" Thomas interrupted. "You've lost me completely. In the first place, if there is any assignment of accounts to be made I'll do it. It will be done on a basis that is fair to the sales reps concerned, and profitable to the company. You know that."

"Dave, I'm only asking for what is fair." Nelson's face was flushed. Thomas noticed that the man he had always believed to be deliberately confident and self-possessed was now so agitated that it was difficult for him to speak. "I don't want my territory chopped up and handed to some green kid!"

Thomas noticed that everybody in the office was now watching Nelson. "Calm down, Cliff," he whispered to the sales rep, indicating with a nod of his head that others were watching.

"Don't talk to me that way!" replied Nelson. "I don't care. A man with 25 years' service deserves some consideration!"

"You're absolutely right, Cliff. You're absolutely right." As Thomas repeated his words, Nelson settled back in his chair. The typewriters started clattering again.

"Now, first of all, Cliff," as Thomas tried to return the conversation to a

---

[2] Nelson's selected accounts are the accounts in parentheses in Exhibit 6.

friendly basis. "Where did you get the idea that your territory was going to be 'chopped up'?"

"You said so yourself. You said it at the sales meeting the other day when you made that speech about how you were going to boost sales in Syracuse." Nelson emphasized his words by pounding the side of the desk with his masonic ring.

Thomas reflected for a moment. He recalled his speech at the sales meeting called, "How We Can Do a Better Job for Puritan Drug." The speech was a restatement of the merchandising policy of the New York office. He had mentioned that getting more profitable business would require that a larger percentage of the purchases of each account would have to come to Puritan Drug; that receiving a larger share of the business from each store would require more selling time in each store; and that greater concentration on each account would require reorganization of the sales territories. He realized that his future plans entailed reorganization of the territories. He had not anticipated, however, Nelson's reaction.

Finally, Thomas said, "I do plan to make some territorial changes—not right away—at least not until I have looked things over pretty darn carefully. Of course, you understand that our first duty is to make greater profits for the company. Some of our territories would be a great deal more profitable if they were organized and handled in a different manner."

"What are you going to do about Harvey's territory?" asked Nelson.

Since Thomas had not yet looked over the information about the territory, he was anxious not to commit himself to any course of action relating to it. "Well, I just haven't had a chance to study the situation yet," he replied. "If I could make the territory more profitable by reorganizing it, I guess that is what they would expect me to do."

"What about the promises the company made to me about letting me choose the accounts I want?" Nelson asked.

"You don't mean the company's promise; you mean Schultz's promise," Thomas corrected him.

"Well, if Schultz wasn't 'the company,' I don't see how you figure that you are!" Nelson's face resumed its flush.

"OK, Cliff. How about giving me a chance to look over the situation. You know that I want to do the right thing. Let me go over the list of the accounts you want. In a few days I can talk intelligently about the matter." Thomas felt that there was no point in carrying the discussion further.

"All right, Dave," said Nelson, rising. The two men walked toward the front entrance of the office. As they reached the top of the steps leading to the front door, Nelson turned to Thomas and offered his hand. "Look, Dave, I'm sorry I got so mad. You just can't imagine what this means to me. I know you'll see it my way when you know the whole story." Nelson's voice sounded strained.

Thomas watched the older man leave. He felt embarrassed, realizing that Nelson's parting words had been overheard by several manufacturers' representatives standing nearby.

A Conversation with the Division Manager

Thomas decided he would immediately discuss his conversation with Nelson with Jackson. He walked over to Jackson's office, and hesitated upon reaching the doorway. Jackson looked up, and indicated with a gesture that Thomas should take a seat.

Thomas sat down and waited for Jackson to speak. Jackson was occupied for the moment unwrapping a cigar. After a few moments of silence, Thomas opened the conversation. "Clifford Nelson just stopped by to speak to me."

"Yeah?" said Jackson, removing bitten flakes of tobacco from the end of his tongue.

"He said something about getting some of Harvey Brooks' accounts when Harvey retired," Thomas said in a deliberately questioning manner.

"Yeah."

Thomas continued, "Well, this idea of his was based on a promise that he said H. L. had made."

"Yeah. He told me that, too."

"Did Schultz make such a promise?" Thomas inquired.

"Hell, I don't know. It sounds like him." Jackson tilted back in his swivel chair.

"What shall I do about it?"

"Don't ask me; you're the sales manager." Jackson paused, holding his cigar away from his lips as if he were about to speak. Just as Thomas was about to say something, Jackson lurched forward to flick the ashes from his cigar into his ash tray. "Look here, Dave. I don't want any morale problems around here. You're the first of the 'wonder boys' to be put in charge of a department in this division. I don't want you to do anything to mess up the morale. We never had any morale problems when Schultz was around. We don't want anything like that in this division."

Thomas was momentarily bewildered. He knew from the way that Jackson used the phrase "wonder boys" that he was referring to the managers brought into the organization by Richard Topping.

Jackson went on, "Why the devil did you tell the reps that you were going to reassign the sales territories without even telling me?"

"But you were there when I said it."

"Said what?"

"Well, at the sales meeting, that one of the ways we were going to get more business was to reorganize the sales territory," Thomas replied.

"I certainly don't remember anything like that. Dave, you gave a good inspirational talk, but I sure can't remember anything about reassigning territories."

"Actually, I just mentioned the reorganization of territories in passing," Thomas smiled.

"I'll be damned. That sort of thing is always happening. Here everybody is frothing at the mouth about something that they think we are going to do and we haven't the slightest idea why they think we're going to do it. You know, probably the real reason Harvey Brooks is retiring, instead of staying on as he planned, was this fear of sales territory reorganization. Both he and Nelson know that their retirement pension is based on earnings from their last five years of active employment. Now that I think of it, three or four of the other sales reps have stopped during the last couple of days to tell me what a fine job they were doing. They probably had this territory reassignment stuff on their minds, too."

Jackson's cigar was no longer burning. He began groping under the papers on his desk for a match. Thomas took advantage of this pause in the conversation. "Mr. Jackson, I think there are some real advantages to be won by adjusting the sales territories. I think—"

"You still think that after today?" the division manager asked in a sarcastic tone.

"Why, yes! The profit made on sales to an individual account is related closely to delivery expense. The larger the total proportion of the account's business we get, the more profit we make because the delivery expense remains more or less constant."

"Look, Dave, you college computer types always have everything figured out, but sometimes that doesn't count. Morale is the important thing. The sales reps won't tolerate having their territories changed. I know that you have four trainees that you'd like to put out on territories. If you put them out on parts of the territories belonging to some of the more experienced reps—bam! God knows how many of our good sales reps would be left. I've never had any trouble with sales force morale since I've been manager of this division. Old Schultz, bless his soul, never let me down. He wasn't any damn Ph.D., but he could handle sales reps. Don't get off on the wrong foot with them, Dave. With the labor situation in the warehouse being what it is, I've just got too much on my mind. I don't want you creating more problems than I can handle. How 'bout it, boy!"

Jackson ground out his half-smoked cigar, looking steadily at Thomas.

Thomas was extremely upset with the division manager's implication that he lacked concern for sales rep morale. He had always thought of himself as very considerate. He realized that at the moment his foremost desire was to get away from Jackson.

Thomas rose from his chair, saying, "Mr. Jackson, you can count on me. I know you are right about this morale business."

"Atta boy," said the division manager. "It does us a lot of good to talk like this once in a while. Now, see if you can make peace with the sales reps. I want you to handle everything yourself."

"Well, thanks a lot," said Thomas, as he backed out of the office door.

As he walked through the office, he saw two manufacturers' representatives with whom he had appointments. His schedule of appointments that day prohibited him from doing more than gathering the material pertaining to the Nelson and Brooks territories.

Thomas Goes Home

Thomas left the office shortly after 5 o'clock to drive to a suburb of Syracuse. It was a particularly hot and humid day. Pre-Fourth of July traffic lengthened the drive home by nearly 20 minutes. When he finally turned into his own driveway, he felt as though his skin were caked with grime and perspiration. He got out of the car and walked around to the terrace at the rear of the house. Beth, his wife, was sitting in a deck chair, working on some papers.

"Hello, Dave. You're late," she said, looking up with a smile.

"I know it. Even the traffic was bad today." He dropped his suit coat on a glass-topped table and sprawled out full length on a chaise lounge. "I'm exhausted. And, boy, I am disgusted with myself."

"Bad day?"

"Awful. You just can't imagine how discouraging it is trying to get this job organized. You would think it would be obvious to everyone that what ails the Syracuse Division is the organization of the sales force," said Thomas, arranging a pillow under his head.

"I didn't realize that you thought anything was wrong with the Syracuse Division."

"Well, what I mean is that we now get only 20 percent of the potential wholesale business. If I could organize the sales force my way—well, God knows, maybe we could get 40 percent of the business. That is what the New York office watches for. The sales manager who increases his division's share of the market gets the promotions when they come along. I know Topping transferred me to this division because he knew these possibilities existed."

"I don't understand. Is Mr. Topping still your boss, or is Mr. Jackson?"

"Beth, it's terribly discouraging. While Jackson is my boss, I'll never get anywhere in Puritan Drug unless Topping and the other people in New York promote me."

"Don't you like Mr. Jackson?"

"I had a run-in with him today."

"You didn't!" she said as she laid her papers aside.

Thomas didn't anticipate his wife's reaction. He gazed up at the awning as if he did not notice her intent expression. "We didn't argue particularly. He just—well, he doesn't know too much about sales management. He put his foot down on my plans to reorganize the territories.''

"I can't understand why you would go and get yourself into a fight with your boss when you haven't even been here two months.''

"Honest, Beth, I didn't have any fight. Everything is OK. He just—well, do you want me to be a divisional sales manager all my life?''

"You're tired,'' she said sympathetically. "Why don't you go up and shower.''

"That sounds wonderful,'' he said, raising himself from the chaise lounge.

An Unexpected Caller

Thomas had just stepped out of the shower when he heard his wife calling to him. "Dave, Fred Taylor is here to see you.''

"Tell him I'll be down in just a minute. Offer him a drink, Beth.''

As he dressed, Thomas wondered why Fred Taylor had chosen the dinner hour to call. During the month since he had moved into his new home, no other sales rep had ever dropped by uninvited.

When Thomas came downstairs, he found Taylor sitting on the living room couch, a gin and tonic in his hand.

"Hello, Fred,'' said Thomas, crossing the room with his right hand extended. "You look as if you had a hot day. Why don't you take off your coat? If we go out to the terrace, you may get a chance to cool off.''

"Thanks, Dave,'' the visitor said as they moved out to the terrace. "I'm sorry to barge in this way, but I thought it was important.''

"Well, what's on your mind?'' asked Thomas as they sat down.

"I heard about what happened at the office today. I thought I'd come over and tell you that we stand behind you 100 percent.''

Thomas was perplexed by Taylor's words. He realized that Taylor probably was referring to his meeting with Nelson. Thomas said, "I'm not sure what you mean, Fred.''

"I heard that you and Nelson had it out this morning about changing the sales territories,'' Taylor replied.

Thomas smiled. Two thoughts entered his mind. He was amused at the proportions that the brief morning conversation had assumed. At the same time, he was curious to know how Taylor, who had presumably been in the field selling, had heard about the incident so quickly. Without hesitation he asked, "Where did you hear about this, Fred?''

"Bill Murray told me! He was down at the warehouse with Walter Miller when I stopped off to pick up a special narcotics order for a customer. They are all excited about this territory business. Murray said Nelson came out to his house at lunch time and told him about it. Everybody figured that you were going to change the territories when you started traveling around with each of the reps, especially after what you said at the sales meeting.''

"Well, the reason I went on the road with each of the reps, Fred," said Thomas, "was so that I could learn more about their selling problems while, at the same time, meet the customers.''

Taylor smiled, "Sure, but when you started filling out a rating sheet on each account, I couldn't help thinking you had some reason for it.''

Thomas realized that Taylor had spoken with irony in his voice, but he thought it was better to let the matter pass. Since he was planning to use the information he had gathered for the reorganization of the sales territories, he decided that he would be frank with Taylor. To find out what the young sales rep's reaction might be to territorial changes, he said, "Fred, I've thought a lot about making some changes in the territories—"

Taylor interrupted him. "That's terrific. I'm sure glad to hear that. I don't like to speak ill of the dead, but old Schultz really gave the trainees the short end of the stick when he put us on territories. He either gave us a territory of uncontacted accounts where it was like beating our heads against a stone wall. Some of us actually quit, like the two guys who trained with me. Or, Schultz gave us replacement territories where some of the best accounts had been handed over to the older reps. Well, I know for a fact that when I took over my territory from Mike Green, Bill Murray and Albert Simpson got 12 of Green's best accounts. And, damn it, I got more sales out of what was left than Green ever did; Murray and Simpson's total sales didn't go up. It took me a while, but I had the laugh at every sales meeting when our monthly sales figures were announced.''

"Is that right?" said Thomas.

"Damn right! And I wasn't the only one. That's why those old duffers are so down on the four of us that have come with the division since the mid-1970s. We've beaten them at their own game.''

"Do you think that Harrington and Howard and Donnelly feel the same way?" asked Thomas.

"Think, hell! I know it! That's all we ever talk about. If you reorganize those territories and give us back the accounts that Schultz took away, you'll see some real sales records. Take, for example, the Medical Arts Pharmacy out by Mercy Hospital. Bill Murray got that one away from my territory and he calls there only once a week. If I could get that one back, I'd get in there three times a week, and get five times as much business.''

Thomas had to raise his hands in a gesture of protest. "Don't you have enough accounts already, Fred, to keep you busy?"

"Dave, I spend 50 hours a week on the road and I love it; but I know damn well that if I put some of the time I spend in the 'two-by-four' stores into some of those big juicy accounts like Medical Arts Pharmacy, I'd do even more business.''

Thomas commented, "I'm not particularly anxious to argue now, but if you start putting time into Medical Arts Pharmacy, what's going to happen to your sales to the two-by-four stores?"

Taylor quickly replied, "Those druggists all know me. They'd go right on buying."

Thomas did not agree with Taylor. He thought that Taylor realized this.

After a moment of silence, Taylor rose from his chair, saying, "I'd better scoot home. My family will be furious with me for being late when we have plans for the weekend."

The two men walked to Taylor's car. As Taylor climbed into his car, he said, "Dave, don't forget what I said. Harrington, Howard, Donnelly, and I stand behind you 100 percent. You won't ever hear us talk about going over to a competitor!"

"Who's talking about that?" asked Thomas.

"Well," said Taylor as he started the motor and shifted into gear, "I don't want to tell tales out of school."

"Sure," Thomas said quickly. "I'm sorry I asked. So long, Fred. I'll see you soon."

Part 7

Pricing Decisions

The cases in the pricing section of this book involve several different kinds of decisions. A firm's pricing strategy is extremely important because of the quickness with which a change can be implemented, because of the importance of price to consumers in their purchase decisions, and because of the direct impact of prices on profits.

The first important consideration in establishing a price for a product is the firm's pricing objectives. A firm striving for growth may utilize a totally different strategy from one who is seeking to discourage others from cutting prices or to desensitize consumers to price. Firms with objectives oriented around maximizing long-run profits may utilize different strategies than firms who are seeking to maximize short-run profits. Thus, the first step in establishing a price should be to clearly identify what the objectives are.

Two alternative strategies often utilized are skimming and penetration. A skimming strategy is one in which a high initial price is set, and the product is sold to all those consumers willing to pay this price. The price is then lowered somewhat, and the product is sold to those consumers willing to pay that price. This process continues for some time, "skimming the cream" off the top of the market with each price change. For example, when electronic calculators were first introduced, they were priced at more than $300. A number of scientific and engineering related organizations were willing to purchase the product at this price. The price was then lowered to the neighborhood of $150 to $200, and a number of other organizations were willing to purchase the product. Later, the price was reduced to the $50 to $100 range, and very many more buyers entered the market. Eventually, the price was lowered still further, and many more consumers entered the market.

A skimming strategy is appropriate when there are no close substitutes for the product and the demand is inelastic with respect to price. It is a very conservative policy allowing the marketer to recover as much of the costs as possible quickly in the event that demand is not that great. It also allows the marketer to accumulate money for aggressive penetration later when competition enters the market. A skimming strategy is an effective way to segment the market, as in the calculator example and in the case of the book market where a skimming strategy is used for hardcover books, and the paperback edition is later introduced using a penetration strategy.

A penetration strategy utilizes a low initial price in the hopes of penetrating a large proportion of the market in a short period of time. This strategy would be used when one or more of the following conditions existed:

a. High short-run price elasticity (for example, the low price of the Model-T Ford allowed many people to purchase a car for the first time).
b. Large economies of scale in production.
c. The probability of quick public acceptance.
d. The probability of quick competitive imitation.

The specific pricing decisions that have to be made include the price level to set, price variation including discount structure and geographic price differences, margins to be given to various intermediaries in the channels of distribution, and the determination of when to change the price structure.

A number of different pricing methods are utilized by organizations. Some use the cost-plus method, whereby a certain percentage is added to the firm's costs to establish their pricing. This method is often used by industrial marketers and by wholesalers and retailers. Other organizations use break-even analysis, marginal cost analysis, and/or marginal revenue analysis to determine their pricing structure. Still other organizations are price followers and use a strategy of meeting the prices of competitors.

The ideal way to determine the price that should be charged involves analyzing a number of variables before actually setting the price. Included would be:

1. *Consumer buying patterns.* What price would consumers expect to pay for this type of product? What are the important price points or price lines that different segments of the market desire?
2. *Product differentiation.* In what ways is the company's product different from the others on the market? What advantages does the product offer the consumer?
3. *What is the competitive structure* of the industry, and what stage of the product life cycle is the product in?
4. *How price sensitive* is total industry demand, and how price sensitive is demand for the individual firm's product? What is the size of the total market and what is the likelihood of economies of scale?
5. *What is the economic climate forecast,* and how sensitive is the demand of the product to changes in the economic climate?

6. *Legal and social considerations.* New interpretations of the Robinson-Patman Act (prohibiting price discrimination) and various state laws governing pricing must be taken into consideration.
7. *Cost structure of the firm.* The relationship between fixed costs and variable costs is extremely important in pricing decisions, as is the cost structure of the firm compared to competitors' pricing structure. Pricing strategy for a hotel, with a very low variable cost ratio, will of necessity be quite different than pricing strategy for a clothing manufacturer, which has a very high variable cost ratio.
8. *The overall marketing strategy for the product.* It is important to recognize that the pricing strategy must be consistent with all the other elements of the firm's marketing strategy.

Case 31

S.C. Johnson and Son, Limited (R)*

Four months ago, in November, George Styan had been appointed division manager of Innochem, at S.C. Johnson and Son, Limited[1] (SCJ), a Canadian subsidiary of S.C. Johnson & Son, Inc. Innochem's sole product line consisted of industrial cleaning chemicals for use by business, institutions, and government. George was concerned by the division's poor market share, particularly in Montreal and Toronto. Together, these two cities represented approximately 35 percent of Canadian demand for industrial cleaning chemicals, but less than 10 percent of Innochem sales. It appeared that SCJ distributors could not match the aggressive discounting practiced by direct-selling manufacturers in metropolitan markets.

Recently, George had received a rebate proposal from his staff designed to increase the distributor's ability to cut end user prices by "sharing" part of the total margin with SCJ when competitive conditions demanded discounts of 30 percent or more off the list price to end users. George had to decide if the rebate plan was the best way to penetrate price-sensitive markets. Moreover, he wondered about the plan's ultimate impact on divisional profit performance. George either had to develop an implementation plan for the rebate plan or draft an alternative proposal to unveil at the Distributors' Annual Spring Convention, three weeks away.

The Canadian Market for Industrial Cleaning Chemicals

Last year, the Canadian market for industrial cleaning chemicals was approximately $100 million at end user prices. Growth was stable at an overall rate of approximately 3 percent per year.

* Copyright © 1987, The University of Western Ontario. This case was written by Carolyn Vose under the supervision of Associate Professor Roger More for the sole purpose of providing material for class discussion at the School of Business Administration. Any use or duplication of the material in this case is prohibited except with the written consent of the School. Used with permission.

[1] Popularly known as Canadian Johnson Wax.

"Industrial cleaning chemicals" included all chemical products designed to clean, disinfect, sanitize, or protect industrial, commercial, and institutional buildings and equipment. The label was broadly applied to general purpose cleaners, floor maintenance products (strippers, sealers, finishes, and detergents), carpet cleaners and deodorizers, disinfectants, air fresheners, and a host of specialty chemicals such as insecticides, pesticides, drain cleaners, oven cleansers, and sweeping compounds.

Industrial cleaning chemicals were distinct from equivalent consumer products typically sold through grocery stores. Heavy-duty industrial products were packaged in larger containers and bulk and marketed directly by the cleaning chemical manufacturers or sold through distributors to a variety of end users. Exhibit 1 includes market segmentation by primary end user categories, including janitorial service contractors and the in-house maintenance departments of government, institutions, and companies.

EXHIBIT 1 Segmentation of the Canadian market for industrial cleaning chemicals

By end user category	
End user category	*Percent total Canadian market for industrial cleaning chemicals (end user value)*
Retail outlets	25%
Contractors	17
Hospitals	15
Industrial and office	13
Schools, colleges	8
Hotels, motels	6
Nursing homes	5
Recreation	3
Government	3
Fast food	2
Full-service restaurants	2
All others	1
Total	100% = $95 million

By product category	
Product category	*Percent total Canadian market for industrial cleaning chemicals*
Floor care products	40%
General purpose cleaners	16
Disinfectants	12
Carpet care products	8
Odor control products	5
Glass cleaners	4
All others	15
Total	100% = $95 million

Building Maintenance Contractors

In Canada, maintenance contractors purchased 17 percent of the industrial cleaning chemicals sold during 1980 (end user price). The segment was growing at approximately 10–15 percent a year, chiefly at the expense of other end user categories. *Canadian Business* reported, "Contract cleaners have made sweeping inroads into the traditional preserve of in-house janitorial staffs, selling themselves on the strength of cost efficiency."[2] Maintenance contract billings reached an estimated $1 billion last year.

Frequently, demand for building maintenance services was highly price sensitive, and since barriers to entry were low (small capitalization, simple technology), competition squeezed contractor gross margins below 6 percent (before tax). Variable cost control was a matter of survival, and only products bringing compensatory labour savings could command a premium price in this segment of the cleaning chemical market.

A handful of contract cleaners did specialize in higher margin services to prestige office complexes, luxury apartments, art museums, and other "quality-conscious" customers. However, even contractors serving this select clientele did not necessarily buy premium cleaning supplies.

In-House Maintenance Departments

Government

Last year, cleaning chemical sales to various government offices (federal, provincial, and local) approached $2 million. Typically, a government body solicited bids from appropriate sources by formally advertising for quotations for given quantities of particular cleaning chemicals. Although bid requests often named specific brands, suppliers were permitted to offer "equivalent substitutes." Separate competitions were held for each item and normally covered 12 months' supply with provision for delivery "as required." Contracts were frequently awarded solely on the basis of price.

Institutions

Like government bodies, most institutions were price sensitive owing to restrictive budgets and limited ability to "pass on" expenses to users. Educational institutions and hospitals were the largest consumers of cleaning chemicals in this segment. School boards used an open-bid system patterned on the government model. Heavy sales time requirements and demands for frequent delivery of small shipments to as many as 100 locations were characteristic.

Colleges and universities tended to be operated somewhat differently. Dan Stalport, one of the purchasing agents responsible for maintenance supplies at The University of Western Ontario, offered the following comments:

---

[2] "Contract Cleaners Want to Whisk Away Ring-Around-the-Office," *Canadian Business*, 1981, p. 22.

Sales reps come to UWO year 'round. If one of us (in the buying group) talks to a salesman who seems to have something—say, a labour-saving feature—we get a sample and test it. Testing can take up to a year. Floor covering, for example, has to be exposed to seasonal changes in weather and traffic.

If we're having problems with a particular item, we'll compare the performance and price of three or four competitors. There are usually plenty of products that do the job. Basically, we want value—acceptable performance at the lowest available price.

Hospitals accounted for 15 percent of cleaning chemical sales. Procurement policies at University Hospital (UH), a medium-sized (450-bed) facility in London, Ontario, were typical. UH distinguished between "critical" and "noncritical" products. Critical cleaning chemicals (i.e., those significantly affecting patient health, such as phenolic germicide) could be bought only on approval of the staff microbiologist, who tested the "kill factor." This measure of effectiveness was regularly retested, and any downgrading of product performance could void a supplier's contract. In contrast, noncritical supplies, such as general purpose cleaners, floor finishes, and the like, were the exclusive province of Bob Chandler, purchasing agent attached to the Housekeeping Department. Bob explained that performance of noncritical cleaning chemicals was informally judged and monitored by the housekeeping staff:

> Just last year, for example, the cleaners found the floor polish was streaking badly. We (the Housekeeping Department) tested and compared five or six brands—all in the ballpark price-wise—and chose the best.

Business

The corporate segment was highly diverse, embracing both service and manufacturing industries. Large volume users tended to be price sensitive—particularly when profits were low. Often, however, cleaning products represented such a small percentage of the total operating budget that the cost of searching for the lowest cost supplier would be expected to exceed any realizable saving. Under such conditions, the typical industrial customer sought efficiencies in the purchasing process itself, for example, by dealing with the supplier offering the broadest mix of janitorial products (chemicals, paper supplies, equipment, etc.). Guy Breton, purchasing agent for Securitech, a Montreal-based security systems manufacturer, commented on the time economies of "one-stop shopping":

> With cleaning chemicals, it simply isn't worth the trouble to shop around and stage elaborate product performance tests. I buy all our chemicals, brushes, dusters, toweling—the works—from one or two suppliers . . . buying reputable brands from familiar suppliers saves hassles—back orders are rare, and Maintenance seldom complains.

Distribution Channels for Industrial Cleaning Chemicals

The Canadian market for industrial cleaning chemicals was supplied through three main channels, each characterized by a distinctive set of strengths and weaknesses:

a. Distributor sales of national brands.
b. Distributor sales of private label products.
c. Direct sale by manufacturers.

Direct sellers held a 61 percent share of the Canadian market for industrial cleaning chemicals, while the distributors of national brands and private label products held shares of 25 percent and 14 percent, respectively. Relative market shares varied geographically, however. In Montreal and Toronto, for example, the direct marketers' share rose to 70 percent and private labellers' to 18 percent, reducing the national brand share to 12 percent. The pattern, shown in Exhibit 2, reflected an interplay of two areas of channel differentiation, namely, discount capability at the end user level and the cost of serving distant, geographically dispersed customers.

EXHIBIT 2 Effect of geography on market share of different distribution channels

Supplier type	Share nationwide	Share in Montreal and Toronto
Direct marketers	61%*	70%
Private label distributors	14	18
National brands distributors	25†	12

* Dustbane	17%
G.H. Wood	13
All others	13
Total	61%
† SCJ	8%
N/L	4
Airkem	3
All others	10
Total	25%

Distributor Sales of National Brand Cleaning Chemicals

National brand manufacturers, such as S.C. Johnson and Son, Airkem, and National Labs, produced a relatively limited range of "high-quality" janitorial products, including many special purpose formulations of narrow market interest. Incomplete product range, combined with shortage of manpower and limited warehousing, made direct distribution unfeasible in most cases. Normally, a national brand company would negotiate with middlemen who handled a broad array of complementary products (equipment, tools, and supplies) by different manufacturers. "Bundling" of goods brought the distributors cost efficiencies in selling, warehousing, and delivery by spreading fixed costs over a large sales volume. Distributors were, therefore, better able to absorb the costs of after-hour emergency service, frequent routine sales and service calls to many potential buyers, and shipments of small quantities of cleaning chemicals to multiple destinations. As a rule, the greater the geographic dispersion of customers, and the smaller the average order, the greater the relative economies of distributor marketing.

Comparatively high gross margins (approximately 50 percent of wholesale price) enabled national brand manufacturers to offer distributors strong marketing support and sales training along with liberal terms of payment and freight plus low minimum order requirements. Distributors readily agreed to handle national brand chemicals, and in metropolitan markets, each brand was sold through several distributors. By the same token, most distributors carried several directly competitive product lines. George suspected that some distributor salesmen only used national brands to "lead" with and tended to offer private label whenever a customer proved price sensitive, or a competitor handled the same national brand(s). Using an industry rule of thumb, George estimated that most distributors needed at least 20 percent gross margin on retail sales to cover sales commission of 10 percent, plus delivery and inventory expenses.

Distributor Sales of Private Label Cleaning Chemicals

Direct-selling manufacturers were dominating urban markets by aggressively discounting end user prices—sometimes below the wholesale price national brand manufacturers charged their distributors. To compete against the direct seller, increasing numbers of distributors were adding low-cost private label cleaning chemicals to their product lines. Private labelling also helped differentiate a particular distributor from others carrying the same national brand(s).

Sizable minimum order requirements restricted the private label strategy to only the largest distributors. Private label manufacturers produced to order, formulating to meet low prices specified by distributors. The relatively narrow margins (30–35 percent wholesale price) associated with private label manufacture precluded the extensive marketing and sales support national brand manufacturers characteristically provided to distributors. Private label producers pared their expenses further still by requiring distributors to bear the cost of inventory and accept rigid terms of payment as well as delivery (net 30 days, FOB plant).

In addition to absorbing these selling expenses normally assumed by the manufacturer, distributors paid salesmen higher commission on private label sales (15 percent of resale) than on national brands (10 percent of resale). However, the incremental administration and selling expenses associated with private label business were more than offset by the differential savings on private label wholesale goods. By pricing private label chemicals at competitive parity with national brands, the distributor could enjoy approximately a 50 percent gross margin at resale list, while preserving considerable resale discount capability.

Private label products were seldom sold outside the metropolitan areas where most were manufactured. First, the high costs of moving bulky, low-value freight diminished the relative cost advantage of private label chemicals. Second, generally speaking, it was only in metro areas where distributors dealt in volumes great enough to satisfy the private labeller's minimum order requirement. Finally, outside the city, distributors were less likely to be in direct local competition with others handling the same national brand, reducing value of the private label as a source of supplier differentiation.

For some very large distributors, backward integration into chemical production was a logical extension of the private labelling strategy. Recently, several distributors had become direct marketers through acquisition of captive manufacturers.

Direct Sale by Manufacturers of Industrial Cleaning Chemicals

Manufacturers dealing directly with the end user increased their gross margins to 60–70 percent of retail list price. Greater margins increased their ability to discount end user price—a distinct advantage in the price competitive urban marketplace. Overall, direct marketers averaged a gross margin of 50 percent.

Many manufacturers of industrial cleaning chemicals attempted some direct selling, but relatively few relied on this channel exclusively. Satisfactory adoption of a full-time direct-selling strategy required the manufacturer to match distributor's sales and delivery capabilities without sacrificing overall profitability. These conflicting demands had been resolved successfully by two types of company: large-scale powder chemical manufacturers and full-line janitorial products manufacturers.

Large-scale powder chemical manufacturers. Economies of large-scale production plus experience in the capital-intensive manufacture of powder chemicals enabled a few established firms, such as Diversey-Wyandotte, to dominate the market for powder warewash and vehicle cleansers. Selling through distributors offered these producers few advantages. Direct-selling expense was almost entirely commission (i.e., variable). Moreover, powder concentrates were characterized by comparatively high value-to-bulk ratios, and so could absorb delivery costs even where demand was geographically dispersed. Thus, any marginal benefits from using middlemen were more than offset by the higher margins (and associated discount capability) possible through direct distribution. Among these chemical firms, competition was not limited to price. The provision of dispensing and metering equipment was important, as was 24-hour servicing.

Full-line janitorial products manufacturers. These manufacturers offered a complete range of maintenance products, including paper supplies, janitorial chemicals, tools, and mechanical equipment. Although high margins greatly enhanced retail price flexibility, overall profitability depended on securing a balance of high- and low-margin business, as well as controlling selling and distribution expenses. This was accomplished in several ways, including:

Centering on market areas of concentrated demand to minimize costs of warehousing, sales travel, and the like.

Increasing average order size, either by adding product lines which could be sold to existing customers, or by seeking new large-volume customers.

Tying sales commission to profitability to motivate sales personnel to sell volume, without unnecessary discounting of end user price.

Direct marketers of maintenance products varied in scale from established nationwide companies to hundreds of regional operators. The two largest direct marketers, G.H. Wood and Dustbane, together supplied almost a third of Canadian demand for industrial cleaning chemicals.

S.C. Johnson and Son, Limited

S.C. Johnson and Son, Limited (SCJ), was one of 42 foreign subsidiaries owned by the U.S.-based multinational, S.C. Johnson & Son, Inc. It was ranked globally as one of the largest privately held companies. SCJ contributed substantially to worldwide sales and profits and was based in Brantford, Ontario, close to the Canadian urban markets of Hamilton, Kitchener, Toronto, London, and Niagara Falls. About 300 people worked at the head office and plant, while another 100 were employed in field sales.

Innochem Division

Innochem (Innovative Chemicals for Professional Use) was a special division established to serve corporate, institutional, and government customers of SCJ. The division manufactured an extensive line of industrial cleaning chemicals, including general purpose cleansers, waxes, polishes, and disinfectants, plus a number of specialty products of limited application, as shown in Exhibit 3. Last year, Innochem sold $4.5 million of industrial cleaning chemicals through distributors and $0.2 million direct to end users. Financial statements for Innochem are shown in Exhibit 4.

Innochem Marketing Strategy

Divisional strategy hinged on reliable product performance, product innovation, active promotion, and mixed channel distribution. Steve Remen, market development manager, maintained that "Customers know our products are of excellent quality. They know that the products will always perform as expected."

EXHIBIT 3 Innochem product line

Johnson Wax is a systems innovator. Frequently, a new product leads to a whole new system of doing things—a Johnson system of "matched" products formulated to work together. This makes the most of your time, your effort, and your expense. Call today and see how these Johnson systems can give you maximum results at a minimum cost.

For all floors except unsealed wood and unsealed cork

Stripper:	**Step-Off**—powerful, fast action
Finish:	**Pronto**—fast-drying, good gloss, minimum maintenance
Spray-buff solution:	**The Shiner Liquid Spray Cleaner or The Shiner Aerosol Spray Finish**
Maintainer:	**Forward**—cleans, disinfects, deodorizes, sanitizes

For all floors except unsealed wood and unsealed cork

Stripper:	**Step-Off**—powerful, fast stripper
Finish:	**Carefree**—tough, beauty, durable, minimum maintenance
Maintainer:	**Forward**—cleans, disinfects, deodorizes, sanitizes

For all floors except unsealed wood and unsealed cork

Stripper:	**Step-Off**—for selective stripping
Sealer:	**Over & Under-Plus**—undercoater-sealer
Finish:	**Scrubbable Step-Ahead**—brilliant, scrubbable
Maintainer:	**Forward**—cleans, disinfects, sanitizes, deodorizes

For all floors except unsealed wood and cork

Stripper:	**Step-Off**—powerful, fast stripper
Finish:	**Easy Street**—high solids, high gloss, spray buffs to a "wet look" appearance
Maintainer:	**Forward**—cleans, disinfects, deodorizes
	Expose—phenolic cleaner disinfectant

For all floors except unsealed wood and unsealed cork

Stripper:	**Step-Off**—for selective stripping
Sealer:	**Over & Under-Plus**—undercoater-sealer
Finishes:	**Traffic Grade**—heavy-duty floor wax
	Waxtral—extra tough, high solids
Maintainer:	**Forward**—cleans, disinfects, sanitizes, deodorizes

General cleaning:
Break-Up—cleans soap and body scum fast
Forward—cleans, disinfects, sanitizes, deodorizes
Bon Ami—instant cleaner, pressurized or pump, disinfects

Toilet-urinals:
Go-Getter—"Working Foam" cleaner

Glass:
Bon Ami—spray-on foam or liquid cleaner

Disinfectant spray:
End-Bac II—controls bacteria, odors

Air freshener:
Glade—dewy-fresh fragrances

Spot cleaning:
Johnson's Pledge—cleans, waxes, polishes
Johnson's Lemon Pledge—refreshing scent
Bon Ami Stainless Steel Cleaner—cleans, polishes, protects

All-purpose cleaners:
Forward—cleans, disinfects, sanitizes, deodorizes
Break-Up—degreaser for animal and vegetable fats
Big Bare—heavy-duty industrial cleaner

Carpets:
Rugbee Powder & Liquid Extraction Cleaner
Rugbee Soil Release Concentrate—for pre-spraying and bonnet buffing
Rugbee Shampoo—for power shampoo machines
Rugbee Spotter—spot remover

Furniture:
Johnson's Pledge—cleans, waxes, polishes
Johnson's Lemon Pledge—refreshing scent
Shine-Up Liquid—general purpose cleaning

Disinfectant spray air freshener:
End-Bac II—controls bacteria, odors
Glade—dewy-fresh fragrances

Glass:
Bon Ami—spray-on foam or liquid cleaner

Cleaning:
Break-Up—special degreaser designed to remove animal and vegetable fats

Equipment:
Break-Up Foamer—special generator designed to dispense Break-Up cleaner

General cleaning:
Forward—fast-working germicidal cleaner for floors, walls, all washable surfaces
Expose—phenolic disinfectant cleaner

Sanitizing:
J80 Sanitizer—liquid for total environmental control of bacteria; no rinse necessary if used as directed

EXHIBIT 3 *(concluded)*

For all floors except asphalt, mastic and rubber tile.
Use sealer and wax finishes on wood, cork, and cured
concrete; sealer-finish on terrazzo, marble, clay, and
ceramic tile; wax finish only on vinyl, linoleum, and
magnesite.

Sealer:	**Johnson Gym Finish**— sealer and top-coater, cleans as it waxes.
Wax finishes:	**Traffic Wax Paste**—heavy-duty buffing wax
	Beautiflor Traffic Wax— liquid buffing wax
Maintainers:	**Forward**—cleans, disinfects, sanitizes, deodorizes
	Conq-r Dust—mop treatment
Stripper:	**Step-Off**—stripper for sealer and finish
Sealer:	**Secure**—fast-bonding, smooth, long-lasting
Finish:	**Traffic Grade**—heavy-duty floor wax
Maintainer:	**Forward or Big Bare**
Sealer-finish:	**Johnson Gym Finish**—seal and top-coater
Maintainer:	**Conq-r-Dust**—mop treatment

Disinfectant spray:
  End-Bac II Spray—controls bacteria, odors
Flying insects:
  Bolt Liquid Airborne or **Pressurized Airborne,**
    P3610 through E10 dispenser
Crawling insects:
  Bolt Liquid Residual or **Pressurized Residual,**
    P3610 through E10 dispenser
  Bolt Roach Bait
Rodents:
  Bolt Rodenticide—for effective control of rats
    and mice, use with Bolt Bait Box

EXHIBIT 4
S.C. JOHNSON AND SON, LIMITED
Profit Statement of the Division
(in thousands)

Gross sales:	$4,682
Returns	46
Allowances	1
Cash discounts	18
Net sales	4,617
Cost of sales	2,314
Gross profit:	2,303
Advertising	75
Promotions	144
Deals	—
External marketing services	2
Sales freight	292
Other distribution expenses	176
Service fees	184
Total direct expenses	873
Sales force	592
Marketing administration	147
Provision for bad debts	—
Research and development	30
Financial	68
Information resource management	47
Administration management	56
Total functional expenses	940
Total operating expenses	1,813
Operating profit	490

At SCJ, performance requirements were detailed and tolerances precisely defined. The Department of Quality Control routinely inspected and tested raw materials, work in process, packaging, and finished goods. At any phase during the manufacturing cycle, Quality Control was empowered to halt the process and quarantine suspect product or materials. SCJ maintained that nothing left the plant "without approval from Quality Control."

"Keeping the new product shelf well stocked" was central to divisional strategy, as the name Innochem implies. Products launched over the past three years represented 33 percent of divisional gross sales, 40 percent of gross profits, and 100 percent of growth.

Mixed Distribution Strategy

Innochem used a mixed distribution system in an attempt to broaden market coverage. Eighty-seven percent of divisional sales were handled by a force of 200 distributor salesmen and were serviced from 50 distributor warehouses representing 35 distributors. The indirect channel was particularly effective outside Ontario and Quebec. In part, the tendency for SCJ market penetration to increase with distances from Montreal and Toronto reflected Canadian demographics and the general economics of distribution. Outside the two production centres, demand was dispersed and delivery distances long.

Distributor salesmen were virtually all paid a straight commission on sales, and were responsible for selling a wide variety of products in addition to S.C. Johnson's. Several of the distributors had sales levels much higher than Innochem.

For Innochem, the impact of geography was compounded by a significant freight cost advantage: piggybacking industrial cleaning chemicals with SCJ consumer goods. In Ontario, for example, the cost of SCJ to a distributor was 30 percent above private label, while the differential in British Columbia was only 8 percent. On lower value products, the "freight effect" was even more pronounced.

SCJ had neither the salesmen nor the delivery capabilities to reach large-volume end users who demanded heavy selling effort or frequent shipments of small quantities. Furthermore, it was unlikely that SCJ could develop the necessary selling and distribution strength economically, given the narrowness of the division's range of janitorial products (i.e., industrial cleaning chemicals only).

The Rebate Plan

The key strategic problem facing Innochem was how best to challenge the direct marketer (and private label distributor) for large-volume, price-sensitive customers with heavy service requirements, particularly in markets where SCJ had no freight advantage. In this connection George had observed:

Our gravest weakness is our inability to manage the total margin between the manufactured cost and consumer price in a way that is equitable and sufficiently profitable to support the investment and expenses of both the distributors and ourselves.

Our prime competition across Canada is from direct-selling national and regional manufacturers. These companies control both the manufacturing and distribution gross margins. Under our pricing system, the distributor's margin at end user list on sales is 43 percent. Our margin (the manufacturing margin) is 50 percent on sales. When these margins are combined, as in the case of direct-selling manufacturers, the margin becomes 70 percent at list. This long margin provides significant price flexibility in a price-competitive marketplace. We must find a way to profitably attack the direct marketer's 61 percent market share.

The rebate plan George was now evaluating had been devised to meet the competition head-on. "Profitable partnership" between Innochem and the distributors was the underlying philosophy of the plan. Rebates offered a means to "share fairly the margins available between factory cost and consumer price." Whenever competitive conditions required a distributor to discount the resale list price by 30 percent or more, SCJ would give a certain percentage of the wholesale price back to the distributor. In other words, SCJ would sacrifice part of its margin to help offset a heavy end user discount. Rebate percentages would vary with the rate of discount, following a set schedule. Different schedules were to be established for each product type and size. Exhibits 5, 6, and 7 outline the effect of rebates on both the unit gross margins of SCJ and individual distributors for a specific product example.

The rebate plan was designed to be applicable to new, "incremental" business only, not to existing accounts of the distributor. Distributors would be required to seek SCJ approval for end user discounts of over 30 percent or more of resale list. The maximum allowable end user discount would rarely exceed 50 percent. To request rebate payments, distributors would send SCJ a copy of the resale invoice along with a written claim. The rebate would then be paid within 60 days. Currently, Innochem sales were sold by distributors at an average discount of 10 percent off list.

Proponents of the plan maintained that the resulting resale price flexibility would not only enhance Innochem competitiveness among end users but would also diminish distributor attraction to private label.

As he studied the plan, George questioned whether all the implications were fully understood and wondered what other strategies, if any, might increase urban market penetration. Any plan he devised would have to be sold to distributors as well as to corporate management. George had only three weeks to develop an appropriate action plan.

EXHIBIT 5 Distributors' rebate pricing schedule: An example using Pronto floor wax

Code: 04055
Product description: Pronto Fast-Dry Finish
Size: 209-Litre
Pack: 1

EFF. DATE: 03-31-81
Resale price list 71 613.750
Distributor price list 74 349.837
Percent markup on cost with carload and rebate

Discount percent[1]	Quote (Federal sales tax included)[2]	Rebate		2%		3%		4%		5%	
		Percent[3]	Dealers[4]	Net[5]	Markup percent[6]	Net	Markup percent	Net	Markup percent	Net	Markup percent
30.0	429.63	8.0	27.99	314.85	36	311.35	38	307.86	40	304.36	41
35.0	398.94	12.0	41.98	300.86	33	297.36	34	293.86	36	290.36	27
40.0	368.25	17.0	59.47	283.37	30	279.87	32	276.37	33	272.87	35
41.0	362.11	17.5	61.22	281.62	29	278.12	30	274.62	32	271.12	34
42.0	355.98	18.0	62.97	279.87	27	276.37	29	272.87	30	269.37	32
43.0	349.84	18.5	64.72	278.12	26	274.62	27	271.12	29	267.63	31
44.0	343.70	19.0	66.47	276.37	24	272.87	26	269.37	28	265.88	29
45.0	337.56	20.0	69.97	272.87	24	269.37	25	265.88	27	262.38	29
46.0	331.43	20.5	71.72	271.12	22	267.63	24	264.13	25	260.63	27
47.0	325.29	21.0	73.47	269.37	21	265.88	22	262.38	24	258.88	26
48.0	319.15	21.5	75.21	267.63	19	264.13	21	260.63	22	257.13	24
49.0	313.01	22.0	76.96	265.88	18	262.38	19	258.88	21	255.38	23
50.0	306.88	23.0	80.46	262.38	17	258.88	19	255.38	20	251.88	22
51.0	300.74	24.0	83.96	258.88	16	255.38	18	251.88	19	248.38	21
52.0	294.60	25.0	87.46	255.38	15	251.88	17	248.38	19	244.89	20
53.0	288.46	26.0	90.96	251.88	15	248.38	16	244.89	18	241.39	19
54.0	282.33	28.0	97.95	244.89	15	241.39	17	237.89	19	234.39	20
55.0	276.19	30.0	104.95	237.89	16	234.39	18	230.89	20	227.39	21

[1] Discount extended to end user on resale list price.
[2] Resale price at given discount level (includes federal sales tax).
[3] Percentage of distributor's price ($613.75) rebated by SCJ.
[4] Actual dollar amount of rebate by SCJ.
[5] Actual net cost to distributor after deduction of rebate and "carload" (quantity) discount.
[6] Effective rate of distributor markup.

EXHIBIT 6   Effect of rebate plan on manufacturer and distributor margins: The example of one 209-litre pack of Pronto floor finish retailed at 40 percent below resale list price

I. Under present arrangements	
Base price to distributor	$349.84
Price to distributor, assuming 2 percent carload discount*	342.84
SCJ cost	174.92
∴ SCJ margin	$167.92
Resale list price	613.75
Resale list price minus 40 percent discount	368.25
Distributor price, assuming 2 percent carload discount	342.84
∴ Distributor's margin	$ 25.41
II. Under rebate plan	
Rebate to distributor giving 40 percent discount off resale price amounted to 17 percent distributor's base price	$ 59.47
SCJ margin (minus rebate)	108.45
Distributor margin (plus rebate)	84.88
III. Competitive prices	
For this example, George estimated that a distributor could buy a private brand "comparable" product for approximately $244.	

* A form of quantity discount, which, in this case, drops the price the distributor pays to SCJ from $349.84 to $342.84.

EXHIBIT 7 Effect of end user discount level on manufacturer and distributor margins under proposed rebate plan: The example of 1 209-litre pack of Pronto Fast-Dry Finish*

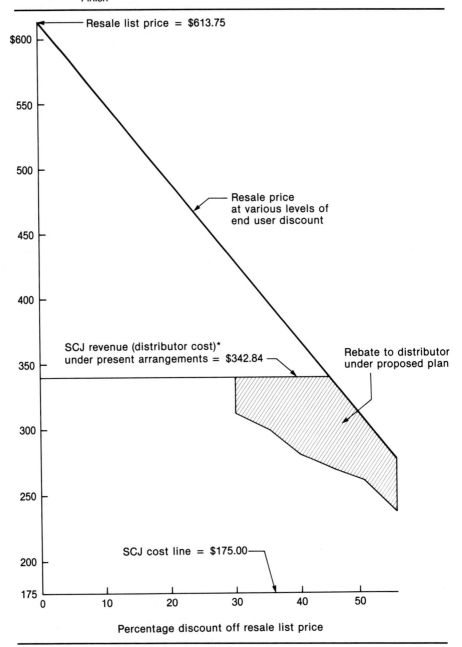

* Assuming 2 percent quantity ("carload") discount off price to distributor.

Case 32

United Techtronics*

In June 1977, United Techtronics faced a major pricing decision with respect to its new video screen television system. "We're really excited here at United Techtronics," exclaimed Mr. Roy Cowing, the founder and president of United Techtronics. "We've made a most significant technological breakthrough in large-screen, video television systems." He went on to explain that the marketing plan for 1978 for this product was now his major area of concern, and that what price to charge was the marketing question that was giving him the most difficulty.

Company History

United Techtronics (UT) was founded in Boston in 1959 by Mr. Cowing. Prior to that time Mr. Cowing had been an associate professor of electrical engineering at M.I.T. Mr. Cowing founded UT to manufacture and market products making use of some of the electronic inventions he had developed while at M.I.T. Sales were made mostly to the space program and the military. Sales grew from $100,000 in 1960 to $27 million in 1976. Profits in 1976 were $3.2 million.

The Video Screen Project

For a number of years beginning in the late 1960s, Mr. Cowing had been trying to reduce the company's dependency on government sales. One of the diversification projects that he had committed research and development monies to was the so-called video screen project. The objective of this project was to develop a system whereby a television picture could be displayed on a screen as big as 8 to 10 feet diagonally. In late 1976, one of UT's engineers made the necessary breakthrough. The rest of 1976 and the first few months of 1977 were spent

---

* This case was written by Thomas C. Kinnear. Copyright © 1980, Thomas C. Kinnear.

producing working prototypes. Up until June 1977, UT had invested $600,000 in the project.

Video Screen Television

Extra-large screen television systems were not new. There were a number of companies who sold such systems both to the consumer and commercial (taverns, restaurants, and so on) markets. Most current systems made use of a special magnifying lens that projected a regular small television picture onto a special screen. The result of this process is that the final picture lacked much of the brightness of the original small screen. As a result, the picture had to be viewed in a darkened room. There were some other video systems that did not use the magnifying process. These systems used special tubes, but also suffered from a lack of brightness.

UT had developed a system that was bright enough to be viewed in regular daylight on a screen up to 10 feet diagonal. Mr. Cowing was unwilling to discuss how this was accomplished. He would only say that the process was protected by patent, and that he thought it would take at least two to three years for any competitor to duplicate the results of the system.

A number of large and small companies were active in this area. Admiral, General Electric, RCA, Zenith, and Sony were all thought to be working on developing large-screen systems directed at the consumer market. Sony was rumored to be ready to introduce a 60-inch diagonal screen system that would retail for about $2,500. A number of small companies were already producing systems. Advent Corporation, a small New England company, claimed to have sold 4,000, 84-inch diagonal units in two years at a $4,000 price. Muntz Manufacturing claimed one-year sales of 5,000, 50-inch diagonal units at prices from $1,500 to $2,500. Mr. Cowing was adamant that none of these systems gave as bright a picture as UT's. He estimated that about 10,000 large-screen systems were sold in 1976.

Cost Structure

Mr. Cowing expected about 50 percent of the suggested retail selling price to go for wholesaler and retailer margins. He expected that UT's direct manufacturing costs would vary depending on the volume produced. Exhibit 1 presents these estimates. He expected direct labor costs to fall at higher production volumes due to the increased automation of the process and improved worker skills. Material costs were expected to fall due to less waste due to automation. The equipment costs necessary to automate the product process were $70,000 to produce in the 0–5,000-unit range, an additional $50,000 to produce in the 5,001–10,000-unit range, and an additional $40,000 to produce in the 10,001–20,000-unit range. The useful life of this equipment was put at five years. Mr. Cowing was sure that production costs were substantially below those of current competitors including Sony. Such was the magnitude of UT's

EXHIBIT 1 Estimated production costs of UT's video screen system

		Volume	
	0–5,000	5,000–10,000	10,001–20,000
Raw materials	$ 480	$460	$410
Direct labor	540	320	115
Total direct costs	$1,020	$780	$525

technological breakthrough. Mr. Cowing was unwilling to produce over 20,000 units a year in the first few years due to the limited cash resources of the company to support inventories, and so on.

Market Studies

Mr. Cowing wanted to establish a position in the consumer market for his product. He felt that the long-run potential was greater there than in the commercial market. With this end in mind he hired a small economic research consulting firm to undertake a consumer study to determine the likely reaction to alternative retail prices for the system. These consultants undertook extensive interviews with potential television purchasers, and examined the sales and pricing histories of competitive products. They concluded that: "UT's video screen system would be highly price elastic across a range of prices from $500 to $5,000, both in a primary and secondary demand sense." They went on to estimate the price elasticity of demand in this range to be between 4.0 and 6.5.

The Pricing Decision

Mr. Cowing was considering a number of alternative suggested retail prices. "I can see arguments for pricing anywhere from above Advent's to substantially below Muntz's lowest price," he said.

Case 33

Big Sky of
Montana, Inc.*

Introduction

Karen Tracy could feel the pressure on her as she sat at her desk late that April afternoon. Two weeks from today she would be called on to present her recommendations concerning next year's winter season pricing policies for the Big Sky of Montana, Inc.—room rates for the resort's accommodation facilities as well as decisions in the skiing and food service areas. The presentation would be made to a top management team from the parent company, Boyne U.S.A., which operated out of Michigan.

"As sales and public relations manager, Karen, your accuracy in decision making is extremely important," her boss had said in his usual tone. "Because we spend most of our time in Michigan, we'll need a well-based and involved opinion."

It'll be the shortest two weeks of my life, she thought.

Background: Big Sky and Boyne U.S.A.

Big Sky of Montana, Inc., was a medium-sized destination resort[1] located in southwestern Montana, 45 miles south of Bozeman, and 43 miles north of the west entrance to Yellowstone National Park. Big Sky was conceived in the early 1970s and had begun operation in November 1974.

The 11,000-acre, 2,000-bed resort was separated into 2 main areas: Meadow and Mountain Villages. The Meadow Village (elevation 6,300 feet) was located 2 miles east of the resort's main entrance on U.S. 191 and 7 miles

---

* This case was prepared by Anne Senausky and Professor James E. Nelson for educational purposes only. It is designed for classroom purposes and not for purposes of research nor to illustrate either effective or ineffective handling of administrative problems. Some data are disguised. Copyright © 1978 by the Endowment and Research Foundation at Montana State University. Used with permission.

[1] Destination resorts were characterized by on-the-hill lodging and eating facilities, a national market, and national advertising.

from the ski area. The Meadow Village had an 800-bed capacity in the form of 4 condominium complexes (ranging from studios to 3-bedroom units) and a 40-room hostel for economy lodging. Additional facilities included an 18-hole golf course, 6 tennis courts, a restaurant, post office, a convention center with meeting space for up to 200 people, and a small lodge serving as a pro shop for the golf course in the summer and cross-country skiing in the winter.

The Mountain Village (elevation 7,500 feet) was the center of winter activity, located at the base of the ski area. In this complex was the 204-room Huntley Lodge offering hotel accommodations, 3 condominium complexes (unit size ranged from studio to 3-bedroom), and an 88-room hostel for a total of 1,200 beds. The Mountain Mall was also located here, next to the Huntley Lodge and within a five-minute walk of 2 of the 3 condominium complexes in the Mountain Village. It housed ticket sales, an equipment rental shop, a skier's cafeteria, two large meeting rooms for a maximum of 700 persons (regularly used as sack lunch areas for skiers), two offices, a ski school desk, and ski patrol room, all of which were operated by Boyne. Also in this building were a delicatessen, drug store/gift shop, sporting goods store/rental shop, restaurant, outdoor clothing store, jewelry shop, a T-shirt shop, two bars, and a child day-care center. Each of these independent operations held leases, due to expire in two to three years.

The closest airport to Big Sky was located just outside Bozeman. It was served by Northwest Orient and Frontier Airlines with connections to other major airlines out of Denver and Salt Lake City. Greyhound and Amtrak also operated bus and train service into Bozeman. Yellowstone Park Lines provided Big Sky with three buses daily to and from the airport and Bozeman bus station (cost was $4.40 one way, $8.40 round trip), as well as an hourly shuttle around the two Big Sky villages. Avis, Hertz, National, and Budget offered rent-a-car service in Bozeman with a drop-off service available at Big Sky.

In July 1976 Boyne U.S.A., a privately owned, Michigan-based operation, purchased the Huntley Lodge, Mountain Mall, ski lifts and terrain, golf course, and tennis courts for approximately $8 million. The company subsequently invested an additional $3 million into Big Sky. Boyne also owned and operated four Michigan resort ski areas.

Big Sky's top management consisted of a lodge manager (in charge of operations within the Huntley Lodge), a sales and public relations manager (Karen), a food and beverage manager, and an area manager (overseeing operations external to the lodge, including the mall and all recreational facilities). These four positions were occupied by persons trained with the parent company; a fifth manager, the comptroller, had worked for pre-Boyne ownership.

Business figures were reported to the company's home office on a daily basis and major decisions concerning Big Sky operations were discussed and approved by "Michigan." Boyne's top management visited Big Sky an average of five times annually, and all major decisions such as pricing and advertising were approved by the parent for all operations.

The Skiing

Big Sky's winter season usually began in late November and continued until the middle of April, with a yearly snowfall of approximately 450 inches. The area had 18 slopes between elevations of 7,500 and 9,900 feet. Terrain breakdown was as follows: 25 percent novice, 55 percent intermediate, and 20 percent advanced. (Although opinions varied, industry guidelines recommended a terrain breakdown of 20 percent, 60 percent, and 20 percent for novice, intermediate, and advanced skiers, respectively.) The longest run was approximately three miles in length; temperatures (highs) ranged from 15 to 30 degrees Farenheit throughout the season.

Lift facilities at Big Sky included two double chairlifts, a triple chair, and a four-passenger gondola. Lift capacity was estimated at 4,000 skiers per day. This figure was considered adequate by the area manager, at least until the 1980–81 season.

Karen felt that the facilities, snow conditions, and grooming compared favorably with those of other destination resorts of the Rockies. "In fact, our only real drawback right now," she thought, "is our position in the national market. We need more skiers who are sold on Big Sky. And that is in the making."

The Consumers

Karen knew from previous dealings that Big Sky, like most destination areas, attracted three distinct skier segments: local day skiers (living within driving distance and not utilizing lodging in the area); individual destination skiers (living out of state and using accommodations in the Big Sky area); and groups of destination skiers (clubs, professional organizations, and the like).

The first category was comprised typically of Montana residents, with a relatively small number from Wyoming and Idaho. (Distances from selected population centers to Big Sky are presented in Exhibit 1.) A 1973 study of four Montana ski areas performed by the advertising unit of the Montana department of highways characterized Montana skiers as:

1. In their early 20s and males (60 percent).
2. Living within 75 miles of a ski area.
3. From a household with two skiers in it.
4. Averaging $13,000 in household income.
5. An intermediate to advanced ability skier.
6. Skiing five hours per ski day, 20 days per season locally.
7. Skiing four days away from local areas.
8. Taking no lessons in the past five years.

Karen was also aware that a significant number of day skiers, particularly on the weekends, were college students.

EXHIBIT 1

A. Population centers in proximity to Big Sky (distance and population)

City	Distance from Big Sky (miles)	Population (U.S. 1970 Census)
Bozeman, Montana	45	18,670
Butte, Montana	126	23,368
Helena, Montana	144	22,730
Billings, Montana	174	61,581
Great Falls, Montana	225	60,091
Missoula, Montana	243	29,497
Pocatello, Idaho	186	40,036
Idaho Falls, Idaho	148	35,776

B. Approximate distance of selected major U.S. population centers to Big Sky (in air miles)

City	Distance to Big Sky*
Chicago	1,275
Minneapolis	975
Fargo	750
Salt Lake City	375
Dallas	1,500
Houston	1,725
Los Angeles	975
San Francisco	925
New York	2,025
Atlanta	1,950
New Orleans	1,750
Denver	750

* Per passenger air fare could be approximated at 20 cents per mile (round trip, coach rates).

Destination, or nonresident skiers, were labeled in the same study as typically:

1. At least in their mid-20s and males (55 percent).
2. Living in a household of three or more skiers.
3. Averaging near $19,000 in household income.
4. More an intermediate skier.
5. Spending about six hours per day skiing.
6. Skiing 11–14 days per season with 3–8 days away from home.
7. Taking ski school lessons.

Through data taken from reservation records, Karen learned that individual destination skiers accounted for half of last year's usage based on skier days.[2] Geographic segments were approximately as follows:

---

[2] A skier day is defined as one skier using the facility for one day of operation.

Upper Midwest (Minnesota, Michigan, North Dakota)	30 percent
Florida	20 percent
California	17 percent
Washington, Oregon, Montana	15 percent
Texas, Oklahoma	8 percent
Other	10 percent

Reservation records indicated that the average length of stay for individual destination skiers was about six or seven days.

It was the individual destination skier who was most likely to buy a lodging/lift package; 30 percent made commitments for these advertised packages when making reservations for 1977–78. Even though there was no discount involved in this manner of buying lift tickets, Karen knew that they were fairly popular because it saved the purchaser a trip to the ticket window every morning. Approximately half of the individual business came through travel agents, who received a 10 percent commission.

The third skier segment, the destination group, accounted for a substantial 20 percent of Big Sky's skier day usage. The larger portion of the group business came through medical and other professional organizations holding meetings at the resort, as this was a way to "combine business with pleasure." These groups were typically comprised of couples and individuals between the ages of 30 and 50. Ski clubs made up the remainder with a number coming from the southern states of Florida, Texas, and Georgia. During the 1977–78 season, Big Sky drew 30 ski clubs with membership averaging 55 skiers. The average length of stay for all group destination skiers was about four or five days.

A portion of these group bookings were made through travel agents, but the majority dealt directly with Karen. The coordinator of the professional meetings or the president of the ski club typically contacted the Big Sky sales office to make initial reservation dates, negotiate prices, and work out the details of their stay.

The Competition

In Karen's mind Big Sky faced two types of competition, that for local day skiers and that for out-of-state (i.e., destination) skiers.

Bridger Bowl was virtually the only area competing for local day skiers. Bridger was a "nonfrills," nonprofit, and smaller ski area located some 16 miles northeast of Bozeman. It received the majority of local skiers including students at Montana State University, which was located in Bozeman. The area was labeled as having terrain more difficult than that of Big Sky and was thus more appealing to the local expert skiers. However, it also had much longer lift lines than Big Sky and had recently lost some of its weekend business to them.

Karen had found through experience that most Bridger skiers usually "tried" Big Sky once or twice a season. Season passes for the two areas were mutually honored at the half-day rate for an all-day ticket, and Big Sky occasionally ran newspaper ads offering discounts on lifts to obtain more Bozeman business.

For out-of-state skiers, Big Sky considered its competition to be mainly the destination resorts of Colorado, Utah, and Wyoming. (Selected data on competing resorts is presented in Exhibit 2.) Because Big Sky was smaller and newer than the majority of these areas, Karen reasoned, it was necessary to follow an aggressive strategy aimed at increasing its national market share.

EXHIBIT 2 Competitors' 1977–1978 package plan rates,* number of lifts, and lift rates

	Lodge double (2)†	Two-bedroom condo (4)	Three-bedroom condo (6)	Number of lifts	Daily lift rates
Aspen, Colo.	$242	$242	$220	19	$13
Steamboat, Colo.	230	230	198	15	12
Jackson, Wyo.	230	242	210	5	14
Vail, Colo.	230	242	220	15	14
Snowbird, Utah	208	none	none	6	11
Bridger Bowl, Mont.	(no lodging available at Bridger Bowl)			3	8

* Package plan rates are per person and include seven nights lodging, six lift tickets (high season rates).

† Number in parentheses denotes occupancy of unit on which price is based.

Present Policies

Lift Rates

It was common knowledge that there existed some local resentment concerning Big Sky's lift rate policy. Although comparable to rates at Vail or Aspen, an all-day lift ticket was $4 higher than the ticket offered at nearby Bridger Bowl. In an attempt to alleviate this situation, management at Big Sky instituted a $9 "chair pass" for the 1977–78 season, entitling the holder to unlimited use of the three chairs, plus two rides per day on the gondola, to be taken between specified time periods. Because the gondola served primarily intermediate terrain, it was reasoned that the chair pass would appeal to the local, more expert skier. A triple chair serving the bowl area was located at the top of the gondola, and two rides on the gondola would allow those skiers to take ample advantage of the advanced terrain up there. Otherwise, all advanced terrain was served by another chair.

However, if Big Sky was to establish itself as a successful, nationally prominent destination area, Karen felt the attitudes and opinions of all skiers must be carefully weighed. Throughout the season she had made a special effort to grasp the general feeling toward rates. A $12 ticket, she discovered, was thought to be very reasonable by destination skiers, primarily because Big Sky was predominantly an intermediate area and the average destination skier was of intermediate ability; also because Big Sky was noted for its relative lack of lift lines, giving the skier more actual skiing time for the money. "Perhaps we should keep the price the same," she thought, "we do need more business. Other destination areas are likely to raise their prices and we should look good in comparison."

Also discussed was the possible abolition of the $9 chair pass. The question in Karen's mind was if its elimination would severely hurt local business or would it sell an all-lift $12 ticket to the skier who had previously bought only a chair pass. The issue was compounded by an unknown number of destination skiers who opted for the cheaper chair pass too.

Season-pass pricing was also an issue. Prices for the 1977–78 all-lift season pass had remained the same as last year, but a season chair pass had been introduced which was the counterpart of the daily chair lift pass. Karen did not like the number of season chair passes purchased in relation to the number of all-lift passes and considered recommending its abolition as well as an increase in the price of the all-lift pass. "I'm going to have to think this one out carefully," she thought, "because skiing accounted for about 40 percent of our total revenue this past season. I'll have to be able to justify my decision not only to Michigan but also to the Forest Service."

Price changes were not solely at the discretion of Big Sky management. As is the case with most larger western ski areas, the U.S. government owned part of the land on which Big Sky operated. Control of this land was the responsibility of the U.S. Forest Service, which annually approved all lift pricing policies. For the 1976–77 ski season, Forest Service action kept most lift rate increases to the national inflation rate. For the 1977–78 season, larger price increases were allowed for ski areas which had competing areas near by; Big Sky was considered to be such an area. No one knew what the Forest Service position would be for the upcoming 1978–79 season.

To help her in her decision, an assistant had prepared a summary of lift rates and usage for the past two seasons (Exhibit 3).

Room Rates

This area of pricing was particularly important because lodging accounted for about one third of the past season's total revenue. It was also difficult because of the variety of accommodations (Exhibit 4) and the difficulty in accurately forecasting next season's demand. For example, the season of 1976–77 had been unique in that a good portion of the Rockies was without snow for the initial months of the winter including Christmas. Big Sky was fortunate in receiving as much snow as it had, and consequently many groups and individuals who were originally headed for Vail or Aspen booked in with Big Sky.

Pricing for the 1977–78 season had been made on the premise that there would be a good amount of repeat business. This came true in part but not as

EXHIBIT 3

A.   1977–78 lift rates and usage summary (136 days operation)

Ticket	Consumer cost	Skier days*	Number season passes sold
Adult all-day all-lift	$ 12	53,400	
Adult all-day chair	9	20,200	
Adult half day	8	9,400	
Child all-day all-lift	8	8,500	
Child all-day chair	5	3,700	
Child half day	6	1,200	
Hotel passes†	12/day	23,400	
Complimentary	0	1,100	
Adult all-lift season pass	220	4,300	140
Adult chair season pass	135	4,200	165
Child all-lift season pass	130	590	30
Child chair season pass	75	340	15
Employee all-lift season pass	100	3,000	91
Employee chair season pass	35	1,100	37

B.   1976–77 lift rates and usage summary (122 days operation)

Ticket	Consumer cost	Skier days	Number season passes sold
Adult all-day	$ 10	52,500	
Adult half day	6.50	9,000	
Child all-day	6	10,400	
Child half day	4	1,400	
Hotel passes†	10/day	30,500	
Complimentary	0	480	
Adult season pass	220	4,200	84
Child season pass	130	300	15
Employee season pass	100	2,300	70

* A skier day is defined as one skier using the facility for one day of operation.
† Hotel passes refers to those included in the lodging/lift packages.

EXHIBIT 4

A.   Nightly room rates,* 1977–1978

	Low season range	High season range	Maximum occupancy
Huntley Lodge			
Standard	$ 42–62	$ 50–70	4
Loft	52–92	60–100	6
Stillwater Condo			
Studio	40–60	45–65	4
One-bedroom	55–75	60–80	4
Bedroom w/loft	80–100	90–100	6
Deer Lodge Condo			
One-bedroom	74–84	80–90	4
Two-bedroom	93–103	100–110	6
Three-bedroom	112–122	120–130	8
Hill Condo			
Studio	30–40	35–45	4
Studio w/loft	50–70	55–75	6

EXHIBIT 4 *(concluded)*

B. Nightly room rates, 1976–1977

	Low season range	High season range	Maximum occupancy
Huntley Lodge			
Standard	$ 32–47	$ 35–50	4
Loft	47–67	50–70	6
Stillwater Condo			
Studio	39–54	37–52	4
One-bedroom	52–62	50–60	4
Bedroom w/loft	60–80	65–85	6
Deer Lodge Condo			
One-bedroom	51–66	55–70	4
Two-bedroom	74–94	80–100	6
Three-bedroom	93–123	100–130	8
Hill Condo			
Studio	28–43	30–45	4
Studio w/loft	42–62	45–65	6

* Rates determined by number of persons in room or condominium unit and do not include lift tickets. Maximums for each rate range apply at maximum occupancy.

much as had been hoped. Occupancy experience had also been summarized for the past two seasons to help Karen make her final decision (Exhibit 5).

As was customary in the hospitality industry, January was a slow period and it was necessary to price accordingly. Low season pricing was extremely important because many groups took advantage of these rates. On top of that,

EXHIBIT 5

A. 1977–1978 Lodge-condominium occupancy (in room-nights*)

	December (26 days operation)	January	February	March	April (8 days operation)
Huntley Lodge	1,830	2,250	3,650	4,650	438
Condominiums†	775	930	1,350	100	90

B. 1976–1977 Lodge-condominium occupancy (in room-nights)

	December (16 days operation)	January	February	March	April (16 days operation)
Huntley Lodge	1,700	3,080	4,525	4,300	1,525
Condominiums‡	600	1,000	1,600	1,650	480

C. Lodge-condominium occupancy (in person-nights§)

December 1977 (1976)	January 1978 (1977)	February 1978 (1977)	March 1978 (1977)	April 1978 (1977)
7,850 (6,775)	9,200 (13,000)	13,150 (17,225)	17,900 (17,500)	1,450 (4,725)

* A room-night is defined as one room (or condominium) rented for one night. Lodging experience is based on 124 days of operation for 1977–78 while Exhibit Three shows the skiing facilities operating 136 days. Both numbers are correct.

† Big Sky had 92 condominiums available during the 1977–78 season.

‡ Big Sky had 85 condominiums available during the 1976–77 season.

§ A person-night refers to one person using the facility for one night.

groups were often offered discounts in the neighborhood of 10 percent. Considering this, Karen could not price too high, with the risk of losing individual destination skiers, nor too low, such that an unacceptable profit would be made from group business in this period.

Food Service

Under some discussion was the feasibility of converting all destination skiers to the American Plan, under which policy each guest in the Huntley Lodge would be placed on a package to include three meals daily in a Big Sky-controlled facility. There was a feeling both for and against this idea. The parent company had been successfully utilizing this plan for years at its destination areas in northern Michigan. Extending the policy to Big Sky should find similar success.

Karen was not so sure. For one thing, the Michigan resorts were primarily self-contained and alternative eateries were few. For another, the whole idea of extending standardized policies from Michigan to Montana was suspect. As an example, Karen painfully recalled a day in January when Big Sky "tried on" another successful Michigan policy of accepting only cash or check payments for lift tickets. Reactions of credit card carrying skiers could be described as ranging from annoyed to irate.

If an American Plan were proposed for next year, it would likely include both the Huntley Lodge Dining Room and Lookout Cafeteria. Less clear, however, were prices to be charged. There certainly would have to be consideration for both adults and children and for the two independently operated eating places in the Mountain Mall (see Exhibit 6 for an identification of eating places in the Big Sky area). Beyond these considerations, there was little else other than an expectation of a profit to guide Karen in her analysis.

The Telephone Call

"Profits in the food area might be hard to come by," Karen thought. "Last year it appears we lost money on everything we sold." (See Exhibit 7.) Just then the telephone rang. It was Rick Thompson, her counterpart at Boyne Mountain Lodge in Michigan. "How are your pricing recommendations coming?" he asked. "I'm about done with mine and thought we should compare notes."

"Good idea, Rick—only I'm just getting started out here. Do you have any hot ideas?"

"Only one," he responded. "I just got off the phone with a guy in Denver. He told me all of the major Colorado areas are upping their lift prices one or two dollars next year."

"Is that right, Rick? Are you sure?"

"Well, you know nobody knows for sure what's going to happen but I think it's pretty good information. He heard it from his sister-in-law who works in Vail. I think he said she read it in the local paper or something."

EXHIBIT 6 Eating places in the Big Sky area

Establishment	Type of service	Meals served	Current prices	Seating	Location
Lodge Dining Room*	A la carte	Breakfast	$2–5	250	Huntley Lodge
		Lunch	2–5		
		Dinner	7–15		
Steak House*	Steak/lobster	Dinner only	6–12	150	Huntley Lodge
Fondue Stube*	Fondue	Dinner only	6–10	25	Huntley Lodge
Ore House†	A la carte	Lunch	.80–4.00	150	Mountain Mall
		Dinner	5–12		
Ernie's Deli†	Deli/restaurant	Breakfast	1–3	25	Mountain Mall
		Lunch	2–5		
Lookout Cafeteria*	Cafeteria	Breakfast	1.50–3.00	175	Mountain Mall
		Lunch	2–4		
		Dinner	3–6		
Yellow Mule†	A la carte	Breakfast	2–4	75	Meadow Village
		Lunch	2–5		
		Dinner	4–8		
Buck's T-4†	Road house restaurant/bar	Dinner only	2–9	60	Gallatin Canyon (2 miles south of Big Sky entrance)
Karst Ranch†	Road house restaurant/bar	Breakfast	2–4	50	Gallatin Canyon (7 miles north of Big Sky entrance)
		Lunch	2–5		
		Dinner	3–8		
Corral†	Road house restaurant/bar	Breakfast	2–4	30	Gallatin Canyon (5 miles south of Big Sky entrance)
		Lunch	2–4		
		Dinner	3–5		

* Owned and operated by Big Sky of Montana, Inc.

† Independently operated.

EXHIBIT 7 Ski season income data (percent)

	Skiing	Lodging	Food and beverage
Revenue	100.0	100.0	100.0
Cost of sales:			
Merchandise	0.0	0.0	30.0
Labor	15.0	15.9	19.7
Maintenance	3.1	5.2	2.4
Supplies	1.5	4.8	5.9
Miscellaneous	2.3	0.6	0.6
Operating expenses	66.2	66.4	66.7
Net profit (loss) before taxes	11.9	7.0	(25.2)

"That doesn't seem like very solid information," said Karen. "Let me know if you hear anything more, will you?"

"Certainly. You know, we really should compare our recommendations before we stick our necks out too far on this pricing thing. Can you call me later in the week?" he asked.

"Sure, I'll talk to you the day after tomorrow; I should be about done by then. Anything else?"

"Nope—gotta run. Talk to you then. Bye," and he was gone.

"At least I've got some information," Karen thought, "and a new deadline!"

Case 34

Midland Industries (A)*

In late 1986, the overall plastics molding industry was operating at less than two-thirds capacity[1] as shown in Exhibit 1. Lin Love, general manager of Midland Industries of Watertown, New York, was evaluating a potential opportunity to use some of his idle molding capacity by supplying plastic flower pots to customers of a large firm, Harris[2] Products of Toledo, Ohio. Harris had invited Midland and other molders to quote on an initial order of injection-molded flower pots, with the understanding that substantially larger orders could follow a successful bid.

Lin believed that the market for plastic flower pots was highly price sensitive at the wholesale level and was convinced that any bid which exceeded Harris' estimated cost of manufacture would likely be rejected. During the next few days, he had to decide whether Midland should bid on the Harris contract and, if so, under what terms. Midland was currently operating at 45 percent of capacity.

Midland Industries

In 1949, the Betty Lou Shoe Company integrated backward into the molding of plastic shoe parts. Nine years later, the captive molding operation of this company was acquired by Shoe Corporation of America, forming a new division, Midland Plastics. While continuing as a captive supplier, Midland began to use its idle machine capacity to solicit contract business outside the firm. Following acquisition by Pacific Petroleum in 1964, Midland's shift from captive to custom molding was complete.

---

[1] Molders minimized high set-up and purge costs by attempting round-the-clock operation. By industry convention, theoretical capacity was calculated for a work week of five 24-hour days (i.e., 120 hours per week).

[2] Disguised name.

EXHIBIT 1 Rate of capacity utilization in the plastics and rubber products industry

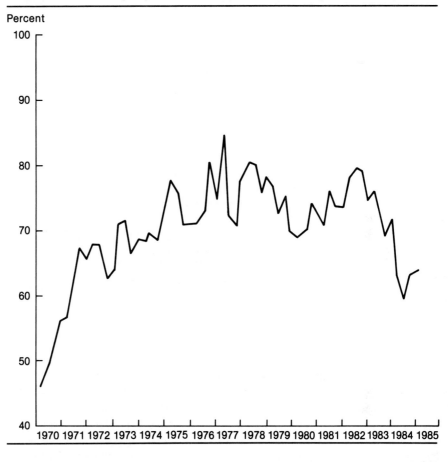

Midland Industries in 1986

Midland was recognized in the plastics molding industry as a leader. According to the trade journal *Plastics:*

> Willingness to experiment—to be first to try something and in the process establish a competitive edge—is the leadership trait that has marked Lin E. Love and the company he heads, Midland Industries, as an innovator in the plastics fields.
>
> For years, he and his company have been in the vanguard of advances in plastics processing—with learned lessons willingly shared among other molders.[3]

Midland had sales of $3.4 million in 1986, and employed 120 full-time hourly plant workers (approximately 40 per shift) plus 31 salaried workers. As

---

[3] Lyn Hamilton, "Taking Yet Another Step in Automatic Molding," *Plastics,* October, 1975, p. 22.

EXHIBIT 2 Plastics fabricating operations: Distribution by size of work force

Number of employees	Percent operations within each category
1–9	30.3%
10–49	45.8
50–99	13.6
100–499	10.1
Over 500	.2
	100.0%

Exhibit 2 shows, Midland had one of the largest work forces in the plastics molding business. The 90,000-square-foot plant shown in Exhibit 3 was roughly allocated as follows:

Production	64,000 square feet
Raw material storage	15,000 square feet
Finished goods storage	5,000 square feet
Office	6,000 square feet

Despite its size, Midland was essentially a custom job shop, molding parts from clock faces to TV cabinets, electric fan blades, and designer tea kettles for 50 or more companies. The median annual business per client was approximately $60,000; however, the largest account approached $750,000 per year. Individual orders ranged in value from $2,000 to $50,000.

Custom molders were frequently very vulnerable to economic downturns, and so many had tried to develop proprietary products and components to boost capacity utilization. Midland, however, had remained strictly a custom contract molder, even through the early 80s recession.

It was no idle boast when Midland claimed to "custom mold plastics of every type into every variety of shape, size, and form utilizing every modern (plastics) manufacturing process." Exhibit 4 lists the varied equipment available for compression, injection, and transfer molding and numerous secondary operations including spray painting, silk screening, hot stamping, heat sealing, welding, and punching. Advanced quality control facilities enabled Midland to guarantee that each product would "consistently meet exact customer specifications." Midland was capable of producing within tolerances of ± .002 inch on many parts it molded.

Specialty molding contracts tended to be low volume. On average, individual runs lasted only two to three days (i.e., 48–72 machine-hours) and were therefore associated with high per unit manufacturing costs, high turnaround costs, substantial investment in raw materials inventory (different types, grades,

EXHIBIT 3 Floor plan of plant showing storage space available for lease to Midland

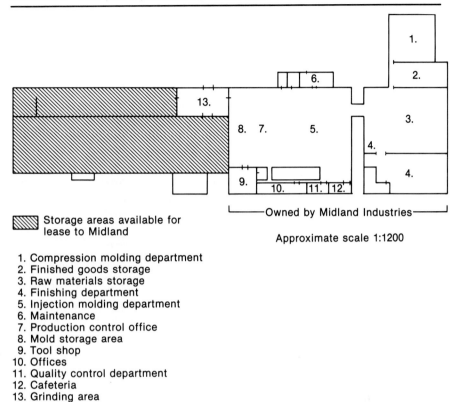

Storage areas available for lease to Midland

—————Owned by Midland Industries—————

Approximate scale 1:1200

1. Compression molding department
2. Finished goods storage
3. Raw materials storage
4. Finishing department
5. Injection molding department
6. Maintenance
7. Production control office
8. Mold storage area
9. Tool shop
10. Offices
11. Quality control department
12. Cafeteria
13. Grinding area

and colors of resin), complicated production scheduling, and frequent work-in-process delays. Competition in the specialty segment was not entirely price based, and gross margins to the molder normally ranged between 15 and 20 percent. Lin identified the nine injection molders listed in Exhibit 5 as the major direct competitors for specialty contracts in New York.

In contrast, competitors were much more numerous in the molded plastic commodities market segment (drinking cups, combs, buttons, caps, closures, and other relatively low-cost standard design items). Almost 150 molders vied for commodity contracts. Relatively low barriers to entry (an active market in secondhand machinery, relatively simple technology, standard product design) favoured ''basement'' shops, which followed a low-capitalization, high-capacity utilization strategy. Conversely, firms such as Midland, with greater investment intensity and higher fixed costs, were seriously handicapped in this price-sensitive, high-volume segment.

EXHIBIT 4

General Description of Plant and Equipment

Plant Size	— 90,000 square feet
Number of Employees	— 150 approximately
Manufacturing Processes	— Injection, Compression, Transfer, SMC, Decorating and Finishing

Injection Equipment – 19 Molding Machines

Quantity	Clamp	Shot Size	Type of Feed	Manufacturer
1	100 ton	3½ oz.	Screw	Trubor
1	175 ton	4 oz.	Screw	Reed-Prentice
1	175 ton	4 oz.	Plunger	Reed-Prentice
2	200 ton	8 oz.	Screw	Reed-Prentice
1	200 ton	14 oz.	Screw	Beloit
1	220 ton	14 oz.	Screw	H.P.M.
1	275 ton	8 oz.	Screw	Reed-Prentice
2	300 ton	20 oz.	Screw	Impco
1	300 ton	20 oz.	Screw	Watson-Stillman
1	325 ton	25 oz.	Screw	Beloit
1	375 ton	24 oz.	Screw	Reed-Prentice
1	375 ton	25 oz.	Screw	Beloit
1	400 ton	48 oz.	Screw	H.P.M.
1	450 ton	50 oz.	Screw	Fellows
1	500 ton	48 oz.	Screw	H.P.M.
1	650 ton	75 oz.	Screw	Fellows
1	750 ton	100 oz.	Screw	Beloit

Compression & Transfer Equipment—8 Molding Machines

1	150 ton		Bradley & Turton
1	250 ton		Biraghi
2	250 ton		Bradley & Turton
3	220 ton		Rodgers
1	350 ton		Viceroy

DECORATING & FINISHING EQUIPMENT

- 12 Spray Painting Booths
- 12 Hot Stamping Machines (up to 20 ton)
- 3 Ultra-Sonic Welding Machines
- 1 Heat Sealing Machine
- 1 Shrink Tunnel
- 1 Wheelabrator Deflasher
- 1 Guyson Deflasher
- Drilling Equipment, Silk Screening
- Punching & Auxiliary Equipment

QUALITY CONTROL LABORATORY EQUIPMENT

1 Profile Projector Comparator	— Nikon
1 Daylight Comparator	— Macbeth
1 Flammability Testing Cabinet	— G.M.
1 Impact Testing Machine	— Tinius Olsen
1 Melt Indexer	— Slocomb
1 Moisture Balance	— Ohaus
1 Notching Machine	— Testing Mach.
1 Heat Testing Oven	— Blue M
1 Cold Testing Freezer	— So Low
Miscellaneous Auxiliary Equipment	

COMPUTER MONITORING AND PROCESS CONTROL EQUIPMENT

 Midland Industries

EXHIBIT 5   Main competitors for specialty molding business in New York

Allied Plastics
General Electric
Somerville Plastics
Progressive Plastics
Plastomer
Custom Plastics
F and H Plastics
Mitchell Plastics
Plastmade

Pricing Policy at Midland Industries

A request for a bid quotation usually represented the starting point of buyer-seller negotiation. Midland submitted bid quotations to prospective buyers on the standard form reproduced in Exhibit 6. A molder's ratio of contracts to bids reflected selectivity in bidding as well as the level of competition from captive and custom molders, both domestic and foreign, and capacity utilization. Six percent of Midland's quotations led to contracts, which was close to the industry average.

At Midland, a quotation normally covered administrative overhead, selling expense, financial expense, and net profit of 20 percent plus "standard factory cost." Standard factory cost computations were made as follows:

1. The physical volume of one piece, computed from blueprint dimensions, was multiplied by the known density of the molding compound to determine weight per thousand and associated resin costs. A scrap allowance was then added to the material cost. In the case of the recyclable thermoplastic resins used in injection molding, the material scrap allowance represented the expected cost of regrinding.

2. In general, the annual budgeted plant overhead (e.g., indirect labour, depreciation, plant salaries, taxes, utilities, repairs) was divided by the anticipated number of hours of machine operation during the year. Adjustments were made in the overhead rates of individual machines to reflect different machine sizes and capabilities. The hourly wages of direct labour were added to this hourly overhead rate, yielding the "machine-hour rate." The expected run length (Cycle times × Number of pieces required × Number of mold cavities) was added to allow for time lost while setting up the mold, starting up the run, molding imperfect parts, and purging the equipment. The total time was multiplied by the machine-hour rate and added to the total resin cost, yielding the standard cost estimate.

Lin outlined the Midland approach to bid pricing in a *Plastics* article reproduced, in part, as Exhibit 7. Implementation of this "realistic full costing"

EXHIBIT 6

 Midland Industries

QUOTATION

TO

Date

Your Enquiry

Attention

MIL Part No.	ITEM:	Description/Blueprint No.	Production Run Quantity	Shipment(s) Release Period	Price /M

In accordance with Para. 1(a) (reverse side), for every $.01 per Kilogram change in resin cost, the above **price(s)** will change by $ _____ per M parts. Prices are based on resins costs as of

MOLD SPECIFICATIONS

Injection ☐   Transfer ☐

Compression ☐

Number of Cavities _____

Complete Mold _____

Cavities and Cores Only _____

Approximate Tool Delivery	Tool Price
Estimated Delivery of Samples For Approval	

DESCRIPTION OF SPECIAL FIXTURES

MATERIAL SPECIFICATIONS

PACKAGING SPECIFICATIONS

QUALITY SPECIFICATIONS

Unless otherwise specified below, this quotation is based on 2.5 A.Q.L. to C.G.S.B. Standard 105 G.P.I. and 105 G.P. 2 Dated July 19, 1965 (U.S.A. MIL-Std. - 105D Dated April 29, 1963.)

TERMS:

1 F.O.B.—Our Plant Midland
2 All taxes extra
3 Merchandise—Net 30 days
4 Tooling—Subject to vendor terms
5 2% per month charged on Overdue Accounts

EXHIBIT 7   Lin Love's views on costing: Excerpts from article published July 1984

Costing or Guessing

Most molders use a machine-hour rate, which includes all plant costs. We can call this "plant overhead," and it would include:

Indirect labor.

Depreciation.

Plant salaries.

Taxes.

Utilities.

Repairs.

It is impossible to go into the details of arriving at machine-hour rates, but generally the total plant overhead is spread over the anticipated hours you expect the plant to operate in a year. Add the direct labor and you have a rate. It sounds simple, but in reality it becomes a real problem because of different machine sizes and capabilities. However, regardless of how you do it, you must recover the total of your fixed and variable costs. All too often molders set their machine-hour rates by the going rate in the marketplace and with no regard for their own costs. What I would like to do is highlight a few areas that are sometimes overlooked and which, if not given serious consideration, may undermine your expected gross profit.

The obvious mechanics of estimating are relatively easy, taking into consideration material cost and packaging supplies. More difficult is estimating the cycle. You will either make money or lose money, depending on how realistic you are at this stage. Of the many variables involved in estimating, all of the major ones involve cycle. These are interrelated, and you must take them all into consideration. To do this, you must know the customer's requirements and quality standards. Otherwise you will find that you cannot perform to standard within the cycle used in your estimate.

Once you have determined the possible cycle, then check for what will be the "average" cycle. These are two entirely different figures and it is the latter one, "the average," that should go into your estimate.

And what about the nasty word *scrap.* Too many molders still think of scrap as a piece of material that can be reclaimed. Stop fooling yourselves about getting all that resin back and especially don't forget you lost machine time and thus lowered your average cycle.

Quantity	1,000	
Scrap	13%	1,130
Cavities		1
Cycle		36
Mlc. size		16 oz.

This first area of scrap allowance is vital if you are going to meet standard costs. Remember, each time you mold a piece of scrap, you must consider the lost machine time as well as lost material. Therefore, if we have a 13 percent scrap factor, we must allow enough machine time to mold 1,130 parts in order to end up with 1,000 good parts. This 13 percent factor is carried through the estimate sheet for material and molding time. How do we get that percentage?

EXHIBIT 7 *(continued)*

Scrap allowance formula

		Class 1 material	Class 2 material
		5%	10%
		Nylon	Acetate
		Polystyrene colors	Polycarbonate
		A.B.S.	Crystal or
		Polyethylene	white materials
High quality	5%	10%	15%
Medium quality	3	8	13
Standard quality	0	5	10

We rate materials and quality requirement of the article. You may not agree with our grouping of materials or scrap allowance. Naturally, if you are fortunate enough to be in production on a single material or exceedingly long runs, this can be modified. But for a custom shop with short runs using many materials, don't sell yourself short. You will need these allowances!

As outlined in the illustration above, if we cross reference a medium quality job with a 3 percent factor and a class 2 material with a 10 percent factor we end up with the 13 percent scrap allowance.

Original preparation costs must be absorbed into the job, regardless of length of run. These preparation costs must include mold set-up time, purging time, and purging material. For each a formula can be developed.

Mold set-up formula

Machine size	Hourly rate	Class 1 (average)	Class 2 (difficult)
4 oz.	$10	1.5 hrs. $15	3.0 hrs. $30
16 oz.	$14	2.5 hrs. $21	5.0 hrs. $70
50 oz.	20	4.0 hrs. 80	8.0 hrs. 160

Note: Rates shown are for example purposes only.

In the illustration above, mold set-ups are divided into two categories, average and difficult. Machine time for mold set-up is lost to you and must be charged to the job. Use your standard machine-hour rate for the size of machine required and multiply it by the number of hours. Thus on the right-hand side, a difficult mold that takes five hours to set up on a 16-oz. machine costs $70, and this becomes one part of your preparatory cost.

Purging formula

Machine size	Hourly rate	Class 1			Class 2		
		Hours	$	Pounds	Hours	$	Pounds
4 oz.	$10	2	20	25	4	40	65
16 oz.	$14	3	$42	50	6	$ 84	80
50 oz.	20	4	80	75	8	160	100

Note: Rates shown are for example purposes only.

In purging we refer back to the class of material previously used, multiply it by the standard machine-hour rate, and obtain the lost machine time during purging. Thus on the right-hand side again, a class 2 material costs $84 of machine time to purge plus 80 pounds of material. This cost must be spread over the total number of parts molded.

EXHIBIT 7 *(continued)*

Short-run penalty 1

Quantity ordered	1M
Hours allowed	15
Total cost	$210.00

You never heard of a short-run penalty? Well, you should have! The estimator correctly figured the mold capable of running at a specific cycle. But how do you get the mold settled down to this cycle if the run will last for only three or four shifts? Here is what you can do.

Short-run penalty

Run hours	Penalty hours	4 oz. $10 hr.	16 oz. $14 hr.	50 oz. $20 hr.
30	5	$ 50	$ 70	$100
26	7	70	98	140
22	9	90	126	180
18	11	110	154	220
14	13	130	182	260
10	15	$150	$210	$300
8	16	160	224	320
6	17	170	238	340
4	18	180	252	360

Note: Rates shown are for example purposes only.

Starting at 30 hours use a reversal procedure. The shorter the run, the more hours you charge. By the time you get down to a 10-hour run you charge 15 hours penalty. If you think this is ridiculous, just put a true job costing on some of those short runs and remember it used just as many technicians and engineers to get it started, as a longer run.

	Pounds per 1,000		Price	
Material 3	Net	Gross	per pound	
G.P. Styrene	480.7	543.2	.15	$81.48
Red No. 2454				
Blue No. 1323				
Less reclaim		62.5	.075	4.69
Total				$76.79

The only point in showing the illustration above is to emphasize the original scrap allowance. We previously said because of a 13 percent scrap allowance we would need to mold 1,130 pieces to get 1,000 good ones. Allow for this material and if you so wish you can credit this area for reclaimed scrap.

	Molding Hours per 1,000			
Cycle seconds	Total	Good	$ Rate	Std. cost
36	10.0	11.3	14.00	$158.20

On molding extend the actual cycle by the time to mold those 130 extra pieces to arrive at the standard cycle for the job.

EXHIBIT 7 *(concluded)*

Quantity		1 000	4 000	10 000
Short-run penalty	1	210 00		
Preparation cost	2	102 75	25 69	10 28
Material	3	76 79	76 79	76 79
Molding	4	158 20	158 20	158 20
Die repair 5% of 158.20		7 91	7 91	7 91
Supplies	5			
Standard cost (000)	6	555 65	268 59	253 18

The recap, above, shows how the short-run penalty in the first column disappears after the quantity goes up in other columns. It also shows how the preparation costs, mold set-up, and purging are reduced as the quantity goes up. It puts the high cost of "getting going" on the short runs where it belongs. All other costs of material and molding remain constant.

Note that an allowance for the mold repair is based on a percentage of the hours the mold is running. This item eats into your gross profit if it is not specifically tied into the job.

Quantity		1 000	4 000	10 000
Preparation cost				
Molding cost	6	555 65	268 59	253 18
Assembly scrap	% of 6	16 67	8 06	7 60
Secondary operations	8	30 30	30 30	30 30
Supplies	9			
Standard cost		602 62	306 95	291 08

Beyond the molding level there may be secondary operations such as hot stamping, spray painting, or assembly. Many molders, starting into these operations in a small way, figure on absorbing their overhead on molding machine-hour rates. Thus they estimate direct labor only for these secondary operations. However, they do have overhead for these operations, such as supervision, floor space, and equipment costs, and it should be assessed to this operation properly.

Be sure to allow for scrap in this area based on the complete molded cost plus any extended labor or materials that have preceded.

Standard cost

```
Indirect labour  ⎫
Plant salaries   ⎪
Fringe benefits  ⎪
Repairs          ⎬   Plant         Direct labour
Plant supplies   ⎪   overhead  +   material      = Standard
Utilities        ⎪                                  cost
Taxes            ⎪
Depreciation     ⎪
Insurance        ⎭
```

Finally, we have a standard cost estimate above. This represents, in our system, the manufacturing cost including all plant expenses mentioned previously.

To arrive at the selling price we must add the following to the cost estimate:

Selling price = Standard cost + Administrative O/H, selling expense, financial expense, profit

These items are handled usually on a percentage basis, relative to your total sales budget forecast. Each firm must make its own decision, to achieve the desired return on investment.

philosophy encountered practical difficulties such as imperfect cost information and competition from molders with lower actual or apparent costs, or molders who were milling, for a particular contract, to bid below their full costs or even their variable costs in order to "win."

To some extent, the terms of their standard molding contract protected Midland from cost overruns. The most important contract provisions dealt with price, quantity and material:

Price

a. We reserve the right to increase our prices at any time if such increase(s) become necessary due to higher labour or material costs, or for other reasons beyond our control. However, unfilled orders or unfilled portions thereof which have been entered by us will be filled at the prices originally agreed upon, provided we are able to make shipment within the calendar quarter of order entry. All or part of an accepted order not shipped within the original calendar quarter will be invoiced at prices in effect during calendar quarter(s) in which shipments are made.

   [For every $0.01 per kilogram change in resin cost, the quoted price(s) will change by $_____ per thousand parts. Prices are based on resin costs as of _____.]

b. We also reserve the right to increase the price on any undelivered portion of any order by the amount seller's costs are affected by changes in federal or provincial sales taxes, duties, or rates or exchange.

c. The prices quoted herein apply only to uninterrupted runs in the quantities specified and are subject to the seller's acceptance when the order is received.

d. This quotation is subject to revision if not accepted within thirty (30) days from the date hereof.

Quantity

Delivery of 5 percent more or less than the quantity ordered shall constitute fulfillment of the order and any excess within this limit shall be accepted and paid for by the purchaser. If no underrun is specified, the overrun allowance will be increased to 10 percent. If no overrun is specified, the underrun allowance will be increased to 10 percent.

Materials

The purchaser is responsible for disclosing at the outset all pertinent engineering and design requirements and restrictions of the part. Any expense incurred by the seller due to failure of the purchaser to comply with the above will be the responsibility of the purchaser. The seller agrees to supply his professional engineering knowledge to advise the purchaser in every way possible and also draw on the specialized facilities of tool makers, designers, and material suppliers, but the final choice of the most suitable plastic material must ultimately be the responsibility of the purchaser.

Contracts were usually negotiated for large quantities to be delivered in several shipments (i.e., individual "orders") over the course of a year. Normally, each order was produced as a separate run. Orders were shipped as completed and clients billed net 30 days from date of shipment. In practice, Midland adopted a flexible policy with respect to total contract quantity.

Lin noted an industrywide tendency to underestimate or ignore costs in pricing decisions, a trend that was particularly prevalent in times of surplus capacity. Claiming that "competition-based pricing" was "spoiling the market," Lin became chief spokesman for "realistic full-costing plus reasonable return" in an address before the Society of Plastic Industries:

> One of the worst fallacies of the plastic processing industry is trying to plug up machine utilization with incremental costing. Naturally, a case can be made for incremental costing to help pick up the high fixed costs of our type of operation. However, the marketplace becomes flooded with the opportunity to buy at incremental prices. At this stage it becomes incremental no more—it becomes suicidal!
>
> Surely making a profit is the only way to stay in business. Surely it is the only way the customer will have a reliable source of supply. If the industry does not earn reasonable returns on investment, it will not continue to attract capital. If any industry needs capital, it is surely ours. Machinery, modernized and automated, adequate building space, research and control methods all take vast amounts of capital. This money can only come from the financial community, and it won't come from there unless we can prove that the return is forthcoming. Keep this in mind when pricing and don't be misled.

Harris Products

Harris Products marketed a line of flower pots to department stores, discount merchandisers, hardware chains, and nurseries across the United States and Canada. The pots were currently molded for Harris by an Ohio-based custom molding company. The current chain of distribution for the flower pots was as follows:

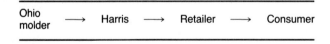

The U.S. market for flower pots and other garden accessories had seen explosive growth. According to *Merchandising Week:*

> It's no secret. Creeping charlies, boston ferns, diffenbachias are big business and the "greening" of housewares is accelerating at a phenomenal rate.
>
> Spurred by intense consumer interest in home horticulture plus the lure of fast turns and a high profit structure, housewares buyers are finding sales of pots, plants, and plant-related accessories sprouting all over the country.

Department stores and mass merchandisers have added or expanded these sections. . . . In fact, the category is growing at such a pace that it merits its own buyer in some stores.

Retail margins can run as high as 70 percent on plants (sometimes higher). . . . Planters can realize margins from 30 percent to 60 percent in assortments including plastic, ceramic, clay, wicker, basket, wood, and glass. Plastic and ceramic are said to be the number one and two most popular sellers. The key to . . . planters seems to be wide assortment with colorful designs balanced by those in natural tones.

A popular retail price point for plastic pots is about $1.50, while it's around $2.50 for ceramic. Baskets are popular near the $2 mark, while clay is good at $1 and under.[4]

The year 1986 had seen "continued strong growth" in U.S. demand and the emergence of a similar pattern in Canada. Harris had found a sales agent to promote and sell in New York State, where sales were weak. The agent predicted that Harris' sales would exceed 1 million flower pots in 1987 in New York, as shown in Exhibit 8. Their sales in 1986 had been 118,000 pots.

EXHIBIT 8 Harris forecast of their New York sales, 1987

Model		Forecast sales (000 units)
BP-11		30
BP-13		25
BP-15		22
LP-3		30
LP-4		55
LP-5		70
LP-6		80
LP-7	(item 1)	45
LP-11	(item 2)	45
#400		25
#430		25
#440		45
#450		40
#470	(item 3)	45
CS-4		65
CS-5		75
CS-6		80
CS-7		80
CS-8		70
CS-11		40
CS-13		30
CS-15		25
CS-17		25
Total		1,072

---

[4] "Pots and Plants Bloom amid the Pots and Pans," *Merchandising Week,* October 6, 1975, p. 1.

Equipped with 19 injection molding machines and a full-time work force of 140 employees, Harris' current Ohio molder could continue to handle the extra pot production caused by this sales growth, at least in the short term.

However, several factors weighed against this approach. Major Harris retail customers were highly price sensitive and demanded fast, direct delivery to minimize their inventory costs. Plastic finished goods from out of state were subject to a New York excise tax of 15 percent, which had to be paid by the retailer. Moreover, Harris was concerned that New York excise tax disagreements would cause competitively disadvantageous delays and expense. Operating a warehouse to service New York customers would add fixed costs on the order of $15,000 per year.

These problems had prompted Harris to consider New York pot manufacture for the New York market. They had sought a long-term relationship with a suitable custom injection molder willing to make, package, store, invoice, and ship flower pots to their retail customers, at an all-inclusive unit price comparable to their laid-in cost from Ohio.

Harris' basic requirements somewhat limited the number of New York molders eligible for bid consideration. Their prerequisites included:

1. A wide range of molding equipment—to accommodate all 23 sizes/styles in the Harris flower pot line.
2. Scheduling flexibility—to "work around" the production timetable of their molder. Harris owned only one set of flower pot molds. These were held in the custody of their molder. Since duplicate molds would cost an additional $15,000 each, Phillips intended to shuttle the molds back and forth across the state line, at an estimated cost of $50 per mold (round trip).
3. Storage space—to house raw materials (i.e., four colours of polypropylene resin and 20 different sizes of paper cartons) plus finished inventory.

In December 1986 Harris asked Midland to submit a quotation on an initial order for three flower pot models for 5,000 units of each. Harris would not guarantee purchase volume beyond this initial order. Lin also knew that Harris wanted a minimum margin themselves of about 20 percent in marketing the flower pots.

The Bid Pricing Decision

Lin Love believed Midland had the range of molding equipment and scheduling flexibility necessary to accommodate Harris. He was also confident that any additional area required to store resins, packaging materials, and finished goods could be leased on neighbouring property. Lin was less sure of Midland's ability to sell at a price agreeable to Harris and still make an acceptable return. As he reviewed the opportunity, he became more aware of the uncertainties in available cost/market information and wondered about the level of risk in the situation. On the other hand, Lin knew that any bid which grossly exceeded the laid-in cost of Ohio-produced pots would be rejected. He had made estimates of the Ohio molder's cost, but did not know its exact selling price to Harris. Harris would not reveal this information to him.

Harris flower pots were molded using a polypropylene resin, which was currently selling at 32.3 cents in New York compared to 26.5 cents per pound in Ohio. Prices of the various resins were volatile, reflecting a complex interplay of factors, including the capacity of resin producers, the demand for different resins, and the prices of petroleum feedstocks, among others.

Harris provided molding cycle times for each flower pot mold based on information from their supplier. Item 1 was molded in a double-cavity die, producing two pots every 46 seconds, while items 2 and 3 were molded singly every 40.6 seconds and 46.4 seconds, respectively. Although Midland had no previous experience molding flower pots, Lin was confident that it would be no more difficult than many other items they were molding.

The three flower pot models would be molded on separate machines, each assigned a different machine-hour rate:

	Variable	Fixed	Machine-hour rate
Item 1	$10.15	$18.95	$29.10
Item 2	7.40	7.80	15.20
Item 3	8.25	10.95	19.20

Lin believed Harris' current supplier's variable processing costs (mostly direct labor) were more comparable to those at Midland. He was also fairly certain that, proportionately, annual fixed overhead was similar for both firms, although higher annual volume would lower the Ohio supplier's fixed costs on a per unit basis. Lin estimated machine-hour rates at the Ohio supplier as below:

	Variable	Fixed	Estimated machine-hour rate
Item 1	$10	$10	$20
Item 2	7	3	10
Item 3	8	4	12

Lin also expected Midland to match the Ohio supplier's "preparation" times (i.e., set-up and purge) but felt that shorter run lengths at Midland would raise per unit costs. The average run at Midland would be 5,000 flower pots, only one third the average run at the Ohio supplier.

Almost entirely variable, Midland's packaging expenses per thousand units were estimated as follows:

Item 1	$37.40
Item 2	40.60
Item 3	47.43

Lin knew packaging was less expensive in Ohio, since a recent study conducted by SPI had shown that New York molders spent approximately 25–30 percent more than their Ohio counterparts for equivalent packaging. Midland had adequate storage space to accommodate the initial order. If, however, sales projections proved accurate, Midland would need approximately 1,000 square feet of additional space to accommodate subsequent orders. Room was available in an adjacent building for $4/square foot on a yearly basis. Storage costs would have to be fully absorbed into the unit price, as Harris refused to pay warehousing charges directly. Exhibit 9 summarizes the factory cost projections for Midland Industries. Similar estimates for Harris' current molder appear in Exhibit 10.

There would likely be no significant differences in selling and administration costs whether the pots were produced in New York or Ohio. Furthermore, the shipping charges on the finished flower pots (borne by Harris customers) were roughly the same FOB the Ohio supplier's plant as FOB Watertown, New York.

Lin questioned whether the differences between Harris' laid-in cost from Ohio and Midland's costs would ensure Midland "reasonable" profit, which he considered should be 20 percent. He reviewed the terms on the quotation sheet and wondered how much Midland could rely on the estimates. Lin had only three days to decide whether Midland should bid for the Harris business, and if so, on what terms. He knew that, given the excess capacity in the industry, competition for the business would be fierce.

EXHIBIT 9 Estimated cost of producing initial order for Midland (cost per 1,000 units expressed in $)

	Item 1	Item 2	Item 3
Resin cost per pound	$ .323	$ .323	$ .323
Pounds of resin required/1,000 units*	580	604	620
Total resin cost/1,000 units	$187.34	$194.90	$200.26
Number of pots/cycle	2	1	1
Standard average cycle time	46 sec.	40.6 sec.	46.4 sec.
Gross molding hours/1,000 units*	6.4 hrs.	11.13 hrs.	12.9 hrs.
Machine-hour rate†	$ 29.10	$ 15.20	$ 19.20
Total machine cost/1,000 units	$186.25	$168.95	$247.70
Preparation time per run‡	1 hr.	1 hr.	1 hr.
Preparation time cost/1,000 units	$ 5.80	$ 3.05	$ 3.85
Packaging cost/1,000 units	$ 37.40	$ 40.60	$ 47.43
Total estimated factory cost	$416.79	$407.50	$499.24

* Includes 5 percent scrap allowance.

†	Item 1	Item 2	Item 3
Variable	$ 10.15	$ 7.40	$ 8.25
Fixed	18.95	7.80	10.95
Total machine-hour rate	$ 29.10	$ 15.20	$ 19.20

‡ Assumes run of 5,000 units.

EXHIBIT 10   Estimated molder cost of producing initial order at the current Ohio molder's plant (cost per 1,000 units expressed in $)

	Item 1	Item 2	Item 3
Resin cost per pound	$ .265	$ .265	$ .265
Pounds of resin required/1,000 units*	580	604	620
Total resin cost/1,000 units	$153.70	$160.05	$164.30
Number of cavities (i.e., pots/cycle)	2	1	1
Gross molding hours/1,000 units*	6.4	11.13	12.9
Machine-hour rate*	$ 26.00	$ 13.50	$ 16.50
Total machine cost	$166.40	$150.25	$212.85
Preparation time per run (hrs.)†	1	1	1
Preparation time cost/1,000 units	$ 1.70	$ .90	$ 1.10
Packaging/1,000 units	$ 29.20	$ 34.45	$ 40.20
Total estimated factory cost	$351.00	$345.65	$418.45

* Includes 5 percent scrap allowance.
† Assumes run of 15,000 units.

Case 35

Consolidated-Bathurst
Pulp and Paper Limited*

On the morning of September 28, 1973, Mr. John Andrew, president of
Consolidated-Bathurst Pulp and Paper Limited, was evaluating the current price
charged for newsprint to U.S. customers. A number of recent developments in
the newsprint market had provoked this evaluation. Newsprint was in much
shorter supply than in previous years due to a large increase in demand in the
last two years. This increase had not been matched by increased industry
capacity to produce. Also, a number of competitors' newsprint mills were shut
down by strikes. Mr. Andrew was considering a change from Consolidated-
Bathurst's current price of U.S. $175 per ton. He was aware that he would have
to carefully consider both the customers' reactions and the competition's reactions to any changes that he might make.

Company Background

Consolidated-Bathurst Pulp and Paper Limited was a wholly owned subsidiary
of Consolidated-Bathurst Limited, a fully integrated, multiproduct paper company. Mr. Andrew was a senior vice president of the parent company, besides
holding the operating responsibility for the newsprint division.

In 1972, Consolidated-Bathurst Limited had sales of $348 million and had
assets of $430 million. The company's sales and earnings performance record
for the period 1966–72 is shown in Exhibit 1. In 1970 and 1971, the company
operated at a loss. Throughout this period the newsprint operation, the firm's
major product line, had remained profitable, but with insufficient return on
investment to warrant the investment of additional capital to purchase a new
newsprint machine. These machines cost about $120,000 per daily ton, if built
at an existing mill site with wood handling facilities available. At a new site, the
costs of developing this wood handling capacity would raise the cost to about
$150,000 per daily ton. Thus, a machine that could produce 500 tons per day

---

* This case was written by Thomas C. Kinnear and Stephen Becker. Copyright © 1974, the
University of Western Ontario. Reproduced with permission.

EXHIBIT 1 Sales and earnings results ($000)

	1972	1971	1970	1969	1968	1967	1966
Net sales	$348,055	$343,362	$353,944	$348,087	$295,472	$242,198	$234,485
Earnings (before extraordinary items)	6,496	442	589	10,554	13,126	17,788	21,108
Per common share*	0.55	(0.45)	(0.42)	1.23	1.69	2.48	3.05
Net earnings (loss) per share after extraordinary items*	0.56	(8.70)	(2.30)	1.40	1.36	2.40	3.00

* Per common share earnings are stated after deducting application of preferred dividend requirements.

would cost about $75 million. Consolidated-Bathurst had made some capital investments in the last few years and as a result anticipated that their capacity would increase by 70,000 tons per year at the end of 1973. This increase in capacity would come from an extension of their Belgo Division Mill in Shawinigan, Quebec. An old newsprint machine had been purchased and modified at a cost of $11 million to give this increase in capacity.

Governments, particularly provincial, had frequently distorted the industry's normal growth pattern. By means of grants and tax incentives, they had promoted expansion when it was not needed, sometimes in a locale which was not and never could be economic. Many of these ventures had proven to be disastrous. (Developments in Newfoundland and Manitoba were outstanding examples of this.)

Mr. Andrew was concerned that increased prices would be an incentive for competitors to develop new mills. The risks were that expansion by competitors would decrease Consolidated-Bathurst's share of the market and also that rapid expansion by many companies could result in significant overcapacity such as had existed some few years before.

In 1972, Consolidated-Bathurst recorded a newsprint sales volume of 912,000 tons, of which about two thirds was sold in U.S. markets. About 10 percent was sold overseas and the rest in Canada. Other Consolidated-Bathurst products included pulp, container board, kraft paper, boxboard, lumber, and packaging products. Overall, the company's total business was 56 percent basic mill products, 41 percent packaging, and 3 percent lumber.

The Newsprint Industry

Consolidated-Bathurst ranked fifth in newsprint capacity in Canada with 9.2 percent of the total capacity. Exhibit 2 shows the capacity and shares of the other Canada-based competitors in the industry. Operating capacity rates for the past nine years, as shown in Exhibit 3, were a major element in pricing decisions by members of the industry. There were also a number of significant U.S. producers of newsprint. Exhibit 4 shows their estimated capacities. The U.S. companies were very important in the pricing process for newsprint. Consolidated-Bathurst sales personnel felt that American publishers attached a

EXHIBIT 2 Canadian newsprint producers (>200,000 tons) in order of size, by capacity and residual total (<200,000 tons) lumped

Producer	Capacity (tons)	Share of industry (percent)
1. MacMillan-Bloedel Ltd.	1,364,100	13.4%
2. Canadian International Paper	1,154,100	11.3
3. The Price Company Ltd.	1,058,400	10.4
4. Abitibi Paper Co. Ltd.	1,044,200	10.2
5. Consolidated-Bathurst Ltd.	936,600	9.2
6. Ontario Paper Co. Ltd.	765,000	7.5
7. Bowaters Canadian Corp. Ltd.	546,200	5.4
8. Domtar Newsprint Ltd.	540,300	5.3
9. Great Lakes Paper Co. Ltd.	432,200	4.2
10. Anglo-Canadian Pulp & Paper	336,800	3.3
11. Spruce Falls Power & Paper Co.	332,100	3.3
12. Ontario-Minnesota Pulp & Paper Co.	322,200	3.2
13. Donohue Co. Ltd.	257,000	2.5
14. Crown Zellerbach Can. Ltd.	254,100	2.5
15. B. C. Forest Products Ltd.	242,700	2.4
Balance of producers (<200,000 ton producers)	607,600	5.9
	10,193,600	100.0

EXHIBIT 3 Canadian newsprint industry: Capacity, operating ratio, production, reserve capacity (1965 through 8 months 1973)

Year	Official capacity*	Indicated operating ratio	Production	Indicated reserve capacity
1965	8,420,800	91.7	7,719,700	701,100
1966	8,878,100	94.8	8,418,800	459,300
1967	9,293,900	86.6	8,051,500	1,242,400
1968	9,655,400	83.2	8,031,300	1,624,100
1969	9,611,500	91.1	8,758,400	853,100
1970	9,718,900	88.6	8,607,500	1,111,400
1971	10,050,400	82.6	8,297,000	1,753,400
1972	10,117,900	85.6	8,660,800	1,457,100
8 months—1973	6,795,100	90.5	6,130,100	665,000
12 months—1973	10,193,600†			

* Capacity figures shown are official, theoretically possible amounts. An approximate 95 percent is considered practically possible. Note also that these figures represent nondutiable (U.S. tariff) grades only and do not incorporate Groundwood Printing and Specialty Grades (dutiable) of which some 500,000 tons per annum are produced. Detailed capacities of the latter are not published and, indeed, some part of the above capacities can be shifted to produce dutiable grades as demand dictates and profit incentives exist.

† Estimated.

EXHIBIT 4 Major U.S. newsprint producers

Producer	Capacity (tons)
Southland Paper	470,000
Kimberly-Clark	420,000
Publishers Paper	360,000
Great Northern	360,000
Boise Cascade	135,000
Boise Price	150,000
Others	<100,000

higher degree of legitimacy to price increases originating with U.S.-based producers. At the present time, only Great Northern, Crown Zellerbach, and Publishers Paper of the U.S. producers were placing their major sales emphasis in the prime market areas of the Canadian producers.

Most pulp and paper companies were experiencing increasing production costs. As shown in Exhibit 5, manufacturing costs as a percentage of sales were

EXHIBIT 5 Ratio of manufacturing costs to gross sales: Index 1965 = 100

Year	Industry
1972	108
1971	107
1970	103
1969	106
1968	108
1967	106
1966	102
1965	100

higher in 1972 than most of the previous seven years. Consolidated-Bathurst's manufacturing costs as a percentage of sales had risen sharply in the previous three years and in 1973 were above the industry average. An increase in the cost of labour in 1974 was expected to increase production costs even more. Although Consolidated-Bathurst did not have any workers on strike, the demands of wage parity with other firms that were on strike would certainly be a major factor in future negotiating sessions. The current industry labour position is shown in Exhibit 6. The seriousness of the situation was reported in the *Globe and Mail* on Friday, September 28, 1973:

EXHIBIT 6 Eastern Canadian newsprint mills—strikes situation as of September 28, 1973

Company	Date strike began	Status
MacMillan Rothesay Ltd. (MacMillan-Bloedel Mill at Rothesay, Quebec)	September 9	Still out
E. B. Eddy	August 29	Ratified Sept. 14
Canadian Cellulose	August 1	Settled Aug. 5
C.I.P.—Gatineau, LaTuque, Trois Rivieres	July 27	Still out
C.I.P.—Hawkesbury	August 3	Still out
New Brunswick International Paper	August 8	Still out
Ontario and Minnesota Pulp and Paper—Fort Frances	July 3	Still out
—Kenora	July 9	Still out
Price Company—Alma and Kenogami	August 10	Still out

Despite recent settlements in Ontario, strikes in the Quebec pulp and paper industry continue to present a bleak contrast to an otherwise rosy prospect for that key Quebec industry.

No end is in sight to strikes involving about 5,000 workers that began several weeks ago at five mills, three of them in Quebec, owned by Canadian International Paper Co. of Montreal, nor to strikes by about 1,800 employees that began in August at two Quebec mills of Price Co. Limited of Quebec City.

Meanwhile, the UPIU (United Paperworkers International Union) has resumed contract negotiations with the Eastern Canada Newsprint Group, which is bargaining on behalf of five mills owned by four Quebec companies and one in Nova Scotia. Negotiations involving several other Quebec mills remain in abeyance in their preliminary stages.

These strikes come at a time when sales have generally been "Terrific" for pulp and paper producers, says Paul E. Lachance, President of the Council of Pulp and Paper Producers of Quebec.

He considers the strikes particularly unfortunate because the industry could have been selling so much. He estimates that between CIP and Price, about $1 million a day of sales are being lost.

Dr. Lachance expects strong markets to continue in 1974.

The Market for Newsprint

About 50 percent of newsprint in the United States was consumed by major metropolitan papers and the rest by much smaller dailies and weeklies. Papers like the *New York Times* and the *Detroit News,* for example, would consume about 400,000 tons and 100,000 tons of newsprint every year, respectively. Consolidated-Bathurst sold mostly to larger papers or groups of papers. Their yearly contracts with the larger papers or groups of papers ranged from 20,000 tons to over 100,000 tons with an average of about 50,000 tons. Consolidated-Bathurst had a total of about 170 accounts with 10 percent of these accounting for almost 70 percent of sales and 25 percent accounting for over 90 percent of sales. In the United States some of the larger contracts were held with the *Baltimore Sun,* The Newhouse Group (including *Long Island Daily* and *Cleveland Plain Dealer*), the Knight Newspapers (including *Miami Herald, Beacon Journal,* Akron, Ohio, *Detroit Free Press*), the *Detroit News, Philadelphia Bulletin, Boston Globe, The Wall Street Journal,* and the *New York Daily News.* Major Canadian customers included *La Presse Trans-Canada Newspapers,* the *Montreal Star,* and the *Toronto Star.* For large accounts, newsprint contracts were negotiated by Mr. Andrew and his immediate subordinates. The publisher and financial vice president usually represented the newspaper in these negotiations. Most other newsprint producers had about the same amount of account concentration as Consolidated-Bathurst.

In determining which newsprint producer received a particular volume of newsprint contract, publishers considered the printability and runability (amount of breakage in the press), delivery time, sales terms, and customer technical service to correct any problems. Personal relationship among negotiators was also considered to be very important. Almost all publishers had two or three sources of supply. Also, they quite often purchased some cut-price newsprint from smaller suppliers in Scandinavia or the United States.

About 85 percent of Canadian newsprint was produced in eastern Canada with the remaining 15 percent being produced in British Columbia. The major western producers were MacMillan-Bloedel Limited, Crown Zellerbach, and B. C. Forest Products. These producers sold mainly in the western United States and the Orient. MacMillan-Bloedel also had about 25 percent of its total capacity at Rothesay in eastern Canada and so competed directly with the eastern producers. The eastern producers sold mainly in the Northeast and Midwest United States, the United Kingdom, South America, and Canada.

Personnel at Consolidated-Bathurst estimated that in 1974, U.S. production would be 3.4 million tons out of a capacity of 3.6 million tons, and that Canadian production would be 9.8 million tons out of a capacity of 10.6 million tons. U.S. exports were expected to be about 100,000 tons while Canadian overseas exports were expected to be about 1.7 million tons. Scandinavian imports into the United States were expected to be about 300,000 tons. Total U.S. demand for 1974 was estimated at 10.5 million tons, while Canadian demand was expected to be 900,000 tons. Another 200,000 tons were expected to be sold for inventory.

Mr. Andrew knew that a few competitors had started marketing a 30-pound grade of newsprint. An important factor was that the thinner sheet produced a 6 percent saving in wood consumption. This saving was important as the pulp and paper industry was quickly approaching the limit of low-cost, accessible wood resources. The impact of this thinner paper on publishers was not yet known.

Consolidated-Bathurst also made higher-quality newsprint grades, which sold at a 3 percent to 10 percent premium over the standard price.

EXHIBIT 7 Outline of U.S. newsprint price changes (1965–1973) in U.S. dollars per ton

Date	Company (in order of announcement)	Announced increase or decrease	Effective price	Effective date	
March 1, 1966 (est.)	Domtar	$10	$145	April 1, 1966	
	Bowater Sales Corp.	10	145	April 1, 1966	
	Consolidated Paper (Consolidated-Bathurst's 1966 name)	10	145	April 1, 1966	
March 23, 1966	Domtar announces rollback	(5)	140	May 16, 1966	
	Bowater Sales Corp.	(5)	140	May 16, 1966	
	Great Lakes Paper	(5)	140	May 16, 1966	
April 20, 1966	All firms change effective date	(5)	140	June 1, 1966	
September 26, 1966	Crown Zellerbach Corp.	4	138	June 1, 1967	
October 25, 1966	MacMillan Bloedel	(3)	137	June 1, 1967	West Coast
November 1, 1966	Crown Zellerbach	3	140	June 1, 1967	United States only
March 15, 1967	Consolidated Paper	3	143	July 1, 1967	
March 17, 1967	International Paper Sales Co.	3	143	July 1, 1967	
September 27, 1968	International Paper Sales Co.	5	148	January 1, 1969	North
		4	147	January 1, 1969	South*
	All others follow immediately after				
September 24, 1969	Bowater Sales Co.	4-5	152	January 1, 1970	Wipes out all price differential—universal price
November 20, 1969	(Consolidated-Bathurst is 4th company to announce price increase)	(1)	152	January 1, 1970	North
	$1 price differential to South reinstated		151	January 1, 1970	South

Date	Company	Increase	Price	Effective	Market
September 8, 1970	Anglo-Canadian	10	162	January 1, 1971	
	Consolidated-Bathurst	10	162	January 1, 1971	
	International Paper	10	162	January 1, 1971	
September 22, 1970	Boise-Cascade	10	162	January 1, 1971	South only
	Boise-Cascade	8	160	January 1, 1971	All markets
November 3, 1970	Abitibi	8	160	January 1, 1971	
November 4, 1970	Southland Paper	7	159	January 1, 1971	South
November 15, 1970	All majors	8	160	November 15, 1970	
December 6, 1970	All majors	8	160	April 1, 1971	Canada only
August 12, 1971	MacMillan-Bloedel	8	168	November 1, 1971	
	Price Company	8	168	November 1, 1971	
	(Consolidated-Bathurst is 5th company to announce price increase)				
August 15, 1971	Nixon imposes wage-price freeze. Price increase dropped.				
December 10, 1971 (Est.)	International Paper Sales Co.	8	168	December 1971	North
	(3.4%, or $5.25 price increase approved	5.25	164.25	December 1971	South
	by U.S. Price Commission)				
	Consolidated-Bathurst	8	168	December 1971	North
December 1, 1972	Great Northern Paper Co.	5	170	February 1, 1973	
	Southland Paper Co.	5	170	February 1, 1973	
	(Consolidated-Bathurst is 4th company to announce price increase (December 19)).				
April 12, 1973	Bowater Sales Co.	5	175	July 1, 1973	
	Kruger Pulp and Paper	5	175	July 1, 1973	
	Consolidated-Bathurst	5	175	July 1, 1973	

* South includes Texas, Oklahoma, Louisiana, Arkansas, Missouri, and Kansas.

History of Price Changes

Because of the competitiveness in the newsprint market, any price changes were made after much deliberation and with full anticipation of possible competitive moves. An outline of pricing activity in the U.S. newsprint market in recent years is shown in Exhibit 7. This exhibit lists only those firms that were in the first group of firms to act on any price change. After a sorting-out period following a price change, most firms sold at the established market price within a particular geographic market. Usually a change was made effective from a future date which allowed both competitors and purchasers time to analyze and react to the change. The North-South distinction in the exhibit refers to the fact that major publishers in the southeastern states had bargained one firm against another to get a lower market price than existed in the northeastern states. This difference existed despite the increased distance and transportation costs.

Most sales contracts were for 5 to 10 years but provisions for price increases were outlined in clauses tying them to "general although not necessarily universal" industry prices. In relation to these contracts, members of the sales staff generally felt that the customer was not bound if the conditions under which the contract was signed should change.

Newsprint represented about 30 percent of the total costs to newspaper publishers, and consequently, newsprint price increases had to be passed on by the publisher, usually to advertisers, if he was to maintain his profitability. Timing of a price increase therefore was critical—if it came just after the publisher had revised his advertising rates (which were usually fixed for a certain period) then he would have no means of recouping the extra cost. Rate cards for major publishers were set at many different times throughout the year.

Newspaper publishers had in the past reacted in several ways to the announcement of a price increase for newsprint. The first reaction was sometimes emotional. Heated telephone calls, letters pleading for reconsideration, or speeches castigating the Canadian newsprint "cartel" were not uncommon.

Publishers could also take direct action by threatening to cancel their contracts. Some contracts actually had been cancelled using the price increase as an excuse, but the real reason might have been something else. More often, customers used the threat of cancellation to extract discounts from suppliers. This pressure was particularly effective when either of the following conditions existed:

a. The market was soft; that is, the industry was in a general state of oversupply. In this case, the customer would likely be able to find supply elsewhere, often at a reduced price.

b. The customer had more than one supplier. If one supplier was willing to grant a discount, the customer could use this as leverage to obtain concessions from the others. A prime example of this type of situation existed in the southern United States where a publisher-controlled newsprint company had influenced the establishment of a market price $2 less than the rest of the eastern United States. Because of this, Canadian mills charged a lower price to southern customers than to those in the North.

In August 1971, President Nixon imposed universal wage and price controls in the United States for 90 days. As of September 1973, the newsprint industry was operating under voluntary restraint on prices. Price increases were allowed, but were subject to review by the Cost-of-Living Council. If this council considered a price increase to be unreasonable, it could order the price rolled back.

The Future

Mr. Andrew was anxious to avoid any losses in the future especially in view of Consolidated-Bathurst's performance in previous years. In evaluating all the factors, Mr. Andrew knew that he would have to decide what the new price should be and when the change was to be made if he decided to make any price change at all. He also wondered if now was the time to make the investment in a new newsprint machine, and if so, what size of machine. He expected that production costs for newsprint on a new machine would be about 10 percent less than the current average total cost. Mr. Andrew knew that he was operating in a basically conservative commodity business. He was anxious to make good decisions both for his company and for his industry.

Part 8

Public Policy and Ethical Aspects of Marketing

The current environment of the marketing manager is undergoing rapid change and transition. Probably the most noteworthy of these developments, whether for better or for worse, is the increasing pervasiveness of public influences on marketing institutions and decision making. In this context, public influences are generally defined to include different levels of government (acting through legislation, regulation, or moral suasion), organized public groups (the consumerism movement, for example), individual advocates of change, and the force of changing public attitudes and opinion.

The cases in this section seek to develop an improved understanding of some of these trends and developments, and to provide practice for students in rendering decisions in the contemporary environment. The specific objectives of the cases are as follows:

1. To improve capacity for marketing decision making in situations where public influences and ethical considerations are involved.
2. To explore the nature and extent of public and ethical influences on marketing institutions and decision making.
3. To develop conceptual foundations leading to an improved understanding of contemporary developments in marketing.

Approaches to decision making in the area of marketing and public policy are not well established. One possible approach makes the following three assumptions:

1. Marketing and public policy decisions are made in a bargaining arena containing many interest groups.
2. Either explicit or implicit bargaining takes place among the interest groups in this arena whenever a marketing decision involves public influences.

3. Better decisions will be made if the objectives, motivations, and behaviors of each interest group are understood.

With these assumptions in mind, we present an approach to decision making in this area:

1. List and/or diagram the interest groups involved in a particular decision context. Note the interrelationships among them.
2. Identify the behavior of each group.
3. Attempt to explain this behavior by examining the objectives, motivations, and values of the people comprising the groups.
4. Identify what each group stands to lose or gain in the bargaining.
5. Identify what each group might be most willing to give up. What would they most want in return?
6. Based upon this analysis, predict the likely strategies of each group.
7. Make a decision based upon the anticipated reaction of each group to the alternatives you are considering. Be sure to have a contingency in case their reactions are not as you anticipated.

The ethical aspects of marketing are varied and complex. They fall in the so-called gray area of marketing decision making and behavior. The decision or behavior is itself legal, but may not be the right thing to do. The development of an approach to marketing ethics falls beyond the scope of this book. However, in this section we do present cases that explicitly raise ethics questions for marketers. Ethical issues are also present in some of the cases in other parts of the book.

Case 36 _____

F&F Sales Company*

Tom Frolik leaned back in his chair and reflected upon the events that had taken place earlier that day. His first day back to work after a long weekend over New Year's had really been hectic. Apparently while he had been on his skiing vacation, an article had appeared in the morning newspaper indicating that the Georgia State Troopers were upset about the effectiveness of radar detectors such as the Fuzzbusters that he marketed, and had encouraged several legislators to introduce a bill for the upcoming General Assembly outlawing these devices in Georgia. The phone had been ringing all day with many people calling to order a Fuzzbuster before their sale became illegal. Recognizing the potential consequences of this act for his company, he decided to develop a complete plan of action in the next few days.

Background on Radar Detector

The first radar detectors were marketed in the early 1960s. Typically, the units were not very high quality and sold for a price between $19.95 and $29.95. These units clipped onto the visor and would emit a beep when police radar was detected, allowing the driver to slow down before being caught in a radar trap. Although these units were relatively unsophisticated, several companies were somewhat successful in marketing them through mail-order advertising. With speed limits of 70 or 75 mph on most highways, however, most people did not have a need for these units.

Things changed dramatically beginning in 1973 with the fuel crisis and oil embargo. Speed limits were reduced nationally to 55 mph and were often enforced. The first response to this development was a dramatic increase in the sale of Citizens Band (CB) radios, which had been in existence for a number of years, but had experienced a very low level of sales. Many truckers purchased these units, and soon thereafter salesmen and other individuals who had to drive

_____
* Written by Kenneth L. Bernhardt. Copyright © 1980 by Kenneth L. Bernhardt.

a great deal began purchasing CB units. By 1975, the general public started buying CB radios in great numbers.

There were several problems with the CB radios as a means of avoiding speeding tickets. First, as more and more amateurs started using their radios, the channels became very cluttered. Often it was hard to hear what people were saying, as many people tried to use the same channel. Second, the CB radio became less and less reliable as the police (Smokey the Bear) put CB radios in their cars also. Thus, they could receive the same messages that truckers and other drivers were sending to each other. Third, the CB radio became much less reliable at night with the users' inability to see the police speed trap in the dark.

In addition to the problems with the effectiveness of CB radios, the state of the art on radar increased substantially about this time. With the old police radar units, about all they could do was set up a radar trap. New mobile radar units were developed that allowed the policemen to get a radar reading on a speeding car while the police car was moving. Another dramatic development was the ability of police radar to determine the speed of a car even though the police car was going in the opposite direction. Thus, a police officer could detect a speeding car going in the other direction, make a U-turn and arrest the speeder, something that was unheard of previously.

It was in this environment of reduced speed limits, increased enforcement, reduced effectiveness of CB radios, and increased effectiveness of police radar that the Fuzzbuster was introduced by the Electrolert Company in 1975. The Fuzzbuster, a military-type, parametric radar receiver, is sensitive to one/one hundredth of one-millionth of one watt, approximately the strength of radar at three miles if not blocked or otherwise attenuated. The Fuzzbuster receives in the 10.5 GHz Amateur (ham microwave) Band.

Drawing less than one quarter of a watt power, the Fuzzbuster can be left on indefinitely. It is installed on the dash of the car and has a self-contained antenna. The unit plugs into the cigarette lighter. When radar is picked up by the receiver, a warning light goes on and at the same time, a high-pitched tone is generated. The tone cuts off after two to three seconds, but the lamp remains bright until the radar signal ceases. The Fuzzbuster provides this identification of radar up to three miles distant. A pamphlet describing the Fuzzbuster is reproduced in Exhibit 1.

Background on Tom Frolik and F&F Sales Company

Tom Frolik first became aware of Fuzzbusters in January 1976, when he was working as a consultant to a large truck stop on Interstate 75 in Georgia. At that time Fuzzbusters had a suggested retail price of $99.95 and were sold to the retailer for $75. The truck stop ordered one dozen and sold them. They then ordered another dozen, and these also sold quite rapidly. Mr. Frolik then contacted the Electrolert Company and worked out an arrangement to become a distributor. The truck stop had a warehouse distribution subsidiary which bought replacement parts for trucks, and this subsidiary became an Electrolert

EXHIBIT 1

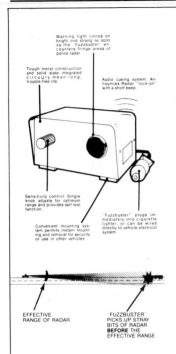

Warning light comes on bright and strong as soon as the "Fuzzbuster" encounters fringe areas of police radar.

Tough metal construction and solid state integrated circuitry mean long. trouble-free life.

Audio cueing system: Announces Radar "lock-on" with a short beep.

Sensitivity control. Single knob adjusts for optimum range and provides self-test function.

Convenient mounting system permits instant mounting and removal for security or use in other vehicles.

"Fuzzbuster" plugs immediately into cigarette lighter, or can be wired directly to vehicle electrical system.

EFFECTIVE RANGE OF RADAR

FUZZBUSTER PICKS UP STRAY BITS OF RADAR **BEFORE** THE EFFECTIVE RANGE

Complete protection for

$109.⁹⁵

FUZZBUSTER

IS MADE EXCLUSIVELY BY

ELECTROLERT, inc.

Troy. Ohio 45373

DISTRIBUTED BY

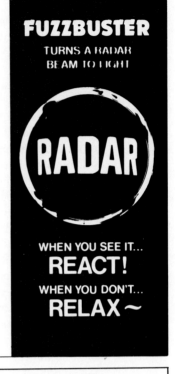

FUZZBUSTER

TURNS A RADAR BEAM TO LIGHT

RADAR

WHEN YOU SEE IT...
REACT!

WHEN YOU DON'T...
RELAX ~

FUZZBUSTER

Parametric Radar Receiver

Put a **Fuzzbuster** on your Dash and you can drive relaxed again. No watching for Radar lurking in the bushes, or trying to make sense out of the C.B. Radio chatter. And you don't have to put up with squeals or growls that warn you too late, or when there isn't any Radar around. Now you can enjoy the drive. anytime. anyplace . . . tension free.

The **Fuzzbuster** has been proven by tens of thousands of truckers over billions of miles, nationwide...so effective it has become a highway legend!

The **Fuzzbuster** was designed by a Speed Radar Manufacturer, and is a thoroughly engineered military type parametric radar receiver. Its performance is absolutely unparalleled. All solid-state integrated circuit construction insures extreme sensitivity and reliability.

The **Fuzzbuster** is equipped with a revolutionary audio cueing system which alerts you with a short beep each time the receiver locks on to a Radar signal. At the same time. the **Fuzzbuster** gives you positive visual indication of stationary or moving Radar ("New Vascar") two to ten times farther than the range of the Radar. You'll have ample time to slow down. With a little practice, the visual indicator can even tell you where and what kind of speed trap you are encountering.

The **Fuzzbuster** mounts quickly on the Dashboard and plugs directly into your cigar lighter, or you can wire it directly. It automatically adapts to positive or negative ground systems. The black matte finish prevents glare, and blends with any interior.

It works!

- **Sensitive** to **1/100th** of a **millionth** of **one watt** microwave energy.
- **Many times** more **sensitive** and **selective** than nearest pretender.
- **Works two** to **ten times** farther than Radar **without** the frequent **false alarms** of other detectors.
- **Draws** less than ¼ **watt...indefinite life.**
- **12 volt positive** or **negative** ground.
- **No antenna — no involved installation.**
- **Receives** all X-Band Radars in **all states.**
- **Especially effective** on new **Moving Radar,** used by 40 states.
- **Works day** or **night...city** or highway.
- **Half the cost** of a good **C.B. Radio.**

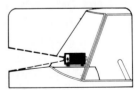

Give the **Fuzzbuster** a good view of the road ahead, and it will spot those electronic ambushes long before the Radar can spot you!

distributor. About this time some product improvements were made, the most important being the introduction of a flashing light in addition to the beep when radar was detected, and the retail price was increased to $109.95. The whole-sale price was $79.

The price to the distributor was $59 per unit, but they had to order in gross (a gross is 144 units). The manufacturer provided sample advertising mats and allowed $3 per unit for co-op advertising allowances. In March 1976, the truck stop ordered its first gross and at the same time, reduced the retail price to $84.95. Mr. Frolik recalled that they sold like hotcakes at this price, but because of complaints from those who had paid $109.95, and a feeling that a higher price would not hurt sales, they decided to raise the price to $89.95.

The truck stop distributor subsidiary made no attempt to sell Fuzzbusters through any other outlets, but did sell them through a second truck stop which they had recently purchased.

By October they had sold five gross (720 units) and were told that they had a big backup on the co-op advertising allowance. At the same time, the owner of the truck stop began to have some guilt feelings about marketing the product and decided he did not want to advertise it using his company name.

In late October, Tom Frolik announced that he was leaving the truck stop company to move to Atlanta to establish his own consulting firm and start several entrepreneurial enterprises. The owner of the truck stop suggested that Frolik market in the Atlanta area some of the products that the truck stop's distributor subsidiary handled. Frolik suggested that he be given the use of the advertising allowance credit for the Fuzzbuster, that he put in the time on the project, and that the truck stop owner and he split the profits on an equal basis. His proposal was accepted by the truck stop owner, and thus F&F Sales Company was created.

In November when Frolik came to Atlanta, the advertising allowance was up to $2,200. The Electrolert Company would pay 50 percent of all advertising expenditures for the Fuzzbuster up to this amount, but they would pay 100 percent of the expenses for newspaper advertising. Because of this provision, Frolik decided to take out some ads in *The Atlanta Journal* and *Constitution*. Exhibit 2 contains the ad that was approved by Electrolert. Mr. Frolik decided to run the ad four times—Sunday, December 12, the evening of December 16, the morning of December 17, and Sunday, December 19. These four ads, at an average of approximately $550 each, would utilize the full co-op advertising allowance available.

After the December 12 ad ran, with minimal response, Mr. Frolik changed the ad by inserting the telephone number of his office where people could call for further information or to place an order which would be charged to a bank credit card (using the truck stop's bank credit card mechanism). The four ads resulted in the immediate sale of 60 Fuzzbusters, with approximately half the people calling in for information before sending in their order. Mr. Frolik indicated that most of these buyers were salesmen, rather than truckers.

Three other outlets in Atlanta were advertising Fuzzbusters at this time. Two of these were retailers which took out small ads at a price of $99.95 and

EXHIBIT 2

$109.95, with both stores requiring the consumer to come to the retail outlet to purchase the Fuzzbuster. The third source was a firm in Alabama that offered a toll-free number together with a coupon in the ad for ordering. This firm, which accepted credit cards, charged $89.95 plus tax and handling ($3.50 for the tax and handling, the same as F&F Sales charged).

Although there were several other companies which marketed similar kinds of products, Mr. Frolik felt that the Fuzzbuster was the best radar detector available on the market. In the Atlanta area, these competitors had virtually no distribution.

Current Situation

As a result of the four ads in the middle of December, Mr. Frolik had been quite optimistic about sales of the Fuzzbuster. He had a number of ideas which he was planning to implement to increase sales, including taking out some classified advertising in the CB radio section of the classified ads. He also knew that Radio Shack stores did not stock Fuzzbusters or competitors, so he planned to write to the 43 Radio Shack store managers in his area and ask them to send any customers who requested this product to him.

Thus, all was very rosy for F&F Sales Company and Mr. Frolik when he left on Friday, December 24 for a 10-day skiing vacation. By the time he returned to the office on January 3, things were quite different. Exhibit 3 contains the article which ran in the morning *Atlanta Constitution* on Friday, December 31, describing the plan by the Georgia State Troopers to outlaw Fuzzbusters. Exhibit 4 contains the proposed legislation that would be introduced in the Georgia legislature. Mr. Frolik had read that the Virginia legislature had banned the devices several years earlier, but that the public outcry against such action had been so strong that legislation lifting the ban on radar detectors was under consideration in that state, and had a high likelihood of passing.

Mr. Frolik realized that his vacation was over and that he would have to develop a plan of action for the next few weeks. His first thought was that none of the cases he had studied during his M.B.A. program at a well-known eastern business school had dealt with this type of problem.

EXHIBIT 3   Fuzzbuster newspaper article

Fuzz Busters Really Work—
Troopers Want Radar Detectors Outlawed

By Keeler McCartney

Georgia state troopers are up in arms over the latest gadgets some motorists are using to detect highway radar speed timers, and they want the upcoming General Assembly to do something about it.

Bill Wilson, information officer of the state Department of Public Safety, said the gadgets in question detect the presence of radar machines and warn drivers before the troopers have a chance to detect speeders.

"It just isn't fair," Wilson said.

He said the warning devices, usually mounted on the dashboards of autos and trucks, can be purchased for $99.95 under the suggestive trade names of "Fuzz Busters," "Bear Finders" and "Trooper Snoopers."

As they approach radar stations, drivers equipped with the devices are alerted by a variety of noises ranging from the wail of an upended talking doll to the buzz of an angry bee and the beep of a telephone answering service.

The safety department has prepared a bill to submit to the next General Assembly which would make it a misdemeanor to possess, manufacture, or sell the devices in Georgia.

Troopers have checked the devices and found that they do, indeed, give the driver ample warning to slow down to the legal 55-mile limit before he enters a radar field, Wilson declared.

State Patrol Capt. R. C. Womack, who conducted a series of the tests in the Thomson and Savannah areas, concluded his findings this way:

"These devices are very demoralizing to the trooper who works the road day after day attempting to enforce the national speed limit. It is also a pathetic situation when a $100 device can counteract a $2,000 piece of equipment being used by law enforcement officers."

The troopers may be down because of the radar warning detectors, but they definitely are not out. They've worked up a trick or two of their own to beat the gadgets.

One of their favorites is to keep the radar speed timer turned off until the driver is well within range and then flick it on.

"The warning device will sound, all right," Wilson grinned. "But it's too late. The driver has already been caught."

And troopers have figured out the Citizens' Band (CB) lingo that goes with the use of radar detectors.

A favorite among truck drivers is, "My bird dogs are barking."

While awaiting legislative action, the troopers are collecting advertisements of the warning gadgets.

"Put a——on your dash and you can drive relaxed again," one ad suggests.

"No watching for radar lurking in the bushes or trying to make sense out of the CB radio chatter," says another. "And you don't have to put up with squeaky bleeps that warn you too late. Now you can enjoy the drive."

Wilson said legislation which the safety department is seeking is similar to laws already passed in the states of Virginia and Connecticut and the cities of Denver, Colo., and Washington, D.C.

EXHIBIT 4 Proposed legislation

H.B. No. 545
By: Representatives Milford of the 13th, Coleman of the 118th, Smith of the 42nd, McDonald of the 12th and Childs of the 51st

A BILL TO BE ENTITLED

AN ACT

To prohibit the use of devices on motor vehicles used to detect the presence of radar upon highways; to prohibit the operation of motor vehicles so equipped; to prohibit the sale of such devices; to provide for penalties; to provide an effective date; to repeal conflicting laws; and for other purposes.

BE IT ENACTED BY THE GENERAL ASSEMBLY OF GEORGIA:

Section 1. Prohibiting use of devices on motor vehicles to detect presence of radar upon highways or operation of motor vehicles so equipped or sale of such devices. It shall be unlawful for any person to operate a motor vehicle upon the highways of this State when such vehicle is equipped with any device or mechanism to detect the emission of radio microwaves in the electromagnetic spectrum, which microwaves are employed by police to measure the speed of motor vehicles upon the highways of this State for law enforcement purposes; it shall be unlawful to use any such device or mechanism upon any such motor vehicle upon the highways; it shall be unlawful to sell any such device or mechanism in this State. Provided, however, that the provisions of this section shall not apply to any receiver of radio waves of any frequency lawfully licensed by any State or federal agency.

Section 2. Any person, firm, or corporation violating the provision of this Act shall be guilty of a misdemeanor and, upon conviction thereof, shall be punished as for a misdemeanor, and any such prohibited device or mechanism shall be forfeited to the court trying the case.

Section 3. The presence of any such prohibited device or mechanism in or upon a motor vehicle upon the highways of this State shall constitute prima facie evidence of the violation of this section. The State need not prove that the device in question was in an operative condition or being operated.

Section 4. This section shall not apply to motor vehicles owned by the State or any political subdivision thereof and which are used by the police of any such government nor to law enforcement officers in their official duties, nor to the sale of any such device or mechanism to law enforcement agencies for use in their official duties.

Section 5. This Act shall become effective upon its approval by the Governor or upon its becoming a law without his approval.

Section 6. All laws and parts of laws in conflict with this Act are hereby repealed.

Case 37

Nestlé and the Infant Food Controversy (A)*

In October 1978, Dr. Fürer, managing director of Nestlé S.A., headquartered in Vevey, Switzerland, was pondering the continuing problems his company faced. Public interest groups, media, health organizations, and other groups had been pressuring Nestlé to change its marketing practices for infant formula products, particularly in developing countries. Those groups had used a variety of pressure tactics, including consumer boycott in the United States over the past eight years. Critics of Nestlé charged that the company's promotional practices not only were abusive but also harmful, resulting in malnutrition and death in some circumstances. They demanded Nestlé put a stop to all promotion of its infant formula products both to consumers and health personnel.

Nestlé management had always prided itself on its high quality standards, its efforts to serve the best interests of Nestlé customers, and its contribution to the health and prosperity of people in developing countries. Nestlé management was convinced their infant formula products were useful and wanted; they had not taken the first signs of adverse publicity in the early 1970s very seriously. By 1978, massive adverse publicity appeared to be endangering the reputation of the company, particularly in Europe and North America. Despite support from some health officials and organizations throughout the world, Nestlé management in Vevey and White Plains, New York (U.S.A. headquarters) were seriously concerned. Dr. Fürer had been consulting with Mr. Guerrant, President of Nestlé U.S.A., in an effort to formulate a strategy. Of immediate concern to Nestlé management was the scheduled meeting of the National

* This case was written by Aylin Kunt, research assistant under the supervision of Professors Christopher Gale and George Taucher in 1979. The earlier work of Professor James Kuhn of Columbia University is gratefully acknowledged. This version is a substantial revision of the earlier case and was prepared by Professor Michael R. Pearce. Copyright © 1981 by l'Institut pour l'Etude des Methodes de Direction de l'Enterprise (IMEDE), Lausanne, Switzerland and The School of Business Administration, University of Western Ontario, London, Ontario, Canada. It is intended for classroom discussion and is not intended as an illustration of good or bad management practices.

Council of Churches (USA) in November 1978. On the agenda was a resolution to support the critics of Nestlé who were leading the consumer boycott against Nestlé products in the United States. The National Council of Churches was an important, prestigious organization which caused Nestlé management to fear that NCC support of the boycott might further endanger Nestlé.

Also of concern was the meeting of the World Health Organization (WHO) scheduled in the fall of 1979 to bring together the infant food manufacturers, public interest groups, and the world health community in an attempt to formulate a code of marketing conduct for the industry. Nestlé management, instrumental in establishing this conference, hoped that a clear set of standards would emerge, thus moderating or eliminating the attacks of the public pressure groups.

Dr. Fürer was anxious to clear up what he thought were misunderstandings about the industry. As he reviewed the history of the formula problem, he wondered in general what a company could do when subjected to pressure tactics by activist groups, and in particular, what Nestlé management should do next.

Nestlé Alimentana S.A.

The Swiss-based Nestlé Alimentana S.A. was one of the largest food products companies in the world. Nestlé had 80,000 shareholders in Switzerland. Nestlé's importance to Switzerland was comparable to the combined importance of General Motors and Exxon to the United States. In 1977, Nestlé's worldwide sales approximated 20 billion Swiss francs. Of this total, 7.3 percent were infant and dietetic products; more specifically, 2.5 percent of sales were accounted for by infant formula sales in developing countries.

Traditionally a transnational seller of food products, Nestlé's basic goal had always been to be a fully integrated food processor in every country in which it operated. It aimed at maintaining an important market presence in almost every nation of the world. In each country, Nestlé typically established local plants, supported private farms and dairy herds and sold a wide range of products to cover all age groups. By the end of 1977, Nestlé had 87 factories in the developing countries and provided 35,610 direct jobs. Nestlé management was proud of this business approach and published a 228-page book in 1975 entitled *Nestlé in Developing Countries*. The cover of this book carried the following statement:

> While Nestlé is not a philanthropic society, facts and figures clearly prove that the nature of its activities in developing countries is self-evident as a factor that contributes to economic development. The company's constant need for local raw materials, processing, and staff, and the particular contribution it brings to local industry, support the fact that Nestlé's presence in the Third World is based on common interests in which the progress of one is always to the benefit of the other.

Although it neither produced nor marketed infant formula in the United States, the Nestlé Company, Inc. (White Plains) sold a variety of products such as Nescafé, Nestea, Crunch, Quik, Taster's Choice, and Libby and McNeil & Libby products throughout the United States.

With over 95 percent of Nestlé's sales outside of Switzerland, the company had developed an operating policy characterized by strong central financial control along with substantial freedom in marketing strategy by local managers. Each country manager was held responsible for profitability. Through periodic planning meetings, Nestlé management in Vevey ("the Centre") reviewed the broad strategy proposals of local companies. One area of responsibility clearly reserved by Vevey was the maintenance of the overall company image, although no formal public relations department existed. Marketing plans were reviewed in part by Vevey to see if they preserved the company's reputation for quality and service throughout the world.

Nestlé and the Infant Formula Industry

The international infant formula industry was composed of two types of firms, pharmaceutically oriented ones and food processing ones. The major companies competing in the developing countries were as follows:

Company	Brands
A. Pharmaceutical	
(U.S.) Wyeth Lab (American Home Products)	SMA, S26, Nursoy
(U.S.) Ross Lab (Abbott Laboratories)	Similac, Isomil
(U.S.) Mead Johnson (Bristol-Myers)	Enfamil, Olac, Prosobee
B. Food processing	
(U.S.) Borden	New Biolac
(Swit.) Nestlé	Nestogen, Eledon, Pelargon Nan, Lactogen
(U.K.) Unigate	

In addition to these six firms, there were about another dozen formula producers chartered in 1978 throughout the world.

The basic distinction between pharmaceutically oriented formula producers and food processing oriented producers lay in their entry point into the formula business. In the early 1900s, medical research laboratories of major pharmaceutical firms developed "humanized formulas," leading their parents into marketing such products. Essentially, a humanized formula was a modification of normal cow's milk to approximate more closely human milk. Generally speaking, the food processing companies had begun offering infant food as an extension of their full milk powdered products and canned milk.

As early as the 1800s, Nestlé had been engaged in research in the field of child nutrition. In 1867, Henri Nestlé, the founder of the company and the great-grandfather of infant formula, introduced the first specifically designed, commercially marketed infant weaning formula. An infant weaning formula is basically a cereal and milk mixture designed to introduce solids to a child of five–six months of age.

As of the 1860s, both Nestlé and Borden had been producing sweetened and evaporated milk. Nestlé very quickly recognized the need for better artificial infant food and steadily developed a full line of formula products in the early 1900s (for example, Lactogen in 1921, Eledon in 1927, Nestogen in 1930). Although it was a food processing company, Nestlé's product development and marketing were supervised by physicians.

In the United States in the early 1900s, the infant formula products developed by the medical laboratories were being used primarily in hospitals. Over time, the industry developed the distinction of formula products for "well babies" versus for "sick babies." In the latter category would be included special nutritional and dietary problems, such as allergies to milk requiring babies to have totally artificial formulas made from soybeans. Approximately 2 percent of industry volume was formula designed for "sick babies."

In the late 19th century and early years of the 20th century, Nestlé had developed a commanding position in the sweetened and evaporated milk market in the developing countries (also referred to as "the Third World"). Demand for these products was initially established among European colonials and gradually spread throughout the world and into the rising middle classes in many nations. Nestlé's early marketing efforts focused on switching infant feeding from the previously common use of sweetened and condensed milk to a more appropriate product, humanized infant formula.

By promoting a full product line through doctors (medical detailing), Nestlé achieved an overwhelmingly dominant market position in the European colonies, countries which later became independent "Third World" countries. Meanwhile, most of the competition developed quickly in the industrialized countries, so much so that Nestlé stayed out of the U.S. formula market entirely. Only late in the 1950s did significant intense competition, mainly from American multinationals, develop in Nestlé's markets in developing countries. These markets with their high birth rates and rising affluence became increasingly attractive to all formula producers. After the entry of American competitors, Nestlé's share of markets began to erode.

As of 1978, Nestlé accounted for about one third to one half of infant formula sales in the developing countries while American companies held about one fifth. The size of the total world market for infant formula was not exactly known because data on shipments of infant formula were not separated from other milk products, especially powders. Some sources guesstimated world sales to be close to $1.5 billion (U.S.), half of that to developing countries.

Traditional Methods of Promotion

Several methods had been used over the years to promote infant products in developing countries. Five major methods predominated:

1. Media advertising—all media types were employed including posters in clinics and hospitals, outdoor billboards, newspapers, magazines, radio, television, and loudspeakers on vans. Native languages and English were used.

2. Samples—free sample distribution either direct to new mothers or via doctors was relatively limited until competition increased in the 1960s. Mothers were given either formula or feeding bottles or both, often in a ''new mother's kit.'' Doctors in clinics and hospitals received large packages of product for use while mother and baby were present. The formula producers believed this practice helped educate new mothers on the use of formula products, and hopefully, initiated brand preference. In some instances, doctors actually resold samples to provide an extra source of income for themselves or their institutions.

3. Booklets—most formula marketers provided new mothers with booklets on baby care which were given free to them when they left the hospitals and clinics with their newborn infants. These booklets, such as Nestlé's *A Life Begins,* offered a variety of advice and advertised the formula products and other infant foods, both Nestlé and home made.

4. Milk nurses—milk nurses (also known as mothercraft nurses) were formula producer employees who talked with new mothers in the hospitals and clinics or at home. Originally, they were all fully trained nurses, instructed in product knowledge, then sent out to educate new mothers on the correct use of the new formula products. This instruction included the importance of proper personal hygiene, boiling the water, and mixing formula and water in correct quantities. These became a major part of many firms' efforts; for example, at one time Nestlé had about 200 mothercraft employees worldwide. The majority of milk nurses were paid a straight salary plus a travel allowance, but over time, some were hired on a sales-related bonus basis. Some companies, other than Nestlé, began to relax standards in the 1960s and hired nonnursing personnel who dressed in nurses' uniforms and acted more in a selling capacity and less in an educational capacity.

5. Milk banks—milk bank was the term used to describe a special distribution outlet affiliated with and administered by those hospitals and clinics which served very low income people. Formula products were provided to low income families at much reduced prices for mothers who could not afford the commercial product. The producers sold products to those outlets at lower prices to enable this service to occur.

PAG 23

Nestlé management believed the controversy surrounding the sale of infant formula in developing countries began in the early 1970s. Many international organizations were concerned about the problem of malnourishment of infants in the developing countries of South Asia, Africa, and Latin America. In Bogota (1970) and Paris (1972), representatives of the Food and Agricultural Organization (FAO), the World Health Organization (WHO), UNICEF, the International Pediatric Association, and the infant formula industry including Nestlé all met to discuss nutrition problems and guidelines. The result was a request that the United Nations Protein-Calorie Advisory Group (PAG), an organization formed in 1955, set guidelines for nutrition for infants. On July 18, 1972, the PAG issued Statement 23 on the "Promotion of special foods for vulnerable groups." This statement emphasized the importance of breast-feeding, the danger of over-promotion, the need to take local conditions into account, the problem of misuse of formula products, and the desirability of reducing promotion but increasing education.

Statement 23 included the following statements:

Breast milk is an optimal food for infants and, if available in sufficient quantities, it is adequate as the sole source of food during the first four to six months of age.

Poor health and adverse social circumstances may decrease the output of milk by the mother . . . in such circumstances supplementation of breast milk with nutritionally adequate foods must start earlier than four to six months if growth failure is to be avoided.

It is clearly important to avoid any action which would accelerate the trend away from breast-feeding.

It is essential to make available to the mother, the foods, formulas, and instructions which will meet the need for good nutrition of those infants who are breast-fed.

Nestlé management regarded PAG 23 as an "advisory statement," so management's stance was to see what happened. None of the developing countries took any action on the statement. Nestlé officials consulted with ministers of health in many developing countries to ask what role their governments wished Nestlé to play in bringing nutrition education to local mothers. No major changes were requested.

At the same time, Nestlé Vevey ordered an audit of marketing practices employed by its companies in the developing nations. Based on reports from the field, Nestlé management in Vevey concluded that only a few changes in marketing were required which they ordered be done. In Nigeria, the Nigerian Society of Health and Nutrition asked Nestlé to change its ads for formula to stress breast-feeding. Nestlé complied with this request, and its ads in all developing countries prominently carried the phrase "when breast milk fails, use . . ."

The British Contribution

In its August 1973 issue, the *New Internationalist,* an English journal devoted to problems in developing countries, published an article entitled "The Baby Food

Tragedy.'' This was an interview with two doctors: Dr. R. G. Hendrikse, Director of the Tropical Child Health Course, Liverpool University, and medical researcher in Rhodesia, Nigeria, and South Africa, and Dr. David Morley, Reader in Tropical Child Health, University of London. Both doctors expressed concern with the widespread use of formula among impoverished, less literate families. They claimed that in such cases, low family incomes prevented mothers from buying the necessary amount of formula for their children. Instead, they used smaller quantities of formula powder, diluting it with more water than recommended. Further, the water used was frequently contaminated. The infant thus received less than adequate nutrition, indeed often was exposed to contaminated formula. The malnourished child became increasingly susceptible to infections, leading to diarrheal diseases. Diarrhea meant the child could assimilate even less of the nutrients given to him because neither his stomach nor intestines were working properly. This vicious cycle could lead to death. The two doctors believed that local conditions made the use of commercial infant formula not only unnecessary, but likely difficult and dangerous. Breast-feeding was safer, healthier, and certainly less expensive.

The article, in the opinion of many, was relatively restrained and balanced. However, it was accompanied by dramatic photographs of malnourished black babies and of a baby's grave with a tin of milk powder placed on it. The article had a strong emotional impact on readers and reached many people who were not regular readers of the journal. It was widely reprinted and quoted by other groups. The journal sent copies of the article to more than 3,000 hospitals in the developing nations.

The two doctors interviewed for the article had mentioned Nestlé and its promotional practices. Accordingly, the editors of the *New Internationalist* contacted Nestlé S.A. for its position. The company response was published in the October issue of the *New Internationalist* along with an editorial entitled ''Milk and Murder.''

Nestlé S.A. responded in part as follows:

We have carefully studied both the editorial and the interviews with Dr. Hendrickse and Dr. Morley published in the August edition of the *New Internationalist*. Although fleeting references are made to factors other than manufacturers' activities which are said to be responsible for the misuse of infant foods in developing countries, their readers would certainly not be in a position to judge from the report the immense socioeconomic complexities of the situation. . . .

It would be impossible to demonstrate in the space of a letter the enormous efforts made by the Nestlé organization to ensure the correct usage of their infant food products, and the way in which the PAG guidelines have been applied by the Nestlé subsidiaries. However, if the editor of the *New Internationalist* (or the author of the article in question) wishes to establish the complete facts as far as we are concerned, then we should be happy to receive him in Vevey on a mutually agreeable date in the near future. We should certainly welcome the opportunity to reply to some of the sweeping allegations made against Nestlé either by implication or by specific references.

The editor of the *New Internationalist* refused the invitation to visit Nestlé's Vevey headquarters. Further they maintained that PAG 23 guidelines were not being observed and did not have any provisions for enforcement.

In March 1974, War on Want published a pamphlet entitled *The Baby Killer*. War on Want was a private British group established to give aid to Third World nations. In particular, they were devoted ''to make world poverty an urgent social and political issue.'' War on Want issued a set of recommendations to industry, governments, the medical profession, and others to deal with the baby formula problem as they saw it. See Exhibit 1.

EXHIBIT 1 War on Want's recommendations

Industry
1. The serious problems caused by early weaning onto breast milk substitutes demand a serious response. Companies should follow the Swedish example and refrain from all consumer promotion of breast milk substitutes in high risk communities.
2. The companies should cooperate constructively with the international organisations working on the problems of infant and child nutrition in the developing countries.
3. Companies should abandon promotions to the medical profession which may perform the miseducational function of suggesting that particular brands of milk can overcome the problems of misuse.

Governments of developing countries
1. Governments should take note of the recommendations of the Protein Advisory Group for national nutrition strategies.
2. Where social and economic conditions are such that proprietary infant foods can make little useful contribution, serious consideration should be given to the curtailment of their importation, distribution, and/or promotion.
3. Governments should ensure that supplies are made available first to those in need—babies whose mothers cannot breast feed, twins, orphans, etc.—rather than to an economic elite, a danger noted by the PAG.

British Government
1. The British Government should exercise a constructive influence in the current debate.
2. The Government should insist that British companies such as Unigate and Glaxo set a high standard of behaviour and it should be prepared to enforce a similar standard on multinationals like Wyeth who export to developing country markets from Britain.
3. The British representative on the Codex Alimentarius Commission should urge the commission to consider all aspects of the promotion of infant foods. If necessary, structural alterations should be proposed to set up a subcommittee to consider broader aspects of promotion to enable the commission to fulfill its stated aims of protecting the consumer interests.

EXHIBIT 1 *(concluded)*

Medical profession

There is a need in the medical profession for a greater awareness of the problems caused by artificial feeding of infants and of the role of the medical profession in encouraging the trend away from breast-feeding.

Other channels

Practicing health workers in the Third World have achieved startling, if limited, response by writing to local medical journals and the press about any promotional malpractices they see and sending copies of their complaints to the companies involved. This could be done by volunteers and others not in the medical profession but in contact with the problem in the field.

In Britain, student unions at a number of universities and polytechnics decided to ban the use of all Nestlés products where they had control of catering following the initial exposé by the *New Internationalist* magazine. Without any clear objective, or coordination, this kind of action is unlikely to have much effect.

However, if the companies involved continue to be intransigent in the face of the dangerous situation developing in the Third World, a more broadly based campaign involving many national organisations may be the result. At the very least, trade unions, women's organisations, consumer groups, and other interested parties need to be made aware of the present dangers.

There is also a clear need to examine on a community scale, how infant feeding practices are determined in Britain today. There is a long history of commercial persuasion, and artificial feeding is now well entrenched.

As has been shown, there are still risks inherent in bottle feeding even in Britain. The available evidence suggests that both mother and child may do better physically and emotionally by breast-feeding. An examination of our own irrational social practices can help the Third World to throw a light on theirs.

The Baby Killer was written by Mike Muller as an attempt to publicize the infant formula issue. Mr. Muller expanded on the *New Internationalist* articles, and in the view of many observers, gave reasonable treatment to the complexity of the circumstances surrounding the use of formula products in the developing countries. On the whole, it was an attack against bottle-feeding rather than an attack against any particular company.

Part of *The Baby Killer* was based on interviews the author had with three Nestlé employees: Dr. H. R. Müller, G. A. Fookes, and J. Momoud, all of Nestlé S.A. Infant and Dietetics Division. These Nestlé officials argued that Nestlé was acting as responsibly as it could. Further, they said that abuses, if they existed, could not be controlled by single companies. Only a drastic change in the competitive system could check abuses effectively. Mr. Muller apparently was not impressed by this argument, nor did he mention Nestlé management's stated willingness to establish enforceable international guidelines for marketing conduct. In *The Baby Killer,* Mr. Muller revealed he was convinced that Nestlé was exploiting the high birth rates in developing countries by encouraging mothers to replace, not supplement, breast-feeding by formula products. Mr. Muller offered as support for his stance a quotation from Nestlé's 1973 Annual Report:

> . . . the continual decline in birth rates, particularly in countries with a high standard of living, retarded growth of the market. . . . In the developing countries our own products continue to sell well thanks to the growth of population and improved living standards.

Dr. Fürer's reaction to *The Baby Killer* was that Mr. Muller had given too much weight to the negative aspects of the situation. Mr. Muller failed to mention, for example, that infant mortality rates had shown very dramatic declines in the developing countries. Some part of these declines were the result of improved nutrition, Dr. Fürer believed, and improved nutrition was partly the result of the use of formula products. Despite his strong belief that Nestlé's product was highly beneficial rather than harmful, Dr. Fürer ordered a second audit of Nestlé's advertising and promotional methods in developing countries. Again, changes were made. These changes included revision of advertising copy to emphasize further the superiority of breast-feeding, elimination of radio advertising in the developing world, and cessation of the use of white uniforms on the mothercraft nurses.

At the same time, on May 23, 1974, WHO adopted a resolution that misleading promotion had contributed to the decline in breast-feeding in the developing countries and urged individual countries to take legal action to curb such abuses.

The Third World Action Group

In June 1974, the infant formula issue moved into Switzerland. A small, poorly financed group called the Third World Action Group located in Bern, the capital of Switzerland, published in German a booklet entitled *Nestlé Kills Babies (Nestlé Totet Kinder)*. This was a partial translation of the War on Want publication *The Baby Killer*. Some of the qualifying facts found in Mr. Muller's booklet were omitted in *Nestlé Kills Babies,* while the focus was changed from a general attack on bottle-feeding to a direct attack on Nestlé and its promotional practices.

Nestlé top management was extremely upset by this publication. Dr. Fürer immediately ordered a follow-up audit of Nestlé's marketing practices to ensure stated corporate ethical standards were being observed. Nestlé management also believed that the infant formula issue was being used as a vehicle by leftist, Marxist groups intent on attacking the free-market system, multinational companies in general, and Nestlé in particular. Internal Nestlé memoranda of the time reveal the material available to management that supported their belief that the issue went beyond infant formula promotion. For example:

Having a closer look at the allies of the AG3W in their actions, we realize that they happen to have the same aim. There are common actions with the leninist progressive organizations (POCH), who are also considered to be pro-Soviet, with the Swiss communist party (PdA) and the communist youth organization (KJV), as well as with the revolutionary marxist alliance (RML). Since the AG3W has tried to coordinate the support of (only pro-communist) liberation movements with representatives of the communist block, it is not surprising that they also participate at the youth festival in Eastern Berlin.[1]

Believing the issue to be clearly legal, Nestlé management brought suit in July 1974 against 13 members of the Third World Action Group and against two newspapers who carried articles about *Nestlé Kills Babies*. Nestlé charged criminal libel, claiming that the company had been defamed because "the whole report charges Nestlé S.A. with using incorrect sales promotion in the third world and with pulling mothers away from breast-feeding their babies and turning them to its products." More specifically, Nestlé management claimed the following were defamatory:

The title "Nestlé Kills Babies."

The charge that the practices of Nestlé and other companies are unethical and immoral (written in the introduction and in the report itself).

The accusation of being responsible for the death or the permanent physical and mental damage of babies by its sales promotion policy (in the introduction).

The accusation that in less developed countries, the sales representatives for baby foods are dressed like nurses to give the sales promotion a scientific appearance.

The trial in Bern provided the Third World Action Group with a great deal of publicity, giving them a forum to present their views. Swiss television in particular devoted much time to coverage of the trial and the issues involved. The trial ended in the fall, 1976. Nestlé management won a judgment on the first of the libel charges (because of lack of specific evidence for the Third World Action Group), and the activists were fined 300 Swiss Francs each. Nestlé management dropped the remaining charges. In his judgment, the presiding judge added an opinion that became well-publicized:

The need ensues for the Nestlé company to fundamentally rethink its advertising practices in developing countries as concerns bottle-feeding, for its advertising practice up to now can transform a life-saving product into one that is dangerous and life-destroying. If Nestlé S.A. in the future wants to be spared the accusations of immoral and unethical conduct, it will have to change its advertising practices.

---

[1] Third World Action Group (AG3W) *Der Zürichbieter,* August 15, 1973.

The Controversy Spreads

While the trial was in process, various interest groups from all over the world became interested and involved in the infant formula controversy. In London, England, Mr. Mike Muller founded the Baby Foods Action Group. Late in 1974, the World Food Conference adopted a resolution recommending that developing-nation governments actively support breast-feeding. The PAG had been organizing a number of international regional seminars to discuss all aspects of the controversy. For example, in November 1974, during the PAG regional seminar in Singapore, the PAG recommended that the infant formula industry increase its efforts to implement Statement 23 and cooperate to regulate their promotion and advertising practices through a code of ethics.

The world health organizations kept up the pressure. In March 1975, the PAG again met:

> to discuss together the problem of deteriorating infant feeding practices in developing countries and to make recommendations for remedying the situation. The early discontinuance of breast-feeding by mothers in low-income groups in urban areas, leading to malnutrition, illness, and death among infants has been a serious concern to all.

In May 1975, WHO at its 14th plenary meeting again called for a critical review of promotion of infant formula products.

In response, representatives of the major formula producers met in Zürich, Switzerland, in May 1975 to discuss the possibility and desirability of establishing an international code of ethics for the industry. Nine of the manufacturers, with the notable exceptions of Borden, Bristol-Myers, and Abbott, created an organization called the International Council of Infant Food Industries (ICIFI) and a code of marketing conduct. This code went into effect November 1, 1975. Some firms also adopted individual codes, including Nestlé, with standards higher than the ICIFI code.

The ICIFI code required that ICIFI members assume responsibility to encourage breast-feeding, that milk nurses be paid on a strict salary basis and wear company uniforms, and that product labels indicate breast milk as the best infant food. At this time, Nestlé began to phase out use of mass media for infant formula in developing countries, but continued to distribute educational materials and product information in the hospitals and clinics. Nestlé management believed such advertising and promotion was of educational value: to ensure proper use of formula and to decrease usage of sweetened and condensed milk for infant feeding.

ICIFI submitted its code of ethics to the PAG who submitted it to a number of third parties. On the basis of their opinions, the PAG refused to endorse the code saying it did not go far enough, that substantial amendments were required. ICIFI rejected these suggestions because of difficult antitrust considerations, so the PAG withheld its approval of the code.

An important exception to ICIFI membership was Abbott Laboratories. While Abbott representatives had attended the meeting that led to the establishment of ICIFI, they decided not to join. Abbott, having recently had difficulties with the U.S. Food and Drug Administration regarding the marketing of cyclamates and artificial sweeteners, felt ICIFI was not an adequate response to the public pressure:

> The most important area is to reduce the impact of advertising on the low-income, poorly educated populations where the risk is the greatest. The ICIFI code does not address this very important issue.
>
> Our company decided not to join ICIFI because the organization is not prepared to go far enough in answering this legitimate criticism of our industry. We feel that for Abbott/Ross to identify with this organization and its code would limit our ability to speak on the important issues.

Abbott acted largely independently of the other producers. Later in 1977, Abbott management announced its intention to commit about $100,000 to a breast-feeding campaign in developing nations and about $175,000 to a task force on breast-feeding, infant formula, and Third World countries.

Developments in the United States

Although Nestlé U.S. neither manufactured nor marketed formula, management found itself increasingly embroiled in the controversy during the mid-1970s. The first major group to bring this matter to the public was the Interfaith Center on Corporate Responsibility (ICCR). The ICCR, a union of 14 Protestant denominations and approximately 150 Catholic orders and dioceses, was a group concerned about the social responsibility behaviour of corporations. The ICCR advised its members on this topic to guide decisions for the members' combined investment portfolio of several billion dollars. Formerly known as the Center of Corporate Responsibility, the ICCR was established under the tax-exempt umbrella of the American National Council of Churches when the U.S. Internal Revenue Service revoked the CCR tax exemption.

The ICCR urged its members to investigate the marketing practices of the leading American formula producers, American Home Products, Abbott Laboratories, and Bristol-Myers. Stockholder groups demanded from these companies, as they were entitled to do by American law, detailed information regarding market shares, promotion and advertising practices, and general company policies concerning the infant formula business.

Nestlé management believed that the ICCR was interested in ideology more than in baby formula. As support, they pointed to a statement made in a January edition of ICCR's *The Corporate Examiner:*

> The motivations, ethos, and operations of transnational corporations are inimical to the establishment of a new economic order. Both justice and stability are undermined in the fulfillment of their global vision.

Perhaps the major vehicle used by ICCR to get attention was a half-hour film entitled *Bottle Babies*. Well-known German filmmaker Peter Krieg began this film shortly after the Bern trial began. Nestlé Vevey management believed that the film was partially sponsored by the World Council of Churches to provide a public defense for the Third World Action Group position. Most of the filming was done in Kenya, Africa, in 1975 in a "documentary" style, although Nestlé management pointed out that the film was scripted and in their opinion, highly emotional and misleading. A letter (Exhibit 2) that Nestlé management later received written by Professor Bwibo of the University of Nairobi supported management's views about the *Bottle Babies* film.

ICCR distributed copies of the *Bottle Babies* film to church groups throughout the United States. Typically, the film was shown to a gathering of church members followed by an impassioned plea to write letters of protest and a request for funds to further the campaign. Since the film singled out Nestlé for attack in its last 10 minutes, Nestlé became symbolic of all that was wrong in the infant formula controversy in the minds of these religious groups. Nestlé management, however, was seldom asked for, or given an opportunity to present, its position on the issues.

While Nestlé felt the growing pressure of *Bottle Babies,* the major American formula producers faced a variety of ICCR-shareholder initiatives. ICCR requested detailed information from American Home Products, Abbott Laboratories, and Bristol-Myers. Each company responded differently.

American Home Products.   After refusing to release all the information ICCR requested, AHP faced a resolution to be included in its proxy statement. ICCR dropped the resolution the day before printing, when AHP management agreed:

To provide the requested information.

To send a report to its shareholders saying that many authorities believe misuse of infant formula in developing countries could be dangerous, that the company promotes breast-feeding while making available formula for mothers who cannot or do not choose to breast-feed, that the company would promote to medical professionals only and that AHP was a member of ICIFI which was developing a voluntary code of promotional practices.

Abbott Laboratories.   After a year and a half of meetings with ICCR, Abbott released most of the information ICCR wanted. Still, to obtain the rest of the data, ICCR shareholders filed a shareholder resolution. This proposal received less than the three percent of the vote required by the Securities and Exchange Commission (SEC) in order to resubmit the proposal at a later time. Thus, it was not resubmitted.

Bristol-Myers.   Bristol-Myers would not cooperate with ICCR so one church shareholder with 500 shares, Sisters of the Precious Blood, filed a

EXHIBIT 2

14th April, 1978

Miss June Noranka
644 Summit Avenue
St. Paul
Minnesota 55105

Dear Miss Noranka:

Following your visit to Kenya and my office I write to inform you, your group, your colleagues, and any other person interested that the film Peter Krieg filmed in this department and the associated teaching areas, did not represent the right aspects of what we participated in during the filming.

The film which was intended to be a scientific and educational film turned out to be an emotional, biased, and exaggerated film—and failed to be a teaching film. It arouses emotions in people who have little chance to check these facts. No wonder it has heated the emotions of the Activists groups in America and I understand now spreading to Europe. I wish I was in an opportunity to be with your groups and we view the film together and I comment.

As a pediatrician, I would like to put on record that I have not seen the Commercial baby food companies pressure anybody to use their brands of milk. As for Nestlé, we have discussed with their Managing Directors, starting much earlier than the time of the film in 1971, as to the best way of approaching baby feeding and discussed extensively advertisement especially the material to be included. The directors have followed our advice and we are happy with their working conditions.

We are interested in the well-being of our children and we are Medical Scientists. So anything of scientific value we will promote but we will avoid imagined exaggerated and distorted views.

I am taking the liberty to copy this letter to Mr. Jones, managing director of Food Specialty in Nairobi who produce and make Nestlé's products here, for his information.

Yours sincerely,

NIMROD O. BWIBO
Professor & Chairman

shareholder resolution in 1975 asking that the information be released. After receiving 5.4 percent of the vote and having aroused the concern of the Ford Foundation and the Rockefeller Foundation, it appeared the resolution would be launched again the next year. In August 1975, Bristol-Myers management published a report "The Infant Formula Marketing Practices of Bristol-Myers Co. in Countries outside the United States." The 1976 proxy included the Sisters' resolution and a statement entitled "Management's Position." The Sisters maintained the statement was false and misleading and filed suit against management; statements appearing in a proxy statement are required by law to be accurate.

In May 1977, a U.S. district court judge dismissed the case, saying the Sisters had failed to show irreparable harm to themselves as the law requires. The judge would not comment on the accuracy of the company's proxy report. The nuns appealed with the support of the SEC. In early 1978, the management of Bristol-Myers agreed to send a report outlining the dispute to all shareholders and to restrictions on company marketing practices including a ban on all consumer-directed promotion in clinics, hospitals, and other public places and a stop to using milk nurses in Jamaica.

In 1977, Abbott management agreed to revise their code of marketing conduct and to eliminate the use of nurses' uniforms by company salespeople despite the fact some were registered nurses.

ICCR and its supporters also persuaded Representative Michael Harrington, Democrat–Massachusetts to cosponsor a federal resolution requiring an investigation of U.S. infant formula producers.

The campaign against the formula producers took on a new dimension in mid-1977. A group called the Third World Institute, led by Doug Johnson at the University of Minnesota, formed the Infant Formula Action Coalition "INFACT" in June 1977. INFACT members were encouraged by ICCR and the Sisters, but felt that significant progress would not be made until Nestlé was pressured to change. INFACT realized that legal and shareholder action against a foreign-based company would be futile, so on July 4, 1977, INFACT announced a consumer boycott against those infant formula companies whose marketing practices INFACT found abusive. Despite the boycott's original target of several companies, Nestlé was the main focal point especially after the other major companies made concessions to ICCR. INFACT began the boycott in front of Nestlé's Minneapolis offices with a demonstration of about 100 people. INFACT urged consumers to boycott over 40 Nestlé products.

Nestlé management in White Plains was not sure what response to take. Nestlé U.S. was not at all involved with infant formula, but was genuinely concerned about the publicity INFACT was getting. Nestlé S.A. management on the other hand originally did not think the boycott campaign would amount to anything, that it was a project of some college kids in the United States based on misinformation about events in other parts of the world.

In September and October 1977, Nestlé senior managers from Vevey and White Plains met with members of INFACT, ICCR, the Ford Foundation, and other interested groups. Nestlé management had hoped to resolve what they thought was a problem of poor communication by explaining the facts. Nestlé management argued the company could not meet competition if it stopped all promotion, which would mean less sales and less jobs in the developing nations. Further, management claimed: "We have an instructional and educational responsibility as marketers of these products and, if we failed in that responsibility, we could be justly criticized." INFACT members stated they found the talks useful in clarifying positions, but concluded Nestlé was unwilling to abandon all promotion of its formula products.

In November 1977, INFACT decided not only to continue the boycott, but also to increase it to a national scale. INFACT held a conference in Minneapolis on November 2–4, for more than 45 organizers from 24 cities. These organizers represented women's groups, college hunger-action coalitions, health professionals, church agencies, and social justice groups. A clearinghouse was established to coordinate boycott efforts and information collection. The group also agreed to assist ICCR in its shareholder pressure campaign and to press for congressional action. Later, INFACT petitioned all U.S. government officials, state and federal, for support of the boycott. On November 21, the Interfaiths Hunger Coalition, a group affiliated with INFACT, demonstrated in front of Nestlé's Los Angeles sales office with about 150 people chanting "Nestlé kills babies." This demonstration received prominent media coverage as did other boycott activities. The combination of INFACT's boycott, ICCR's shareholder efforts, the exhibition of *Bottle Babies,* and the strong support of other U.S. activists (including Ralph Nader, Cesar Chavez, Gloria Steinem, and Dr. Benjamin Spock), resulted in an increasingly high profile for the infant formula controversy, even though Nestlé management believed there had been as yet no adverse effect on sales.

In early 1978, an unofficial WHO working group published the following statement:

> The advertising of food for nursing infants or older babies and young children is of particular importance and should be prohibited on radio and television. Advertising for mother's milk substitutes should never be aimed directly at the public or families, and advertising for ready-made infant food preparations should show clearly that they are not meant for less than three-month-old infants. Publicity for public consumption, which should in any case never be distributed without previous recommendation by the competent medical authority, should indicate that breast milk should always constitute the sole or chief constituent of food for those under three months. Finally, the distribution of free samples and other sales promotion practices for baby foods should be generally prohibited.

Nestlé management met again with INFACT representatives in February 1978. No progress was made in reconciling the two sides. Nestlé management could not accept statements from INFACT such as:

The corporations provide the product and motivate the people to buy it, and set into motion a process that may cause the death of the baby. The corporations are responsible for that death. When the outcome is death, the charge against the corporation is murder.

Nonetheless, management learned what INFACT wanted:

Stop all direct consumer promotion and publicity for infant formula.

Stop employing "milk nurses" as sales staff.

Stop distributing free samples to clinics, hospitals, and maternity hospitals.

Stop promoting infant formula among the medical profession and public health profession.

To further publicize their campaign, INFACT representatives and their allies persuaded Senator Edward Kennedy, Democrat–Massachusetts, to hold Senate hearings on the infant formula issue in May 1978. CBS decided to make a TV report of the entire affair. To prepare for the hearings, INFACT organized a number of demonstrations across the United States. At one meeting on April 15, 1978, Doug Johnson said:

The goal of the Nestlé's Boycott Campaign and of the entire infant formula coalition is to get the multinationals to stop promotion of infant formula. We're not asking them to stop marketing; we're not asking them to pull out of—out of the countries; we're simply asking them to stop the promotion, and in that I think we're—we're in agreement with a number of prestigious organizations. The World Health Organization recently asked the corporations to stop consumer advertising and to stop the use of free samples, and the International Pediatric Association did that several years ago. So, I think we're asking a very reasonable thing: to stop promoting something which is inappropriate and dangerous.

CBS filmed these demonstrations, but did not air them until after the Kennedy hearings.

The Kennedy Hearings and CBS Report

Senator Kennedy was chairman of the Subcommittee on Health and Scientific Research on Infant Nutrition. Both critics and members of the infant formula industry appeared before the Kennedy Committee in May 1978. Nestlé S.A. management decided not to send headquarters management or management from Nestlé U.S. Instead, they asked R. Oswaldo Ballarin, president and chairman of Nestlé, Brazil, to represent Nestlé at the hearings. Dr. Ballarin began with a statement prepared by Nestlé U.S., but Senator Kennedy soon interrupted him as the following excerpt from the testimony indicates:

Dr. Ballarin: United States Nestlé's Company has advised me that their research indicates this is actually an indirect attack on the free world's economic system: a worldwide church organization with its stated purpose of undermining the free enterprise system is at the forefront of this activity.

Senator Kennedy: Now you can't seriously expect . . . [Noise in background: gavel banging] We'll be in order . . . we'll be in order now please. We'll be in order. Uh, you don't seriously expect us to accept that on face value, after we've heard as . . . as you must've, Doctor . . . if I could just finish my question . . . the . . . the testimony of probably 9 different witnesses. It seemed to me that they were expressing a very deep compassion and concern about the well-being of infants, the most vulnerable in this . . . face of the world. Would you agree with me that your product should not be used where there is impure water? Yes or no?

Dr. Ballarin: Uh, we give all the instructions . . .

Senator Kennedy: Just . . . just answers. What would you . . . what is your position?

Dr. Ballarin: Of course not. But we cannot cope with that.

Senator Kennedy: Well, as I understand what you say, is where there's impure water, it should not be used.

Dr. Ballarin: Yes.

Senator Kennedy: Where the people are so poor that they're not gonna realistically be able to continue to purchase it, and which is gonna . . . that they're going to dilute it to a point, which is going to endanger the health, that it should not be used.

Dr. Ballarin: Yes, I believe . . .

Senator Kennedy: Alright, now . . . then my final question is . . . is what do you . . . or what do you feel is your corporate responsibility to find out the extent of the use of your product in those circumstances in the developing part of the world? Do you feel that you have any responsibility?

Dr. Ballarin: We can't have that responsibility, sir. May I make a reference to . . .

Senator Kennedy: You can't have that responsibility?

Dr. Ballarin: No.

Dr. Ballarin's testimony continued (for example of excerpts, see Exhibit 3), but Nestlé management believed little attention was paid to it. Mr. Guerrant, president of Nestlé U.S., was very angry and wrote a letter to Senator Kennedy on May 26, 1978, protesting against the way he had treated Dr. Ballarin (Exhibit 4).

CBS aired its program on July 5, 1978. Again, Nestlé management was upset. In their view CBS had selected portions of the testimonies to make Nestlé management look inept and confused. Mr. Guerrant wrote a letter of protest to CBS president Richard Salant (Exhibit 5).

Following the Kennedy hearings, representatives of Nestlé S.A., Abbott, Bristol-Myers, and American Home Products met privately with Senator Kennedy to explore a suggestion for a further hearing. Meanwhile, the president of ICIFI wrote Kennedy, pointing out that this was an international and not a U.S. domestic issue—and should therefore be discussed at a forum sponsored by WHO. Kennedy accepted ICIFI's suggestion and requested the Director Gen-

EXHIBIT 3 Further excerpts from Dr. Ballarin's testimony

Nestlé recognized that even the best products will not give the desired results if used incorrectly. We, therefore, placed great weight on educational efforts aimed at explaining the correct use of our product. Our work in this field has received the public recognition and approval of the official Pediatric Associations in many countries. Such educational efforts never attempt to infer that our product is superior to breast milk. Indeed, we have devoted much attention to the promotion of breast-feeding, and educational material has always insisted that breast-feeding is best for the baby.

Nevertheless, many factors militate against exclusive breast-feeding in the rapidly growing cities of Brazil as well as other developing countries, and our products are seen today as filling a valid need, just as they did when they were first introduced over 50 years ago. In recognition of this, all such products are subject to strict price control, while in many countries which do not have a local dairy industry, they are classified as essential goods and imported free of duty. In many cases, official agencies establish what they consider to be a fair margin for the manufacturers.

It must be stressed that many problems remain to be solved. Our production is far from reaching the total needs of the population. Hence, many mothers in the poorer population groups continue to supplement breast-feeding with foods of doubtful quality. Owing to the lack of adequate medical services, especially in the rural areas, misuse of any supplement can occur and we are very conscious of the need to improve our efforts. These efforts depend on continued cooperation between the infant food industry and health professionals. We have to be more and more conscious of our responsibility to encourage breast-feeding while researching new foods and safer methods for feeding babies who cannot be exclusively breast-fed. The dilemma facing industry and the health service alike, is how to teach these methods without discouraging breast-feeding.

EXHIBIT 4 Excerpts from Mr. Guerrant's letter to Senator Kennedy

I am angry but more important deeply concerned about the example of our governmental processes exhibited this week by the Human Resources Subcommittee on Health and Scientific Research.

It was the general consensus of several people in the audience that your position toward the manufacturers was "you are guilty until you prove your innocence." Objectivity would have been more becoming, Senator.

Secondly, it seemed equally probable that prior to the hearing the prepared statements were reviewed and you were quite prepared to rebuff Dr. Ballarin on his statement "undermining the free enterprise system." Unaccustomed to television and this type of inquisition, Dr. Ballarin, who appeared voluntarily, was flustered and embarrassed.

Probably, for this gathering, the statement was too strong (though nothing to compare with their theme "Nestlé kills babies") and should have been more subtle. But the point is well made, and your apparent denial of this possibility concerns me.

As you may know, this whole issue gained its greatest momentum a few years ago in Europe fostered by clearly identified radical leftist groups. Their stated purpose is opposition to capitalism and the free enterprise system. I submit that they are not really concerned with infants in the Third World but are intelligent enough to know that babies, especially sick and dying, create maximum emotional re-

EXHIBIT 4 *(concluded)*

sponse. Further, they are clever enough to know that the people most easy to "use" for their campaign, to front for them, are in churches and universities. These are good people, ready to rise against oppression and wrong-doing without, regrettably, truthful facts for objective research. I know, as my father is a retired Presbyterian minister, and I have a very warm feeling toward members of the church, Protestant and Catholic.

People with far left philosophies are not confined to Europe and are certainly represented in many accepted organizations here and abroad. (Please take the time to read the enclosed report of the 1977 Geneva Consultation of the World Council of Churches.) Associated with the World Council is the National Council of Churches, and one of their units is the Interfaith Centre for Corporate Responsibility. One of their major spokespersons appears to be Leah Margulies, who was present in your hearing.

Now, just briefly to the very complex infant food issue. As the U.S. Nestlé Company does not manufacture or sell any infant food products, we are unhappy with the attempted boycott of our products—at least 95 percent of these manufactured in the United States. The jobs and security of about 12,000 good U.S. employees are being threatened.

From our associates in Switzerland, and Nestlé companies in the Third World, we have gathered hundreds of factual documents. Neither Nestlé nor the U.S. companies in this business claim perfection. Companies are comprised of human beings. However, virtually every charge against Nestlé has proved to be erroneous. Distorted "facts" and just pure propaganda have been answered by people with undeniable integrity and technical credentials. Quite some time ago, because of the accusations, Nestlé world headquarters in Switzerland studied every facet of their total infant food business, made immediate changes where warranted and established new and very clear policies and procedures regarding the conduct of this business.

I might add that Nestlé infant foods have undoubtedly saved hundreds of thousands of lives. There is not even one instance where proof exists that Nestlé infant food was responsible for a single death. The products are as essential in the Third World as in the industrialized world. Though the accusers use some statements by apparently qualified people, there is an overwhelming amount of data and number of statements from qualified medical, technical, and government representatives in the Third World confirming Nestlé's position.

At your hearing this week were the same identical charges made against Nestlé and the others years ago. These people will not recognize the changes made in marketing practices nor the irrefutable facts of the real infant health problems in the Third World. They continue to push the U.S. Nestlé boycott and continue to distribute the fraudulent film "Bottle Babies." (Please read Dr. Bwibo's letter enclosed.) Sincere, well-meaning church people continue to be used, as they have not had all the real facts available for analysis.

The above situation made me believe that the organizers must have some motivation for this campaign other than what appears on the surface. If it could possibly be what I think, then our representatives in government should proceed with caution, thorough study, and great objectivity, as your ultimate position can be of critical consequence. I am not a crusader, but I do feel the free enterprise system is best.

EXHIBIT 5   Excerpts from Mr. Guerrant's letter to CBS President Salant

In the first minute of the program the infant formula industry has been tried and convicted of causing infant malnutrition. The remainder of the program is devoted to reinforcing Mr. Myer's conclusion. Tools of persuasion include the emotionality of a needle sticking in a child's head and the uneasy answers of cross-examined industry witnesses who are asked not for the facts but to admit and apologize for their "guilt."

But CBS Reports chose to concentrate on the "rhetoric of concern" and the claims which permeate the rhetoric. Industry's response to the rhetoric is not glamorous but hits into the root causes of infant malnutrition—the poverty, disease, and ignorance existing in the areas of developing and developed countries. Those conditions are not easy for anthropologists, economists, scientists, or medical people to trace or explain. And certainly the reasons for them are not as identifiable as a major corporation. But in 30 minutes Mr. Myers and Ms. Roche identified four companies as a major reason for infant malnutrition.

One way Nestlé has attempted to meet the responsibility is by making capital investments in and transferring technology to the developing countries. Nestlé began this effort in 1921 in Brazil and now has almost 40,000 local employees working in 81 manufacturing facilities in 25 developing countries. Not only does Nestlé have a beneficial impact on those directly employed, the company also encourages and assists the development of other local supporting industries, such as the dairy industry and packaging plants.

Another way Nestlé meets its responsibility is to work with local governments and health authorities in educating consumers. Clinics, pamphlets, posters, books, and product labels emphasize the superiority of breast-feeding, demonstrate proper sanitation and diet for breast-feeding, and show in words and pictures how to correctly use formula products.

Neither of these positive approaches was covered in CBS Reports nor was there mention of the fact that infant mortality has declined worldwide over the past 30 years, nor that lack of sufficient breast milk is a major cause of infant malnutrition, nor that tropical diseases cause millions of deaths per year in developing countries. Any one of these facts would have provided some balance to the Myers-Roche report.

---

eral of WHO to sponsor a conference at which the question of an international code could be discussed.

A consensus emerged that a uniform code for the industry was required and that Kennedy and ICIFI would suggest that WHO sponsor a conference with that aim in mind. The conference would be comprised of WHO officials, ICIFI members and other companies, health and government officials from the developing countries, and all appropriate concerned public groups. WHO accepted the idea and announced the conference date in the fall of 1979. Shortly after Nestlé management met with Kennedy, the National Council of Churches, comprised of about 30 major religious groups in the United States, announced that the question of supporting INFACT and ICCR would be discussed and decided at the NCC national conference in November 1978.

The Situation in October 1978

Dr. Fürer knew all senior Nestlé management felt personally attacked by critics of the industry. Not only was this the first major public pressure campaign ever encountered by Nestlé, but also Nestlé management felt its critics were using unfair tactics. For example, again and again they saw in boycott letters and articles a grotesque picture of a wizened child with a formula bottle nearby. Eventually this picture was traced to Dr. Derrick Jeliffe, an outspoken critic of the industry. He admitted to *Newsweek* he had taken the picture in a Caribbean hospital in 1964. Even though it seemed the media and many respected companies were against Nestlé, Dr. Fürer stated publicly:

> No one has the right to accuse us of killing babies. No one has the right to assert that we are guilty of pursuing unethical or immoral sales practices.

Nonetheless, under U.S. law a company is regarded as a public person which meant that the First Amendment applied; that is, Nestlé could not get legal relief against charges made by the critics unless the company could prove those charges were both wrong and malicious.

Further, Dr. Fürer was struck by the fact that all the demands for change were coming from developed countries. In fact, Nestlé had received many letters of support from people in the developing countries (Exhibit 6). Mr. Ernest Saunders, Nestlé vice president for infant nutrition products summarized his view as follows:

> Government and medical personnel tell us that if we stopped selling infant foods we would be killing a lot of babies.

EXHIBIT 6 Examples of support for Nestlé

1. I have been associated with the medical representatives of Nestlé in Kenya for the last five years. We have discussed on various occasions the problems of artificial feeding, in particular the use of proprietary milk preparations. We have all been agreed that breast-feeding should always come first. As far as I am aware, your representatives have not used any unethical methods when promoting Nestlé products in this country.

   M. L. Oduori, Senior Consultant
   Pediatrician
   Ministry of Health
   Kenyatta National Hospital, Nairobi
   Kenya, Dec. 23, 1974

2. You are not "killing babies," on the contrary your efforts joined with ours contribute to the improvement of the Health Status of our infant population.

   We consider your marketing policies as ethical and as not being opposite to our recommendations. We note with pleasure that you employ a fully qualified nurse and that during discussions with mothers she always encour-

EXHIBIT 6 *(continued)*

ages breast-feeding, recommending your products when only natural feeding is insufficient or fails.

> Dr. Jerry Lukowski
> Chief Gynecologist, Menelik Hospital
> Ethiopia, Dec. 3, 1974

3. Over several decades I have had direct and indirect dealings with your organisation in South Africa in relation to many aspects of nutrition among the nonwhite population who fall under our care, as well as the supply of nutriments to the hospital and peripheral clinics.

   I am fairly well aware of the extent of your Company's contributions to medical science and research and that this generosity goes hand in hand with the highest ethical standards of advertising, distribution of products, and the nutrition educational services which you provide.

   At no time in the past have my colleagues or I entertained any idea or suspicion that Nestlé have behaved in any way that could be regarded as unethical in their promotions, their products or their educational programmes. On all occasions when discussion of problems or amendments to arrangements have been asked for, full cooperation has been given to this department.

   Your field workers have given and are giving correct priorities in regard to breast feeding, and, where necessary, the bottle feeding of infants.

   The staff employed to do this work have shown a strong sense of responsibility and duty towards the public whom they serve, no doubt due to the educational instruction they have themselves received in order to fit them for their work.

> S. Wayburne, Chief Pediatrician
> Baragwanath Hospital
> Associate Professor of Pediatrics,
> Acting Head of Department of
> Pediatrics, University of
> Witwaterbrand/South Africa
> Dec. 18, 1974

4. I have read about the accusation that "Nestlé Kills Babies" and I strongly refute it, I think it is quite unjustifiable.

   On my experience I have never seen any mother being advised to use artificial milk when it was not necessary. Every mother is advised to give breast foods to her baby. It is only when there is failure of this, then artificial foods are advised.

   I, being a working mother have brought up my five children on Nestlé Products and I do not see anything wrong with them. I knew I would have found it difficult to carry on with my profession if I had nothing to rely on like your products.

   Your marketing policies are quite in order as I knew them and they are quite ethical. As they stress on breast milk foods first and if this is unobtainable then one can use Nestlé's Products.

> Mrs. M. Lema, Nursing Officer
> Ocean Hospital
> Dar-es-Salaam/TANZANIA
> Dec. 16, 1974

EXHIBIT 6 *(concluded)*

5. On behalf of the Sisters of Nazareth Hospital, I thank you heartily for your generous contribution in giving us the Nestlé products in a way that we can assist and feed many undernourished children freely cured and treated in our hospital.

   Trusting in your continuous assistance allow me to express again my sincerest thanks, and may God bless you.

   Nazareth Hospital
   Nairobi, Kenya
   September 9, 1978

6. I am very grateful for this help for our babies in need in the maternity ward.

   Another mission has asked me about this milk gift parcels, if there would be any chance for them. It is Butula Mission and they have a health centre with beds and maternity and maternal child health clinics. There is a lot of malnutrition also in that area, so that mothers often do not produce enough milk for their babies. It would be wonderful if you could help them also.

   Nangina Hospital
   Medical Mission Sisters
   Funyula, Kenya
   June 15, 1976

7. As a doctor who has practiced for 18 years in a developing country, I was angered by the collection of half-truths, judiciously mixed with falsehoods put out by the Infant Formula Action Coalition as reported in the *Newsweek* article on breast-feeding. Whether we like it or not, many mothers cannot or will not resort to breast-feeding. I do not believe that advertising has played any significant part in their decision. It is an inescapable necessity that specific, nutritionally balanced formulas are available. Otherwise, we would witness wholesale feeding with products that are unsuitable.

   I carry no brief for companies like Nestlé, but have always found it to be a company with the highest regard to ethical standards. Infant formulas have saved many thousands of lives. What alternative are their critics proposing?

   D. C. Williams, M.D.
   Kuala Lumpur
   Malaysia

8. Surely, Nestlé is not to blame. There have been similar problems here but through the efforts of the Save the Children Fund and government assistance, feeding bottles can only be purchased through chemists or hospitals by prescription. In this way, the decision of whether to breast-feed or not is decided by qualified personnel.

   I would think that Americans would have better things to do than walk around disrupting commerce with placards.

   Gail L. Hubbard
   Goroka, Papua New Guinea

Dr. Fürer also believed that the scientific facts underlying the breast versus bottle controversy were not being given adequate attention (for example, see Exhibit 7) nor were the changes Nestlé and the other companies had made. Nestlé's policies regarding infant formula products were apparently not well known. Exhibit 8 includes excerpts from the latest edition, dated September 1, 1977.

EXHIBIT 7 Examples of supplementary information on breast-feeding versus bottle-feeding

1.   Findings of the Human Lactation Center (HLC).

The HLC is a scientific research institute, a nonprofit organization dedicated to worldwide education and research on lactation. The HLC entered the breast/bottle controversy between the infant formula industry and the anti-multinational groups in an attempt to clarify certain issues. Eleven anthropologists, all women, studied infant feeding practices in 11 different cultures, ranging from a relatively urbanized Sardinian village to a very impoverished Egyptian agricultural village. Their findings:

Poverty is correlated with infant morbidity (disease). Child health is associated with affluence.

Infant mortality had decreased in the three decades prior to 1973 when food prices began to escalate.

Breast milk is the best infant food but breast-feeding exclusively for most *undernourished* women in the less developed countries is inadequate beyond the baby's third month. Lack of sufficient food after this time is a major cause of morbidity and mortality whether or not the infant is breast-fed.

Mixed feeding is an almost universal pattern in traditional cultures; that is, breast-feeding and supplementary feeding from early on and often into the second year.

The preferred additional food for the very young child is milk. Most milk is fresh milk, unprocessed.

Most women still breast-feed though many do not. The popular assumption that breast-feeding is being reduced has not been verified.

Third World women with the least amount of resources, time or access to health care and weaning foods, have no choice but to breast-feed.

More than half the infants they bear do not survive due to lack of food for themselves and their children.

Women who are separated from close kin, especially the urban poor, lack mothering from a supportive figure. They find themselves unable to lactate adequately or lose their milk entirely. Without suitable substitutes, their infants die.

Middle class women in the less-developed countries, market women, the elite and professional women are moving towards bottle feeding with infant formula in much the same way women turned from breast to bottle feeding in the western countries.

EXHIBIT 7 *(continued)*

The current literature on breast-feeding in the developing countries is mea-ger. Information on mortality, the incidence of breast-feeding, the content of infant food, and the amount of breast milk, tend to be impressionistic re-ports by well-meaning western or western trained persons often unaware of the complexities of feeding practices and insensitive to the real-life sit-uation of the mothers. Judgments for action based on these inconclusive data could be dangerous.

Mothers have a sensitive and remarkable grasp of how best to keep their in-fants alive. Neither literacy nor what has been called "ignorance" deter-mine which infants live and which die except as they are related directly to social class.

In seeking solutions to the problems of infant well-being in the developing world, we must listen to the mothers and involve them in the decisions which will affect their lives.

2. *The Feeding of the Very Young: An Approach to Determination of Policies*, re-port of the International Advisory Group on Infant and Child Feeding to the Nu-trition Foundation, October 1978:

"Two basic requirements of successful feeding are: (1) adequate milk during the first four to six months of life, and (2) adequate complementary foods during the transition to adult diets. It is imperative that all societies recognize these re-quirements as a major component of nutrition policy. The extent to which mothers are able to meet both of these requirements will vary under different cultural and sociological circumstances. In all societies there will be some proportion of moth-ers who will not be able to meet them without assistance, and policy must be de-veloped to protect those children who are at risk of malnutrition resulting from inadequacy in either one or both of these basic requirements."

Source: Nestlé memoranda.

EXHIBIT 7 *(concluded)*

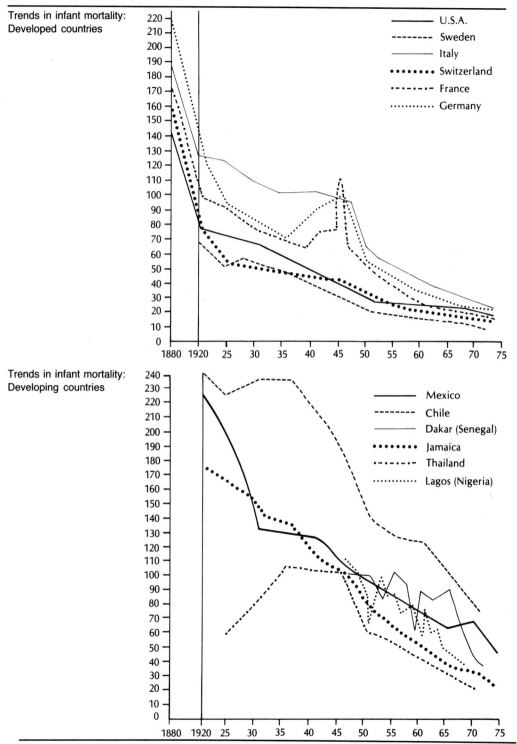

Trends in infant mortality:
Developed countries

Trends in infant mortality:
Developing countries

Source: Demographic Yearbook, United Nations.

EXHIBIT 8 Excerpts from Nestlé directives on infant and dietetic products policy

---

Infant milks

It is recognized that breast milk is the best food for a baby. Our baby milks are therefore not intended to compete with breast milk, but to supplement breast feeding when the mother's own milk can no longer cover the baby's needs or to replace it when mothers cannot, or elect not to breast feed.

Three to four months after birth, the quantities of breast milk produced by the average mother become insufficient to satisfy the growing needs of the baby. The baby needs a supplement of water and food. From this moment on, in the poor communities of developing countries this baby is in danger because water is sometimes polluted and local foods, like plantain or manioc, are nutritionally inadequate. They are starchy foods with little food value and a young baby cannot digest them. Thus the highest infant mortality occurs precisely in areas where babies receive only mother's milk plus a supplement of unboiled local water and/or starchy decoctions.

This is not a Nestlé theory. This is a fact known by every Third World doctor and recently scientifically demonstrated by British researchers working in Africa.

The alternative to traditional local supplement is a properly formulated breast milk substitute, preferably a humanized formula. It is true that there is a risk of misuse, but these risks exist with a local supplement too, although the baby has a better chance of survival when the starting point is of high quality.

It is precisely to reduce the risks of misuse and thereby increase the chances of survival that we had developed over the years a comprehensive programme of information and education: contact with doctors, educative advertising, booklets, nurses; all this had the purpose of making the alternative to local supplements known and ensuring a proper and safe use of our products when needed. Nestlé policies are designed to avoid the unnecessary replacement of breast milk.

The real issue is not breast milk versus formula, as so often pictured, but breast milk plus formula plus education versus traditional foods like manioc.

Products must be in line with internationally recognized nutritional criteria and offer definite consumer benefits.

Distribution policy

It is a rule that PID products are never sold to mothers directly by us; distribution aims at making products available to prescribers and users under optimum safety and price conditions.

Within the limits set by the law and by the distribution structure, we practice mixed distribution (pharmacies and general food stores) and use the normal market channels. On the other hand, dietetic specialties and products designed for delicate or sick babies, which are basically sold on medical prescription, are sold only through pharmacies, unless special local conditions warrant mixed distribution.

Communication policy—direct contact with mothers

Medical representatives must not enter into direct contact with mothers, unless they are authorized to do so in writing by a medical or health authority and provided that they are properly qualified. Films may be shown with the agreement of the medical or public health authorities concerned.

EXHIBIT 8 (concluded)

Visits to mothers in their homes are not allowed unless the responsible medical authority has made a written request for a visit to take place.

Personnel policy

The main task of the medical promotion personnel consists in contacting the medical and paramedical professions and hospitals. They are not concerned with direct sales to mothers and cannot sell dietetic products other than, exceptionally and exclusively, to the trade or institutions.

Specialized training must be given to such staff, to enable them to render a genuine service to the medical and paramedical professions and give them scientific and unbiased information on product characteristics and utilization.

No sales-related bonus will be paid to any staff engaged in medical promotion or having direct contact with mothers. If a bonus is to be paid, it must depend on elements other than sales, such as personal qualities and qualifications.

Many members of management believed the attack against Nestlé was ideologically based. They gathered information about and quotations from many of the activist groups to support their position (for example, see Exhibit 9). Whatever their foundation, the critics seemed to Dr. Fürer to be gaining publicity and momentum. INFACT claimed at least 500 separate action committees in the United States, support in about 75 communities in Canada, as well as support in about 10 other countries. "The movement is snowballing," reported Gwen Willens of INFACT. "We're getting over 300 letters of support every day."

As Dr. Fürer consulted with senior management in Nestlé, he wondered what further steps Nestlé might take to deal with the controversy surrounding the marketing of infant formula products in the developing countries.

EXHIBIT 9 Examples of comments concerning the ideology of the activist group

---

Sue Tafler and Betsy Walker, "Why Boycott Nestlé?" in *Science for the People,* January/February 1978.

> Unfortunately, the power in many developing countries is not held by the people themselves, and local ruling elites often want to encourage corporate investment. . . . What the boycott will not do is overthrow capitalism. . . . The boycott can unite well-meaning groups that see themselves as apolitical with more openly political groups. . . . We can have the effect of politicizing others working in the coalition. If Nestlé does make some concessions to the demands of the boycott, the sense of victory can give encouragement to the organizers of the boycott to continue on to larger struggles.

T. Balasusiya, Centre for Society and Religion, Colombo, Sri Lanka, participant at the World Council of Churches meeting, January 1977.

EXHIBIT 9 *(concluded)*

> The capitalist system is the main cause of the increasing gap and within that system multinationals are a main form. Ideology of wealth is the practical religion of capitalist society. Churches are legitimizers of the system, so their first job is self-purification. There can be no neutrality between money and God.
>
> Our function is not to judge persons, but we have to judge systems. . . . What alternative solutions do countries propose that have rejected the capitalist system, e.g., USSR, China, Cuba, Tanzania? Capitalism is inherently contradictory to the Gospel.

M. Ritchie, at a conference, "Clergy and Laity Concerned," August 1978.

> It's not just on babies, it's not just multinational corporations, it's class conflict and class struggle. Broadening the constituency both of people interested in the infant formula issue . . . how the infant formula campaign and the people there link up completely in terms of support and action with other types of campaigns. . .
>
> I think ultimately what we're trying to do is take an issue-specific focus campaign and move it in conjunction with other issue-specific campaigns into a larger very class-wide very class-conscious campaign and reasserting our power in this country, our power in this world.

Douglas Johnson of INFACT, at an address in Washington, September 1978.

> Our hope is that we can use this [boycott] campaign as the forerunner of legislation for control of multinational corporations.

Source: Nestlé internal memoranda.

Case 38

Country Lass Fashions*

As New England regional manager for Country Lass Fashions, Jonathan Frank recognized that he was low man on the totem pole. Having recently earned his masters in retailing from Columbia University, he knew that his opinion was not regarded very highly yet in the organization, but he also knew that his company was in trouble.

Country Lass had been in business for over 30 years. With a reputation for good-quality products, the company's sales had slowly grown to over $9 million. But while its founders understood production and sales, Country Lass exhibited very little understanding of the market. Through ignorance or neglect, it appeared to violate all the standard practices of the industry. Country Lass made no funds available for cooperative advertising, permitted no returns of unsold merchandise, and had a policy of no markdown allowances. Its promotion was limited to advertising in high-circulation national magazines and major metropolitan newspapers. In short, in an industry known for good relations between manufacturers and retailers, Country Lass was conceding nothing.

This negative internal attitude was complicated by external pressures. Foreign producers, with much lower material and labor costs, were flooding the market with high-quality, inexpensive goods. Tariffs designed to keep foreign competitors away from the United States market also drove up the cost of imported fabric and textile machinery. In any event, these tariffs were replete with loopholes and were being scaled down and repealed by the federal government ostensibly to achieve a free-market economy. Finally, popular-priced competitors were offering stylish products which were currently very successful.

In this environment Frank had to try to sell women's fashion goods. Inventory was piling up, especially blouses. Frank decided to take a chance with an idea he had been considering for some time. He had a good working relationship with Mary Blake, fashion editor for the *Boston Times*. If Blake

* This case was prepared by Mort Ettinger, Salem State College and Daniel Lindley, Bentley College. Used with permission.

could write a fashion page featuring Country Lass blouses, Frank was sure he could sell two pages of advertising to retailers who carried Country Lass blouses. Retailers who purchased space would be eager to order blouses in advance of the publicity and tie-in advertising. Fliers could be prepared by the *Times* based on the story and the ads and sent to the retailers for display and distribution in their stores.

After talking with Blake and *Times* advertising manager Art Lester, Frank was sure he was on to something. The *Times* had once been a major newspaper in the Boston area, but it had suffered at the hands of its two major competitors, the *Globe* and the *Herald*. In fact, its single biggest advertiser was Lambert and Vaccaro, a large Boston department store, and one of Country Lass' largest accounts. Frank, Blake, and Lester were convinced that this idea would benefit all parties.

The next task facing Frank was to sell the advertising. The cost of display advertising was $74.65 per column inch; each page contained five 14-inch columns. The cost of two full pages came to $10,451. Frank figured that the top of each page could carry two 2½ by 3½ display ads at $653 each. The rest of each page could be divided into 35 boxes (1 by 1½) and sold for $112 each.

Frank decided to sell the four display ads himself. Convinced that Lambert and Vaccaro would buy, Frank decided to save that store until last. The three remaining major department stores in Boston were easy to sell. Emmanuel's and Truman's did not want to be excluded. Flutey's was eager to be represented if Lambert and Vaccaro would be in the ad. But when Frank called on Muriel Lincoln, the head buyer for Lambert and Vaccaro, he ran into a problem he had not anticipated. Lincoln said she wanted nothing to do with the ad if Flutey's would appear in it.

By now nearly all the small ads had been sold. Many participating advertisers had already received tear sheets of the ad to display on the shopping floor and in dressing rooms of their stores and to send to preferred customers. Frank was in a tough spot. An idea came to him. He walked over to Flutey's and went straight to the buyer's office. "I'm in trouble," he said and explained the problem. Flutey's buyer reacted as he had hoped; she offered to buy the space that had been reserved for Lambert and Vaccaro in addition to the space already purchased.

Frank wasted no time in getting over to the *Boston Times* composing room. Within 30 minutes he had a final mock-up of the ad. Taking a short-cut to his office through Lambert and Vaccaro, Frank ran into Muriel Lincoln. He could not resist showing her the story and the accompanying ad. "Look how impressive this is. And to think, you could have been in it," he told her. She gave him an icy stare as they parted company.

When Jonathan Frank returned to his office there was an urgent phone message to call Art Lester. He could tell there was trouble when Lester's secretary forwarded the call. "I've got bad news," Lester started. "We have to pull the ad. Don't ask me why; I can't tell you. You have to trust me that there are important reasons. Don't take this personally."

Frank could not believe what he was hearing. After arguing, pleading, and, finally, reminding Lester of their close professional relationship over the years, Frank learned that Lincoln had threatened to discontinue advertising with the *Times* if the ad and story ran. By now, inventory had been shipped. Retailers were planning in-store promotions and tie-ins to correspond to the advertising. If no large consumer response materialized, loyal retailers risked getting stuck with a large volume of perishable fashion merchandise, and salespeople risked antagonizing good customers.

Frank made two more phone calls. His attorney advised, ''Never sue a newspaper.'' His insurance broker was only too happy to sell him a $1 million liability policy.

Case 39

California Valley Wine Company*

Introduction

On a March night in 1988, Maxwell Jones, new products/special project manager for California Valley Wine Company, leaned back in his chair in the office headquarters in Fresno, California. He glanced at the clock. It was already 10:30 P.M. on Wednesday. Max had been in the office since morning, but he was not sure that he was any closer to resolving the dilemma. Max had to make a recommendation which would shape the future of California Valley Wine Company (CVWC).

In recent years the company experienced diminishing sales and declining profitability (Exhibit 1). Several new product ideas were under consideration by CVWC management. Max received instructions to make a recommendation on what the new product was to be. For several months Max worked on the new product project and struggled with the decision. He gathered a large amount of information from trade sources, field salespeople, and executives at CVWC. By the end of the week, Max's recommendation was due to the New Product Evaluation Committee.

EXHIBIT 1 Sales and Profit for CVWC, 1980–1987 ($ millions)

Year	1980	1981	1982	1983	1984	1985	1986	1987
Sales	18.2	19.6	21.9	22.0	21.1	21.2	20.9	19.5
Earnings before taxes	2.1	1.8	1.9	1.6	.9	1.0	(.5)	.05

Background of California Valley Wine Company

CVWC was established in early 1934, shortly after the repeal of Prohibition. The founders, two cousins, George and Frank Lombardi, grew table grapes in

---

* This case was prepared by John E. Bargetto, MBA student, and Patrick E. Murphy, professor of marketing, University of Notre Dame. This case is written to facilitate classroom discussion rather than to illustrate either effective or ineffective corporate decision making. Copyright © 1990 by Patrick E. Murphy. Used with permission.

Fresno, California, and saw the sudden demand in wine as a good opportunity to enter the wine business. The Lombardis purchased an old winery that had been vacated during Prohibition and they began fermenting in the fall of 1934. In the early years they sold their wines mainly in barrels to restaurants, hotels, and liquor stores. In 1950 they constructed a major, modern winery on the outskirts of Fresno and planted additional vineyards.

In 1988 CVWC owned 1,600 acres of grapes, mostly Chenin Blanc, Thompson Seedless, and Ruby Cabernet. They marketed the wines in 1.5 and 3.0 liter bottles which retailed for $3.59 and $6.79, respectively. The three wines sold were Chenin Blanc (a white wine made from Chenin Blanc grapes), a Mountain Burgundy (a red wine made from Ruby Cabernet grapes), and a Mountain Rose (a rose wine made from a blend of red wine and Thompson Seedless).

Contemporary Wine Industry Conditions

In recent years the wine business in California (where 90 percent of U.S. wine is produced) experienced particular difficulties. The so-called wine boom of the 1970s, when consumption levels of wine rose steadily, was over; per capita wine consumption recently declined (see Exhibit 2). The highest-ever consumption level occurred in 1985 and 1986, at 2.43 gallons per capita. However, in 1987 for the first time in 25 years, per capita consumption of wine decreased. Max knew well the reasons for the decline: growing health consciousness in society, greater awareness of physical problems associated with alcohol consumption, stiffer DUI laws and a rising drinking age, and the popularity of soft drinks with the younger generation. After 15 years of solid growth, total wine consumption (including coolers) in 1987 slipped to 581 million gallons.

EXHIBIT 2 Apparent wine consumption in the United States 1934–1987

	Population*		Wine consumption†		Per capita wine consumption	
Year	1,000 Persons	Percent Change	1,000 Gallons	Percent Change	Gallons	Percent Change
1934	126,374	—	32,674	—	0.26	—
1935	127,250	0.7%	45,701	39.9%	0.36	38.5%
1936	128,053	0.6	60,303	32.0	0.47	30.6
1937	128,825	0.6	66,723	10.6	0.52	10.6
1938	129,825	0.8	67,050	0.5	0.52	0.0
1939	130,880	0.8	76,647	14.3	0.59	13.5
1940	131,954	0.8	89,664	17.0	0.68	15.3
1941	133,121	0.9	101,445	13.1	0.76	11.8
1942	133,920	0.6	133,038	11.4	0.84	10.5
1943	134,245	0.2	97,501	−13.7	0.73	−13.1
1944	132,885	−1.0	98,955	1.5	0.74	1.4
1945	132,481	−0.3	93,975	−5.0	0.71	−4.1
1946	140,054	5.7	140,316‡	49.3	1.00‡	40.8
1947	143,446	2.4	96,660‡	−31.1	0.67‡	−33.0
1948	146,093	1.8	122,290	26.5	0.84	25.4

EXHIBIT 2 *(concluded)*

Year	Population* 1,000 Persons	Percent Change	Wine consumption† 1,000 Gallons	Percent Change	Per capita wine consumption Gallons	Percent Change
1949	148,665	1.8	132,567	8.4	0.89	6.0
1950	151,235	1.7	140,380	5.9	0.93	4.5
1951	153,310	1.4	126,514	−9.9	0.83	−10.8
1952	155,687	1.6	137,620	8.8	0.88	6.0
1953	158,242	1.6	140,796	2.3	0.89	1.1
1954	161,164	1.8	142,156	1.0	0.88	−1.1
1955	164,308	2.0	145,186	2.1	0.88	0.0
1956	167,306	1.8	150,039	3.3	0.90	2.3
1957	170,371	1.8	151,881	1.2	0.89	−1.1
1958	173,320	1.7	154,633	1.8	0.89	0.0
1959	176,289	1.7	156,224	1.0	0.89	0.0
1960	179,979	2.1	163,352	4.6	0.91	2.2
1961	182,992	1.7	171,632	5.1	0.94	3.3
1962	185,771	1.5	168,082	−2.1	0.90	−4.3
1963	188,483	1.5	175,918	4.7	0.93	3.3
1964	191,141	1.4	185,625	5.5	0.97	4.3
1965	193,526	1.2	189,677	2.2	0.98	1.0
1966	195,576	1.1	191,176	0.8	0.98	0.0
1967	197,457	1.0	203,403	6.4	1.03	5.1
1968	199,399	1.0	213,658	5.0	1.07	3.9
1969	201,385	1.0	235,628	10.3	1.17	9.3
1970	203,984	1.3	267,351	13.5	1.31	12.0
1971	206,827	1.4	305,221	14.2	1.48	13.0
1972	209,284	1.2	336,985	10.4	1.61	8.8
1973	211,357	1.0	347,481	3.1	1.64	1.9
1974	213,342	0.9	349,465	0.6	1.64	0.0
1975	215,465	1.0	368,029	5.3	1.71	4.3
1976	217,563	1.0	376,389	2.3	1.73	1.2
1977	219,760	1.0	400,972	6.5	1.82	5.2
1978	222,095	1.1	434,696	8.4	1.96	7.7
1979	224,567	1.1	444,375	2.2	1.98	1.0
1980	227,255	1.2	479,628	7.9	2.11	6.6
1981	229,637	1.0	505,684	5.4	2.20	4.3
1982	231,996	1.0	514,045	1.7	2.22	0.9
1983	234,284	1.0	528,076	2.7	2.25	1.4
1984	236,477	0.9	554,510	5.0	2.34	4.0
1985	238,736	1.0	580,292	4.6	2.43	3.8
1986	241,096	1.0	587,064	1.2	2.43	0.0
1987§	243,400	1.0	580,933	−1.0	2.39	−1.6

* All ages resident population in the United States on July 1.

† All wine, including wine coolers, entering distribution channels in the United States.

‡ Figures reflect excessive inventory accumulation by consumers and the trade in 1946, and subsequent inventory depletion in 1947; therefore, data for these years do not accurately reflect consumption patterns.

§ Preliminary.

Sources: Prepared by Economic Research Department, Wine Institute, on behalf of the California Wine Commission. Based on data obtained from reports of Bureau of Alcohol, Tobacco, and Firearms, U.S. Treasury Department, and Bureau of the Census, U.S. Department of Commerce.

During the 1970s, with its steady growth and romantic appeal, the wine industry drew many interested investors. The number of California wineries grew from 240 in 1970 to over 600 by 1980. While most of these were smaller wineries with whom CVWC did not compete directly, some aggressive competitors did enter the market. For example, in 1977 Coca-Cola purchased Taylor California Cellers and employed the same sophisticated marketing techniques— segmentation and slick advertising campaigns—used to sell Coke. (Coke sold Taylor to Seagrams in 1983 but Coke left behind the impact of much greater advertising expenditures by the entire wine industry.) With all of these new entrants, inventories swelled in most wineries and the industry suffered from excess supply.

To make matters worse, during the first half of the 1980s the dollar was overpriced in international markets. The wine market became flooded with inexpensive foreign wines, mainly from Italy, France, and Germany. In 1984, imports held 25.7 percent of the total wine market in the United States. Italian wines (such as the well-known brands of Riunite and Soave Bolla) dominated in the United States with 51 percent of the imported wine market.

During the 1980s consumption of hard booze such as whiskey and vodka dropped significantly. At the same time, low-alcohol wines (7–9 percent) as well as nonalcoholic wines entered the market. These changes reflected a growing concern about the need for greater moderation regarding the consumption of alcoholic beverages. Increased desire for good health and concern about the high caloric content of alcoholic beverages also discouraged alcoholic beverage consumption in the United States during the 1980s. In fact, a Gallup Poll taken in 1987 showed that 63 percent of Americans "occasionally drink alcohol" while a 1989 poll indicated that the percentage fell to 56 percent.

Social activist groups had recently directed consumers' attention toward the need for more moderate alcohol consumption. The growing attention about the dangers of alcohol use while driving gave rise to organizations such as MADD (Mothers Against Drunk Driving) and SADD (Students Against Driving Drunk). One organization, Stop Marketing Alcohol on Radio and Television (SMART), embarked on a major lobbying effort to restrict advertising of beer and wine because of health problems associated with alcoholic beverages and the companies' appeal to younger and underage drinkers.

From his vantage point within the industry, Max was clearly aware that all these factors pointed to the changing attitude that Americans had toward the use of all alcoholic beverages. CVWC's sales had been affected by all of these developments. The sales of its red, white, and rose table wines bottled under the brand name California Valley continued to lose market share (Exhibit 3). It was time that CVWC did something and it was Max's responsibility to evaluate new product possibilities. He had been with CVWC since 1962 when he joined as a sales representative. Over the years he was promoted to sales manager and eventually became the western states regional director of sales.

EXHIBIT 3 CVWC market share of jug wines (1980–1987)

	Market Share
1980	14.0%
1981	15.0
1982	15.1
1983	14.9
1984	14.1
1985	14.6
1986	13.2
1987	10.4

Two Possible Products

After considering several possible products, including sparkling wines, fruit wines, and blush wines, Max narrowed the field to two: a wine cooler or an inexpensive dessert wine. A wine cooler is a blend of carbonated water, fruit juice, and wine with an alcohol level of 4–6 percent. While wine coolers had been consumed for years, sometimes in the form of sangria, the surge in popularity had been a recent phenomenon (Exhibit 4). Coolers were first introduced as a commercial beverage in the early 1980s by California Cooler

EXHIBIT 4 Total cases of wine coolers sold, 1981–1987 (millions)

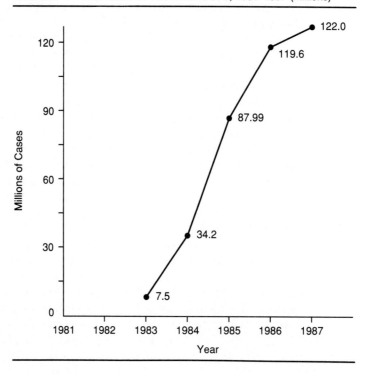

and there were numerous brands on the market. One concern expressed by the president at CVWC was the relatively high caloric content (225 per 12-ounce bottle) of the wine cooler. By 1987, the wine cooler segment of the wine industry had swelled to a $1.7 billion business representing 20 percent of the wine market.

The majority of the cooler market was divided between five market leaders. In 1987, Seagram's Wine Cooler and Gallo's Bartles and Jaymes together commanded nearly 48 percent of the market (Exhibit 5). Miller Brewing Company made a major product introduction of Matilda Bay malt-based cooler in 1987. Max was uncertain whether wine coolers were merely a fad or if they would become a permanent beverage option for consumers.

EXHIBIT 5 Wine cooler market share (1987)

Cooler	Share
Seagrams	24.0%
Bartles & Jaymes	23.4
California Cooler	13.1
Sun Country	9.2
White Mountain	7.1
All others	23.2
Total	100.0%

Although the rapid growth of the cooler market had ended, it represented a tremendous potential for sales. However, if CVWC were to enter this market, it would meet tough competition. A large advertising budget would be required to take market share from those brands already established, such as Bartles & Jaymes and Seagrams. For instance, Gallo allotted $80 million in 1985 to introduce its new cooler product.

CVWC could easily produce wine coolers from excess bulk wine. Other ingredients needed to make coolers are easily obtained. The same wine wholesalers through which CVWC sold its table wine can be utilized to distribute the cooler product. For example, the company used wholesalers and also sold directly to large retailers such as the Liquor Barn (a chain of California discount liquor stores) and out-of-state distributors in other places.

The Dessert Wine Option

Wines containing more than 14 percent alcohol are known as fortified or dessert wines because brandy has been added during the fermentation process to yield a beverage with higher alcohol content than table wines. Dessert wines can be contrasted with table wines that usually have an alcohol content of 10–14 percent. The most important advantage of the fortified wine option is profitability; the 22 percent net margins on these wines were larger than the 13 percent net margin on wine coolers. The varieties of grapes that CVWC grew were ideal for fortified wines, both for making the wine and the brandy required. Max had estimated that for $20,000 CVWC could set up an in-house brandy distillery which could supply all the brandy required to make fortified wines.

Although the same distributors could be used to get this product onto the market, Max was aware that some of the biggest liquor stores in California refused to carry low-end dessert wine products. In the words of a manager at one Liquor Barn, "We don't carry those products because we do not want that clientele in our store."

Dessert wines included a whole range of products from high-end Portugese ports ($15/bottle) to low-end muscatels ($1.99 bottle). During the 1940s and 1950s, these sweet ports and sherries represented a sizable portion of the wine consumed and they continued to grow until about 1970. The tastes of typical wine consumers for these sweet wines moved to a preference for drier table wines and the market for fortified wines began to erode. In recent years, the majority of the fortified wines consumed were inexpensive brown bag purchases by street drunks. Although the image of these wines has changed, dessert wines have a noble past.

History of fortified wines. Fortifying wine with the addition of brandy is a practice that dates back to the Roman period. The fortification process solved a practical problem of wine spoilage in ancient times. Wine spoilage especially posed a problem for those traveling who did not have the luxury of a cool cellar to protect the wine from damaging heat. Winemakers of that early era discovered that if wine was fortified by adding a concentrated spirit (like brandy) it would age longer. This practice was copied by the British living in Madeira, Portugal, who found that this fortification process allowed the wine to hold up better for the long sea journey home.

During the decades following the repeal of Prohibition in 1933, fortified wines such as sherries and ports represented a major portion of the wine consumed in the United States. These wines were typically enjoyed as an aperitif or as a dessert. However, as tastes changed and the variety of wines available broadened, wine drinkers began to consume more table wines. In 1970 dessert wines represented 27.7 percent of the wine market, but by 1986 they accounted for only 7.5 percent of the total wine market. Inexpensive fortified wine products are classified as special natural wines. As measured in volume, consumption of this product has been quite steady during the years 1968–1986 (Exhibit 6). Table wines saw a big increase in consumption during the 1970s and represented the vast majority of the nearly 600 million gallons consumed in the United States.

The Dilemma

Max was well aware, however, of the problems involved with entering the fortified wine market. Fortified wines presently available in the market were typically associated with the type of wines consumed by the destitute alcoholics

EXHIBIT 6 Wine consumption in the United States, 1968–1986

Year	U.S.-produced other special natural wine over 14 percent alcohol consumed in the United States	All U.S.-produced wine consumed in the United States (1,000 gallons)	Percent of type
1968	12,591	191,447	6.6%
1969	12,221	210,936	5.8
1970	11,665	237,328	4.9
1971	11,631	269,065	4.3
1972	11,823	289,942	4.1
1973	10,944	292,041	3.7
1974	9,653	298,071	3.2
1975	10,918	318,071	3.4
1976	11,994	317,470	3.8
1977	12,396	331,766	3.7
1978	11,104	340,620	3.3
1979	10,084	352,206	2.9
1980	10,008	377,120	2.7
1981	10,288	390,971	2.6
1982	10,293	391,956	2.6
1983	11,055	397,070	2.8
1984	10,807	412,099	2.6
1985	11,724	441,034	2.7
1986	13,698	477,891	2.9

who roamed the streets. Max was struck by an article he read some time ago in *The Wall Street Journal*. He reached for a copy of the article he placed in a file folder and reread it closely. (The text of the article is shown in Exhibit 7).

He was particularly sensitive about alcoholism because his father had suffered from the disease. He knew that many street drunks depended on these inexpensive fortified wines because it was the cheapest source of alcohol available. However, Max was not really sure what percentage of fortified wines were purchased by public drunks.

Max had wondered for some time about the ramifications of offering a fortified product to the market and whether or not it would add to the serious problem of alcoholism in this country. After reading *The Wall Street Journal* article, Max contacted the Wine Institute in San Francisco. The Wine Institute is an industry-funded organization whose purpose is to represent the California wineries and promote their wines. The reply regarding this question of the so-called misery market came in a written letter.

We reject the notion, however, that availability of "over 14 percent wine" encourages and/or causes abuse of the product. We know from a wide range of literature that alcohol abuse is a complex medical and social problem evolving from a vast array of generic biochemical predispositions, cultural norms, behaviors, expectations, and beliefs. We believe the most effective way to address alcoholism is through intervention, education, treatment, and prevention programs.

EXHIBIT 7

Misery Market

Winos & Thunderbird Are a Subject Gallo Doesn't Like to Discuss

It, Other Vintners Disavow Wines' Appeal to Drunks, But the Money Is Good

Night Train to the Bowery

By Alix M. Freedman
Staff Reporter of The Wall Street Journal

NEW YORK—In the dim light of a cold February morning, a grizzled wino shuffles into the Bowery Discount liquor store muttering, "Thunder-chicken, it's good lickin.'" Fumbling for some change, he says: "Gimme one bird." Raymond Caba, the store clerk, understands the argot and hands over a $1.40 pint of Thunderbird, the top seller in what he calls "the bum section."

The ritual is repeated a thousand times a day in dead-end neighborhoods across the country. Cheap wines with down-and-dirty names—and an extra measure of alcohol—are the beverage of choice among down-and-out drunks. But winos are a major embarrassment to the big companies that manufacture these wines. With rare exceptions, they aren't eager to acknowledge their own products.

Thunderbird and Night Train Express are produced by the nation's largest wine company, E.&J. Gallo Winery, though you'll not learn that from reading the label on the bottle. MD

20/20 is made by Mogen David Wine Corp., a subsidiary of Wine Group Ltd., which refuses to talk about its product. Richards Wild Irish Rose Wine, the very best seller in the category, is produced by Canandaigua Wine Co. Canandaigua is volubly proud of the wine but quick to point out that it enjoys wide popularity with people who aren't alcoholics.

The Biggest Bang

People concerned about the plight of street alcoholics are critical of the purveyors of dollar-a-pint street wines made with cheap ingredients and fortified with alcohol to deliver the biggest bang for the buck. At 18% to 21% alcohol, these wines have about twice the kick of ordinary table wine, without any of the pretension.

The consumption of alcohol in the U.S. *is* declining in virtually every category, but the best selling of the low-end brands keep growing, in large part be-
(Continued)

EXHIBIT 7 (*continued*)

cause customers can't stop drinking. Says Paul Gillette, the publisher of the Wine Investor in Los Angeles: ''Makers of skid-row wines are the dope pushers of the wine industry.

Vintners generally try hard to filter their wines through the imagery of luxury and moderation, stressing vintage, touting quality. So they are understandably reluctant to be associated in any way with what some call a $500 million misery market.

Suppliers deny that the most popular street wines sell as well as they do because they appeal to dirt-poor, hard-core drinkers. Companies contend that their clientele is not like that at all, and, besides, any alcoholic beverage can be abused. (The wine people say they face stiff competition from high-alcohol malt liquor and 200-milliliter bottles of cheap vodka.) The future for the high-proof business, vintners say, isn't particularly rosy in any case. The wine category they call ''dessert'' or ''fortified''— sweet wines with at least 14% alcohol— has lost favor with drinkers.

Markedly Profitable

Wino wines are inexpensive to produce. They come in no-frills, screw-top packaging and require little or no advertising. Although they generally aren't the major part of vintners' product lineups, they are especially profitable. All told, net profit margins are 10% higher than those of ordinary table wines, Canandaigua estimates. Gallo says that isn't true for its products, but it won't say what is true.

The wines are also a rock-solid business. Of all the wine brands in America, the trade newsletter Impact says, Wild Irish Rose holds the No. 6 spot, Thunderbird is 10th and MD 20/20 is 16th. In contrast to the lackluster growth of most other wine brands, unit sales of the leading cheap labels, Wild Irish Rose and Thunderbird are expected to be up 9.9% and 8.6% respectively this year, Jobson's Wine Marketing Handbook estimates.

So unsavory is this market that companies go to great lengths to distance themselves from their customers. If suppliers are willing to talk about the segment—and few are—they still don't acknowledge the wino's loyal patronage. Gallo and Canandaigua leave their good corporate names off the labels, thus obscuring the link between product and producer.

The 'No-Name Market'

''This is the market with no name,'' says Clifford Adelson, a former executive director of sales at Manischewitz Wine Co., which once made low-end wines and was recently acquired by Canandaigua. ''It's lots and lots of money, but it doesn't add prestige.''

Cheap wines typically aren't even sold in many liquor stores. For instance, Frank Gaudio, who owns the big Buy-Rite Twin Towers Wine & Spirits store in New York's World Trade Center, doesn't stock any of these brands, though many homeless alcoholics spend their days just outside his door. ''We don't want that clientele in our store,'' he says. ''We could sell [fortified wines] and probably make money, but we don't.'' The wines, however, are staples of the bulletproof liquor stores of low-income neighborhoods. While you can't say the whole market for items like Thunderbird and Night Train consists of derelicts, down-and-outers do seem to be its lifeblood. Fifty current and reformed drinkers interviewed for this article claim to have lived on a gallon a day or more of the stuff.

EXHIBIT 7 (continued)

Misery Market: Catering to Winos Isn't a Subject Vintners Discuss

"The industry is manufacturing this for a select population: the poor, the homeless, the skid-row individual," says Neil Goldman, the chief of the alcoholism unit at St. Vincent's Hospital in Manhattan's Greenwich Village.

* * *

Dawn finds a small bottle gang near the Bowery, chasing away the morning shakes with a bottle of Thunderbird they pass from hand to hand. Mel Downing tugs up the pant leg of his filthy jeans to reveal an oozing infection on his knee. He is drinking, he says, to numb the pain of this "wine sore" and other ones on his back before he goes to the hospital later in the morning. "We're used to this stuff," the 39-year-old Mr. Downing quickly adds. "We like the effect. We like the price."

A cheap drunk is the main appeal of the wines that winos call "grape" or "jug," but most often just "cheap." Winos say that these wines, even when consumed in quantity, don't make them pass out as readily as hard liquor would.

Walter Single, a recovering alcoholic, recalls that on a daily diet of nine pints of Wild Irish Rose, he still was able "to function well enough to panhandle the money he needed to drink all day and still have enough left for a wake-up in the morning."

Some drinkers say the high sugar content of the wines reduces their appetite for food, so they don't have to eat much. Others say they still can drink wine even after their livers are too far gone to handle spirits. Still others appreciate the portability of pint bottles.

"I feel more secure with a pint," explains Teddy Druzinski, a former carpenter. "It's next to me. It's in my pocket." Canandaigua estimates that low-end brands account for 43 million gallons of the dessert category's 55 million gallons and that 50% is purchased in pints.

Many people in the wine industry eschew producing skid-row wines. "I don't think Christian Brothers should be in a category where people are down on their luck—where some may be alcoholics," says Richard Maher, the president of Christian Brothers Winery in St. Helena, Calif. Mr. Maher, who once was with Gallo, says fortified wines lack "any socially redeeming values."

"The consumers are we alcoholics," agrees Patrick Gonzales, a 45-year-old wino who is undergoing a week of detoxification at a men's shelter on New York's Lower East Side: "You don't see no one sitting at home sipping Mad Dog [MD 20/20] in a wine glass over ice."

Market Profile

Major producers see their customers otherwise. Robert Huntington, the vice president of strategic planning at Canandaigua, says the Canandaigua, N.Y., company sells 60% to 75% of its "pure grape" Wild Irish Rose in primarily black, inner-city markets. He describes customers as "not super-sophisticated," lower middle-class and low-income blue-collar workers, mostly men.

Daniel Solomon, a Gallo spokesman, *(continued)*

EXHIBIT 7 (*continued*)

maintains that Thunderbird "has lost its former popularity in the black and skid-row areas" and is quaffed mainly by "retired and older folks who don't like the taste of hard products."

According to accounts that Gallo disputes, the company revolutionized the skid-row market in the 1950s after discovering that liquor stores in Oakland, Calif., were catering to the tastes of certain customers by attaching packages of lemon Kool-Aid to bottles of white wine. Customers did their own mixing at home. The story goes that Gallo, borrowing the idea, created citrus-flavored Thunderbird. Other flavored high-proof wines then surged into the marketplace. Among them: Twister, Bali Hai, Hombre, Silver Satin and Gypsy Rose. Gallo says that the Kool-Aid story is "a nice myth" but that Thunderbird was "developed by our wine makers in our laboratories."

Vintners advertised heavily and sought to induce skid row's opinion leaders—nicknamed "bell cows"—to switch brands by plying them with free samples. According to Arthur Palombo, the chairman of Cannon Wines Ltd. and one of Gallo's marketing men in the 1950s and '60s, "These were clandestine promotions." He doesn't say which companies engaged in the practice.

Today, such practices and most brands have long since died out. Companies now resort to standard point-of-sale promotions and, in the case of Canandaigua, some radio and television advertising. There still is an occasional bit of hoopla. In New Jersey, Gallo recently named a Thunderbird Princess, and Canandaigua currently is holding a Miss Wild Irish Rose contest. But to hear distributors tell it, word of mouth remains the main marketing tool.

The market is hard to reach through conventional media. Winos will drink anything if need be, but when they have the money to buy what they want, they tend to hew to the familiar. (Sales resistance may help explain why the handful of low-end products that companies have tried to launch in the past 20 years mostly have bombed.) Besides, "it would be difficult to come up with an advertising campaign that says this will go down smoother, get you drunker and help you panhandle better," says Robert Williams, a reformed alcoholic and counselor at the Manhattan Bowery Corp.'s Project Renewal, a half-way house for Bowery alcoholics.

Companies see no reason to spend a lot of money promoting brands they don't want to be identified with. "Gallo and ourselves have been trying to convey the image of a company that makes fine products," says Hal Riney, the president of Hal Riney & Associates, which created the TV characters Frank Bartles and Ed Jaymes for Gallo's wine cooler. "It would be counterproductive to advertise products like this."

Richards Wild Irish Rose purports to be made by Richards Wine Co. The label on a bottle of Gallo's Night Train reads "vinted & bottled by Night Train Limited, Modesto, Ca." Gallo's spokesman, Mr. Solomon, says "The Gallo name is reserved for traditional [table] wines."

Industry people chime in that it isn't at all uncommon for companies to do business under a variety of monikers. But they also agree with Cannon's Mr. Palombo: "Major wine producers don't want to be associated with a segment of the industry that is determined to be low-end and alcoholic."

Winos have their own names for what they buy, Gallo's appellations notwithstanding. When they go to buy Night Train, they might say, "Gimme a ticket." They call "Thunderbird "pluck," "T-Bird" or "chicken." In street lingo, Richards Wild Irish Rose is
(continued)

EXHIBIT 7 (concluded)

known as "Red Lady," while MD 20/20 is "Mad Dog."

If skid-row wines are cheap to market, they are even cheaper to make. They are generally concocted by adding flavors, sugar and high-proof grape-based neutral spirits to a base wine. The wine part is produced from the cheapest grapes available. Needless to say, the stuff never sees the inside of an oak barrel.

"They dip a grape in it so they can say it's made of wine," says Dickie Gronan, a 67-year-old who describes himself as a bum. "But it's laced with something to make you thirstier." Sugar probably. In any event, customers keep on swigging. Some are so hooked that they immediately turn to an underground distribution system on Sundays and at other times when liquor stores are closed. "Bootleggers," often other alcoholics, buy cheap brands at retail and resell them at twice the price. The street shorthand for such round-

the-clock consumption is "24-7."

At nightfall, Mr. Downing, the member of the bottle gang with the leg infection, is panhandling off the Bowery "to make me another jug," as he puts it. As his shredded parka attests, he got into a fight earlier in the day with his buddy, Mr. Druzinski, who then disappeared. Mr. Downing also got too drunk to make it, as planned, to the hospital for treatment of his "wine sores."

A short while later, Mr. Druzinski emerges from the shadows. He has a bloodied face because he "took another header," which is to say he fell on his head. Nevertheless, in the freezing darkness, he joins his partner at begging once again.

"I'm feeling sick to my stomach, dizzy and mokus," Mr. Downing says. "But I still want another pint." He scans the deserted street and adds: "Another bottle is the biggest worry on our minds."

In doing some more research about the social implications of fortified beverages, Max had found an article in the *British Journal of Addiction*.[1] The article was titled, "A Ban of Fortified Wine in Northwestern Ontario and Its Impact on the Consumption Level and Drinking Pattern." The article described an experiment in which fortified wines were removed from store shelves in 10 communities in Ontario. The brands removed were those in the lower-price category, and considered to be the more popular beverage of public inebriates, many of whom were Native Indians. The researchers sought to compare the drinking patterns of people living in these 10 delisted communities with those in 18 communities where these fortified wines continued to be available. The researchers found that the ban of these fortified wines only led to an increased consumption of table wines, vodka, and Liquor Board wines and in some cases created additional social problems. Max felt that the presence of fortified wines in the American market did not cause alcoholism, but felt bothered by the idea

---

[1] "A Ban of Fortified Wine in Northwestern Ontario and its Impact on the Consumption Level and Drinking Patterns," *British Journal of Addiction*, 76 (1981), pp. 281–88.

that a large proportion of the customers for a CVWC fortified product might be these public drunks.

Marketing Strategy

Whether Max recommended CVWC to enter the fortified wine market or the wine cooler market, he would be responsible for developing the appropriate marketing strategy. Max had a fairly clear vision in his mind of what the two potential products could be. In the case of the fortified wine, it would be made from the Thompson Seedless and French Colombard grapes and would contain about 15 percent sugar while having 18 percent alcohol. He thought perhaps the product could have an added orange or cherry flavor.

Given the potential image problems that a market for a fortified product could create for CVWC, Max felt that if they were to enter this market it would be best for CVWC to utilize an alternative brand name and a DBA (doing business as). The DBA is the name of the producer which, by law, has to be listed on the label. To protect the image of California Valley Wine Company, the bottom of the label could read ''Produced and Bottled by CVWC Cellars,'' thereby disguising the producer of the wine. In addition to the DBA, as the *TWSJ* article mentioned, many wineries in California used second labels in order to protect the image of their main brand. For example, Gallo bottles its wines under a whole myriad of brand names: Carlo Rossi, Andre, and Polo Brindisi. Exhibit 8 lists the brand names, producers, and market shares of the leading fortified wine products. Although Max had not given much consideration to possible brand names for the fortified wine, Warm Nights had been tossed around by some of the salespeople.

EXHIBIT 8   U.S. fortified wine industry (fortified wines are sweet wines with at least 14 percent alcohol.)

Wine	Producer	Market share (percent)
Wild Irish Rose	Canandaigua	22%
Thunderbird	Gallo	18
All other Gallo dessert wines		16
MD 20/20	Wine Group Ltd.	7
Cisco	Canandaigua	4
Night Train Express	Gallo	3
All others: imported dessert wines, other domestic brands		30

Source: Industry estimates.

Max felt that perhaps an upscale product with a distinctive label could be developed, one that commanded a higher price in the market and which in turn would yield a greater margin. It could be bottled in 750 milliliter bottles and positioned distinctively away from the low-end competition of MD 20/20 and Thunderbird. Examples of packaging options are shown in Exhibit 9. Certainly

EXHIBIT 9

part of the reasons these wines were favorites of the public drunks was the inexpensive price. A 375-milliliter bottle of Night Train retailed for $1.09. The 750-milliliter bottles of Thunderbird and Wild Irish Rose could be purchased for as little as $1.99 and $2.32, respectively.

He wondered if the flat-shaped, pint-size bottle of Night Train had been intentionally designed to fit into a coat pocket. He thought that CVWC—in order to avoid the misery market—could market a product packaged with a fancy label in a corked bottle, and sell it for a higher price, for example, $5.50. It could be positioned more as a sophisticated dessert wine. But then Max questioned whether or not customers would be willing to pay for this.

Max believed that the fortified wine was a liquor store item. Perhaps it would be feasible to selectively market this product, focusing on suburban stores. In this way the inner-city liquor stores, often frequented by public drunks, could be avoided. Max knew that once the product is out on the store shelves, the producer cannot influence who buys the product or how it is used. One idea that came to mind was that CVWC could print on the bottom of the labels "ENJOY IN MODERATION" like some other alcoholic beverage producers had done.[2] Perhaps this would help discourage abuse of the product. Max had bounced the idea off one of the salespeople, who replied, "Hey, Max, that's not our responsibility."

Promotion of fortified wines posed a particularly difficult problem. Max wondered how CVWC could promote the product and which product attributes could be highlighted. Max pulled out his *Code of Advertising Standards* that wine industry members were to voluntarily abide by. The following is a paragraph from the first section:

> Subscribers shall not depict or describe in their advertising: The consumption of wine or wine coolers for the effects their alcohol content may produce or make direct or indirect reference to alcohol content or extra strength, except as otherwise required by law or regulation.

There were certainly problems with promotion of this product, but one thing was certain. If CVWC was not able to promote the product it would be difficult to take market share away from the competition.

Of course, if Max were to recommend entering the wine cooler business, the problems associated with fortified wines would be avoided. If CVWC was to be successful in the wine cooler business, it would require some innovation. Max had thought that CVWC could develop a cooler with new flavors, for example, pomegranate or wild berry. They could be packaged in six packs potentially leading to greater sales over the typical four pack. He believed women could be targeted for this new product which could be sold as low calorie. Max considered whether CVWC might get some nationally known TV star to endorse the new product.

---

[2] "Alco Beverage Company and Moderation Advertising," HBS case 9–387–070.

EXHIBIT 10   Projected CVWC sales (1989–1991)

	Wine Cooler		
	1989	1990	1991
Sales (millions)*	5.00	6.00	7.00
Expenses			
Cost of goods sold	3.00	3.60	4.20
Selling and administrative	0.20	0.20	0.20
Salaries	0.15	0.17	0.19
Advertising	0.90	0.90	0.90
Interest	0.20	0.25	0.25
Total expenses	4.45	5.12	5.74
Earnings before taxes	0.55	0.88	1.26
	Fortified Wine		
Sales (millions)†	2.50	3.50	5.50
Expenses			
Cost of goods sold	1.00	1.40	2.20
Selling and administrative	0.20	0.20	0.20
Salaries	0.10	0.11	0.12
Advertising	0.20	0.20	0.20
Interest	0.15	0.15	0.15
Total expenses	1.65	2.06	2.87
Earning before taxes	0.85	1.44	2.63

* Based on $11.42/case selling price.
† Based on $14.75/case selling price.

He turned on the PC near his desk and stared at the projections for both the fortified wine and wine cooler options. Exhibit 10 contains the actual numbers generated by the spreadsheet program. Both alternatives seemed to be viable and would help the bottom line of CVWC. He thought the numbers might even be a bit conservative.

Max was even more confounded by all of these considerations. But then again it was his responsibility to give the recommendation to the committee. Not only was he expected to present his recommendation regarding the new product to the New Product Evaluation Committee but he was also asked to discuss his strategy with the Social Responsibility Committee. This committee had been established in 1976 to oversee the activities of the various departments at CVWC because of its involvement in the alcoholic beverage industry.

When looking for some misplaced statistics on his cluttered desk, Max found a memo he had received from the vice president of marketing earlier in the day. The memo was marked "urgent" in red ink. It instructed Max to have his recommendation available by noon tomorrow. The memo concluded with a "Are there any other new product options you haven't explored? Max, see me in the morning." Max took a long breath and reached for the articles on the wine industry that covered his desk. Thumbing through them he hoped that a clear strategy would come to mind, one that he could sleep with.

Part 9

Marketing Programs and Strategy

This section contains seven cases which are comprehensive in nature, requiring the student to make a number of decisions in several different marketing decision areas. Thus, a great deal of integration is necessary. A decision in one of the marketing areas may have a significant impact on the other decisions which must be made to complete the marketing program.

In developing a complete marketing program for a product, one must start with the firm's overall goals and objectives. Then all the environmental factors such as demand, competition, marketing laws, distribution alternatives, and cost structure must be analyzed. At this point, a number of opportunities as well as potential problems will have been identified, and specific marketing objectives can be established.

The marketer must make a clear definition of the target market(s) to be served. This can be determined only after a thorough evaluation of all the alternative segments of the market, their needs, wants, attitudes and behavior, the strengths and weaknesses of the firm's products and those of competitors, and the potential profitability of various alternatives.

The next step in developing the marketing program is to search for the optimal marketing mix; that is, what is the best combination of product strategy, pricing strategy, promotion strategy, and distribution strategy? Typically, there will be a number of possible alternatives for each of these, so the marketer must determine the interrelationships among them and choose the optimal combination based upon a complete situation analysis.

The last step in the development of a marketing program is to create a plan for implementing the program. Without adequate implementation, even the best-designed plans will fail.

Case 40

Roboprint*

It was 5:30 P.M. on Friday, August 20, 1989. Walt Morgan, newly appointed vice president marketing for Roboprint, Inc. sat pondering his first assignment. Morgan's boss was the president of Roboprint, Dave Padgitt. "Morgan," Padgitt said, "I want a complete marketing program for our new product line on my desk by September 5. I want the works: target segments, choice of distribution channel, advertising and promotion campaigns, sales projections, and analysis on competitive products." Morgan was dazed but undaunted.

Industry Background

Roboprint, Inc. designs and builds heavy-duty, industrial-quality printers that can interface with most computer hardware systems. The following description, provided in *The Printer Buyer's Guide and Handbook* (vol. 6, no. 5), succinctly describes this segment of printer users.

> While some offices use printers primarily for correspondence and the occasional memorandum, others need to produce high-volume output on a constant basis. For them, the term *heavy-duty* means being able to print a month's worth of statements (on six-part forms), shift to a passable near-letter quality (NLQ) mode for a couple of hundred mail-merged letters, and then, with the wide paper loaded, churn out inventory reports and sales projections.
>
> Clearly, such users have no need for even the finest conventional printer, no matter how beautifully formed its NLQ characters are or how crisp and colorful its graphics can be. Rather, they need a real battleship of a printer.

Roboprint is focusing its products on this market segment. In addition to its standard printer line, Roboprint also manufactures printers with custom soft-

* This case was written by Richard S. Aiken under the supervision of Thomas C. Kinnear. The casewriter gratefully acknowledges the permission of David Padgitt and Great Lakes TAAC, without whose original work this report would not have been possible. Copyright © 1990 by Thomas C. Kinnear.

ware features for customers that order in large quantities (usually greater than 25 units). All of Roboprint's printers are wide-carriage (132-column) models.

Product Design Technology

There are several different types of computer printers. In the broadest sense, printers can be divided into three categories; *page printers, line printers,* and *character printers.* Page printers are printers that can print an entire page at once, typically using either a *xerographic* or *electrostatic* imaging process. Xerographic printing is the most common image transfer technology, with electrostatic printers losing popularity except in specialized large-format multi-color applications such as computer-aided design (CAD).

Laser printers are probably the most common type of page printer. They use a laser to sensitize a xerographic toner drum. Once limited primarily to drafting and graphic applications, as a result of advances in technology and reductions in cost, laser printers are now the technology of choice for most page printing applications.

Line printers are printers that can print an entire line of characters or dots at once. They are quickly losing ground to the advances in laser printer technologies, but still exist. They are used primarily for high-speed applications where character quality and low cost are secondary factors. Line printers are typically shared by several users and are often found in a company's data processing center.

There are two primary line printer categories, *impact* and *nonimpact.* There are several obsolete impact line printer technologies such as *chain printers* and *band printers.* The most popular impact line printer technology still being used is probably *dot-impact* line printing.

Two types of nonimpact line printers are *thermal line printers* and *ink-jet line printers.* Thermal line printers require a special heat-sensitive type of printer paper. The thermal print head is a linear array that must make direct contact with the thermal paper. Ink-jet line printers accelerate charged droplets of ink through an electric field, propelling them onto the paper's surface.

There are two general types of serial computer printer; *serial impact printers,* and *serial nonimpact printers.* Serial impact printers print a single character or column of dots at a time, as their printhead moves serially across the piece of paper. The printhead forms an image on the paper by impacting a printer ribbon. Serial impact printers can usually be used with multipart carbon forms, although the number of layers that they can accommodate may vary. The two most popular types of serial impact printers are *daisy wheel printers* and *dot-matrix printers.*

Daisy wheel printers have the advantage of *letter quality* (LQ) type and low cost, but they are generally relatively slow. Dot matrix printers are fast and inexpensive, but their character quality is generally lower. Dot matrix printers use a printhead usually made up of either 9 or 24 pins in a column and can provide *near letter-quality* (NLQ) text. The latter type of dot matrix printer creates higher-quality text but is generally more expensive than the former. Unlike daisy wheel printers, most dot-matrix printers are capable of printing graphics as well as text.

Serial nonimpact printers differ from serial impact printers in that the printing mechanism does not require striking an inked ribbon. They are, therefore, not suitable for multipart carbon forms. There are two primary types of serial nonimpact printers, *serial thermal printers* and *serial ink-jet printers.* Serial thermal printers are relatively slow, require special paper, generally have low-quality print, but are relatively noise-free. Serial ink-jet printers are similar, except that they do not require special paper.

Company Background

Management. Roboprint, Inc., a Florida corporation, was founded and incorporated in November 1980. Roboprint's management is well qualified to develop and market computer printers. Several of Roboprint's managers come from previous positions involved with electronic product development. Roboprint's organization chart is shown in Exhibit 1.

EXHIBIT 1 Roboprint organizational chart

	Dave Padgitt President / CEO	
Walt Morgan Vice President Marketing and Sales	Donna Sallee Vice President Finance / CFO and General Manager	Robert Geisler Director Technical Services
Sales	Financial Planning	Design Engineering
Sales Forecasting	Accounting	Service / Tech
Strategic Marketing	Personnel	Manufacturing
Product Planning	Production	Material
Marketing Support	Quality Control	Purchasing

Existing Product Line. Roboprint's product line is currently made up of seven basic models. All seven are dot matrix, wide-carriage printers (132 columns) and are intended for heavy-duty industrial use. Important charac-

EXHIBIT 2 Competitive printer feature comparisons

MAKE/MODEL	CPS DRAFT	CPS LQ	BIT-MAPPED GRAPHICS	BI-DIR.	INTERNAL MEMORY	PAPER FEED	SHEET FEEDER OPTION	CARRIAGE	INTER-FACE	NUMBER OF PRINT WIRES	PRICE
DATASOUTH											
DS 180	180	N/A	Y	Y	4K	T	N	Wide	S,P	-	$1,395
DS 220	90/220	40	Y	Y	2K	F,T	N	Wide	S,P	-	1,695
DS 220 AF	90/220	40	Y	Y	2K	F,T	Y	Wide	S,P	-	1,895
TX 5180	180	N/A	N	N	4K	T	N	Wide	P	-	2,995
TX 5220	220	40	N	N	2K	F,T	Y	Wide	P	-	3,495
CX 3180	180	N/A	N	N	4K	T	N	Wide	P, IBM	-	3,195
CX 3220	220	40	N	N	2K	F,T	Y	Wide	P, IBM	-	3,695
DATAPRODUCTS											
9030	300	33	Y	Y	2K	T,cut sheet	Y	Std.	P,S(opt)	9 wire	$649
9040 (opt)	300	83	Y	Y	2K	T,cut sheet	Y	Wide	P,S(opt)	9	799/899
9034	300	33	Y	Y	32K	T,cut sheet	Y	Std.	P,S	24	899
9044 (opt)	300	83	Y	Y	32K	T,cut sheet	Y	Wide	P,S	24	1,099/1,199
8070 PLUS	400	300/100	Y	Y	4K	T,F	Y	Wide	P/S	9	1,695-1,795
FACIT											
B3100	250	60	Y	Y	12K	F,T	Y	Std	S,P	9	$695
B3150	250	60	Y	Y	12K	F,T	Y	Wide	S,P	9	895/965
B3350	200	100	Y	Y	12K	F,T	Y	Wide	S,P	18	995/1,040
4528-T	165	82	Y	Y	2K/+6K	F,T	N	Both	S,P	9	1,225-1,275
B3450	250	80	Y	Y	16K	F,T	Y	Wide	S,P	24	1,295
Documate 3000	200	100	Y	Y	-	F,T	Y	Std.	S,P	9	1,495
4528-V	165	82	Y	Y	6K/+12K	T	N	Both	S,P	9	1,625-1,675
4528-D	165	82	Y	Y	6K/+12K	T	N	Both	S,P	9	1,775-1,875
C6510	300	75	Y	Y	6K	F,T	Y	Wide	S,P	9	1,795
C6520	300	75	Y	Y	6K	F,T	Y	Wide	P,S	9	1,795
C7500	400	100	Y	Y	4K	F,T	Y	Wide	S,P	18	2,195
4542	250	250	Y	Y	.766K-8K	T	N	Wide	S,P IEEE	9 flex hammers + int'fce	3,395
4544	225	225	Y	Y	4K-8K	T	N	Wide	S,P IEEE	9 flex hammers + int'fce	3,595
INFOSCRIBE											
1000	200/100	N/A	Y	Y	3.4K	T	N	Wide	S,P	9	$1,390
1100	200/100	40	Y	Y	3.4K	F,T	Y	Wide	P,S,Com.	9	1,590
1200	200/100	40	Y	Y	3.4K	T	N	Wide	S,P	9	1,995
1400	400/200	80	Y	Y	32K	T	N	Wide	P,S,Cmdr.	18	1,845
800	200/100	40	Y	Y	3.4K	T	N	Wide	S,P,Cmdr.	9	1,795
103X	200/100	40	Y	Y	3K	T	N	Wide	IBM,Twinax	9	3,199
143X	400/200	80	Y	Y	32K	T	N	Wide	IBM,Twinax	18	3,499
83X	200/100	40	Y	Y	3K	T	N	Wide	IBM,Twinax	9	3,199
GENICOM											
1025 (color opt)	200	100	Y	Y	2K/8K (opt)	F,T	Y	Std.	S,P	18	$1,029
1020	200	100	Y	Y	2K/8K	F,T	Y	Wide	S,P	18	1,195
1040 (color opt)	360	90	Y	Y	56K	F,T,pin	Y	Wide	S,P	24	1,799
3210	240	60	Y	Y	2K/8K	T	Y	Wide	S,P	9	1,495
3310	300	90	Y	Y	.512K-6K	T	Y	Wide	S,P	9	1,645
3310 Color	300	90	Y	Y	.512K-6K	T	Y	Wide	S,P	9	2,295
3320 Quiet	300	180	Y	Y	.512K-6K	T	Y	Wide	S,P	18	1,965
3410	400	120	Y	Y	.512K-6K	T	Y	Wide	S,P	18	2,160
3410 Quiet	400	120	Y	Y	.512K	T	Y	Wide	S,P	18	2,325
3510/3520	300	90	Y	Y	4K	T	Y	Wide	IBM coax/twin	9	3,620/3,590
3530/3540	400	120	Y	Y	4K	T	Y	Wide	IBM coax/twin	18	4,270/4,240
OTC											
2142	1200	180	Y	Y	8K	T	N	136	P	21	$4,995
850XL	850	106	Y	Y	8K	T	N	136	S,P	9	2,495
850 Printnet	850	106	Y	Y	256K	T	N	136	S,P	9	2,995
888XL	850	106	Y	Y	8K	T	N	136	Twin AX,P	9	3,795
889XL	850	106	Y	Y	8K	T	N	136	CO-AX, P	9	3,995
2142-Serial Model	1200	180	Y	Y	8K	T	N	136	S/P	21	5,190
2142-Twin-AX Model	1200	180	Y	Y	8K	T	N	136	S/P, Twin-AX	21	6,290
2142-Coax Model	1200	180	Y	Y	8K	T	N	136	S/P,Coax	21	6,290
2162	1800	270	Y	Y	8K	T	N	136	P	21	6,750
2162-Serial/ Parallel Model	1800	270	Y	Y	8K	T	N	136	S,P	21	6,945
2162-Coax Model	1800	270	Y	Y	8K	T	N	136	S,P, coax	21	8,045
2162-Twin-AX Model	1800	270	Y	Y	8K	T	N	136	S,P, Twin-AX	21	8,045

EXHIBIT 2 *(concluded)*

MAKE/MODEL	CPS DRAFT	CPS LQ	BIT-MAPPED GRAPHICS	BI-DIR.	INTERNAL MEMORY	PAPER FEED	SHEET FEEDER OPTION	CARRIAGE	INTER-FACE	NUMBER OF PRINT WIRES	PRICE
PRINTEK											
TH 9010	200	40	Y	Y	2K	T	N	Wide	S,P	9	$1,325
XLD9030	200	80	Y	Y	2K	F,T	Y	Wide	S,P, Diabalo	18	1,695
TH9020	340	80	Y	Y	2K	T	N	Wide	S,P	18	1,895
FP 20--	200	45	Y	Y	8K	T	N	Wide	S,P	9	2,095
TEXAS INSTRUMENTS											
Omni 810 Forms Printer	150	N/A	N	Y	256 char	T	N	Wide	S,P	9	1,645
Omni 820 RO	150	N/A	N	Y	.250K-2K	F	N	Wide	S,P	9	1,995
Omni 820 KSR	150	N/A	N	Y	.250K-2K	F	N	Wide	S,P	9	2,165
880 AT Forms Printer	300	75	Y	Y	2K-16K	T	N	Wide	S,P	9	2,195
880 Forms Printer	300	75	Y	Y	2K-16K	T	N	Wide	S,P	9	2,195
880 DP Forms Printer	300	150	Y	Y	2K-16K	T	N	Wide	P,S	9	2,195
Omni 885	300	75	Y	Y	6K-22K	T	N	Std	S,P	9	2,295

teristics of the printers are listed below. The product characteristics are summarized and compared to competing products in Exhibit 2.

TH9010. The TH9010 is Roboprint's basic model for the low end of the general heavy-duty printer market. It offers speeds of 200 characters per second (CPS) in draft mode and 45 CPS in letter-quality mode. It has bit-mapped graphics capabilities, bidirectional printing, and 2 kilobytes of internal memory. Paper feed is accomplished through a tractor mechanism (consequently, no sheet feeder option is available). The printer features a wide carriage, serial and parallel interfaces, and has a nine-pin printing head (meaning the dot matrix is made up of nine print wires). The retail selling price is $1,325, with a one-year warranty on the printer and a two-year warranty on the printhead.

TH9020. The TH9020 is very similar to the TH9010 except for certain features that position it at the high end of the general heavy-duty printer market. It offers higher speeds than the TH9010 (340 CPS in draft mode and 80 CPS in letter-quality mode). It also has bit-mapped graphics capabilities, bidirectional printing, 2 kilobytes of internal memory, paper feed through a tractor mechanism (no sheet feeder option), a wide carriage, and serial and parallel interfaces like the TH9010. But it has an 18-pin printing head (giving the dot matrix much better definition than the 9-pin head). The retail selling price is higher at $1,895, with a one-year warranty on the printer and a two-year warranty on the printhead. The TH9010 and TH9020 are positioned toward the general heavy-duty printer market, the TH9010 being at the lower end in terms of quality/performance and the TH9020 at the high end.

XLD9030. Roboprint describes the XLD9030 as an executive-quality printer, with fine print reproduction and graphics capabilities. Its performance and technical features place it between the TH9010 and the TH9020. It offers

200 CPS in draft mode and 80 CPS in letter-quality mode. It has bit-mapped graphics capabilities, bidirectional printing, and 2 kilobytes of internal memory (like the two TH printers) but offers a friction paper feed in addition to the tractor mechanism. This allows the XLD9030 to come with a sheet feeder option (a sheet feeder is a tray of individual sheets of paper, as is used in most laser printers and copiers). It also has serial and parallel interfaces, like the TH models, but offers Diablo compatible software controls as well. It has an 18-pin printing head (giving higher resolution than a 9-pin head). The retail selling price is $1,695, with a two-year warranty on the printhead. The XLD9030 is positioned as an executive-quality printer to be used primarily for word processing and presentation graphics applications by the busy executive. It evolved from the model 930 which started shipping toward the latter half of 1983. The XLD suffix was added in 1985 to reflect a software change which provided better print quality. In terms of quality and performance, the XLD9030 lies somewhere between the TH9010 and the TH9020.

FP2009.   The FP2000 series consists of four heavy-duty printers that have the striking force necessary to print on multipart forms (up to nine sheets). Accordingly, it is positioned toward the heavy-duty demand document and multipart forms printing market. The FP2000 series prints at 200 CPS in draft mode and 45 CPS in letter-quality mode. It has bit-mapped graphics capabilities, bidirectional printing, and 8 kilobytes of internal memory. Paper feed is accomplished via tractor mechanism (thus no sheet feeder option is available). All four models come with a wide carriage and serial and parallel interfaces. The 2009 has a nine-inch printing head and is intended for heavy-duty, high-volume data processing printing needs. It sells for $2,095 retail, with a one-year warranty on the printer and a two-year warranty on the printhead.

FP2018.   The FP2018 differs from the 2009 in that it has an 18-pin printhead, which makes it suitable for bar code printing (the 18-pin head gives the higher resolution that is required by bar code scanning devices). In its other essential features, it is the same as the 2009. The retail selling price is $1,295, with a one-year warranty on the printer and a two-year warranty on the printhead.

FP2009 TX.   The 2009 TX and 2018 TX are variations of the 2009 and 2018, respectively. These printers emulate the IBM 4214, 5225, and 5256 printers, and offer direct attachment to the IBM system 3X computers without requiring a protocol convertor. (However, they still have the standard RS232 serial interface that allows them to be connected to a standard personal computer or terminal.) The *TX* stands for the *twin-axial* connectors that allow direct attachment to the IBM system. The 2009 TX has a nine-pin printhead and sells for $3,495 retail, with a one-year warranty on the printer and a two-year warranty on the printhead.

FP2018 TX.   The FP2018 TX differs from the 2009 TX in the same way that the 2009 differs from the 2018. It offers higher resolution printing through its 18-pin printing head than the 2009 TX. The retail selling price is $3,595, with a one-year warranty on the printer and a two-year warranty on the printhead.

Designed to handle nine-part forms with minimal waste, the FP2009 has become Roboprint's best selling printer. Exhibits 3 through 5 break down Roboprint's sales by product for 1987 and 1988 and illustrate that Roboprint has become increasingly reliant on the 2000 series for both unit and dollar volume. Roboprint management estimates that the majority of sales (both units and dollar volume) is attributable to the FP2009. Sales of the TH9010, TH9020, and XLD9030 are expected to decrease further in 1989 as they continue on their path toward obsolescence.

Product Cost Issues. Since printers are manufactured on an assembly line/batch flow basis, the cost accounting system does not capture cost data by job. On the other hand, a limited number of customer orders require customizing and are manufactured on a job order basis. Roboprint accumulates costs by major components: material, labor, and overhead. Direct costs (material and labor) are not available by product line. Overhead expenses are accumulated by department/cost center and have a direct relationship to managerial responsibil-

EXHIBIT 3 Roboprint's 1987 and 1988 sales

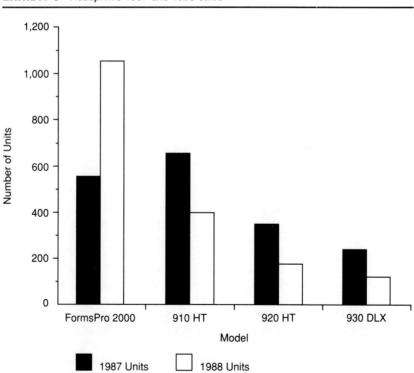

EXHIBIT 4   Roboprint's 1987 sales by product

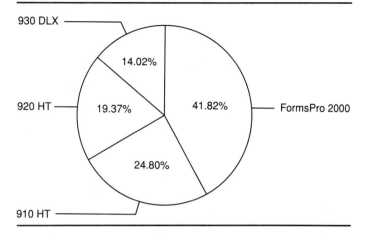

930 DLX

14.02%

920 HT   19.37%   41.82%   FormsPro 2000

24.80%

910 HT

EXHIBIT 5   Roboprint's 1988 sales by product

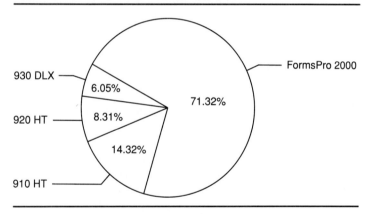

FormsPro 2000

930 DLX

6.05%   71.32%

920 HT   8.31%

14.32%

910 HT

ity. A standard cost approach is used for material only. Material usage/cost is based upon the engineering department's bills of material. Since labor costs are about 8 percent of sales, management does not feel that much time should be devoted to determining and controlling labor costs. Direct labor is calculated monthly to determine if the costs fall within range of the budgeted labor costs.

Since printers are, for the most part, built for inventory, rather than for a specific customer, a list price is determined for the basic printer and also for options. Generally, prices are based upon total manufacturing cost, plus a markup of about 45 percent, regardless of marketing channel. Prices range from $807 for the model TH9010 to $1,538 for the new FP2000 printer. Competitive pricing of printer features is also factored into the final listed price. Roboprint's printers are considered to be high-end printers, which probably accounts for its higher price level. The average wholesale price for serial impact printers was $1,052 during 1988.

Marketing. Unlike a number of small manufacturing firms that emphasize engineering over marketing, Roboprint's marketing staff is roughly equal to its engineering staff. Its management is generally more sensitive to marketing issues than other electronic manufacturing firms of its size. Roboprint presently has two management-level employees assigned to sales and marketing functions. Their titles are vice president of sales and marketing, and assistant marketing manager.

Roboprint's vice president of marketing and sales is responsible for all of Roboprint's sales and marketing activities including long-term strategic planning and day-to-day operational aspects of sales. Roboprint's assistant marketing manager is primarily involved with assisting the vice president of marketing and sales with the development of new sales literature and training materials and coordinating direct mail activities.

According to Roboprint's management, because of limited resources, Roboprint's marketing personnel are unable to "do things the way big companies do," such as formal market research. Prior to Roboprint's restructuring, there were many products that were half finished, with no focus or clear strategy. Lead largely by Roboprint's vice president of marketing and sales, Roboprint adopted its current marketing strategy of "differentiating itself from the larger printer manufacturers," while not spreading itself too thin. This resulted in making some hard decisions and ultimately dropping some of the uncompleted projects.

Roboprint saw one of its competitors, Datasouth, develop a laser printer that was obsolete before it made it to market and did not want to follow in its footsteps. As a result, it dropped both laser printers and color printers that would compete directly with products made by the big manufacturers, from its development program. It chose instead to focus on the heavy-duty industrial market segment, and more recently on the multipart form and bar code market niches. The FP2000 series is the successful result of this strategy, and the new line which will be available in early 1990 is expected to take over where the 2000 series left off.

Distribution Channels. Roboprint distributes printers through three primary distribution channels: distributors, systems houses, and value added resellers (VARs). Secondary distribution channels, which account for a very small portion of sales, include dealers, representatives (reps), and original equipment manufacturers (OEMs). Collectively these primary and secondary distribution channels are often referred to as Roboprint's *resellers*. The similarities, differences, and characteristics of Roboprint's primary distribution channels are discussed below.

Roboprint's distributors are generally large firms that sell a number of different computer products and carry a number of competing computer printers. Distributors generally have a trained sales force which sells Roboprint's printers directly to the end users, which are almost exclusively businesses rather than individuals. Because distributors sell to a large number of customers, they tend to sell the most printers compared with systems houses and VARs.

Roboprint's systems houses sell minicomputer systems for particular applications. The printers that they sell are usually bundled with a minicomputer system. The systems houses are likely to purchase a larger number of printers over a given period of time than VARs. The printers are typically used repeatedly for a standard application. An example of such an application would be an airline ticket system to be installed at an airline's ticket counters throughout the country. OEMs are similar to systems houses but are more likely to require a customized product (special font characters, form lengths, or custom labeling of the printer housing).

Roboprint's VARs are similar to its system houses. Its VARs are primarily sellers of smaller computer systems. A Roboprint printer is one of several components bundled with such a system. Although generally smaller than minicomputer-based systems, the systems tend to be costly, and the VARs tend to be smaller firms. The VARs generally have a low sales volume and may order a single Roboprint printer every few months. A customized hospital patient billing system is one example of a computer system that would typically be sold by a VAR.

Promotion. Roboprint's primary promotional channel is direct mail. Feedback provided by surveys and conversations with members of each of Roboprint's distribution channels (distributors, systems houses, and VARs) is used to isolate target industries that have multipart form and bar code applications. Roboprint's present strategy, which has resulted from such feedback, is to focus on the following three industries:

- Electronic parts wholesalers.
- Customs brokers.
- Freight forwarders.

Roboprint targets the end users in these industries with direct promotional mailings. These mailings typically include an industry-specific cover letter, an industry-related case study providing a success story of a similar customer, and product literature. The approach is a pull strategy, which focuses promotion on the end user to create demand for the product. In line with this approach, Roboprint has recently introduced two secondary promotional channels to reach end users: reader response cards and magazine advertising.

Roboprint is also focusing promotional efforts on resellers, both existing and potential resellers. It publishes a newsletter every two months which is sent to roughly 100 key resellers and a few large end users. The newsletters keep the resellers informed of new developments and new products. In an effort to attract new resellers, Roboprint direct-mails literature to potential distributors, systems houses, and VARs.

Marketing Research. In November 1988, Roboprint commissioned a group of students from Slippery Rock University to perform a market study to measure the attitudes of resellers, existing customers, and potential customers. The study was based on data collected by the group through qualitative, open-ended telephone surveys. In general, the study indicated favorable response to the FP2000 series, with less favorable responses to the TH9010, TH9020, and XLD9030. The competitive advantages of the FP2000 series of printers appear to be its forms handling capability, ease of use, and durability. Its major disadvantage appears to be its limited speed, seconded by its high noise level. Roboprint appears to be integrating some of the marketing research feedback into its new product line. The major findings of this study are given in Exhibit 6.

Target Segments. The printer industry may be segmented by printing technologies: serial impact and nonimpact, line impact and nonimpact, and page printers. From a marketing perspective, it is more useful to segment the printer market by end-user usage. The printer market in general, and more specifically the serial dot matrix impact printer market, can be segmented into four usage groups: data processing, text processing, office information, and electronic publishing. This is the segmentation model that Roboprint's management uses. Roboprint is focusing primarily on the data processing segment of the market. Roboprint management focused on technology, product features, sales and distribution, and competition in order to determine its strategic fit in the data processing market segment. This segment depends largely on impact technology, and more specifically dot matrix, for the required ruggedness and multipart forms capability. The sales and distribution requirements are highly applications-oriented, and largely for that reason, the dominant competitors are domestic manufacturers. The types of companies that have the greatest need for demand document printers are: wholesale distributors, freight forwarders/customs brokers, hospitals, manufacturing companies, hotels/motels, airlines/airline agents, car rental companies, trucking and railway companies, financial brokerage companies, and car dealers/car service departments.

Product Life Cycle. The product life cycle of computer printers is similar to the product life cycle of computers. Generally this averages around five years, depending on the particular application. Life cycles for mainframes and minicomputers tend to be longer than the life cycles for microcomputers, for example. New computers are constantly being introduced, often based on new design and manufacturing technologies, with more features and lower prices than preceding models.

EXHIBIT 6 Demand document printer customers' needs

Type	Carriage	Speed	Impact force	Noise level	Bar coding
Wholesale distributors	Wide or Narrow	200–400 cps	3 to 4 parts	Somewhat important	Important
Freight forwarders	Wide	200–400 cps	8 to 9 parts	Somewhat important	Somewhat important
Hospitals	Narrow	200 cps	4 to 7 parts	Very important	Somewhat important
Manufacturing companies	Wide	200–400 cps	4 to 7 parts	Somewhat important	Important
Hotels	Narrow	200 cps	2 to 3 parts	Important	
Airlines	Narrow	200–300 cps	9 to 12 parts	Important	
Car rental agencies	Narrow	200 cps	4 to 6 parts	Important	Important
Trucking companies	Wide	200–400 cps	4 to 7 parts	Somewhat important	
Financial companies	Narrow	200–400 cps	2 to 3 parts	Important	
Car dealers	Wide	200–300 cps	3 to 5 parts	Somewhat important	

The same goes for computer printers, but to a lesser degree. Whereas computing performance or memory capacity of new computers is often an order of magnitude (factor of 10x) greater than preceding models, a 50 percent or lower increase in computer printer speed over the preceding model is typical. More frequently, new printer models will support new features such as added font capacity or paper handling capabilities rather than an enormous speed increase. Assessing the desirability of these features by the customer is a critical marketing function.

Because of the high development costs associated with complex electronic products such as computers and printers, both in terms of engineering costs and tooling costs, the short life cycle puts added financial constraints on new product development. Products must either be designed to cover these costs completely during their short life cycles, or they must be designed so that their life cycles can be extended by using pieces of the present line in the next-generation products.

Competition

Genicom

Established in 1983, Genicom Corporation manufactures a number of different printers using several different technologies which appeal to various market niches. Its product lines include teleprinters, tempest printers, daisy wheel printers, laser printers, and line printers, as well as heavy-duty dot matrix printers. According to a company marketing representative, Genicom holds approximately a 15 percent market share of the total computer printer industry. Genicom offers a comprehensive nationwide service program that includes the following five services:

1. Service-on-site by 134 metro service areas.
2. Emergency service parts.
3. Lease option.
4. Repair and return.
5. Factory fixed depot repair.

Genicom's 1000 series of desktop printers are targeted for desktop and demand document use competing with Roboprint's 900 series of printers. Genicom's 3000 series of business-class printers offer higher speeds and additional interfaces and emulation capabilities not found in its 1000 series.

Texas Instruments

Texas Instruments, headquartered in Dallas, Texas, has been in business since 1930 and has been designing and building computers and computer products for more than 30 years. TI's product line of industrial-grade printers is based on the Omni 810 Forms Printer which is the workhorse industry standard. It supports up to nine-part forms. According to product literature, ''hundreds of thousands'' of customers have purchased the Omni 810. Its design dates from either the late 1970s or early 1980s. The Omni 810 probably competes with Roboprint's 900 series of printers.

TI's 880 series of printers are descendants of the Omni 810. They share the same basic mechanical platform but have faster drive electronics and motors to support the higher print speeds. The 880 series probably competes with Roboprint's FP2000 series of printers.

TI's latest industrial printer is the Omni 885. It was introduced late in 1986 or early in 1987. It was not built on the standard Omni 810 platform but appears to be a completely new design. It has the styling of a laser printer or small office copier. Roboprint's new line of printers appears to be positioned against the Omni 885.

Facit, Inc.

Founded in Sweden in 1413, Facit AB is one of the world's oldest companies. In 1971 Facit introduced its first printer. According to a company marketing representative, Facit holds approximately 1 percent market share of the total computer printer industry. Facit manufactures a full line of dot matrix, thermal, and laser printers, as well as a wide range of numerical control products.

Facit's B3450 is a multicapability 24-pin printer with a demand document paper path and zero tear-off. It has several paper handling options and supports a four-color ribbon and font cards. Its cabinet styling is consistent with the lower-end units in the line. It probably competes with Roboprint's 900 series of printers.

Facit's Documate 3000 is specifically targeted toward demand document and bar code/label applications. It supports zero tear-off, six-part form handling, and 11 bar code formats are built in. It supports variable-sized characters from 1/10 to 9.6 inches, as well as character rotation. It probably competes with Roboprint's 2000 series of printers.

Output Technology Corporation

Output Technology Corporation (OTC) was established in 1983. According to company literature, OTC prides itself in being the American manufacturer of the world's fastest serial dot matrix printers. OTC's success is said to lie in its commitment to serving its customers through:

1. A technical support hotline.
2. Depot service and on-site maintenance through nationally recognized third-party firms.
3. Worldwide service through the U.S. factory located in Spokane, Washington, as well as the international service facility in Amsterdam.
4. On-site technical training and a technical sales support team.
5. Extended warranty programs.

OTC is focusing on the very-high-speed segment of the industrial-grade printer market. It accomplishes high throughput by using not one but three printheads in its "TriMatrix" print mechanism found in such printers as its 850XL.

Dataproducts

Dataproducts is a 27-year-old company based in Woodland Hills, California. Dataproduct's product line includes band, line matrix, dot matrix, laser, solid ink, and thermal transfer printers. Dataproducts designs, manufactures, and markets a comprehensive range of printer technologies. By providing such a range, Dataproducts is not only targeting industrial-grade printers but the entire printer market. Dataproducts offers many application-specific printing solutions for the following markets:

1. Electronic desktop publishing.
2. CAD/CAM/CAE/graphics.
3. Data processing.
4. Office automation.
5. Bar coding/industrial marking.
6. TEMPEST.

Dataproducts is well-established in the OEM marketplace, having several major computer companies as customers. Dataproducts also markets printers through industrial distributors, value-added distributors, value-added resellers (VARs), value-added dealers (VADs) and directly to select end users.

Dataproducts manufactures band printers, line matrix printers, daisy wheel printers, and laser printers, as well as dot matrix printers. Its dot matrix printer products consist of the 9000 series and the 8070 Plus. The 9000 series is targeted toward business applications, specifically word processing, business graphics, and spreadsheets. Dataproducts 8070 Plus is specifically targeted toward the heavy-duty printer market. It is a high-speed (400 CPS) product, with six-part form capability, and optional character sets, font styles, bar code fonts, and sheet feeder. Priced competitively, it is likely to compete against Roboprint's FP2000 series.

Datasouth

Datasouth Computer Corporation, located in Charlotte, North Carolina, was founded in 1977. The company manufactures five series of high-performance matrix printers. Datasouth printers are available nationwide through a network of sales/service distributors, enabling Datasouth to secure a strong presence in the industry.

Datasouth manufactures heavy-duty dot matrix printers primarily for demand document and bar code applications. All of Datasouth's printers appear to share a similar injection-molded case and probably share the same mechanical platform. Datasouth's basic product is the DS 180 Plus. The "180" indicates that the printer's speed is 180 characters per second (CPS). The DS 220 prints at 220 CPS, and the DS 400 at 400 CPS. Datasouth's DS 220 is essentially a higher-speed version of a DS 180 that also supports letter-quality and bar code printing. The DS 220 AF is essentially a DS 220 with an optional single-sheet feeder.

Infoscribe

Infoscribe has designed and manufactured a range of heavy-duty printers since 1980. Its manufacturing and sales office are both located at its headquarters in Reston, Virginia. According to a company marketing representative, Infoscribe's market share is close to 2 percent in the heavy-duty printer market. Its primary customers are the federal government, the medical market, and professional services.

Infoscribe manufactures two classes of heavy-duty industrial-grade dot matrix printers; the series 100 class and the series 8 class. The series 100 class of printers is targeted toward general heavy-duty uses including multipart form and bar code applications. The series 8 class of printers is targeted toward demand document applications.

Epson

Epson, Inc. was founded in 1975. Its headquarters is located in Torrance, California. Epson is beginning to pose a threat to industrial-grade printer manufacturers. Because of its experience in the consumer-grade printer market, it brings strong manufacturing, marketing, and financial resources to the industrial niche. In the near future, Epson may become a primary player in this market niche as it is already in the consumer market.

Although not currently one of Roboprint's main competitors, Epson has recently introduced a printer for the heavy-duty market segment. Epson's DFX–5000 is a high-volume serial dot matrix printer that can print at up to 533 characters per second. It provides two separate paper paths which are selectable at the touch of a button, eliminating the manual changeover from one form to another. It handles up to six-part carbonless forms, automatically adjusts for different thicknesses, and supports zero tear-off. Roboprint is designing its new line of printers in part to compete with Epson's DFX–5000.

Epson's entry into the heavy-duty industrial-grade printer market may well be a turning point in the history of the computer printer market. As the computer printer market reaches maturity, it can be expected that the large players will begin to move into smaller market niches in order to continue growth as overall demand begins to flatten out. The continuing advancements in laser printer technology, which compete with dot matrix technology in a number of applications, have contributed greatly to this leveling off of demand for dot matrix printers. Because Japanese manufacturers are generally market-share-oriented, it is likely that other Japanese competitors will follow Epson's move

EXHIBIT 7 Comparison of competitors

Company	Sales volume (millions)	Employees	Square feet	Strengths
Genicom Corporation	$302	3,600	433,000	Broad product line. 14 regional sales offices. Comprehensive nationwide service program. Strong and broad international presence. Worldwide distribution network. Expanded domestic customer base. Dedicated to R&D.
Texas Instruments, Inc.	967 (Digital Products Segment)	78,000 (Total)	n/a	Extensive worldwide service network. Strengthened financial condition. Broad product line. Strong global presence. Good, cost-effective program. Brand name.
Facit, Inc.	350	2,500	27,000	Subsidiary of one of the world's oldest companies. Sales and service in over 90 countries. Offers third-party service through world's largest third-party organization. Several Facit-owned service centers. Privately owned. Specialized applications.
Output Technology Corporation	16	100	n/a	World's fastest serial dot matrix printers. Worldwide service through U.S. factory and an international service facility. Focuses on medium-priced high-speed printers. Strong commitment to serving its customers.
Dataproducts	345	4,200	110,000	World's leading independent supplier of computer printers. Designs, manufactures, and markets a comprehensive range of printer technologies. Well established in the OEM marketplace. Three depot facilities to repair and remanufacture all its products and subassemblies. Extensive sales network.
Datasouth Computer Corporation	19	170	60,000	Nationwide sales/service distributors. Manufactures five series of high-performance matrix printers. Experienced management team. One unified printer operation, worldwide. Centralized engineering management.
Infoscribe	4	30	70,000	Manufactured in the United States. Lowest cost of ownership.
Epson, Inc.	640	850	40,000	New entrant into the industrial-grade printer market. Strong experience in the consumer-grade printer market.

Sources: *Dun and Bradstreet's Million Dollar Directory, Dun and Bradstreet's Corporate Identifiers*, telephone inquiries, company literature, and trade magazines.

shortly. Aggressive pricing is likely to follow, ultimately followed by a consolidation. The primary thrust of these competitors' marketing plans are summarized in Exhibit 7.

Market Shares

Based on recent market surveys, the market shares of the primary competitors in the demand document segment are:

	1988 Units	Share of the market
FormsPro 2000	1,100,000	7%
Datasouth	1,500,000	10
Facit	2,000,000	13
Others (Infoscribe, etc.)	1,000,000	7
Texas Instruments	9,400,000	63

New Products

Roboprint is currently developing seveal new printers to replace its aging 900 series of printers. Sales of the existing FP2000 series are expected to continue after the introduction of the new models. Roboprint hopes to have working prototypes of its new units developed by August of 1989, with first shipments beginning in the first quarter of 1990. A matrix showing the tentatively planned features of this new line of printers is shown in Exhibit 8. There are three new models: the FormsPro 2080, 4000, and 4080.

The new products provide several features not found in previous Roboprint printers. These features were based, in part, on customer feedback. The major new feature, according to Roboprint's management, is the addition of narrower 80-column printers which accept standard 8 1/2-inch fanfold paper.

EXHIBIT 8 New product line

Model #	Est. % of Sales	80 col	132 col	200 cps	≤ 400 cps	9 pin	18 pin	Comments
2080	15%	■		■		■		Low-end, multi-part, 80 col.
4000	60%		■		■		■	High-end, multipart 132 col. with barcode
4080	10%	■			■		■	High-end, multipart 80 col. with barcode

Previous models were all wider units which accepted up to 14-inch fanfold paper.

Roboprint's new 80-column units provide a lower cost and smaller footprint, which in some customer applications will eliminate the need for a separate printer stand, allowing for desktop and countertop use. All of these new units feature push-tractor technology allowing demand-document handling capability, meaning that a single form can be printed out and torn off without waste.

The cases for Roboprint's new printers will be primarily made from extruded aluminum, rather than injection-molded plastic used in its previous models. Extrusion will allow the same tooling to be used for both the 80- and 132-column models. Their styling resembles a cross between an office copying machine and a small laser printer. The higher-end units feature a liquid crystal display used for printer setup.

Another important new feature is higher-speed printing. Roboprint's older series of printers topped out at roughly 340 CPS in draft mode for one of its units, with 200 CPS being standard for the rest of its models. The new units have one entry-level model at 200 CPS, and the rest at just under 400 CPS. This move toward a higher-speed product line was prompted by the general trend toward higher-speed printing, and specifically by the recent entry of an Epson printer with 480 CPS, and the anticipated entry of a Genicom printer with 500 CPS.

A three-tractor option will be featured on a number of Roboprint's new units. This feature will be included primarily on Roboprint's high-end units. The three-tractor option will allow three different types of fanfold forms to be threaded through the printer, allowing quick and easy changing of forms without rethreading the printer. This idea is similar to a two-tractor printer developed by Epson. The relative strengths and weaknesses of the new product line are enumerated in Exhibit 9.

Morgan had been told that the new product would still be targeted toward the heavy-duty printer segment. However, he was charged with developing a list of target industries that might be users of the new product. Once this was developed, he needed a cost-effective promotional strategy to reach these customers. Morgan was unsure of the effect launching the new product would have on the existing product line and whether to drop the old line or risk cannibalizing it. He wrestled with many questions: What advertising media to use? What about a direct sales force? What changes, if any should be made to the existing promotion strategy?

EXHIBIT 9 New product analysis

Planned products	Price	Speed	Carriage width	Relative strengths	Relative weaknesses
FormsPro 2080	$1,995	200 cps	Narrow	• Narrow width • High impact • Ease of use • Reliability • Durability • Warranty	• One set of tractors • Price/speed ratio (compared to new Epson & Genicom)
FormsPro 4080	$2,395	400 cps	Narrow	• Narrow width • Speed • Ease of use • Reliability • Durability • Warranty • Bar codes	• Impact force • One set of tractors • Price/speed ratio (compared to new Epson & Genicom)
FormsPro 4000	$2,495	400 cps	Wide	• High impact • Fast speed • Programmable • Bar codes • Quiet • Warranty • Reliability	• Price/speed ratio

Case 41

Dutch Food Industries Company (A)*

In early September, Jan de Vries, product manager for Dutch Food Industries' new salad dressing product, was wondering what strategy to follow with respect to this new product. His assistant had prepared information concerning alternative promotional methods to use to introduce the new product, and he was concerned with exactly which of these he should recommend for the product's introduction. He also wondered what price the new product should retail for and when the company should introduce the new product. Mr. de Vries had to decide these issues in the next couple of days, as his report containing his recommendations on the introduction of the new salad dressing was due on the desk of the director of marketing the following Monday.

Company Background

The Netherlands Oil Factory of Delft, The Netherlands, was founded in 1884. This firm, which supplied edible oils to the growing margarine industry, merged in 1900 with a French milling company. The new firm then operated under the name Dutch Food Industries Company (DFI).

From this origin, the brand name DFI became increasingly strong and was eventually given to all of the company's branded products. More recently, the name was registered for use internationally.

In the course of the 1920s, DFI became an important factor in the margarine market. The company was a troublesome competitor for the Margarine Union, the company formed by the merger in 1927 of the two margarine giants, Van den Bergh and Jurgens. In 1928, an agreement was reached by which DFI joined the Margarine Union.

In 1930, the interests of the Margarine Union were merged with those of International Industries Corporation—a large, diversified, and international

---

* This case was written by Kenneth L. Bernhardt and James Scott assisted by Jos Viehoff, graduate student, Netherlands School of Economics. Copyright © 1990 by Kenneth L. Bernhardt.

organization. It was in this way that DFI became a part of the International Industries complex of companies.

International Industries Corporation (IIC) is a worldwide organization with major interests in the production of margarine, other edible fats and oils, soups, ice cream, frozen foods, meats, cheeses, soaps, and detergents.

The total sales of IIC were more than $1 billion.[1] Profits before taxes were $56 million.

Within IIC, DFI proceeded with its original activities after its margarine factory was closed, namely developing its exports of oils and fats, its trade in bakery products, as well as a number of branded food products. The following list indicates the range of consumer products which the company marketed: table oil, household fats, mayonnaise, salad dressing (several varieties), tomato ketchup, peanut butter, and peanuts.

DFI's total annual sales were between $14 million–$28 million. Profits before taxes were between $1.4 million–$2.8 million.

Background on the Dressing Market

A large and growing percentage of Holland's population eats lettuce, usually with salad dressing, with their meals. Estimates indicated that 82 percent of the people ate lettuce with salad dressing regularly. The salad dressing market has extreme seasonal demand as shown in Exhibit 1. This seasonal pattern coincides with the periods of greatest production of lettuce in Holland. Thus, 50 percent of the total year's volume for the salad dressing market occurs in the four months beginning in April. During this period, lettuce is plentiful and sells for approximately $0.46 per head.

The total salad dressing market was growing at approximately 7 percent per year. DFI's share of the market had declined from 20.7 percent to 16.6 percent over the last five years. The total market for salad dressings at manufacturer's level was currently estimated at between $7 million and $8.4 million. The company was looking for ways to halt the decline in market share and, in fact, increase DFI's share of the growing market.

Historically, the salad dressing market was composed of two segments. The first was a 25 percent oil-based salad dressing, which comprised 90 percent of the total market. The other 10 percent of the market consisted of 50 percent oil-based salad dressing, a slightly creamier product. Previously, DFI, in an effort to increase its market share, had introduced a new product which was 50 percent oil based. Up to that time, DFI sold only 25 percent oil-based salad dressing. The product, called Delfine, was not successful in obtaining the desired volume and profit. While DFI still marketed Delfine, almost all of DFI's volume came from its 25 percent oil-based product, Slasaus.

A research study was conducted to help the DFI marketing executives determine why Delfine was not successful. Several reasons emerged:

---

[1] All financial data in this case are presented in U.S. dollars.

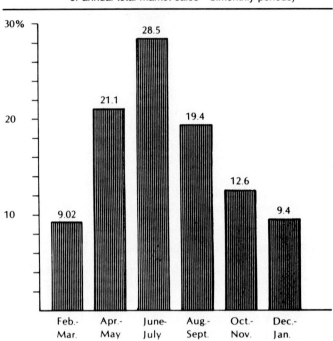

EXHIBIT 1 Seasonal analysis of salad dressing market (percentage of annual total market sales—bimonthly periods)

1. The potential of the 50 percent oil-based market was much smaller than originally anticipated, and only a small percentage of the total population was even interested in this product.
2. The consumers could detect only a small difference between the 25 percent oil-based and the 50 percent oil-based varieties when blind-tested. The difference was not noticeable enough for the consumers to prefer the 50 percent oil-based product.
3. The 50 percent oil-based salad dressing was more expensive, and the consumer was not willing to pay the difference for an apparently almost imperceptible difference.

   Because the Delfine sales were well below expectations, DFI removed the heavy promotion support which it had been giving the product. The executives decided to wait for a significant breakthrough of a product with unique advantages. The Delfine experience indicated to them that it would take a totally new type of product for DFI to increase its market share significantly.

Background and Development of Slamix

Every two years, the company conducted a housewives' habits study in which a panel of 700 consumers was asked about their household and their food preparation habits. In August two years before, the company received the most recent study, called PMC-11. The housewives were asked how they prepared their lettuce and what ingredients they used. The results showed that an extremely large percentage of the housewives added not only salad dressing to lettuce, but also added other ingredients such as salt, pepper, eggs, onion, gherkins, and so on. Thus DFI executives got the idea that putting some of these ingredients in the salad dressing would result in a real convenience for the housewife, and DFI would have the significant new product for which they had been searching. The laboratory, in August of the same year, began developing a "dressed" salad dressing which included some of the ingredients which many housewives were accustomed to adding.

Early in the next year, a committee called the Slamix Committee,[2] was formed to make sure that every part of the company was involved in the development of this new product. The committee, which was headed up by the product manager, had representatives from various parts of the company, including development, production, and marketing. The committee studied production problems, laboratory findings, and in general, was charged with the responsibility of seeing that the development progressed as scheduled. The committee did not have decision-making powers but either invited decision makers to important meetings or wrote reports to the people who were in a position to make the required decisions.

After several product tests concerned with taste and keeping properties were conducted at the factory, the company, one year after laboratory work began, undertook its first consumer test of the new "dressed" salad dressing. A panel of housewives was shown a bottle of the new product which was a salad dressing containing pieces of gherkins, onions, and paprika. Several conclusions emerged from this study:

1. The "dressed" salad dressing was seen by the housewives as more than a salad dressing with ingredients. It was seen as a completely new product.
2. There were two sides to this newness:
   a. By looking at the product, they thought that it had a new taste.
   b. The convenience aspect was strongly stressed by the housewives.
3. The housewives thought that the new product would be good for decorating the lettuce. With its new color (light red with colorful ingredients), they thought that they could decorate the lettuce much better than with present salad dressings which were creme-colored and very similar to mayonnaise.
4. When asked about the ingredients, one half of the housewives were favorable toward paprika, and half were against it. This apparently was a troublesome ingredient. However, because of the convenience aspect, gherkins and onions were favored by the housewives.

Later, a second consumer study was conducted by the Institute of Household Research in Rotterdam. A sample of 140 housewives who actually used

---

[2] Literally translated, Slasaus means "lettuce sauce," and Slamix is literally "lettuce mix."

salad dressing on lettuce was given a bottle of the new product to take home. Then, they were visited in their homes. Much useful information emerged from this study. After looking at the product, but before trying it, the housewives said that it looked like a fun product, it made them happy, and they thought that it would taste good. When asked what they thought the product contained, they said tomatoes, red paprika, celery, gherkins, and green paprika.

However, the company was disappointed with the housewives' overall evaluation of the product. Only 20 percent of the housewives said that they thought the product was very good, 11 percent did not like the product, and 69 percent of the housewives said that there were some favorable and some unfavorable aspects of the product. The main reason for the 80 percent unfavorable reaction was the consistency of the new salad dressing. It was too thin. The housewives could pour it too easily and it rapidly went to the bottom of the bowl. Because it fell to the bottom, the housewives said that it was much harder to decorate their salad. It was also uneconomical because they felt that they would put too much on if the product was that thin. There were also problems with taste. Many of the housewives thought it was too sour or too sharp. The paprika was the main reason for the dissatisfaction.

In spite of the above problems, there were several aspects of the study which encouraged the company to proceed with the development of this new product. When asked how they would change the ingredients in the "dressed" salad dressing, only 47 percent of the housewives suggested changes. Most recommended that more onions be added. The housewives were asked for their preference between DFI's Slasaus and the new "dressed" salad dressing. As shown in Exhibit 2, the housewives preferred the new product, except for its consistency. Sixty percent of the housewives said that they would buy the product if it were possible to buy it in the store. Since this was a very high positive response, the company was very encouraged.

EXHIBIT 2   Preference test: Slasaus versus "dressed" salad dressing

Prefer	Taste	Appear-ance	Decoration aspects	Con-sistency	Con-venience
"Dressed" salad dressing	59%	73%	46%	18%	50%
Slasaus	38	20	44	65	20
No preference/no difference	3	7	10	17	30
	100%	100%	100%	100%	100%

The marketing, production, and development groups, coordinated by the Slamix Committee, began work on incorporating the required changes made evident by this consumer study. DFI's development group experimented with changes in the consistency, taste, and ingredients. The production group experimented with a new production process. DFI had intended to introduce the new "dressed" salad dressing in a few months. However, the top corporate executives decided that, before the new product could be introduced, an extensive test of its keeping properties (vulnerability to deterioration) would have to be conducted.

The keeping-properties test showed that after several months the light red-colored product changed to a pink color. The difference in color was only slight, but DFI executives thought that the consumer reaction to this change should be tested. They decided that at the same time they would conduct a consumer test to find a name for this new product. A sample of 180 housewives from the Institute of Household Research was used to get at these questions. Only 2 out of the 180 housewives saw that there was a difference in color between the two bottles of the new product. When they were told that there was a slight difference and were shown the two bottles together, most of the housewives could not see the color change, and those that could were not unhappy about it.

The housewives were then asked what the name for this product should be. The phrase "mixed salad dressing" kept coming up. The housewives were then asked what they thought of two names which the company had screened, "Slamix" (lettuce mix) and "Spikkeltjessaus" (sauce with little spots). Eighty-one percent thought that Slamix was a very good name. Only 26 percent thought that Spikkeltjessaus was a good name. The name Slamix was chosen for the new product. Interestingly, that was the name that the company had used internally for the new product when it was first being developed.

A short time later, DFI had solved the color-change problem. The company now thought that it had a product ready to be marketed, so a final consumer test was undertaken to test the effect of all of the changes that had been made during the previous year.

Two versions of Slamix, a white one and a pink one, were tested at the Institute for Household Research. One hundred eighty housewives were asked what they thought of the product and whether they would buy it or not. The negative reactions to the product were minimal. Almost no negative comments were voiced. The problems of consistency, color, taste, and ingredients had apparently been solved. When asked if they would buy the product, 76 percent of those shown the pink product, and 70 percent of those shown the white product responded in a positive manner. After tasting the two versions of Slamix, the housewives revealed a strong preference for the pink Slamix. The DCI executives felt that the product was now ready to be marketed.

DFI executives next reviewed the financial projections prepared by Mr. de Vries, the product manager. Almost no capital investment would be required as the Slamix would be produced by using present production facilities. Only a few machines, at a total cost of $11,000, would be required.

At an early stage in the development of the product, Slamix sales had been forecasted at 3.7 percent of the total market at the end of the first year. Encouraged by the results of the consumer tests, DFI executives revised their estimate of sales. The new forecast was for approximately 6.7 percent of the market. (See Exhibit 3.)

EXHIBIT 3 Forecast sales of Slamix

Year	Share of market (percent)
Original estimates	
Year 1	3.7%
Year 2	3.9
Year 3	4.4
Revised estimates	
Year 1	6.7
Year 2	11.7

The directors of the company thought that they finally had the product for which they had been waiting. The consumer tests were complete, and the product had found very high favor with the consumers. There was significant technological development involved in the product, and DFI executives thought that it would take considerable time for the competition to duplicate the product. The product manager's projected sales seemed reasonable. Mr. de Vries was asked to prepare a comprehensive report concerning the introductory marketing strategy to be used to introduce the new product.

Pricing Strategy

The first problem that the product manager had to resolve concerned the suggested retail price that the company should charge for Slamix. To help Mr. de Vries make his recommendation, the assistant product manager had made a list of the following considerations:

1. The company's total cost for a 0.30-liter-size bottle of Slamix was $0.20. This was 20 percent higher than DFI's regular salad dressing, Slasaus.
2. The gross margin for Slasaus was 22 percent. Because of the unique qualities of Slamix, large development costs, and possible substitution with Slasaus, a higher gross margin for Slamix might be considered.
3. DFI gave the wholesalers a 12.5 percent margin and retailers a 14.3 percent margin for Slasaus. Possibly these should be increased for Slamix to encourage greater acceptance and promotion by the trade channels of distribution.
4. The two leading salad dressings, Salata by Duyvis and Slasaus, both had a retail price of $0.28 for the 0.30-liter bottle. The retail price for the 0.60-liter bottle was $0.48. Private label salad dressings were $0.22 for a 0.30-liter bottle. The average price for all salad dressings was approximately $0.26.
5. DFI had conducted some research on the optimal price of Slamix. After using a sample of the product, 140 housewives were asked what price they would be willing to pay for Slamix. Their responses, by percent, were:

	Percent
$0.31 or less	45%
Between $0.31 and $0.40	41
$0.40 or more	14
Total	100%

The average price mentioned was $0.34.

The assistant product manager also prepared the table shown in Exhibit 4. The first column shows the retail price, and gives data that allows one to calculate trade margins and gross margin for Slasaus. The remaining six columns show alternative retail prices for Slamix, resulting from different trade margins and gross margins. Mr. de Vries wondered which of these prices he should recommend to the board of directors.

EXHIBIT 4 Alternative prices for Slamix*

		Slamix					
	Slasaus	1	2	3	4	5	6
Retail price	$0.28	$0.32	$0.34	$0.34	0.36	$0.37	$0.38
Price to retailer	0.24	0.28	0.28	0.29	0.295	0.31	0.316
Price to wholesaler	0.21	0.25	0.25	0.26	0.26	0.28	0.28
Cost	0.165	0.20	0.20	0.20	0.20	0.20	0.20

* Selected figures in this table have been disguised.

Promotion Alternatives

The board of directors told the product manager that he had $203,000 for his promotion budget. Of this, $7,000 was to be allocated as Slamix's share of the general corporate advertising which aided all DFI products. The $203,000 was determined by using a percentage of the "expected gross profit of the first year" for Slamix.[3] DFI's policy was to break even in the third year of the new product, attaining a total payback within five years. The company was generally willing to spend the gross profit for the first year as part of the total investment.

The company had already given considerable thought to the sales message and the brand image desired for Slamix. The information below was sent to the advertising agency to help in planning the promotional program of the company:

> *Sales message.* It is now possible, in a completely new way, to make delicious salad. Sla + Slamix = Sla Klaar. (Lettuce + Slamix = Lettuce Ready)

---

[3] It was possible that the percentage could be greater than 100 percent. This would mean that the company was willing to spend more than the first year's gross profit for initial promotion.

Supporting message. Slamix is a salad dressing with pieces of onion, gherkins, and paprika.

Desired brand image. With Slamix you can make, very easily and very quickly, a delicious salad that also looks nice. Slamix is a complete, good, handy product. DFI is a modern firm with up-to-date ideas.

Thus, the company wanted to get across three principal points. They are (1) that Slamix is a completely new product, (2) that it is convenient, and (3) that it is a salad dressing with ingredients making it a complete salad dressing.

The product manager was undecided as to how to divide the $196,000 among the following alternatives:

1. Television.
2. Radio.
3. Newspaper advertising.
4. Magazines.
5. Sampling.
6. Coupons.
7. Price-off promotion.
8. Key chain premiums.
9. Trade allowances.

Television

The product manager thought that television would be advantageous because of the ability to show the product in actual use—a housewife pouring Slamix onto the lettuce. The cost of using the television medium is shown in Exhibit 5. The company did not have a choice among the seven blocks of time, but had to take whatever was available. For planning, however, they figured an average cost of a 30-second ad would be $1,800. Mr. de Vries felt that at least 25 advertisements were necessary before the TV advertising would have maximum impact.

EXHIBIT 5 Data on Dutch television media

Station	Block number	Time	Cost of 30-second ad
Nederland 1	1	Before early news	$2,300
Nederland 1	2	After early news	2,300
Nederland 1	3	Before late news	2,950
Nederland 1	4	After late news	2,950
Nederland 2	5	After early news	500
Nederland 2	6	Before late news	840
Nederland 2	7	After late news	840
Average cost per 30-second TV ad			$1,800
Production cost for a TV ad			7,000

TV coverage per 1,000 households = 850 or 85 percent. Only about one half of the homes can receive Nederland 2.

Radio

The chief attraction of radio was its extremely low price. Each 30-second radio ad cost $126 on Radio Veronica, a popular station during the daytime. Production costs for a radio ad were approximately $840. Only 60 percent of the households could receive Radio Veronica, mainly in the western part of the country. Mr. de Vries felt that if radio were used, a minimum of 100 spots should be purchased.

Newspapers

Mr. de Vries thought the main advantages of newspapers would be the announcement effect and its influence with the local trade. Nationally, the cost of each half-page insertion would be $14,000.

Magazines

Magazines would be a desirable addition to the promotional program for several reasons. Due to the ability to use color, the company could show the product as it actually looked on the shelf. By using several women's magazines, the company could reach a select audience of people reading the magazine at its leisure. Data on selected Dutch magazines are shown in Exhibit 6. Mr. de Vries thought that if they were to use a magazine campaign, at least 10 insertions would be necessary before the advertising would be very effective. Of the possibilities in Exhibit 6, the agency thought that the combination of *Eva*,

EXHIBIT 6 Data on selected Dutch magazines

Magazines	Type	Circulation	Frequency	Price for full-page ad Black and white	Color	Cost per 1,000 circulation*
Eva	Women's	375,000	Weekly	$ 770	$1,408	$3.75
Margriet	Women's	825,000	Weekly	2,100	3,440	4.15
Libelle	Women's	570,000	Weekly	1,416	2,340	4.10
Prinses	Women's	213,000	Weekly	660	1,175	5.55
Panorama	General	403,000	Weekly	1,300	2,150	5.40
Nieuwe Revu	General	261,000	Weekly	920	1,540	5.90
Spiegel	General	175,000	Weekly	710	1,325	7.55
Het Beste	Digest	325,000	Monthly	965	1,615	4.90
Studio	TV guide	575,000	Weekly	1,525	2,420	4.20
NCRV-gids	TV guide	482,000	Weekly	1,420	2,290	4.75
Vara-gids	TV guide	504,000	Weekly	1,500	2,370	4.70
AVRO-Televizier	TV guide	950,000	Weekly	2,600	3,870	4.05
Combination of Eva, Margriet, and AVRO-Televizier				4,900	7,785	3.65

* Cost of one-page color ad, divided by circulation in thousands. With *Eva* as an example, cost per 1,000 circulation = $1,408/375 = $3.75.

Margriet, and *AVRO-Televizier* would be most effective for DFI, since the combination would reach a large number of people at a relatively low cost.

Sampling

Although he realized that it was very expensive, Mr. de Vries considered the use of direct-mail sampling. A small 12 cm. by 18 cm. (approximately 5 × 7 inches) folder could be mailed to Holland's 3.7 million households for $20,000. The cost, however, would increase substantially if a small bottle of the product were to be included in the direct mailing. This cost would be 20 cents for handling, plus 75 cents for the actual sample. Thus, it would cost $980,000 to sample the whole country.

Coupon

Mr. de Vries was considering whether or not to include a coupon good for $0.04 off the purchase of Slamix with one of the other DFI products—mayonnaise, for example. He estimated that 900,000 coupons would be distributed. At a redemption rate of 5 percent, the cost would, thus, be approximately $1,700.

Price-Off Promotion

DFI made use of a reduced retail price for most of its new product introductions. Thus, the product manager thought it quite normal to consider the use of reducing the retail price by U.S. $0.07 per bottle and identifying this price reduction on the label of the product. It was felt that this reduced price would encourage the housewives to try Slamix. It was also quite normal to follow up this sales promotion with a similar price reduction approximately five months after the product was introduced. This would encourage those who had still not tried the product to purchase a bottle and would encourage those who had already bought one bottle to continue purchasing the new product. The cost of this price-off promotion is shown in Exhibit 7.

EXHIBIT 7

Introduction:	
720,000 bottles at 25 cents (U.S. $0.07) off each	$50,400
Handling and display materials	2,800
Total	$53,200
Follow-up five months later:	
600,000 bottles at 25 cents (U.S. $0.07) off each	$42,000
Handling and display materials	2,800
Total	$44,800

Key Chain Premium

It was very unusual to use a free premium to introduce a new product, but Mr. de Vries was considering this alternative for several reasons. Many products in Holland at this time were using key chains as a premium. As shown in Exhibit 8, an extremely large percentage of the people in Holland were collecting key chains. The details of the research showed that mothers and daughters were more likely to collect key chains, especially if the children were between 8 and 11 years of age. Mr. de Vries felt that if he used key chains as premiums for the introduction of Slamix he could have a follow-up promotion five months later using either key chains or price-off deals. Selected cost information on the key chain promotion is shown in Exhibit 9.

EXHIBIT 8 Percentage of households collecting key chains

	June	July	September
Households with children	45	n.a.	n.a.
Households without children	5	n.a.	n.a.
Total (weighted average)	34	37	41

n.a. = not available.

EXHIBIT 9

Introduction:	
720,000 bottles = about 220 metric tons	
750,000 key chains at $0.056	$42,000
Handling costs and display materials	16,800
Total	$58,800
Follow-up five months later:	
600,000 bottles = about 180 tons	
625,000 key chains at $0.056	$35,000
Handling costs and display materials	14,000
Total	$49,000

Trade Allowances

The product manager also considered the use of trade allowances to encourage the retailers to accept and promote the new product. The company traditionally offered $0.28 per case of 12 bottles. Thus, if it was decided that trade allowances were desirable, the cost would be $16,800 for the initial introduction and an additional $14,000 used during the follow-up promotion five months later. Trade allowances could be used together with either the price-off promotion or the key chain promotion. The product manager felt that trade allowances would not be very effective without one of the two consumer sales promotions.

Distribution

Outside of the question of what trade margins to use and whether or not to use trade allowances during the consumer sales promotions discussed above, Mr. de Vries did not see any problems with distribution. DFI had a sales force of approximately 50 persons who regularly called on 10,000 outlets in Holland. It was felt that the sales force could handle the introduction of the new product with no problem.

The last problem the product manager faced concerned the timing of the introduction of Slamix. The product would be ready for introduction in October. Mr. de Vries wondered whether the seasonal nature of the demand for the product would make it more desirable to hold off the introduction until March of the next year.

Case 42

The Toronto–Dominion Bank: Green Line Investor Services*

In August 1988, Keith Gray, senior vice president of the Toronto–Dominion Bank and president of Green Line Investor Services Inc., was considering a number of alternatives to stimulate the growth and profitability of the TD Bank's discount brokerage business. Green Line Investor Services had been launched in 1984 and by 1988 had captured an approximately 60 percent share of the discount brokerage business in Canada.

The rapid growth of the business had been interrupted by the market crash on Black Monday in October 1987. Trading volume after October 19 was dramatically lower and this had put severe pressure on Green Line's profitability. Mr. Gray was anxious to stimulate business growth and move the business back toward profitability.

General Background on the Brokerage Business

The securities industry in Canada consisted of approximately 120 investment dealers involved in underwriting and distributing security issues. The industry had grown substantially since the beginning of the bull market in 1983 from revenues of $1.8 billion in 1983 to $3.5 billion in 1987 (Exhibit 1). This growth included both the full-service and discount brokerage firms. Typically, a full-service firm would charge commission rates for not only performing a trade for a client but also offering investment advice and distributing research reports. On the other hand, at a discount brokerage firm lower commissions (up to 80 percent less than full-service rates) were charged. These lower rates could be charged as a result of the larger volume of transactions, the absence of commis-

* This case was written by James Henderson, research assistant, and Professor Adrian B. Ryans as a basis for class discussion rather than to illustrate either effective or ineffective handling of an administrative situation. Nonpublic data have been disguised in order to protect the confidentiality of competitive information.

EXHIBIT 1 Aggregate income statement for Canadian investment dealers, 1982–1987 ($ millions)

	1983	1984	1985	1986	1987
Revenues					
Underwriting	$ 533.5	$ 510.6	$ 719.5	$ 893.6	$ 903.9
Brokerage comission*	821.5	669.7	903.1	1,180.9	1,645.3
Interest	441.5	484.0	566.0	665.9	792.0
Other	59.5	67.1	94.1	93.9	201.2
Total revenues	$1,856.0	$1,731.4	$2,282.7	$2,834.3	$3,542.4
Expenses					
Salaries/commissions	879.5	786.8	1,065.2	1.335.0	1,812.5
Communications	97.7	81.5	112.4	132.2	168.7
Interest	375.4	413.0	494.9	566.2	675.4
Rent	59.2	72.6	81.1	97.4	114.7
Other	289.0	329.8	396.6	512.2	668.4
Total expenses	$1,700.8	$1,683.7	$2,150.2	$2,643.0	$3,439.7
Net income before tax	$ 155.2	$ 47.7	$ 132.5	$ 191.3	$ 102.7

* Includes both retail and institutional commissions.
Source: Statistics Canada, *Financial Institutions*, 61006.

sioned salespersons, lower overheads, and no research department. For an average broker, a large part of the savings came from the use of salaried employees (30–40 percent) and the absence of a research department (5–10 percent). The consolidated statement of earnings for Midland Doherty Financial Corporation, one of Canada's largest full-service retail firms, is shown in Exhibit 2.

EXHIBIT 2 Midland Doherty Financial Corporation consolidated statement of earnings ($ thousands)

	1987	1988
Revenues		
Commissions	$ 69,048	$ 75,635
Interest	52,933	63,433
Principal transactions	21,822	26,778
Underwriting and syndication	22,024	20,481
Other	10,066	9,876
Total revenues	$175,893	$196,203
Expenses		
Employee compensation and benefits	79,588	89,088
Interest	44,515	54,601
Administrative and marketing	21,998	23,687
Communications	8,890	8,654
Occupancy and equipment rental	7,715	8,588
Depreciation and amortization	2,540	2,867
Total expenses	$165,246	$187,485
Earnings before income taxes	10,647	8,718
Provision for income taxes	5,400	4,079
Net earnings for the year	$ 5,247	$ 4,639

For years ending March 31, 1987, and March 31, 1988.
Source: Midland Doherty Financial Corporation, 1988 Annual Report.

The discount brokerage industry began in the United States with the deregulation of commission rates in 1975. In essence, the fixed commission rates on all securities transactions executed by investment dealers were eliminated. Price competition became a factor in the brokerage industry and, as a result, the discount brokers emerged on the scene. By 1987, the discount brokerage industry had grown to a substantial 25 percent of the total volume of securities traded. The major player in the U.S. market was Charles Schwab with a 33 percent share of the commission revenues of all discount brokers. By the end of 1986, the firm had 95 branches and 1,600,000 accounts of which almost 1 million were active. Exhibit 3 shows the growth of the discount brokerage industry in the United States, and Exhibit 4 presents selected financial and other data for Charles Schwab.

In Canada, the Ontario Securities Commission, following the United States' lead, deregulated commission rates in 1983. Several discount brokerage firms were set up as operating arms of existing full-service investment dealers, while others were independently owned. Charles Schwab submitted an applica-

EXHIBIT 3 Estimated growth of discount brokers in the United States

Total brokerage market

	1979	1982	1984	1985	1986
Total retail commissions ($ millions)	$1,795	$1,570	$2,266	$2,639	$3,345
All discount brokers					
Commissions revenues ($ millions)	$ 10	$ 129	$ 326	$ 443	$ 655
Pretax income	n/a	n/a	6	69	163
Number of firms	n/a	n/a	120	117	122

EXHIBIT 4 Charles Schwab financial highlights, selected years

Income statement data (US$ thousands)	1982	1984	1986
Revenues			
Commissions	$49,300	$ 90,200	$213,600
Interest	17,600	57,200	87,100
Other	500	1,100	7,600
Total revenues	$67,400	$148,500	$308,300
Expenses			
Compensation and benefits	$18,300	$ 37,900	$ 81,600
Interest	8,300	36,400	51,600
Communications	9,200	21,700	27,700
Occupancy and equipment	4,100	14,200	19,600
Depreciation and amortization	2,200	6,200	10,000
Other operating expenses	15,100	30,300	51,500
Total expenses	$57,100	$146,700	$242,100
Income before taxes	$10,300	$ 1,800	$ 66,200
Taxes on income	5,100	800	34,000
Net income	$ 5,200	$ 1,100	$ 32,200
Other data			
Number of branches	52	89	95
Number of accounts	400,000	900,000	1,600,000

tion to the Foreign Investment Review Agency requesting permission to set up an operation in Canada but was denied access. By 1988, the three largest discount firms in Canada accounted for approximately 10 percent of the total volume of securities traded and 97 percent of the total commission revenues of the discount brokerage industry.

Origins, Initial Strategy, and Growth of GLIS

The Toronto-Dominion Bank was formed through the amalgamation in 1955 of the Bank of Toronto, established in 1855, and the Dominion Bank, established in 1869. It had since grown into Canada's fifth largest chartered bank in terms of total assets. By 1988, it had over 950 branches scattered across Canada and around the world. The TD employed 21,000 people, and its deposits held had grown substantially each year to a total of $44 billion by the end of 1987. Traditionally, the TD had earned profit margins almost double that of the other major Canadian banks. It was one of two major North American banks that was accorded an AAA rating for its long-term debt and deposits by Moody's Investor Service. Net income for 1987 was $53 million, down from previous years because of the writedowns for Third World loans. However, it was the only major Canadian bank to report a profit for the year.

The TD did provide stock trading services prior to 1983. However, because of federal government regulations designed to maintain the ''four pillars'' of the financial industry (banking, trusts, insurance, and investment dealers), the TD was unable to promote this service. The Bank Act stated that banks could act as agents of a vendor or purchaser of equity securities only if the trade was effected by a broker or dealer. Many within the bank viewed the service as a loss leader which was necessary to attract customer deposit business.

Unlike the other banks, the TD entered the brokerage business early in 1984. In late 1983, after the deregulation of the investment dealer commission rates, Equity Trading Inc., a discount brokerage arm of the full-service Toronto investment dealer, Loewen, Ondaatje, McCutcheon and Co., approached the TD with the suggestion that the two organizations join forces. The proposal was to make discount rates available to the bank's customers who did their securities business through the bank and in return to promote the services and channel transactions through Equity. Out of this proposal evolved the Green Line Investor Service (GLIS). The name was chosen to link the service with the other ''Green'' services offered by TD such as the Green Machine (TD's automated banking machines) and the Green Card (TD's VISA card). Ultimately, TD purchased Equity's account base of 800.

Discount brokerage, as opposed to full-service brokerage, was chosen because of the regulations stipulated in the Bank Act, and the investment required. In 1984, the TD could operate a discount brokerage arm under the regulations of the Bank Act without being registered as an investment dealer. At that time it could not operate a full-service arm, because it could not provide investment counsel or portfolio management services as stated in the Bank Act.

As opposed to a full-service broker, a discount brokerage operation required neither large investments in sales representatives' comissions, nor large investments in a research department.

Green Line Investor Service, 100 percent owned by the Toronto-Dominion Bank, began operations in 1984 with eight people, a telephone line, and very little knowledge of the brokerage business. The initial concept of GLIS was a package of investor services consisting primarily of a toll-free telephone hotline that would enable existing TD clients and the new Equity client base to directly contact a central order-taking desk located at the Toronto head office. In addition to the hotline, the bank had planned to offer its members periodic and detailed statements to assist them in monitoring their stock-trading activities, safekeeping services, and margin accounts. The initial objectives for GLIS were unclear because of the newness of the discount brokerage business. However, GLIS executives hoped to have 25,000 accounts open and to increase the number of trades per day to approximately 750 by 1990. GLIS management soon found that the investments in automation and the telephone systems to support this increasing number of trades and accounts were high.

In 1984 GLIS served only the Ontario market. Initially, only equity trading was offered, but other new products were soon added and the phone service was broadened to serve other areas of Canada. Exhibit 5 describes the evolution of GLI's product line and geographical coverage.

In 1987 the TD Bank became the first bank to purchase a seat on the Toronto Stock Exchange. The seat cost the TD Bank $190,000, the highest price paid for a seat since the 1929 stock market crash. By mid-1987 Green Line

EXHIBIT 5 The Toronto-Dominion Bank Green Line Investor Services: Chronology of Products Offered and Regions Covered

1984	Equity trading Regions: Ontario
1985	Quebec Stock Saving Plan Mortgage Fund Canadian Index Fund Self-directed RRSPs Regions: Quebec and Saskatchewan
1986	Self-directed RRIFs Mortgages in self-directed RRSPs and RRIFs United States Index Fund Green Line Direct Quote Regions: Nova Scotia, New Brunswick, Prince Edward Island, Newfoundland, Manitoba, British Columbia
1987	Other firms mutual funds Regions: Alberta
1988	Trading Plus Money market instruments Options Bonds Precious metals Green Line Investment Management Correspondent Brokerage

was enjoying a 45 percent market share in the discount brokerage industry. However, until June 1987 it was restricted in the trading and promotions it could do. As stipulated in the Bank Act, GLIS had to distribute its trade orders through other brokerage houses, who were referred to as "jitney brokers." Also, each trade had to be settled through each broker rather than through the usual clearing center, the Canadian Depository for Securities (CDS). When the financial services industry was partially deregulated on June 30, 1987, GLIS became a fully registered broker. GLIS could then trade and have its own backroom operations. However, it was not until February 1988 that GLIS began to use its own traders.

Purchase of Gardiner Group

Mr. Gray had heard rumors in the fall of 1987, that the Canadian Imperial Bank of Commerce (CIBC) was interested in buying Gardiner Group, the third largest discount broker in Canada with a 12 percent market share. Mr. Gray called the head of Gardiner, George Gardiner, on Tuesday, October 14, 1987, but his call was not returned. The CIBC had tabled an offer to purchase Gardiner Group, and this offer was under active consideration at the time of Mr. Gray's call. Mr. Gray called again on Wednesday and was able to arrange a meeting for that afternoon. At 6 P.M. on Thursday, October 16, 1987, the night before the deal was to be signed with CIBC, GLIS completed an agreement to purchase the Gardiner Group.

The resources and skills that Gardiner brought to GLIS included:

1. The management group at Gardiner had a stockbroking background, unlike the bank's personnel. This helped GLIS personnel understand the business better.
2. Gardiner provided an electronic order entry system for trading. Orders no longer had to be phoned to the floor to initiate a trade. The order could simply be put into the system.
3. The additional investment products that Gardiner offered, namely options and short selling, could be incorporated into the GLIS product line.
4. Gardiner provided trading expertise on the Toronto and Vancouver stock exchanges and soon after on the Montreal Exchange.
5. Gardiner offered correspondent brokerage services. This service handled other brokerage houses' backroom operations. It included the settlement and clearing of accounts and the safekeeping of securities.
6. Gardiner had 11 offices across Canada to sell investment products on a more personal basis.

The deal was finalized in December 1987, but it was not until February 1988 that the Gardiner Group fully merged with GLIS. For the Gardiner Group, the amalgamation was a shock. Approximately 25 percent of the Gardiner personnel left voluntarily because of the differences in work environments. The Gardiner people were used to a paternalistic small business environment run by Mr. George Gardiner. The company had been run quite informally. This atmosphere changed as they moved to the more bureaucratic, large company environment at the Toronto-Dominion Bank.

Organization

About 375 employees worked at Green Line Investor Services' headquarters in Toronto, Ontario. The company had 10 offices located across Canada in each major city.

Keith Gray headed up GLIS along with three other operations within the bank. He was the senior vice president of cash management and investor services. Within his group, Mr. Ed Kukiel, previously a Gardiner Group

EXHIBIT 6   The Toronto-Dominion Bank Green Line Investor Services: Partial Organization Chart

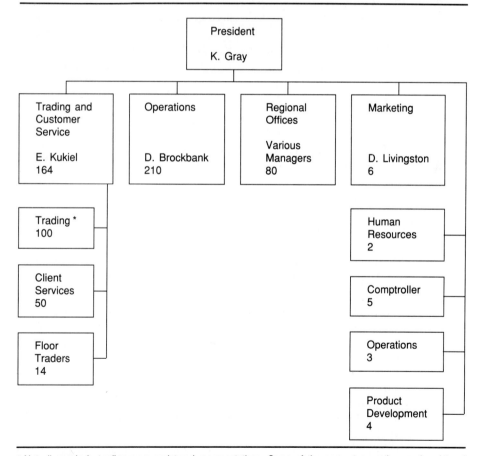

* Not all people in trading were registered representatives. Some of the account executives and registered representatives were in the regional offices.

executive, managed the trading operations and customer service, Mr. Doug Brockbank directed the backroom operations, and Mr. David Livingston was responsible for Marketing. A partial organization chart is given in Exhibit 6.

Service and Products Offered

GLIS offered four different services for its customers: Direct Trading, Trading Plus, Correspondent Brokerage, and Green Line Investment Management.

Direct Trading was the original service provided by GLIS and still was the service used by approximately 80 percent of the accounts. It provided the client the basic service of a toll-free line, all investment products, safekeeping of the securities, and monthly reports of the client's stock-trading activity. The client, therefore, could call in during GLIS's hours of operation (15 hours per day, seven days a week) and was connected with any available representative to place an order. The average transaction value was $12,000, which generated an average commission fee of $60.

Trading Plus evolved after the purchase of Gardiner Group. The philosophy at Gardiner was to offer trading services at a discount but with personal service. They believed that clients still preferred to have their own personal account executive similar to a full-service firm but without the advice. As a result, Gardiner prices were slightly higher than the other discount firms. This service was maintained when Gardiner was acquired by GLIS. Trading Plus at GLIS was offered through 10 offices across Canada at a $10 higher per trade commission fee than Direct Trading.

GLIS also acted as a correspondent broker for other brokerage firms. It provided the backroom operations, such as clearing and settling the trades, billing the clients, and the safekeeping of the securities and accounts for other firms. In August 1988, it was serving four brokers. GLIS received about 20 percent of the commissions generated by the brokerage firms using its correspondent brokerage service.

In June 1988, GLIS introduced a new service, Green Line Investment Management (GLIM). It was designed for investors with portfolios of more than $100,000. An annual fee of 1.25 percent of the average daily market value of the portfolio was charged for the service. The portfolio was administered by GLIS and managed by Hodgson Roberton Laing Limited, investment counselors. By the end of June, GLIS was administering five accounts.

In addition to these major services, GLIS offered Direct Quote. Direct quote was an electronic voice service available 24 hours per day, seven days per week. Approximately one third of all calls were for this service. It provided daily stock prices on the TSE, ME, VSE, ASE, NYSE, AMEX and NASDAQ. It was free of charge.

Within the Direct Trading and Trading Plus services, GLIS traded a full range of investment products: equities, bonds, options, guaranteed investment certificates (GICs), money market instruments, precious metals, GLIS mutual funds (United States Index Fund, Canadian Index Fund, Mortgage Fund, Canadian Balanced Fund, Canadian Bond Fund, Canadian Equity Fund, Canadian Money Management Fund, and United States Money Management Fund), other firms' mutual funds, self-directed RSPs, self-directed RIFs, and Quebec Stock Savings Plan (QSSP). The breakdown of trades by type of product in early 1988 was:

Equities	82%
Options	8
Money market	8
Other (bonds, precious metals, and mutual funds)	2

With the addition of new products and services, GLIS grew from a small regional discount broker operating only in Ontario to the biggest discount broker in Canada, enjoying a 57 percent market share. Volumes grew by 220 percent between 1986 and 1987 to 1,700 trades per day. The original objective of 25,000 accounts by 1990 was easily surpassed. By late 1987, the number of accounts was 100,000. A summary of GLIS's income statements for 1987 and 1988 is given in Exhibit 7.

EXHIBIT 7   The Toronto-Dominion Bank Green Line Investor Services: Financial statements ($ thousands)

	1987	(Projected) 1988
Income		
Trading revenue	$17,300	$17,600
Net interest revenue	5,300	11,000
Other revenue	1,300	2,200
Gross income	$23,900	$30,800
Operating expenses		
Personnel	$ 9,000	$13,300
Systems and equipment	4,500	6,700
Premises	1,100	2,900
Communications	2,800	4,600
Marketing	3,200	2,800
Clearing/brokerage	3,000	1,800
Other	800	1,400
R&D	500	600
Total expenses	$24,900	$34,100
Net income	($ 1,000)	($ 3,300)

For years ending October 31, 1987, and October 31, 1988.
Source: Company records.

Operations

The backroom operations included the settling of the trades each day and the management of the cash resources of GLIS to minimize interest expenses. Settlement of trades involved a five-day process from the initiation of the trade to the settlement of the trade by the client. When the trade was phoned in, the registered representative would enter the order. The order would be directed electronically to a trading system, such as the Canadian Automated Trading System (CATS), where the trade would be filled automatically or sent electronically to the floor traders where it would be filled manually. The process used depended on the type of trade initiated. Then the backroom would be informed in order to start the five-day process to clear and settle the trade. On the fifth day, the trade would be ready for settlement. The typical trade would be settled through the Canadian Depository for Securities. However, for GLIS, this convenience only occurred after June 1987, when it became a fully registered brokerage house. Prior to that date, GLIS had to settle separately with each brokerage house.

The backroom also provided safekeeping services for clients. At GLIS, the backroom had over $1 billion of securities to manage. Safekeeping services for each client included holding of the client's securities and the management of dividends, interest, tax information, proxies and company information, and a monthly statement. No fees were charged to the client for these services, which was consistent with the practice of the rest of the industry.

Customers in 1988

The demand for investments in Canada had grown since 1984. In 1984, 13 percent of adults in Canada owned shares in publicly traded companies or stock mutual funds. That figure could be broken down further into 12 percent owning common and preferred stocks and 2 percent owning stock mutual funds. By 1987, the size of the market had grown by 40 percent. About 20 percent of adults in Canada owned shares—15 percent common or preferred shares and 5 percent stock mutual funds.

With the rapid growth in the number of customers through October 1987, little attention had been paid to the types of customers represented in the customer base. Of the new investment accounts opened in Canada, about 20 percent were with discount brokers. At the time, GLIS had not segmented its customer base and had little knowledge about the types of customers buying particular products and services. However, it was known that the typical GLIS investor was someone knowledgeable about investing. He (80 percent were male) was over 50 with approximately $20,000 to invest. He usually made approximately three trades per year; however, this figure would grow to seven trades in bull markets. Typically, the GLIS investor had a relationship with both a full-service broker and a discount broker. This type of investor was ideal for GLIS because of his trading activity and because he did not expect any advice or research from GLIS. Mr. Gray felt, though, that the average age of the typical investor would decline. The baby boomers would have more money to invest in the future as they grew into the 40 to 50 age bracket.

With the end of rapid growth in October 1987, the need for better information on the customer base became more critical. Formal market research was performed by Green Line in early 1988 to find out more about its customers and its performance as a discount broker. Some results from this survey of active Green Line customers are contained in Exhibit 8.

EXHIBIT 8   The Toronto-Dominion Bank Green Line Investor Services: 1988 Customer survey results

- 81 percent male and 19 percent female.
- Average age 52 with 61 percent over 50.
- 56 percent have more than 20 years' investment experience.
- Investment knowledge:
  12 percent limited
  58 percent average
  30 percent sophisticated
- Investment objectives:
  50 percent safety of principal
  58 percent long-term capital gain
  42 percent income
  43 percent short-term capital gain
- 61 percent of transactions were less than $10,000 with an average of $12,000.
- Average portfolio size was $175,000 with 51 percent less than $100,000. (There was some evidence that a high percentage of Green Line customers had the majority of their portfolios with another broker or brokers).
- 63 percent had accounts with full-service brokers.
- 37 percent had a net worth in excess of $500,000, and 92 percent had a net worth in excess of $100,000.
- 37 percent had incomes in excess of $75,000 with an average of $50,000.
- 62 percent lived in Ontario.
- 34 percent of clients had learned about Green Line from the *Globe and Mail* and 28 percent from TD branches.
- 91 percent used Green Line for equity trading, 5 percent for mutual fund trading, and 8 percent for bond trading.
- GLIS service quality was as likely to be considered better than at a full-service firm as it was to be considered worse. Among those customers that felt that GLIS's service was worse than that of full-service brokers, the major reasons cited were lack of research, lack of advice, and fewer products/services.
- Over 70 percent of respondents stated they used GLIS for more than 60 percent of their trading activity.

Competition in 1988

In 1984 GLIS followed several firms into the discount brokerage business in Canada. These other firms included Marathon Brown and Disnat.

Marathon Brown, a division of a publicly traded full-service firm, First Marathon, was GLIS's biggest threat, with an approximately 30 percent share of the discount brokerage market in 1988. By 1985, it was earning a profit from its 10 branches located across Canada. In 1987, half of the discount arm was acquired by Central Capital, to give the firm increased financial credibility. Central Capital, through its two trust companies Guaranty Trust and Central Trust, operated approximately 165 branches serving over 300,000 accounts across the country. The partnership planned to develop facilities to provide Marathon's discount brokerage services to this client base and to provide savings and loans services to the Marathon Brown client base.

The services offered by Marathon Brown were similar to GLIS with the following exceptions:

1. Account opening requirement: Marathon Brown had an account opening balance requirement of $5,000 in cash or securities.
2. Settlement policy: "Money in your account when you buy and securities in your account when you sell" for all transactions.
3. Twenty-four hours a day, seven days a week service.
4. Guaranteed Investment Certificates (GIC) Center: Marathon Brown had put together a selection of GICs from financial institutions from which its customers could choose.
5. Marathon Brown did not have its own traders. It used the trading services of its parent company, First Marathon.

Disnat, the other major discount broker in Canada, was the first to start up operations after the deregulation of commission rates. Because of its origins in Quebec, Disnat had a stranglehold on that province's market, enjoying a 60 percent market share in Quebec which resulted in an overall 10 percent share of the Canadian market. Blocks of the company had subsequently been purchased by various organizations in Quebec. The ownership of the company in 1988 was 33 percent by Crédit Desjardins, 33 percent by McNeil Mantha, a full-service brokerage house, and 33 percent by Financières Entraide Coopérants, an insurance cooperative. This backing gave it the financial resources it needed as well as access to a large potential customer base. Crédit Desjardins had over 1,200 branches across Quebec. Disnat's commission revenues in 1987 were $6.7 million, up 88 percent from the previous year and net income was $1.4 million. It had opened an office in Toronto in 1987. However, since the crash, the firm was struggling to be profitable as a result of the decreased volumes of transactions.

The commission and fee structure for GLIS, Marathon Brown, and Disnat were similar. Exhibit 9 refers to the commission rates charged by the three firms for listed and over-the-counter stock trades.

Charles Schwab, the largest of the approximately 120 discount brokers in the United States, was approximately 10 times the size of Green Line Investor Service. During the October 1987 crash it lost one half of its capital base of $150 million. For Schwab, the cost of a broad entry into the Canadian discount brokerage market would be very high because of the required investment in new systems and marketing.

Other financial institutions were getting into the discount brokerage business. Several of the chartered banks had expressed their intent to enter before the crash, but little had happened since these announcements. National Bank

EXHIBIT 9 The Toronto-Dominion Bank Green Line Investor Services: Commission and Fee Schedules

	Commission per order		
Price per share	Marathon Brown	Green Line Direct Trading	Disnat
$ 0–1.00	$30 + 1.5¢/share	$35 + 1¢/share	$35 + .5¢/share
$ 1.01–5.12	$30 + 2¢/share	$35 + 2¢/share	$35 + 2.5¢/share
$ 5.13–10.12	$30 + 4¢/share	$35 + 3¢/share	$35 + 3.5¢/share
$10.13–20.12	$30 + 5¢/share	$35 + 4¢/share	$35 + 4.5¢/share
$20.13–30.12	$30 + 6¢/share	$35 + 5¢/share	$35 + 5.5¢/share
$30.13 +	$30 + 7¢/share	$35 + 6¢/share	$35 + 6.5¢/share

Notes:
1. Green Line Trading Plus had a $45 base fee.
2. There was a flat charge for all orders of $2,000 or less. In mid-1988 these were: Marathon Brown: $30; Green Line Direct Trading: $35; and Disnat: $35.

had set up Investel as their discount brokerage arm. Green Line executives felt that this service might pose a real threat to GLIS. However, in June 1988, the bank purchased 73 percent of Levesque Beaubien, a full-service firm. As a result, their commitment to the discount brokerage industry appeared to diminish. Similarly the Royal Bank announced its intentions to formalize its existing trading services to clients in its branches by developing a discount brokerage arm. However, in December 1987, the Royal Bank purchased 75 percent of Dominion Securities, a full-service firm. Again, its interest in discount brokerage seemed to wane. The Bank of Nova Scotia had also discussed setting up a discount brokerage service. In November 1987, they purchased 100 percent of McLeod Young Weir, another full-service brokerage house. In August 1988, all of the banks were still absorbing their acquisitions. Exhibit 10 summarizes the recent takeovers by the banks of full-service firms.

EXHIBIT 10 Takeovers of Canadian brokerage firms by chartered banks

Banks	Royal Bank	CIBC	Bank of Montreal	Bank of Nova Scotia	TD Bank	National Bank
Assets	$102 billion	$88 billion	$87 billion	$71 billion	$54 billion	$33 billion
Purchase	75% Dominion Securities	10% Gordon Capital 65% Wood Gundy	75% Nesbitt Thompson	100% McLeod Young Weir	100% Gardiner Group	73% Levesque Beaubien
When	Dec. 1987	Nov. 1987 Jan. 1988	Sept. 1987	Nov. 1987	Oct. 1987	May 1988
Capital	$252 million	$155 million $194 million	$210 million	$210 million	Not publicly available	$66 million
Value	$385 million	$40 million $190 million	$290 million	$419 million	Not publicly available	$100 million

Emerging Environmental Forces in 1988

Brokerage businesses were very difficult to manage because of the volatility of the stock markets and the uncertainty of new regulations.

Before the October 19, 1987, crash on the stock market, GLIS had been making approximately 1,700 trades and answering approximately 10,000 calls per day. However, during the day of the crash the number of trades increased to 3,500 and the number of calls to 22,000. After the crash, trading volumes decreased to an average of 1,100 per day. Option trading, which was included in the 1,100 trades per day, decreased by 60 percent from pre-crash volumes. Equity and bond trading remained flat in 1988. However, money market trading was up significantly.

The securities industry was heavily regulated. Each investment dealer was regulated through the Investment Dealers Association of Canada or one of the stock exchanges (TSE, ME, ASE, VSE). These organizations, in turn, were regulated by the provincial securities commissions, such as the Ontario Securities Commission. Regulations in the industry included certain capital requirements for each investment dealer, training requirements for the registered representatives, and trading and reporting requirements. However, the regulatory environment was in a state of flux. After June 1987, the four pillars of the Canadian financial services industry began to break down. For example, any Canadian chartered bank could now own a life insurance company or an investment dealer. After June 1988, any foreign institution could own a brokerage house in Canada. These regulatory changes were the result of actions by the federal government. By 1988, the six largest chartered banks, governed by the Federal Bank Act, each operated brokerage arms, which were regulated provincially. Each province had competing legislation for the securities industry that made it even more difficult for the banks to manage. Expectations in the industry were that changes would be made to improve the prevailing situation.

Despite these uncertainties, there were several areas that Keith Gray felt would have positive effects on the brokerage industry: federal government actions, aging baby boomers, and telecommunications.

Several federal government actions improved the investment climate in Canada. Following Britain's lead, the federal government seemed to be stepping up its privatization efforts with the sale of DeHavilland to Boeing and the proposed sale of part of Air Canada. Capital gains of up to $100,000 over a person's lifetime were now tax free which encouraged further investing. In Quebec, in the early 80s, the Quebec Stock Savings Plan (QSSP) was introduced which stimulated equity investments in Quebec ventures.

The average age of the population had an effect on investment behavior. By the late 1980s on average at the age of 42 people had a positive investable net cash flow of approximately $1,400. By the age of 50, this positive investable cash flow increased substantially. As the baby boomers aged into the 40–50 age bracket, Keith Gray saw that the amount of total investing would increase significantly.

Investing would become easier as the use of telecommunications increased. With the introduction of cellular telephones and personal computers in the home, Mr. Gray again saw this as stimulating total investment activity.

The Situation in August 1988

Objectives of GLIS

Since the crash in October, the levels of trading activity had decreased by 40 percent in the industry. The objectives of GLIS, therefore, changed from keeping up with the growth in demand for the service, to growing the overall market by finding methods to attract new clients, and to maintaining its market share of 57 percent. Mr. Gray was quite confident that the Canadian discount brokerage market could grow to 25 percent of the total volume of securities traded, as it had in the United States.

However, the executives were concerned that new business might have to come from clients who wanted not only the discount rates but also the investment advice and the research reports offered by full-service firms. Attracting clients was becoming increasingly costly. The average cost for attracting a new client in 1988 was about $200 and this figure was rising.

Mr. Gray wanted to make GLIS as flexible an organization as possible, so that the trading room could easily switch from 1,000 trades per day to 2,000 trades per day or vice versa. Without additional staff or capital expenditures he believed that GLIS could handle 2,000 trades per day in August 1988.

GLIS executives also had several service standard objectives. With the telephone system installed, several statistics could be extracted such as abandoned calls and the wait times clients encountered. When someone hung up before being answered by an available trader, it was counted in the statistics as an abandoned call. The wait times referred to the number of seconds the clients had to wait before their calls were answered by a registered representative. The tolerance level for abandoned calls was 4–5 percent and for wait time was one minute. For customer service, the turnaround time for answering a customer complaint was 48 hours. Mr. Gray wanted to decrease the turnaround time to same-day service. Customer investigations were taking up to 14 days. He wanted to shorten this process to five days.

The Role of GLIS

The TD executives saw the nature of banking evolving over time. In the 1960s banking was traditionally conducted through the branches. However, this had changed during the late 70s and early 80s with the introduction of automated banking machines and the increased usage of credit, debit, and travel and entertainment cards. Access to funds was easier. The TD saw the emergence of the telephone as the next major advance in banking. GLIS was an important element of this advance. Similar to traditional banking, it provided a financial service that handled financial transactions for individuals every day. The next step would be home banking using personal computers or other types of terminals in the home or the workplace.

Resources and Skills of GLIS

GLIS had 10 offices located in all the major cities across the country with additional investor centers in Toronto, Montreal, and Vancouver. The 23 account executives of the Trading Plus service were located in the 10 offices. In addition, the 90 registered representatives for Direct Trading were located in four of these offices with the vast majority of them being located in Toronto. Each sales representative had to be licensed, at the minimum, by taking the Canadian Securities Course and the registered representative examinations. For options trading, another course had to be taken in order for the representative to be registered. In the future, Mr. Gray wanted all sales representatives to be registered for options trading so that all types of trading could be performed by all representatives. In 1988, customers calling in for options trading had to be transferred to the options department. Unlike the full-service firms, all salespeople were paid on a salary basis with team-based bonuses for achieving certain trade volume targets or service objectives. GLIS has 14 floor traders on the TSE, ME, and the VSE.

In May 1988, because of the decreased volume of trades, Green Line released 100 contract employees and reassigned 50 other employees to other bank divisions.

GLIS benefited from the large financial resource base of the Toronto–Dominion Bank. Like most other banks, it had electronic systems in place in order to move large sums of money within seconds. During the crash, GLIS was able to support all the margin calls.

Strategic and Tactical Options

Even though GLIS had close to a 60 percent market share, Mr. Gray was concerned about GLIS's lack of profitability. A number of options that would impact either margins or volumes were under consideration, and he was anxious to make a decision and begin implementing the chosen strategy. The major options under consideration were

1. **Further segmentation of the existing and potential customer base and the pursuit of new segments.** No formal segmentation of the customer base had been conducted to date because there was neither the data available nor the resources to devote to this activity as GLIS struggled to keep up with the growth in the business. However, after the crash, the need for more customer information became apparent. Mr. Gray wondered how to segment the market, and what the differences were between the full-

service investor and the discount brokerage investor. How could he induce full-service investors to trade through GLIS? How much would it cost to attract these clients?

2. **Additional services for, and education of, the current customer base.** Keith Gray felt that there was a spectrum of brokerage services from the most inexpensive service such as Direct Trading to the most expensive service, a full-service brokerage house. He realized that GLIS was a victim of the ups and downs of the stock market, but he wondered how much GLIS would have to improve its service to induce more trading from its existing client base and to educate them to make their use of GLIS more efficient. Among the options under consideration were the following:

   a. Increasing the hours available from 15 hours per day seven days a week to 24 hours a day seven days a week. Marathon Brown already offered this service. This would involve no additional capital costs.

   b. Educating the clients to do market orders as opposed to limit orders. Market orders were trades that were initiated based on the market price. Limit orders, on the other hand, had a stipulated price. Therefore, the representative had to wait for the price either to increase or decrease depending on a buy or sell situation before he or she could initiate a trade. Such orders could not be confirmed immediately. In Canada, 75 percent of the trades initiated were limit orders compared to 25 percent in the United States. By increasing the market orders, the phone lines could be freed up for more incoming calls and the representatives' productivity increased.

   c. Developing a clearinghouse system for research reports and industry reports. By offering a service that would distribute the research of independent research firms to its customers, GLIS could compete more directly with the full-service firms. For example, Financial Post Cards would cost the customer $15 each, research reports $5 each, and a full-year's research on a selection of firms would cost $250. The service could be easily instituted. The GLIS representatives would simply pass a customer's order to the respective information sources for a 10 percent markup. Mr. Gray wondered whether the service should be a profit maker or a promotional tool to encourage more trading.

   d. Offering advice to clients. Mr. Gray was concerned about the possible effects this move would have on his sales staff. He also wondered if they were qualified.

   Mr. Gray was concerned about possible competitive reactions, not only from the discount brokers but also from the full-service firms, if he were to offer any of these services.

3. **Offer more products.** Mr. Gray thought that there were many other products or services that GLIS could offer. Some of the products under consideration were:

a. Other financial institutions' GICs.

b. Banking by telephone services, for example, mortgage applications or personal loan deposits.

c. Personal insurance products.

4. **Pricing.** There were several options available to increase prices:

a. Increase the base fee for each trade. This increase would discourage small share volume traders.

b. Increase the fees as the size of the trade increased.

c. Institute a service charge on safekeeping services. No brokerage firm to date charged for safekeeping services. However, for GLIS, if a client did not trade, the firm still had to spend money for the safekeeping services. For example, if the customer did a certain amount of trading then the fee would be waived. How much, Keith Gray wondered, could he charge per year per customer?

d. Increase the minimum fee GLIS would charge for any trade. A high percentage of trades with discount brokers involved gross amounts of less than $2,000, and this would incur the minimum fee.

Mr. Gray wondered how much the price changes would erode the customer base, if at all.

Mr. Gray was anxious to move the business toward profitability, but was unsure about what to do next. While he was under increasing pressure from the TD Bank to produce profits at GLIS, he knew that the bank was willing to continue to invest in the business, as long as it was convinced that the investment would produce a reasonable return. He hoped to present his recommendations for changes at a planning meeting taking place in less than one month. Or, he wondered, was he simply being too impatient—was the GLIS business just a victim of the normal stock market cycles and should he just "ride out the bear market," rather than making significant changes in strategy now?

Case 43

The Stroh Brewery Company*

In April 1985, the headline in the *Detroit News* asked, "Why Can't Stroh Tap More of the Home Market?" The text went on to explain that while other leading brewers enjoy a generous share of the beer market on their home turf, the Stroh Brewery Company of Detroit, Michigan, had settled into a very distant third place in Detroit and Michigan, behind Budweiser and Miller. (See Exhibit 1 for state of Michigan beer sales.) "It's hard to describe why Stroh is not number one in Detroit," said Don Hill, president of City Marketing, Inc., a Detroit area beer distributor. "If you were to randomly call people and ask them which beer is number one here, they would say Stroh's," Hill said. "If you ask

EXHIBIT 1 State of Michigan beer sales, top 13 brands *(barrels)*

	Brand	Percent total	1984 Sales	1984 Percent change	1983 Sales	1983 Percent change	1982 Sales
1.	Miller	15.9	1,074,375	−9.0	1,180,674	−9.5	1,304,621
2.	Budweiser	14.3	966,310	+12.4	859,993	+10.2	780,408
3.	Miller Lite	13.1	888,407	−1.7	903,405	+4.7	862,603
4.	**Stroh***	**11.5**	**779,712**	**−8.2**	**849,209**	**+3.9**	**817,373**
5.	Pabst	8.2	557,152	−23.0	723,874	−9.3	798,071
6.	**Schlitz†**	**4.5**	**305,520**	**−22.5**	**374,144**	**+13.7**	**328,967**
7.	Michelob	4.1	275,444	+12.8	244,082	−15.5	288,693
8.	Busch	3.2	215,828	+140.8	89,646	−11.2	100,908
9.	Michelob Light	3.2	213,581	−6.9	199,782	−11.3	255,227
10.	Budweiser Light	3.1	212,239	+31.4	162,011	+22.0	132,815
11.	Blatz	2.9	193,242	+24.7	203,727	+26.2	161,454
12.	Altes	1.8	121,488	−15.6	144,028	+22.5	177,566
13.	Colt 45	1.8	119,242	−12.7	136,560	+5.2	129,841

* Includes all Stroh brands.
† Includes all Schlitz brands.
Source: *The Michigan Brewery Record,* Investment Statistics Company, Detroit, 1985.

---

* This case was prepared from public sources by Susan A. Johnstal, under the supervision of Thomas C. Kinnear. Copyright © 1987 Thomas C. Kinnear.

them what they drink, they'll name something else.'' During 1984, the Stroh brewery's total sales by volume declined 8.2 percent in the state of Michigan.

Along the East and West Coasts, Stroh's beer, the flagship brand of the Stroh brewery, had a ritzy appeal similar to imported beers because of its unique fire-brewing process. It has been said that a case of Stroh's could be traded for any two cases of anything else in the East. In the Midwest, however, Stroh's was not a new name, and the hometown brew enjoyed no such mystique. In the Michigan home base, Stroh's was just another blue-collar thirst quencher. Bolstering the Midwest image of Stroh's and increasing share in its home market were priorities to Stroh management, as was the successful expansion of the flagship brand across the country.

However, the status of Stroh's national expansion was also a question. Stroh began to break out of its traditional Midwest distribution area by taking its flagship labels, Stroh's and Stroh Light, to a national level in 1984. Stroh advertised the two brands heavily with television commercials and outdoor billboards, further developed its wholesaler network, installed on-premise taps in bars and taverns, and sponsored local charity events. As a result, the Stroh geographic distribution area grew. By the end of 1984, Stroh officials were pleased with the preliminary results of the expansion effort. But Stroh's brand, as well as the entire list of Stroh brands, faced a faltering demand for beer in the United States (down .6 percent in 1984), and Stroh's nationwide 1984 beer sales by volume declined 1.6 percent. (See Exhibit 2 for Stroh production by brand.)

EXHIBIT 2 Stroh production by brand (millions of barrels)

	1982	1983	1984
Old Milwaukee (popular priced)	6.0	7.6	7.1
Stroh (premium)	5.4	5.5	5.3
Schaefer (popular priced)	2.5	3.0	4.0
Schlitz Malt (malt liquor)	2.6	2.6	2.1
Schlitz (premium)	4.1	3.2	1.7
Old Milwaukee Light (popular light)	0.8	1.0	1.5
Stroh Light (premium light)	0.6	0.7	0.8
Goebel (popular priced)	0.3	0.3	0.6
Schlitz Light (premium light)	0.4	0.3	0.1
Erlanger (super premium)	0.1	—	—
Other	0.1	0.1	0.7
Schaefer L.A. (popular LA)			
Schaefer Light (popular light)			
Signature (super premium)			
Piels (premium)			
Piels Light (premium)			
Silver Thunder (malt liquor)			
Primo (premium)			
Total	22.9	24.3	23.9

Note: Capacity total = 29.5 million barrels.
Source: *Beverage Industry,* January 1985.

In addition to falling sales, management was concerned about several industry changes expected during the rest of the century. Consumer tastes were changing in the types of beer they preferred; imports and light beers were gaining sales volume at the expense of premium beers. Consumers' changing lifestyles included more often choosing wines and bottled water over beer. Demographic trends, including an aging society, threatened the popularity of beer as the number of people in the 18-to-35-year-old age bracket decreased. Increased consciousness of alcohol abuse brought about proposed legislation on banning beer advertising on television and radio. Within the beer industry, traditional beer wholesaler policies of exclusive territories were in question because of their anticompetitive nature. Finally, the efficiencies of national marketing and distribution were dictating that regional-only breweries could no longer compete as effectively against well-financed national brands, while consolidation of smaller brewers continued. These industry changes and Stroh's weakening position in its home market and lack of solid penetration in its new markets threatened to unseat Stroh from its 1985 number three spot on the list of largest national beer brewers.

History and Past Marketing Strategy

The Stroh family started brewing beer in the United States over 130 years ago. Bernhard Stroh, a German immigrant, opened his first successful brewery in 1865 in Detroit, Michigan. He brewed the beer in copper kettles over direct fire, a process that originated in Europe, while other brewers in America brewed over steam. The company grew in the Detroit area as a family business by delivering the brew to residents and local taverns. During Prohibition, the company survived by producing ice cream, malt extract, near beer, soft drinks, and ice. At the end of Prohibition, Stroh became a successful Midwestern beer brewer. Roger Fridholm, president of the Stroh brewery, attributes this success to quality, consumer service, packaging, and advertising. Also contributing to growing beer sales was the postwar baby boom, which produced 28 million additional Americans in beer brewers' prime age bracket, 18 to 35 years old. Stroh, as well as the entire beer-producing industry, could not help but grow as total beer consumption doubled in the next two decades.

In the 1960s, Stroh's was a popular-priced beer with a reputation for quality and taste generated by its fire brewing. Consumers were loyal to Stroh's because they believed, for the most part, that they were getting a premium beer at popular prices. Until 1979, Stroh had one brewery and essentially one brand: Stroh's (Bohemian style beer).

But during the 1970s, as the national brewers—Anheuser-Busch of St. Louis, Missouri, and the Miller Brewing Company of Milwaukee, Wisconsin—began to dominate the beer industry with tremendous advertising budgets, consolidation of smaller brewers sliced the number of beer producers in the country from approximately 171 to 45. In 1973, Stroh began raising the prices of Stroh's brand in hopes of repositioning it as a premium beer to compete directly with Budweiser and Miller. In the early 1980s, Anheuser-Busch (A-B) and Miller continued to grow without the aid of acquisition and forced many smaller brewers out of business. The Stroh brewery was forced to take on a defensive marketing strategy at that time. Stroh struggled to hold onto its existing Midwestern market and tried to offset the lack of sales growth by expanding into other beer segments and by producing new beer products. Stroh Light was introduced in 1979 as the first internally developed new product in the company's history, but serious production growth was severely hampered by the limits of Stroh's sole brewing plant.

"We woke up in the late 1970s to what was going on around us," says Chairman Peter Stroh, and that is when the brewery began its very aggressive expansion campaign. In 1979, Stroh acquired the F&M Schaefer Corporation, of Allentown, Pennsylvania, the eleventh largest brewer at the time. "We didn't buy a brand, we bought a brewery," explains Hunter Hastings, vice president of brand management. Although Stroh did not abandon the Schaefer brand, Stroh invested over $35 million to convert Schaefer's plant to fire brewing so that it could increase production of Stroh's brands. The Schaefer acquisition became Stroh's first move to dramatically expand the company.

In the summer of 1982, after a bitter battle, the Stroh Brewery Company, the seventh largest brewer in the nation, jumped to number three almost overnight when it acquired the Jos. Schlitz Brewing Company of Milwaukee, Wisconsin. Stroh borrowed $336 million to acquire the third largest brewer, thereby tripling its number of brewing plants to better compete at the national level. Stroh gained 1,250 wholesalers, 7,000 employees, and two very strong brand names: Old Milwaukee and Schlitz Malt Liquor.

Newspapers at the time quoted Peter Stroh's admiration for the Schlitz management. "I've been very impressed by their progress in overcoming the problems they inherited," exclaimed Peter. He was referring to the fact that during the five years before the merger, Schlitz's annual volume slid 35 percent, primarily because of quicker production techniques that noticeably cheapened the beer's quality. Peter Stroh believed his future as an independent brewer was in jeopardy, and the Schlitz failing position made it a prime candidate for takeover. With expansion for the Stroh brewery in mind, management concluded that acquisition was much cheaper than building new facilities. Building a brand new plant would have cost Stroh approximately $60 to $80 per barrel of plant capacity. Purchasing Schlitz cost only $25 per barrel. Schlitz's strategically located plants (see Exhibit 3 for a list of Stroh breweries) and its national, well-established distribution channels, including on-premise accounts in bars, off-premise network of retail stores, and wholesalers and distributors, were a few of the major reasons for Stroh's interest in Schlitz.

Stroh used the additional Schlitz plants nationwide to take advantage of economies of scale in production, distribution, and, probably most important, in advertising. Prior to 1982, as a regional brewer, Stroh had to pay a 50 percent premium on spot television to get the same results as A-B and Miller, who

EXHIBIT 3 Stroh's breweries

Location	Capacity (million barrels)
Detroit, Michigan*	7.25
Allentown, Pennsylvania†	3.5
Longview, Texas‡	3.8
Van Nuys, California‡	2.95
Memphis, Tennessee‡	5.5
Winston-Salem, North Carolina‡	5.0
St. Paul, Minnesota§	1.5
Total	29.5

* Closed June 1985.
† Original Schaefer brewery.
‡ Original Schlitz brewery.
§ Exchanged with Pabst after Schlitz acquisition.

advertised nationally. "Every time we are forced to buy prime time regional spots, we take it on the chin," explained John Bissell, group vice president of marketing. To make up for this inefficiency prior to the Schlitz acquisition, Stroh and the Adolph Coors Company, a regional brewer out of Golden, Colorado, cleverly bought television air time together in the 1970s and split it down the Mississippi River; Stroh commercials aired in the East, and Coors commercials aired in the West. After the Schlitz acquisition, as a national competitor Stroh could get even better representation on network television.

The Stroh brewery management proved its commitment to the growth of the company through its bold takeover of Schlitz. In reference to building the company as a national competitor, corporate Planning and Development Vice President Christopher W. Lole said, "You'd have to give credit to Peter. He's the visionary." But the fact remains that sales of Stroh products, both nationally and at home, have been falling, and Stroh management must further develop its marketing strategy to ensure the future of this independent family business.

Industry Environment

The Competition

The U.S. beer industry is highly competitive. In 1985, there were about 45 national, regional, and local brewers. Beer is an extremely mature product in the product life cycle, and as the industry shakeout continues, national brands are growing only at the expense of the smaller brewers.

Anheuser-Busch has traditionally dominated the beer industry through its sheer size and financial muscle. "The King of Beers" has been the largest brewer for over 25 years, and in 1984, A-B captured approximately 35.9 percent of the beer market, up from 33.6 percent the previous year. (See Exhibit 4 for brewers' estimated market shares.) A-B is the only domestic brewer to

EXHIBIT 4 Brewers' estimated market shares

	1979	1981	1983	1984E
Anheuser-Busch	26.8%	30.0%	33.6%	35.9%
Miller	20.8	22.2	20.8	21.3
Stroh*	**15.3**	**12.9**	**13.5**	**13.4**
Heileman	6.6	7.7	9.7	8.6
Coors	7.5	7.3	7.6	7.5
Pabst	12.3	10.5	7.1	6.6
Genesee	2.0	2.0	1.8	1.7
Schmidt	2.2	1.6	1.7	1.6
Pittsburgh	0.4	0.5	0.6	0.5
Others†	6.1	5.3	3.6	1.9
Total	100.0%	100.0%	100.0%	100.0%

* Includes Schlitz and Schaefer totals for all years.
† Includes imports and excludes tax-free sales.
Source: *Beverage Industry,* January 1985.

have meaningful growth in 1984: 6 percent growth in a total domestic market that declined 1.1 percent (or .6 percent, including imports). A-B's flagship brand, Budweiser, topped the most popular beer brands list in 1984 with 24.2 percent of the total beer sales, up from 22.8 percent in 1983. (See Exhibit 5 for the 1984 top 10 beer brands.) Also on the top 10 list was Michelob, the dominant super premium beer brand. New in 1984, Budweiser LA (without periods after the initials; LA is a logo protected by a trademark after Stroh unsuccessfully tried to use it for the Schaefer brand) is a low-alcohol brand with full-scale marketing support in the A-B lineup, with spending equivalent to all other A-B brands except Budweiser.

EXHIBIT 5 1984 Top 10 beer brands

Rank	Brand (brewer)	Market share	1984 Brand growth	Production (million barrels)
1	Budweiser (A-B)	24.2%	+3.7%	44.3
2	Miller Lite (Miller)	9.9	+.1	18.0
3	Miller High Life (Miller)	7.9	−14.7	14.5
4	Coors (Coors)	4.8	−10.0	8.7
5	**Old Milwaukee (Stroh)**	**3.9**	**−6.6**	**7.1**
6	Michelob (A-B)	3.7	−4.3	6.7
7	Pabst (Pabst)	3.6	−12.2	6.5
8	**Stroh (Stroh)**	**2.9**	**−3.6**	**5.3**
9	Old Style (Heileman)	2.8	−12.1	5.1
10	Coors Light (Coors)	2.5	+31.2	4.5

Source: *Beverage Industry,* January 1985.

The Miller Brewing Company, a subsidiary of Philip Morris, was in a strong number two position. Miller's clever advertising and timely product development of Miller Lite, the first successful low-calorie beer, gave Miller almost 21.3 percent of the total beer market in 1984. The trend-setting Miller Lite brand beat its older brother, Miller High Life, for second position on the

1984 top 10 list of beer brands. Overall, Miller had a volume increase, up 1.3 percent in 1984, thanks to Miller Lite and Miller's new popular priced brands, Meisterbrau and Milwaukee's Best. Miller's flagship brand, Miller High Life, experienced declining sales, however, dropping from 17 million barrels in 1983 to 14.5 million in 1984. Problems with this brand have been widely speculated on. Some beer experts believe Miller used the "It's Miller Time" campaign long after its effectiveness had peaked, barely altering it for 10 years. Miller also raised the price of Miller High Life in 1980 in a slumping economy. Although Budweiser eventually followed, the higher price may have permanently driven countless High Life drinkers to Budweiser. In 1985, Miller reviewed several ad agencies in an attempt to pump life back into the brand's sagging sales. J. Walter Thompson USA won the six-month-long competition, and began promoting Miller with a "Made the American Way" campaign.

Although Miller had reported operating profits since being acquired by Philip Morris, according to *Fortune* (March 3, 1985) these profits have been so paltry that they have covered only the interest on the roughly $1 billion Philip Morris borrowed to build breweries and bottling plants in the 1970s. Miller had a $450 million brewery that it had never used as of 1985, and there was widespread speculation on Wall Street that Philip Morris would sell Miller. Yet, many brewing analysts believed The Miller Brewing Company was still the only serious competition A-B had in terms of market share and financial backing.

While A-B and Miller had faced little real competition in previous years, they had to contend in the 1980s with a trio of second-tier companies who were breaking out of their traditional regional boundaries in order to avoid losing market share. These brewers included Stroh, G. Heileman Brewing Company of La Crosse, Wisconsin, and the Adolph Coors Company. Like Stroh, Heileman and Coors were becoming more adept at competing with the leaders.

During the past decade, Heileman jumped from 15th place to 4th in the beer industry. The company has built its empire chiefly by acquiring and successfully revitalizing regional brands, including Old Style, its lead brand among the 24 brands it had. A strong brand identity was important for Old Style, which sought new markets as a means of improving brand share and becoming a national brand. Heileman had nine breweries and a mammoth wholesaler network. Overall, Heileman's marketing strategy, based on brand acquisitions and heightened price competition, added up to a rough year in 1984: Heileman sales declined over 11 percent.

Heileman also tried to merge with Schlitz in 1982, but the move was blocked by the Justice Department on antitrust grounds. In 1984 and 1985, Heileman attempted to acquire the ailing Pabst Brewing Company, the sixth largest brewer. This move was blocked by federal injunction after Stroh and the Christian Schmidt Brewing Company of Philadelphia, the number nine brewer, began a lawsuit alleging unfair competition.

Despite shrinkage of sales in its western base, Coors expanded outside of its traditional market into the Southeast in the 1980s. With a renewed financial position (Coors traditionally has no debt) after a disastrous labor strike in 1977,

Coors established itself in a strong number five position among national beer brewers. Coors benefited from very strong brand identification for its premium Coors and Coors Light labels. These brews are unpasteurized and always shipped in refrigerated compartments, which contribute both to the brands' quality image and to customer confusion. Consumers were hesitant about buying Coors from unrefrigerated retail displays during large holiday promotions. As a result, in the summer of 1985, Coors advertised that while refrigeration certainly was desirable, it was not necessary to ensure the purity of Coors's taste.

1984 marked the first year that Coors had its two major brands in the list of top 10 most popular beer brands. Coors has not competed significantly in other beer segments. It seems the major limitation to Coors's expansion is that the company produces beer at a lone brewery in Golden, Colorado.

Beer Segmentation and the Consumer

For the first time in almost three decades, beer consumption in the United States declined in 1984. Consumption was 182.7 million barrels, down from 1983's 183.8 million barrels. Most industry researchers attribute this decline to changing lifestyles and social pressures. As brewing analysts predicted overall growth in domestic beer consumption to continue at 1 percent annually or less for the rest of the century, beer brewers sought to gain a larger portion of a steady-size pie through segment proliferation. Since many experts feel there really is no significant perceived difference among beer brands, especially after the first taste, brewers attempted to appeal to all different consumer backgrounds and introduced a brand image for almost every lifestyle, income, and taste.

1984 was a good year for light beer (for the more health-conscious consumer), popular priced beer (code term meaning inexpensive), and imported beers. Light beer sales increased its total industry share by 8 percent, moving up to 36.4 million barrels, or 19.9 percent of the total. Popular priced brands, the second most important segment, moved up to 42 million barrels, or 23 percent of the total. Imports accounted for 3.9 percent of total consumption, or 7.1 million barrels. (See Exhibit 6 for industry beer sales by market segment.)

EXHIBIT 6 1984 Industry beer sales by market segment

	Barrels (millions)	Percent
Light beer	36.4	9.9%
Popular priced	42.0	23.0
Imports	7.1	3.9
Premium priced	82.3	45.0
Super premiums	9.1	5.0
Other (Malts, LA)	5.8	3.0
Total	182.7	100.0

Source: *Beverage Industry*, January 1985.

However, the gains in these segments did not make up for the losses in the super premium segment (expensive beers of perceived higher quality), the premium segment (generally a brewer's flagship brand), and the malt liquor segment (beers with high alcohol content). Premium priced products, by far the largest beer segment, accounted for 82.3 million barrels sold, or 45 percent of the total in 1984. Super premiums, generally priced higher on a par with imports, were down 1.3 million barrels, accounting for 9.1 million barrels in sales, or 5 percent of the total market. Stroh had representation in every beer segment and was committed to continuing this strategy.

The majority (83 percent) of the nation's beer drinkers are males. They are usually between the ages of 18 and 34, with per capita consumption declining rather steadily with age (see Exhibit 7). Demographic trends were less than favorable for beer producers in the 1980s as the postwar baby boom generation moved beyond the prime beer drinking age. The 18-to-34 age group was predicted to decline by 4 million people before 1990. Stroh reacted to this unfortunate trend by seeking national market penetration.

EXHIBIT 7 Consumer characteristics

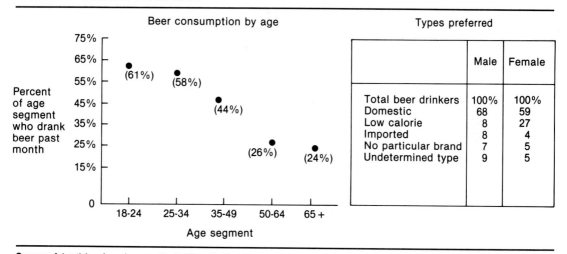

Source: *Advertising Age,* January 16, 1984, p. M-10.

Changes in eating and drinking habits also impeded growth in beer sales. The most prevalent change centered around our society's health concerns. Light beers have been very successful in addressing consumer demands for low-calorie foods since Miller introduced Miller Lite in the mid-1970s. During the 10 years following Miller Lite's introduction, light beer sales grew to account for over 20 percent of total beer sales and two thirds of the total growth in beer consumption for the period. Stroh markets almost one third of its brands with light labels, including Stroh Light, Old Milwaukee Light, Schlitz Light, Schaefer Light, and Piels Light.

A large threat to increasing beer sales in this country in the 1980s was increased concern over alcohol abuse. Various community groups, especially Mothers Against Drunk Driving (MADD), opposed brewers for allegedly glamorizing drinking in their advertising. Peter Stroh said the drinking/driving problem was probably the single most important issue he faced in 1984. While many states raised the drinking age from 18 to 21, lawmakers also stiffened the penalty for driving while drunk. "This is an issue the beer industry cannot back away from. It is in the brewers' best interest to assist in educational efforts aimed against alcohol abuse," says Peter Stroh. Stroh has been very closely associated with efforts at Johns Hopkins and other leading universities to study health-related alcohol abuse effects.

On a related issue, consumer groups like SMART (Stop Marketing Alcohol on Radio and TV) were attempting to ban all alcoholic beverage advertising from TV and radio. Coalitions formed on both sides of the issue, and at Stroh, management felt brewers should work to shape any serious activity in this critical area rather than leaving the future of advertising laws only to the politicians. Stroh certainly did not want to see higher excise taxes to fund the fight against alcohol abuse, cigarette-type warning labels, or taglines on beer commercials warning consumers about the damage of abusing alcoholic beverages. Brewers traditionally imposed their own advertising standards, such as having actors in their ads who were over 25 years of age and never actually drank the beer on camera. Brewers claimed that there has been no credible scientific evidence to show that advertising encourages alcohol abuse and that the Supreme Court has previously ruled that truthful advertising has Constitutional protection. On the other hand, many legal scholars profess that a ban on advertising beer and wine on radio and television will withstand Constitutional law, and they point out the cigarette ruling as an example.

A-B addressed the alcohol-related issues by introducing a low-alcohol brand beer in 1984. Stroh quickly followed with Schaefer L. A. but was only distributing it on a limited basis until October 1985. In mid-1985, although A-B declined to give sales numbers for its low-alcohol beer, A-B called its LA "the bar call of the 80s" and did say that off-premise sales had been stronger than anticipated. Since exact sales figures on low-alcohol brands are not readily available, experts can only estimate that low-alcohol beers had only a negligible share of the beer market in their first year after introduction. Many analysts predict low-alcohol beers will not become a major market segment.

Advertising

"The Big Two," A-B and Miller, have capitalized on their high volumes with economies of scale in both production and distribution. This has allowed them to increase advertising expenditures well beyond what others can afford. (See Exhibit 8 for some national advertising expenditures by brand.) In an industry where savvy marketing is a key success factor, A-B and Miller secured the major live-action sports telecasts in the early 1980s with exclusive network

EXHIBIT 8 Some national advertising expenditures by brand ($000s)

Brand	Medium	1982	1983	1984
Budweiser and Bud Light (A-B)	Magazines	$ 2,560	$ 5,208	$ 2,907
	Newspapers	1,929	2,242	2,246
	Network TV	50,479	68,165	93,421
	Spot TV	21,905	30,094	29,087
	Network radio	4,572	4,052	2,179
	Spot radio	20,261	19,804	17,660
	Outdoor	3,191	2,217	2,123
Total		$104,897	$131,782	$149,623
Miller High Life and Miller Lite (Miller)	Magazines	$ 1,555	$ 1,352	$ 1,870
	Newspapers	490	1,556	1,279
	Network TV	74,651	84,082	104,930
	Spot TV	19,868	22,374	18,514
	Network radio	—	—	—
	Spot radio	16,051	5,194	17,449
	Outdoor	661	470	657
Total		$113,276	$125,028	$144,699
Michelob and Michelob Light (A-B)	Magazines	$ 13,993	$ 6,371	$ 2,040
	Newspapers	11,657	980	812
	Network TV	22,355	19,760	49,566
	Spot TV	14,653	2,209	6,643
	Network radio	—	503	2,017
	Spot radio	1,867	7,746	3,445
	Outdoor	74	30	252
Total		$ 64,599	$ 37,602	$ 64,775
Coors and Coors Light (Coors)	Magazines	$ 56	$ 29	$ 46
	Newspapers	1,153	1,016	657
	Network TV	7,069	9,746	11,218
	Spot TV	11,367	18,658	24,398
	Network radio	—	—	—
	Spot radio	8,081	21,209	18,528
	Outdoor	451	547	517
Total		$ 28,179	$ 51,205	$ 55,364
Stroh's and Stroh Light (Stroh)	**Magazines**	**$ 260**	**$ 255**	**$ 1,988**
	Newspapers	**113**	**242**	**450**
	Network TV	**3,578**	**24,962**	**27,780**
	Spot TV	**7,649**	**7,014**	**5,936**
	Network radio	**—**	**—**	**—**
	Spot radio	**1,842**	**3,472**	**6,141**
	Outdoor	**610**	**951**	**2,642**
Total		**$14,052**	**$36,896**	**$44,937**
Heineken (Van Munching)	Magazines	n/a	$ 4,708	$ 5,006
	Newspapers		15	150
	Network TV		2,895	3,004
	Spot TV		5,532	7,143
	Network radio		1,645	548
	Spot radio		7,659	12,983
	Outdoor		—	—
Total			$ 22,454	$ 28,834

EXHIBIT 8 *(concluded)*

Brand	Medium	1982	1983	1984
LA (A-B)	Magazines			$ 742
	Newspapers			1,618
	Network TV			19,218
	Spot TV			783
	Network radio			2,036
	Spot radio			558
	Outdoor			872
Total				$ 25,827
Lowenbrau (Miller)	Magazines	$ 111	$ 130	$ 454
	Newspapers	131	81	18
	Network TV	16,096	15,918	12,387
	Spot TV	6,412	4,748	5,762
	Network radio	—	—	—
	Spot radio	1,359	4,020	3,045
	Outdoor	6	18	14
Total		$ 24,115	$ 24,915	$ 21,680
Meister Brau (Miller)	Magazines		—	—
	Newspapers		$ 1,028	$ 41
	Network TV		8,300	18,336
	Spot TV		2,887	2,906
	Network radio		—	—
	Spot radio		—	—
	Outdoor		9	25
Total			$ 12,224	$ 21,308

Source: *Marketing and Media Decisions,* 14th Annual Report, "The Top 200 Brands."

advertising contracts that prohibited other beer competitors from airing their ads. The audience that watches live-action sports is the audience beer makers everywhere strive to attract: males aged 18 to 35. Stroh believed that network exclusive pacts hurt company business. "We have all the tools to compete, except for access to these sporting events. We have made offers to purchase time based on the terms and conditions customary to the television industry," explained Christopher Lole. The inability to reach a target audience through major network sports programs has critical trade implications also. Not having a presence on major sporting events makes it harder for local wholesalers to compete against those wholesalers whose product gets plenty of national exposure, and therefore it is more difficult to get ample shelf space from retailers.

After persistent efforts by Stroh management, including Peter Stroh himself, lengthy negotiations with the networks, and an investigation by the Department of Justice, the networks changed their policies on ad exclusivity in 1984. While no lawsuits were actually filed, Stroh made it clear that it would sue the networks on a restraint of trade basis if the two sides could not come to an agreement. Stroh was able to buy enough network time in 1984 to put off litigation over the matter. In fact, the networks actually offered Stroh more time than it could afford, according to Hunter Hastings, vice president of brand management. Stroh contracted to sponsor ABC's "Monday Night Baseball" on a nonexclusive basis for 1984. In addition, Stroh bought time on two NBC boxing matches and a CBS auto racing series.

In June 1985, the Stroh brewery introduced the "Stroh's Circle of Sports." For two hours every weekend for 13 weeks, Stroh's pursued a strategy of "going where the big guys ain't" on the USA cable network and a broadcast TV syndicate. The show featured interviews, analyses, opinions, historical flashbacks, and an "event of the week" shown from the perspective of a sports participant. The "Stroh's Circle of Sports" signaled that the brewer would look for advertising niches instead of always going head-on against A-B and Miller. This also represented the first example of Stroh's efforts to target audiences at a lower cost by creating its own programming. Stroh spent an estimated $200 million for advertising and sales promotions in 1985, but still could not match the spending of A-B and Miller.

Domestic beer brewers spent an estimated $575 million on advertising their products in 1984, which does not include the costs of promotion and distribution. Beer has gone from emphasizing traditional taste and quality claims to heavy consumer imagery. Certainly quality is an important factor in selling beer (as Schlitz found out only too late), but advertising, especially on TV, is the strategy of choice for the big beer makers.

Promotion

Brewers' promotional tactics came in many forms. Sporting events around the country throughout the year were usually the events of choice for national brewers—again, as a way of attracting young beer drinkers to their brands. Stroh sponsored the "Stroh Thunderfest," a hydroplane race in Detroit in which *Miss Budweiser* was often the boat favored to win. Other sponsorships by major brewers included bowling teams, auto races, rodeos, and track-and-field events. Budweiser was the official beer of the 1984 Olympics.

Many brewers sponsored special events such as rock concerts or symphonies to associate their beers with the lifestyles of those who participated in the events. Signature was the official beer of the 1982 World's Fair in Knoxville, Tennessee. Many brewers also sponsored charity events, including raising money for the renovation of the Statue of Liberty and making local donations to children's hospitals.

Brewers, in cooperation with local distributors, were very aggressive in providing quality point-of-purchase displays in retail outlets. Brewers attracted consumers in liquor and party stores with permanent and temporary illuminated prestige signs, nonilluminated plaques, and neon signs. Decorated mirrors with company logos were universally found in taverns and bars.

Stroh's very successful retail merchandising programs included the 10-year-old "Stroh a Party" campaign, which Stroh implemented to build sales of Stroh's and Stroh Light during the high-volume, peak summer selling season. The "Strohman"—a large plastic, stand-alone snowman—gave retailers a high-visibility display for Stroh's and Stroh Light during the winter holiday season. The "Strohman" program included not only the familiar snowman but also six-pack toppers, price cards, and cooler stickers for use in every display setting.

Super premium beers and malt liquors generally did not discount their prices to wholesalers in order to protect their upscale image. However, premium beers and popular priced brands often discounted their prices to wholesalers who in turn passed the savings on to retailers who, hopefully, sold the beers at sale prices during promotional campaigns. One of the wholesaler's jobs was to keep tabs on retail prices. Old Milwaukee offered periodic cents-off coupons, mail-in refund offers, and sweepstakes. These promotions were offered through newspapers, point of purchase, and direct mail.

Distribution and Pricing

Stroh brands, like all beers, were distributed through a three-tiered distribution system:

1. The brewery sold to wholesalers, who were independent, local businesspeople.
2. Wholesalers sold to retailers (bars and stores).
3. Retailers sold to consumers.

A brewery could not legally sell to retailers or to consumers.

Stroh officials, as described in a company document, believed the three-tiered system worked well because wholesalers agreed to provide service to all accounts, from mom-and-pop stores to high-volume chain stores. The wholesalers must maintain Stroh's strict standards of product quality by never selling beer over 90 days old and by keeping the product in temperature-controlled warehouses. In return, Stroh signed territorial agreements with wholesalers, giving them exclusive rights to sell Stroh products in their territories. From the brewery's point of view, this meant that the company did not have to pit wholesalers against one another. This industrywide practice was controversial because of its anticompetitive aspects.

Brewers set their prices of low-margin, popular priced beers to wholesalers based on a cost plus profit method. Brewers set prices of super premium beers, on the other hand, on a more consumer-oriented approach. Wholesalers and retailers were free to set their own prices based on their usual markups, but brewers hit certain price points by establishing a price to the wholesalers that, when marked up by the wholesalers and retailers, would match the desired retail price. (See Exhibit 9 for 1985 typical domestic retail beer brand prices.)

Laws governing promotional pricing varied widely from state to state. When a brand offered a lower promotional price, some states required it to stick with that price for as long as 120 days. For regular retail prices, most brands followed the segment leader's pricing strategy in any particular geographical market.

EXHIBIT 9 1985 Typical retail beer brand prices (six-pack of 12-ounce bottles or cans)*

Brand	Brewer	Price
Popular priced		
Blatz	Heileman	$2.50
Busch	Anheuser-Busch	2.49
Carling Black Label	Heileman	2.50
Goebel	**Stroh**	**2.25**
Meisterbrau	Miller	2.49
Natural Light	Anheuser-Busch	2.49
Old Milwaukee	**Stroh**	**2.39**
Old Milwaukee Light	**Stroh**	**2.39**
Premium		
Budweiser	Anheuser-Busch	$2.98
Bud Light	Anheuser-Busch	2.98
Miller High Life	Miller	2.98
Miller Lite	Miller	2.98
Old Style	Heileman	2.98
Pabst	Pabst	2.98
Schlitz	**Stroh**	**2.98**
Schlitz Light	**Stroh**	**2.98**
Stroh	**Stroh**	**2.98**
Stroh Light	**Stroh**	**2.98**
Super premium		
Erlanger	**Stroh**	**$3.39**
Lowenbrau	Miller	3.49
Michelob	Anheuser-Busch	3.39
Signature	**Stroh**	**3.39**
Malt Liquor		
Colt 45	Heileman	$2.98
Schlitz Malt Liquor	**Stroh**	**2.98**

* Price does not include sales tax or bottle deposit.

Current Marketing Strategy and Brand Management at Stroh

The Stroh Brewery Company's objective in 1985 was to keep a strong and growing number three position in the beer industry, with the ultimate goal of unseating the second largest industry leader, Miller. Industry experts predicted that consolidation of brewers in the next few decades would leave only four or five major beer producers. Although the company policy in 1985 did not include long-term planning of five years or more, Stroh was determined to be one of those few.

With the purchase of Schaefer, Stroh became a company in transition. Hunter Hastings said the company had to "make the switch from being a production company to a marketing company." In 1985, the entire marketing department was only six years old. The company recruited many young marketing MBAs, but most of the senior marketing executives came from other marketing-oriented firms. J. Wayne Jones, formerly with Coca-Cola, accepted the newly created position of executive vice president of sales and marketing in 1984, and John Bissell, group vice president of marketing, came from General Mills. Before the mid-1970s, Stroh did not bring outside talents into the company.

A-B and Miller relied on the ''block buster brand'' approach to the beer market for many years with their hugely successful Budweiser and Miller brands, respectively. Stroh, on the other hand, used the portfolio theory of brands after gaining so many different brands from acquisitions, and focused on the many segments in the beer market. Stroh had a brand of beer for all popular beer segments in the 1980s: popular priced, premium, malt liquor, etc. Stroh also concentrated on special niches, including demographics (Blacks and Hispanics) and geographics (targeting different states and cities with unique campaigns).

In 1984, Stroh concentrated its energy on taking its flagship brands—Stroh's and Stroh Light—nationwide. Stroh planned to market Schaefer nationwide in 1985 and have Signature not far behind. Other brands, such as Schlitz Malt Liquor and Old Milwaukee, already made Stroh a national firm through the Schlitz acquisition. But in 1984, Roger Fridholm hoped Stroh's brand penetration nationwide would broaden its 13.4 percent market share to 15 percent. Fridholm did not, however, pin down a time frame for this objective.

The Stroh marketing strategy contained six priorities for the company:

1. Maintain and grow Stroh's and Stroh Light as national competitors.
2. Maintain Old Milwaukee as the market leader in the popular priced segment.
3. Maintain and grow Schlitz Malt Liquor as the clear leader in the malt liquor segment.
4. Maintain leadership as the only beer company to specifically target the needs of Blacks and Hispanics.
5. Establish a super premium beer brand.
6. Continue the company's effort in new product development.

To support these six priorities, Stroh devoted almost 75 percent of its financial budget to 6 of its 15 brands: Stroh's, Stroh Light, Old Milwaukee, Old Milwaukee Light, Schlitz Malt Liquor, and Signature.

Stroh's and Stroh Light

For the best possible financial efficiencies, Stroh's and Stroh Light came under the same brand manager, had the same budgets, and were advertised in the same advertising campaigns (a strategy that had worked well with Old Milwaukee and Old Milwaukee Light). Stroh gave these flagship brands the same consumer positioning as the heavyweights in the premium beer category, Budweiser and Miller High Life. But Stroh wanted this image to carry a few discerning characteristics. Stroh's and Stroh Light were brewed with Stroh's unique fire-brewing process, which the company believed gave these beers the finest taste. In the 1980s, Stroh's and Stroh Light targeted what the company called the "type A" beer drinker. This was someone who drank at least a case of beer per week: the heavy user. Therefore, Stroh was careful to package the Stroh's brands in colorful, bright cartons and cans to attract this young, fun-loving consumer. Beginning in 1969, Stroh's used the advertising theme "From One Beer Lover to Another, Stroh's." In 1984, Stroh's was extremely successful with its clever "Alex the Dog" television advertising campaign (see Exhibit 10 for a copy of Stroh's television photoboard). Stroh believed humor makes these brands more memorable. Budweiser and Miller High Life did not use humor to advertise in this premium segment. Budweiser long used its familiar tagline, "For all you do, this Bud's for you!" and Miller began using a new theme song for its television commercials in 1985; "Miller's made the American Way, born and brewed in the USA, just as proud as the people who are drinking it today, Miller's made the American Way!"

In May 1984, Stroh's and Stroh Light became nationally distributed in Stroh's big push to become a national brewer. 1984 consumption of Stroh's and Stroh Light was 6.1 million barrels, which captured 7.4 percent of the national premium market. The two beers became available in all 50 states, but total sales for these two brands were down over 1 percent nationally in 1984, and sales in Michigan were off 8.2 percent for the same year.

Taking Stroh's and Stroh Light national had an advantage in that it allowed the company to address the key Hispanic populations in the West like no one else had before. Stroh appointed a new national manager of Hispanic market development in 1984 and spent over $4 million in the ethnic market with heavy advertising in radio, outdoor displays, and newspapers. Other brewers also attempted to capture the Hispanic market in the West and Southwest, but Stroh was emerging with the first major effort to court the Hispanic market. Stroh's success in this area is yet to be evaluated.

Old Milwaukee and Old Milwaukee Light

Old Milwaukee (OM) and Old Milwaukee Light (OM Light) was the best-selling duet of Stroh brands at 8.6 million barrels in 1984. The goal for these two original Schlitz brands was to continue to dominate the popular priced beer brands with a national image that says OM and OM Light have everything premium but the price. Stroh spent heavily to create this image and has attracted drinkers from other competitors. In a stagnant industry, OM's brands grew 16.9 percent in 1983. OM was the fifth most popular brand in 1984, climbing from number seven the previous year. OM and OM Light's large volumes were very important for assuring the utilization of full plant capacities, but at their popular prices, OM and OM Light did not provide very large profit margins.

Stroh emphasized image and taste rather than price when advertising OM on radio and television. Stroh believed Miller was making a mistake when it

EXHIBIT 10

CLIENT: Stroh Brewery Co.
TITLE: Alex the dog

COMMERCIAL NUMBER: OUSB 3301
LENGTH: 30 seconds

POKER PLAYER: I'd sure like another Stroh's.
HOST: No, wait. Alex!

DOG: ARF

HOST: Two cold Stroh's.

DOG: ARF
HOST: Wait till you see this.

(SFX REFRIGERATOR DOOR OPENING)
He just opened the refrigerator.

(SFX BOTTLE OPENING)

He just opened one bottle.
(SFX BOTTLE OPENING)
He just opened the other.

(SFX STROH'S BEING POURED INTO GLASS)
Now he's pouring yours.

(SFX OTHER STROH'S BEING POURED)
Now he's pouring mine.
(SFX DOG DRINKING)

Alex, you better be drinking your water.

From one beer lover to another.

MUSIC

mentioned low prices in the advertising of its new popular priced Meisterbrau, OM's chief competition from Miller. Meisterbrau ended its television commercials in the early 1980s by claiming Meisterbrau "Tastes as good as Budweiser, at a better price!" Stroh believed advertising low prices did not reflect the proper image for quality.

OM and OM Light came in premium packages: tall bottles with colorful cartons and cases. (For pictures of OM and OM Light containers as well as of the rest of the Stroh line, see Exhibit 11.) They were carefully merchandised with premium point-of-purchase signs and premium print advertising. In television ads, Stroh differentiated OM through a "hard play/reward" theme rather than the "hard work/reward" style of Meisterbrau. The characters in those OM television commercials were younger, vibrant types who enjoyed stone crab fishing in the Gulf of Mexico or bar-hopping in New Orleans, just the type of

EXHIBIT 11 Stroh bottles and cans

Source: Stroh media pamphlet.

events that are capped off with Old Milwaukee. At the end of each commercial, the characters observed, "It doesn't get any better than this!" (See Exhibit 12.)

OM used many techniques to promote the beer. Charles Powell, brand manager for OM and OM Light, explained that "While a lot of beer is consumed by men, it's actually bought [off premise] by women. So we try to provide incentives for women to buy our beer." OM capitalized on the gatekeeper effect by stressing refunds and product discounts. OM set trends with coupons on a more extensive basis than had been seen before. OM sponsored five in-store promotions each year, including sweepstakes and give-aways. OM ran ads on all three networks in prime time slots during big league sporting events. OM also constantly tried to get retail trade attention through heavy advertising in trade publications.

Schlitz Malt Liquor

Schlitz Malt Liquor (SML) was clearly the brand leader in the malt liquor segment with a 40 percent market share in 1984 and 2.1 million barrels sold. Schlitz achieved this position with a superior product, and Stroh maintained it with ongoing taste tests to achieve the best flavor in this segment. Stroh stressed specific consumer targeting techniques for SML. Blacks consume almost 75 percent of this specialty product, so Stroh featured top Black pop groups like Kool and the Gang in television commercials. Malt liquors contain more alcohol and have a fuller, more robust flavor. For many years Schlitz used the strength of a bull crashing through a brick wall to create this imagery. All of SML's advertising copy showed celebration and times when people want more alcohol. (See Exhibit 13 for a sample Schlitz Malt Liquor television photoboard.) Because it produced the dominant product in malt liquors, Stroh used leadership pricing techniques and never resorted to discounts. However, SML sales were down .5 percent in 1984 as were sales of the entire malt liquor segment.

Signature

Signature was introduced in 1982 as the second new internally developed product in Stroh's history. Only in limited distribution in 1985, Stroh planned to expand this super premium product on a national level in the near future. The objective was to gain a significant share of the super premium segment. This segment, however, has traditionally been completely dominated by A-B's very popular Michelob brand, which sold almost 74 percent of the beer in this segment in 1984. Miller's Lowenbrau sold another 13 percent.

Signature, brewed from 100 percent European hops through the Stroh fire-brewing process, closely targeted the high-priced super premium segment with what the company believed was a fine-tasting product (200 recipes were rejected before Signature was personally chosen by Peter Stroh) that combined drinkability with a definite, distinctive flavor that was smoother and less bitter

EXHIBIT 12

BBDO

Batten, Barton, Durstine & Osborn, Inc.

Client: **STROH BREWERY**

Product: **OLD MILWAUKEE DUAL BRAND**   Title: **"SUMMER SKIING"**

Time: **30 SECONDS**   Comml. No.: **SZDB 4053**

VO: Mount Hood, Oregon and
Old Milwaukee

both mean something
great to these guys.

Mount Hood means the
best summer skiing

in America.

And Old Milwaukee
means a great beer.

Cold, crisp Old Milwaukee beer.

And smooth, golden

Old Milwaukee Light.

SONG: OLD MILWAUKEE

VO: And Old Milwaukee Light.

SONG: TASTE AS GREAT
AS THEIR NAME.

GUY: Man, it doesn't get
any better than this.

EXHIBIT 13

B&B

BENTON & BOWLES
909 THIRD AVENUE
NEW YORK, N.Y.
(212) 758-6200

CLIENT: SCHLITZ
PRODUCT: MALT LIQUOR
TITLE: "BACHELOR PARTY/FP"
COMM'L NO.: SZML 0108
LENGTH: 30 SECONDS

(MUSIC UNDER)
FOUR TOPS SING: Tonight you're still a bachelor, tomorrow's almost here.

So while you're still a free man, let's bring on the beer . . .

KOOL AND THE GANG: Bull!

FOUR TOPS: Bull???

KOOL AND THE GANG SING: On this night to remember, it's so clear.

You deserve to celebrate with more taste than beer.

The bull's got a taste so big, so bold, so smooth.

Let's all party with the Schlitz Malt Liquor Bull.
ALL SING: Don't say beer, say Bull.

BACHELOR: Hey Gang how about another Bull?

(SFX: CRASH)

(SFX: CRASH)

ALL SING: No one does it like the Bull!

than other premiums. Signature tried to be distinctive not only in flavor but on other levels as well. Although Signature was on a parity pricing schedule with Michelob, Signature really focused on packaging, and Stroh proclaimed that Signature had a better shelf life than Michelob. Signature came in a uniquely shaped, old-fashioned-type bottle with gold foil around the top and elegant gold-trimmed labels. This package won Signature the coveted Clio award for packaging.

Signature bears the signature of former Chairman John W. Stroh, and the Stroh family history told through print ads (see Exhibit 14) conveyed to consumers why they should pay more for this product.

Michelob specifically targeted the yuppie crowd (young, urban professionals). This was quite evident in Michelob television advertising, which professed, ''There's a style in your life, no one can ever deny. You're on your way to the top, and along the way you've always known just who you are. Where you're going, it's Michelob!''

Signature concentrated on the same young, financially stable age group in a somewhat different fashion with television commercials that featured independent, bearded role models who left corporate America to become entrepreneurs in such exciting fields as scuba diving and car racing. (See Exhibit 15 for a sample of Signature television advertising.) John Bissell, group vice president of Stroh marketing, described the target audience for Signature as ''carefree, independent, self-confident, well-educated, and successful young men and women—the people who tend to dress differently than others, go into business for themselves, and, while viewed as responsible individuals, are definitely free-thinkers.''

All the Rest

The Stroh Brewery Company had 11 other brands in 1985: Goebel, Schaefer, Schaefer Light, Schaefer L.A., Piels Beer, Piels Light, Schlitz, Schlitz Light, Erlanger, Silver Thunder, and Primo. These brands combined received only 25 percent of all the financial support of the company. Most of the brands competed on price, especially Goebel.

Stroh was repositioning its super premium beer, Erlanger (a label originated by Schlitz), for the 1980s as a specialty beer parity priced with imported beers. Erlanger management planned to make its brew available on a limited basis in upscale retail and on-premise accounts. Erlanger planned for three new labels on a rotating schedule and a new bottle in order to take advantage of high gross margins in this segment, although total industry sales in this segment declined in 1984.

Stroh took advantage of regional tastes, making Piels brands available in the East, Primo in Hawaii, and Goebel in the Midwest. As of the summer of 1985, Stroh intended to expand the popular priced Schaefer brands' distribution area, breaking them out of their original distribution area in 14 eastern states.

EXHIBIT 14

EXHIBIT 15

STROH SIGNATURE

"CAR BUILDER"

MAN: (VO) I gave up a great job with an auto company

to do what I always wanted--design and build race cars.

(MUSIC)
SINGERS: WHEN A MAN HAS SOMETHING EXTRA DEEP INSIDE HIS SOUL. . .

IT SHINES LIKE A DIAMOND

AND IT'S WORTH MORE THAN GOLD.

MAN: (VO) This is the way to make a living.

SINGERS: SO HERE'S TO THE MAN

WHO LOOKS DEEP INSIDE.

AND HERE'S TO THE MAN

WHO FINDS SOMETHING EXTRA.

ANNCR: (VO) Stroh Signature is something extra.

You have our name on that.

MCA ADVERTISING, LTD.

The Schlitz Problem

One of Stroh's biggest challenges after the Schlitz acquisition was to develop a new marketing program to breathe life into the ailing Schlitz brands, which sold only 1.8 million barrels in 1984. Stroh management monitored Schlitz sales, which slumped 26 percent in 1982, the first year under Stroh. Christopher Lole noted that "the first step to revitalizing the brand is to slow the erosion." Analysts say "The Beer That Made Milwaukee Famous" lost over one million faithful Schlitz drinkers after the company reformulated the Schlitz brewing process, which made the brew taste "funny." Schlitz again revised the brew's formula and claimed that it was even better than the original Schlitz product. However, despite Schlitz's extensive advertising efforts, the old crop of regular Schlitz drinkers did not return.

Stroh began the new Schlitz campaign with a makeover of the Schlitz packaging. The new Schlitz brand marketing team replaced the "government-issue" yellow packing cartons with a more colorful design and also redesigned the Schlitz logo and bottle configuration. "The major change was just brightening it up so it didn't look like it was only available for people over the age of 60," said Marketing Vice President John Bissell. "I don't think we spent more than $25,000 on the research, because we needed to move fast."

Apparently, Stroh did not pump big money into Schlitz until revitalization signs warranted more financial backing. Stroh did, however, continue to support promotional efforts in Schlitz's 28 strongest southern states, especially in Texas. Although many analysts thought Stroh was merely milking Schlitz, management insisted in 1984 that it would not drop the Schlitz name. "Any brand that can generate some reasonable sales and profits determines its own viability," said Bissell.

Special Products Division

The Stroh Brewery Company instituted a new special products division at corporate headquarters in 1985. Although Stroh had continually marketed Stroh's ice cream since Prohibition, Stroh was definitely less diversified than the other major brewers, who owned everything from a major league baseball team (Anheuser-Busch owned the St. Louis Cardinals as well as many other nonbeer ventures) to cigarette companies (Miller, for example, was a subsidiary of Philip Morris, the tobacco company that also owned 7UP). Stroh was very busy developing a nonbeer beverage in early 1985: White Mountain Cooler. It is a flavored malt beverage similar to a wine cooler, targeted especially at women and nonbeer drinkers. Stroh was also investigating an all-natural flavored water beverage and the possibility of producing baked goods or snack foods since these products all require essentially the same ingredients Stroh already used in beer and could be distributed through some of the same retail beer channels.

Position in Home Market

The lag in home market sales was a puzzle for Stroh officials. In 1984, all Stroh brands captured approximately 16 percent of the Michigan market, down 10 percent from 1983. This compares unfavorably with a 28.91 percent Michigan market share for the Miller Brewing Company and 28.9 percent for Anheuser-Busch. Meanwhile, A-B commanded a 51 percent share of the market in its native Missouri in 1984. In Wisconsin, Miller beat another local brewer, G. Heileman Brewing Company, for the top slot, gaining 28.6 percent of the market to Heileman's 27.8 percent: a total of 56.4 percent for the home team.

Stroh closed its original brewery in Detroit in June 1985, which greatly disappointed many Stroh loyalists, although Stroh had long been a conscientious corporate citizen and involved in Michigan special events. Previous to the brewery's closing, Stroh had not been a firm that sought headlines. Detroit newspaper writers attributed this to the low profile Chairman Peter Stroh traditionally took because he didn't want to pat himself on the back. But during

EXHIBIT 16

We Are Still Here

Dear Michigan Consumers and Retailers,

The Stroh Brewery Company was founded in Detroit in 1950. Since then, the names "Stroh" and "Detroit" have become linked in the minds of people throughout the United States and, in fact, throughout the world.

Our difficult decision to close the least-efficient plant in our seven-brewery system was not a severance of that link. It was a decision made to ensure our future in a highly competitive industry. That future will show that the Stroh Brewery Company's commitments to Detroit and to Michigan remain as strong, if not stronger, than before.

Possibly the most visible sign of our sustaining commitment is our River Place corporate headquarters, a major development along the Detroit waterfront that will be a long-term asset to this city and its people. When the offices, shops, restaurants, and residences open at River Place, our 750 corporate employees will be joined by thousands of Detroiters sharing in the beauty and excitement River Place offers.

Other Stroh commitments are seen in our support of civic and cultural events. If you enjoy the Detroit-Montreux Jazz Festival or the Signature concerts at Meadowbrook; if you're in the stands for the hydroplane "Thunderfest" or the Detroit Formula One Grand Prix; if you watch "Late Night America" or "Michigan Outdoors;" if you attend the Detroit Symphony, or visit the Detroit Institute of Arts; then you are touched by the Stroh commitment to our home.

These are but a few of our commitments to Detroit and to Michigan. There is one more, which is perhaps the most important of all. That is our commitment to you that the brewing of fine beers will continue to be our top priority. Our Michigan distributors will continue to provide this state with the finest, and we intend to share it with the people of Michigan regardless of where you may live.

Sincerely,

Peter W. Stroh
Chairman
The Stroh Brewery Company

the summer the local brewery closed, Stroh published full-page ads in the Detroit area enumerating Stroh's community activities, apparently responding to Michigan consumers' anger. (See Exhibit 16 for a reprint of those advertisements.)

As the Stroh Brewery Company pondered the current state of the beer industry, both at home and nationally, management knew that it could institute long-range and risky plans without worrying about impressing any shareholders since the company was privately owned. The corporate management style was open and aggressive. But as the company grows, in Peter Stroh's words, "The thing to keep our eyes on is not so much our size, but the size of the guys we're up against."

It was against this background that the management at the Stroh Brewery Company developed its strategy to slow the erosion of sales in the home market. At the same time, meaningful penetration of the Stroh and Schaefer brands in the national market was certainly one of Stroh's top objectives, and further refinement of its implementation techniques was appropriate. Stroh's market planners knew where they wanted their expansion strategy to take them: closer to the top of the list of national competitors. However, while analyzing the effectiveness of the national expansion efforts thus far (see Exhibit 17), Stroh did not have the financial strength to take on all potential successful projects at once. Stroh had to establish which alternatives claimed the highest priorities, while balancing them against a declining beer market and powerful competition.

EXHIBIT 17
THE STROH BREWING COMPANY
Selected Financial Data*
Year Ended March 31
(amounts in $000s)

	1983	1982	1981
Barrels of beer sold	22,900	9,100	8,900
Brewery capacity	29,550	12,250	11,000
Sales	$1,535,126	$593,444	$561,578
Sales net of excise taxes	1,317,986	499,124	467,292
Earnings (loss) from operations	1,228	(6,172)	2,973
Discontinued operations	—	—	4,863
Change in accounting principles	—	11,774	—
Net earnings	1,228	5,602	7,836
Pro forma net earnings (loss)	1,288	(6,172)	10,716
Depreciation	39,868	19,724	15,918
Working capital	45,666	14,369	22,891
Year-end working capital	(46,502)	(19,370)	25,946
Property, plant, equipment	456,876	168,210	139,882
Total assets	721,142	263,433	231,588
Long-term debt†	321,328	72,996	69,648

* Includes operations for Schlitz from 1982 and Schaefer from 1980.
† Includes redeemable preferred shares of Schaefer.
Source: The Stroh Brewery Company 1983 Form 10-K.

Case 44

Canadair Challenger Jet*

Mr. James Taylor and Mr. Harry Halton were taking a last-minute look at the marketing strategy developed for Canadair's new Challenger business jet. Mr. Taylor was head of Canadair Inc., the Challenger's marketing arm located in Westport, Connecticut. Mr. Halton, the executive vice president, was the chief engineer, responsible for the design and production of the Challenger at Canadair's Montreal plant. The Challenger was being touted as the world's most advanced business aircraft, incorporating the latest technologies to achieve high speed, longest range, greatest fuel economy, and greatest seating space and comfort. It was early July 1976, and the president of Canadair, Mr. Fred Kearns, wanted senior management's consensus on product design, pricing, advertising, and approach to selling.

The preliminary design of the Challenger was generally complete, but Mr. Halton continued to receive suggestions for additional features from Mr. Taylor and his marketing group, from prospective customers, and from project engineers. Rather than build prototype models by hand, Mr. Halton had decided to begin setting up a full-scale production line. Eventually, three preproduction models of the Challenger would be constructed for testing and demonstration.

Canadair management was considering a number of pricing options. Some executives advocated a very competitive initial price to hasten customer orders, with subsequent price increases. Another group of top executives believed that the Challenger should bear a premium price to reflect its superiority and to recover $140 million in development costs. The advertising agency's proposed copy for the Challenger's print advertisements was feared to be too controversial and the marketing group wondered whether some "softening" of the copy might be advisable. Selling direct to customers, selling direct to customers with a supplementary dealer network, or selling entirely through a dealer network

* This case was prepared by Mr. Larry Uniac, research assistant, under the direction of Professor Kenneth G. Hardy. Case material of the Western School of Business Administration is prepared as a basis for classroom discussion. Copyright © 1979, The University of Western Ontario.

were three possible approaches to sales. Finally, executives recognized that plans for service facilities required to maintain the Challenger "in the field," which could mean anywhere in the world, were very sketchy.

Canadair executives wanted 50 orders by September 30, 1976, before committing fully to the Challenger program. However, the major marketing decisions had to be finalized before the sales blitz could begin. If sales by September 30 fell in the range of 30 to 40 units, management might grant an extension on the deadline. However, sales of fewer than 30 units probably would result in scrapping the Challenger program.

General Background

Canadair's objective was to sell 410 units, or 40 percent of the market for large business jets over the period from 1978 to 1988. Business jets were changing the way companies conducted business, as executives learned the competitive advantages that a corporate aircraft could provide. What critics had once scorned as a "toy of executive privilege" was increasingly seen as a desirable and advantageous management tool. "Probably more than ever, most businessmen agree with Arco's vice chairman Louis F. Davis, that 'there's nothing like face-to-face communications to keep a business running.' "[1] One observer commented:

> As big as corporate flying has become in recent years, there are strong signs that its role will continue to expand rapidly in years to come. Of the largest 1,000 U.S. companies, only 502 operate their own airplanes versus 416 five years ago. That leaves a sizable virgin market, which sales people from a dozen U.S. and foreign aircraft builders are tripping over each other to develop.[2]

Competitors were skeptical that the Challenger could meet its promised specifications. The unloaded Challenger would weigh only 15,085 pounds compared to 30,719 for the Grumman Gulfstream II (GII), a head-on competitor that was the biggest corporate jet flying, yet still provide a wider cabin. The Challenger would be propelled by less powerful engines than the GII, yet theoretically would fly faster and consume only 50 percent as much fuel. "The Canadians seem to know something the rest of the industry doesn't," commented Ivan E. Speer, group vice president of Aerospace at Garret Corp., the major builder of corporate jet engines.[3] The Challenger was to be powered by Avco-Lycoming engines, a competitor to the Garret Corp.

More simply, it was not known how well the Challenger would fly. Although Canadair had made jets for the military, the company had never built a business jet. Beyond these concerns, production problems could arise with a project of this nature and magnitude, but little could be done to anticipate how and when these problems would occur.

---

[1] "Corporate Flying: Changing The Way Companies Do Business," *Business Week*, February 6, 1978, p. 64.

[2] Ibid., p. 62.

[3] Ibid., p. 64.

Company Background

Originating as the aircraft division of Canadian Vickers Ltd. in the 1920s, Canadair assumed its own identity in 1944 following a reorganization brought about by the Canadian government. In 1947, Canadair was acquired by Electric Boat Company of Groton, Connecticut, forming the basis for an organization that became General Dynamics Corp. in 1952. Canadair reverted to Canadian government ownership in January 1976 under a government plan for restructuring the Canadian aerospace industry. In 1975, *Interavia* magazine described Canadair as follows: "Once a flourishing company, Canadair is the 'sick man' of the national aerospace industry; employment has steadily dropped since 1970, when 8,400 were on the books, and could fall below 1,000 sometime this year unless new work is found rapidly."[4]

However, uneven employment was characteristic of the entire aircraft industry. In terms of deliveries, quality, innovation, and steady profits, Canadair had an enviable record. Located at Cartierville Airport in St. Laurent, Quebec, approximately 10 miles from the center of Montreal, the plant was one of the largest and most versatile aerospace-manufacturing facilities in Canada. Canadair's activities included the design and development of new aircraft, and contracting for major modifications to existing types of aircraft. Subcontracts for the manufactured component parts and subassemblies for military and commercial aircraft in production such as the Boeing 747 accounted for a substantial volume of the company's business (Table 1). Exhibit 1 supplies data on earnings for Canadair from 1973 to 1976. Canadair's President reflected on the activities of the company:

> We at Canadair are not really known as a major influence in the international aerospace industry. For various reasons, we have been a major subcontractor or producer of other people's aircraft over a large span of our existence, and our native designs have not been more than a small portion of our overall effort. You may imagine that the elder statesmen of the aerospace industry smiled indulgently when they heard about this radical new aircraft that Canadair was developing.

TABLE 1   Canadair's estimated sales from 1973 through 1976 by class of business

	1976		1975		1974		1973	
	Dollars (000)	Percent	Dollars (000)	Percent	Dollars (000)	Percent	Dollars (000)	Percent
Aircraft	20,410	46	15,520	42	38,808	68	22,006	63
Component subcontracts	7,783	17	6,716	18	2,945	5	2,967	9
Surveillance systems	9,367	21	6,958	19	9,620	17	8,542	25
Other	7,034	16	7,938	21	5,744	10	1,113	3
Total	44,954	100%	37,132	100%	57,117	100%	34,628	100%

[4] *Interavia*, February 1975, p. 150.

EXHIBIT 1

CANADAIR LIMITED AND SUBSIDIARIES
Consolidated Statement of Income
($000)

	Year Ended December 31			
	1976*	1975	1974	1973
Sales	$44,594	$37,132	$57,117	$34,628
Cost of sales	41,325	42,421	53,264	31,702
Income (loss) from operations	3,269	(5,289)	3,853	2,926
Other income (expense):				
Interest income	240	260	248	356
Miscellaneous income	9	30	61	71
Interest expense	(2,056)	(3,203)	(1,755)	(1,001)
	(1,807)	(2,913)	(1,446)	(574)
Income (loss) from operations before provision for income taxes, loss on discontinued operations of a subsidiary, extraordinary items and share of earnings of Asbestos Corporation Limited	1,462	(8,202)	2,407	2,352
Provisions for federal and provincial income taxes	642	6	1,122	1,056
Income (loss) before loss on discontinued operations of a subsidiary, extraordinary items and share of earnings of Asbestos Corporation Limited	820	(8,208)	1,285	1,296
Loss on discontinued operations of a subsidiary	(385)	(165)	(260)	(280)
Income (loss) before extraordinary items and share of earnings of Asbestos Corporation Limited	435	(8,373)	1,025	1,016
Extraordinary items:				
Income tax reduction	638	—	1,100	1,041
Gain on exchange	—	1,957	—	—
Provision for disposal of a subsidiary company's assets	(988)	—	—	—
Total extraordinary items	(350)	1,957	1,100	1,041
Income (loss) before share of earnings of Asbestos Corporation Limited	85	(6,416)	2,125	2,057
Share of earnings of Asbestos Corporation Limited	—	7,368	6,063	520
Net income	$ 85	$ 952	$ 8,188	$ 2,577

Consolidated Statement of Earned Surplus (deficit—$000)

	Year Ended December 31			
	1976*	1975	1974	1973
Balance at beginning of year	$(14,059)	$ 49,683	$41,495	$38,918
Net income	85	952	8,188	2,577
	(13,974)	50,635	49,683	41,495
Dividend paid	—	25,000	—	—
Unrecovered portion of investment in Asbestos Corporation Limited, representing the excess of carrying value over the amount paid by General Dynamics Corporation	—	39,694	—	—
	—	64,694	—	—
Balance at end of year	$(13,974)	$(14,059)	$49,683	$41,495

* Estimated results for 1976.

The Canadian Aerospace Industry[5]

The Canadian aerospace-manufacturing industry had specialized capabilities for the design, research and development, production, marketing, and in-plant repair and overhaul of aircraft aero-engines, aircraft and engine subsystems and components, space-related equipment and air and ground-based avionic systems and components.

Approximately 100 companies were engaged in significant manufacturing work, but 40 companies accounted for 90 percent of the industry's sales in 1975. Three companies (including Canadair) were fully integrated, having the capability to design, develop, manufacture, and market complete aircraft or aero-engines. With aggregate sales of $785 million in 1976, the Canadian aerospace industry shared fifth place in western world sales with Japan, after the United States, France, the United Kingdom, and the Federal Republic of Germany.

It was economically impractical for Canadian industry to manufacture all the diverse aerospace products demanded on the Canadian market. Through selective specialization, the Canadian industry had developed product lines in areas related to Canadian capabilities and export-market penetration. In 1975, 80 percent of the industry's sales were in export markets, an achievement attained under strong competitive conditions.

The Canadian industry was fully exposed to the competitive forces of the international aerospace market. In some cases, its hourly labour rates were higher than those in the United States. The industry's export-market penetration was vulnerable to the economic forces associated with competitors' industrial-productivity improvements. The industry, like most world aerospace industries, was manufacturing high-cost and high-risk products. There were many hazards: a relatively long-term payback cycle, sporadic government purchasing decisions, tariff and nontariff barriers, monetary inflation, and rapid technological obsolescence.

Aerospace industries throughout the world generally received government support, particularly in the areas of research, development, and equipment modernization. For example, the U.S. aircraft industry benefitted from the annual $10 billion Department of Defense budget and the annual $6 billion NASA budget. By contrast, during the nine years ended March 31, 1976, the Government of Canada had provided $349 million to the Canadian aerospace industry through several programs. In short, the Canadian aircraft industry was not subsidized.

There were indications in 1976 that the Canadian aerospace industry was entering a growth cycle. The trend lines of Canadian sales and exports encouraged an optimistic outlook.

---

[5] Source: Chairman D. C. Lowe, *A Report by the Sector Task Force on the Canadian Aerospace Industry*, June 30, 1978.

The Business Jet Industry

Continued expansion of business-aircraft activities was expected to continue into the 1980s in what business aviation officials described as the "best growth climate in years."[6] Booming sales of business aircraft in Europe, the Middle East, and Africa were giving rise to a belief that the business aircraft was becoming a true business tool in these regions, much as it had in the United States about a decade earlier.

All forecasts pointed to an enormous upsurge in the sale of business jet aircraft. Exhibit 2 graphs the trends in the U.S. business jet industry from 1956 to an estimate of 1976 and beyond. Exhibit 3 illustrates the trends in world deliveries of all corporate aircraft from 1965 to 1975, with delivery estimates through 1981. Many factors were contributing to increase the desire for private business aircraft:

> Commercial airlines were reducing service drastically as they added the "jumbo" jets. In six years, the number of U.S. cities served by commercial airlines dropped from 525 to 395.

EXHIBIT 2 Growth trends in U.S. business flying (semilog paper)

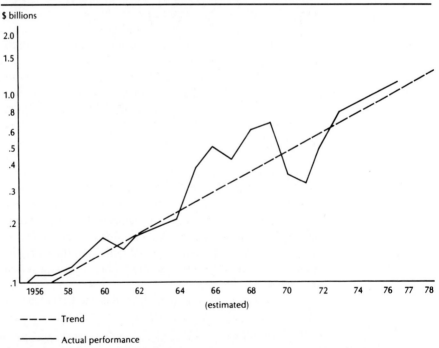

Source: *Aviation Week and Space Technology.*

---

[6] *Aviation Week and Space Technology*, September 11, 1978, pp. 46–56.

EXHIBIT 3 Unit worldwide corporate jet deliveries (all models)

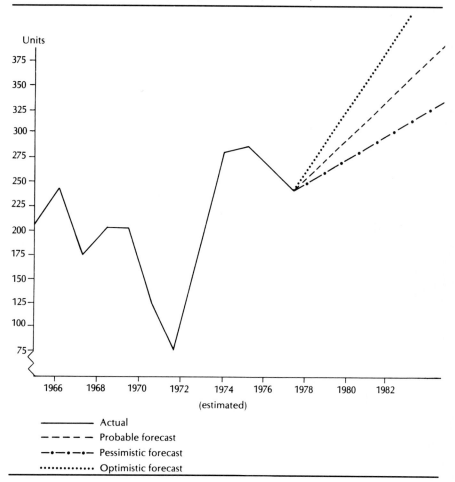

Units

Actual

Probable forecast

Pessimistic forecast

Optimistic forecast

Ninety-seven percent of all scheduled-air-carrier passengers in the United States flew out of only 150 airports.

Flights were packed with tourists and other occasional travelers. This made it difficult to obtain reservations and impossible to work en route. The amount of executive time spent traveling was increasing and most of this travel time was being wasted.

Corporate planes provided the management of many companies with new flexibility and shortened reaction time in special situations.

Cost savings could be achieved; for example, Xerox flew 15,000 employees per year on a company-owned shuttle plane between its Stamford headquarters and its Rochester (N.Y.) plant, saving $410,000 annually over commercial air fares.

There was growing concern for the security and protection of top executives from the growing incidence of airplane hijackings.

Finally many organizations were trading up to newer or larger aircraft to replace outdated, older equipment. Essentially, technology permitted such improvements over the aircraft of 10 years earlier (for example in fuel economy) that the buyers could easily justify the update.

To cash in on the business jet bonanza, several manufacturers were planning to introduce new models. The following business jets would be on the market in some fashion by 1979:

Canadair's Challenger (large category).

Dassault-Breguet Falcon 50 (medium category).

Grumman Gulfstream III (large category).

Rockwell's Sabreliner 80A (medium category).

Cessna's Citation III (medium category).

Gates Learjet's 54/55/56 series (medium category).

Corporate Aircraft Categories

More than 100 different aircraft models were offered to the business flyer.[7] Hence, the selection of the right aircraft for an individual company was a complex task. John Pope, Secretary of the National Business Aircraft Association, emphasized this advice: "Any aircraft selected involves a compromise, because the worst error you can make is buying more aircraft than you need and underutilizing it."[8] The general categories in order of performance and price were: single-engine piston, multiengine piston, turboprop, turbojet, and turbofan.

Single-engine piston aircraft, while not usually considered "corporate," did provide starting points for many smaller companies, as well as individuals who combined business and pleasure flying. . . . Multiengine piston aircraft were the next step up, offering the additional security and performance afforded by a second engine. . . . Piston-engine twins were considered excellent entry-level aircraft for smaller corporations, with a relatively high percentage owner-flown. . . . Turboprop aircraft were referred to by some as "turbojets with propellers attached." . . . Turboprops used significantly less fuel than pure jets but could easily cost more than $1 million.[9]

Turbojet and turbofan aircraft flew faster and, for the most part, farther than the other aircraft. A turbojet was not usually a first-time purchase for a smaller company. Prices in this category ranged from $1 million to $7.5

---

[7] "Corporate Aviation: The Competitive Edge," *Dun's Review,* January 1979, p. 89.
[8] Ibid.
[9] Ibid.

million. The turbofans offered greater low-altitude efficiency than the turbojets. The Challenger, JetStar II, Falcon 50, GII, and GIII were turbofans.

The following rules of thumb were often used to determine the suitability of different planes for different flying needs:

Average distance per flight	Appropriate type of aircraft for this distance
150– 200 miles	Single-engine piston
200– 500 miles	Multiengine piston and smaller turboprop
500– 750 miles	Turboprops and small turbojets
750–1,000 miles	Small turbojets
1,000–2,000 miles	Medium-size turbojets
2,000–4,000 miles	Large turbofans and large turbojets

Corporate Jet Competition

The Falcon 50, Gulfstream II and III, and JetStar II seemed to compete directly against the Challenger. Exhibit 4 summarizes sales by segment and model from 1965 to 1975. A schematic layout of each competitive plane is shown in Exhibits 5 and 6. Exhibit 7 compares the salient product differences for the Challenger and its competitors.

EXHIBIT 4 Worldwide corporate jet deliveries (units)

Model	1965	1966	1967	1968	1969	1970	1971	1972	1973	1974	1975	1976 prices (000s)
Small jet market												
Citation 1								52	81	85	69	$ 918
Falcon									1	21	26	1,905
Lear 23	80	18	1									—
Lear 24		24	26	28	33	20	10	16	21	22	18	—
Lear 25				18	25	18	10	23	45	40	14	1,315
Lear 35/36										4	47	1,679
Hansa			3	6	14	4	1	1	5			—
Sabre 40	26	31	5	5	1	6						—
Corvette										6	5	—
Westwind #1151/52/54	30	50	25	10	12	5	4	11	12	12	4	—
Total small jets	136	123	60	67	85	53	29	103	165	190	183	
Medium jet market												
Hawker Siddely 125	43	58	20	32	39	32	18	24	24	25	13	2,075
Sabre 60			11	20	14	6	9	4	4	20	9	2,200
Sabre 75								6	1	10	19	2,406
Falcon 20	14	43	63	38	25	18	7	24	46	17	29	3,005
Total medium jets	87	101	94	90	78	56	34	60	75	72	70	
Large jet market												
JetStar	18	22	18	18	11	2	4	10	6	1	0	5,035
Gulfstream			2	35	36	17	14	14	17	18	20	5,500
Total large jets	18	22	20	53	47	19	18	24	23	19	20	
Grand total	211	246	174	210	210	128	77	194	284	290	273	

EXHIBIT 5 Cabin floor outline

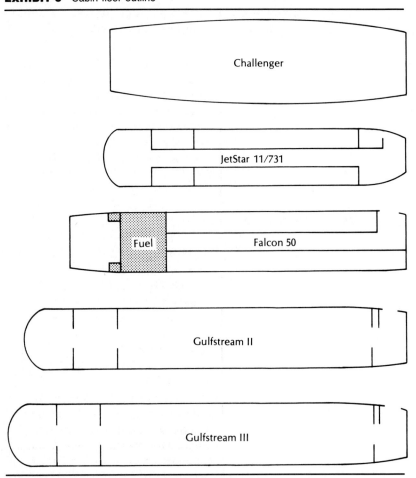

Challenger

JetStar 11/731

Fuel   Falcon 50

Gulfstream II

Gulfstream III

Note: Challenger data based on engineering statistical analysis. For performance guarantees see Technical Specification.

The new Dassault-Breguet Falcon 50, with its flight testing scheduled for completion by October 1978 and certification expected in December 1978, was slightly ahead of the Challenger program. The Challenger would probably not be certified until August 1979. Flight tests of the Falcon 50 had shown that its performance figures were better than expected in terms of landing strip required and rate of climb. The Falcon 50 was essentially a modification of the medium-sized Falcon 20, which had been introduced 14 years earlier.

The new Falcon 50 would be available for delivery by March 1979 and its performance in terms of projected operating cost per mile and range was second only to the Challenger. The print advertisement for the Falcon 50 claimed that it would be the fastest business jet in the world, although this statement was

EXHIBIT 6

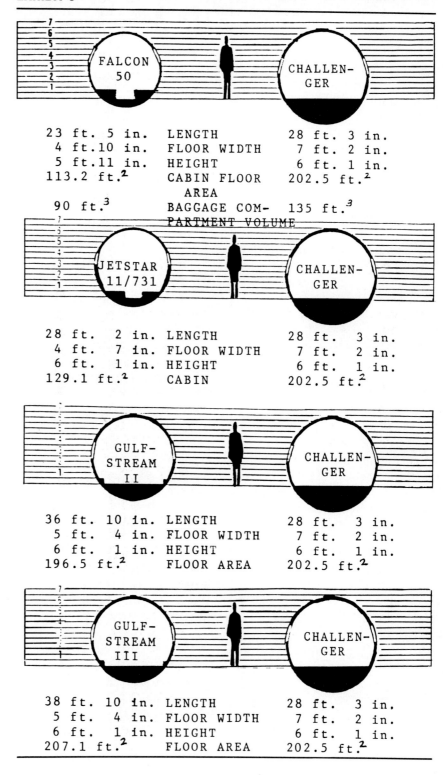

23 ft. 5 in.	LENGTH	28 ft. 3 in.
4 ft.10 in.	FLOOR WIDTH	7 ft. 2 in.
5 ft.11 in.	HEIGHT	6 ft. 1 in.
113.2 ft.^{2}	CABIN FLOOR AREA	202.5 ft.^{2}
90 ft.^{3}	BAGGAGE COM-PARTMENT VOLUME	135 ft.^{3}

28 ft. 2 in.	LENGTH	28 ft. 3 in.
4 ft. 7 in.	FLOOR WIDTH	7 ft. 2 in.
6 ft. 1 in.	HEIGHT	6 ft. 1 in.
129.1 ft.^{2}	CABIN	202.5 ft.^{2}

36 ft. 10 in.	LENGTH	28 ft. 3 in.
5 ft. 4 in.	FLOOR WIDTH	7 ft. 2 in.
6 ft. 1 in.	HEIGHT	6 ft. 1 in.
196.5 ft.^{2}	FLOOR AREA	202.5 ft.^{2}

38 ft. 10 in.	LENGTH	28 ft. 3 in.
5 ft. 4 in.	FLOOR WIDTH	7 ft. 2 in.
6 ft. 1 in.	HEIGHT	6 ft. 1 in.
207.1 ft.^{2}	FLOOR AREA	202.5 ft.^{2}

EXHIBIT 7 Comparative specifications

	Operating cost per nautical mile	Maximum range	Cruising speed	Fuel consumption 100 nm at cruise speed	Noise decibles* Take-off	Noise decibles* Sideline	Noise decibles* Approach
Challenger†	$ .93	3,900 nm.	547 mph	4,160 lb.	78	87	90
JetStar II	$1.25	2,800 nm.	538 mph	7,250 lb.	n.a.	n.a.	n.a.
Gulfstream III	$1.16	3,600 nm.	534 mph	6,410 lb.	90	102	98
Gulfstream II	$1.26	3,187 nm.	541 mph	7,723 lb.	90	102	98
Falcon 50	$1.06	3,550 nm.	528 mph	6,200 lb.	87	94	97

* 1979 FAA 36 Regulation = Take-off: 89, Sideline: 94, and Approach: 98.

† Initial proposal for first 50 units.

Source: Canadair comparative advertising material (based on statistical analysis).

disputed by the calculations made by Canadair engineers. Messrs. Halton and Taylor believed that the Falcon 50 would be around for some time, although its fuel consumption would be a major competitive disadvantage.

Gulfstream II and III

The Gulfstream II first flew in October 1966 and represented the latest technology at the time of its certification. Its turbojet engines were powerful, but consumed considerably more fuel than used in the more recent high-bypass turbofans used by the Challenger. In addition, engine noise was high both inside and outside the cabin. Since 1966, 173 Gulfstream IIs had been sold around the world.

Grumman had accelerated developmental work on a new Gulfstream III to replace the Gulfstream II in response to new demands on the market and the news of the Challenger. The Gulfstream III would be an aerodynamically modified version of the Gulfstream II, but it would use the same engines. The first prototype of the Gulfstream III was scheduled for completion in August 1979 and the first production unit was scheduled for delivery in March 1980. A print advertisement showing the Gulfstream III is shown in Exhibit 8.

JetStar II

The JetStar II, available since January 1976, was a re-engineered version of the original JetStar which had been certificated in 1961. Although the new engines of the JetStar were turbofans, they were medium-bypass fans and not as efficient as high-bypass fans in minimizing fuel consumption. More than 112 JetStars had been sold since 1961.

According to a company spokesman, Lockheed-Georgia anticipated no new changes to its JetStar II in order to meet forthcoming competition from the Challenger, Falcon 50, and Gulfstream III. Lockheed was still attempting to determine its market share in the larger-cabin business fleet, with the performance and acceptance of the three new aircraft still unknown. JetStar IIs were being built at the rate of one per month and the earliest promised delivery date was June 1978.[10]

The Challenger Program

Early in 1976, much of Canadair's subcontract work was nearing completion, and Canadair was not selling enough of its own CL-25 water bombers to fill the gap. Canadair executives needed an ambitious project if they were to meet government demands for eventual self-sufficiency. Mr. Halton commented:

> We knew that we needed to do something in the general-aviation business and a market-research study indicated that business aviation would be a growth market.

[10] *Aviation Week and Space Technology,* September 11, 1978.

EXHIBIT 8   Gulfstream III ad

The faster the Gulfstream III flies, the farther behind it leaves every other executive jet.

If you drive any kind of vehicle, you know that speed impacts how far it's going to travel. Automobiles or airplanes, the law is the same: the higher the speed, the shorter the range.

For example, the long range cruise speed of the Gulfstream III is Mach .77, or about 510 mph. At that speed, the Gulfstream III has an NBAA IFR range of 4,205 statute miles.

That's more than enough range for the Gulfstream III to fly non-stop routinely between London and New York in about 8 hours with at least 8 passengers and baggage. (No other executive jet can do that.)

Boost the cruise speed of the Gulfstream III to its maximum—Mach .85, or over 560 mph—and its NBAA IFR range becomes 3,226 statute miles with the same payload.

That's still enough range to fly at least 8 people at *top speed* from Boston to London or between any two airports in the continental United States in less than 6 hours. (No other executive jet can do that, either. The fact is, the Gulfstream III can fly more people farther faster than any executive jet.)

But we're not advocating speed. We're talking about *productivity.*

The Gulfstream III offers such unique flexibility in trade-offs between speed, range and payload that it can fly virtually any kind of mission—and do it with optimum productivity.

At a time when the world's businesses are placing increased emphasis on maximizing every investment, it is little wonder that the thoroughly proven Gulfstream III continues to dominate the market for long-range executive transports.

If you are planning for the acquisition of an aircraft that can help make your organization more effective and productive, now is the time to look into the Gulfstream III.

A full-scale demonstration of this remarkable airplane on one of your upcoming business trips at home or abroad could shape your thinking about business jets for years to come.

The man to talk to is Charles G. Vogeley, Senior Vice President of Gulfstream Marketing. Call him at (912) 964-3274; or write to him at Gulfstream American Corporation, P.O. Box 2206, Savannah, Georgia 31402 U.S.A.

He can show you why the Gulfstream III continues to leave its challengers farther and farther behind.

The Gulfstream III. The Ultimate.

Gulfstream American
Member GAMA

In November 1975, Fred Kearns talked with Bill Lear about his concept of an advanced business aircraft based on two known pieces of technology, the supercritical wing used on military aircraft and the high-bypass fanjet engine. In January 1976, I met with Bill Lear and by March 1976 we were negotiating options on the Lear design. Jim Taylor was hired in April 1976 to head up the marketing for the new aircraft and by May he had arranged a selling seminar to which he invited 200 chief pilots and senior corporate officers to Canadair's plant to unveil the Challenger concept.

Bill Lear, who built the first business jet in 1961, had developed the original concept of the Challenger around an 88-inch diameter fuselage. Representatives of the business market for the jet responded to the design encouragingly. However, Canadair decided to change the rear design drastically for a number of reasons, one of them a fuel-tankage problem. Also, at the original meeting with 200 chief pilots and executive officers, potential customers expressed demands for roominess. Consequently, Canadair engineers redesigned the jet with a 106-inch fuselage. As it happened, the extra width made the plane capable of seating four abreast. Lear disassociated himself from the Challenger program in response to this change and dubbed the Canadair design "Fat Albert." Canadair executives recognized the possibility of creating a "stretch" version of the Challenger that perhaps could carry up to 50 passengers.

It was clear at the beginning of 1976 that in order to finance the project, at least $70 million would have to be raised in addition to the company's own $70 million. Projects with this degree of leverage were not uncommon in the aerospace industry and the Canadian government agreed to *guarantee* a $70-million Eurobond for Canadair. A forecast schedule of investment outlays is shown in Exhibit 9.

The Challenger's most salient product benefits as conceived by Canadair's marketing and engineering staff were:

Large wide-body cabin: excellent size for executive, air taxi, third-level carriers, and cargo.

Fuel economy: lowest operating cost per nautical mile compared with direct competition.

Long range: long single-stage flight or numerous short-stage flights without refueling.

Competitive speeds: very competitive, high cruise speed in long-range configuration.

Low noise levels: most closely meets FAA standards for 1979.

Market forecast

Canadair was already building a test model for fatigue tests, a test model for static tests, and three preproduction models for the eventual production plan which would be as follows:

EXHIBIT 9

CL 600 CHALLENGER

Pro Forma* Cash Flow Profile as of June 1976
($000)

	Sept. 76–Dec. 79 not assignable	Dec. 77–Oct. 80 lot #1 aircraft 1–50	Apr. 79–Aug. 81 lot #2 aircraft 51–100	Feb. 80–Apr. 82 lot #3 aircraft 101–150	Oct. 80–Jan. 83 lot #4 aircraft 151–200	Jul. 81–Dec. 83 lot #5 aircraft 200–250	Total
Labor, overhead cost	$ 86,400	$ 72,460	$ 28,350	$ 26,350	$ 24,980	$ 25,315	$ 264,855
Material, equipment cost	20,925	81,148	94,970	107,450	113,045	126,100	543,638
Other costs (rentals, service)	21,600	17,550	925	713	760	750	42,298
Program support cost	6,075	18,936	10,440	11,100	12,784	14,475	73,810
Marketing		5,030	2,744	2,938	3,390	3,836	17,938
Finance		31,326	10,700				42,026
Total cost	$135,000	$226,450	$149,129	$148,551	$154,959	$170,476	$ 984,565
Revenue		$205,000	$225,500	$238,500	$253,000	$268,000	$1,190,000
Cumulative	$(135,000)	$(156,450)	$(80,079)	$ 9,870	$107,911	$205,435	$ 205,435
Date #1 aircraft ordered		Jul. 76					
Anticipated date last aircraft ordered		Nov. 76	Apr. 78	Oct. 79	Apr. 81	Oct. 82	
Delivery date #1 aircraft		Nov. 79					
Anticipated date last aircraft delivered		Sept. 80	Aug. 81	June 82	May 83	Apr. 84	
Assumed average price per aircraft		4,100	$4,510	$4,770	$5,060	$5,360	$4,750

* These data are presented for case study purposes only and do not purport to represent actual estimating data.

1979— 6 units
1980—50 units
1981—80 units

The first test unit was expected to fly by April 1978 and the preproduction models were to be available for delivery by the end of 1979. This production plan was adopted in response to an analysis of the market trends for this category. Table 2 traces the market history of jet sales in the medium and large categories.

TABLE 2 Market history (units): Sales of medium and large size jets (Gulfstream II, JetStar, Falcon 20, HS 125)

1966:	123	1971:	43
1967:	103	1972:	72
1968:	123	1973:	93
1969:	111	1974:	62
1970:	69	1975:	51

10-year total: 850 units

The United States was the major market for corporate aircraft. Table 3 summarizes the geographic distribution of corporate-aircraft sales during 1966–1975:

TABLE 3 Distribution of sales, 1966–1975 (all corporate planes)

	Units	Percent
North America	565	66.5
Europe	189	22.2
Central and South America	25	2.9
Asia	24	2.8
Africa	37	4.4
Oceania	10	1.2
	850	100.0

On the basis of this history, Canadair's marketing staff first calculated pessimistic, probable, and optimistic worldwide sales forecasts for the medium and large jet category from 1978 to 1988, judged to be the Challenger's sales life (Table 4).

Canadair executives then narrowed this down to a forecast for Challenger sales only (Table 5).

TABLE 4 Worldwide business-jet sales forecast, 1978–1988
(Challenger category, executive configuration only)

	Pessimistic	Probable	Optimistic
North America	600	625	675
Europe	200	225	275
Central and South America	25	40	65
Asia	25	40	65
Africa	50	75	95
Oceania	10	15	20
	910	1,020	1,195

TABLE 5 Challenger sales forecast, 1978–1988 (executive
configuration only)

	Pessimistic	Probable	Optimistic
North America	150	250	300
Europe	55	80	105
Central and South America	15	20	25
Asia	15	25	35
Africa	20	30	50
Oceania	5	5	10
	260	410	525

The most-probable-sales estimate for this period represented a 40 percent share of the probable world market during 1978–88. In the midterm, Canadair executives could consider a stretched version of the Challenger for the commuter and freight market. Adding this version would raise the probable forecast to 560 units, the pessimistic to 333, and optimistic to 750 units. The average variable cost per unit for the first two hundred units was projected to be $4.1 million per jet but variable costs per unit were expected to show some improvement because of the experience curve effect after the first 200 jets. Exhibit 9 shows a pro forma cash flow for the first 250 Challengers that might be produced. No cost or investment data had been generated on the stretched Challenger model.

Pricing

The marketing staff had prepared several pricing options for the Challenger. It was necessary to finalize pricing for the first 50 orders and work out a *general* pricing plan for the rest of the projected sales. Exhibit 10 contains data on the existing competitive prices and the marketing staff's best estimate of future pricing moves by the competition.

One pricing option for the first 50 orders was to undercut the competition by $1.2 million, setting the price at $4.1 million per Challenger. To some executives, a $1.2 million discount seemed large for such a superior product, even though the Challenger had flown only ''on paper.'' They pointed out that all

EXHIBIT 10 Expected pricing movement in the large-jet market ($000)

	1976 current price*	Expected BCA price†								
		1977	1978	1979	1980	1981	1982	1983	1984
Challenger‡	$4,100								
JetStar II	5,345	$5,195	$5,611	$6,057	$6,544	$7,068	$7,633	$8,244	$8,900
Gulfstream III	6,200	?	—	—	—	—	—	—	—
Gulfstream II	5,500	5,900	6,354	6,844	7,371	7,938	8,549	9,208	9,910
Falcon 50	5,750	5,750	5,750	5,750	6,153	6,583	7,044	7,537	8,060

* Average BCA equipped prices.
† Smith and Taylor were less certain of pricing activity after 1980.
‡ Initial proposal for first 50 units.
Source: Company records.

new aircraft faced this issue of confidence and that most buyers understood the process of designing an all-new aircraft and the process of gearing up a volume production system. Because the breakeven volume under the low-price option was larger than the probable-sales forecast, the price was expected to rise after the first 50 orders.

Alternatively, the Challenger could be priced at parity with the competition. In this case, the price would probably increase in step with inflation and the pricing of competitive products.

Some executives suggested that the Challenger's superior product characteristics required a premium price even in the short run. They believed that the Challenger could maintain a premium over competitive prices in the long run.

The purchase price for each Challenger would include training for captains, maintenance training for mechanics, programmed maintenance assistance from Montreal, and service and support from any of the three planned service facilities. Bill Lear, who had done the initial Challenger design, would receive 5 percent of the *sale* price of the first 50 units sold, 4 percent on the second 50, and 3 percent on all orders beyond the first hundred.

The following terms of purchase were proposed:

1. Each customer would be required to make a 5 percent deposit for each plane ordered. All deposits would be placed in escrow with accrued interest at the Canadian prime rate (10 percent in 1976).
2. One year before delivery, the customer would pay 30 percent of the purchase price.
3. Six months before delivery, the customer would pay 30 percent again.
4. The customer would pay the final 35 percent of the purchase price upon delivery.

Service

After-sale service was an important purchase criterion for the customer. Canadair executives tentatively had decided to build three factory-owned service centres which would service only Challengers. Their cost, $4.5 million each, was included in the planned $140 million investment. One centre would be located in Hartford, Connecticut, where Canadair's U.S. sales office was located, one in the southwestern United States, and one in Europe. The selection of these locations was based on the projection that these areas would provide the majority of Challenger sales. Only technical personnel would operate from these facilities.

The service facilities would have to be completed in time to service the first jets as they were sold at the end of 1979. Canadair would have to service early Challenger buyers very well to enhance its credibility and improve sales prospects. There was some concern at Canadair about whether factory-owned centres were the best way to provide service. Some corporate jet manufacturers such as Gulfstream and Hawker-Siddely utilized service distributors. Hence, the 200 Hawker-Siddely 125s in the United States were serviced by a distributor network of 14 outlets. This method of servicing, if chosen by Canadair, would eliminate the $4.5 million investment in each service facility, but because the Challenger was technically more advanced than its competition, special in-house expertise might offer certain advantages and would not require handing over technical information to distributors who serviced competitive aircraft.

Advertising and Promotion

The advertising and promotion budget for the Challenger program in 1976 was set at about $2.5 million. Because the Challenger was a new and unproven airplane, the marketing staff and its advertising agency had decided to mount a print advertising campaign in the leading technical and business magazines to support the sales force's personal selling activities. Domestic and international advertising campaigns were planned for journals such as *Professional Pilot, Business Week, Business and Commercial Aviation, Interavia,* and *The Wall Street Journal.* All of the Challenger's competitors advertised in these journals, trying to reach the executive in charge of purchasing a business jet and the pilot who would be flying the jet.

To achieve high readability scores for their advertising, Canadair executives were prepared to use a bold, confident, and "challenging" theme. Examples of the proposed advertisements are shown as Exhibits 11, 12 and 13. This copy differed markedly from what the competition typically employed. Of the total advertising and promotion budget, $625,000 was to be allocated to print advertising.

Studying the competition's advertising copy, Mr. Taylor sensed that the competition had already begun to react to the Challenger program. This was particularly evident in the Gulfstream II and JetStar II advertisements. Still, the Canadair marketing group was worried that its own bold campaign could backfire and damage the credibility of the Challenger by taking pot shots at the competition, especially when the Challenger had no flight tests to back it up. If

EXHIBIT 11

This business jet design is so advanced, it's making the competition airsick.

Enter the Canadair Challenger. Not just another business jet, but the first new concept in business jets in about 20 years.

And we're not just saying that with empty words.

We're sending forth this solid challenge:

We challenge any business jet to fly as fast.
We challenge any business jet to offer as much range.
We challenge any business jet to fly as efficiently.
We challenge any business jet to match our wide-body comfort.

And now, we'd like to plunge into some specifics, demonstrating why our competition is feeling a bit queasy at the moment.

The Challenger challenges the JetStar II.

The Challenger is really much more of a star than the JetStar II. It will carry 17% less fuel, yet travel 1,400 statute miles further.

The Challenger will be faster, quieter, 40% less expensive to operate. As well as a sprawling 25 inches wider.

The Challenger challenges the Falcon 50.

Compared to the Challenger, the Falcon 50 is a bird of a different feather. The Challenger will fly up to 35 mph faster (New York to Los Angeles in 5 hours and 11 minutes).

The Challenger will also fly 1,000 miles further, be quieter, and burn 20% less fuel while doing so. And as for the inside story, the Challenger will have 42% more cabin volume than the Falcon 50, and 76% more baggage space.

The Challenger challenges the Gulfstream II.

The Challenger will carry 40% less fuel, yet travel 900 miles further.

The Challenger will be about ⅓ less expensive to operate.

And the Challenger will be easy to take in still another way. Noise. We'll be significantly quieter than the Gulfstream II. And because we'll be 10 inches wider, we'll even challenge their cabin for passenger comfort and room.

How we're meeting the challenge.

We're meeting the challenge of the Challenger by discarding the hand-me-down technology that the competition uses.

Our business jet will incorporate the most sophisticated and proven technology currently available.

That includes the Lycoming ALF-502 turbofan with a 5 to 1 high bypass ratio. Its power will provide us with the best thrust-to-weight relationship of any commercially obtainable plane.

We also bring you a new wing. An advanced, yet proven, airfoil concept that will delay the formation of shock waves.

So prepare yourself for this shock: we'll not be just faster than any business jet, we'll be faster than a DC-10.

The company that's behind all this is Canadair, makers of over 3,800 aircraft, 580 supersonic.

For more information on the Challenger, formerly known by the drawing board name LearStar, write to Jim Taylor at Canadair Inc., Dept. T, 274 Riverside Avenue, Westport, Conn. 06880. Or call him at (203) 226-1581.

You'll become convinced that the Challenger, the business jet that's making the competition airsick, can be a very healthy investment for your company.

canadair Challenger

We challenge any business jet to match it.

*All performance figures in this advertisement for CHALLENGER are based upon wind tunnel tests and engineering statistical analysis with flight testing to begin in early 1978.

EXHIBIT 12

Our competition wastes a lot of energy. And they'll be wasting a lot more when they try to explain these figures.

On a 1,000 nautical mile trip, the CHALLENGER will burn:

- **36% less fuel than a JetStar II.**
- **45% less fuel than a Gulfstream II.**
- **20% less fuel than a Falcon 50.**
- **11% less fuel than a Falcon 20F.**

These are the numbers that add up to trouble for the competition.

The numbers that prove the Challenger will be the business jet that not only outperforms all the rest, but outconserves all the rest of the full-cabin business jets.

The environment will save. You will save. And with fuel costs taking off even faster than a Challenger, we don't have to tell you what the savings will be.

Our economy isn't a con.

The same engine that will let us go so fast (Montreal to London in 5 hours, 29 minutes) is also what will use up our fuel so slowly. It's the Lycoming ALF-502 turbofan with a 5 to 1 high bypass ratio. This design means exceptional fuel efficiency.

So does our new wing. An advanced configuration that will delay the formation of shock waves. So drag, which is such a drag, won't drag as much. And lift will be lifted. So the Challenger will fly faster, further, and more economically than any other business jet.*

Our economy will also apply to maintenance. The Challenger's engine is fully modular for on-airframe servicing. Meaning our engine is a snap to fix. You won't be paying $1,000 for labor to replace a $50 part.

Tomorrow's plane without yesterday's technology.

Scratch the twenty-year-old technology the competition embraces. The Challenger is being built from scratch.

Incorporating all the latest proven aspects of both design and technology.

Even our cabin is a big idea. The Challenger will be the first wide-body business jet. Almost a full foot wider than any other, and two spacious feet wider than most.

Now who's behind all this, you ask? Canadair. Canadair has built over 3,800 aircraft, 580 supersonic.

There's much more detailed information on the Challenger, formerly known by the drawing board name LearStar, and Jim Taylor has it. Write to him at Canadair, Dept. T, P.O. Box 6087, Montreal, Canada H3C3G9. Or call him at (514) 744-1511.

He'll spend all the time you need talking about the plane that will expend so little energy.

canadair challenger
We challenge any business jet to match it.

*All performance figures in this advertisement for CHALLENGER are based upon wind tunnel tests and engineering statistical analysis with flight testing to begin in early 1978.

EXHIBIT 13

Finally, the first new concept in business jets in twenty years. The Canadair Challenger. We hereby challenge any business jet to match it.

The Canadair Challenger is the class business jet that's in a class by itself.

Respectfully dismissing twenty-year-old technology, it's being built from scratch.

In fact, the engineering of this aircraft is so brilliantly eclectic that it lets us hurl forth the Canadair Challenger Challenge.

We challenge any business jet to fly as fast.*

We challenge them to offer as much range.*

We challenge them to fly as efficiently.

We challenge them to match our wide-body comfort.

And now we'd like to tell you just how we've engineered the best business jet yet.

We bring you a new wing.

Our newly designed wing is why the Challenger will outperform all the rest. This advanced configuration delays shock waves. So drag, which is such a drag, doesn't drag as much. And lift is lifted. What's more, the wing weighs less. The result:

The Challenger can fly from Montreal to London in 5 hours and 29 minutes. Faster than a 747!

*Guaranteed speed and range.

Room to move while you're moving.

Stretch your legs and stoop no more —the Challenger is the first wide-body business jet. Almost a full foot wider than all the rest. With six feet of head-room and a flat floor.

The Lycoming ALF. It's the best engine going.

The Challenger's engine is the Lycoming ALF 502 Turbofan with a 5 to 1 high bypass ratio. (These fans make the Challenger efficient.) On a 1,000 nautical-mile trip it will burn 54% less fuel than the JetStar I and 20% less than the Falcon 50.

After you take off, we don't take off.

Our service and support is as disciplined as our engineering. There'll be

Company Owned and Operated Service Centers. There'll be other Authorized Service Stations. And a year of computerized maintenance comes free.

But let us not forget the company that's behind all this. Canadair. Canadair has built over 3,800 aircraft, 580 of them supersonic.

For more information on the Challenger, formerly known by the drawing board name LearStar, write to Jim Taylor at Canadair Inc., P.O. Box 6087, Montreal, Canada H3C3G9. Or call him at (514) 744-1511.

canadair Challenger

We challenge any business jet to match it.

COPYRIGHT CANADAIR

their theme proved inappropriate, they could quickly develop other themes and advertisements. In any case, the advertising agency would be paid 10 percent of the expenditures for media space.

To reinforce the print advertising campaign, brochures and other sales literature were printed. An active direct mailing program could be used to solicit inquiries from potential prospects. The Challenger would also be promoted through press releases and press conferences, pilot seminars, photography, and newsletters, so that magazine articles would chronicle the progress of the Challenger engineering and marketing activities.

All competitors generally used this kind of promotion, but with varying degrees of intensity and success. The Falcon 50 marketers had used comparative advertising but had made no mention of the Challenger in their advertising. Canadair executives believed this obvious exclusion was an attempt by the Falcon 50 people to present the Challenger as unworthy of consideration. The JetStar II and Gulfstream II advertising did not use comparative approaches.

Exhibit 14 contains rate and reach data for full-page advertisements (the typical size in the large-jet business) in publications typically used by corporate-airplane advertisers. Media space could be purchased as early as the third week in July.

The Selling Task

President Kearns described the selling process this way:

> Each sale *is* different. It isn't like going to the military with a proposal and finding that you have just won a competition and the armed forces are going to buy 225 of your airplanes in the very first contract. It isn't like going to the airlines and selling batches of 10 or a dozen transports at once, all to the same specifications, with the same number of seats and the same colours inside and on the tail! It is, in fact, a matter of doing a complete presentation and proposal for every single prospect you approach. We start out with a prospect list made up of present business-aircraft operators plus other major corporations throughout the world who do not yet operate any aircraft. These organizations often have the need but we in the industry have yet to prove it to them. We gather data on the companies. We get an idea of their current needs by talking to their pilots, or we make some estimates if they have never operated an aircraft.
>
> We study the trips their people make, the points they routinely travel between, the longest and shortest flights, how many go on each trip, etc. Gradually a picture emerges to show us each prospect's specific requirement. And armed with that study, we approach the prospects with our sales proposals.

The first pitch was usually made to a firm's pilot. He generally had only veto power and not purchase power, but his acceptance was crucial. The salesman had to determine how much he would be able to use the pilot to make the sale. Mr. Taylor described three possibilities:

EXHIBIT 14 Print advertising rate data[1]

Publication	Edition	Circulation (000s)	Distribution	Full page (1 time)	Half page	Frequency discount 7 times	13 times
The Wall Street Journal	Eastern	606	Daily	$14,101	$ 7,050		
	Midwest	458		11,366	5,683		
	West	289		7,958	3,534		
	Southwest	168		4,049	2,024		
	North America	1500		36,265	18,132		
Business Week	International	59	Weekly	$ 2,450			
	European	31		1,710			
	Northeast	218		6,180			
	Midwest	182		5,120		10%	5%
	Pacific Coast	131		3,640			
	Southwest	51		1,480			
	Southeast	66		1,900			
	North America	738		9,000			
Fortune	North America	600	Biweekly	$13,710			
	Eastern	201		7,000		8%	4%
	Midwestern	159		5,130			
	Southeastern	60		2,610			
	Southwestern	48		2,210			
	Western	115		3,820			
	International	70		4,020			
	European	46		3,070			
Forbes	North America	665	Monthly	$10,990		7%	4%

Publication	Edition	Circulation (000s)	Distribution	Full page (1 time)	Frequency discount 3 times	5 times	7 times	13 times
Dun's Review	Eastern	90	Monthly	$3,405				
	Central	86		2,665	7%	6%	5%	
	Southern	32		1,515				
	Western	40		1,160				
	All	248		5,405				
Aviation Week and Space Technology	All North America	97	Weekly	$4,343	2.5%	1.8%		4%
Business and Commercial Aviation	All North America	50	Monthly	$2,850		11%		6%
Flight International*	All	47	Weekly	$1,670		6%		6%
Interavia*	All	3	Monthly	$ 390	14%	22%		

Notes: * International circulation.

[1] All rates are for black-and-white ads and are noncontract rates.

Source: Standard Rate and Data Service.

1. The pilot is strongly in your favour. He would act like an in-house salesman for you.
2. The pilot is unsure. The first task is to move him to neutral and then improve his and management's attitudes.
3. The pilot is against the product right off, clearly the least-preferred situation. The first task here is to cool him off and try to get to the chief
   executive officer and sell him first.

The salesman had to be very perceptive in assessing to what degree the
influencers on the selling decision would be involved, and finding out who exactly would make the final decision.

Prospects were identified with the assistance of a *Business and Commercial Aviation*[11] study that measured the impact of company aircraft in the U.S.
top 1000 industrials as compiled by *Fortune* magazine.

This summary of the business performance of the Fortune 1000 industrials
showed that the aircraft operators, for whatever reason, were more efficient.
The 514 aircraft-operating companies controlled 1,778 aircraft in 1975, an increase of 125 over 1974. This study concluded that:

> . . . nearly one half of the nation's biggest corporations are not operators even
> though their dollar volume of business indicates a cash flow that would support
> capital equipment such as an aircraft. In some cases, the nature of a firm's activi-
> ties precludes the need for travel to locations not well served by public transporta-
> tion; for others, the scheduling flexibility and effective utilization of personnel
> afforded by business aviation is not a strong incentive in the firm's type of
> business endeavors. But there are many corporations, we suspect, where the
> concept of business aircraft still is not appreciated or fully understood, and it is in
> this area that a greater knowledge of corporate aviation is needed.[12]

Hence, part of the selling task involved giving a potential customer an education
in the advantages of corporate-owned aircraft in general before making a pitch
for a particular model.

Another study identified companies owning the most expensive and largest fleets in the United States (Table 6).

TABLE 6 The most expensive corporate fleets

Company	Number of airplanes	Fleet value ($ millions)
Coca-Cola	5	$17.2
3M Co.	7	16.2
Rockwell International	21	15.6
Mobil	28	14.4
IBM	9	13.2

[11] Arnold Lewis, "Business Aviation and the Fortune 1,000," *Business and Commercial
Aviation*, December 1978, pp. 1–4.

[12] Ibid.

TABLE 6 *(concluded)*

Company	Number of airplanes	Fleet value ($ millions)
Atlantic Richfield	20	13.0
General Motors	14	12.8
United Technologies	14	12.3
Exxon	16	11.3
Tenneco	26	11.1
ITT	13	10.9
Shell	24	9.7
Diamond Shamrock	3	9.0
Gannett	4	8.9
General Dynamics	5	8.8
U.S. Steel	4	8.8
Conoco	19	8.7
Texaco	8	8.3
Time	9	8.2
Johnson & Johnson	7	8.1
Marathon Oil	14	8.0

Data: Aviation Data Service Inc.

The People behind the Selling Task

Mr. James Taylor, 55, had been hired by Canadair in April 1976 to market the Challenger concept to the corporate market. Mr. Taylor's fascination with aircraft went back many years. His father had been a test pilot in both World War I and World War II. James Taylor had scored successes for the Cessna Aircraft Corp. and the French-based Dassault-Brequet Aircraft Corp. When Mr. Taylor joined Dassault in 1966, the "Fan Jet Falcon 20" soon became the industry sales leader in terms of both units and dollars. In 1966, Lear had sold 33 jets worldwide through 200 dealers, but in 1967, Mr. Taylor and his four salesmen sold 45 Falcon 20s in North America without the assistance of any dealers. Mr. Taylor believed in direct sales rather than a dealer network because, as he put it: "It is a narrowly defined market. When I sell direct, I have better control over hiring, training, the territory, and the price. I like to bring prospects in for seminars, take a mock-up to key cities, and make extensive use of direct mail."

Joining Cessna in March 1969, he became the architect behind the highly successful "Citation" marketing and product-support programs which transformed the aircraft into the world's most successful business jet in its initial four years of production.

Mr. Taylor brought three key people with him to Canadair. Mr. Bill Juvonen had been with Mr. Taylor on three previous marketing programs including the Falcon 20 and the Citation. He became the vice president of sales responsible for Canada and the United States west of the Mississippi. Mr. Dave Hurley had spent five years with Cessna and had worked with Mr. Taylor on two programs. He became the vice president of sales responsible for the eastern half of the United States. Barry Smith had been the director of corporate marketing services for Atlantic Aviation, a company that serviced and distributed such corporate jets as the Gulfstream II, the Hawker-Siddely 125 and the Westwind. He had later worked for James Taylor in the same capacity on the successful Cessna Citation program. Mr. Taylor immediately hired him as vice president, marketing services. Mr. Smith would be responsible for advertising, direct mail, and all the "inside" marketing services. These four men made up the marketing team that would have to sell 50 Challengers before September 30th, 1976.

Final Question

The Challenger's design was undergoing constant modification. Mr. Taylor described the chief engineer, Mr. Halton, as "the most open-minded engineer I've ever met. For example, one of our customers suggested an APU (auxiliary power unit) system to assure power to the cabin electricals in flight. Harry designed in the APU system. Similarly, traditional aircraft use DC electricals but there are customer advantages in using AC. Harry put in AC. When Harry cannot accommodate one of our design suggestions, he always has good reasons and he takes the time to tell us. Normally, a chief pilot would not want you talking to his boss, but with the Challenger, some pilots not only are talking to their bosses, they are relaying information to us and to them." However, it was time to finalize the design and move ahead on a production system that would produce 80 aircraft per year.

Although Mr. Taylor had been very successful using a direct sales approach, other companies made extensive use of dealer networks, particularly in foreign countries. The "five percenters" (agents) in foreign countries also raised the issue of controlling their selling practices, especially in countries where mordida[13] was almost a standard practice.

The pricing strategy and promotion strategy would have to provide fairly rapid market penetration. Advertising and service expenditures already comprised $16 million of the investment budget; changes in these expenditures would have to promise compensating paybacks. There had to be a high probability that the proposed marketing plan would deliver the sales forecast for the Challenger. Mr. Taylor smiled and commented wryly to his aides: "This is going to have to be the biggest selling job in history. I think we can count on working 6 days a week, 14 hours a day, from now until September 30."

Two manufacturers were rumoured to be looking at the Challenger statistics to see how best to compete with this wide-body turbofan. Messrs. Taylor, Halton, and Kearns sat down on the morning of July 4, 1976, to review the Challenger strategy for the next three months and the longer term.

---

[13] Mordida represents payments to government officials in return for favors.

Case 45

Quaker State*

OIL CITY, PA   In the ultracompetitive motor-oil market, cutthroat discounting has become a way of life. So when Quaker State decided a year ago to stop slashing prices and emphasize quality, it was a big gamble.

The early results are in, and they aren't pretty. The company's nine-month revenue fell 9 percent, and fourth-quarter earnings are expected to show a big decline from a year earlier. The stock isn't far from its 52-week low. Wall Street is disenchanted.

The Wall Street Journal, Heard on the Street column, January 8, 1990

It has been three years since the devastating loss of 1987, and the Quaker State marketing strategy has been reworked again and again. With greater competition and new entrants, it appears Quaker State's future for the 1990s is in jeopardy. The relatively small independent oil company in Oil City has been repeatedly rumored as a takeover candidate. Management at Quaker State realize they need to regain past levels of profitability and market share to maintain their independence. There is no more room to gamble with the company's future and lose. The marketing strategy for the next year, 1991, and subsequent years, needs to identify and meet consumer needs.

The Passenger-Car Motor-Oil Market

The passenger-car motor-oil (PCMO) market can be characterized as a very competitive mature market with very little growth. Subsequently, the market is very price sensitive, and new product developments are closely watched by all competitors. The market is made up of the motor-oil specialist companies who produce and market strictly motor oil and the gasoline companies who primarily market gasoline. Traditionally, the motor-oil specialists have been the market share leaders based on their distribution networks and their product innovation.

---

* This case was written by Craig F. Ehrnst under the supervision of Thomas C. Kinnear. The authors wish to thank the people at Quaker State without whose assistance this case would not have been possible. Copyright © 1990 by Thomas C. Kinnear.

However, during recent years the gasoline companies have increased their efforts to capture market share through mass merchandisers and other distribution channels formerly dominated by the motor-oil specialists.

Influenced by the automotive manufacturers, motor-oil quality has been increased to meet the performance needs of engines built in recent years. The higher quality standards have required increased research among motor-oil industry producers. These standards have been met with new additive packages to further prevent rust, corrosion, and sludge buildup. Most motor oil producers reformulated their products to meet the new industry standards during the mid-1980s. However, due to the nature of the competitive market, the full costs associated with the new additive packages have not been passed on to consumers. The reformulated products offered to consumers provide a higher-quality product to consumers and a lower margin for producers.

After reformulating their products, motor-oil producers took very aggressive positions to reintroduce their products. Advertising expenditures have essentially doubled, from estimates of $50 million in 1984 to well over $100 million in 1988 (see Exhibit 1). Promotional expenditures have also increased at a similar rate. The heavy advertising and promotional expenditures have been

EXHIBIT 1   Advertising and promotion expenditures

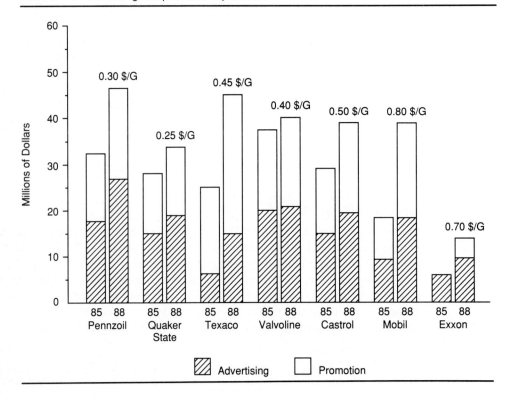

led by the motor-oil specialists. Their dependence on brand awareness is essential to pull their products through the distribution chain of mass merchandisers and auto parts stores.

Motor Oil Classifications

The consumer is quality conscious but is probably unaware of measures to distinguish real quality from perceived quality motor oil. Fortunately, classification systems have been developed to measure motor-oil viscosity and engine service requirements (see Appendix A). First, the motor-oil viscosity standards, developed by the Society of Automotive Engineers (SAE), provides a guide for users to select motor oil according to the climate conditions of their automobiles. For example, a multigrade motor oil 5W–30 would perform better in subzero temperatures than a multigrade motor oil grade of 10W–30. Next, the engine service classification system, developed by motor-oil industry specialists, defines characteristics of a motor oil to help the consumer with the selection of appropriate products. Motor oil manufacturers label their product with a letter classification system according to recommended engine service requirements. For example, the motor oil with the letter designation "SG" is the recommended motor oil with the highest standards acceptable for 1989 gasoline engine warranty maintenance service. There are several other lower grades of motor oil, but the "SG" grade would be preferred because of its superior quality and because it can be substituted for other grades of motor oil.[1]

Both systems can provide the consumer with useful information, but typical consumers are probably not aware of the systems and they are most likely confused by the mix of numbers and letters used in the classification systems. Consumers will often rely on friends, their mechanics, or a salesperson when deciding which brand of motor oil to purchase. Appendix A provides a detailed overview of the two classification systems.

The Consumer Markets

The PCMO market is segmented by consumer usage into two principal areas—the do-it-yourselfer (DIYer) or the installed segments. Exhibit 2 illustrates the breakdown between the two primary market segments and their respective subsegments. The DIYers prefer to purchase their motor oil and install it themselves (or with the assistance of friends). There has been a decline in the DIYer market, from 70 percent in 1985 to 66 percent in 1988. In contrast, the installed segment has shown continued signs of growth, as service and convenience have influenced the buying perspectives of consumers.

---

[1] Quaker State, "Oil and Lubricants Vital to Your Vehicle's Survival," May 1, 1989, pp. 6–9.

EXHIBIT 2   Distribution channel structure

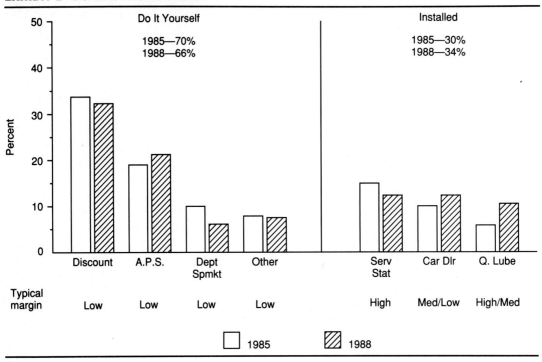

The Do-It-Yourself Market

The DIYer has been the single largest market for two primary reasons: First, the DIYer wants to ensure that the oil change is done correctly. An individual's investment in an automobile is typically a substantial part of his or her income. Therefore, it is worthwhile to protect their investments with the necessary motor oil changes. In addition, the DIYers are generally very proud of their cars and they don't mind changing their motor oil, but they don't particularly like it either. Rather, they change their own oil so they can be sure that it's done right. Second, the DIYers prefer changing their motor oil because they are price sensitive. Promotional discounts have been a common tradition in recent years, and thus the DIYers have become accustomed to discounted product prices.

Past industry surveys indicate that half of the DIYers are brand loyal for a variety of reasons. Perceived product quality and reliability are two reasons for maintaining this loyalty, but there is also a mixing problem that forces brand loyalty. The brand-loyal DIYer will purchase motor oil by the case, particularly if the brand is on sale. As the case empties, all of the single quart bottles may not be used up prior to the next oil change. The brand-loyal DIYer will consider the potential negative impacts of mixing two different brands of motor oil and thus, remain brand loyal to the last remaining quart of motor oil, rather than discarding it.

Approximately half of the DIYers are switchers who either switch and stick or switch less on the basis of quality and more based on price. The switch and stick DIYers switch brands of motor oil because of concerns with product quality or because they purchased a new car. Most automobile manufacturers have extended the life of engine warranties and are now more inclined to recommend specific brands of motor oil. With the combination of a new car purchase and the extended engine service warranties, it has become increasingly more important to maintain a single brand of motor oil throughout the ownership of the auto. The switch and stick DIYers are willing to try other motor oils perceived to better preserve and protect their automotive investment. The price-driven switchers see no problem in switching brands because they perceive no difference in the various brands of motor oil. The lowest price motor oil will virtually guarantee their next purchase decision.

DIYers can be characterized as either brand loyal or switchers. They install their own motor oil not because they enjoy the task, but rather because they want to make sure that it is done right. DIYers are generally very price sensitive and more likely to become switchers when their preferred brand is not on sale. This market segment continues to be the larger of the two consumer markets, but the DIYer market has been declining and future growth is considered unlikely.

The "Installed" Market

The installed market consists of those consumers who have their cars' motor oil changed at service stations, car dealerships, or at quick-lube centers. Exhibit 2 shows the 4 percent growth in recent years of the installed market, as well as the rapid growth of the quick-lube centers, primarily at the expense of service stations. Price has not been as great a factor as convenience to these buyers. Based on consumer research, the installed market prefers a high-quality brand of motor oil that is expeditiously installed. Convenience to the consumer has become increasingly more important, as demographic trends indicate that more and more dual-income families have less free time available to do such things as changing their own motor oil.

The quick-lube centers have been one of the newest developments in the motor-oil industry. The rapid growth of quick-lube centers, which specialize in fast motor-oil changes (10 minutes or less), could be attributed to their convenience and expertise based on volume. The traditional quick-lube service center performs only motor oil changes in a three- to four-bay building. These buildings are frequently located near high-traffic centers, and some are converted service stations. The quick-lube service's bay doors are located in the front and back of the building in order for customers to drive in and out easily. The quick-lube centers also have a pit below the automobile service bay area for technicians to perform service without raising the car on a service platform, typical of most service stations. The pit reduces service time and provides added customer convenience since customers do not have to leave their cars.

Roughly half of the quick-lube centers are independently owned and they have been one of the fastest-growing businesses of the automotive service sector. Motor-oil specialist companies have been very aggressive in acquiring and building quick-lube centers. However, several major gasoline companies have been experimenting with building their own quick-lube centers, as well as modifying existing service stations.

Service stations have historically had the largest market share of the installed market, but they have lost market share to the quick-lube centers. Most service stations have not been regarded as very convenient to customers, nor have they been particularly price competitive. It is difficult for service stations to justify having a highly paid mechanic perform motor oil changes. Other service and preventive maintenance performed at service stations are preferred because of their higher profit margins. In addition, traditional service stations have been designed without pits because service platforms used to raise and lower cars are more desirable for other forms of maintenance. The service platforms are particularly advantageous because mechanics can obtain easier access to perform tire, brake, transmission, and other undercarriage repairs. The choice of a pit or a service platform is mutually exclusive. The pit requires a basement below the garage floor, while the service platform base is typically embedded in the garage floor.

Some industry analysts feel that the car dealerships offer another area of potential market growth. Extended engine service warranties are valid only with performed preventive maintenance, including frequent motor oil changes. The car dealerships have access to a large customer base, and they perform the majority of the manufacturers' service guarantees.

Growth in the installed market has also been fueled by environmental concerns about used motor oil and proposed legislation. Legislators have become increasingly concerned with the means of disposal of used motor oil, particularly by the typical DIYer. Currently, there is little incentive for a DIYer to return used motor oil to a community collection point, nor is there an incentive to create a collection point. While it is advantageous to recycle used motor oil, it is difficult to distinguish used motor oils from other more hazardous oils. There are significant health risks associated with unknowingly handling contaminated motor oil that may be a more harmful hazardous waste. Greater environmental awareness could lead to direct legislation affecting the DIYer and the future handling of used motor oil.

The installed market consumer prefers a high-quality motor oil conveniently installed. The recent growth in market share of quick-lube centers, and the frequency of discussed environmental legislation, make the installed market an attractive market for future growth.

Distribution

Motor-oil products are distributed from the blending plants to both mass merchandisers and motor-oil distributors. The mass merchandisers include discount and department stores such as K mart, Montgomery Wards, Wal-Mart, Zayres, and others. The distributors handle distribution to smaller accounts such as individual quick-lube centers, service stations, grocery stores, drug stores, and hardware stores. Depending on the purchase volume, the accounts of auto parts stores could be handled as either mass merchandisers or distributors.

Generally, mass merchandisers purchase directly from the manufacturer and sell the motor oil by offering discounted prices to consumers. It is not uncommon for mass merchandisers to have their own private-label brands priced slightly less than the name-brand motor oils. The private-label brand is usually produced and packaged by a major oil company. The mass merchandiser's consumers are DIYers who are very price sensitive. Therefore, the mass merchandisers negotiate larger discounted volume purchases to resell name-brand motor oils at discounted prices across the country.

The distributors resell either a single company's products (as exclusive distributors) or they handle several different brands of motor-oil products for resale. This depends on the distributors' relationship with their suppliers. Some distributors are independently owned, while others are managed by motor oil companies. The relationship with the motor oil supplier may provide preference on whether the distributor handles more than one brand of motor oil. The distributors' consumer markets include both the DIYer and installed consumer. Pricing is extremely important to the independent distributors, as they are often in direct competition with the mass merchandisers for business.

Pricing

As a result of the cutthroat competition in the motor-oil industry, pricing has left most firms remaining in the industry with very small margins. The product pricing decisions are driven by competition for additional motor-oil market share. Although raw material cost may vary significantly from month to month, these price fluctuations are not passed on to consumers. There are a variety of reasons for current industry pricing practices, including factors affecting distribution channels, market share, and product image.

Mass merchandisers and large discounters have been particularly skillful in obtaining large volume discounts from most motor-oil producers. However, discounted volume sales to mass merchandisers can alienate the independent distributors. The independent distributors supply motor oil to both the installed and the DIYer consumer markets, while the mass merchandisers supply motor oil primarily to the DIYers. The pricing dilemma for motor-oil producers is extremely difficult. Independent distributors are very astute about product prices, and they sell motor oil to hundreds of service operations daily. Discounted motor oil offered at the mass merchandisers directly undercuts the distributors' price and is considered a threat to future business. As a result, motor-oil producers often deal with negotiated product pricing issues on a daily basis.

Market share is also an important factor in product pricing. The firms with large market shares—typically the motor oil specialists—have followed a more consistent pricing strategy ranging well within 50 cents per gallon of each other (see Exhibits 3 and 4). The gasoline companies, generally with lower market shares, have a larger variance in price range, as noted in Exhibit 4. Gasoline companies have virtually perfected instant price changes at the fuel pump, and they have not been afraid to frequently change the prices of their motor oil. Some firms with low market share have discounted their product price to tempt DIYers to switch brands. Havoline, owned by Texaco, has been particularly successful in gaining market share with this strategy, but it has been very costly. Depending on the firm's market share, pricing can influence the frequency of price changes and the price level.

Product image and positioning also significantly influence motor-oil pricing decisions. The motor-oil specialists have been the most successful in developing premium-brand images. The premium image commands a higher price and typically a higher demand. However, some gasoline companies have

EXHIBIT 3 PCMO market share

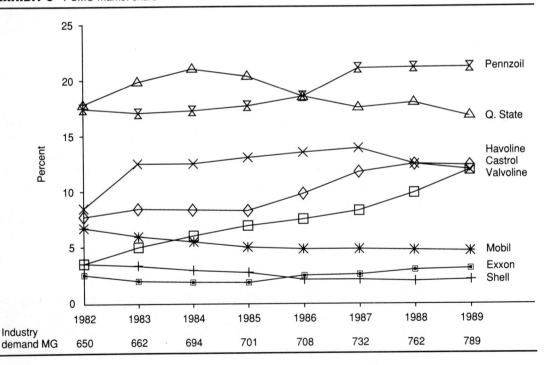

EXHIBIT 4   Retail pricing trends—Do it yourself

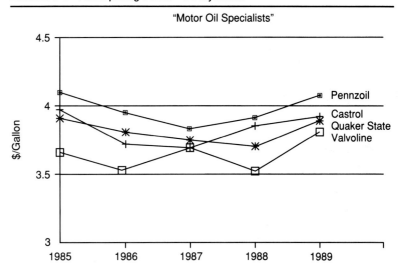

"Motor Oil Specialists"

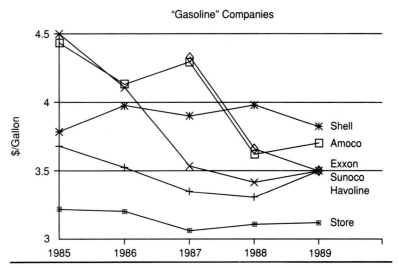

"Gasoline" Companies

+ Market leader averaging 0.80 $/gallon above store brand.

followed premium price strategies even though their product was not perceived to be a premium product.

Product pricing has been further complicated by product discounts offered to consumers and distributors. In the mid-1980s the motor-oil industry quickly caught onto the concept of offering product coupon discounts to consumers. Rebates were readily available to most consumers by virtually all motor-oil producers in an effort to protect or capture market share. This rebating reduced margins and increased the intensity of competition among the key players. Overall, product pricing decisions must carefully weigh the trade-offs within distribution channels and brand-quality perceptions.

The PCMO Competitors

The competitors in the PCMO industry have each carefully positioned their products to meet specific market niches or to address future growth potential. Pennzoil and Quaker State have been successful in maintaining market leadership, but others such as Castrol and Havoline have successfully increased their respective market shares. A brief summary of all the key PCMO players follows.

Pennzoil

Pennzoil displaced Quaker State in 1986 as the market-share leader by capturing 21 percent of the PCMO market (see Exhibit 3). Their marketing strategy has been to remain as market leader by pushing their product hard into the quick-lube services. Pennzoil has approached the quick-lube market by franchising their name and flooding the quick-lube markets with their products. In 1988, Pennzoil claimed to have supplied about two-thirds of the motor oil sold in the booming U.S. quick-lube business. Pennzoil also has a long-term commitment with Jiffy Lube, the largest U.S. quick-lube franchise. The Pennzoil-Jiffy Lube relationship developed partly out of necessity, since Pennzoil was one of their largest creditors and Jiffy Lube had overbuilt their operations too quickly. Pennzoil stepped in with much needed cash, and over the following years Pennzoil has gained a greater controlling interest in Jiffy Lube.

Pennzoil has emphasized quality and brand loyalty to maintain their premium price level. As a result, Pennzoil users are brand loyal and less likely to become switchers. The 1988 annual report summarized part of their market approach:

> While motor oil sales were healthy in 1988, they failed to match the record levels of 1987. One major reason was deep discounting on the part of competitors, a tactic that tends to make motor oil a commodity. Pennzoil avoided this trap, unlike some of its competitors, and managed to hold market share, thanks to strong brand loyalty on the part of Pennzoil consumers. It finished the year comfortably ahead of its nearest competitor by a margin of several points.[2]

The motor oil and automotive products segment of Pennzoil had revenues of $1,312.2 million and an operating income of $110.8 million (excluding a $122 million write-down of assets) in 1988. Pennzoil earned a profit of $115.9 million and $168.7 million in 1987 and 1986.

---

[2] Pennzoil, 1988 Annual Report, p. 14.

Pennzoil's advertising and promotion has been directed at building their installed market position, while maintaining their DIYer position. Their advertising theme has stressed the multidimensional aspect of their motor oil to handle thermal breakdown, lubrication, and reduced friction; that is, ''world-class protection.'' Given Pennzoil's strong cash position and their market leadership, Pennzoil will adamantly defend their market share against competitor's threats.

Castrol

Castrol has been one of the most successful marketers of PCMO in recent years. This is evidenced by their rise in market share from 5 percent in 1983 to almost 10 percent in 1988. Castrol has focused their product on the small car users, emphasizing their product as a high-performance motor oil developed for small-car engine needs. Their users are considered younger and more upscale and tend to drive cars with four-cylinder engines. Castrol users are in a class by themselves, with high brand loyalty and a specific market.

Castrol developed their market by focusing on the small-car DIYer and aggressively marketing the car dealers. Castrol has not directed any investment at the quick-lube business. Castrol has established their market niche as ''an oil for small engine protection'' tied to the advertising theme ''engineered for smaller cars.''

Havoline

Havoline has progressively increased its market share on a consistent basis. First, Havoline successfully dropped its name association with Texaco in the mid-1980s. Gasoline company motor oils in general are perceived negatively compared to their rivals, the motor-oil specialist. Second, Havoline has maintained a clear low-price strategy to obtain market share. While this strategy has been costly—a $25 million estimated loss in 1988 alone—market share has increased almost 2 percent for each of the last three years.

The Havoline users tend to be switchers who perceive their motor oil as a second choice, not as good as Pennzoil or Castrol, but effective. Havoline seems to be used because of price and product availability. Their advertising message has emphasized the formulation's ability to reduce sludge with the theme ''more protection than you'll ever need.''

Valvoline

Valvoline has had significant trouble in recent years, resulting in estimated break-even performance. Valvoline, owned by Ashland Oil, has been the price leader, but they have lost market share primarily due to the aggression of Texaco. Valvoline consumers are not as brand loyal as Pennzoil or Castrol consumers. When prices began to decline in the mid-1980s, Valvoline consumers departed.

Valvoline obtained brand awareness in the 1970s with their advertising theme using "Val the chimp" to make Valvoline a household name.[3] Television commercials and print advertising showing Val performing an oil change with Valvoline made it look easy. Clearly targeted at the DIYer, it was a creative advertisement that caught the public's attention. Today, Valvoline has switched its emphasis to the motor oil's product quality and brand image. The current advertising utilizes aggressive comparison advertising aimed specifically at the market leaders, such as Quaker State. Valvoline advertises that their motor oil is the highest-quality oil recommended by car manufacturers, with the theme "People who know, use Valvoline."

Others

The gasoline companies, Mobil, Exxon, Shell, and others, round out the rest of the PCMO business with break-even profits at best. Only Mobil has successfully utilized the gasoline company name with its name brand motor oil, particularly Mobil 1. Exxon has made some efforts recently to revitalize their brand, SUPERFLO, with heavy advertising and the building of experimental quick-lubes. Shell has introduced a reformulated motor oil specifically aimed at the rapidly expanding small truck market. The product, called Truckguard, offers the protection needed for small trucks, but there are no preliminary results to indicate success or failure of this product.

The PCMO industry remains a very competitive industry, and throughout the next few years margins are expected to remain low. The threat of new entrants is highly unlikely; however, there are clear opportunities for consolidations or external acquisitions in order to capture market share. Niche market segments have been successfully developed at the DIYer level to foster and maintain brand loyalty.

Finally, another factor to consider is the potential for a revolutionary development in the PCMO market. Environmental concerns about the illegal disposal of used motor oil have been increasingly brought to the attention of legislators. Legislation may be created to address this concern, possibly leading to the development of an engine sealed for life, with no oil added after the purchase of the car. Another possibility to consider is the usage of alternative fuels, such as methanol, requiring different lubrication needs. Any significant investment in this competitive industry should consider external factors which may affect the product life cycle of PCMO.

Quaker State—Background

Established in 1931, Quaker State has always been known as a leader in product innovation and in establishing motor oil standards. The founders of Quaker

---

[3] "Val the Chimp Made Valvoline a Household Name," *The Oil Daily,* April 20, 1988, p. B–9.

State pioneered one of the first brands of motor oil which was the oil of choice in the early days of the automobile. However, the PCMO environment has changed, and today Quaker State has lost both market share and past profit performance. In 1987, the company reported its first loss ever, $1.82 a share, and surrendered its number one market position to Pennzoil (See Exhibit 5).

EXHIBIT 5 Quaker State stock price

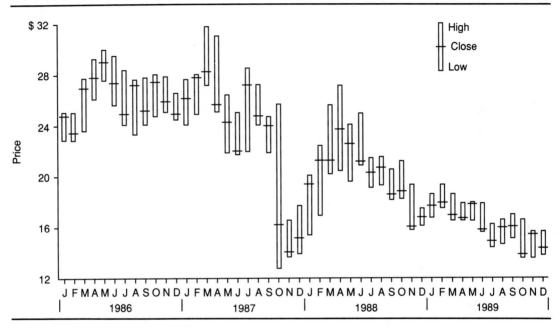

Overall, operating margins collapsed from 12.9 percent to 6.0 percent, reflecting deep product discounting. Quaker State's net income has fallen from profits of $50.3 million in 1986 to $14.9 million in 1988. The 1989 profits have fallen even further to $11.8 million on declining sales of $734.7 million. Within a 15-month period, the company switched chief executives three times.[4] These results have been disturbing for Quaker State and the marketing issues have not been resolved to restore past market share and operating profit performance.

Similar to other oil companies, Quaker State used the benefits of their abundant cash flow over the years to diversify their business away from the volatile motor oil business. Through various acquisitions, the firm is divided into five separate business units:

---

[4] Kerry Hannon, "Run over by the Competition," *Forbes*, September 5, 1988, p. 80.

	Percent		
1989 Data	Sales	Profit	Assets
1. Motor oil/auto	59%	41%	31%
2. Coal operations	13	22*	11
3. Insurance group	11	17	32
4. Truck-lite	7	20	6
5. Minit-lube, Inc.	10	0	20

* Includes +29 percent unusual item less −7 percent from operations.

The petroleum operations still provide the majority of sales, profits, and proportionate assets. In order for Quaker State to have a successful recovery, the core motor oil business needs to be turned around.

Quaker State's roots go back to the oil fields of Pennsylvania, first discovered at the turn of the century. The superior Pennsylvania, crude oil enabled Quaker State to offer a premium-quality product, with refineries located near the producing fields in Pennsylvania. Today, the Pennsylvania fields are not nearly as productive as in prior years, and now Quaker State must obtain most of their raw materials from other sources.

Manufacturing

Motor oil is produced from a refined barrel of crude oil into a specialty product called a lube basestock. Typically refinery production of lube basestock is less than 30 percent of all refinery output. The remaining 70 percent of the output is made up of gasoline, kerosene, and fuel oil, which can be sold to other consumer markets. The lube basestock is then blended with Quaker State's unique additive package and filled in the appropriate containers for consumer usage.

Quaker State's manufacturing facilities were designed to maximize motor-oil production, but overall this method of production is considered extremely inefficient. Essentially 70 percent of their output is resold as undesirable products with a break-even margin, at best. The major gasoline companies, on the other hand, maximize output streams by separating these streams and further refining the outputs into more valuable products.

Quaker State's cost structure on motor oil production has increased. The production inefficiencies have become more apparent as the availability of Pennsylvania-based crude oil has decreased and their outside purchases have increased. Recently it has been more efficient for Quaker State to purchase their lube basestock needs from the major gasoline companies and blend the motor oil at Quaker State packaging facilities. As a result, the future need of Quaker State's three refineries is extremely questionable. The 1987 loss included a $30 million write-down of assets related to the closure of the Ohio Valley Refinery.

Their other refineries and some related plants have also been rumored to be on the auction block. Currently, it appears Quaker State's future will primarily be directed at blending and packaging their motor oil and marketing the product to consumers. Without raw material advantages, it is expected that this will increase their cost basis. However, it is probably the most attractive opportunity given the alternative—inefficiently producing motor oil with higher raw material costs and transportation costs.

Quaker State Marketing Strategies

In 1987, Quaker State realized the early results of a disastrous marketing strategy when it lost its number one market share to Pennzoil. With the assistance of the outside consulting firm, McKinsey & Co., management tried to force their distribution subsidiaries to carry Quaker State products exclusively, and to increase sales to mass merchandisers.[5] The company's profits plunged as its distributors lost business to competitors with a larger variety of brands. In addition, distributors became increasingly upset with the company as the firm offered deep discounts to the mass merchandisers. The relationship between the motor oil distributors and Quaker State was significantly weakened in 1986.

Distribution

Jack W. Corn, a former distributor of the company's products, was brought in to turn the company around, as the new president of Quaker State. He increased the company's investment in the firm's Minit-Lube shops, and he has attempted to patch up relations with the distributors. As noted in the 1988 annual report, Jack Corn stated:

> The first move we made was to change our program direction so that selling Quaker State would be attractive and profitable to independent distributors. In my opinion, that is the part of our business that has built consumer brand image and demand over the years. The independent distributors create the demand for the big mass merchandisers. And future demand depends on having a strong independent marketing force in as many markets as we can possibly have.[6]

In 1986, the company had 223 independent distributors handling their product. By 1988, the number of distributors dropped to 202. The firm appealed to their distributors by reversing past discount pricing strategies offered to the mass merchandisers. However, it is difficult to assess the extent of the damage done to the company's distribution network.

---

[5] Michael Schroeder, "Quaker State Switches into a Quick-Change Artist," *Business Week,* October 16, 1989, p. 126.
[6] Jack W. Corn, Quaker State, 1988 Annual Report, p. 15.

Pricing

In an effort to smooth the problems with the independent distributors, pricing policy became a critical issue. While pricing problems have always been a thorn in Quaker State's side, they became a larger problem. After discounting the company's products in 1986–87 and having several different price schedules for different consumers, Quaker State moved toward a uniform pricing policy. This meant that all customers, mass merchandisers and distributors, would pay comparable prices for the Quaker State products. However, in order to appease each of the distribution channels, Quaker State has priced their product in the low end of the motor oil price range (see Exhibit 4).

Products

The Quaker State product mix is illustrated in Appendix D. The product strategy for Quaker State has been to be a leader in product quality across all of their products. In 1988, the firm completed upgrading all of their motor oils to the highest standards.[7] In 1989, Quaker State's 5W–30 and 10W–30 grades completed tests confirming that they qualify as "Energy Conserving II." This certified that these grades allowed motorists to achieve at least 2.7 percent greater mileage than a standard motor oil.[8]

Quaker State continues to improve product quality on a regular basis, and they anticipate matching any new product innovations that appear in the motor-oil market.

Packaging

Quaker State was one of the first major motor oils to change their product package from the can to the plastic bottle. In 1985, Quaker State also came up with an astute marketing innovation—a new easy-pour container. But its plastic can was round and hard to stack on store shelves. Pennzoil, 18 months later, produced a square container that fit more product on a tight shelf space. Quaker State was pushed aside, as it was less convenient to stack and reshelf.[9]

Minit-Lube Operations

Quaker State chose to expand its efforts in the quick-lube market with the additional acquisitions of quick-lube service centers. As of year-end 1989, the firm had over 450 Minit-Lube outlets either franchised or company owned. Mr. Corn has indicated that they would like to maintain a 60/40 percent owner/franchisee relationship.

---

[7] Quaker State, 1988 Annual Report, p. 6.
[8] Quaker State, 1989 Annual Report, p. 6.
[9] Hannon, "Run over by the Competition," p. 80.

The Minit-Lube outlets have focused their efforts on increasing the quality of service provided to customers. Quaker State is planning on a premium service worth a premium price. Quaker State has increased the prices at Minit-Lube operations to meet the high costs of the physical facilities.

Promotion

The promotion strategy for Quaker State has a focus for both the DIYer market and the installed market. First, the company continues to sponsor a racing program to demonstrate the high-quality attributes of the motor oil at major race events. Quaker State feels that the DIY user of motor oil is a "car-caring person who is intensely interested in auto racing."[10] The racing program has sponsored a number of racing events in NASCAR competition and international road races. The racing program emphasizes to DIYers the quality of Quaker State motor oil which can work for professionals, and therefore, "it can work for you, too."

Second, the company moved to enhance its position in the installed market by offering a lubrication limited warranty, available for new cars and good for 250,000 miles or 10 years (whichever comes first to the original owner)—see Appendix B. The warranty provides for repair or replacement of lubricated engine parts, provided certain rules are followed. The primary rule requires the owners to have their motor oil changed over 4,000 miles or four months by a professional installer who uses Quaker State.

Advertising

The emphasis on quality has been reduced in the 1990 print and commercial advertisements to stress Quaker State is "One Tough Motor Oil." This is supported with several different television advertisements emphasizing the 250,000-mile guarantee, NASCAR racing, and company testing of the product—sample advertisements are in Appendix B.

Appendix A   SAE Classifications

Over the years, the Society of Automotive Engineers (SAE) developed a classification system (Crankcase Oil Viscosity Classification—SAE J300–JUN 86) based on viscosity measurements. Thick, slow-flowing oils are assigned high numbers; thinner oils that flow more freely receive low numbers. Modified several times, the system establishes distinct motor oil viscosity grades: SAE 0W, SAE 5W, SAE 10W, SAE 15W, SAE 20W, SAE 25W, SAE 20, SAE 30, SAE 40, and SAE 50.

---

[10] Quaker State, 1988 Annual Report, p. 12.

Viscosity: A measure of how much a fluid resists flowing. Motor oil is more viscous than water.

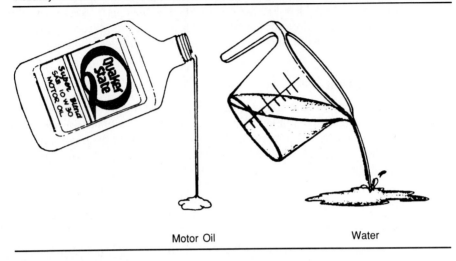

Motor Oil   Water

SAE: Society of Automotive Engineers

The "W" in the SAE grades stands for winter. Viscosity grades with the W classification are based on their maximum viscosity and borderline pumping temperatures at specific low temperatures. The W grades also are based on the minimum viscosity at +100°C. These oils are tested to ensure that they have proper flow characteristics and are suitable for use in cold seasons and climates. Oils without the W classification, on the other hand, are tested to ensure the proper viscosity at +100°C only. Although SAE 20 and SAE 20W oils are separate classifications, each will generally meet the viscosity requirements of the other. Those that do meet the requirements are classified SAE 20W–20. This simple form of multigrading is one of the few possible without adding a viscosity index improver.

The viscosity index is an arbitrary scale in which oil from Pennsylvania crude is typically 100 and oils from naphthenic crudes are placed in the 0 to 70 range. These numbers are not related to the actual viscosity of the oil or its SAE number. Viscosity index numbers measure the change in viscosity as the operating temperatures change; the higher the number, the smaller the change. Motor oils used in a wide range of operating temperatures may have viscous polymers or polymeric compounds added to decrease this rate. Called "viscosity index improvers" because they raise the index number, these additives make possible the multigrade or "all-season" oils that have been marketed by U.S. oil companies for more than four decades.

Because the multigrades, such as SAE 5W–30, 10W–30, and 10W–40, are light enough to crank easily at low temperatures and heavy enough to perform well at high temperatures, they are among the most widely used motor oils.

Table 1 shows single and multigrade oils and the lowest temperatures at which they can be expected to perform satisfactorily.

TABLE 1 SAE grades of motor oil*

Lowest temperature	Singlegrade oils	Multigrade oils
32°F/0°C	20, 20W, 30	10W-30, 10W-40, 10W-50, 15W-40, 20W-40, 30W-50
0°F/−18°C	10W	10W-30, 10W-40
Below 0°F/−18°C	5W	5W-20, 5W-30, 5W-40

* "Motor Oil Guide," American Petroleum Institute, Washington D.C., 1982.

These grades refer to viscosity only and provide no information about the type or quality of an oil or its intended purpose. For this reason, another system was needed to take other factors into account. An early classification system developed by the American Petroleum Institute (API) classified engine oils as regular, premium, and heavy duty. A later API effort, in conjunction with the Society of Automotive Engineers (SAE) and the American Society for Testing and Materials (ASTM), described and classified the various service/engine-operating conditions as a basis for selecting the proper crankcase oil.

Engine Service Classifications

The changing requirements of the automobile industry, along with the need for more effective communication among engine manufacturers, the oil industry, and the consumer, led to a new API Engine Service Classification System. This system, developed by API, ASTM, and SAE, allows engine oils to be defined on the basis of performance characteristics and their intended types of service (see Table 2). Together, the API and SAE systems define the characteristics of a

TABLE 2 Service classification

Letter Designation	API Engine Service Description
SG	1989 gasoline engine warranty maintenance service. For passenger cars, vans, and light trucks beginning with the 1989 model year operating under manufacturer's recommended maintenance procedures. These oils provide improved control of engine deposits, oil oxidation, and engine wear relative to oils developed for previous categories. These oils also provide protection against rust and corrosion; they can be used where SF, SE, SF/CC, or SE/CC are recommended.
SF	1980 gasoline engine warranty maintenance service. For passenger cars and some trucks, beginning with 1980 models operating under engine manufacturers' warranties. These oils provide increased oxidation stability and better antiwear performance than the oils that meet the minimum requirements for the SE classification.

TABLE 2 (concluded)

Letter Designation	API Engine Service Description
SE	1972 gasoline engine warranty maintenance service. For passenger cars and some trucks, beginning with 1972 (and some 1971 models) operating under engine manufacturers' warranties. These oils provide better protection than SC- and SD-classified oils.
SD	1968 gasoline engine warranty maintenance service. For passenger cars and some truck models operating under engine manufacturers' warranties in effect for model years 1968 through 1970, plus some 1971 or later models. These oils provide better protection than SC-classified oils.
SC	1964 gasoline engine warranty service. For passenger cars and some truck models operating under engine manufacturers' warranties in effect for model years 1964 through 1967.
SB	Minimum duty gasoline engine service. For engines operating under conditions mild enough to require only minimum protection through compounding.
SA	Formerly for utility gasoline and diesel engine service. For engines operated under conditions so mild that they do not need the protection of compounded oils; there are no performance requirements.
CE	Service typical of turbocharged or supercharged heavy-duty diesel engines manufactured since 1983 and operated under both low-speed, high-load and high-speed, high-load conditions. Oils designed for this service may also be used when previous API engine service categories for diesel engines are recommended.
CD-II	Service typical of two-stroke cycle diesel engines requiring highly effective control over wear and deposits. Oils designed for this service also meet all performance requirements of API Service Category CD.
CD-Diesel	Severe duty diesel engine service. For certain naturally aspirated, turbocharged, or supercharged diesel engines in which effective control of wear and deposits is essential or when fuels ranging widely in quality (including high-sulfur content) are used. These oils provide protection from bearing corrosion and high-temperature deposits.
CC-Diesel	Moderate-duty diesel and gasoline engine service. For certain naturally aspirated, turbocharged, or supercharged diesel engines in moderate- to severe-duty service; also used for some heavy-duty gasoline engines.
CB-Diesel	Moderate-duty diesel engine service. For light- to moderate-duty diesel engines operating with lower-quality fuels that require greater protection against wear and deposits; occasionally used for light-duty gasoline engines.
CA-Diesel	Light-duty diesel engine service. For light- to moderate-duty diesel engines using high-quality fuels; sometimes used for gasoline engines in mild service.

motor oil to help consumer selection of appropriate products. Table 3 shows the API classifications and SAE grades of Quaker State motor oils.

Oil manufacturers are responsible for ensuring that a given motor oil has the performance characteristics essential for the recommended service classification(s). Engine manufacturers, on the other hand, are responsible for evaluating the class of service applicable to the engine's design and intended use and

TABLE 3 Quaker State motor oils: SAE grades and API classifications

Product	SAE Grade	API Classification
Sterling	10W-30	SG-SF/CC-CD
Deluxe	10W-40	
Deluxe Performance	5W-30, 20W-50	
Super Blend	10W-30, 20W-40	SG-SF/CC-CD
HD	10W, 20W-20, 30, 40	
Turbo	10W-30	SG-SF/CC-CD
Regular	30	
Motorcycle Motor Oil (4-cycle)	20W-50	
HDX Universal Fleet	10W, 20W-20, 30, 40, 50 15W-40	CE, CD II, CD/SG-SF

recommending the appropriate classification of oil for the engine. The consumer's responsibility lies in being aware of the engine manufacturer's recommendation and purchasing the proper oil.

Appendix B Quaker State advertising

EXHIBIT B-1

ONE TOUGH MOTOR OIL ANNOUNCES ONE TOUGH GUARANTEE...

250,000

TWO HUNDRED FIFTY THOUSAND MILES OR TEN YEARS.

Use Quaker State exclusively in your new car, and our limited guarantee will cover lubricated engine parts for 250,000 miles or ten years, whichever comes first.

How tough is today's Quaker State?

Tough enough to make this promise: Use only Quaker State in your new car's engine, and if any lubricated engine part not covered by the manufacturer's warranty or extended-service contract suffers an oil-related break-down during its first 250,000 miles or ten years, Quaker State will pay for the repair.

We'll guarantee lubricated parts in engines of all sizes—domestic or imported.

Quaker State's limited guarantee covers lubricated parts in engines of every single imported and domestic car or light truck sold in the United States. It even covers the deductible on any extended warranty you might have purchased from your new-car dealer. Enrollment is absolutely free.

See a copy of lubrication limited warranty and enrollment details at participating service centers.

Complete details and enrollment forms for the Quaker State 250,000-mile or ten-year guarantee are available at participating Quaker State service centers. These include many new-car dealers, automotive service centers and fast lubes nationwide.

To participate in the guarantee program, enroll your new car at a participating service center within six months or 6,000 miles of purchase. Use only Quaker State Motor Oil, and have your oil and filter changed at a service center according to manufacturer's instructions for severe driving conditions but not to exceed 4,000 miles or four months between changes. Save your receipts.

How can Quaker State make a guarantee this tough?

Today's Quaker State has proven its toughness over and over again in the most rigorous tests that the world's auto makers have thrown at it. The result: Quaker State actually exceeds lubrication speci-fications for every single car sold in the United States. It takes a tough oil to offer a guarantee this tough. But Quaker State is One Tough Motor Oil.

The Big Q is One Tough Motor Oil.

©1990 Quaker State Corporation.   DON'T POLLUTE. PLEASE DISPOSE OF USED MOTOR OIL PROPERLY.

EXHIBIT B-2

QUAKER STATE---
ONE TOUGH MOTOR OIL
BRINGS YOU A TOUGH NEW
ADVERTISING CAMPAIGN!

EXHIBIT B-3

QUAKER STATE
ONE TOUGH MOTOR OIL
PRESENTS
A TOUGH ADVERTISING CAMPAIGN.

LEADERSHIP LEVELS OF QUAKER STATE
IMAGE ADVERTISING BEHIND OUR
"ONE TOUGH MOTOR OIL" THEME

- We will <u>dominate</u> television auto racing with our
  year round motor oil exclusivity on ESPN <u>and</u>
  major network races.

- We will <u>dominate</u> consumer magazines –
  automotive enthusiast, do-it-yourselfer,
  and outdoor publications.

- We will <u>dominate</u> broadcast advertising in
  major ADI's covering the U.S.

QUAKER STATE'S MEDIA SPENDING WILL BE UP +63% VERSUS 1989!

EXHIBIT B-4

"GUARANTEE"

LENGTH: 30 SECONDS

COMM'L NO.: QOAZ 0133

ANNCR: One tough motor oil announces one tough guarantee.

The Quaker State

250,000 mile or 10 year guarantee.

Register your new car at a participating service center.

Then use only Quaker State.

Have oil and filter changed as directed at a service center

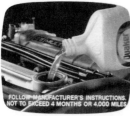

and if any lubricated engine part suffers an oil related break down

within 250,000 miles

or 10 years

you're covered. Quaker State guarantees it in writing.

The Big Q

is one tough motor oil.

EXHIBIT B-5

"TESTED TOUGH"

LENGTH: 30 SECONDS

COMM'L NO.: QOAZ 0063

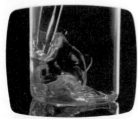

ANNCR: It's one of the most technologically advanced, most rigorously tested fluids on earth.

Relentlessly measured for maximum protection against the friction...(SFX)

the wear

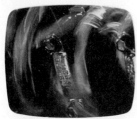

and tear...(SFX)

the heat and stress of today's engines.

It is today's Quaker State.

In Europe, in Japan, in America

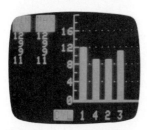

Quaker State quality has passed the most demanding tests

auto makers can throw at it.

At Quaker State we don't just say we're tough, we're tested tough.

The Big Q

is one tough motor oil.

EXHIBIT B-6

"TOUGH ENGINES"

LENGTH: 30 SECONDS

COMM'L NO.: QOAZ 0043

ANNCR: What makes a Quaker State engine so tough? One tough motor oil.

And being tough takes more than just talking tough.

There's a brand that says it's been engineered for smaller engines.

Well, Quaker State

has been tested tough for small engines

in Japan, in Europe and in America.

In fact, Quaker State has toughed out the most demanding specs

for every size engine in every size car sold in the U.S.

What makes any size Quaker State engine so tough?

Quality engineered Quaker State.

The Big Q

is one tough motor oil.

EXHIBIT B-7

"NASCAR"

LENGTH: 30 SECONDS

COMM'L NO.: QOAZ 0083

ANNCR: They got the green flag at Daytona.

Roared through Talladaga.

Left Darlington in the dust.

And which car piled up the most tough NASCAR miles in '89?

The Quaker State King Racing Buick.

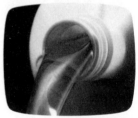

Its engine getting maximum protection

from one tough motor oil. The same Quaker State you buy right off the shelf.

Only one car was tough enough to stack up NASCAR's highest mileage total.

Only one oil was tough enough to tough it out every single one of those miles.

Quaker State.

The Big Q

is one tough motor oil.

EXHIBIT B-8

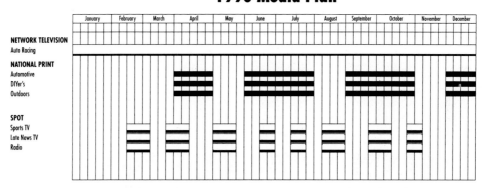

Ordering of Co-op Advertising Materials

To order materials call Customer Service at 1-800-759-2525 and give them the appropriate advertising material code number.

The following co-op advertising materials are available at no charge for use by case goods or bulk retailers:

Lube Warranty	Order Code Number
20 Second Television	3000559
45 Second Radio	3000560
30 Second Radio	3000561
16 1/2" x 11 1/4" Black & White Newspaper Ad	3000562
8 1/4" x 11 1/4" Black & White Newspaper Ad (Available 4/15)	3000563
Tested Tough (Beaker)	
20 Second Television	3000564
45 Second Radio	3000565
30 Second Radio	3000566
Tough Engines (Tested for all size engines)	
15 Second Television	3000568
45 Second Radio	3000569
30 Second Radio	3000570
Reprints of this Storyboard Handout	3000571
Copy of 1990 Ad Campaign Videotape	3000572

Retailers will have to produce their remaining portion of the co-op ad; plus buy and place the media. **All tags for these ads still must receive copy approval by Quaker State Marketing.** Please refer to the 1990 Retailer Merchandising Program for more information and details.

EXHIBIT B-9

IT TAKES A TOUGH OIL TO OFFER AN ADVERTISING CAMPAIGN THIS TOUGH.

BUT QUAKER STATE IS ONE TOUGH MOTOR OIL.

Appendix C

Annual income statement ($ millions)

	Dec. 1988	Dec. 1987	Dec. 1986	Dec. 1985	Dec. 1984
Sales	$869.104	$847.952	$899.065	$974.251	$924.630
Cost of goods sold	626.390	611.501	642.930	731.336	721.022
Gross profit	242.714	236.451	256.135	242.915	203.608
Selling, general, and administrative expense	190.977	183.958	139.716	132.037	114.780
Operating income before depreciation	51.737	52.493	116.419	110.878	88.828
Depreciation, depletion, and amortization	39.201	39.467	35.675	36.416	34.777
Operating profit	12.536	13.026	80.744	74.462	54.051
Interest expense	9.048	6.977	8.926	13.509	12.922
Non-operating income/expense	8.341	11.744	18.070	18.752	10.322
Special items	5.804	− 122.000	.000	1.887	− 24.695
Pretax income	17.633	− 104.207	89.888	81.592	26.756
Total income taxes	2.700	− 56.150	39.600	35.700	9.000
Minority interest	.000	.000	.000	.000	.000
Income before extraordinary items and discontinued operations	14.933	− 48.057	50.288	45.892	17.756
Extraordinary items	.000	.000	.000	.000	.000
Discontinued operations	.000	.000	.000	.000	.000
Net income	14.933	− 48.057	50.288	45.892	17.756
Preferred dividends	.000	.000	.000	.000	.000
Available for common	14.933	− 48.057	50.288	45.892	17.756
Savings due to common stock equivalents	.000	.000	.000	.000	.000
Adjusted available for common	$ 14.933	$ − 48.057	$ 50.288	$ 45.892	$ 17.756

Appendix D **Quaker State's product mix**

EXHIBIT D-1

Case 46

Guest Quarters: Frequent Flyer*

In January 1986, John Vernon, vice president of marketing for Guest Quarters, a firm of all-suite hotels, decided that Guest Quarters should join at least one of the frequent flyer programs conducted by the major airlines. He knew that some action needed to be taken immediately to increase occupancy and profits at Guest Quarters, particularly the new units in Tampa, Florida, and Charlotte, North Carolina. The newest hotels, the ones that lenders looked to in making determinations of financial strength, were experiencing problems in developing the kind of acceptance that Guest Quarters had gained in its older locations. Despite the fact that almost no data substantiating the benefits or costs of frequent flyer programs were available, Mr. Vernon believed that participation in such a program could help remedy the firm's situation, but many options were open as to how and when to implement this strategy.

Background

Guest Quarters, the pioneer in the all-suite segment of the hotel industry, was founded in 1972 when real estate developer George Kaufman bought a garden apartment complex in Atlanta, Georgia. Originally positioned as temporary housing for relocated families, it evolved into a new concept: the all-suite hotel. By 1985, Guest Quarters had grown to a total of nine properties: three in the Washington, D.C., area; two in Atlanta; one each in Houston, Tampa, Charlotte, and Greensboro. Two other units were under construction in Bethesda, Maryland, (bringing to four the number of units in the Washington, D.C., area) and in Austin, Texas. Since 1972, Guest Quarters had experienced a compound annual growth rate of revenues in excess of 25 percent. The 1984 operating margin was 37 percent. All-suite properties typically delivered gross margins in

* This material was written by Professor Eleanor G. May based on a Directed Business Study written by Mary Haggerty, James T. Jervey, Allan McAllister, and Christopher Morrissey. Copyright © 1986 by The Colgate Darden Graduate Business School Sponsors, Charlottesville, Virginia WP3106C. Used with permission.

EXHIBIT 1 Guest quarters's advertisement

THE HOUSTON GUEST QUARTERS SUITE. AT $116, IT'S A LUXURY YOU CAN AFFORD. AT $85, IT'S A VALUE YOU CAN'T AFFORD TO MISS.

We're so convinced the spacious charms of a Guest Quarters suite will make you a regular Guest Quarters guest, we're making this unprecedented introductory offer to get you here in the first place. So if you already have a reservation at the Westin Oaks, the Inn on the Park, the Westin Galleria, the Hyatt, the Hilton or any of the other fine hotels in Houston, consider this.

Now through Sept. 1, 1983*, you can spread out, rest up and luxuriate in one of our spacious suites. For about the price of their small single.

So, if you plan to spend $85 or more for a hotel room in Houston, you can't afford *not* to spend it for a Guest Quarters suite.

GUEST QUARTERS
THE ALL SUITE HOTELS

Call toll free
800 424-2900
In Washington, DC, call 861-0610
or call your travel consultant

*Sorry, this offer is not valid April 29-May 5.

GUEST QUARTERS—GALLERIA WEST 5353 Westheimer Road
GUEST QUARTERS—GALLERIA EAST 2929 Post Oak Blvd.
Other Guest Quarters Hotels in Washington, DC, Alexandria, VA, Atlanta, GA, Greensboro, NC.

a range between 35 percent and 60 percent, compared with 25 percent for standard hotels.

The Guest Quarters product concept was originally that of a ''home away from home,'' blending the convenience of a hotel with the space and freedom found in a personal residence. The first Guest Quarters in Atlanta (Roswell

Road) continued to present this image, catering to salespeople and middle management executives who had extended assignments in the Atlanta area and also still serving as temporary housing for executives' families transferring to Atlanta.

In the newer Guest Quarters units, however, the service package was closer to that of a full-service hotel with food and beverage operations, common areas for meetings, and so on. Guest Quarters suites typically consisted of a living room, dining area, and a fully equipped kitchen, in addition to a bathroom and one or two bedrooms. To make them more distinctive and more homelike, each suite was decorated with original prints and live plants. (See Exhibit 1 for a sample advertisement that shows a mockup of a Guest Quarters suite.)

Guest Quarters primarily targeted the business traveler. In 1985, 70 percent of all Guest Quarters revenues were generated from the individual corporate traveler, while an additional 25 percent of revenues were derived from guests attending meetings or conventions. Recent research conducted for Guest Quarters indicated that the typical Guest Quarters customer spent more time on the road than did the typical frequent traveler.

Guest Quarters rates varied according to location, depending on the competition and on the level of luxury and amenities of the building and the suite, but in general a Guest Quarters suite was priced equivalent to a single room in a full-service hotel. One-bedroom suite per diem rates varied from $85 to $150; two-bedroom suites ranged from $90 to $235. (See Exhibit 2 for a full list of rates.)

In many ways Guest Quarters resembled a holding company of nine independent hotels rather than a chain of similar units. The geographic expansion of the firm had been determined by the availability of real estate rather than

EXHIBIT 2   Guest Quarters's room rates, 1985

	1-Bedroom suite		
Location	Single	Double	2-Bedroom suite
Washington area			
Alexandria	$ 97	$112	$134
Pennsylvania Avenue	130	150	235
New Hampshire Avenue	130	150	235
Houston	105	125	185
Atlanta area			
Perimeter Center	120	140	182
Roswell Road	88	99	109
Greensboro	70	85	90
Charlotte	95	107	145
Tampa	110	120	160

by a coordinated plan to position the hotel for a particular market. Growth of the company had occurred both by acquiring existing buildings and by constructing new ones. The hotels varied in size from 101 suites at New Hampshire Avenue in Washington, D.C., to 335 suites at the Galleria in Houston. There was no standard facility design, and individual suites varied in size and layout by facility. Properties also varied in physical appearance as well as in services available. Exhibit 3 describes some of the variations among the locations.

EXHIBIT 3 Guest Quarters's service packages

Suites	Size (sq. ft.)	Availability
Studio	484	Alexandria only
1 bedroom	600–800	All locations
Executive suite	900	Greensboro only
2 bedroom	996–1,560	All locations
3 bedroom	1,350	Roswell Road only
Penthouse	1,400	Alexandria only

Dining room
Available at all locations except New Hampshire Avenue, Pennsylvania Avenue, and Greensboro.

Lounge
Available at Perimeter, Charlotte, Tampa, and Houston. Included in dining room at Roswell Road and Alexandria. Not available at New Hampshire Avenue, Pennsylvania Avenue, and Greensboro.

Suite service (room service)
24-hour service available at Perimeter, Charlotte, Tampa, and Houston. 7 A.M. to 11 P.M. service available at Roswell Road, Alexandria, New Hampshire Avenue, and Pennsylvania Avenue. Continental breakfast only at Greensboro.

Swimming pool on site*
Available at all locations except Pennsylvania Avenue.

Jacuzzi and sauna on site*
Available at Perimeter, Charlotte, Tampa, and Greensboro only.

Fitness/exercise area on site*
Available at Perimeter, Charlotte, Tampa, Houston, and Greensboro.

Airport parking/courtesy car
Varies by location.

* Some locations have affiliations with off-site facilities.

The Guest Quarters service package varied by facility. In 1985, restaurants, suite (room) service, and meeting and banquet facilities were found at most locations. Additional special services, such as a lending library of best-sellers, cable television, exercise facilities, secretarial services, and a grocery shopping service, were also available depending on location.

In the spring of 1985, the average Guest Quarters occupancy rate ranged from 73 percent at Pennsylvania Avenue to 43 percent at Charlotte. Furthermore, like all hotels that catered to business travelers, Guest Quarters occupancy rates were much higher Monday through Thursday than Friday through

EXHIBIT 4   Guest Quarters's average daily occupancy by hotel, January–June 1985

	Mon.	Tues.	Wed.	Thurs.	Fri.	Sat.	Sun.	Avg.
Washington area								
Alexandria	70%	69%	71%	67%	59%	56%	57%	64%
New Hampshire Avenue	66	69	74	68	51	53	57	62
Pennsylvania Avenue	79	83	84	78	61	66	66	73
Houston	54	56	54	48	35	33	39	46
Atlanta area								
Perimeter Center	80	81	83	77	37	36	49	53
Roswell Road	71	77	76	62	45	48	56	62
Greensboro	73	72	71	73	56	56	59	66
Charlotte	46	55	59	50	32	33	28	43
Tampa	66	78	79	70	42	39	42	59
Average	67%	71%	72%	66%	46%	46%	50%	60%

EXHIBIT 5   Guest Quarters's seasonal demand by hotel, January–June 1985

	Peak	
Hotel	Month/day	Occupancy rate
Washington area		
Alexandria	April, Saturday	100%
New Hampshire Avenue	June, Tuesday	87
Pennsylvania Avenue	June, Tuesday	87
Houston	May, Monday	72
Atlanta area		
Perimeter Center	June, Tuesday	97
Roswell Road	June, Wednesday	87
Greensboro	April, Thursday	94
Charlotte	March, Wednesday	76
Tampa	March, Tuesday	99

Sunday. (See Exhibits 4 and 5 for details of occupancy and demand.) Occupancy rates were major indicators of profitability of hotels as a result of the low variable cost per room—$2 to $3 per night. Many of the corporate travelers, however, were allowed corporate discounts and thus did not pay the full "rack" rate.

Guest Quarters Marketing

National marketing and advertising promotions for Guest Quarters were conducted out of national headquarters in D.C. (Exhibit 6 shows the total marketing and sales budget for Guest Quarters for 1986.) The national marketing staff consisted of one man, the director of marketing, Mickey Rowley, who reported to John Vernon. Mr. Rowley's responsibilities included: developing all print and media advertisements; designing and administering direct mail campaigns; managing the 800 reservation number; acting as the national sales director; and supervising the Guest Quarters regional sales office in New York. As national

EXHIBIT 6 Guest Quarters's 1986 marketing budget

Advertising	$1,330,000
Regional sales offices	229,000
Toll-free telephone service	313,000
Sales payroll at hotels	790,000
Sales expense at hotels	258,000
	$2,920,000

sales director, Mr. Rowley took salespeople to implement sales "blitzes" in cities where Guest Quarters did not have hotels. In this capacity, he also managed national accounts and developed joint promotions with such companies as Hertz Car Rentals and Ask Mr. Foster Travel Agency (a national agency).

One direct mail campaign had been very effective. Guest Quarters had mailed 500,000 cards to major credit unions giving 20 to 40 percent discounts on weekend stays at Guest Quarters. The credit unions distributed the cards to their members as a benefit of membership. Mr. Vernon claimed that in one hotel 18 percent of one month's revenue had been generated through this campaign.

Guest Quarters advertised in all in-flight magazines in every other issue. It advertised about 20 times a year in *The Wall Street Journal*. Guest Quarters also arranged "trade-outs" with Cable News Network. CNN provided Guest Quarters with free advertising in return for hotel accommodations.

The regional sales office in New York City, staffed by two people, was responsible for calling on the headquarters of major accounts and large travel agencies. The staff arranged free accommodations for travel agents on tours, for which airlines, hotels, and car rental agencies donated travel accommodations. John Vernon, however, questioned the effectiveness of promoting to travel agencies. He believed that at least 80 percent of business travelers either knew where they wanted to stay or received recommendations from someone they knew.

Each Guest Quarters hotel had a marketing or sales staff of four people. A staff that consisted of a director of marketing, two directors of sales, and a secretary was responsible for calling on all potential customers in its area—it had a free rein in providing discounts to attract sales.

The Lodging Industry

In 1985, there were 54,000 lodging establishments in the United States with a capacity of 2.7 million rooms; average occupancy during 1985 was just over 64 percent. The industry was considered mature; changes in demand usually occurred only when the general economy shifted. However, a significant oversupply had developed in a number of metropolitan areas. Industry experts predicted that by 1992 there would be 3.1 million rooms and thus the oversupply would continue. Demand was forecast to increase at the rate of 1 to 3 percent per year, keeping pace with the 2 percent supply increase, therefore maintaining occupancy rates at the mid-60 percents.

The maturity of the lodging industry had led to consolidation among firms in an attempt to maintain the historical double-digit growth rates and to gain economies of scale. For instance, in 1985 Marriott acquired Howard Johnson's and Holiday Inn purchased both Residence Inns and Embassy Suites.

Industry segmentation had also accelerated as large chains perceived a need to differentiate themselves if they were to maintain their market shares. The all-suite segment had grown rapidly as part of this trend. The 300 all-suite hotels represented less than 2 percent of the total room inventory in 1985, but industry experts predicted that this supply would grow at the rate of 20 to 25 percent annually in the next few years. By 1990, there would be an estimated 1,000 all-suite facilities offering almost 150,000 suites. In addition to Guest Quarters, in 1985 all-suite chains included Embassy Suites, Residence Inns, L'Hermitage, Lexington, and Park Suite Hotels. Several large hotel chains like Doubletree Inns and the Radisson Hotel Corporation were experimenting with all-suite properties, and Marriott was poised to enter the market. Exhibit 7 describes the major participants in the all-suite segment of the industry in 1985.

Advertising and promotion in the lodging industry was not standardized among firms either by type or by amount. Hyatt, for example, was conducting a $2 million nationwide print and broadcast advertising campaign, while Marriott was spending $16 million on its ''honored guests'' awards program. Promotions and advertising typically were not carefully evaluated because of the unavailability of accurate, broad-based consumer data.

Some lodging executives thought that a major problem in the industry was the lack of product differentiation. It was believed that, within a similar price range, guests perceived that many hotels looked alike and offered similar benefits. James Collins, senior vice president for marketing at Hilton Hotels Corp., said, ''We all have happy people [employees], we all have good facilities, we all have good service.''

In evaluating the marketing efforts in the lodging industry, Michael Levin, president and chief operating officer of Days Inn of America, stated: ''I call it marketing by necessity—for survival.''

Airline Frequent Flyer Programs

Airline frequent flyer programs were born in the 1979–1980 recession. Airline industry profit performance, which had been adversely impacted by deregulation, was further damaged by decreasing load factors, the air traffic controllers' strike, and by increases in both interest rates and fuel prices. The airline industry traditionally suffered under the burden of high operating leverage; therefore, it was extremely important for the airlines to try to maintain volume.

EXHIBIT 7 Composition of the suite hotel industry, 1985

Company	Average room rate	Existing		Under Construction		Announced plans
		Sites	Rooms	Sites	Rooms	
Amberley Suites	$52.50	2	354	3	450	Open 20 properties by 1988
Doubletree Suites	$82.50	1	221	1	220	Open 30 properties by 1990
Granada Royale/Embassy Suites	$70–$75	43	9,260	37	7,950	Open 150 to 200 properties by 1988
Guest Quarters	$87–$120	9	1,729	1	189	Open 3 to 5 properties per year
Hawthorne Suites	$70	6	554	0	0	Open 200 properties nationwide
Hotel Corp of Pacific	$60–$100	19	4,463	0	0	
L'Hermitage	$154	7	1,089	1	80	
Lexington	$39–$69	13	2,184	2	240	Open 5 to 7 properties per year
Marriott						Will become major competition in 1986
Park Suite Hotels	$70	8	1,857	3	885	Open 12 to 15 properties per year
Quality Inns	$45–$85	0	0	5	700	Open 300 properties during next 5 years
Radisson Hotels	$75	1	150	3	759	
Residence Inns	$65	55	6,448	25	2,500	Open 500 properties by 1990
Royce Hotel Suites	$75–$100	2	305	14	2,100	Open an average of 2 per month
Totals		166	28,604	95	16,073	

Prior to this time, airlines attempted to maintain volume through special fares and through other promotional programs designed to increase customer loyalty and repeat business.

American Airlines was the first airline to develop a frequent flyer program—the AAdvantage program, introduced in 1981. Such programs offered flyers "mileage points"—awards of free travel on future flights—for miles traveled on the airline beyond a certain minimum. Other airlines soon followed suit, and the programs expanded as other travel businesses (hotels, rental cars, cruise lines) recognized the benefits to be derived from frequent traveler programs and became affiliated with one or more airline programs. The programs gained momentum in 1983 when United Airlines offered extra bonus coupons to flyers as part of an effort to regain business lost during the strike. By 1985, each of the 13 major trunk-line carriers had developed frequent flyer programs. These programs included 16 hotels, 9 rental car agencies, and 17 associated airlines. Exhibit 8 lists the major airlines' programs and their hotel and rental car affiliations as of January 1986.

EXHIBIT 8 Frequent flyer program affiliations, January 1986

Airline	Hotels	Car rentals
American Airlines	Inter-Continental	Avis
	Sheraton	
Continental	Marriott	Thrifty
Delta	Preferred Hotels	National
	Marriott	Alamo
Eastern	Marriott	Hertz
		Dollar
		General
New York Air	Resorts International	Avis
Northwest Orient	Stouffer	National
	Hilton	Thrifty
	Omni/Dunfey	
	Preferred Hotels	
	Radisson/Colony	
Pan Am	Inter-Continental	Hertz
	Sheraton	
Piedmont	Stouffer	Hertz
Republic Airlines	None	Hertz
		National
TWA	Hilton	Hertz
	Marriott	
United Airlines	Hyatt	Hertz
	Westin	Budget
	Meridien	
	Kempinski	
Western Airline	Sheraton	Budget
	Village Resort Condominiums	

There were a number of factors that could affect the future of frequent flyer programs and of the airline industry:

1. Intense competition within the airline industry.
2. Costs of implementing and operating frequent flyer programs.
3. Availability of marketing information.
4. Ethical problems surrounding frequent flyer programs.
5. Tax liability issue surrounding frequent flyer programs.

The airline industry as a whole had not fully recovered from the downturn which accompanied the recession and the oversupply of seats after deregulation. Although fuel prices and interest rates had fallen, load factors remained low. Furthermore, no abatement was expected in the level of industry competition. Deregulation had resulted in the major airlines revamping their route structures as they had their competitive strategies. A fairly common strategy was to establish hubs at additional locations in order to provide tie-ins to a greater number of destinations.

Expansion by the major airlines had served to further aggravate the problem of excessive seat capacity. Industry load factors slipped 1½ percentage points in 1985, to approximately 55 percent, the lowest level in five years. Price wars led to a 22 percent drop in yield per passenger mile and a decline in operating profits. Industry sources believed that the fare structure would continue to deteriorate, and operating profits for 1986 were expected to fall approximately 8.5 percent from 1985 levels to $700 million.

There appeared to be little evidence as to whether frequent flyer programs were a cost-effective method of maintaining customer loyalty. While the airlines were not forthcoming about the revenues and expenses associated with frequent flyer programs, it was clear that the programs were costly both to develop and to operate. Frequent flyer programs were, in effect, price-cutting measures. Each of the major airlines provided similar bonuses to their customers, and so the industry as a whole ended up simply offering the customer, in effect, rebates on tickets, reducing the airlines' gross margins. The long-term profitability of the programs had yet to be determined, and the absolute effect was not easy to quantify, because a major part of the cost was postponed until redemption. There were no figures on how many people actually cashed in their bonuses. Nor was it known how many people used free tickets for flights they would have taken anyway, or how many took unplanned trips to use their free tickets.

It was also unclear whether frequent traveler programs actually influenced business travelers' decisions. For instance, the head of travel administration for Bankers Trust International was doubtful about the efficacy of such programs. According to him, most frequent business travelers are well-paid executives who do not have the time to worry about changing their plans to win free mileage points. However, a straw poll by *Economy Magazine* taken among bankers suggested otherwise. Many respondents to the poll said that they were members of schemes for Pan Am, American Airlines, or TWA—some bankers belonging to more than one. Those bankers who belonged to programs said they would be influenced in favor of using an airline to which they belonged, when there was a choice.

Apparently, the only quantifiable public information on participation in frequent flyer programs was in a 1985 study of the frequent flyer as a lodging guest conducted by Market Facts, Chicago, for the American Hotel and Motel Association. The study surveyed 1,055 travelers who were selected from among a representative panel of 30,000 men and women on the basis of their travel histories. Only 30 percent of the respondents were involved in some type of frequent flyer program; 21 percent were enrolled in some type of frequent traveler plan. No information on if and how much the frequent-flyer programs had increased business was available from the airlines which were developing and promoting the programs.

A possible controversy concerning frequent flyer bonus programs had been raised by some employers, who questioned whether awarding bonuses to business travelers for travel that had been paid for by the employer was ethical and legal. According to proponents of frequent flyer programs, however, many businesses took the position that business travel was a significant personal inconvenience to the employee; therefore, any such benefits should accrue to the traveler. Others believed that the bonuses should go to the employer rather than the employee since the employer paid for the original ticket and, therefore, in effect paid for the bonus.

In addition, abuse of frequent flyer programs was occurring, such as taking a circuitous route in order to accumulate extra bonus points on a specific airline. Some flyers arranged trips to their advantage by not taking the most direct route and arranging stops. Many companies were taking steps to prevent such abuse. Systems and requirements were being developed to require that both time and money efficiency be applied in flight planning. At some firms, in-house travel services have been made responsible for implementing such a policy. For others, travel agencies offered services that would guarantee efficiency in travel arrangements. Other companies were dealing with the problem by attempting to get the benefit to accrue to the business itself rather than to the individual. Such a procedure required the cooperation of the airlines, since the systems were designed originally to restrict the bonus to the specific flyer and his or her family.

A tax liability issue had also cropped up. Representative Harold Ford (Democrat, Tennessee) introduced a bill into Congress requiring that frequent flyer bonuses be reported as income to the individual. According to Congressman Ford, the cost of frequent flyer programs accounted for as much as 7 percent of the $66.5 billion that corporations paid for travel.

Lodging Involvement in Frequent Flyer Programs

Hotel companies could participate in the earnings and/or the awards segments of airline frequent flyer promotions. As an earnings partner, a hotel chain offered members of a specific airline frequent flyer program the opportunity to earn mileage points when staying at one of its hotels; mileage points could also be redeemed for services at that hotel chain. In contrast, an awards partner permitted redemption of mileage points earned elsewhere (through rental cars or air travel) for lodging.

All the major upscale hotel companies were affiliated with at least one frequent flyer promotion, either through the earnings or awards portions or both. Some companies had joined as many as four. In addition, a number of smaller upscale hotels had formed a coalition called preferred hotels through which they participated in these programs. Typically, lodging companies participated in both the earnings and awards segments of at least two frequent flyer programs. Sometimes, some units of a chain, such as resort locations, would be exempted from the program.

Typically, the airline approached the hotel company to join a frequent flyer program. It usually was important that the locations of the hotel properties be sufficiently compatible with the airline route structure for the airline to want to have the specific hotel chain in its program.

It appeared that little or no analysis was made by the hotel companies to determine the effect of a program on profits. The decision to join apparently was a defensive measure as well as a means of gaining information about and dialogue with high-frequency users.

The costs to the hotels were negotiated with the airlines. Generally, no initial program initiation fee was charged to the hotel company. Transaction costs to the lodging chain for the earnings portion of a frequent flyer program were based by the airline on a mileage equivalency. For example, a hotel might give 2,000 miles "credit" to the frequent traveler for each overnight stay. When the visit was recorded with the airline program, a fee was charged to the hotel (possibly one cent for each mile credited to the guest). Miles offered by hotels to guests varied between 500 and several thousand. Hence the cost to the hotel might be $2,000 \times \$.01$ or \$20 per guest using the frequent flyer program. Some hotel chains allowed awards for each night of the stay, others gave "mileage" only once for each visit to the hotel.

Additional costs were incurred by the hotel, of course, when bonus points, which typically had not been acquired at the hotel, were redeemed for free accommodations.

It appeared that hotel chains were joining programs not in response to evidence that the program would increase profitability but because other hotel chains were participating in a program. While no hotel company provided any figures, some believed that their involvement in frequent flyer programs had improved occupancy, primarily by stimulating repeat business. None of the companies were willing to state that it induced new customers to try the hotel. Tracking was not generally utilized in the industry and most companies did not have the information required to measure the costs and benefits of participating in the program. Of the major hotel chains, only Sheraton reported experiencing incremental profits attributable to participation in frequent flyer programs.

All-Suite Chains and Frequent Flyers

In early 1986, no all-suite hotel chain was affiliated with an airline frequent flyer program nor did it appear that any had plans to join one in the near future. According to a spokesperson at Embassy Suites, ''Our marketing dollars are better spent on advertising to induce trial than on a promotion such as frequent flyer programs that encourage repeat business.'' This opinion was typical of other companies, with the exception of Marriott. Marriott's all-suite hotels, when introduced, reportedly would be included in existing Marriott hotel frequent flyer affiliations.

Some hotel groups had opted to develop and implement their own frequent traveler programs. Holiday Inns, after reputedly losing millions on its frequent traveler program, made major changes in it, limiting its use and benefits to Holiday units. Ramada Inns was developing a ''business card'' plan with restricted bonuses, and Marriott Hotels had instituted its ''honored guests program.''

Conclusion

John Vernon believed that the Guest Quarters' decision to enter a frequent flyer program should be implemented promptly, if the firm was to continue to be profitable. He was unsure, however, what program should be adopted and what benefits should be offered. In any event, he knew that steps had to be taken right away to increase occupancy at Tampa and Charlotte.